UNJUST ENRICHMENT

Unjust enrichment is one of the least understood of the major branches of private law. This book builds on the 2006 work by the same authors, which examined the developing law of unjust enrichment in Australia. The refinement of the authors' thinking, responding to novel issues and circumstances that have arisen in the maturing case law, has required many chapters of the book to be completely rewritten. The scope of the book is also much broader. It concerns the principles of the law of unjust enrichment in Australia, New Zealand, England and Canada. Major decisions of the highest courts of these jurisdictions in the last decade provide a fertile basis for examining the underlying principles and foundations of this subject. The book uses the leading cases, particularly in England and Australia, to distil and explain the fundamental principles of this branch of private law. The cases discussed are current as of 1 May 2016 although the most recent could only be included in footnotes.

Unjust Enrichment

Second Edition

James Edelman and Elise Bant

·HART·
PUBLISHING
OXFORD AND PORTLAND, OREGON
2016

Hart Publishing
An imprint of Bloomsbury Publishing Plc

Hart Publishing Ltd
Kemp House
Chawley Park
Cumnor Hill
Oxford OX2 9PH
UK

Bloomsbury Publishing Plc
50 Bedford Square
London
WC1B 3DP
UK

www.hartpub.co.uk
www.bloomsbury.com

Published in North America (US and Canada) by
Hart Publishing
c/o International Specialized Book Services
920 NE 58th Avenue, Suite 300
Portland, OR 97213-3786
USA

www.isbs.com

First edition published in 2006. Second edition first published in 2016.

British Library Cataloguing-in-Publication Data
A catalogue record for this book is available from the British Library.

ISBN: PB: 978-1-84113-318-8
ePub: 978-1-78225-562-8

Library of Congress Cataloging-in-Publication Data

Names: Edelman, James, author. | Bant, Elise, author.

Title: Unjust enrichment / James Edelman and Elise Bant.

Other titles: Unjust enrichment in Australia

Description: Second edition. | Oxford ; Portland, Or. : Hart Publishing, 2016. | Includes bibliographical references and index.

Identifiers: LCCN 2016016402 (print) | LCCN 2016016702 (ebook) | ISBN 9781841133188 (pbk. : alk. paper) | ISBN 9781782255628 (Epub)

Subjects: LCSH: Unjust enrichment—English-speaking countries. | Restitution—English-speaking countries.

Classification: LCC K920 .E34 2016 (print) | LCC K920 (ebook) | DDC 346/.1521029—dc23

LC record available at https://lccn.loc.gov/2016016402

Typeset by Compuscript Ltd, Shannon
Printed and bound in Great Britain by
Lightning Source UK Ltd

CONTENTS

TABLE OF CASES

European Union

Australia

Canada

Hong Kong

Ireland

New Zealand

Singapore

United Kingdom

United States

TABLE OF LEGISLATION

Treaties

Australia

Canada

France

Germany

New Zealand

United Kingdom

Statutory Instruments

Part I

The Action For Unjust Enrichment

1

Introduction

In *Jones v Randall*[1] Lord Mansfield said that 'the law of England would be a strange science indeed if it were decided upon precedents only. Precedents serve to illustrate principles, and to give them a fixed certainty.' The *raison d'être* of this book is to explain the principles underlying the law of unjust enrichment, by exegesis from the precedents.

Although this book is the second edition of *Unjust Enrichment in Australia,* the book now focuses heavily on English law as well as Australian law. At relevant points it also contains discussion of the law in the United States, Canada, and New Zealand. There is a reason for our expanded focus. In 2006 when we published *Unjust Enrichment in Australia* our focus was on the underdeveloped law of unjust enrichment in Australia. We wrote *Unjust Enrichment in Australia* as a blueprint for the future development of the subject in Australia, drawing from precedent and principle. Since that edition, Australian law has developed substantially. In some respects, including the recognition of the concept of a right to retain, it provides a model for the development of English law. In other respects, such as explanation of the elements of the reductionist enquiry into the components of an unjust enrichment claim, English law has developed more rapidly. The ability for these two jurisdictions to learn and borrow from each other is a strong reason for the expanded scope and comparative focus of this new edition. The question marks which still hang over the existence of the subject in Australia provides a further basis for critical examination of central propositions which are taken for granted in English law, and approached, in some cases, differently in Canada.

At the boundaries of any subject there is scope for different jurisdictions to take different approaches. But we consider that developments in England and Australia emphasise that the core of unjust enrichment is truly *common* law based on shared underlying principles. To write a book today which is concerned only with the Australian common law of unjust enrichment would be parochial and insular. This new edition of the book, many chapters of which have been completely rewritten, is conceived as a true consideration of the *common* principles of the law of unjust enrichment. The differences between English and Australian law of unjust enrichment, including the different constitutional contexts, generally fade into the background when compared with the vast number of truly common issues raised within the subject, including those which the courts of neither country have yet considered. As Lord Neuberger said in *FHR European Ventures LLP and others v Cedar Capital Partners LLC*,[2] it is 'highly desirable for all those jurisdictions to learn from each other, and at least to lean in favour of harmonising the development of the common law round the world.'

[1] *Jones v Randall* (1774) 1 Cowp 37, 39, 98 ER 954, 955.

[2] *FHR European Ventures LLP and others v Cedar Capital Partners LLC* [2014] UKSC 45, [2015] AC 250, 273 [45]. See also *Starbucks (UK) Ltd v British Sky Broadcasting Group plc* [2015] UKSC 31 [50] (Lord Neuberger).

Although there are differences between unjust enrichment in English law and in Australian law, as Professor Häcker has explained this minor degree of variance between common law systems[3]

> is not merely tolerable, but positively desirable, provided that certain minimum conditions securing overall compliance are met. To avoid a break-up such as befell the *ius commune* from the late 18th century onwards, plunging continental legal systems into national isolation (which they are now trying to overcome), it is essential that common lawyers maintain and nurture a climate where one jurisdiction takes cognisance of the developments in another and where intellectual exchange can thrive.

Despite the exponential growth of learning in this subject in recent decades, there are many details of the law of unjust enrichment which have yet to be worked out by Australian and English courts. One reason for this is that in the life of the law, the law of unjust enrichment is still an infant. Our common law of contract and torts only began to emerge in a coherent form in England and the United States in the second half of the nineteenth century. There was a heavy civilian influence. The law of trusts had emerged a little earlier. But, as Frederick Pollock explained, the 'scientific' treatment of principles of English law began in 'that classical period of our jurisprudence' between 1852 and 1875.[4] In contrast, unjust enrichment did not emerge as a recognised branch of the law of obligations until the later twentieth century: 1954 in Canada,[5] 1987 in Australia[6] and 1991 in England.[7] Some of the brilliant writers, such as James Barr Ames, who were part of the formative processes for the law of contract and the law of torts had also written on the law of unjust enrichment. But they were the exceptions. Academic writing on unjust enrichment was sparse until the mid-twentieth century. The subject was hidden in the interstices of the law of contract, in forms of actions in *indebitatus assumpsit,* and in particular bills in equity.

In the development of the law of contract and the law of torts in the late nineteenth century, judges were heavily influenced by academic writing. From the mid-twentieth century, there was an era of prolific scholarship in unjust enrichment. The explicit judicial recognition of the law of unjust enrichment was also based on academic writing. And academic writing devoted to exposing the principles of the law of unjust enrichment kept moving ahead of the cases. But there is now a vast corpus of case law and, as emphasised recently by the Court of Appeal in *Investment Trust Companies (In Liquidation) v Revenue and Customs Commissioners*,[8] it is that case law which forms the primary source material for development of the law. For that reason, this book focuses first and foremost on the cases, although we draw from academic writing in areas where case law is deficient, or where academic writing has provided additional clarity concerning the underlying principle, or where underlying principles cannot be drawn from the cases.

[3] B Häcker, 'Divergence and Convergence in the Common law—Lessons from the *Ius Commune*' (2015) 131 *LQR* 424, 453.

[4] F Pollock, *The Law of Torts: A Treatise on the Principles of Obligation Arising from Civil Wrongs in the Common Law* (London, Stevens and Sons, 1887) vii.

[5] *Deglman v Guaranty Trust Co of Canada* [1954] SCR 725.

[6] *Pavey & Matthews Pty Ltd v Paul* [1987] HCA 5, (1987) 162 CLR 221; *David Securities Pty Ltd v Commonwealth Bank of Australia* [1992] HCA 48, (1992) 175 CLR 353.

[7] *Lipkin Gorman v Karpnale Ltd* [1991] 2 AC 548.

[8] *Investment Trust Companies (in liq) v Revenue and Customs Commissioners* [2015] EWCA Civ 82 [47] (the Court).

Although this book focuses heavily on the principles as extracted from the cases, we reiterate the vast influence that academic scholarship has had on the development of this area of law, from the most fundamental issues in this branch of private law to the most mundane. Like the leading cases, our scholarship in this book, and the exegetical exercise in which we are engaged, owes a vast debt to the leading, and pioneering, academic works of three scholars of the twentieth century. They are Robert Goff (later Lord Goff), Gareth Jones, and Peter Birks. It was the books by these authors in 1966 and 1985 which became the bedrock upon which the modern law of unjust enrichment developed in England and Australia.[9] Other commentators have shone further light on the tributaries of the river mapped by Goff and Jones and Birks. In England those writers include Professors Burrows, Virgo, Mitchell, Mitchell and Watterson. In Australia the writers include Professors Mason, Carter, and Tolhurst. In Canada they include Professors Maddaugh, McCamus, and McInnes. Although we differ from these writers in some respects, and occasionally in major respects, this book owes much to these writers and their explanations of the law of unjust enrichment.

Although this book's primary focus is the cases, it is not a compendium of cases. With the proliferation, and increasing sophistication, of search engines, blogs, and online indices of cases, there is little place for such books today. Nor is this book merely an exercise in what is sometimes pejoratively described as 'top-down reasoning'. Although this label can be misleading because almost all analogical reasoning in law involves a top-down aspect, we are not engaged in an exercise of supposing what the law should be and then identifying cases with results which might fit that picture. Instead, the function of this book for an English and Australian audience is to set out the principles of the law of unjust enrichment which emerge from the norms as reflected in the broad pattern of cases, including both the reasoning and results. However, in many of the older cases there is no judicial reasoning to explain why a defendant was unjustly enriched. We use those cases, as well as modern, sometimes conflicting, decisions to explicate the principles by which the law of unjust enrichment has developed and by which it should develop. Throughout, our focus is on the matrix of private law. It is on coherence within the law of unjust enrichment and also between unjust enrichment and the broader private law of obligations. For these reasons, although our examination is heavily rooted in the case law, there are occasions where we explain that even some judicial decisions in the highest courts in Australia or England cannot be justified.

Apart from the increased focus on English law, there are other major changes that have led to much of the first edition of this book being completely rewritten. For instance, a significant departure from the previous edition is that we explain that when asking whether an enrichment was unjust, it is necessary to ask *both* whether there was an 'unjust factor' *and* whether there is any juristic reason to retain the enrichment. We came close to this view in the first edition, noting the strong views of Dr Kremer drawn from the older cases. More recent cases have further elucidated the essential nature of this underlying principle. The new edition of *Goff and Jones* under the editorship of Professor Charles Mitchell, Professor Paul Mitchell and Dr Watterson also adopts a similar approach.

Some matters have not changed from the previous edition of this book. In particular, we continue to follow the powerful framework first adopted by *Goff and Jones* which

[9] See R Goff and G Jones, *The Law of Restitution* (London, Sweet & Maxwell, 1966); P Birks, *An Introduction to the Law of Restitution* (Oxford, Clarendon Press, 1985).

deconstructed the law of unjust enrichment into essential questions by which it could be understood. That framework was given great focus by Birks, and later adopted in many cases. The framework provides a helpful manner of focusing the mind on many of the issues that arise in a claim for unjust enrichment. It requires consideration of four questions in any unjust enrichment case:

1. Was the defendant enriched?
2. Was the enrichment at the plaintiff's expense?
3. Was the enrichment unjust?
4. What defences apply?

None of these labels ('enrichment', 'at the expense of', 'unjust') involves words which must be interpreted as though they were contained in a statute. But this reductionist enquiry provides a prism through which to understand and examine the central questions presented by this subject. Within each area there are sub-questions and sub-sub-questions. As we will see in the next chapter, even those courts which sometimes appear to deny the utility of the reductionist approach to unjust enrichment in Australian law inevitably find it necessary to consider the same issues, sometimes even using the same reductionist labels such as 'unjust factor' and 'enrichment'.

The chapters in Part II consider these questions in sequence. But, before we turn to the detail of the law of unjust enrichment, the first three chapters of this book, which comprise Part I, begin with a structural overview of the subject. After this chapter's introduction, Chapter 2 explains the nature of the law of unjust enrichment. We will see that even today the foundations of the law of unjust enrichment are not secure. Chapter 3 then explains the nature of the remedy of restitution. The law's response, when a plaintiff is unjustly enriched, is to require restitution. But we will see that there are at least eight different senses in which the word 'restitution' is used to describe a remedy. Five of these are responses to unjust enrichment. The focus of the remainder of the book is upon only one restitutionary response to unjust enrichment, albeit the one which occupies almost all of the case law: restitution of value.

2

The Nature of an Action Based on Unjust Enrichment

Contents

I. Introduction

One dominant, but false, account of the status of unjust enrichment in Australia goes something like this. About 25 years ago, the common law was approaching maturity. The objective theory of contract had largely triumphed.[1] A conceptual model of torts had emerged which, whilst not particularly elegant,[2] had provided structure and some clarity to the law of torts. Then, at this time of maturity, an alien intruder disrupted the careful development of the common law. The alien intruder was the law of unjust enrichment. For some, this belated recognition of the law of unjust enrichment in Australia[3] and England[4] (although earlier in Canada)[5] is one of those embarrassing things of the 1980s and early 90s, like pop music or mullet hairstyles. In 1997, Peter Birks and Robert Chambers recounted a conversation with a leading Australian judge, Meagher JA, which was consistent with this

[1] *Taylor v Johnson* [1983] HCA 5, (1983) 151 CLR 422.

[2] See the discussion in J Edelman, J Goudkamp and S Degeling (eds), 'The Foundations of Torts in Commercial Law' in *Torts in Commercial Law* (Pyrmont, NSW, Thomson Reuters, 2011).

[3] *Pavey & Matthews Pty Ltd v Paul* [1987] HCA 5, (1987) 162 CLR 221. See also *Australia and New Zealand Banking Group Ltd v Westpac Banking Corp* [1988] HCA 17, (1988) 164 CLR 662, 673; *David Securities Pty Ltd v Commonwealth Bank of Australia* [1992] HCA 48, (1992) 175 CLR 353.

[4] *Lipkin Gorman v Karpnale Ltd* [1991] 2 AC 548.

[5] *Deglman v Guarantee Trust Co of Canada* [1954] SCR 725.

account of the law of unjust enrichment. This former judge was a great equity lawyer and legal historian. Birks and Chambers said that this judge remarked to one of them: 'We don't need a law of restitution. It is no more than a neo-Marxist conspiracy to upset law that has always been perfectly well understood under the familiar headings of the common counts.'[6]

As Birks and Chambers recognised, Meagher JA was one of the few lawyers who truly understood the origins of the common counts. He could have explained the different species of assumpsit. He knew the difference between assumpsit and debt. He could also have exposited the difference between assumpsit and case, and when an eighteenth-century plaintiff would be non-suited. But there are not many lawyers today who carry in their heads the history and precedents of the forms of action. And even if lawyers today generally did think in terms of forms of action, the first part of this chapter seeks to expose the fallacy that it was a wrong turning for the law of unjust enrichment to break free from the forms of action. In a short historical account we show that the law of unjust enrichment has a heritage at least as distinguished as our modern conception of the law of contract or torts even though the modern law of unjust enrichment took longer to break free from the forms of action.

It has been accepted in a number of cases that the following construct is a helpful guide to determine whether liability arises for unjust enrichment:

(1) the defendant is enriched;
(2) the defendant's enrichment is at the expense of the plaintiff; and
(3) the defendant's enrichment is unjust or, in other words, an 'unjust factor' causes or contributes to the transaction by which the defendant is enriched; and
(4) whether any defences apply.

This reductionist enquiry provides important protection against the law of unjust enrichment degenerating into an exercise of idiosyncratic discretion.[7] These four questions have been endorsed as the appropriate approach to unjust enrichment many times in Australian decisions.[8] And they have been endorsed by the highest English courts.[9] They form the structure of this book, although recent cases have cast doubt upon whether such an enquiry is legitimate in Australian law.[10]

[6] P Birks and R Chambers (eds), *Restitution Research Resource*, 2nd edn (Oxford, Mansfield Press, 1997) 1.

[7] *Pavey & Matthews Pty Ltd v Paul* [1987] HCA 5, (1987) 162 CLR 221, 256–57 [14] (Deane J).

[8] See *Roxborough v Rothmans of Pall Mall Australia Ltd* [2001] HCA 68, (2001) 208 CLR 516, 568 fn 257, [139] fn 229 (Kirby J): 'generally accepted analysis'. See also *Torpey Vander Have Pty Ltd v Mass Constructions Pty Ltd* [2002] NSWCA 263, (2002) 55 IPR 542, [34] (Spigelman CJ); *Hollis v Atherton Shire Council* [2003] QSC 147, (2003) 128 LGERA 348 [9], [10] (Jones J); *Say-Dee Pty Ltd v Farah Constructions Pty Ltd* [2005] NSWCA 309 [222] (Tobias JA); *Ideas Plus Investments Ltd v National Australia Bank Ltd* [2006] WASCA 215, (2006) 32 WAR 467 [65] (Steytler P), [96] (McLure JA); *Ethnic Earth Pty Ltd v Quoin Technology Pty Ltd (in liq) (No 3)* [2006] SASC 7, (2006) 94 SASR 103, 117 [65] (Bleby J); *Natuna Pty Ltd v Cook* [2007] NSWSC 121 [155] (Biscoe AJ); *ABL Custodian Services Pty Ltd v Smith* [2010] VSC 548 [54] (Croft J); *Australian Financial Services and Leasing Pty Ltd v Hills Industries Ltd* [2011] NSWSC 267 [21] (Einstein J); *Henderson v McSharer* [2013] FCA 414 [73] (Barker J); *Equuscorp Pty Ltd v Haxton; Equuscorp Pty Ltd v Bassat; Equuscorp Pty Ltd v Cunningham's Warehouse Sales Pty Ltd* [2012] HCA 7, (2012) 246 CLR 498 [30] (French CJ, Crennan and Kiefel JJ).

[9] *Crown Prosecution Service v Eastenders Group* [2014] UKSC 26, [2015] AC 1 [102] (Lord Toulson, with whom Lady Hale and Lords Kerr, Wilson and Hughes agreed); *Benedetti v Sawiris* [2013] UKSC 50, [2014] AC 938 [10] (Lord Clarke, with whom Lords Kerr and Wilson agreed); *Banque Financière de la Cité v Parc (Battersea) Ltd* [1998] UKHL 7, [1999] 1 AC 221, 227 (Lord Steyn).

[10] *Southage Pty Ltd v Vescovi* [2015] VSCA 117, (2015) 321 ALR 383 [49] (the Court); cf [51] and *Australian Financial Services and Leasing Pty Ltd v Hills Industries Ltd* [2014] HCA 14, (2014) 253 CLR 560 [136] (Gageler J).

II. History of Unjust Enrichment

Although the law of unjust enrichment is sometimes thought to be a very modern and new category of law, the truth is precisely the opposite. Roman law, from which much of the development of the modern law of obligations borrowed, recognised unjust enrichment alongside contract and delict. In the formulary period of Roman law, unjust enrichment was concealed within the praetor's formula for relief. But it emerged generally during the classical period, described as an obligation *quasi ex contractu*: 'obligations which cannot strictly be seen as arising from contract but which, because they do not owe their existence to wrongdoing, are said to arise as though from a contract.'[11] There was later recognition that 'quasi contract' was not the best name for this category of law. In one text in the Digest, attributed to Pomponius, it was said that *iure naturae aequum est neminem cum alterius detrimento et injuria fieri locupletiorem* ('by the law of nature it is fair that no one become richer by the loss and injury of another').[12]

The English history of unjust enrichment followed a similar pattern of development to that of Roman law. During the period of the forms of action, common law claims for unjust enrichment were brought as writs of debt or account. The nature of the action was concealed behind a bare plea that the defendant owed the money as a debt or must account for it. For instance, an action for debt was brought against the abbot of a monastery where a monk purchased goods which were used by the monastery.[13] When the nature of these actions was discussed, they often were referred to by the use of the Roman quasi-contract.

After a misinterpretation of a decision of the Court of Exchequer Chamber in 1648,[14] the common law courts began to allow plaintiffs to plead unjust enrichment cases in forms of action known as *indebitatus assumpsit* (a species of 'assumpsit', or promise) rather than in debt.[15]

These pleadings involved an allegation by the plaintiff that the defendant, being indebted (*indebitatus*), had promised to pay the debt (*assumpsit*) but failed to pay.[16] This form of action was preferable to debt because, unlike debt, a defendant could not wage his law. He could not defend the case by finding witnesses or compurgators (often paid for the service) to swear to his innocence. *Indebitatus assumpsit* cases lay for anything that could give rise

[11] P Birks and G McLeod (trs), *Justinian's Institutes* (London, Duckworth, 1987) 117 [3.27]. The Latin text of 'said to arise as though from a contract' is *quasi ex contractu nasci videntur.* In another Digest extract from Pomponius, the reference to the obligation not to unjustly enrich oneself at the expense of another appears without the words *et injuria* (unjust): CH Monro (tr), *The Digest of Justinian*, vol II (Cambridge, Cambridge University Press, 1909) 12.6.14.

[12] A Watson (tr), *The Digest of Justinian*, vol IV (Philadelphia, University of Pennsylvania Press, 1985) 50.17.206. Discussed in D Ibbetson, 'Unjust Enrichment in English Law' in E Schrage (ed), *Unjust Enrichment and the Law of Contract* (Netherlands, Kluwer Law International, 2001) 35.

[13] DJ Ibbetson, *A Historical Introduction to the Law of Obligations* (Oxford, Oxford University Press, 1999) 266 citing YB T.22 Edw III f.8 pl.16.

[14] *Slade's Case* (1648) Style 138, 82 ER 592.

[15] Although only initially including money counts, from the mid-nineteenth century counts of *quantum meruit and quantum valebat*, for the value of services and goods, were also pleaded as *indebitatus assumpsit*: JH Baker, 'The History of Quasi-Contract in English Law' in WR Cornish, R Nolan, J O'Sullivan and G Virgo, *Restitution, Past, Present and Future: Essays in Honour of Gareth Jones* (Oxford, Hart Publishing, 1998) 41.

[16] E Lawes, *Practical Treatise on Pleading in Assumpsit* (London, W Reed, 1810) 418–503.

to a debt. A number of common counts arose which alleged the circumstances in which the debt arose.[17]

One of the common counts of *indebitatus assumpsit* was the common count of money had and received. The pleading of an action for money had and received was borrowed from the old writ of account against a receiver, and alleged that the defendant 'had' money that in law had been 'received to the use of the plaintiff'. Like the other counts in *indebitatus assumpsit*, money had and received was originally brought for a genuine promise. The defendant 'had and received' money to the use of the plaintiff and had to pay it over because that was what he had promised to do. The count for money had and received moved 'very slowly outwards from a genuinely contractual core'[18] to fictional promises. The fictional promise cases included claims that we would now recognise as claims for restitution of value obtained by unjust enrichment. For instance, where a plaintiff overpaid money to a defendant by mistake, the plaintiff could recover the amount of the overpayment on a count of money had and received in *indebitatus assumpsit*.[19] The implied promise fiction was obvious, because the defendant had never promised to return the money; indeed, the defendant might not even have realised that the money was paid by mistake.[20] But the fiction persisted and these actions in *indebitatus assumpsit* were generally known as quasi-contract. This language, borrowed from the Romans, meant 'as though from' (*quasi*) contract because of the 'implied' or fictitious promise.

English law almost broke free from the fiction of implied contract in the mid-eighteenth century when Lord Mansfield explained that the basis of restitutionary recovery was specific reasons for injustice (referred to in the modern law as 'unjust factors').[21] In a celebrated passage from *Moses v Macferlan*,[22] Lord Mansfield said that:

> If the defendant be under an obligation, from the ties of natural justice, to refund; the law implies a debt, and gives this action, founded in the equity of the plaintiff's case, as it were upon a contract ('quasi ex contractu,' as the Roman law expresses it). This species of assumpsit, ('for money had and received to the plaintiff's use,') lies in numberless instances ...[23]

English law could have immediately followed Lord Mansfield's lead and recognised (as it now does) a law of unjust enrichment which insisted upon a particular reason why restitution should be awarded, or as we now say, an 'unjust factor'. This was the course proposed by Sir William Evans.[24] However, Lord Mansfield's valiant attempt at classification was overshadowed by the publication of Sir William Blackstone's comprehensive *Commentaries on the Laws of England*,[25] which entrenched the dominant language of the Roman quasi-contract.

[17] DJ Ibbetson, *A Historical Introduction to the Law of Obligations* (Oxford, Oxford University Press, 1999) 148.

[18] ibid 272.

[19] Eg *Kelly v Solari* (1841) 9 M & W 54, 152 ER 24.

[20] FW Maitland, *The Forms of Action at Common Law* (AH Chaytor and WJ Whittaker eds, Cambridge, Cambridge University Press, 1965) 70.

[21] See *Lindon v Hooper* (1776) 1 Cowp 414, 416, 98 ER 1160, 1162; *Moses v Macferlan* (1760) 2 Burr 1005, 1012, 97 ER 676, 681 (Lord Mansfield comparing the action to a bill in equity).

[22] *Moses v Macferlan* (1760) 2 Burr 1005, 97 ER 676.

[23] ibid, 1008, 678.

[24] W Evans, 'An Essay on the Action for Money Had and Received' in W Evans, *Essays: On the Action for Money Had and Received, on the Law of Insurances and on the Law of Bills of Exchange and Promissory Notes* (Liverpool, Merrit & Wright, 1802, reprinted in [1998] *Restitution Law Review* 1).

[25] W Blackstone, *Commentaries on the Laws of England* (first published 1765–69, Chicago, The University of Chicago Press, 1979) Books I–IV.

When, in the mid-nineteenth century, a series of procedural reforms[26] abolished the need to specify a form of action and therefore abolished the requirement to plead the (often) fictitious promise in *indebitatus assumpsit,*[27] unjust enrichment actions remained widely known as quasi-contract. An error then began to occur. The Latin 'as though from a contract' morphed into the erroneous expression 'implied contract'. This error was described as 'erroneous and very unfortunate'.[28] The high-water mark of the quasi-contract approach was *Sinclair v Brougham,*[29] a decision not explicitly overruled until 1996.[30] In that case, Viscount Haldane LC said that when the common law 'speaks of actions arising *quasi ex contractu* it refers merely to a class of action in theory based on a contract which is imputed to the defendant by a fiction of law.'[31]

One of the most significant influences for the development of the modern Anglo-Australian law of unjust enrichment was the writing of Professor James Barr Ames.[32] Ames was a civilian scholar writing at the time of the great formative development of the common law of obligations. He lectured that '[t]he equitable principle which lies at the foundation of the great bulk of quasi-contracts, namely, that one person shall not unjustly enrich himself at the expense of another, has established itself very gradually in the Common Law'.[33] In an article in 1888, Ames referred to three categories of quasi-contract: judgment debts, statutory (and customary) dues, and 'the fundamental principle of justice that no one ought unjustly to enrich himself at the expense of another'.[34] The latter was the largest of all.

A colleague of Ames, Professor Keener, drew from Ames' work,[35] and in an extremely influential monograph explained that the instances of quasi-contractual liability rested 'upon the doctrine that a man shall not be allowed to enrich himself unjustly at the expense of another.'[36] In a text on quasi-contract, which followed Keener's in 1913, the first two categories of Ames' were quietly abandoned and quasi-contract was treated as synonymous with unjust enrichment.[37] Fifty years later, this view was confirmed with the authority of the United States *Restatement of the Law of Restitution.*[38]

Following academic and judicial dissatisfaction with the notion of quasi-contract,[39] a turning point for unjust enrichment in England came in Lord Wright's speech in the House of Lords in *Fibrosa Spolka Akcyjna v Fairbairn Lawson Combe Barbour Ltd.*[40] Lord Wright knew the *Restatement of the Law of Restitution* very well; he had published a lengthy review

26 *Common Law Procedure Act 1852* (15 & 16 Vict c 76) which followed the 1832 Hilary Rules.

27 ibid s 49.

28 *Re Rhodes* (1890) 44 Ch D 94, 105 (Cotton LJ).

29 *Sinclair v Brougham* [1914] AC 398.

30 *Westdeutsche Landesbank Girozentrale v Islington London Borough Council* [1996] UKHL 12, [1996] AC 669.

31 *Sinclair v Brougham* [1914] AC 398, 415.

32 See esp JB Ames 'The History of Assumpsit: Implied Assumpsit' (1888) 2 *Harvard Law Review* 53.

33 JB Ames, *Lectures on Legal History and Miscellaneous Legal Essays* (Cambridge, Harvard University Press, 1913) 162.

34 JB Ames 'The History of Assumpsit: Implied Assumpsit' (1888) 2 *Harvard Law Review* 53, 64.

35 That it was Keener drawing from Ames, and not vice versa, is explained in A Kull, 'James Barr Ames and the Early Modern History of Unjust Enrichment' (2005) 25 *Oxford Journal of Legal Studies* 297.

36 WA Keener, *A Treatise on the Law of Quasi-Contracts* (New York, Baker and Voorhis & Co, 1893) 19.

37 FC Woodward, *The Law of Quasi Contracts* (Boston, Little Brown & Co, 1913).

38 WA Seavey and AW Scott, *Restatement of the Law of Restitution* (St Paul, Minn, American Law Institute, 1937) 14–15.

39 See eg *United Australia v Barclays Bank* [1941] AC 1, 29: 'These fantastic resemblances of contracts invented in order to meet requirements of the law as to forms of action which have now disappeared' (Lord Atkin).

40 *Fibrosa Spolka Akcyjna v Fairbairn Lawson Combe Barbour Ltd* [1942] UKHL 4, [1943] AC 32.

of it in 1938.[41] The *Fibrosa* case was the first explicit English judicial recognition of the law of 'unjust enrichment'. The plaintiff was a Polish company that had made an advance payment for a contract for the delivery of machinery from Britain in 1941. War broke out. The House of Lords held that the contract had been frustrated, and that the Polish company was entitled to repayment of the advance as 'money had and received' in *indebitatus assumpsit*.[42] The action for money had and received could not, without a fiction, be based upon a contractual agreement to repay, nor upon any wrongdoing by the defendant. Lord Wright saw this and, echoing Lord Mansfield, explained that the reason for restitution in the context of a claim based upon failure of consideration was an obligation to pay arising from the circumstances.[43] Later he explained that '[t]he obligation is a creation of the law, just as much as an obligation in tort. The obligation belongs to a third class, distinct from either contract or tort, though it resembles contract rather than tort.'[44] As for the category that this 'creation of law' fell into, Lord Wright said that 'any civilized system of law is bound to provide remedies for cases of what has been called unjust enrichment ... Payment under a mistake of fact is only one head of this category of the law.'[45]

Apart from Lord Wright's opinion, there was another powerful force operating against the implied contract theory. This was an extraordinary English treatise by Goff (later Lord Goff) and Jones (later Professor Jones, the Downing Professor of the Laws of England) in 1966.[46] At the same time there had begun a series of rejections of the theory of implied contract by Australian judges.[47] By 1987 in Australia,[48] and 1991 in England,[49] it was conclusively recognised by the highest courts that unjust enrichment at the expense of another was a legal concept. The first comprehensive Australian text on the subject (covering restitution for unjust enrichment as well as restitution for wrongdoing) was published in 1995.[50]

The recognition of unjust enrichment as a category of law then required an understanding of its operation and meaning. There were two broad possibilities. The first possible approach to the concept of unjust enrichment might have been to see it merely as a vague principle of justice.[51] Much of the writing and decisions on unjust enrichment in the United States is characterised by this idea that 'Unjust enrichment is an indefinable idea in the same way that justice is indefinable'.[52] Unjust enrichment in the United States is commonly treated as a 'loose framework as well as an invitation for a normative inquiry'.[53] This United States approach cannot be solely attributed to the *Restatement of the Law of Restitution* of 1937. As we saw above, that Herculean work succeeded in breaking unjust enrichment free

[41] RAW Wright, Review of *Restatement of the Law of Restitution* (1937) 51 *Harvard Law Review* 369.

[42] Overruling *Chandler v Webster* [1904] 1 KB 493.

[43] *Fibrosa Spolka Akcyjna v Fairbairn Lawson Combe Barbour Ltd* [1942] UKHL 4, [1943] AC 32, 62. See also ibid 47 (Viscount Simon LC), 55 (Lord Atkin).

[44] ibid 62.

[45] ibid 61.

[46] R Goff and G Jones, *The Law of Restitution* (London, Sweet & Maxwell, 1966).

[47] *Watney v Mass* (1954) 54 SR (NSW) 203, 206 (Street CJ), 222 (Herron J); *Mason v New South Wales* [1959] HCA 5, (1959) 102 CLR 108, 146 [18] (Windeyer J); *Deposit & Investment Co Ltd v Kaye* (1963) 63 SR (NSW) 453, 457, [1963] NSWR 833, 837 (Walsh JA).

[48] *Pavey & Matthews Pty Ltd v Paul* [1987] HCA 5, (1987) 162 CLR 221. See also *Australia and New Zealand Banking Group Ltd v Westpac Banking Corp* [1988] HCA 17, (1988) 164 CLR 662, 673 [11].

[49] *Lipkin Gorman v Karpnale Ltd* [1991] 2 AC 548.

[50] K Mason and J Carter, *Restitution Law in Australia* (Sydney, Butterworths, 1995).

[51] *Baylis v Bishop of London* [1912] 1 Ch 127, 140 (Hamilton LJ).

[52] GE Palmer, *The Law of Restitution*, vol 1 (Boston, Little Brown & Co, 1978) 5.

[53] H Dagan, *The Law and Ethics of Restitution* (Cambridge, Cambridge University Press, 2004) 26.

from the fiction of implied contract. And although the *Restatement* did not elaborate on the nature or operation of unjust enrichment in detail, the reporters of the *Restatement* knew that the principle of unjust enrichment would need to be further refined and developed.[54]

The second approach was adopted in England and Australia. This approach is to explain the legal concept of unjust enrichment as a category of law. Like the legal conception of torts, it provides an organising conception for various different instances of liability. By the time of the *Restatement of the Law (Third) Restitution and Unjust Enrichment,*[55] the reporter, Professor Kull, referred to 'unjust enrichment as an independent basis of liability in common-law legal systems—comparable in this respect to a liability in contract or tort[s]…'.

In 1966, the opening pages of the first edition of Goff and Jones' *The Law of Restitution* seemed to suggest that unjust enrichment ought to be seen in the first manner, as a vague principle: '"[u]njust enrichment" is, simply, the name which is commonly given to the principle of justice'[56] and, 'in a search for unifying principle at this level we should not expect to find any precise "common formula", but rather an abstract proposition of justice.'[57] But the authors went on to say that '[t]he search for principle should not be confused with the definition of concepts'.[58] The legal concept of unjust enrichment was introduced two pages later:

> The principle of unjust enrichment is capable of elaboration. It presupposes three things: first, that the defendant has been enriched by the receipt of a benefit; secondly, that he has been so enriched at the plaintiff's expense; and thirdly, that it would be unjust to allow him to retain the benefit.[59]

It is this second approach which has now achieved dominance in England and Australia. In a passage which was later quoted by five justices of the High Court of Australia,[60] Deane J said that unjust enrichment is

> a unifying legal concept which explains why the law recognizes, in a variety of distinct categories of case, an obligation on the part of a defendant to make fair and just restitution for a benefit derived at the expense of a plaintiff and which assists in the determination, by the ordinary processes of legal reasoning, of the question whether the law should, in justice, recognize such an obligation in a new or developing category of case.[61]

The High Court of Australia unanimously confirmed this approach in *Bofinger v Kingsway Group Ltd*[62] explaining that '[t]he concept of unjust enrichment may provide a means for comparing and contrasting various categories of liability.' It may also 'assist in the determination by the ordinary processes of legal reasoning of the recognition of obligations in a new or developing category of case'.[63] As Deane J had said earlier,[64] the use of unjust enrichment is an 'informative generic label for purposes of classification, in Australian law' of a 'notion

[54] WA Seavey and AW Scott, 'Restitution' (1938) 54 *Law Quarterly Review* 29, 29.

[55] American Law Institute, *Restatement of the Law (Third) Restitution and Unjust Enrichment*, vol 1 (St Paul, Minn, American Law Institute Publishers, 2011) 3. The second *Restatement* was never completed.

[56] R Goff and G Jones, *The Law of Restitution* (London, Sweet & Maxwell, 1966) 11.

[57] ibid 12.

[58] ibid 12.

[59] ibid 14.

[60] *David Securities Pty Ltd v Commonwealth Bank of Australia* [1992] HCA 48, (1992) 175 CLR 353, 379 [46].

[61] *Pavey and Matthews Pty Ltd v Paul* [1987] HCA 5, (1987) 162 CLR 221, 256–57 [14].

[62] *Bofinger v Kingsway Group Ltd* [2009] HCA 44, (2009) 239 CLR 269 [88].

[63] ibid [89].

[64] *Muschinski v Dodds* [1985] HCA 78, (1985) 160 CLR 583, 617 [10].

underlying a variety of distinct categories of case … [in which] a benefit [is] derived at the expense of a plaintiff.' More recently, in *Equuscorp Pty Ltd v Haxton; Equuscorp Pty Ltd v Bassat; Equuscorp Pty Ltd v Cunningham's Warehouse Sales Pty Ltd,*[65] French CJ, Crennan and Kiefel JJ said that unjust enrichment 'has a taxonomical function referring to categories of cases in which the law allows recovery by one person of a benefit retained by another.'

The same approach is dominant in England. That approach was adopted in 2011, when the eighth edition of Goff and Jones' classic work, now edited by Professor Charles Mitchell, Professor Paul Mitchell and Dr Watterson, became known as *Goff and Jones' The Law of Unjust Enrichment*. At the start of the book[66] the passage above from Deane J is quoted. The editors of *Goff and Jones* explain that unjust enrichment is therefore 'an organising concept that groups decided authorities on the basis that they share a set of common features'.[67] The Australian and English approach to the legal concept of unjust enrichment focuses on the ordinary processes of analogical legal reasoning. That approach was pioneered by Goff and Jones, and the subject of an immensely detailed analysis by Birks.[68] It directed attention to three issues, and a fourth concerning defences:

(1) the defendant must be enriched;
(2) the enrichment must come at the expense of the plaintiff;
(3) the enrichment must be unjust; and
(4) a court should consider if any defences apply.

The 'generally accepted analysis' is that liability for unjust enrichment, subject to defences, is refined by a focus, before defences, upon the first three questions.[69] Each of these enquiries raises extremely difficult issues. For instance, the boundaries of what will count as an unjust factor are not fixed.[70] Examples of unjust factors were given by Lord Mansfield in *Moses v Macferlan*:

> money paid by mistake; or upon a consideration which happens to fail; or for money got through imposition, (express, or implied;) or extortion; or oppression …[71]

A quarter of a millennium later, although it is well established that liability in unjust enrichment requires the existence of an 'unjust factor',[72] it is difficult to find judicial recognition

[65] *Equuscorp Pty Ltd v Haxton; Equuscorp Pty Ltd v Bassat; Equuscorp Pty Ltd v Cunningham's Warehouse Sales Pty Ltd* [2012] HCA 7, (2012) 246 CLR 498 [30].

[66] C Mitchell, P Mitchell and S Watterson (eds), *Goff and Jones: The Law of Unjust Enrichment*, 8th edn (London, Sweet & Maxwell, 2011) 6–7 [1-08].

[67] ibid 7 [1-08].

[68] P Birks, *An Introduction to the Law of Restitution*, rev edn (Oxford, Oxford University Press, 1989) 21.

[69] See above n 8. Cf *Southage Pty Ltd v Vescovi* [2015] VSCA 117 [49] (the Court).

[70] *Equuscorp Pty Ltd v Haxton; Equuscorp Pty Ltd v Bassat; Equuscorp Pty Ltd v Cunningham's Warehouse Sales Pty Ltd* [2012] HCA 7, (2012) 246 CLR 498 [30] (French CJ, Crennan and Kiefel JJ).

[71] *Moses v Macferlan* (1760) 2 Burr 1005, 1012, 97 ER 676, 681.

[72] *David Securities Pty Ltd v Commonwealth Bank of Australia* [1992] HCA 48 [46]–[47], (1992) 175 CLR 353, 379 (Mason CJ, Deane, Toohey, Gaudron and McHugh JJ); *Wasada Pty Ltd v State Rail Authority of New South Wales (No 2)* [2003] NSWSC 987 [16] (Campbell J) citing K Mason and J Carter, *Restitution Law in Australia* (Sydney, Butterworths, 1995) 59–60; *Matland Holdings Pty Ltd v NTZ Pty Ltd* [2004] FCA 710 [171] (Kenny J); *Ideas Plus Investments Ltd v National Australia Bank Ltd* [2005] WASC 51 [81] (Commissioner Siopis SC); *SCI Operations Pty Ltd v Commonwealth* (1996) 69 FCR 346, 397 (Sackville J), an appeal to the High Court did not affect this obiter dictum: *Commonwealth v SCI Operations Pty Ltd* [1998] HCA 20, (1998) 192 CLR 285; *Farah Constructions Pty Ltd v Say-Dee Pty Ltd* [2007] HCA 22, (2007) 230 CLR 89 [156] (Gleeson CJ, Gummow, Callinan, Heydon and Crennan JJ); *Haxton v Equuscorp Pty Ltd (formerly Equus Financial Services Ltd) (ACN 006 012 344)* [2010]

of purely common law unjust factors beyond those in this list.[73] But these may be matters of detail with which the subject will evolve in the manner in which the common law has always evolved. Although we are approaching two centuries since the abolition of the forms of action, we still see pleadings, almost on a daily basis, which plead little more than 'money had and received', 'money paid to the defendant's use', '*quantum meruit*', or '*quantum valebat*'.

III. Taxonomy

A. The Controversy

As we explained above, in *Equuscorp Pty Ltd v Haxton; Equuscorp Pty Ltd v Bassat; Equuscorp Pty Ltd v Cunningham's Warehouse Sales Pty Ltd*,[74] French CJ, Crennan and Kiefel JJ said that unjust enrichment 'has a taxonomical function referring to categories of cases in which the law allows recovery by one person of a benefit retained by another.' This may have been a subtle endorsement of a theme inherent in the prolific writing by Peter Birks on the place of unjust enrichment within a taxonomy of private law.

Birks proposed a taxonomy of private law which separated legal events from legal responses and integrated equity and the common law claims into events of consent, wrongs, unjust enrichment and other events.[75] His scheme was represented diagrammatically as follows. The horizontal axis contains legal categories of events. The vertical axis reflects the different goals of remedies given by a court within each legal category.[76]

	Consent	Wrongs	Unjust enrichment	Other
Compensation			×	
Restitution	✓	✓	✓	✓
Punishment			×	
Other responses			×	

As Birks acknowledged, he was not the first to propose a taxonomy of private law. His work developed the classificatory schemes of the second-century Roman jurist Gaius and the

VSCA 1, (2010) 28 VR 499 [261] (Dodds-Streeton JA); *Chidiac v Matouk* [2010] NSWSC 386 [216] (Ward J); *Lahoud v Lahoud* [2010] NSWSC 1297 [152]–[164] (Ward J); *Crown in the Right of New South Wales v Anthony Gevaux* [2011] NSWSC 608 [96] (Ward J).

[73] The reference to 'illegality' as an unjust factor is mistaken for the reasons we explain in Ch 13. And we will see in Ch 10 that the taking of undue advantage is better treated as wrongdoing, not as part of the law of unjust enrichment.

[74] *Equuscorp Pty Ltd v Haxton; Equuscorp Pty Ltd v Bassat; Equuscorp Pty Ltd v Cunningham's Warehouse Sales Pty Ltd* [2012] HCA 7, (2012) 246 CLR 498 [30].

[75] Peter Birks has been compared with Friedrich Karl von Savigny and the modern Pandectist school. See J Getzler, 'Am I My Beneficiary's Keeper? Fusion and Loss-Based Fiduciary Remedies' in S Degeling and J Edelman (eds), *Equity in Commercial Law* (Sydney, Thomson LBC, 2005) ch 10.

[76] Birks labelled these axes 'events' and 'responses': P Birks, 'Definition and Division: A Mediation on *Institutes* 3.13' in P Birks (ed), *The Classification of Obligations* (Oxford, Clarendon Press, 1997) ch 1.

eighteenth-century jurist and judge, Sir William Blackstone. Gaius and Blackstone both wrote that the private law was comprised of contract, delict, quasi-contract and quasi-delict. Birks adapted this to a taxonomy of consent, wrongs, unjust enrichment and other events.

Birks' taxonomy of private law attracted furious debate. One objection, by Professor Hedley, was to dismiss Birks' work as a Panglossian ordered and formal law that envisages far too little discretion for the judge and which constrains legal innovation by reference to abstract concepts.[77] Similarly, in *Bofinger v Kingsway Group Ltd*,[78] a joint judgment of the High Court of Australia responded to Birks' views that there is no place for a separate taxonomical category of 'equity' and said that 'the experience of the law does not suggest debilitation by absence of a sufficiently rigid taxonomy in the application of equitable doctrines and remedies.'

This debate about taxonomy is at a high level of abstraction. It is abstracted from the issues arising on the facts of particular cases. But there are three important points which must be made. The first concerns the essential need that the law has for taxonomy. The second point is that taxonomy is a servant, not a master. Taxonomic reasoning assists in promoting understanding and analogies between cases, but it should not usually dictate a result. The third point concerns the need to include equitable actions within unjust enrichment and equitable remedies within restitutionary remedies.

B. The Need for a Taxonomy, and the Flaws in our Existing Taxonomy

It is impossible to argue rationally against *any* form of classification or taxonomy. The human mind operates by classifying and comparing. The rule of law requires that like events be treated alike. To have any real understanding of how the law fits together, we need a mental taxonomy of the law. Most law schools divide private law into a taxonomy which includes principal subjects of contract, torts, trusts, and property. There is also judicial support for the view that the three great sources of obligation in private law are contract, tort and trust.[79] These are incomplete taxonomies, but they are nevertheless taxonomies. Three points should be made about them.

First, in the history of private law obligations our existing taxonomies are very young indeed. Although the trust arose from the ashes of the executed use in the sixteenth and seventeenth centuries,[80] the modern law of contract did not completely emerge from its foundations of *assumpsit* until the mid-nineteenth century when, following publication of a translation of Pothier's *Traité des Obligations*,[81] key English cases such as *Hadley v Baxendale* and *Smith v Hughes*[82] developed the will theory of contract. And the law of tort,

[77] See S Hedley, 'Rival Taxonomies within the Law of Obligations: Is There a Problem?' in S Degeling and J Edelman (eds), *Equity in Commercial Law* (Sydney, Thomson LBC, 2005) ch 4.

[78] *Bofinger v Kingsway Group Ltd* [2009] HCA 44, (2009) 239 CLR 269 [93].

[79] *Roxborough v Rothmans of Pall Mall Australia Ltd* [2001] HCA 68, (2001) 208 CLR 516 [64] (Gummow J).

[80] For the evolution of the trust after the Statute of Uses 1535 (27 Henry VIII c 10), see JH Baker, *An Introduction to English Legal History*, 4th edn (London, Butterworths, 2002) 248–58, 280–97.

[81] W Evans, *A Treatise on the Law of Obligations or Contracts by M Pothier* (London, A Strahan, 1806).

[82] *Hadley v Baxendale* (1854) 9 Ex 241, 156 ER 145; *Smith v Hughes* (1871) LR 6 QB 597. See AWB Simpson, 'Innovation in Nineteenth Century Contract Law' in AWB Simpson, *Legal Theory and Legal History. Essays on the Common Law* (London, Hambledon Press, 1987) 171–202, and DJ Ibbetson, *A Historical Introduction to the Law of Obligations* (Oxford, Oxford University Press, 1999) chs 12 and 13.

in the form we understand it today, did not emerge until the mid-twentieth century after *Donoghue v Stevenson*[83] began the process of generalising a duty of care. Most relevantly for this book, unjust enrichment only emerged from the miscellany of other legal obligations in 1954 in Canada,[84] in 1987 in Australia,[85] and in 1991 in England.[86]

Secondly, the common taxonomies of our private law are neither continuous nor complete. They are not continuous because they include contract alongside trust. But a contract could be the source of a trust. Two persons can contract in terms which create a trust. The taxonomies are also incomplete because there are many obligations which arise other than by contract, tortious act, or creation of a trust. Statute is a prolific example: for instance, the obligation to pay tax. Another example is a unilateral bond or a letter of credit. In relation to the former, after the decline of covenant this was one of the most common obligations. The obligation was created by deed, which commonly recited, in Latin, 'Know all men etc. that I, *AB*, am firmly bound to *CD* in £*n* to be paid at Michaelmas next following.'[87]

Thirdly, the existing category of 'torts' has its boundaries drawn in an irrational place. The inclusion only of civil wrongs arising at common law, and the exclusion of civil wrongs arising in equity, is irrational. Why should the law of torts be confined to civil wrongs whose jurisdictional origin is common law rather than equity? There is no rational answer to this rhetorical question. For instance, it has been recognised for more than a century that the common law tort of deceit is identical to the equitable wrong of deceit. As Lord Chelmsford explained of deceit in equity, 'It is precisely analogous to the common law action for deceit. There can be no doubt that Equity exercises a concurrent jurisdiction in cases of this description, and the same principles applicable to them must prevail both at Law and in Equity.'[88]

C. Weaknesses in Taxonomic Reasoning

There are significant weaknesses in Birks' taxonomy. Most of these weaknesses were recognised by Birks. It is sufficient to focus only on three. First, to the eye of a scientific taxonomer, Birks' taxonomy appears to leave little discretion for the judge and to constrain legal innovation by reference to abstract, intangible concepts.[89] It was, perhaps, for this reason that in *Bofinger v Kingsway Group Ltd*,[90] a joint judgment of the High Court of Australia said, in relation to the absence of a category for 'equity' that 'the experience of the law does not suggest debilitation by absence of a sufficiently rigid taxonomy in the application of equitable doctrines and remedies.' Another joint judgment of the High Court subsequently described Birks' approach to the law concerning restitution of unjust enrichment as 'a mentality in which considerations of ideal taxonomy prevail over a pragmatic approach to legal

[83] *Donoghue v Stevenson* [1932] AC 562.

[84] *Deglman v Guaranty Trust Co of Canada* [1954] SCR 725.

[85] *Pavey & Matthews Pty Ltd v Paul* [1987] HCA 5, (1987) 162 CLR 221; *David Securities Pty Ltd v Commonwealth Bank of Australia* [1992] HCA 48, (1992) 175 CLR 353.

[86] *Lipkin Gorman v Karpnale Ltd* [1991] 2 AC 548.

[87] JH Baker, *An Introduction to English Legal History*, 4th edn (London, Butterworths, 2002) 323.

[88] *Peek v Gurney* (1873) LR 6 HL 377, 393.

[89] See S Hedley, 'Rival Taxonomies within the Law of Obligations: Is There a Problem?' in S Degeling and J Edelman (eds), *Equity in Commercial Law* (Sydney, Thomson LBC, 2005) ch 4.

[90] *Bofinger v Kingsway Group Ltd* [2009] HCA 44, (2009) 239 CLR 269 [93] (the Court).

development'.[91] As Associate Professor Low has said, the difficulty of a taxonomy of a social science is that there are no observable facts by which a classification can be tested and the classification is not independent of its subject matter.[92] For instance, in the original edition of *Systema Naturae*, Linnaeus misclassified a whale as a fish. But when this misclassification was corrected based on observable facts, the reclassification did not physically affect any whales. In contrast, Birks' taxonomy of law was intended to affect its subject matter directly. For instance, as we explain below, the classification of actions in equity for actual fraud as 'wrongs' to be treated alike with common law actions for deceit is a classification which suggests that the actions should be aligned.

A second, and related, weakness in Birks' taxonomy, which Justice Leeming has described,[93] is the absence of any role for statute. Legislation need not, and does not always, respect taxonomic boundaries. Legislation and common law are inextricably intertwined. A coherent system of law cannot treat the two (in Lord Justice Beatson's metaphor) as 'oil and water'.[94] The common law and statute law 'coalesce in one legal system'.[95] As Justice Gageler has observed, 'The meaning of a statutory text is also informed, and reinformed, by the need for the courts to apply the text each time, not in isolation, but as part of the totality of the common law and statute law as it then exists'.[96]

A third weakness in Birks' taxonomy is the absence of a number of internal boundaries which are essential markers in many areas of private law. One boundary is between personal rights and property rights. Birks' taxonomy did not differentiate them. So an obligation to transfer title to, say, a car is an obligation created by consent,[97] but the property right that the purchaser obtains to the car is generated by a different and subsequent event of conveyance. The latter event generating the purchaser's property right needs to be classified separately as either arising by consent (even though the conveyance is something that the vendor is legally obliged to do) or as an 'other event'. Another internal boundary which is concealed by Birks' taxonomy is the distinction between primary and secondary rights.[98] For instance, Birks' taxonomy treats wrongs and unjust enrichment as the same level of event. But the law only recognises a wrong if it has already recognised a pre-existing duty. Furthermore, Birks' taxonomy of private law has no place for a person's duty not to assault another, not to commit trespass, not to defame another, and so on. The only 'event' which gives rise to those rights is a person's birth. Birks was left to say that these fundamental rights are 'superstructural' to his taxonomy. A final internal boundary which is not recognised in Birks' taxonomy is the boundary between different types of right: claim rights, immunities,

[91] *Farah Constructions Pty Ltd v Say-Dee Pty Ltd* [2007] HCA 22, (2007) 230 CLR 89 [154].

[92] K Low, 'The Use and Abuse of Taxonomy' (2009) 29 *Legal Studies* 355, 359.

[93] M Leeming, 'Theories and Principles Underlying the Development of the Common Law' (2013) 36 *University of New South Wales Law Journal* 1002, 1028.

[94] J Beatson, 'Has the Common Law a Future?' (1997) 56 *Cambridge Law Journal* 291, 308.

[95] *R v Secretary of State for the Home Department, Ex parte Pierson* [1997] UKHL 37, [1998] AC 539, 589 (Lord Steyn); WMC Gummow, *Change and Continuity: Statute, Equity, and Federalism* (Oxford, Oxford University Press, 1999) 1.

[96] S Gageler, 'Common Law Statutes and Judicial Legislation: Statutory Interpretation as a Common Law Process' (2011) 37(2) *Monash University Law Review* 1, 1–2.

[97] See discussion in R Stevens, *Torts and Rights* (Oxford, Oxford University Press, 2007) 285–86.

[98] Eg P Birks, 'Equity in the Modern Law: An Exercise in Taxonomy' (1996) 26 *University of Western Australia Law Review* 1, 10.

privileges, and powers. The different nature and character of those 'rights' is essential to understand their interaction as a recent decision of the High Court of Australia has vividly illustrated.[99]

There is sometimes a fourth argument made against Birks' taxonomy. This fourth argument should be rejected. It is the argument that the taxonomy is drawn from the long-distant past of Roman law with no contemporary place in the law. This misunderstands both the contribution and the significance of Roman law to our law today. Not only is Roman law the source of much of our private law, but it continues to have direct influence. As Mr Lee has observed,[100] Roman law was relied upon in three of the most important private law decisions given by the House of Lords in the last 15 years: in 2001,[101] 2002[102] and 2007.[103] In the first case, the late, brilliant, Lord Rodger drew from the conflicting views of Ulpian and Julian in relation to the complex question of causation in the law of torts. In the second case, Lord Hoffmann and Lord Hope of Craighead drew from Roman law the principles concerning *confusio* (and the writings of Iavolenus and Ulpian) to try to resolve the question of tracing of mixed funds. In the third, Baroness Hale referred to the development in Roman law of the *vindicatio* action in her revolutionary dissent concerning whether conversion as a tort extended to intangibles. To put the influence of these Roman scholars in perspective, it would be as if something that one of us had written today on a single point of law, and published extrajudicially, was relied upon as an important authority by a court in the year 3800.

D. The Category of Unjust Enrichment is Independent of Civil Wrongs or Contract

We do not suggest that the taxonomy proposed by Birks is ideal. As we have seen, there are difficulties with it. But, one benefit of Birks' taxonomy is that it illustrates powerfully the independence of the law of unjust enrichment. In particular, one of the most fundamental points in this chapter is to emphasise that the law of unjust enrichment is independent of the law of civil wrongs (including torts) or the law of contract.

Imagine a situation in which a victim pays $100 to a fraudster as a result of a fraudulent misrepresentation. The victim could bring an action against the fraudster for compensation *or* for restitution of the $100 based on the tort of deceit. Alternatively, the victim could bring an action against the fraudster for restitution of unjust enrichment arising from the victim's mistake in his payment to the fraudster. That is the nature of concurrent liability.[104]

[99] For an important recent example see *Western Australia v Brown* [2014] HCA 8, (2014) 88 ALJR 461. There is a basic difference between freedoms from liability which almost never conflict (eg from liability for trespass to minerals by a mining licence and freedom from trespass to land by native title) and competing claim rights or claim rights and freedoms (eg to 'exclusive' possession) which almost always do and require one to give way to the other.

[100] J Lee, 'Confusio: Reference to Roman Law in the House of Lords and the Development of English Private Law' (2009) 5 *Roman Legal Tradition* 24. See also *SZOXP v Minister for Immigration and Border Protection* [2015] FCAFC 69 [47].

[101] *Fairchild v Glenhaven Funeral Services* [2002] UKHL 22, [2003] 1 AC 32.

[102] *Foskett v McKeown* [2000] UKHL 29, [2001] 1 AC 102.

[103] *OBG Ltd v Allan* [2007] UKHL 21, [2008] 1 AC 1.

[104] *Hill v Van Erp* [1997] HCA 9, (1997) 188 CLR 159, 231 (Gummow J).

In many cases, courts have identified whether a particular action is for unjust enrichment or for wrongdoing. As we will see in Part II of this book, the highest courts in Australia and England have explained that claims for restitution based on mistake, duress, undue influence, and failure of consideration are independent of wrongdoing.[105] These are examples of claims in unjust enrichment.

Unlike unjust enrichment, the common element of wrongs is that they are a breach of duty.[106] Even when restitution is the remedy awarded for the wrong, the action is based on the wrong—the breach of duty—not the unjust enrichment of the defendant. An example is *Yakamia Dairy Pty Ltd v Wood*,[107] an unequivocal case of restitution for wrongdoing. The defendants committed the tort of trespass by wrongfully depasturing cattle upon land belonging to the plaintiff. To a claim for trespass to land, the District Court of Western Australia held that the plaintiff had suffered no financial loss as a result of the trespass and could therefore recover no substantial damages. The plaintiff appealed to the Full Court of the Supreme Court of Western Australia and the court unanimously held that a 'reasonable remuneration' should be awarded to represent the value of the use of the land *wrongfully* gained by the defendant from the plaintiff's assets.[108] It was clear that the wrong of trespass was central to the action for restitution. Moving from torts to civil wrongs in equity, in *Farah Constructions Pty Ltd v Say-Dee Pty Ltd*,[109] a joint judgment of the High Court of Australia emphasised that principles concerning breach of fiduciary duty have 'been said to be foreign to unjust enrichment notions because the unjust factors are commonly concerned with vitiation or qualification of the intention of a claimant'. Similarly, in England, in a case where the Court of Appeal recognised that restitution was available for a breach of contract the Court emphasised that the action was not for unjust enrichment. Lord Justice Mance said in the leading judgment:

> the law gives effect to the instinctive reaction that, whether or not the appellant would have been better off if the wrong had not been committed, the wrongdoer ought not *to gain an advantage for free*, and should make some reasonable recompense.[110]

More recently, the difference between restitution for wrongdoing and restitution for unjust enrichment was emphasised by Lord Nicholls in *Sempra Metals Ltd v Inland Revenue Commissioners*.[111] It was also used by Lord Clarke in *Benedetti v Sawiris*,[112] who

[105] *David Securities Pty Ltd v Commonwealth Bank of Australia* 1992] HCA 48, (1992) 175 CLR 353; *Australian Financial Services and Leasing Pty Ltd v Hills Industries Ltd* [2014] HCA 14, (2014) 88 ALJR 552 [83] (Hayne, Crennan, Kiefel, Bell & Keane JJ); *Benedetti v Sawiris* [2013] UKSC 50, [2014] AC 938 [175] (Lord Neuberger).

[106] See J Edelman, *Gain-Based Damages* (Oxford, Hart Publishing, 2002) ch 2; P Birks, 'The Concept of a Civil Wrong' in D Owen (ed), *Philosophical Foundations of Tort Law* (Oxford, Clarendon Press, 1995); P Benson, 'The Basis for Excluding Liability for Economic Loss in Tort Law' in D Owen (ed), *Philosophical Foundations of Tort Law* (Oxford, Clarendon Press, 1995) 427; N McBride, 'Duties of Care: Do They Really Exist' (2004) 24 *Oxford Journal of Legal Studies* 417; SR Perry, 'Protected Interests and Undertakings in the Law of Negligence' (1992) 42 *The University of Toronto Law Journal* 247; BC Zipursky, 'Rights, Wrongs and Recourse in the Law of Torts' (1998) 51 *Vanderbilt Law Review* 1. In *Stubbings v Webb* [1993] AC 498, the House of Lords accepted that a breach of duty was the basis of a tort but held that the phrase in the Limitation Act 1939 was restricted to certain non-intentional torts because of its juxtaposition in a sentence with negligence and nuisance.

[107] *Yakamia Dairy Pty Ltd v Wood* [1976] WAR 57.

[108] ibid 58 (Jackson CJ).

[109] *Farah Constructions Pty Ltd v Say-Dee Pty Ltd* [2007] HCA 22, (2007) 230 CLR 89 [150].

[110] *Experience Hendrix LLC v PPX Enterprises Inc* [2003] EWCA Civ 323, [2003] 1 All ER (Comm) 830 [26] (emphasis added).

[111] *Sempra Metals Ltd v Inland Revenue Commissioners* [2007] UKHL 34, [2008] 1 AC 561, 606 [116].

[112] *Benedetti v Sawiris* [2013] UKSC 50; [2014] 1 AC 938, 959 [24] (Lord Clarke).

emphasised the danger of analogising between cases of restitution for wrongdoing to cases of restitution for unjust enrichment. Difficulty also arises in the case of actions that have not been conclusively classified as an action for unjust enrichment or an action based on wrongdoing and which might be *capable* of being characterised as either. For example, consider an action for restitution of the value of a gift by a plaintiff who was subject to undue influence in the making of the gift. Is this an action based on the wrong of breaching a duty not to unduly influence another? Or is it an action based on unjust enrichment, as Lord Neuberger has suggested?[113] We will see in Chapter 10 that although the action for undue influence is best seen as part of the law of unjust enrichment, there is strong support for the concurrent recognition of a wrong of abuse of influence or wrongful influence. That equitable wrong is very similar to, and might ultimately be submerged within, the equitable wrong of unconscionable dealing which requires 'proof of a predatory state of mind'.[114]

E. Unjust Enrichment Includes Equitable Actions

We will see in Chapter 3 that the remedy of restitution was available in law as well as in equity, and that it makes no sense to separate restitution at law from restitution in equity. The same is true of the event which generates those rights. Where the claim for restitution is sought because of unjust enrichment it should not, and does not, matter whether the unjust enrichment arises at common law (based on a common law unjust factor) or in equity (based on an equitable unjust factor). Indeed, when the *Restatement of the Law of Restitution* was published in 1937, it treated claims for unjust enrichment in equity in the same way as unjust enrichment claims at common law. The Reporters emphasised at the start that '[t]he principles by which a person is entitled to restitution are the same whether the proceeding is one at law or in equity'.[115] Commenting on the *Restatement* in 1938, Sir Percy Winfield said that

> it is immaterial to the draftsmen [of the *Restatement*] whether the remedy be at law or in equity provided it be for unjust enrichment ... It may be a dreadful shock to the pure common lawyer and to the pure equity lawyer to find themselves compelled to embrace each other, but it is high time that they should realize that there is but one principle in this branch of the system ...[116]

Lord Denning made the same point in 1948, stating that 'This principle [of unjust enrichment] has been evolved by the courts of law and equity side by side ... It is no longer appropriate, however, to draw a distinction between law and equity.'[117] The same approach was advocated by Goff and Jones in 1966,[118] and, by 2002, was elevated to the second sentence

[113] ibid 938 [175] (Lord Neuberger). See also *Hart v Burbidge* [2014] EWCA Civ 992 [43] (Vos LJ; Richards and Black LJJ agreeing).

[114] *Kakavas v Crown Melbourne Ltd* [2013] HCA 25, (2013) 250 CLR 392 [161] (the Court).

[115] American Law Institute, *Restatement of the Law of Restitution: Quasi Contracts and Constructive Trusts* (St Paul, Minn, American Law Institute, 1937) 4. The Reporters qualify this statement by saying that sometimes there were limitations at law which did not exist in equity and sometimes equity did not allow claims because they were adequate at law.

[116] P Winfield, 'The American *Restatement* of the Law of Restitution' (1938) 54 *Law Quarterly Review* 529, 532. See also A Kull, 'James Barr Ames and the Early Modern History of Unjust Enrichment' (2005) 25 *Oxford Journal of Legal Studies* 297.

[117] *Nelson v Larholt* [1948] 1 KB 339, 343.

[118] R Goff and G Jones, *The Law of Restitution* (London, Sweet & Maxwell, 1966).

of their text.[119] In 1985 Professor Birks also argued that 'By whatever name they are to be known, restitutionary rights *in personam* cannot continue to be driven into separate categories according to their jurisdictional origin.'[120]

This approach to unjust enrichment, including both common law and equity, was implicitly taken in a joint judgment of five justices of the High Court in *David Securities v Commonwealth Bank of Australia*, where their Honours referred to 'compulsion' (common law) and 'undue influence' (equity) interchangeably when speaking of liability for unjust enrichment.[121] In England, the Court of Appeal has said that unjust enrichment is the 'juridical basis of the grant of relief in respect of transactions impugned by undue influence'.[122] Another example is the joint judgment of three justices in *Roxborough v Rothmans of Pall Mall Ltd*,[123] which referred to cases of failure of consideration in equity as well as common law. The implicit justification for treating equitable doctrine as part of unjust enrichment was made explicit in 1992, less than four months after the decision in *David Securities*, in a joint judgment in *Baltic Shipping Co v Dillon*, by Deane and Dawson JJ:

> [I]n a modern context where common law and equity are fused with equity prevailing, the artificial constraints imposed by the old forms of action can, unless they reflect coherent principle, be disregarded where they impede the principled enunciation and development of the law. In particular, the notions of good conscience, which both the common law and equity recognized as the underlying rationale of the law of unjust enrichment, now dictate that, in applying the relevant doctrines of law and equity, regard be had to matters of substance rather than technical form.[124]

Another example of the obvious need to assimilate both common law and equity in the law of unjust enrichment is the unjust factor of mistake, which is the most common circumstance in which claims for unjust enrichment are brought. A claim for restitution of a mistaken payment or a mistaken transfer of a chattel or land was historically often brought at common law. But it could also be brought in equity. Equity always had a jurisdiction concurrent with the common law to provide restitution in cases of mistake. In *Bingham v Bingham*[125] the defendant purported to sell to the plaintiff an estate which the plaintiff already owned. Both parties were mistaken and the agreement was void. The plaintiff brought an action in equity seeking, inter alia, restitution of his purchase price. The Lord Chancellor held that 'there was a plain mistake, such as the court was warranted to relieve against, and not to suffer the defendant to run away with the money in consideration of the sale of an estate, to which he had no right'.[126] *Bingham v Bingham* is part of a long line of authority.[127] As Professor Ibbetson observed, although this equitable jurisdiction in relation to mistake was most commonly exercised where reconveyance of land was sought, this

[119] G Jones (ed), *Goff and Jones: The Law of Restitution*, 6th edn (London, Sweet & Maxwell, 2002) 3: 'Restitutionary claims are to be found in equity as well as at law'.

[120] P Birks, *An Introduction to the Law of Restitution*, rev edn (Oxford, Oxford University Press, 1989) 33.

[121] *David Securities Pty Ltd v Commonwealth Bank of Australia* [1992] HCA 48, (1992) 175 CLR 353, 374 [36].

[122] *Hart v Burbidge* [2014] EWCA Civ 992 [43] (Vos LJ; Richards and Black LJJ agreeing). See also *Benedetti v Sawiris* [2013] UKSC 50, [2014] AC 938 [175] (Lord Neuberger).

[123] *Roxborough v Rothmans of Pall Mall Australia Ltd* [2001] HCA 68, (2001) 208 CLR 516 [16].

[124] *Baltic Shipping Co v Dillon* [1993] HCA 4, (1993) 176 CLR 344, 376 [8].

[125] *Bingham v Bingham* (1748) 1 Ves Sen 126, 27 ER 934.

[126] *Bingham v Bingham* (1748) 1 Ves Sen 126, 127, 27 ER 934, 934.

[127] *Walker v Armstrong* (1856) 8 De GM & G 531, 44 ER 495; *Re Walton's Settlement, Walton v Peirson* [1922] 2 Ch 509 (Ch); *Meadows v Meadows* (1853) 16 Beav 401, 51 ER 833; *Ellis v Ellis* [1909] 1 Ch 618 (Ch); *Phillipson v Kerry* (1863) 11 WR 1034; *Gibbon v Mitchell* [1990] 3 All ER 338, 341–43; *Dent v Dent* [1996] 1 All ER 659, 669.

narrow circumstance 'was not the consequence of any formal limitation'.[128] In one case involving a claim for restitution of money paid under a mistaken belief that there was an obligation to do so, Hall VC said that 'Nothing can be clearer than this ... that the [equity] Court would, even in the case of a completed contract, give relief against a common mistake in the same way as it would against fraud'.[129]

There are two arguments that are sometimes advanced against assimilating any equitable action into a category with the common law (as unjust enrichment purports to do). The first argument was stated in *Re Hallett's Estate; Knatchbull v Hallett*, by Sir George Jessel MR:

> [I]t must not be forgotten that the rules of Courts of Equity are not, like the rules of the Common Law, supposed to have been established from time immemorial. It is perfectly well known that they have been established from time to time—altered, improved, and refined from time to time. In many cases we know the names of the Chancellors who invented them.[130]

In other words, equity and common law must be treated separately because they are of a fundamentally different nature: the common law has been established from 'time immemorial', whereas the body of rules that comprise of 'equity' is made by judges and changed from time to time. This argument historically had the support of Sir William Blackstone[131] and Sir Matthew Hale.[132] But the notion of a common law which has been established from time immemorial has very few modern supporters.[133] In *Kleinwort Benson Ltd v Lincoln County Council*,[134] all Law Lords sitting in the House of Lords rejected this declaratory theory of the common law. Lord Goff referred to the famous speech given by Lord Reid in 1974 that this declaratory theory is a 'fairy tale':

> There was a time when it was thought almost indecent to suggest that judges make law—they only declare it. Those with a taste for fairy tales seem to have thought that in some Aladdin's cave there is hidden the Common Law in all its splendour and that on a judge's appointment there descends on him knowledge of the magic words Open Sesame. Bad decisions are given when the judge has muddled the pass word and the wrong door opens. But we do not believe in fairy tales any more.[135]

A second argument sometimes made in favour of treating the common law and equity separately is that there are different value systems that underpin the rights which arise at common law from those which arise in equity. There are different versions of this argument. One version, supported by Sir Anthony Mason and Justice Gummow, is that the jurisprudence of equity, deriving from the court of Chancery, involves a flexibility and discretion in application which is not present at common law.[136] A different version of

[128] DJ Ibbetson, *A Historical Introduction to the Law of Obligations* (Oxford, Oxford University Press, 1999) 273–74.

[129] *Jones v Clifford* (1876) 3 Ch D 779, 792.

[130] *Re Hallett's Estate; Knatchbull v Hallett* (1880) 13 Ch D 696 (CA), 710.

[131] W Blackstone, *Commentaries on the Laws of England* (first published 1765–69, Chicago, The University of Chicago Press, 1979) vol 1, 17 and vol 3, 49.

[132] M Hale, *The History of the Common Law of England* (London, 1713).

[133] See K Hayne, 'Letting Justice Be Done Without the Heavens Falling' (2001) 27 *Monash University Law Review* 12, 17.

[134] *Kleinwort Benson Ltd v Lincoln City Council* [1998] UKHL 38, [1999] 2 AC 349.

[135] JSC Reid, 'The Judge as Lawmaker' (1972) 12 *Journal: Society of Public Teachers of Law* 22, 22.

[136] WMC Gummow, *Change and Continuity: Statute, Equity, and Federalism* (Oxford, Oxford University Press, 1999) 53–54, quoting from A Mason 'The Place of Equity and Equitable Remedies in the Contemporary Common Law World' (1994) 110 *Law Quarterly Review* 238, 239. See also A Mason, 'Fusion' in S Degeling and J Edelman (eds), *Equity in Commercial Law* (Sydney, Thomson LBC, 2005) ch 1; P Millett, 'Equity's Place in the Law of

this argument is made by Professor Smith who rejects discretion or conscience as material differences between equity and common law but argues that a different set of moral norms nevertheless underlie equitable principles.[137] These different norms are said to be exemplified by equity's unique conversion of personal rights into property rights (a moral norm he describes as respect for other people's obligations) and the justiciability of motive in equity. Smith argues that these two unique characteristics lie at the core of equity's central institution of the trust.

Strong voices speak against either version of the argument that equity is based on a different morality from common law.[138] Further, even if either version of the argument were accepted, it does not require rejection of the integration of equitable unjust factors into the category of unjust enrichment. This is because even those that espouse this view do not dispute that equity and the common law have a history of integration and mutual learning and can develop concurrently or fuse by analogy.[139] Coherence in legal doctrine is hindered by the notion that, within the law of obligations, different doctrines asking the same question could develop based on different moral norms.

The conclusion that the category of unjust enrichment spans both equity and common law should be unassailable. Even in Australia where the antagonists to this view speak loudest, the view is supported by some judgments in decisions of the High Court of Australia. The view is soundly based in historical decisions of the courts of Chancery which allowed restitution for identical reasons (such as mistake) as the common law. It is a requirement dictated by the need for coherence in the law. And it draws strength from the underlying principle of justice that like cases must be treated alike. In the various chapters which consider unjust factors in this book, the operation of unjust factors in equity and common law are considered together.

IV. Unjust Enrichment and Unconscionable Conduct

One school of thought that might be thought to oppose the recognition of unjust enrichment as a distinct category of claim alongside categories such as tort (wrongs) or contract argues that all the instances of 'unjust enrichment' are better described as 'unconscionability'. In *Roxborough v Rothmans of Pall Mall Australia Ltd,*[140] Gummow J adopted extrajudicial remarks of Finn J and said that 'the concept of unjust enrichment may "contrive legal

Commerce' (1998) 114 *Law Quarterly Review* 214, 216. See also P Finn, 'Equitable Doctrine and Discretion in Remedies' in WR Cornish, R Nolan, J O'Sullivan and G Virgo (eds), *Restitution: Past, Present and Future: Essays in Honour of Gareth Jones* (Oxford, Hart Publishing, 1998) 267 *et seq.*

[137] L Smith, 'Fusion and Tradition' in S Degeling and J Edelman (eds), *Equity in Commercial Law* (Sydney, Thomson LBC, 2005) ch 2

[138] See, for instance K Mason, 'Fusion: Fallacy, Future or Finished?' in S Degeling and J Edelman (eds), *Equity in Commercial Law* (Sydney, Thomson LBC, 2005) ch 3; P Birks, 'Equity, Conscience and Unjust Enrichment' (1999) 23 *Melbourne University Law Review* 1; A Burrows, 'We Do This at Common Law but That in Equity' (2002) 22 *Oxford Journal of Legal Studies* 1, and also A Burrows, 'Remedial Coherence and Punitive Damages in Equity' in S Degeling and J Edelman (eds), *Equity in Commercial Law* (Sydney, Thomson LBC, 2005) ch 15.

[139] See J Edelman and S Degeling, 'Introduction' in S Degeling and J Edelman (eds), *Equity in Commercial Law* (Sydney, Thomson LBC, 2005).

[140] *Roxborough v Rothmans of Pall Mall Australia Ltd* [2001] HCA 68, (2001) 208 CLR 516, 543 [70].

analysis"' and that it 'is capable of concealing rather than revealing why the law would want to attribute a responsibility to one party to provide satisfaction to the other.' For this reason, his Honour argued, the concept of unconscionable conduct has achieved greater currency in Australian law than unjust enrichment.[141] Again, in *Australian Financial Services and Leasing Pty Ltd v Hills Industries Ltd*, Hayne, Crennan, Kiefel, Bell and Keane JJ said of a submission that relief should be refused because a defendant had been 'disenriched':

> This approach seeks to give effect to an understanding of unjust enrichment as a principle of direct application, which operates by measuring the extent of enrichment or, where a defence of change of position is invoked, the extent of disenrichment subsequent to that receipt. Such a 'principle' does not govern the resolution of this case because the concept of unjust enrichment is not the basis of restitutionary relief in Australian law.[142]

There are three ways in which these remarks might be understood. First, they might be thought to be a suggestion that restitution can arise from obligations other than unjust enrichment so that to accept a principle of unjust enrichment that explains all restitutionary obligations can contrive legal analysis. As Gummow J earlier explained, there is a need for 'caution in judicial acceptance of any all-embracing theory of restitutionary rights and remedies founded upon a notion of "unjust enrichment"'.[143] This is undoubtedly correct. Restitutionary remedies can indeed be awarded for reasons other than unjust enrichment. Further, the remedy of money had and received was not always a restitutionary remedy. It was originally based on a genuine promise and the formula was borrowed from the formula of account against a receiver: as a receiver of money an agent always impliedly promised to be accountable for the money.[144] However, the nature and intention behind the remarks appears to go further than merely the point that restitution can be awarded for reasons other than unjust enrichment.

A second manner in which the remarks might be understood is as a rejection of the category of unjust enrichment altogether. In *Vickery v JJP Custodians*[145] Austin J said that '[the recognition of unjust enrichment] remains the position in Australia in 2002, although Gummow J's judgment in *Rothmans* could be taken to suggest a preference for equitable concepts such as the concept of unconscionability'. On this argument all equitable actions form a single category in which the 'overriding aim ... is the prevention of unconscionable behaviour'.[146] To these equitable actions could be added those common law actions such as for money had and received which Gummow J, borrowing from Lord Redesdale, described as equitable in nature.[147] On this view, equitable actions, together with those common law

[141] P Finn, 'Equitable Doctrine and Discretion in Remedies' in WR Cornish, R Nolan, J O'Sullivan and G Virgo (eds), *Restitution: Past, Present and Future: Essays in Honour of Gareth Jones* (Oxford, Hart Publishing, 1998) 252.

[142] *Australian Financial Services and Leasing Pty Ltd v Hills Industries Ltd* [2014] HCA 14, (2014) 253 CLR 560 [78].

[143] *Roxborough v Rothmans of Pall Mall Australia Ltd* [2001] HCA 68, (2001) 208 CLR 516 [72].

[144] *Retchford v Spurlinge* (1591) B & M 500; *Wilkins v Wilkins* (1689) Comb 149, 1 Salk 9.

[145] *Vickery v JJP Custodians* [2002] NSWSC 782, (2002) 11 BPR 20,333 [134].

[146] *Australian Competition and Consumer Commission v CG Berbatis Holdings Pty Ltd* [2000] FCA 2, (2000) 96 FCR 491 [14] (French J). See also *Legione v Hateley* [1983] HCA 11, (1983) 152 CLR 406, 444 [29]; *Thompson v Palmer* [1933] HCA 61, (1933) 49 CLR 507, 537; *Commonwealth v Verwayen* [1990] HCA 39, (1990) 170 CLR 394, 441 [16].

[147] *Roxborough v Rothmans of Pall Mall Australia Ltd* [2001] HCA 68, (2001) 208 CLR 516 [98]–[99]. See *Spect v Spect* (1891) 26 P 203, 205. Further instances of the common law imitating or adopting equity procedures are given in M Macnair, *The Law of Proof in Early Modern Equity* (Berlin, Duncker & Humblot, 1999) 278–79.

actions that are based on equitable notions, should be classified together as part of a category of 'unconscionability' rather than separated into categories such as unjust enrichment, wrongs or actions to enforce consensual obligations. The Victorian Court of Appeal has taken a similar approach to the remarks in cases like *Roxborough* and *Hills Industries* and suggested that a 'liability to make restitution' does not depend on establishing matters such as an unjust factor, enrichment, or that the enrichment was at the expense of the plaintiff.[148] But, in that case, the Court of Appeal in the next paragraph emphasised that restitution required that a factor such as mistake be established.[149] Later, the Court of Appeal turned to the enrichment received and its valuation.[150] Even if the labels of 'unjust factor', 'enrichment', or 'at the expense of' were to be abandoned, it is inevitable that a court will ask the same questions to which those labels direct attention.

A third possibility, and one which we favour, is that the comments extracted above were concerned to emphasise the nature of unjust enrichment as a category which requires consideration of underlying principles at a lower level of generality. So, by comparison with the category of torts, a plaintiff cannot plead that a defendant is liable for having committed a 'tort'. 'Torts' describes the category not the action (which might be assault, battery, conversion etc).[151] Further, as we will see in Chapter 6, one of the enquiries at the lower level of generality is into whether an enrichment is 'unjust' and this enquiry requires consideration of whether there is a juristic reason to retain the enrichment. Sometimes that question is expressed as whether it is 'unconscionable to retain' the enrichment.

This debate about the use of 'unjust enrichment' as a conceptual category is not a new debate. The path of using 'unconscionability' as the category was almost taken at the inception of the subject. But that path was abandoned. Ames himself in the first edition of the *Harvard Law Review* wrote of 'grounds of obvious justice, [by which] it is unconscientious for him to retain [an enrichment] at another's expense'.[152] But in his famous article the following year, 'unconscientious' was dropped in favour of 'unjust', as Pomponius had preferred. The same approach was taken by the High Court of Australia in *David Securities* in the judgment of Mason CJ, Deane, Toohey, Gaudron and McHugh JJ.[153]

There are three reasons why it would be a misstep for the law to adopt unconscionable conduct as the foundational basis for liability which has now been recognised as part of the law of unjust enrichment.

First, it is undoubtedly right that, on its own, and as a general principle, unjust enrichment is indeed vague and capable of concealing the nature of liability rather than revealing it. Indeed, for that reason the Australian and English approach to unjust enrichment (described above) is far more preferable to the United States approach. The conceptual four-fold inquiry in Australian, Canadian, New Zealand and English law has the purpose of *revealing* the nature of the liability.[154] But the substitution of 'unconscionable' for 'unjust enrichment' would be a significant step back for the law. As we will see in Chapter 6,

[148] *Southage Pty Ltd v Vescovi* [2015] VSCA 117, (2015) 321 ALR 383 [49] (the Court).
[149] ibid [50] (the Court).
[150] ibid [84] (the Court).
[151] *Lampson (Australia) Pty Ltd v Fortescue Metals Group Ltd (No 3)* [2014] WASC 162 [45]–[55].
[152] J Ames, 'Purchase for Value Without Notice' (1887) 1 *Harvard Law Review* 1, 3.
[153] *David Securities Pty Ltd v Commonwealth Bank of Australia* [1992] HCA 48, (1992) 175 CLR 353, 378 [45].
[154] P Birks, 'Failure of Consideration and Its Place on the Map' (2002) 2(1) *Oxford University Commonwealth Law Journal* 1, 10.

'unjust' directs attention to the requirement of an unjust factor or reason for restitution and the absence of any juristic reason to retain the enrichment. But 'once a proper basis for "injustice" has been satisfied, it adds nothing to say that the defendant's retention of benefit is unconscionable.'[155] The High Court has emphasised that an assessment of unjust enrichment is *not* to be conducted 'by reference to a subjective evaluation of what is unfair or unconscionable: recovery rather depends on the existence of a qualifying or vitiating factor falling into some particular category.'[156]

A reference to 'unconscionability' by itself is a statement of a conclusion. This observation has been made in a number of High Court decisions, including by Gummow J on several occasions. In one case, Gummow and Hayne JJ said (quoting from French J) that 'unconscionable conduct' is 'better described than defined.'[157] And in *Garcia v National Australia Bank*,[158] Gaudron, McHugh, Gummow and Hayne JJ, after using the label 'unconscionable' to describe a case of mistake, acknowledged that 'the statement that enforcement of the transaction would be "unconscionable" is to characterise the result rather than to identify the reasoning that leads to the application of that description.' Finally, in *ACCC v C G Berbatis Holdings Pty Ltd*[159] Gummow and Hayne JJ approved remarks of John McGhee QC that the broad use of terms like unconscionable and unconscientious 'may have masked rather than illuminated the underlying principles at stake.'[160]

Secondly, there is a real danger that use of a term like 'unconscionable' will mislead and confuse. In its ordinary sense, it suggests fault or dishonesty, notions which are irrelevant to strict-liability unjust factors in unjust enrichment.[161] Even when the concern of the law is with fault, terms like 'unconscionability' impose an uncertain standard. In *Royal Brunei Airlines v Tan*[162] the Privy Council was asked to apply a test for 'unconscionability' to determine whether the wrong of assistance in a breach of trust had been committed. In delivering the advice of the Board, Lord Nicholls emphasised that 'unconscionable is not a word in everyday use by non-lawyers'.[163] He continued, saying that, as a touchstone for liability, it is better avoided because if it 'means no more than dishonesty, then dishonesty is the preferable label. If unconscionable means something different, it must be said that it is not clear what that something different is.' The same criticism of this label was made by the Supreme Court of Canada in discussing the use of the term 'unconscionable' to describe actions in equity based on promissory or representation-based estoppels.[164]

[155] K Mason and J Carter, *Restitution Law in Australia* (Sydney, Butterworths, 1995) 66.

[156] *Farah Constructions Pty Ltd v Say-Dee Pty Ltd* [2007] HCA 22, (2007) 230 CLR 89 [150] (the Court); *Australian Financial Services and Leasing Pty Ltd v Hills Industries Ltd* [2014] HCA 14, (2014) 253 CLR 560 [20] (Hayne, Crennan, Kiefel, Bell and Keane JJ).

[157] *Australian Competition and Consumer Commission v CG Berbatis Holdings Pty Ltd* [2003] HCA 18, (2003) 214 CLR 51 [44] (Gummow and Hayne JJ, quoting from French J).

[158] *Garcia v National Australia Bank* [1998] HCA 48, (1998) 194 CLR 395 [34].

[159] *Australian Competition and Consumer Commission v CG Berbatis Holdings Pty Ltd* [2003] HCA 18, (2003) 214 CLR 51 [43].

[160] See also K Hayne, 'Letting Justice Be Done Without the Heavens Falling' (2001) 27 *Monash University Law Review* 12, 16.

[161] *David Securities Pty Ltd v Commonwealth Bank of Australia* [1992] HCA 48, (1992) 175 CLR 353, 378–79 [46].

[162] *Royal Brunei Airlines v Tan* [1995] UKPC 4, [1995] 2 AC 378.

[163] ibid 392.

[164] *Ryan v Moore* 2005 SCC 38, [2005] 2 SCR 53 [74].

Thirdly, as we will see in Chapter 6, although there is some support in Australian law for a single concept of 'unconscionable retention of benefit', this notion should not replace the remainder of the developed doctrine of unjust enrichment. To effect such a wholesale replacement would be inconsistent with the approach taken to unjust enrichment in the dominant corpus of cases. On numerous occasions judges in the High Court have recognised that unjust enrichment is an 'informative generic label for purposes of classification, in Australian law' of a 'notion underlying a variety of distinct categories of case in which … a benefit [is] derived at the expense of a plaintiff.'[165] Or that unjust enrichment 'has a taxonomical function referring to categories of cases in which the law allows recovery by one person of a benefit retained by another'.[166] Or, that '[t]here is now no longer any question that there is in this country a law of restitution based upon the concept of unjust enrichment'.[167] The concept of 'unconscionable retention' or, as we prefer, 'a juristic reason to retain' has a place in the law of unjust enrichment (Chapters 6 and 7), but it must not displace the whole of the subject.

V. Coherence Between Unjust Enrichment and Other Areas

Although unjust enrichment is a cause of action which has only been explicitly recognised by the common law in the last half-century, it is an action that must be treated as a part of a coherent private law. Much of the focus of this book is on the coherence of unjust enrichment both internally and externally within private law. We have already seen how coherence requires that unjust enrichment include actions which had their origins in the common law courts and the courts of probate, as well as those that had their origins in the courts that applied equity. There are at least three other significant areas in which coherence is essential to the operation of the law of unjust enrichment.

First, as to whether an enrichment is 'unjust', coherence in private law requires that it will not be unjust for a defendant to retain an enrichment if the defendant is entitled to it by the operation of some other area of law. For instance, suppose a defendant is entitled to be paid $1000 under a contract, but the plaintiff mistakenly pays that defendant, intending to pay another creditor first. The plaintiff cannot obtain restitution for his mistaken payment, because the defendant had another juristic reason to keep the payment. The operation of juristic reasons as a right to retain a benefit is considered in Chapters 6 and 7.

Secondly, there is the example of the award of restitution for policy reasons, considered in Chapter 13. Suppose a plaintiff makes a payment to a defendant in circumstances where the plaintiff intended to make the payment. The plaintiff's intention was not vitiated. It was not qualified or conditional. There cannot be any action for unjust enrichment because *as between the parties* there is no injustice in permitting the defendant to keep the payment.

[165] *Muschinski v Dodds* [1985] HCA 78, (1985) 160 CLR 583, 617 [10] (Deane J).

[166] *Equuscorp Pty Ltd v Haxton; Equuscorp Pty Ltd v Bassat; Equuscorp Pty Ltd v Cunningham's Warehouse Sales Pty Ltd* [2012] HCA 7, (2012) 246 CLR 498 [30] (French CJ, Crennan & Kiefel JJ).

[167] *Australian Financial Services and Leasing Pty Ltd v Hills Industries Ltd* [2014] HCA 14, (2014) 253 CLR 560 [132] (Gageler J); *David Securities Pty Ltd v Commonwealth Bank of Australia* [1992] HCA 48, (1992) 175 CLR 353, 401 (Dawson J).

But restitution might nevertheless be awarded for policy reasons, including reasons of coherence with other areas of the law.

Thirdly, there may be reasons of coherence why a defence to unjust enrichment, such as change of position, is denied. In Chapter 14 we consider the defence of change of position. Even if all of the elements of the defence are proved by a defendant, the defendant might still be denied the defence if other policy reasons mean that allowing that defence would stultify the operation of another area of the law.

VI. Conclusion

The single most important point of this chapter is that unjust enrichment is a cause of action and restitution is a remedy. Restitution might be a remedy for torts or equitable wrongs or other events. But this book is concerned only with unjust enrichment. For this reason, this book is entitled *Unjust Enrichment*. It is not called *Restitution*. It is not concerned with the award of restitution for reasons other than unjust enrichment. Although restitution and unjust enrichment are commonly used as interchangeable terms, a wrong turn occurred in 1936 when the American Law Institute published the *Restatement of Restitution*. The Reporter for the Third Restatement, Professor Kull, has said that the last-minute decision to excise 'unjust enrichment' was a mistake.[168] The *Restatement* should, more accurately, have been entitled the *Restatement of Unjust Enrichment* rather than the *Restatement of Restitution*. This point was noticed almost immediately after its publication by Professor Jackson, who observed in his review of the 1937 *Restatement*:

> [S]hould we adopt the tripartite grouping accepted by the *Restatement*? [ie contract, tort, restitution] I very much doubt whether we should find it acceptable. On this scheme, contract and tort are marked off by the source of the obligation, whilst the third group is distinguished by the remedy that is available: the trichotomy is not contract, tort, and unjust [enrichment], but contract, tort and restitution. It is theoretically as unsound as a classification of birds and mammals by their structure and fishes as things that swim in water, although the student of Blackstone who knows that whales are 'royal fish' might perhaps find that this new science confirms the wisdom of the common law.[169]

Professor Birks, in one of his final articles, made a similar point, saying that it is a 'nursery school truth that a series which begins with contract and wrongs must finish with categories of the same kind—categories of causative event, not categories of response.'[170]

Another essential point which we make in this chapter is that a determination that a defendant has been unjustly enriched, and is liable to make restitution, focuses upon four central issues:

(1) the defendant must be enriched;
(2) the enrichment must come at the expense of the plaintiff;

[168] A Kull, 'James Barr Ames and the Early Modern History of Unjust Enrichment' (2005) 25 *Oxford Journal of Legal Studies* 297.
[169] R Jackson, 'The Restatement of Restitution' (1938) 10(2) *Mississippi Law Journal* 95, 95–96.
[170] P Birks, 'A Letter to America: The New Restatement of Restitution' (2003) 3(2) *Global Jurist Frontiers* 1, 20.

(3) the enrichment must be unjust; and
(4) a court should consider if any defences apply.

In the next chapter we turn to the meaning of the remedy of restitution. We will see that as a remedy, restitution has five different meanings in the law of unjust enrichment. These correspond with five different measures of enrichment: value, rights, things, discharged existing duties, and discharged future duties.

3

The Remedy of Restitution

Contents

I. Introduction

In Chapter 2 we explained the nature and origins of unjust enrichment as an independent cause of action. The most fundamental point that we made was that unjust enrichment is a cause of action for which the remedy is restitution. In this chapter we explain the nature of the remedy of restitution. The most fundamental point is that, as Lord Clarke expresses the point, a claim for restitution of unjust enrichment is 'not a claim for compensation for loss, but for recovery of a benefit unjustly gained [by a defendant] … at the expense of the claimant'.[1] Or, as the point has been expressed in the High Court of Australia in relation to a claim in unjust enrichment: 'Restitutionary relief … does not seek to provide compensation for loss. Instead, it operates to restore to the plaintiff what has been transferred

[1] *Benedetti v Sawiris* [2013] UKSC 50, [2014] AC 938 [13] (Lord Clarke, Lord Kerr & Lord Wilson agreeing). See also *Sempra Metals Ltd (formerly Metallgesellschaft Ltd) v Inland Revenue Commissioners* [2007] UKHL 34, [2008] 1 AC 561 [28] (Lord Hope).

from the plaintiff to the defendant.'[2] However, what is rarely appreciated is that there are at least five different types of orders commonly made to ensure recovery of a benefit unjustly gained by a defendant at the expense of a plaintiff.

II. The Core Meaning of 'Restitution'

As we have explained in the introduction to this chapter, awards of restitution of unjust enrichment are usually described in a manner involving one fundamental element in common. They are concerned with giving back to someone something that came from that person. Sometimes this is expressed as reversing a 'transfer of value'. We will see in Chapter 5 that a more precise terminology is that the enrichment acquired by the defendant was caused or contributed to by a defective transaction with the plaintiff. In *Kingstreet Investments Ltd v New Brunswick*, the Supreme Court of Canada described the nature of a restitutionary award for unjust enrichment by explaining:

> Restitution is a tool of corrective justice. When a transfer of value between two parties is normatively defective, restitution functions to correct that transfer by restoring parties to their pre-transfer positions. In *Peel (Regional Municipality) v. Canada*, [1992] 3 S.C.R. 762, McLachlin J. (as she then was) neatly encapsulated this normative framework: 'The concept of "injustice" in the context of the law of restitution harkens back to the Aristotelian notion of correcting a balance or equilibrium that had been disrupted.'[3]

And in *Roxborough v Rothmans of Pall Mall Australia Ltd*,[4] Gleeson CJ, Gaudron and Hayne JJ said that restitution 'operates to restore to the plaintiff what has been transferred from the plaintiff to the defendant whereby the defendant has been unjustly enriched'.

Whether we focus on a 'transfer of value' between the plaintiff and defendant or, as we prefer in Chapter 5, 'a defective transaction which causes or contributes to the defendant's enrichment', one point is clear. Restitutionary remedies do not require a financial loss to the plaintiff. This has been iterated and reiterated by the courts in Australia and England.[5] Indeed, the leading cases in Canada and Australia which first explicitly recognised restitutionary liability for unjust enrichment both involved circumstances in which no financial loss was proved. They were cases where the plaintiff sought restitution of the value of services performed rather than money paid. In both cases, services were performed under a putative contract, which the parties later discovered was unenforceable due to lack of writing.[6] The Supreme Court of Canada and the High Court of Australia both made an

[2] *Roxborough v Rothmans of Pall Mall Australia Ltd* [2001] HCA 68, (2001) 208 CLR 516 [26] (Gleeson CJ, Gaudron and Hayne JJ) quoting *Commissioner of State Revenue (Vic) v Royal Insurance Australia Ltd* [1994] HCA 61, (1994) 182 CLR 51, 75 [41] (Mason CJ).

[3] *Kingstreet Investments Ltd v New Brunswick (Finance)* 2007 SCC 1, [2007] 1 SCR 3 [32]. See further, J Edelman, *Gain-based Damages* (Oxford, Hart Publishing, 2002) ch 3.

[4] [2001] HCA 68, (2001) 208 CLR 516, 529 [26] quoting from *Commissioner of State Revenue (Vict) v Royal Insurance Australia Ltd* [1994] HCA 61, (1994) 182 CLR 51, 75 (Mason CJ).

[5] *Kleinwort Benson Ltd v Birmingham City Council* [1997] QB 380, 400; *Mason v New South Wales* [1959] HCA 5, (1959) 102 CLR 108, 146 [18] (Windeyer J), approved in *Commissioner of State Revenue (Vic) v Royal Insurance Australia Ltd* [1994] HCA 61, (1994) 182 CLR 51.

[6] *Deglman v Guaranty Trust Co of Canada* [1954] SCR 725; *Pavey & Matthews Pty Ltd v Paul* [1987] HCA 5, (1987) 162 CLR 221.

award of restitution to give back the value of the plaintiff's labour that had benefited the defendant. Professor Ames[7] wrote that the 'liability to make restitution is the same in reason' whether the claim is for return of money, for the value of services rendered, or for the value of goods appropriated from the plaintiff.[8]

III. Three Awards of 'Restitution' which are not for Unjust Enrichment

The word 'restitution' causes great confusion in private law. The difficulty arises because the word is used to describe various concepts. The *Oxford English Dictionary*[9] provides six different definitions. Etymologically the word is capable of supporting all meanings. But the concern of this book is only with instances where restitution describes a response to unjust enrichment. We begin with those uses of 'restitution' (sometimes in a very loose sense) with which this book is *not* concerned. In summary, those senses of restitution which are not relevant to the law of unjust enrichment are:

(1) restoring a person to a position before a loss was suffered;
(2) restitution in criminal law; and
(3) disgorgement of the profits of wrongdoing.

A. Restoring a Person to a Position Before a Loss was Suffered

The first use of 'restitution' which should be eschewed is restitution of a person to a position prior to when a loss was suffered. This uses 'restitution' as a synonym for compensation. The first and fourth definitions in the *Oxford English Dictionary* explain restitution as bearing this meaning: 'making reparation to one for loss or injury' or, more specifically, 'the action of restoring a person or persons to a previous status or position'. This echoes Lord Blackburn's classic definition of compensation in *Livingstone v Rawyards Coal Company*:[10] 'that sum of money which will put the party who has been injured, or who has suffered, in the same position as he would have been in if he had not sustained the wrong'. Although 'restitution' is sometimes used to describe loss-based remedies both at common law and in equity,[11] restitution for unjust enrichment is never concerned with compensating for loss.

[7] See, further, Ch 4.

[8] JB Ames, *Lectures on Legal History and Miscellaneous Legal Essays* (Cambridge, Harvard University Press, 1913) 165.

[9] JA Simpson and ESC Weiner (prep), *The Oxford English Dictionary*, 2nd edn (Oxford, Clarendon Press, 1989) 753.

[10] *Livingstone v Rawyards Coal Company* [1880] UKHL 3, (1880) 5 App Cas 25, 39.

[11] See also *The Ability of every Man that shall be impanelled in any Inquest or Attaint in London 1494* (11 Hen 7 c 21) s 21: '[F]or the Recovery and Restitution of the same Debt, Damages, and Costs, the Plaintiff … may … sue'. See also *Hodgkinson v Simms* [1994] 3 SCR 377, 440.

B. Restitution in Criminal Law

Another usage which is not relevant to this book is restitution in criminal law. Sometimes restitution is used to describe the 'just deserts' theory of punishment. On this view, the purpose of punishment is restitution in the sense of restoring the 'relationship' between the offender and the victim.[12] In criminal law, restitution is also sometimes used to describe a payment made to a victim of a crime. These 'restitution orders' describe payments to be made by a criminal to the state or to a victim upon commission of an offence. Sir William Blackstone wrote of the 'restitution in blood' made to 'the criminal's family' following the reversal of a bill of attainder by Parliament, usually for reasons of compassion.[13] Once again, this order in criminal law is not restitution in the sense of a response to unjust enrichment.

C. Disgorgement of the Profits of Wrongdoing

A third usage of 'restitution' is to describe profit-stripping remedies, such as an account of profits, which are made to deter a defendant from wrongful activity or a breach of duty.[14] The most common instances where disgorgement of profits were awarded was in equity following the taking of an account of profits. Sometimes this was described as 'restitution'. However, to the extent that recent decisions in England and Australia have modernised the old Chancery language of account, they have usually avoided the use of 'restitution', in this sense of profit-stripping awards. More common is the use of 'disgorgement'.[15] That label is preferable because it is important to distinguish between the two forms of relief. An account and disgorgement of a defendant's profits is not a restitutionary remedy. As we will see in Chapter 5, restitution requires a *transaction* with the plaintiff, while an account of profits requires only a causal link between a defendant's wrongful conduct and profits made.[16] For this reason, Heydon JA said in *Harris v Digital Pulse Pty Ltd*[17] that 'the rules relating to an account of profits are not restitutionary in the sense that they do not rest on

[12] C Abel and F Marsh, *Punishment and Restitution: A Restitutionary Approach to Crime and the Criminal:* (Westport CT, Westwood Press, 1984) 59–69. See also the discussion in L Zedner 'Reparation and Retribution: Are they reconcilable' (1984) 57 *Modern Law Review* 228.

[13] W Blackstone, *Commentaries on the Laws of England*, Book IV (first published 1765–69, Chicago, The University of Chicago Press, 1979) 385.

[14] P Birks, *Introduction to the Law of Restitution*, rev edn (Oxford, Oxford University Press, 1989) 313; A Burrows, *The Law of Restitution*, 2nd edn (London, Butterworths, 2002) 461–62; Law Commission, *Aggravated, Exemplary and Restitutionary Damages* (Law Com No 247, 1997); G McMeel, *The Modern Law of Restitution* (London, Blackstone, 2000) 327; IM Jackman, 'Restitution for Wrongs' (1989) 48 *The Cambridge Law Journal* 302; *Attorney General v Blake* [1997] EWCA Civ 3008, [1998] Ch 439, 457–59 (Lord Woolf MR); *Jaggard v Sawyer* [1994] EWCA Civ 1 [40], [1995] 1 WLR 269, 281 (Bingham MR); G Virgo, *The Law of Restitution*, 3rd edn (Oxford, Oxford University Press, 2015) 418–19.

[15] *Attorney General v Blake* [2000] UKHL 45, [2001] 1 AC 268, 291, 292 (Lord Steyn); *United Pan-Europe Communications NV v Deutsche Bank AG* [2000] 2 BCLC 461; *Kuwait Airways Corporation v Iraqi Airways Co* [2004] EWHC 2603 (Comm) [387] (Creswell J); *Westminster City Council v Porter* [2002] EWHC 2179 (Ch), [2003] Ch 436 [3] (Hart J); *Hospitality Group Pty Ltd v Australian Rugby Union Ltd* [2001] FCA 1040, (2001) 110 FCR 157 [159] (Hill and Finkelstein JJ); *Harris v Digital Pulse Pty Ltd* [2003] NSWCA 10, (2003) 56 NSWLR 298 [362], [380], [404], [407] (Heydon JA); *Anderson v McPherson (No 2)* [2012] WASC 19 [221]–[226] (Edelman J).

[16] *Boardman v Phipps* [1967] 2 AC 46.

[17] *Harris v Digital Pulse Pty Ltd* (2003) 56 NSWLR 298, 409 [414].

giving back something which the plaintiff had'. Or as Romaine J said in *Maximum Financial Services Inc v 1144517 Alberta Ltd*,[18] disgorgement 'relief is not available in an action in unjust enrichment, but only if [the defendant] is liable for a civil wrong, and an order requiring it to give up its wrongfully-obtained gains is appropriate'.

Sometimes in a claim for disgorgement of profits a limit might be imposed on the extent of recoverable causal profits.[19] But the profits need not be at the expense of the plaintiff, in the sense of deriving from any transaction with the plaintiff. An example is the United States case of *Frank Music Corp v Metro-Goldwyn Mayer Inc*.[20] The defendant hotel, in breach of copyright, had included a segment from the defendant's musical in its revue. The 9th Circuit Court of Appeals awarded the plaintiff 12 per cent of the profits from the revue (being a total of 9 per cent after an allowance to the hotel). The claimants argued that they were also entitled to (i) a share of the profits from the hotel and its gaming operations, because the revue enticed people to the hotel and increased those profits, and (ii) a share of additional 'downsteam corporate benefits' received by the hotel's parent corporation. The 9th Circuit held that the first set of indirect profits could be recovered but that the second were too remote.

In summary, an award of disgorgement of profits (which follows an account of profits) strips the defendant's profits, irrespective of their source. But a personal award of restitution for unjust enrichment is, in loose terms, 'concerned with giving back to someone something that has been taken from them'.[21]

IV. Five Possible Meanings of Restitution as an Order in Response to Unjust Enrichment

There are at least five different orders which have a claim to be remedies to reverse unjust enrichment. In academic analyses of this subject, these different types of order are often conflated. This is unfortunate. In the world of litigation, disputes are resolved by orders. Perhaps the most important part of any party's case is the orders sought. It is incontrovertible that the five situations below represent different orders that can be sought. Hence, when a person claims to be entitled to restitution of unjust enrichment it is of fundamental importance that there is clarity in the type of order that the person says is represented by the demand for restitution. The five types of 'restitution' or, more accurately, the five legal responses to unjust enrichment, are as follows below.

(1) Restitution from a defendant to a plaintiff of *value* obtained from the plaintiff. Here, an order is made for payment of money to the plaintiff.

[18] *Maximum Financial Services Inc v 1144517 Alberta Ltd* [2015] ABQB 646 [84]. See also *Indutech Canada Ltd v Gibbs Pipe Distributors Ltd* [2011] ABQB 38 [512] (Romaine J).

[19] *Warman International Ltd v Dwyer* [1995] HCA 18, (1995) 182 CLR 544.

[20] *Frank Music Corp v Metro-Goldwyn Mayer Inc* 886 F 2d 1545 (1989 9th Cir CA).

[21] *Citadel General Assurance Company v Lloyds Bank Canada* [1997] 3 SCR 805 [30] (La Forest, Gonthier, Cory, McLachlin, Iacobucci and Major JJ). See also *Sempra Metals Ltd (formerly Metallgesellschaft Ltd) v Inland Revenue Commissioners* [2007] UKHL 34, [2008] 1 AC 561 [116]–[117] (Lord Nicholls); *Anderson v McPherson (No 2)* [2012] WASC 19 [226] (Edelman J).

(2) Restitution from a defendant to a plaintiff of a *physical thing* obtained from the plaintiff. Here, an order is made for transfer of the thing to the plaintiff.
(3) Restitution from a defendant to a plaintiff of a *right* obtained from the plaintiff. Here, an order is made for conveyance of the right or an order is made declaring that the defendant has a power to obtain conveyance.
(4) Restitution from a defendant to a plaintiff of a *duty* which a defendant owed to a third party, but which was discharged by the plaintiff. Here, an order is made declaring that the duty exists and is owed to the plaintiff.
(5) Restitution from a defendant of '*future rights*' *or rights subject to a condition precedent* against the plaintiff. Here, an order is made declaring that a contract has terminated.

There are very few examples of courts using the language of unjust enrichment to describe an order for restitution other than (1). One reason for this may be that only (1) uses 'restitution' in a natural sense of the word. A second reason is that in almost every case an award of restitution of value (ie order (1)) will be sufficient for a plaintiff. Plaintiffs generally bring actions for unjust enrichment to recover money. Where a defendant is solvent, then an award of money will almost invariably satisfy the plaintiff. A third reason is that the common law (including equity) has traditionally required that money remedies be inadequate before ordering more specific relief. For instance, the minimum condition for an order of specific performance is that the innocent party should have a legitimate interest extending beyond pecuniary compensation for the breach.[22] Other than in circumstances in which a plaintiff transfers unique rights to a defendant (land, unique chattels, shares in a private company) it is very difficult to defend an award of restitution of the specific rights transferred rather than restitution of their value.

For these reasons, this book focuses primarily on the first category. But the five different responses to unjust enrichment can be illustrated with the following examples:

(1) A transfers title to bearer shares in a private company to B as a consequence of B's undue influence. An order might be made requiring B to make restitution of the value of the shares to A. As we will see in Chapter 4, there is an important question concerning the date for valuation of the shares. The order for restitution of value is the primary focus of this book.
(2) B steals bearer share certificates held by A in a private company. An action for 'specific restitution' can sometimes be brought by the victim (A), and orders for specific restitution of the bearer share certificates might be made.[23] Historically, an action for specific restitution was brought in the Court of Chancery, which would compel the return of the thing.[24] The Common Law Procedure Act 1854, s 78, gave the same power to common law courts without the option for the defendant, such as that which existed in an action in detinue, to pay the value of the chattel. If the chattel could not be found upon an order of execution then the defendant's land or goods could be distrained.
(3) Suppose A transfers title to shares in a private company to B as a consequence of B's undue influence. A might obtain an order requiring re-conveyance of B's rights to the

[22] *Cavendish Square Holdings v Makdessi* [2015] UKSC 67 [30] (Lord Neuberger and Lord Sumption).
[23] *Takamore v Clarke* [2011] NZCA 587, [2012] 1 NZLR 573 [324] (Chambers J).
[24] *Re Scarth* (1874) LR 10 Ch App 234, 235 (Mellish LJ).

shares to A, or an order declaring that A had, and retains, the power to demand conveyance of the rights. These orders are commonly described as involving, respectively, an award of a 'trust' or 'rescission'.

(4) Suppose that, also as a result of undue influence, A discharges a secured debt owed by B to C. In order to reverse the benefit obtained by B, a court might make a declaration that a new debt is created, owed by B to A, on the same terms as the previous debt. This order is generally described as subrogation. But the word 'subrogation', meaning 'substitution', is a misleading metaphor. A is not 'substituted' as B's creditor. Nor is the discharged debt 'revived'. A new debt is created.

(5) A and B enter a contract which contains no express or implied term concerning B's right to terminate. For instance, a simple agreement is entered between A and B for the supply of machinery from A to B for a price. On its proper construction the payment of the price is a condition of the performance of the agreement. An event occurs which has the effect that this condition fails. The event might be the outbreak of war which prevents A from paying the price. Or the event might be A's refusal to pay the price. In either case, the condition upon which B's performance is dependent has failed. B's obligation to perform, if continued, will unjustly enrich A. To reverse that unjust enrichment B's future obligations are discharged. These restitutionary orders are commonly addressed through concepts of 'termination' and 'frustration'. The same idea underlies rescission of an executory contract.

Each of these five scenarios is considered below.

A. The First Type of Restitution Order: Restitution of Value

As we have explained, the first meaning of restitution, namely restitution of value, is by far the most common, and often the only measure that can be justified. Restitution of value is generally the only order sought, even when a plaintiff claims that a defendant has been unjustly enriched by transfer of a right to the defendant (scenario (3)) or discharge of a debt owed by the defendant (scenario (4)). It is therefore the nearly exclusive sense in which the term 'restitution' is used in the cases to describe a remedy for unjust enrichment. For those reasons, although this book is concerned with restitution for unjust enrichment generally, it focuses very heavily upon restitution of value.

B. The Second Type of Restitution Order: Restitution of a Thing

A second meaning of restitution is to speak of restitution of a thing to a person. For instance, a court has power to order specific restitution of an heirloom, unique item or some thing for which money would not be adequate to restore the plaintiff.[25] This remedy would therefore only be exercised in equity where damages were not adequate.[26] As Lord Talbot LC explained in a case involving an old silver altarpiece with a Greek inscription, 'nothing can be more reasonable than that the man who by wrong detains my property, should be compelled to

[25] *Pusey v Pusey* (1684) 1 Vern 272, (1684) 23 ER 465; *Re Scarth* (1874) LR 10 Ch App 234, 235 (Mellish LJ).
[26] *Fells v Read* (1796) 3 Ves Jun 70, (1796) 30 ER 899.

restore it to me again *in specie*; and the law being defective in this particular, such defect is properly supplied in equity.'[27] The remedy was made available at common law in 1854.[28]

An order for restitution of a specific thing is not concerned with the value of the thing. Indeed, one of the very reasons for specific restitution is that an order for payment of the value would not be adequate to restore the plaintiff. Nor is the order concerned with restitution of rights to the plaintiff. For instance, the thing about which restitution is sought might be owned by the plaintiff although detained by the defendant. The plaintiff, as owner, already has the best right to possession.

It is rare for these claims for restitution of a thing to be described as part of the law of unjust enrichment. But, as a matter of principle, these orders for restitution can arise as a result of the same factors that we consider in this book concerning restitution of its value. A century ago, Professor Ames explained that cases involving claims for recovery of chattels after the death of a bailee, such as where the chattels were provided as consideration for a promise the defendant failed to perform, 'the plaintiff is seeking restitution from the defendant, who is trying to enrich himself unconscionably at the expense of the plaintiff'.[29]

C. The Third Type of Restitution Order: Restitution of Rights

A third meaning of restitution is now commonly recognised in academic writing as a response to unjust enrichment, although it is rarely recognised in judicial decisions. This is a claim for restitution of a right. It arises where the plaintiff has transferred a right to the defendant but seeks restitution of that right. For instance, a plaintiff who mistakenly conveys title to land to a defendant might bring a claim for restitution of that title. The process of restitution might be engaged by recognising that the defendant holds the title on trust for the plaintiff.[30] Alternatively, the method of restitution might be an order for rescission and re-conveyance of the right. Although there are differences between the two concepts, both ultimately result in restitution of rights. In *Stump v Gaby*[31] Lord St Leonards equated rescission with the trust saying that a person with the right to rescind a transaction for fraud 'remains the owner' in equity, by which he meant that the person is a beneficiary. And, as Sir Peter Millett once said, eschewing the awkward label of 'mere equity', 'It probably does not matter if we say that the relationship is not a trust relationship, so long as we call it something else. The trouble is that we have no other name for it.'[32] In many cases the bare trust sought is 'akin to orders for [re]conveyance'.[33] But a power to assert reconveyance of a right is far less commonly available than claims for restitution of value. Also, as the High

[27] *Duke of Somerset v Cookson* (1735) 3 P Wms 390, 391, (1735) 24 ER 1114, 1114.

[28] Common Law Procedure Act 1854, s 78.

[29] JB Ames, *Lectures on Legal History and Miscellaneous Legal Essays* (Cambridge, Harvard University Press, 1913) 234–35.

[30] *Leuty v Hillas* (1858) 2 De G & J 110, (1858) 44 ER 929; *Craddock Bros Ltd v Hunt* [1923] 2 Ch 136.

[31] *Stump v Gaby* (1852) 2 De GM & G 623, 630, (1852) 42 ER 1015, 1018. See also *Gresley v Mousley* (1859) 4 De G & J 78, 93, (1859) 45 ER 31, 36 (Turner LJ); and R Chambers, *Resulting Trusts* (Oxford, Clarendon Press, 1997) 172–74.

[32] PJ Millett, 'Restitution and Constructive Trusts' (1998) 114 *Law Quarterly Review* 399, 404.

[33] *Giumelli v Giumelli* [1999] HCA 10, (1999) 196 CLR 101 [5] (Gleeson CJ, McHugh, Gummow & Callinan JJ).

Court of Australia has suggested, the trust might be withheld if the circumstances require it such as where another remedy is capable of doing full justice.[34]

Although there is academic support for a 'restitutionary trust' as a response to unjust enrichment,[35] there is almost no authority in which a court has explicitly recognised that a trust is a response to unjust enrichment. Usually, when a plaintiff seeks restitution of a right which has been transferred to a defendant by an unjust transaction, the claim is pleaded and argued as a claim for rescission or for a constructive or a resulting trust. The reasons for decision are almost never expressed in terms of unjust enrichment. But the labels of 'rescission', 'constructive trust' or 'resulting trust' do not reveal anything about the reason why the trust is being imposed. Indeed, those remedies can be imposed for reasons other than unjust enrichment.

The benefit of acknowledging that a trust might be a restitutionary remedy for unjust enrichment is that this explains *why* the rescission or trust is being recognised. Too often, constructive trusts are imposed without explanation of why they are being imposed. One judicial decision that recognised that a trust can be a restitutionary response to unjust enrichment is the decision of the Supreme Court of Canada in *Kerr v Baranow*.[36] In that case Cromwell J, writing for the court, said that '[a] successful claim for unjust enrichment may attract either a "personal restitutionary award" or a "restitutionary proprietary award"'.[37] The language of 'personal' and 'proprietary' restitutionary awards is unhelpful because it introduces further ambiguities concerning what is meant by 'proprietary'. However, Cromwell J explained that by 'restitutionary proprietary award' he meant an award of a constructive trust when a monetary award is inappropriate or insufficient.[38] As we have explained, the experience of the common law is that it is very rarely the case that a plaintiff has a legitimate interest in a claim to anything other than a pecuniary award. Hence, it should be rare that a trust is needed as a restitutionary response because a monetary award is inappropriate or insufficient as an award of restitution.

Although neither Australian nor English case law has yet explicitly recognised the trust as an institution which can provide a legal response to unjust enrichment, there is a line of authority in England and Australia which recognises that a trust arises in circumstances involving a transfer of title where the plaintiff did not intend the defendant to benefit from transaction. One example from this line of authority is the imposition of a resulting trust where an attempt to create an express trust fails.[39] The transferor does not intend to create

[34] *Bathurst City Council v PWC Properties Pty Ltd* [1998] HCA 59, (1998) 195 CLR 566, [42] (Gaudron, McHugh, Gummow, Hayne and Callinan JJ) giving a priority dispute in insolvency as an example.

[35] See especially P Birks, 'Restitution and Resulting Trusts' in S Goldstein (ed), *Equity: Contemporary Legal Developments* (Jerusalem, Hebrew University of Jerusalem, 1992) 335; R Chambers, *Resulting Trusts* (Oxford, Clarendon Press, 1997); B McFarlane, *The Structure of Property Law* (Oxford, Hart, 2008) 314–31; C Mitchell, P Mitchell and S Watterson (eds), *Goff and Jones: The Law of Unjust Enrichment*, 8th edn (London, Sweet & Maxwell, 2011) 834–35 [38]–[36].

[36] *Kerr v Baranow* 2011 SCC 10, [2011] 1 SCR 269.

[37] ibid [46].

[38] ibid [50].

[39] See the discussion in *Knudsen v Kara Kar Holdings Pty Ltd* [2000] NSWSC 715 [49] (Austin J); and *Yard v Yardoo Pty Ltd* [2006] VSC 109 [298] (Cummins J), discussion not considered on appeal in either *Yard v Yardoo Pty Ltd* [2007] VSCA 35 or *Kara Kar Holdings Pty Ltd v Knudsen* [2001] NSWCA 276. See also JD Heydon and MJ Leeming, *Jacobs' Law of Trusts in Australia*, 7th edn (Chatswood, LexisNexis Butterworths, 2006) 236 [1205].

a trust in favour of himself or herself, but a trust 'automatically' arises because of the lack of intention, usually by the immediate transferor, to enter a transaction that enriches the recipient.[40] Another example is the line of cases where a trust is imposed upon a recipient's title to a transferred asset or a causally related transaction where the 'transferor was entirely unaware' of the transaction.[41] Although none of these English and Australian cases has explicitly recognised unjust enrichment as the source of the trust, there is a reason why the reasoning in some of these cases concerning 'automatic resulting trusts' has been reconsidered and re-explained by academic commentators as an award on the basis of unjust enrichment. This is because the actual reasoning in many of these cases cannot be correct. Some of these cases suggest that the trust arises because the transferor held both a legal and equitable interest and divested only the legal interest.[42] But the holder of the original legal right held no equitable right at all. When the trust is created, a *new* equitable interest arises in favour of the settlor.[43] Unless these decisions, and many others like them, are to be overturned, the reasoning must be refined. Unjust enrichment has been suggested as a possibility for such a re-evaluation. The trusts discussed above are imposed as a legal response to prevent the recipient having the use and enjoyment of rights for his or her own benefit where the plaintiff did not intend to confer the benefit of that use and enjoyment on the defendant through the impugned transaction.[44] It may not be a significant step from this reasoning to conclude that the imposition of a trust in these cases is concerned with preventing unjust enrichment. Lord Millett suggested extrajudicially, endorsing the thesis of Professor Chambers:[45] 'the development of a coherent doctrine of proprietary restitution for subtractive unjust enrichment is impossible unless it is based on the resulting trust as traditionally understood'.[46]

Another example of restitution of rights, which might be characterised as based upon unjust enrichment, is the award of rectification. Rectification might be based upon common mistake which permits rescission of that part of the mistaken agreement by which rights were mistakenly conferred, and replacement with the correct agreement.[47] Rectification might also be based upon unilateral mistake. An example is a contract between the plaintiff and the defendant requiring the plaintiff to convey 100 acres of Blackacre to the defendant. If the contract is induced by a misrepresentation, the plaintiff has a right to rescission of the transaction. But suppose the parties entered into a contract in which the

[40] *Robb Evans of Robb Evans & Associates v European Bank Ltd* [2004] NSWCA 82, (2004) 61 NSWLR 75 [111]–[113] (Spigelman CJ) citing R Chambers, *Resulting Trusts* (Oxford, Clarendon Press, 1997); *Air Jamaica Ltd v Charlton* [1999] UKPC 20, [1999] 1 WLR 1399, 1412 [45] (Lord Millett).

[41] *Robb Evans of Robb Evans & Associates v European Bank Ltd* [2004] NSWCA 82, (2004) 61 NSWLR 75 [111]–[113] (Spigelman CJ).

[42] W Swadling, 'Explaining Resulting Trusts' (2008) 124 *Law Quarterly Review* 72, 99–100 discussing *Vandervell v Inland Revenue Commissioners* [1966] UKHL 3, [1967] 2 AC 291, 313 (Lord Upjohn), 329 (Lord Wilberforce). See also *Air Jamaica Ltd v Charlton* [1999] UKPC 20 [45], [1999] 1 WLR 1399, 1412 (Lord Millett).

[43] *DKLR Holding Co (No 2) Pty Ltd v Commissioner of Stamp Duties (NSW)* [1982] HCA 14, (1982) 149 CLR 431, 463 [7] (Aickin J); *Commissioner of Taxation v Linter Textiles Australia Ltd (in liq)* [2005] HCA 20, (2005) 220 CLR 592 [30] (Gleeson CJ, Gummow, Hayne, Callinan and Heydon JJ); *Peldan v Anderson* [2006] HCA 48, (2006) 227 CLR 471 [37] (Gummow ACJ, Kirby, Hayne, Callinan & Crennan JJ).

[44] *Anderson v McPherson (No 2)* [2012] WASC 19 [103] (Edelman J).

[45] R Chambers, *Resulting Trusts* (Oxford, Clarendon Press, 1997).

[46] PJ Millett, 'Restitution and Constructive Trusts' (1998) 114 *Law Quarterly Review* 399, 410.

[47] *Frederick E Rose (London) Ltd v William H Pim Junior & Co Ltd* [1953] 2 QB 450; *Ryledar Pty Ltd & Anor v Euphoric Pty Ltd* [2007] NSWCA 65 [122] (Campbell JA). See also Lord Hoffmann 'Rectification and other Mistakes', Lecture to the Commercial Bar Association (3 November 2015).

written instrument, as a result of a unilateral mistake known to the defendant, and induced by the defendant, misdescribed Blackacre by 10 acres, expressing the size as 110 acres. The plaintiff might seek to rectify the contract, to have the instrument corrected and the right to the 10 additional acres retrospectively revested in the plaintiff. As in cases of rescission there may, of course, be defences to this claim such as if the defendant sold the land to a bona fide purchaser.[48] On one view, there would still be a need for a previous outward accord before a contract for sale of 100 acres could be enforced.[49] On another view, the mistake is sufficient not merely to rescind the contract for sale of 110 acres, but also to create a new contract for sale of 100 acres which was mistakenly believed to have been agreed, by a known mistake.[50] An understanding of rectification as concerned with rescission of part of an existing agreement strongly supports the former view.

There is a significant reason for the reluctance of courts to accept that an order which recognises rescission of rights or which declares that a right is held on trust is a response to unjust enrichment which should attract the label 'restitution'. This is that the awards do not involve 'restitution' in the same sense as the most common instances involving restitution of value. The use of 'restitution' to describe rescission or the recognition of a trust in response to unjust enrichment is strained. The order recognising a trust, or the power to rescind that arises as a consequence of mistake, does not 'give back' or restore a right to the plaintiff. It usually gives the plaintiff only the *power* to obtain a conveyance of the right. The natural sense of restitution describes the restoration of something to the plaintiff which derived from the plaintiff. Hence, restitution of value restores value to the plaintiff which the defendant obtained and which derived from the plaintiff. And restitution of a thing restores the physical thing to the plaintiff. There are some cases where restitution of rights fits this pattern. For instance where a plaintiff mistakenly conveys land to the wrong person, an order for a constructive trust can be described as restitution of a right which derived from the plaintiff where the label 'constructive trust' conceals a single order for reconveyance.[51]

If courts were to move to using the language of 'restitution' to describe awards which restore rights, it would be important to do so with awareness that the label is being used in different senses from the restoration of value or the restoration of a thing. In many cases the imposition of a trust, or the recognition of a power of rescission, will be by a court order which is one step removed from making restitution of the right because it acknowledges only that the plaintiff has the *power* to obtain restitution of a right. However, the benefit of an unjust enrichment explanation is that it focuses attention upon *why* the trust or rescission of the right is ordered. And with the focus on that reason, it will often suggest that an award of the value of the benefit is not merely sufficient but is a much more appropriate remedy for unjust enrichment. For instance, in *Alesco Corporation Ltd v Te Maari*,[52] the first defendant misappropriated funds from the plaintiff company. The money was paid for various purposes including to the second defendant, to acquire and develop a property, and to repay debt on another property. The plaintiff corporation sought orders including that

[48] *Garrard v Frankel* (1862) 30 Beav 445, (1862) 54 ER 961; *Smith v Jones* [1954] 2 All ER 823 (Ch).

[49] *RCR Tomlinson Ltd v Russell* [2015] WASCA 154 [53] (the Court).

[50] *Roberts & Co Ltd v Leicestershire County Council* [1961] Ch 555; *Riverlate Properties Ltd v Paul* [1975] Ch 133; *Thomas Bates & Son v Wyndhams Lingeries Ltd* [1988] 1 WLR 505; *Agip Spa v Navigazione Alita Italia Spa* [1984] 1 Ll LR 353; *Commissioner for New Towns v Cooper (Great Britain) Ltd* [1995] Ch 259.

[51] *Giumelli v Giumelli* [1999] HCA 10, (1999) 196 CLR 101 [3]–[4].

[52] *Alesco Corporation Ltd v Te Maari* [2015] NSWSC 469.

the properties were held on trust. One ground for those orders was that the plaintiff's rights had been used without its authority to acquire the properties. But the trial judge held that restitution of the value was sufficient, secured by a charge over the properties.[53] Perhaps the most fundamental difficulty in describing rescission as restitution of a right is where the right rescinded is a purely contractual right. We consider that in Section E in relation to discharge of future duties.

D. The Fourth Type of Restitution: Restitution of a Discharged Debt

The fourth type of response to unjust enrichment has been historically described as 'subrogation'. 'Subrogation' simply means 'substitution'. Many cases of subrogation have nothing to do with unjust enrichment. For example, an insurer that has paid the insured victim of a tort and who wishes to exercise rights to take over the victim's litigation, is usually entitled to do so because of an agreement with the victim. The subrogation remedy in these cases derives from contract. It is not a response to unjust enrichment.

Although subrogation usually has nothing to do with unjust enrichment, there are two types of situation in which equity gives a plaintiff a right under the label 'subrogation' which might be described as a restitutionary response to unjust enrichment.

The first situation in which subrogation might give rise to rights as a response to unjust enrichment is where the plaintiff discharges an obligation of the defendant in circumstances in which the discharge is due to some unjust factor. Those cases commonly involve a plaintiff who pays money to a third party to discharge the defendant's debt, although it might also involve discharge of a non-monetary obligation.[54] In these cases, if the discharge of the obligation is unjust, then unjust enrichment might explain the reason for the recognition by the courts that the obligation is fictionally 'revived'.[55] Unjust enrichment can provide the explanation for why the plaintiff is entitled to recover the value of his performance from the defendant as if the defendant were the third party to whom the defendant owed the obligation.

The second situation in which the operation of subrogation might be described as a response to unjust enrichment is where the plaintiff performs the defendant's obligation but the obligation of the defendant to a third party is *not* discharged. Again, if the performance by the plaintiff is due to an unjust factor then the subrogation of the plaintiff to the rights of the third party can be explained on the basis of unjust enrichment.[56]

The House of Lords in *Banque Financière de la Cité v Parc (Battersea) Ltd* explicitly recognised subrogation in these cases as involving a restitutionary remedy to prevent unjust enrichment.[57] The earlier English academic work of Professor Mitchell provided strong support for this conclusion.[58] The same approach was taken by the United Kingdom Supreme Court in *Menelaou v Bank of Cyprus UK Ltd*.[59]

[53] *Bathurst City Council v PWC Properties Pty Ltd* [1998] HCA 59, (1998) 195 CLR 566 [42] (Gaudron, McHugh, Gummow, Hayne and Callinan JJ).

[54] *Macclesfield Corporation v Great Central Railway* [1911] 2 KB 528, 540. See Ch 12, pp 296–97.

[55] Professor Mitchell calls this 'reviving subrogation': C Mitchell, *The Law of Subrogation* (Oxford, Clarendon Press, 1994).

[56] Professor Mitchell calls this 'simple subrogation': ibid.

[57] *Banque Financière de la Cité v Parc (Battersea) Ltd* [1998] UKHL 7, [1999] 1 AC 221.

[58] C Mitchell, *The Law of Subrogation* (Oxford, Clarendon Press, 1994).

[59] *Menelaou v Bank of Cyprus UK Ltd* [2015] UKSC 66.

In contrast with the English approach, in Australia, in *Bofinger v Kingsway Group Ltd*[60] a joint judgment of the High Court expressly denied this to be the case. This is not merely a matter of labelling. There can be very substantive differences. In England, where the focus of non-contractual subrogation is the law of unjust enrichment, it is easy to see why a subrogated plaintiff is entitled to recover the interest on the plaintiff's payment at the same rate as the discharged debt. That is the extent of the defendant's enrichment.[61] In contrast, if the basis for non-contractual subrogation is not to reverse or prevent the unjust enrichment of the defendant, there is no reason why that should be the rate of interest. Australian decisions have therefore applied a standard court or trustee rate.[62]

In the joint judgment in *Bofinger*, two reasons were given for rejecting the English approach. The first reason given in *Bofinger* was that subrogation cases involve multilateral rather than bilateral relationships which create difficulty in identifying the 'unjust' element of unjust enrichment.[63] In a footnote, the joint judgment referred to the comments of Goff and Jones[64] that 'it is not always easy to determine whether it is B or C who has been enriched and why a court should conclude that the enrichment is an unjust enrichment'. But this problem is not unique to cases of subrogation. In the seminal English and Australian cases which recognised the law of unjust enrichment[65] these courts both recognised that the defendants had been unjustly enriched, but did not identify the reason why the enrichment was unjust, ie the 'unjust factor'. As we saw in Chapter 2, it is now well recognised that an unjust factor must be identified. This makes the law, and the reasons for ordering restitution, more transparent, not less so. Further, the paradigmatic unjust enrichment case involves a mistaken payment from the payer to a bank's customer, by instruction from the payer to her bank and then from her bank to the customer's bank. In some circumstances it is not easy to determine the party who is enriched. Is the enrichee the customer's bank? Is it the customer (even when the account entry might be easily reversed)? Or is it both? There is considerable dispute concerning the circumstances in which the defendant to the action can be the customer's bank.[66]

The second reason given in *Bofinger* for rejecting unjust enrichment as the foundation of a claim based on subrogation is that unjust enrichment does not provide 'an explanation for the mortgagor's being treated as bound, in equity, to treat the person who paid off the previous mortgage as entitled to security under it.'[67] There are three answers to this objection.

[60] *Bofinger v Kingsway Group Ltd* [2009] HCA 44, (2009) 239 CLR 269.

[61] *Filby v Mortgage Express (No 2) Ltd* [2004] EWCA Civ 759 [63]–[67] (May LJ).

[62] *McColl's Wholesale v State Bank of NSW* [1984] 3 NSWLR 365, 379 (Powell J); *Titles Strata Management Pty Ltd v Nirta* [2015] VSC 187 [106]–[132] (Daly AJ).

[63] *Bofinger v Kingsway Group Ltd* [2009] HCA 44, (2009) 239 CLR 269 [97].

[64] R Goff and G Jones, *The Law of Restitution*, 7th edn (London, Sweet & Maxwell, 2007) 132.

[65] *Lipkin Gorman v Karpnale Ltd* [1991] 2 AC 548; *Pavey & Matthews Pty Ltd v Paul* [1987] HCA 5, (1987) 162 CLR 221.

[66] See Chs 4 (enrichment) and 15 (defence of ministerial receipt). See also *Australia & New Zealand Banking Group Ltd v Westpac Banking Corporation* [1988] HCA 17, (1988) 164 CLR 662, 675 [14]; M Bryan, 'Recovering Misdirected Money from Banks' in FD Rose (ed), *Restitution and Banking Law* (Oxford, Mansfield Press, 1998); *Uzinterimpex JSC v Standard Bank plc* [2008] EWCA Civ 819, [2008] Bus LR 1762 [39]–[40] (Moore-Bick LJ; Laws LJ and Clarke MR agreeing); R Stevens, 'Why Do Agents "Drop Out"?' [2005] *Lloyd's Maritime and Commercial Law Quarterly* 101; *Agip (Africa) Ltd v Jackson* [1990] Ch 265, 292 (Millett J); C Mitchell, P Mitchell and S Watterson (eds), *Goff and Jones: The Law of Unjust Enrichment*, 8th edn (London, Sweet & Maxwell, 2011) 710 [2810].

[67] *Bofinger v Kingsway Group Ltd* [2009] HCA 44, (2009) 239 CLR 269 [97] citing *Challenger Managed Investments Ltd v Direct Money Corporation Pty Ltd* [2003] NSWSC 1072, (2003) 59 NSWLR 452, (2003) 12 BPR 22,257, 22,269 [50] (Bryson J).

The first answer is that, as the High Court has recognised on numerous occasions,[68] a claim for unjust enrichment does not require loss by the plaintiff. A plaintiff might recover in a claim for unjust enrichment against a defendant even if the plaintiff has suffered no loss, so that restitution would confer a profit on the plaintiff from the transaction. So it should not necessarily be an objection that the plaintiff would acquire a new secured right when prior to the unjust enrichment the plaintiff had no security.

The second answer is that subrogation might be permitted without giving the plaintiff a secured right. In other words, it is possible for the plaintiff to be subrogated to a creditor's rights to payment but not be subrogated to the creditor's security rights. Historically, the subrogation cases justified the conclusion on the basis that the security was 'kept alive' because the plaintiff who paid off the security was 'presumed in equity' to intend to keep it alive. But this involves two fictions. The security is not 'kept alive'. A new security is created by the court. Nor is there any basis for a presumption that the plaintiff intended to make the payment to obtain the benefit of the security. In *Paul v Speirway Ltd*,[69] Oliver J held that subrogation to a secured right would not be possible where the discharge was intended only to create an unsecured loan. More recently, *Banque Financière de la Cité*[70] is a good example of this. In that case, the plaintiff, mistakenly thinking that it held a valid letter of postponement, paid money to discharge a debt of its subsidiary. The debt was secured by a first charge over the subsidiary's property. The plaintiff's claim was not brought against the subsidiary even though the subsidiary was enriched by the plaintiff's mistaken discharge of the subsidiary's debt. Instead, the plaintiff's claim was brought against the company that held a second charge over the property of the subsidiary. The plaintiff said that the company had been enriched by improving its priority, from a second charge to a first charge. The House of Lords held that the plaintiff was entitled to be subrogated to the ('revived') first charge against its subsidiary to obtain priority over the second chargee. But the plaintiff had never intended to obtain a secured right when it discharged the subsidiary's debt. In the leading speech, Lord Hoffmann explained that this new 'charge' would only operate against the second chargee.[71] It would not operate against any other person.

The third answer to the objection by the High Court of Australia is that if unjust enrichment is rejected as the explanation for subrogation, then why does subrogation exist? How are we able to ascertain its boundaries or the scope of its operation? As we have seen, many of the cases were based on an obvious fiction that the plaintiff intended to keep the security alive. Stripped of the fiction, unjust enrichment is the only rationale for permitting subrogation. In *Orakpo v Manson Investments Ltd*, Lord Diplock said 'Some rights by subrogation … appear to defeat classification except as an empirical remedy to prevent a particular kind of unjust enrichment.'[72]

The approach by the High Court of Australia in rejecting unjust enrichment as an explanation of non-contractual subrogation might be supported on the basis that until very recently, no case had suggested that unjust enrichment was the explanation for these cases. This argument would assert that the historical cases should not be reinterpreted by reference to some modern concept of unjust enrichment, even though it is accepted that

[68] See section IIIA above, and chapter five, section II.

[69] *Paul v Speirway Ltd* [1976] Ch 220.

[70] *Banque Financière de la Cité v Parc (Battersea) Ltd* [1998] UKHL 7, [1999] 1 AC 221.

[71] ibid 235–36.

[72] *Orakpo v Manson Investments Ltd* [1978] AC 95 (HL), 104.

the older cases are based on a fiction. But this argument, if accepted, would also undermine much of what is now well accepted to be part of the law of unjust enrichment. As we saw in Chapter 2, historically even a simple case of recovery of a mistaken payment was sometimes based upon a fiction that the action was one for implied contract. Further, why should such an argument that treating subrogation as part of the law of unjust enrichment is ahistorical stop at unjust enrichment? Why not argue that the category of 'contract' is illegitimate because it was a nineteenth-century reinterpretation of the forms of action including assumpsit, covenant and debt?

A better, and more transparent, approach is to recognise that instances of non-contractual subrogation are a response to unjust enrichment but that they involve restitution in a different sense from that in which the remedy is usually understood. A plaintiff who is subrogated to a discharged, secured debt generally obtains a new secured right which did not derive from the plaintiff. Once again, the use of 'restitution' is strained as a description of this remedy for unjust enrichment.

E. The Fifth Type of Restitution: Restitution by Extinguishing Past or Future Rights

The fifth scenario has never been recognised by courts as a case of restitution of unjust enrichment. It has almost never been recognised by commentators. Courts have developed principles concerning the discharge of a plaintiff's future duties under the labels 'termination' and 'frustration'. But no court has clearly enunciated the basis upon which those principles were developed and are applied.

One view is that unjust enrichment can provide an explanation for why a defendant's future rights are discharged. We consider that the basal principle is the same as rescission of executory contractual rights (which operates both prospectively and retrospectively). On this approach, termination occurs because a plaintiff establishes that the basis of her contractual rights has failed due to a failure of a basis of the contract which the plaintiff does not waive (termination for breach) or cannot waive (frustration).[73] This point was made effectively by Floyd LJ (Laws and Bean LJJ agreeing) in *Gartell & Son (a firm) v Yeovil Town Football & Athletic Club Ltd*.[74] His Lordship said that the 'significance of the finding of total failure of consideration was that Yeovil was discharged from its obligation to pay the price'. And then his Lordship observed that the same conclusion is reached by saying that 'there has been a breach of a condition, or of an intermediate term where the breach was so serious as to deprive Yeovil of substantially the whole benefit of the contract'.

An understanding of the doctrines of termination for breach or termination for frustration might significantly benefit from an appreciation of this underlying basal principle of unjust enrichment. For instance, a conceptual difficulty which was only finally resolved in Australia in 2007,[75] concerned whether a plaintiff has a power to terminate for a sufficiently serious breach of an 'intermediate' term which cannot be characterised

[73] C Langley and R Loveridge, 'Termination as a Response to Unjust Enrichment' [2012] *Lloyd's Maritime and Commercial Law Quarterly* 65, relying in part on arguments by J Edelman, 'Liability in Unjust Enrichment Where a Contract Fails to Materialise' in A Burrows and E Peel (eds), *Contract Formation and Parties* (Oxford, Oxford University Press, 2010).

[74] *Gartell & Son (a firm) v Yeovil Town Football & Athletic Club Ltd* [2016] EWCA Civ 62 [33].

[75] *Koompahtoo Local Aboriginal Land Council v Sanpine Pty Ltd* [2007] HCA 61, (2007) 233 CLR 115.

as necessarily a condition or a warranty at the time of contracting. In that case, Kirby J dissented, arguing that 'the classification of a contractual term as "intermediate" is nothing more than a function of *ex post facto* evaluation of the seriousness of the breach in all of the circumstances', so that the label itself is meaningless. It is not assigned on the basis of characteristics internal to, or inherent in, a particular term but is imprecise and is 'imposed retrospectively, in consequence of the application of the judicial process'.[76] An understanding of the basis of termination for breach as lying in the concept of unjust enrichment for failure of consideration might justify why a defendant's rights could be brought to an end by a plaintiff where the basis for the conferral of those rights fails *ex post facto* even if such a determination could not have been known at the time of contracting.

F. The Focus of this Book

The primary focus of this book is on the first category of restitution: restitution of value. This is the most comfortable sense in which the word 'restitution' is appropriately used to describe the remedy for unjust enrichment. As we have explained, restitution is most easily explained as a 'giving back'[77] or, as the High Court expresses it, a 'restoration' of 'what has been transferred from the plaintiff to the defendant'.[78] In each of the other areas, the differences in the nature of the order might justify the different terminology such as specific restitution (scenario 2) rescission, constructive or resulting trusts (scenario 3), subrogation (scenario 4) or frustration or termination (scenario 5). But the future development of the law would be assisted by an understanding that the ultimate basis for the orders in some cases is unjust enrichment. For that reason, although we focus primarily on the dominant restitutionary remedy involving restitution of value, in considering the law of unjust enrichment we also consider cases involving 'restitution' of present and future rights, and discharged duties.

V. The Different Labels Historically Used to Describe Orders for Restitution of Value

A. Different Common Law Labels Concerning Restitution of Value

Historically, restitution was awarded at common law under a number of different names: wayleaves, common counts of *indebitatus assumpsit*[79] (money had and received, money paid to the use of the defendant as well as *quantum meruit* and *quantum valebant* awards),[80]

[76] ibid [107].

[77] *Citadel General Assurance Company v Lloyds Bank Canada* [1997] 3 SCR 805 [30].

[78] *Roxborough v Rothmans of Pall Mall Australia Ltd* [2001] HCA 68, (2001) 208 CLR 516 [26] approving *Commissioner of State Revenue (Vic) v Royal Insurance Australia Ltd* [1994] HCA 61, (1994) 182 CLR 51, 75 [41] (Mason CJ). See also a similar statement in *Hill v Van Erp* [1997] HCA 9, (1997) 188 CLR 159, 226–27 (Gummow J). See also American Law Institute, *Restatement of the Law of Restitution: Quasi Contracts and Constructive Trusts* (St Pauls, Minn, American Law Institute Publishers, 1937) 12 [s 1(a)].

[79] E Lawes, *Practical Treatise on Pleading in Assumpsit* (London, W Reed, 1810) 418–503.

[80] From the mid-nineteenth century these forms were pleaded as *indebitatus assumpsit*: JH Baker, 'The History of Quasi-Contract in English Law' in WR Cornish, R Nolan, J O'Sullivan and G Virgo (eds), *Restitution: Past, Present and Future: Essays in Honour of Gareth Jones* (Oxford, Hart Publishing, 1998) 41.

mesne profits, reasonable royalties and awards simply labelled 'damages' and assessed according to a 'user principle'.

Several examples from different areas of law show the variety of different common law techniques used to describe restitutionary remedies. Matters were further confused because many of these techniques were described in the cases as based on a fiction of 'implied contract'. The history of the abolition of this fiction of implied contract and the decline of the forms of action which disguised many of these restitutionary remedies were discussed in Chapter 2.[81]

The first example of a restitutionary remedy, concealed in the historic language of the forms of action, involves restitution of money to the plaintiff. Historically, the restitution of money to the plaintiff was concealed within *indebitatus assumpsit* counts of money had and received and money paid. The count of money had and received was expressed as follows:

> [N]ot regarding his said several promises and undertakings, but contriving and fraudulently intending, craftily and subtilly, to deceive and defraud [the plaintiff], hath not yet paid the said several sums of money, or any part thereof, ... [and] hath hitherto wholly refused, and still refuses ...[82]

A second example involves restitution of the value of services provided by the plaintiff. Historically the form of action for *quantum meruit* was used in circumstances which included restitution of the value of services. Sometimes the claim for the value of services was sought as an implied term in a genuine contract. But on other occasions there was no contract and restitution of the value of services can only be understood as what is now called restitution of unjust enrichment. As we saw in Chapter 2, it is now recognised that where the claim is based on unjust enrichment, the label *quantum meruit* ('as much as it was worth') could conceal the award of restitution of unjust enrichment. An example is *Pavey & Matthews Pty Ltd v Paul.*[83] Mrs Paul had engaged builders to do building work for her. The contract was oral and unenforceable due to legislation in New South Wales. The High Court of Australia recognised that there was a non-contractual action in unjust enrichment for restitution of the value of the services provided. The High Court acknowledged that historically this remedy had not been described as restitution but instead was pleaded and decided as a form of action in *indebitatus assumpsit*,[84] in particular a 'count' of *quantum meruit*[85] for the fair value of the services performed.

A third example involves restitution of the value of goods. An example of this can be seen where the plaintiff's goods had been stolen by the defendant. Restitution of the value of the goods was commonly awarded in other *indebitatus assumpsit* counts such as of 'goods sold and delivered' or *quantum valebat* counts. In *Russell v Bell* Lord Abinger said that

> if a stranger takes my goods, and delivers them to another man, no doubt a contract may be implied, and I may bring an action either of trover for them, or of assumpsit. ... [There is a] right to waive the tort, and bring an action of assumpsit for goods sold and delivered.[86]

This is now recognised as a claim for restitution of unjust enrichment.

[81] Ch 2 pp 9–15.
[82] HJ Stephen, *A Treatise on the Principles of Pleading in Civil Actions: Comprising a Summary View of the Whole Proceedings in a Suit at Law*, 2nd edn (London, John Butterworth and Son, 1827) 313–14.
[83] *Pavey & Matthews Pty Ltd v Paul* [1987] HCA 5, (1987) 162 CLR 221.
[84] 'Being indebted, he promised.'
[85] 'A fair amount.'
[86] *Russell v Bell* (1842) 10 M & W 340, 352, (1842) 152 ER 500, 506. See also *Hill v Perrott* (1810) 3 Taunt 274, (1810) 128 ER 109.

B. Different Labels in Equity Concerning Restitution of Value

The approach taken in this book is to treat restitutionary awards in equity and at common law together, provided only that the event for which the restitutionary remedy is given (whether at law or in equity) is unjust enrichment. The principle underlying this fusionist approach is explained in detail in Chapters 2 and 4. It is not a new approach. Almost 100 years ago, Professor Hohfeld argued that to treat equity as a separate system from law is 'unscientific, both from the point of view of analysis and from that of educational expediency'.[87] He later said:

> Since, in any sovereign state, there must, in the last analysis, be but a single system of genuine law, since the various principles and rules of that system must be consistent with one another, and since, accordingly, all genuine jural relations must be consistent with one another, two conflicting rules, the one 'legal' and the other 'equitable', cannot be valid at the same moment of time.[88]

When the *Restatement of the Law of Restitution* was published in 1937, it recognised that restitution was a remedy given in equity as well as at law. The full title of the Restatement was *Restatement of the Law of Restitution: Quasi Contracts and Constructive Trusts*. The same approach was taken by Goff and Jones in 1966,[89] and their reference to the concurrent availability of restitution at law and in equity is now emphasised from the outset of their text.[90] Almost every writer on unjust enrichment now recognises that restitution is an equitable remedy as well as a common law one.[91]

Unlike the common law courts, the courts of equity did not develop a litany of labels to describe the remedy of restitution. When the remedy was a personal remedy, equity simply ordered a payment of money. As Professor Ibbetson has observed, although equity was often concerned with rescission of transfers of title to land (made by mistake, fraud, duress or extortion), cases involving personal restitutionary remedies were simply expressed as claims for money.[92] For example in *Attorney-General ex rel Ethery v Hunton*[93] a chief constable had received mistaken overpayments of rates from local ratepayers. He was held liable to the ratepayers for the value of those payments. Today this remedy would be described as restitution (for unjust enrichment arising from the mistaken payment), whether at common law or in equity. Another example is the restitution of value as part of the process of rescission of title.

There are numerous other examples of actions in which equity gave a restitutionary remedy but simply described it as an order for payment. Another such example is in

[87] WN Hohfeld, 'The Relations between Equity and Law' (1913) 11 *Michigan Law Review* 537, 538, quoting from Professor Cook, who referred to the fact that equitable 'modifications' such as specific performance should be taught as part of contract and not as part of 'equity'.

[88] ibid 557 (original emphasis omitted).

[89] R Goff and G Jones, *The Law of Restitution* (London, Sweet & Maxwell, 1966).

[90] C Mitchell, P Mitchell and S Watterson (eds), *Goff and Jones: The Law of Unjust Enrichment*, 8th edn (London, Sweet & Maxwell, 2011) 6 [1-06].

[91] P Birks, *Unjust Enrichment*, 2nd edn (Oxford, Oxford University Press, 2005) 292–93; K Mason and J Carter, *Restitution Law in Australia* (Sydney, Butterworths, 1995); A Burrows, *The Law of Restitution*, 3rd edn (Oxford, Oxford University Press, 2011) 25–26; K Mason, JW Carter and GJ Tolhurst, *Mason & Carter's Restitution Law in Australia*, 2nd edn (Sydney, LexisNexis Butterworths, 2008) xv, 4–6 [103]–[105]; G Virgo, *The Principles of the Law of Restitution*, 3rd edn (Oxford, Oxford University Press, 2015) ch 2.

[92] DJ Ibbetson, *A Historical Introduction to the Law of Obligations* (Oxford, Oxford University Press, 1999) 274.

[93] *Attorney-General ex rel Ethery v Hunton* (1739) West temp Hardwicke 703, (1739) 25 ER 1158.

circumstances in which a plaintiff has discharged, or was liable to discharge, a common liability of a co-obligor or a liability which was secondary to that of the principal debtor. The action for restitution from the co-obligor or principal debtor has usually been described as an award of 'contribution' or 'recoupment' respectively, and the remedy awarded is just described as a payment 'for contribution' or 'recoupment'. There are now a large number of authorities which recognise that these awards of contribution and recoupment, whether at common law or in equity, are awards of restitution based on unjust enrichment.[94] In Chapter 12, the nature of these awards of unjust enrichment is explained. The simple point is that the award is restitutionary: 'A right of indemnity is a right of restitution.'[95] The 'contribution' or 'recoupment' award gives back to the plaintiff what courts describe as the 'practical benefit' that the defendant receives from the discharge of his debt.

Although equity made money awards of restitution of value, a more common restitutionary response in equity was restitution of rights (recognition of trusts or rescission of rights). These cases involve a claimant electing to rescind a transaction and revest rights to a tangible thing that has come from the plaintiff's assets. However, another example of personal restitution in equity is when rescission is unavailable: the particular right of which restitution is sought might have been sold to a third party, or destroyed or fundamentally altered. In such cases equity might give a judgment for a money sum in place of an award designed to restore the right. This money remedy in place of rescission has itself been referred to in a number of different ways. Monetary awards of restitution in equity have been described as 'pecuniary rescission',[96] or 'the monetary equivalent of a rescissionary remedy',[97] or 'rescissory damages'.[98] With the qualification we have explained above, concerning the strain in the use of 'restitution' in cases involving restitution of rights, this book describes these awards as 'restitution' together with all other remedies, whether at common law or in equity, that give effect to a plaintiff's legal right to the return of the benefit received by the defendant at the expense of the plaintiff.

VI. Conclusion

The single most important point of this chapter is that the most dominant, and most comfortable, use of 'restitution' is a remedy that operates to restore to the plaintiff value that derives from the plaintiff. It is a remedy available both at law and in equity. Historically it

[94] *Fitzpatrick v Waterstreet* (NSWCA, 17 December 1998), [2000] ANZ ConvR 15 (Mason P); *Trade Practices Commission v Manfal Pty Ltd (No 3)* [1991] FCA 650, (1991) 33 FCR 382; *Austotel Management Pty Ltd v Jamieson* (FCA, 20 December 1995); *Halgido Pty Ltd v DG Capital Co Ltd* [1996] FCA 1123, (1996) 34 ATR 582; *Balkin v Peck* (1998) 43 NSWLR 706, 712; *James Hardie & Co Pty Ltd v Wyong Shire Council* [2000] NSWCA 107, (2000) 48 NSWLR 679 [36] (Giles JA; Handley JA concurring); *Cockburn v GIO Finance Ltd (No 2)* [2001] NSWCA 177, (2001) 51 NSWLR 624 [23]–[24] (Mason P; Davies AJA and Ipp AJA concurring); *AMP Workers' Compensation Services (NSW) Ltd v QBE Insurance Ltd* [2001] NSWCA 267, (2001) 53 NSWLR 35 [22] (Handley JA; Mason P and Beazley JA agreeing); *Belan v Casey* [2003] NSWSC 159, (2003) 57 NSWLR 670 [71] (Campbell J); *Burke v LFOT Pty Ltd* [2002] HCA 17, (2002) 209 CLR 282 [112] (Kirby J); *Lukey v Corporate Investment Australia Funds Management Pty Ltd* [2005] FCA 298 [335] (Emmett J).

[95] *Owen v Tate* [1976] QB 402, 409.

[96] P Birks, 'Unjust Factors and Wrongs: Pecuniary Rescission for Undue Influence (*Mahoney v Purnell*)' [1997] *Restitution Law Review* 72.

[97] *Hodgkinson v Simms* [1994] 3 SCR 377, 384, also referring to this approach as 'restitutionary': ibid 383.

[98] *Randall v Loftsgaarden* 478 US 647, 649 (1986).

has been described with a multitude of labels. But this is not the only remedy for unjust enrichment. If the remedy of restitution is stretched, then it can be used to describe at least four other responses to unjust enrichment. None of these is the usual response to unjust enrichment. None is usually described as restitution. But an appreciation that each is a response to unjust enrichment can help us understand the nature and contours of the subject.

Another very important point is one that was made in the previous chapter. Restitution is not a synonym for unjust enrichment. Unjust enrichment is a legal category of event and restitution is a remedy, just as tort is a legal category of event and compensation is a remedy. Restitution might respond to events other than unjust enrichment such as torts or equitable wrongs. This book is not concerned with those events. They should be the subject of books concerned with those events. This book is concerned with the event of unjust enrichment. For this reason, this book is entitled *Unjust Enrichment*, and not *Restitution*. Instances in which restitution is awarded for reasons other than unjust enrichment (such as for reasons of legal policy or for wrongdoing) are considered only for the purpose of explaining the boundaries of the subject of unjust enrichment. So, just as a book on tort law is not concerned with the circumstances in which compensation is awarded for a breach of contract, so too this book is not concerned with the circumstances of the award of restitution for reasons other than unjust enrichment. For 70 years the dominant reference to this topic has been to 'the law of restitution'. Almost every common law text until 2003 on unjust enrichment was entitled 'Restitution'.[99] In renouncing 'Restitution' as a title in favour of 'Unjust Enrichment' in his final book, Professor Birks wrote:

> To be properly understood unjust enrichment needs books to itself. That is not to deny that it will always occupy a large part of any book on the law of restitution, but only to assert that its distinctive nature as an independent causative event cannot be securely made apparent unless and until it is treated in isolation from other instances of gain-based recovery.[100]

We agree.

[99] One exception is Professor Dawson's comparative study: JP Dawson, *Unjust Enrichment: A Comparative Analysis* (Boston, Little, Brown and Company, 1951).

[100] P Birks, *Unjust Enrichment*, 2nd edn (Oxford, Oxford University Press, 2005) 4–5.

Part II

Elements of Unjust Enrichment

4

The Enrichment Enquiry

Contents

I. Introduction

The first element in a claim for 'unjust enrichment at the expense of another' is that the defendant must have been enriched. In the cases upon which this book focuses, namely where a plaintiff seeks restitution of value obtained by a defendant, the label 'enrichment' is a useful construct to focus attention upon three related requirements. Those requirements are: (1) a benefit; (2) circumstances which show that the benefit that was provided by the plaintiff was chosen by the defendant; and (3) the choice has been made by the defendant as the principal, not an agent. This chapter examines each of these requirements in turn and then considers the manner in which the benefit is valued and the time at which the valuation is conducted.

The same three requirements do not apply where a different measure of restitution is sought, such as restitution of rights, things, discharged debts, or future duties. For instance, the considerations discussed in this chapter concerning a defendant's choice of a benefit that arise in cases of restitution of value do not arise in cases where a plaintiff seeks restitution of a right or a thing held by the defendant. This is because in the case of restitution of value, a person should not be required to pay for a benefit obtained which is not chosen and which could place her in a worse position than she occupied prior to her receipt of the value. That concern is absent in cases such as restitution of a right or restitution of a thing at least where there has been no change of position. Although some academic works on unjust enrichment are developing the different rules of enrichment for each of these categories of restitution,[1] we have left the rules for recovery in these cases to specific monographs such as those on trusts, subrogation, termination, and frustration. As we explained in Chapter 3, the primary focus of this book is upon restitution of value.[2]

As to the first requirement for enrichment (a benefit), courts take a broad approach which includes the following as benefits: money, services, contractual rights, and opportunities to use and exchange land, chattels and money. The second requirement, that the benefit provided by the plaintiff has been chosen by the defendant, focuses upon the concern in the cases for the autonomy of defendants. A defendant's right to free choice means that he should not be considered enriched unless the benefit is chosen by him. Importantly, this question of choice is independent of the value which a defendant places on the provided benefit. The third requirement, of personal receipt or provision for the defendant, means that an enrichment does not include the exceptional cases in which a defendant receives a benefit ministerially based upon the choice of another person, accounting immediately to that other person.

The final sections of this chapter show that once a defendant is shown to be enriched, the cases have treated the defendant's subjective views about the particular *value* of his enrichment as irrelevant. Valuation of a proved enrichment is carried out on an objective basis; namely, the value to a reasonable person in the position of the defendant. The valuation is conducted at the time the benefit is chosen.

II. A Benefit

Although the concept of a benefit to the defendant lies at the heart of the law of unjust enrichment, there is relatively little discussion in the case law about what is capable of being a benefit, for the purpose of an actionable enrichment. It is convenient to discuss these

[1] See, particularly, A Lodder *Enrichment in the Law of Unjust Enrichment and Restitution* (Oxford, Hart Publishing, 2012) esp 60–64 dealing with enrichment by rights and enrichment by release of a debt.

[2] See Ch 3 pp 35–37.

issues concerning whether particular matters are capable of being a benefit for the purposes of a claim for restitution of value separately from whether they are a benefit *to the defendant*. The issue of whether something is of value and capable of being a benefit for a claim for restitution of the value is a different question from whether the benefit must be chosen by the defendant. But an overarching point should be made at the outset. The notion of 'benefit' to the defendant must be understood in a broad sense in the law of unjust enrichment. So, for instance, if a defendant requests a plaintiff to perform a service for, or make a payment to a third party, then the performance of that service, or the making of that payment by the plaintiff, is a benefit to the defendant.[3] In *Goss v Chilcott*,[4] a lender paid money to a third party who discharged a loan of the borrowers. The payment was held to be an enrichment of the borrowers, whose loan was void. The advance of money to the third party essentially involved a payment at the request of the borrowers to their third-party creditor.

A. Money

The word 'money' describes a medium of exchange which is the measure of value. As Robert Goff J said, 'Money has the peculiar character of a universal medium of exchange.'[5] Although economists subdivide money into different classes depending upon its fungibility, we use the term here to describe only the most liquid forms of exchange: notes and coins, instantly accessible bank debts due to a plaintiff, and so on.

Money, as a measure of value, is therefore a benefit. Arguments for exceptions to this rule are rare. One argument sometimes ventilated in academic environments concerns when the money involved is a stolen physical banknote or bearer instrument. As we will see below in relation to chattels, the thief is enriched at the moment he or she steals the banknote or instrument, even though the owner still has title to the banknote or instrument. The thief is unjustly enriched by the value he receives at the owner's expense: 'someone who receives stolen money is placed under a legal obligation to hand it, or an equivalent sum, back to the rightful owner. If he does not, he will be unjustly enriched.'[6] But the thief will usually be the only person who is unjustly enriched by the receipt of the money. A peculiarity of money is that it is one of the few examples at common law where a bona fide purchaser of a stolen thing will not be liable to the true owner. The passage of money into currency by its use extinguishes the title of the true owner. This rule would be subverted if the bona fide purchaser from the thief, who obtains a benefit, did not have a defence of bona fide purchase.

B. Services

The performance of a service can constitute a benefit of value. Two arguments are sometimes made against services necessarily being a benefit. First, it has been argued that there must be some accretion to the defendant's net *wealth* for services to be beneficial.

[3] *Crown Prosecution Service v Eastenders Group* [2014] UKSC 26, [2015] AC 1; *Riverwood Legion & Community Club Ltd v Repaja & Co Pty Ltd* [2015] NSWSC 383 [210] (Stevenson J).

[4] *Goss v Chilcott* [1996] UKPC 17, [1996] AC 788.

[5] *BP Exploration Co (Libya) Ltd v Hunt (No 2)* [1979] 1 WLR 783, 799.

[6] *Barros Mattos Junior v MacDaniels Ltd* [2004] EWHC 1188 (Ch), [2005] 1 WLR 247 [15] (Laddie J).

Professor Beatson (as Beatson LJ was then) argued that a benefit must have an 'exchange-value' and that this is not the case if a service leaves no valuable end product.[7] Beatson accepted only that pure services which save the defendant from otherwise necessary expenditure are beneficial.[8] Beatson's 'economic benefit' approach has not been applied and pure services have been held to be enriching in a significant number of cases.[9] A good example is *Brenner v First Artists' Management Pty Ltd.*[10] In that case, Byrne J expressly rejected the contention that '"benefit" for the purpose of the rule of restitution for services must be an economic benefit'.[11] That case concerned a claim for restitution of the value of management services provided to a former pop star (Daryl Braithwaite) as part of a campaign to revive the singer's career. Justice Byrne held that it was of benefit to the project simply that it was publicly known that one of the plaintiffs, Fenner, was Braithwaite's manager. Fenner also '[made] himself agreeable' to executives within the music industry, thereby 'oiling … the wheels' for Braithwaite's comeback.[12] Another of Fenner's most valuable tasks was to lift Braithwaite's spirits and ensure his concentration on the task at hand, at a time when Braithwaite may have been despondent or depressed. None of these benefits were tangible or economic in nature, yet all of them were benefits for the purpose of the claim in unjust enrichment.

A second objection to services being relevant benefits is that they cannot be restored to a plaintiff in the same way as money.[13] Once a plaintiff has performed a service, his labour is expended and cannot be returned. For this reason, Professors Grantham and Rickett deny that pure services can be the subject of a claim for restitution.[14] However, as we saw in Chapter 3, most restitutionary remedies have the purpose of restoring *value* to the plaintiff from the defendant personally rather than restoring to the plaintiff rights or restoring a thing.[15] Provided the service performed has a value, that value can be restored.

Perhaps the most significant difficulty lies in cases that involve both services *and* tangible rights as end products.[16] Is the benefit of value the services or the rights to the end product, or both? Professor Virgo argues that where services result in an end product, the services are superseded by the end product.[17] A better approach, which is more consistent with the cases, is to consider the circumstances surrounding the request or acceptance and

[7] J Beatson, *The Use and Abuse of Unjust Enrichment: Essays on the Law of Restitution* (Oxford, Clarendon Press, 1991) 21, 31–33. Cf discussion in G Virgo, *The Principles of the Law of Restitution*, 3rd edn (Oxford, Oxford University Press, 2015) 77.

[8] An example of benefit found on this basis is *Monks v Poynice Pty Ltd* (1987) 8 NSWLR 662, following *Craven-Ellis v Canons Ltd* [1936] 2 KB 403.

[9] Eg *Monks v Poynice Pty Ltd* (1987) 8 NSWLR 662; *Independent Grocers Co-operative Ltd v Noble Lowndes Superannuation Consultants Ltd* (1993) 60 SASR 525; *Brenner v First Artists' Management Pty Ltd* [1993] 2 VR 221; *Damberg v Damberg* [2001] NSWCA 87, (2001) 52 NSWLR 492; *Andrew Shelton & Co Pty Ltd v Alpha Healthcare Ltd* [2002] VSC 248, (2002) 5 VR 577; *Cobbe v Yeoman's Row Management Ltd* [2008] UKHL 55, [2008] 1 WLR 1752.

[10] *Brenner v First Artists' Management Pty Ltd* [1993] 2 VR 221.

[11] ibid, 257.

[12] ibid, 265.

[13] *BP Exploration Co (Libya) Ltd v Hunt (No 2)* [1979] 1 WLR 783, 799 (Robert Goff J).

[14] R Grantham and CEF Rickett, *Enrichment and Restitution in New Zealand* (Oxford, Hart, 2000) 61; see also general discussion at 20–21 and 60–61.

[15] Ch 3 pp 35–37.

[16] *BP Exploration Co (Libya) Ltd v Hunt (No 2)* [1979] 1 WLR 783, 801 (Robert Goff J), discussed in *Brenner v First Artists' Management Pty Ltd* [1993] 2 VR 221, 258 (Byrne J); also *Sunstar Fruit Pty Ltd v Cosmo* [1995] 2 Qd R 214, 228–29 (Derrington J).

[17] G Virgo, *The Principles of the Law of Restitution*, 3rd edn (Oxford, Oxford University Press, 2015) 76–77

to ask whether what was being conferred was an end product or a service. In cases where the defendant has requested the benefit, the answer will simply depend upon whether the benefit requested was the service or the end product. The enrichment will be measured by the value of the particular benefit chosen (the service or the end product).

This approach to enrichment is also compelling in principle. As Byrne J noted in *Brenner*,[18] if a defendant requested the services of a mineral prospector, selling broker, or artist's manager, the value of the service might bear little or no proportion to the end product. A mining prospector might, with little effort, discover a rich resource or, with much effort, be entirely unsuccessful. In each services case the nature of the benefit (service or end product) received falls to be assessed by reference to the circumstances surrounding the conferral of the benefit.

C. Transferred Contractual Rights and the Release from Contractual Obligations

The most obvious example of recognition of contractual rights as a benefit of value is a mistaken payment from A to B in the banking system. B has increased the value of his rights against his bank, which is the debt that B's bank now owes to him. That increased value of the debt is almost always treated as a benefit, apart from exceptional cases discussed later in this chapter.

If the acquisition of contractual rights is a benefit of value, it must also follow that the release of contractual duties is also a benefit of value. For instance, we will see in Chapter 12 that there are numerous cases which recognise that a compelled payment of another's debt is part of the law of unjust enrichment.[19] The benefit that the defendant receives in such cases is the release from contractual obligations. Another circumstance in which we can see how the release from contractual obligations is treated as a restitutionary claim is where an award of restitution is required following rescission of a contract. So, in *Newbigging v Adam*,[20] when Newbigging sought to rescind his contract of partnership, Bowen LJ explained (in dissent, but not on this point) that the discharge of a defendant's obligations, or the assumption by the plaintiff of the defendant's obligations, are 'advantages' for which restitution must be made.

By recognising the release of contractual duties as a benefit, we avoid having to draw distinctions between (i) purely executory contract rights; (ii) contract rights described by the High Court as 'quasi-proprietary';[21] (iii) contractual rights which involve an executed demise;[22] and (iv) contractual rights which create rights to other things. In all cases, the passage of valuable rights or release from onerous duties is a benefit. As we saw in Chapter 3, restitution might take the form of restoring those rights, subrogating the plaintiff to a new

[18] *Brenner v First Artists' Management Pty Ltd* [1993] 2 VR 221, 258.

[19] Ch 12 pp 291–92.

[20] *Newbigging v Adam* (1886) 34 Ch D 582, 594–95. See also *Winefield v Clarke* [2008] NSWSC 882.

[21] *Zhu v Treasurer of the State of New South Wales* [2004] HCA 56, (2004) 218 CLR 530, 572–83 [124]–[147] (Gleeson CJ, Gummow, Kirby, Callinan and Heydon JJ).

[22] *Willmott Growers Group Inc v Willmott Forests Ltd (Receivers and Managers Appointed) (in liq)* [2013] HCA 51, (2013) 251 CLR 592 [39] (French CJ, Hayne and Kiefel JJ), [67] (Gageler J).

duty matching the duty which was extinguished or, most commonly and the subject of this chapter, restitution of the value of the benefit obtained.

D. Transferred Rights to Chattels and Land

Rights to chattels and land are valuable benefits that are capable of being enrichments in the law of unjust enrichment. There are many examples where the receipt of rights to chattels or land is treated as a benefit for the law of unjust enrichment. Three brief examples are *Cressman v Coys of Kensington (Sales) Ltd*,[23] where the benefit was the rights to a car's licence plate, *Weatherby v Banham*,[24] where the benefit was rights to a 'gentlemen's magazine', and *Southage Pty Ltd v Vescovi*,[25] where the receipt of title to a property was a prima facie enrichment.

E. Factual Possession of Things Stolen or Taken

Where a defendant receives legal title to a chattel or land which has value, there can be no doubt that the receipt of this benefit is capable of amounting to an enrichment. As we have seen in Chapter 3, there are different claims which can be brought in unjust enrichment. In some circumstances a claim can be brought for restitution of the *thing*. Another claim that might be brought is a claim for restitution of the rights which have been transferred to the defendant. But by far the most common claim, and the subject of this chapter, is a claim for restitution of the value received by the defendant.

In some circumstances where a defendant obtains factual possession of a thing there can be no claim for restitution of the thing nor any claim for restitution of any rights. For instance, suppose a thief steals an ordinary chattel, such as a standard model car. In that case, there will be no claim for restitution of the thing, because money is an adequate award. Nor is there any need for a claim for restitution of rights because there is no transfer of any of the owner's rights. The owner's rights remain unaffected. But the thief does obtain value at the expense of the owner of the car. This is because the thief obtains the fact of possession which the owner loses by the theft. That fact of possession creates a valuable opportunity for the thief to sell, use, or exchange the rights to the car. The value obtained by the thief has come at the expense of the owner, who will obtain very little, or nothing, when he attempts to sell his rights to the car of which he has no factual possession. In contrast, the value of the thief's ability to transfer rights is due to the thief's possession of the physical car, even if that value might be discounted by a purchaser due to uncertainty which might surround whether there are others with better possessory rights to the car. As Professor McInnes has said, 'only a cold technicality can deny … that a thief is enriched by the car that he steals. While title to the vehicle remains in the victim, it is the thief who need not walk to work.'[26]

[23] *Cressman v Coys of Kensington (Sales) Ltd* [2004] EWCA Civ 47, [2004] 1 WLR 2775.

[24] *Weatherby v Banham* (1832) 5 Car & P 228, (1832) 172 ER 950.

[25] *Southage Pty Ltd v Vescovi* [2014] VSC 141; [2015] VSCA 117, (2015) 321 ALR 383.

[26] M McInnes, 'Restitution, Unjust Enrichment and the Perfect Quadration Thesis' [1999] *Restitution Law Review* 118, 125 fn 38. See also P Birks, 'Property and Unjust Enrichment: Categorical Truths' [1997] *New Zealand Law Review* 623, 647–49, 654.

Apart from the value that the thief receives from the fact of possession, the law also recognises that the factual possession of a thief means that even a thief has a *right* to possess.[27] That possessory right is good against the whole world except the true owner or a person with a better possessory title.[28] But the focus of a claim for restitution of value is the value that the defendant has received. In this case, the value obtained by the defendant derives from the physical possession of the chattel, not the rights that the defendant has to the chattel. Hence, if the car is taken by force from the thief, then the thief will still have his possessory rights. But he will not have any value.

In theory, the measure of the thief's enrichment in an unjust enrichment claim should be the objective exchange value of his factual possession of the chattel which is less than the true market value because he is not the owner. This is the same as the approach in a claim for conversion where the focus upon the *plaintiff's* right shows that the right was conditional. For instance, in *Brierly v Kendall*,[29] Brierly assigned his household chattels to the defendants to secure a debt owed. A term of the agreement was that Brierly was entitled to possess and use the goods without any hindrance from the defendants until default in payment after the due day. The defendants served Brierly with a notice to pay before the due day, and when he did not they took possession of the goods. Brierly brought a claim for damages for conversion for the loss suffered from the sale of his goods. Lord Campbell CJ (with whom Patteson and Wightman JJ concurred) said that he had 'little doubt that the value of the goods [was] not the proper measure of damages'.[30] The measure of damages was assessed at the lower value of Brierly's interest in the goods, which was defeasible if he did not pay the debt by the due date. The same is true for measures of value in unjust enrichment.

F. Opportunity to Use Money

Australian law is currently in a state of uncertainty concerning whether the opportunity to use money is a benefit which is capable of being an enrichment. Cases are pulling in different directions. A line of cases has recognised that a claim for restitution of money must include the use value of the money (interest).[31] As Brooking J has observed, 'interest is the ordinary fruits derived from the enjoyment of money, and those fruits should be

[27] *Bride v Shire of Katanning* [2013] WASCA 154 [72] (Edelman J; Newnes JA agreeing); *Costello v Chief Constable of Derbyshire Constabulary* [2001] EWCA Civ 381, [2001] 1 WLR 1437 [22] (Lightman J; Keene and Robert Walker LJJ agreeing); *Government of the Islamic Republic of Iran v The Barakat Galleries Ltd* [2007] EWCA Civ 1374, [2009] QB 22 [15] (the Court); *McMillan Properties Pty Ltd v WC Penfold Ltd* [2001] NSWSC 1173, (2001) 40 ACSR 319 [44] (Young CJ in Eq); *Fistar v Riverwood Legion and Community Club Ltd* [2016] NSWCA 81 [37] (Leeming JA).

[28] *Costello v Chief Constable of Derbyshire Constabulary* [2001] EWCA Civ 381, [2001] 1 WLR 1437; *Gollan v Nugent* [1988] HCA 59, (1988) 166 CLR 18, 28 [9] (Brennan J): 'there is clear authority that a right of recovery founded on possession is not affected by illegality in the manner in which the plaintiff acquired possession.' See also *Field v Sullivan* [1923] VLR 70, 82–84 (Macfarlan J); *Gatward v Alley* (1940) 40 SR (NSW) 174, 180 (the Court); *Perpetual Trustees & National Executors of Tasmania Ltd v Perkins* [1989] Aust Torts Reports 80-295, 69,201-2 (Green CJ).

[29] *Brierly v Kendall* (1852) 117 ER 1540.

[30] ibid 1543.

[31] *Production Spray Painting and Panel Beating Pty Ltd v Newnham (No 2)* (1992) 27 NSWLR 659; *TCN Channel 9 Pty Ltd v Antoniadis (No 2)* [1999] NSWCA 104, (1999) 48 NSWLR 381; *Meerkin & Apel v Rossett Pty Ltd (No 2)* [1999] VSCA 10, [1999] 2 VR 31; *Heydon v NRMA (No 2)* (2001) 53 NSWLR 600, [2001] NSWCA 445; *Road & Traffic Authority v Ryan (No 2)* [2002] NSWCA 128; *Cornwall v Rowan (No 2)* [2005] SASC 122.

"restored" ... by the person who has enjoyed, or was in a position to enjoy, them.'[32] But two judges of the High Court of Australia have doubted whether on the current state of authority there is any general principle which permits restitution of the use value of money other than in cases of money obtained and retained by fraud and money withheld or misapplied by a trustee or fiduciary.[33]

In contrast, the principle that the opportunity to use money is a benefit is now well established in English law. An important House of Lords decision on this point is *Sempra Metals Ltd (formerly Metallgesellschaft Ltd) v Inland Revenue Commissioners*.[34] Sempra was the lead claimant in group litigation which arose after Sempra's success in the European Court of Justice.[35] The European Court of Justice held that the UK had acted contrary to European law by permitting UK resident corporate groups to postpone the time at which they paid corporation tax, while withholding this advantage from corporate groups with subsidiaries resident in the UK and parent companies resident elsewhere in the EC. Such groups had to pay advance corporation tax. The ECJ directed the UK courts to provide disadvantaged groups with 'an effective legal remedy in order to obtain reimbursement or reparation of the financial loss which they [had] sustained and from which the authorities [had] benefited'.[36] One question for the House of Lords was whether the IRC was unjustly enriched by their free use of Sempra's payment.[37] The House of Lords held that they were.

In the minority in *Sempra*, Lord Scott asserted that the restitutionary award was 'wholly conceptual'.[38] One commentator has also described the award as 'illusory'.[39] The English Court of Appeal in *Littlewoods* also assumed that the benefit received from a free opportunity to use money is the interest or profits *subsequently* earned, saying that 'an innocent recipient of an overpayment should not have to make restitution of more than he actually received, not knowing it was an overpayment, unless he freely accepted the benefit of having an overpayment and the obligation to pay for it at market rates'.[40] All these statements are incorrect. The subsequent use to which the receipt of money is put is not a benefit arising from the relevant transaction. The benefit that arises from the transaction is the *opportunity* to use the money. The Revenue in *Sempra* did not merely choose the payment of the taxation. It chose that payment on an earlier basis than when the payment was otherwise required. It received the opportunity to use the money earlier than it should have done. The opportunity to use millions of pounds without cost is not an illusory benefit, even if it later turns out that no profit was made from the use of the money. The free opportunity

[32] *National Australia Bank Ltd v Bond Brewing Holdings Ltd* [1991] 1 VR 386, 594.

[33] *Commonwealth v SCI Operations Pty Ltd* [1998] HCA 20, (1998) 192 CLR 285 [74] (McHugh and Gummow JJ).

[34] *Sempra Metals Ltd (formerly Metallgesellschaft Ltd) v Inland Revenue Commissioners* [2007] UKHL 34, [2008] 1 AC 561.

[35] *Joined Cases C-397 and 410/98*, Metallgesellschaft Ltd v Inland Revenue Commissioners, Hoechst AG v Inland Revenue Commissioners [2001] ECR I-1727, [2001] Ch 620.

[36] ibid [96].

[37] The question of the period during which the unjust factor of mistake had been operative had earlier divided the House of Lords in *Deutsche Morgan Grenfell Group Plc v Inland Revenue Commissioners* [2006] UKHL 49, [2007] 1 AC 558.

[38] *Sempra Metals Ltd (formerly Metallgesellschaft Ltd) v Inland Revenue Commissioners* [2007] UKHL 34, [2008] 1 AC 561 [145] (Lord Scott).

[39] P Ridge, 'Pre-Judgment Compound Interest' (2010) 126 *Law Quarterly Review* 279, 289.

[40] *Littlewoods Ltd v HM Revenue and Customs* [2015] EWCA Civ 515 [193].

to use money is an immediate benefit irrespective of the use to which the money is put.[41] It would be a great surprise to any lender of money that a defendant who obtained the opportunity to use money without paying for it did not immediately obtain any benefit. A bank does not waive interest charges if the borrower squanders the money. As we will see later, the focus on the value of the opportunity to use the money explains why the rate of interest is assessed objectively. In the words of the Full Court of the South Australian Supreme Court:[42]

> The rate of interest is not dependent upon the rate which the payee in fact earned (if any) on the amounts paid, nor on the rate which the payer could have earned on the money if retained. It is to be determined at a rate which provides appropriate restitution to the appellants.

However, if it turns out that the borrower does not take subsequent advantage of the opportunity benefit—the money is squandered—a defence of subsequent change of position might arise.[43] The availability of such a defence will also depend on factors such as the legality of the defendant's subsequent actions or the defendant's good faith or the defendant's knowledge of the circumstances.

G. Opportunity to Use Land or Chattels

Historically there were claims for restitution for the value of money, land or chattels received in the forms of action in *indebitatus assumpsit*. But, historically, there was no common law claim for the *opportunity to use* money, land or chattels. Bemoaning the lack of recognition of an *indebitatus assumpsit* count in cases involving enrichment through the opportunity to use another's property rights, Professor Ames wrote that

> one is often bound by those same ties of justice and equity to pay for an unjust enrichment enjoyed at the expense of another, although no money has been received. The quasi-contractual liability to make restitution is the same in reason, whether, for example, one who has converted another's goods turns them into money or consumes them.[44]

As we saw in Chapter 2, the law has now broken free from the constraints of the forms of action.[45] Without the constraints of the forms of *indebitatus assumpsit* it is now beyond doubt that the opportunity to use the plaintiff's land or chattels is a benefit that can amount to an enrichment. No loss is required.[46] As Lord Denman CJ explained 'he who holds my

[41] *Littlewoods Retail Ltd & Ors v HM Revenue & Customs* [2014] EWHC 868 (Ch) [372] (Henderson J). Cf *Littlewoods Ltd & Ors v HM Revenue & Customs* [2015] EWCA Civ 515 [186] (the Court).

[42] *Cornwall v Rowan (No 2)* [2005] SASC 122 [39]. See further, J Edelman and D Cassidy, *Interest Awards in Australia* (Sydney, LexisNexis Butterworths, 2003) ch 5.

[43] *Sempra Metals Ltd (formerly Metallgesellschaft Ltd) v Inland Revenue Commissioners* [2007] UKHL 34, [2008] 1 AC 561 [119] (Lord Nicholls). See also *Test Claimants in the FII Group Litigation v HM Revenue & Customs* [2014] EWHC 4302 (Ch) [414] (Henderson J).

[44] JB Ames, *Lectures on Legal History and Miscellaneous Legal Essays* (Cambridge, Harvard University Press, 1913) 164–65.

[45] Ch 2 pp 9–15.

[46] *BP Exploration Co (Libya) Ltd v Hunt* (No 2) [1979] 1 WLR 783, 799 (Robert Goff J); *ABB Power Generation Ltd v Chapple* [2001] WASCA 412, (2002) 25 WAR 158 discussed in Ch 5 p 91. Contrast *Strang Patrick Stevedoring Pty Ltd v The Owners of the Motor Vessel 'Sletter' (Formerly the 'Hibiscus Trader')* [1992] FCA 513, (1992) 38 FCR 501.

premises without an express bargain agrees to pay what a jury may find the occupation to be worth.'[47] Support for the treatment of the opportunity to use land or chattels as a benefit for the purposes of the law of unjust enrichment can be seen in cases involving the restitution of the benefit of the value of land or chattels following the process of rescission[48] which, as we saw in Chapter 3, is capable of being understood as part of the law of unjust enrichment.[49]

If I steal your car and return it after a month, I am enriched by the opportunity to use it that has come from my possession of the car at your expense. In *Dimond v Lovell,*[50] the House of Lords considered a case where a hire car was provided under an unenforceable agreement. Lord Hoffmann, in the leading speech, said that Mrs Dimond 'has had 8 days use of a Ford Mondeo for nothing. She has certainly been enriched at the expense of 1st Automotive'.[51] The claim only failed because the policy underlying the illegality of the agreement precluded a claim for unjust enrichment.[52]

We saw above that there is dispute concerning what must be proved to show that a defendant has obtained the use of money. The best answer, as explained above, is that the benefit is the *opportunity* to use the money, even if it is not used to obtain any profit. The same applies to the use of land, or the hire of chattels. A defendant who obtains the opportunity to use land or chattels without paying for the opportunity obtains a benefit even if the land or chattels are not commercially fruitful.[53] A car hire company does not refund the cost of the hire if the hiring party decides not to drive the car. A lessor does not return the rent if the lessee chooses not to move in. However, as with money, if it turns out that the hirer or lessee does not take subsequent advantage of the benefit—the car is not used or the money is squandered or the premises are not occupied—a defence of subsequent change of position might arise.[54]

III. The Benefit Provided must be Chosen by the Defendant

A. The Requirement of an Objective Manifestation of Choice

It is not enough to establish enrichment to show that a benefit was provided for the defendant in a personal capacity. A further, and essential, element of enrichment is that the benefit was chosen by the defendant by some manifested words or action. The reason for this requirement is that different (and equally reasonable) people have different desires. A person should not be required to pay for a benefit obtained which is not chosen. Think of a

[47] *Mayor of Thetford v Tyler* (1845) 8 QB 95, 100, (1845) 115 ER 810, 812.
[48] *Alati v Kruger* [1955] HCA 64, (1955) 94 CLR 216; *Koutsonicolis v Principe (No 2)* (1987) 48 SASR 328; *F & B Transport Ltd v White Truck Sales Manitoba* (1964) 47 DLR (2d) 419.
[49] Ch 3 p 48.
[50] *Dimond v Lovell* [2000] UKHL 27, [2002] 1 AC 384.
[51] ibid, 397.
[52] See further Chs 7 and 15.
[53] *Lewisham LBC v Masterson* (2000) 80 P & CR 117, 123 (Buxton LJ).
[54] For an example of a case consistent with this analysis in the context of rescission, see *Coastal Estates Pty Ltd v Melevende* [1965] VR 433.

decorator who, to surprise his friend, decorates and refurnishes the friend's house while the friend is on holiday, in fine taste, but using very expensive materials.[55] The horrified friend might have idiosyncratic taste and might think that he is not benefited at all by the goods and services he has received. Or he might have preferred his old furnishings. Respect for the defendant's autonomy and freedom of choice must mean that in such a case, the mere receipt of a benefit cannot be enough to prove enrichment.[56] That benefit must have been chosen. It is an elementary principle of justice that people should not be liable to pay for things that they did not choose.

Proof that a defendant has chosen the benefit is assessed objectively. Although we sometimes follow the shorthand reference to 'choice' which is used in the cases, those cases have never been concerned with a person's unexpressed, subjective opinions. Defendants have never given evidence in trials about their unexpressed choices. Nor should they. For instance, suppose a defendant signs a letter to a plaintiff requesting the provision of a commercial service as part of the plaintiff's business. Suppose also that although no contract is concluded, the defendant performs the service. It is not open to the defendant to disprove choice by saying that he did not want the service, and only signed the letter of request to the plaintiff as a harmless prank. The defendant manifested a choice for the service; his subjective thoughts are irrelevant.

In *Lord Cawdor v Lewis*,[57] the requirement of objective manifested choice was overlooked. Lord Cawdor made improvements to buildings under the mistaken impression that the land was his own. The court held that he was entitled to bring a claim (for set-off in separate proceedings) for the value of the improvements, although there was no suggestion of any conduct by the defendant manifesting any choice of the benefit. On these limited facts, this decision is wrong. It has been criticised for a long time. In the first edition of *Mayne on Damages* in 1856, Mayne wrote of *Lord Cawdor*:[58]

> The improvements may be very valuable, but they may be quite unsuited to the use which the plaintiff intends to make of his land. Even if they are such as he would have wished to make, they may also be such as he could not have afforded to make. To compel him to pay for them ... is quite as unjust as it would be to lay out money in any other investment for a man, and then compel him to adopt it, *nolens volens*.

The requirement that a defendant objectively choose the benefit that is obtained is also consistent with principles of the law concerning disclaimer. A recipient of a gift is entitled to disclaim the gift by objective conduct within a reasonable time of her becoming aware of it.[59] In the same way, until a person has manifested some choice of the benefit, he will not be enriched: 'he is free to choose whether to avail himself of it or not until such time as he has either unequivocally disclaimed or unequivocally accepted the gift.'[60]

[55] The original version of this example was given in *BP Exploration Co (Luther) Ltd v Hunt (No 2)* [1979] 1 WLR 783, 803 (Robert Goff J).

[56] See *Leigh v Dickeson* (1884) 15 QBD 60; *Taylor v Laird* (1856) 25 LJ Ex 329, 332.

[57] *Lord Cawdor v Lewis* (1835) 1 Y & C Ex 427, (1835) 160 ER 174.

[58] JD Mayne, *A Treatise on the Law of Damages: Comprising Their measure, the Mode in Which They Are Assessed and Reviewed, the Practice of Granting New Trials, and the Law of Set-off, and Compensation under the Lands Clauses Act* (London, H Sweet, 1856) 255.

[59] *Standing v Bowring* (1885) 31 Ch D 282; *Re Paradise Motor Company Ltd* [1968] 2 All ER 625, [1968] 1 WLR 1125; N Crago, 'Principles of Disclaimer of Gifts' (1999) 28 *University of Western Australia Law Review* 65.

[60] *Re Stratton's Deed of Disclaimer* [1958] Ch 42, 54, [1957] 2 All ER 594, 599.

There can be difficult issues about how to characterise the benefit that the defendant has chosen. This exercise in characterisation is important, because the defendant is not enriched unless he or she obtains that chosen benefit. For instance, what has been chosen when a mistaken provision of a service is accepted by a defendant who had expressed his understanding that it was offered gratuitously? Or if the defendant accepted the service mistakenly believing, and manifesting to the plaintiff, that it was provided at half-price as an introductory offer? The better view, as Lord Reed explains in *Benedetti v Sawiris*,[61] is that the characterisation of the benefit is based on the conduct of the defendant. That characterisation of the benefit requires consideration of the circumstances in which the choice was made which includes the conduct of the defendant. In each example above, the choice is of a gratuitous service, or a half-price service. That is the benefit chosen by the defendant's conduct. That is the benefit which must be valued. In the examples above, the chosen benefit is a 'free service' and a 'half-price service'.

The cases establish that the essential requirement that the benefit obtained was chosen by the defendant can be proved in a number of ways. It can be proved by a presumption that the defendant has manifested a choice of the benefit, such as when the defendant receives money. It can also be proved by direct evidence of objective choice, such as an express or implied request or by the receipt and retention of a benefit which is readily returnable. Each of these situations is considered below.

B. Situations in which a Manifested Choice of Benefit is Presumed

i. Receipts of Money

There are some circumstances in which a presumption will arise that the defendant has manifested a choice for the provided benefit. The most common of these circumstances is where the benefit is money. Since money is the medium of exchange, anyone who chooses anything which has a price will generally choose to have money. The presumption arises because almost everyone desires things and most things cost money. Because almost everyone, almost everyday, manifests choices for money, it will be sufficient simply to show that money was received for a conclusion that the defendant manifested a choice for the money. But this presumption is rebuttable. There are some cases where a defendant can say that the mere receipt of money, in his or her circumstances, is insufficient for an inference of manifested choice to be drawn.

Although the proper approach is for the receipt of money to be treated, rebuttably, as having been a benefit objectively chosen by the defendant, the rebuttable nature of the presumption is sometimes forgotten because courts and commentators have used the misleading label 'incontrovertible benefit' or 'inevitable benefit'. For instance, Robert Goff J said that '[m]oney has the peculiar character of a universal medium of exchange. By its receipt, the recipient is inevitably benefited'.[62] It has also been said that a defendant will be incontrovertibly benefited by the receipt of a benefit equivalent to money such as a service which causes a saving of a necessary expense, since 'no reasonable person could be heard to

[61] *Benedetti v Sawiris* [2013] UKSC 50, [2014] AC 938 [115].

[62] *BP Exploration Co (Libya) Ltd v Hunt (No 2)* [1979] 1 WLR 783, 799.

deny that the service constitutes an enrichment.'[63] In the leading judgment in the Supreme Court of Canada in *Peel (Regional Municipality) v Canada*,[64] McLachlin J said that 'While the principle of freedom of choice is ordinarily important, it loses its force if the benefit is an incontrovertible benefit, because ... the defendant would not have realistically declined the enrichment.' The remarks quoted above, and the misleading label 'incontrovertible benefit', seem to suggest that the receipt of any benefit in a particular category will always be an enrichment. This is an error. Three examples can be given where the presumption might be rebutted.

The first example imagines a circumstance where a defendant has assets amounting to $95,000 in value. The defendant receives $15,000 annually in government income support. One condition of the annual income support is that the defendant's assets are valued at less than $100,000. The defendant subsequently receives a mistaken payment of $6,000. This mistaken payment has the effect of removing the $15,000 annual benefit. There is no longer a basis to presume that the defendant manifested a choice of the money benefit. Its net effect would be to reduce the defendant's income support substantially. There is no enrichment of the defendant from the mistaken payment.

A second, more difficult, example is the decision of the New South Wales Court of Appeal in *Ford v Perpetual Trustees Victoria Ltd*.[65] In that case Perpetual Trustees lent $200,000 to Mr Ford, secured over his residential property. Mr Ford was intellectually disabled and had no understanding of the transaction he entered into or the documents he signed. He was manipulated by his son, who took the benefit of almost all of the funds paid to Mr Ford. Only $24,857 remained in Mr Ford's account when the action was brought. The defence of change of position was not pleaded. The trial judge found that Mr Ford was unjustly enriched because he had received money.[66] The New South Wales Court of Appeal overturned this decision. In a joint judgment, Allsop P and Young JA explained that Mr Ford did not 'receive the benefit of funds in circumstances that would make it unjust for him not to pay to Perpetual Trustees the balance of the loan'.[67] There was some focus by their Honours on the question of the benefit 'retained' by Mr Ford, which we explain in Chapter 6 (the requirement of injustice). It suffices at this point to say that Mr Ford had rebutted the presumption that merely by receipt he had manifested such a choice. Their Honours pointed to four matters which demonstrated this. First, in substance, there was no written request by him for a loan of the money that was advanced. Secondly, the loan was not for necessaries but was for the benefit of Mr Ford's son. Thirdly, Perpetual Trustees made no enquiry of Mr Ford and was prepared to lend pursuant to documentation that requested the loan be assessed without documentary evidence of his financial position. Although these three matters might not, by themselves, be sufficient to rebut the presumption of a manifested choice of money, their Honours relied upon a fourth matter which was decisive. This was that the objective approach in the law of unjust enrichment, like the objective approach in

[63] *Andrew Shelton & Co Pty Ltd v Alpha Healthcare Ltd* [2002] VSC 248, (2002) 5 VR 577 [101] (Warren J) approving M Bryan, 'Equity and Restitution' in P Parkinson (ed), *The Principles of Equity* (Sydney, Lawbook Co, 2003); *Monks v Poynice Pty Ltd* (1987) 8 NSWLR 662, 664 (Young J); *Cadorange Pty Ltd (in liq) v Tanga Holdings Pty Ltd* (1990) 20 NSWLR 26, 35 (Young J).

[64] *Peel (Regional Municipality) v Canada* [1992] 3 SCR 762, 795.

[65] *Ford v Perpetual Trustees Victoria Ltd* [2009] NSWCA 186, (2009) 75 NSWLR 42.

[66] *Perpetual Trustees Victoria Ltd v Ford* [2008] NSWSC 29, (2008) 70 NSWLR 611 [126] (Harrison J).

[67] *Ford v Perpetual Trustees Victoria Ltd* [2009] NSWCA 186, (2009) 75 NSWLR 42 [128].

the law of contract, sometimes has to give way to principles of coherence. In particular, if an order for restitution of unjust enrichment were made in these circumstances it would undermine the doctrine of non est factum by effectively permitting a lender to enforce an unenforceable contract. We consider these notions of coherence in more detail in Chapter 7.

A third example in which a defendant can rebut a presumption arising from the receipt of money to the effect that it was manifestly chosen is where the defendant shows that he was not aware of the receipt and did not have access to the money when he became aware of it. An example is the decision of the High Court of Australia in *National Commercial Banking Corporation of Australia Ltd v Batty*.[68] In that case, a partner in a firm of two accountants misappropriated cheques that were to be paid to a third party. The fraudulent partner paid the cheques into the partnership account with the National Commercial Bank. He then withdrew them from that account and appropriated them to his own use. The bank brought a claim against the innocent partner for money had and received. As we saw in Chapter 2, since the recognition of unjust enrichment, this claim would now be brought as a claim based on unjust enrichment.[69] The High Court held that the innocent partner was not liable. This result should be explained on the basis that he was not enriched because he had not manifested a choice of the benefit. He did not know of the receipt of the money in the partnership account and could not be held liable under the primary claim. Chief Justice Gibbs (with whom Wilson J agreed) said:

> where the defendant has not had the benefit of the money, has not played any part in disposing of it and was ignorant of the fact that it was theoretically under his control, he should not be liable in the absence of fault on his part.[70]

The conclusion that the innocent partner in *Batty* had not chosen the money and was not enriched is easily reached. More difficult is the possibility raised by Gibbs CJ that a person who is unaware of the receipt, but who is at 'fault', might be unjustly enriched. The word "fault" here is slippery. It has connotations of wrongdoing. But it should not be understood in that way. The reference to fault is best understood as indicating that a sufficient degree of notice of a receipt of money will usually be sufficient to prevent a plaintiff from rebutting the presumption that the money received had been chosen. In *Heperu Pty Ltd v Belle*,[71] the New South Wales Court of Appeal likewise asked whether the recipient of funds 'ought' to have known of the receipt in the sense that the receipt was a matter

> '(a) of which he would have received notice if he had made the investigations usually made in similar transactions; and (b) of which he would have received notice had he investigated a relevant fact which has come to his notice and into which a reasonable man ought to have inquired.'[72]

The reason of precedent why this possibility of notice (awkwardly labelled "fault") short of actual knowledge being sufficient was left open by Gibbs CJ may have been that the same

[68] *National Commercial Banking Corporation of Australia Ltd v Batty* [1986] HCA 21, (1986) 160 CLR 251, 268–69 [19] applied in *Micro Minerals Pty Ltd v Grossberg* [1998] FCA 1795. Cf *Custom Coaches (Sales) Pty Ltd v Frankish* [2002] NSWSC 795, which viewed the rule as a defence, rather than going to the issue of enrichment.

[69] Ch 2 pp 9–15. As Dawson J observed, 'what matters is whether the Bank by reason of the fraud paid money to the firm under a mistake of fact': *National Commercial Banking Corporation of Australia Ltd v Batty* [1986] HCA 21, (1986) 160 CLR 251, 299 [4].

[70] ibid [19], 269. See also *Fistar v Riverwood Legion and Community Club Ltd* [2016] NSWCA 81 [64] (Leeming JA).

[71] *Heperu Pty Ltd v Belle* [2009] NSWCA 252, (2009) 76 NSWLR 230.

[72] ibid [75] (original emphasis omitted) (Allsop P; Campbell JA and Handley AJA agreeing).

suggestion was made 150 years earlier by the common law judges advising the House of Lords in *Marsh v Keating.*[73] In that case, Mrs Keating's stock had been sold by a partner in a firm who had forged a power of attorney. Mrs Keating disclaimed any title to the shares which had been sold without her consent and asserted that the firm was liable for money had and received for the proceeds that they had received from the sale. As the House of Lords explained a century and a half later, the form of action for money had and received in these circumstances is based on the cause of action for unjust enrichment.[74] The firm in *Marsh* argued that it should not be liable because it had not received the proceeds. Their Lordships rejected this argument. They advised that it was sufficient that the money had been paid into the firm's bank account and that the firm had actual knowledge *or means of knowledge* of this receipt. This type of restitutionary liability in unjust enrichment is therefore for the receipt of money where there is presumed to be a manifest choice of the money. Although the defendant might be able to show some objective circumstances suggesting that he was unaware of the receipt, that evidence will be insufficient to rebut the presumption of manifested choice if the overall evidence reveals that a reasonable defendant would have known of the receipt.

ii. Discharges of Necessary Expenses

A second situation in which a benefit is sometimes presumed to be an enrichment, and again sometimes described by the misleading label 'incontrovertible benefit', is where the receipt of a benefit saves the plaintiff necessary expense.[75] There are two kinds of necessary expense. An expense can be *legally* necessary. For example, if a plaintiff discharges a defendant's debt, she discharges an obligation that the defendant was legally required to satisfy.[76] Legally, the defendant could not avoid the necessity of paying. In *Anaconda Nickel Ltd v Tarmoola Australia Pty Ltd,*[77] Anaconda Nickel sought restitution of pre-contractual expenditure on Tarmoola Australia's mining tenements. Anaconda Nickel had carried out exploration for nickel deposits on the tenements. Although Tarmoola Australia was a gold mining company, and did not mine nickel, it was under statutory obligations to make minimum expenditure on the tenements each year. It included some of Anaconda Nickel's exploration expenditure in its report. Tarmoola Australia argued that it could have applied for exemptions from that required expenditure, so that it was not, strictly speaking, 'necessary' to incur expenditure on a yearly basis. The trial judge rejected Tarmoola Australia's argument because it had still been relieved from the expense of seeking such an exemption which it would have chosen.[78] In contrast, in a Canadian case a plaintiff paid the salaries of employees of a company that did not have sufficient funds to pay them. The plaintiff later sought restitution of the

[73] *Marsh v Keating* (1834) 2 Cl & Fin 250, (1834) 6 ER 1149.

[74] *Lipkin Gorman v Karpnale Ltd* [1991] 2 AC 548.

[75] J Beatson, *The Use and Abuse of Unjust Enrichment: Essays on the Law of Restitution* (Oxford, Clarendon Press, 1991) 21, 31–33.

[76] *Young v ACN 081 162 512 (formerly Dallen Design Pty Ltd)* (2005) 218 ALR 449, [2005] NSWSC 139; *Exall v Partridge* (1799) 8 TR 308, (1799) 101 ER 1405; *Peel (Regional Municipality) v Canada* [1992] 3 SCR 762; *Canadian-Automatic Data Processing Services Ltd v Syntecor Ltd* [2003] BCSC 798, (2003) 15 BCLR (4th) 295. For an example of a non-monetary legal obligation, see *Macclesfield Corporation v Great Central Railway* [1911] 2 KB 528.

[77] *Anaconda Nickel Ltd v Tarmoola Australia Pty Ltd* (WASC, 24 February 1999).

[78] The Full Court overturned the decision on the unrelated ground that there was a contract: *Anaconda Nickel Ltd v Tarmoola Australia Pty Ltd* [2000] WASCA 27, (2000) 22 WAR 101.

payments from a corporate officer of the company, arguing that the payments had discharged the officer's statutory liability for the company's debt to its employees. A majority of the British Columbia Court of Appeal held that the defendant was not enriched because although the defendant might have been liable under the legislation (depending on various defences), the defendant's liability was not 'inevitable'.[79]

An expense also can be factually necessary.[80] In *Monks v Poynice Pty Ltd*,[81] Young J accepted that management services provided by a receiver and manager appointed to the defendant company were necessary expenses of the company. On the other hand, in *Peel (Regional Municipality) v Canada*[82] the Supreme Court of Canada held that payments by a municipality for the care and upkeep of young offenders did not incontrovertibly benefit the federal or provincial governments because it was not inevitable, legally or factually, that either government would have otherwise provided for the children.

Although the enquiry in all of these cases focuses upon the necessity of the expenditure, legally or factually, the reason why the enquiry is being undertaken should not be forgotten. The reason for the enquiry is to ensure that the defendant manifested conduct which amounted to a choice of the benefit. Hence, although 'factual necessity' will usually be sufficient, and although such situations effectively involve a presumption that the benefit was chosen, it remains open for a defendant to prove that based on objective conduct a factually necessary expense was not treated as necessary by the defendant and would not have been chosen.

C. Proving Choice by Express or Implied Request

Cases which involve active choice of benefits are commonly characterised by an explicit request.[83] Once the benefit has been chosen by the defendant it does not matter whether its provision is for the defendant or a third party. The provision of the service as requested will be a benefit. For instance, in *Crown Prosecution Service v Eastenders Group*,[84] Lord Toulson (with whom Lady Hale, and Lords Kerr, Wilson and Hughes agreed) held that where the Crown Prosecution had requested the services of a receiver to be performed for various companies, the Crown Prosecution Service was enriched and was liable to pay the reasonable value of those services when the basis on which they were conferred failed.[85]

Although many cases involve express requests, choice can also be proved by implied request where the implication arises from the defendant's words or acts. For example, in *Angelopoulos v Sabatino*,[86] a hotel business was run by a long-term tenant who went into liquidation. While in possession of the hotel, the liquidator removed all plant, stock and

[79] *Canada Automatic Data Processing Services Ltd v Bentley* [2004] BCCA 408, (2004) 242 DLR (4th) 250.

[80] See also *Re Pearl Maintenance Services Ltd* [1995] 1 BCLC 449, 458 (Carnwath J); *Sutherland v Take Seven Group Pty Ltd* [1998] NSWSC 538, (1998) 29 ACSR 201.

[81] *Monks v Poynice Pty Ltd* (1987) 8 NSWLR 662 following *Craven-Ellis v Canons Ltd* [1936] 2 KB 403. See also *Re Berkeley Applegate (Investment Consultants) Ltd; Harris v Conway* [1989] Ch 32, 50–51 (Edward Nugee QC).

[82] *Peel (Regional Municipality) v Canada* [1992] 3 SCR 762.

[83] *Brenner v First Artists' Management Pty Ltd* [1993] 2 VR 221, 258 (Byrne J).

[84] *Crown Prosecution Service v Eastenders Group* [2014] UKSC 26, [2015] AC 1.

[85] *Crown Prosecution Service v Eastenders Group* [2014] UKSC 26, [2015] AC 1 [114].

[86] *Angelopoulos v Sabatino* (1995) 65 SASR 1.

equipment. The defendant owner wanted to use the hotel for a major motor sport event only one month after the removal. So the plaintiffs, who were prospective tenants, took on the urgent renovation project in the expectation that, in due course, they would become tenants on favourable terms. In the leading judgment on appeal, Doyle CJ found that a number of benefits had been conferred on the defendant owner,[87] including incurring less expense than it otherwise would have done in restoring the premises.[88] The defendant owner had actively and overtly encouraged, without expressly requesting, certain expenditure by the plaintiffs on hotel premises. By itself this implied request is sufficient.[89] Limiting the test of benefit to cases of explicit request would ignore the fact that encouragement of a plaintiff to confer a thing or service on the defendant also represents exercise of choice.

In *ABB Power Generation Ltd v Chapple*,[90] ABB had contracted to supply industrial equipment to certain premises. The equipment needed cladding and ABB entered into a contract with the second respondent (CIS) to perform this task. CIS then subcontracted with the first respondent, Fremantle Scaffolding, to provide the necessary scaffolding for the cladding process. The scaffolding work required was more extensive and expensive than that for which the contract had provided. Under time pressure to complete the project, ABB requested Fremantle Scaffolding to do any extra work required and said that Fremantle Scaffolding should have no concerns over payment. ABB later refused to pay, and argued that it had never had any intention to pay Fremantle Scaffolding *itself*. It had told Fremantle Scaffolding that they should recover from CIS. A claim against ABB for restitution of the reasonable value of the work done at ABB's request (but not work done at the request of CIS) was allowed by the Full Court of the Supreme Court of Western Australia. The work had been requested by ABB for its own benefit in order to ensure that the project as a whole was completed on time.

Where a defendant requests, and obtains, goods or services, the receipt will be an enrichment. As Byrne J explained in *Brenner*, proof of a request means that the law is entitled to view the services received as beneficial, even if no other person would agree.[91] Although some commentators have argued that the subjective views of the defendant should be taken into account,[92] the principle governing the whole of this area is an objective one: are the circumstances of the defendant's receipt and retention of the benefit such that the benefit was chosen by the defendant?

Sometimes it is difficult to determine what it was that the defendant requested. Consider the case of *Planché v Colburn*.[93] In that case, Colburn requested that Planché (who was the most distinguished British playwright of his generation) write two children's books.[94] After Planché carried out a lot of research and wrote half of the first volume (for which he had

[87] The trial judge also found that the owner actively encouraged the plaintiffs to carry out the renovations and were left with premises better equipped for letting out.

[88] *Angelopoulos v Sabatino* (1995) 65 SASR 1, 13.

[89] *Lumbers v W Cook Builders Pty Ltd (in liq)* [2008] HCA 27, (2008) 232 CLR 635 [89]–[90] (Gummow, Hayne, Crennan and Kiefel JJ).

[90] *ABB Power Generation Ltd v Chapple* [2001] WASCA 412, (2002) 25 WAR 158.

[91] *Brenner v First Artists' Management Pty Ltd* [1993] 2 VR 221, 258.

[92] G Virgo, *Principles of the Law of Restitution* 3rd edn (Oxford, Oxford University Press, 2015) 65, 69–72 Cf AS Burrows, *The Law of Restitution*, 3rd edn (Oxford, Oxford University Press, 2011) 94–95.

[93] *Planché v Colburn* (1831) 8 Bing 14, (1831) 131 ER 305.

[94] For a detailed history of the case and the decision see C Mitchell and C Mitchell, '*Planché v Colburn* (1831)' in C Mitchell and P Mitchell (eds), *Landmark Cases in the Law of Restitution* (Oxford, Hart Publishing, 2006).

been promised £100), Colburn abandoned the project. Planché was awarded restitution of £50 as the reasonable value of his services. The editors of *Goff and Jones* suggest that this case cannot be explained today as a claim based on unjust enrichment.[95] We agree. It seems from the circumstances that the request was for the completed manuscript. It was not a request for a service of writing. The payment was conditional on receiving the entire text.[96] Further, there is even doubt as to whether the claim was for a *quantum meruit*.[97] This case should not be treated as authority in the law of unjust enrichment.[98]

Another difficult scenario can arise where the defendant requests an end product to be provided as a result of services, but the services are not completed and the end product is not finished. Has the defendant, by choosing the whole, chosen the part? Some cases suggest that he has, particularly if he later completes the work himself and obtains the end product.[99] Professor Burrows suggests that there should be a rebuttable presumption to this effect.[100] However, the cases have not adopted such a presumption and it is clear that anything short of proof that the plaintiff, by the time of the hearing, has obtained the end product requested will not be sufficient proof that the benefit obtained has been chosen. For example, in *Oliver v Lakeside Property Trust Pty Ltd*,[101] Barrett J held that the use by the defendants of plans prepared and work done by the plaintiffs did 'not affect the fact that they had no choice whether to accept or reject the plaintiffs' work at the relevant time.'[102] His Honour also approved[103] *Munro v Butt*,[104] where the plaintiff builder, who was in breach of his contract to perform work on houses of the defendant, failed to recover restitution of the value of his partial performance because the defendant's possession of the land did not amount to a choice of the benefit. Lord Campbell said:

> ... in the case of an independent chattel, a piece of furniture for example ... if the party for whom it was to be made had yet accepted it, an action might, upon obvious grounds, be maintained ... it does not seem to us that there are any grounds from which the same conclusion can possibly follow in respect of a building to be erected, or repairs done, or alterations made, to a building on a man's own land, from the mere fact of his taking possession.[105]

Two other cases can be contrasted to illustrate the importance of characterising the benefit that has been requested, and therefore chosen. The first is *Fibrosa Spolka Akcyjna v Fairbairn Lawson Combe Barbour Ltd*.[106] In that case, the House of Lords considered that the

[95] C Mitchell, P Mitchell and S Watterson (eds), *Goff and Jones: The Law of Unjust Enrichment*, 8th edn (London, Sweet & Maxwell, 2011) 119 [5–25].

[96] See above p 64.

[97] C Mitchell and C Mitchell, '*Planché v Colburn (1831)*' in C Mitchell and P Mitchell (eds), *Landmark Cases in the Law of Restitution* (Oxford, Hart Publishing, 2006).

[98] GH Treitel, *The Law of Contract*, 11th edn (London, Sweet & Maxwell, 2003) 944.

[99] *Lodder v Slowey* [1904] AC 442 affirming *Slowey v Lodder* (1900) 20 NZLR 321; *Renard Constructions (ME) Pty Ltd v Minister for Public Works* (1992) 26 NSWLR 234. See also the discussion of the unjust factor in these cases in Ch 11 pp 274–76.

[100] AS Burrows, *The Law of Restitution*, 3rd edn (Oxford, Oxford University Press, 2011) 355.

[101] *Oliver v Lakeside Property Trust Pty Ltd* [2005] NSWSC 1040.

[102] ibid [88].

[103] ibid [82].

[104] *Munro v Butt* (1858) 8 El & Bl 738, (1858) 120 ER 275. See also *Nicholson v Burnett* (1922) 25 WALR 101, 104 (Burnside J, Northmore J agreeing).

[105] *Munro v Butt* (1858) 8 El & Bl 738, 752–53, (1858) 120 ER 275, 280.

[106] *Fibrosa Spolka Akcyjna v Fairbairn Lawson Combe Barbour Ltd* [1942] UKHL 4, [1943] AC 32.

basis or consideration for a payment which failed was that a Polish company would receive machines promised by an English company. The English company did not deliver the promised machines and war broke out, frustrating the contract. The English company was held to be enriched by the full value of the money paid by the Polish company, notwithstanding that it had done some work and performed part of the assembly. Although some work had been done by the English company in exchange for the payment by the Polish company, the benefit was characterised as the *machines* not the work. Since the Polish company had not received any of the machines it had not received any of the benefit which it had requested. The English company was enriched and the Polish company received nothing in return for its enrichment of the English company. By contrast, in *Stocznia Gdanska SA v Latvian Shipping Co*[107] the House of Lords held that an instalment payment was not recoverable in a contract for the design, building and delivery of a ship because the contract was for 'design and construction of the vessel', and not just the end product.[108]

D. Proving Choice from the Defendant's Conduct Other than Request

i. Retention of a Readily Returnable Benefit

In the context of the common count of *quantum valebant* (fair value of goods), it was long established that, as Parke B said in *Read v Rann*:[109]

> where a special contract has been made for goods, and goods sent, not according to the contract, are retained by the party, there a claim for the value on a quantum valebant may be supported[.]

In *Weatherby v Banham*[110] a publisher sent copies of a magazine to a gentleman for many years. After the gentleman died, the publisher, unaware of his death, continued to send the magazine to his address. The defendant was the successor to the gentleman's property and received the magazine for two years but did not return it or notify the publisher that the gentleman had died. Lord Tenterden CJ held that the common law action for goods sold and delivered could be brought for restitution of the value of the magazines delivered to the defendant.[111] In the language of the modern law of unjust enrichment, this means that where a defendant retains a benefit which is easily returnable, he has been enriched by that choice.

In *Cressman v Coys of Kensington (Sales) Ltd*,[112] the respondents were auctioneers who, contrary to the seller's instructions, sold his personalised number plate when they auctioned his car. Although the sale of the plates was without the seller's consent, the buyer became the legal owner of them when he registered the car. By the time the buyer registered the car, he knew that the seller had not intended to sell the plates. In the leading judgment in the English Court of Appeal, Mance LJ held that the defendant's refusal to return a readily returnable asset suggested that the defendant valued the asset, an inference supported by his

107 *Stocznia Gdanska SA v Latvian Shipping Co* [1998] 1 WLR 574.
108 ibid 588. See also *Hyundai Heavy Industries Co Ltd v Papadopoulos* [1980] 1 WLR 1129.
109 *Read v Rann* (1830) 10 B & C 438, 441, (1830) 109 ER 513, 514.
110 *Weatherby v Banham* (1832) 5 Car & P 228, (1832) 172 ER 950.
111 ibid 229, 951.
112 *Cressman v Coys of Kensington (Sales) Ltd* [2004] EWCA Civ 47, [2004] 1 WLR 2775.

subsequent act of giving the plates to his partner.[113] Although the defendant never had any intention of paying for the benefit, the circumstances surrounding his receipt and retention (and later his gift of it to his partner) were sufficient for a finding that he had chosen the benefit and was enriched. Although Mance LJ described the readily returnable approach by the misleading label 'incontrovertible benefit',[114] the better understanding of the test is that it is concerned with whether the defendant has chosen the benefit. Cases involving retention of a 'readily returnable' benefit involve considering whether a benefit can be easily and freely returned so that, as Mance LJ explained, '[b]y refusing to effect a retransfer ... [the defendant] was exercising a deliberate preference'.[115]

ii. Realisation in Money of a Benefit Obtained

The same focus upon whether a defendant has chosen a benefit explains why a defendant has been enriched in cases where a defendant realises a benefit which is not readily returnable into one which can easily be returned such as money. In other words, by realising the benefit the defendant turns the enrichment into money. In many cases involving services this will be extremely difficult to prove. Where work has been done on an asset which is later sold, it can be very hard to prove that the work done was a direct cause of a part of the increased price paid. But it is not impossible. In *Hughes v Molloy*[116] the plaintiff tenants engaged in improvements to the rented property to the knowledge of the owner. The property was proved to have been sold for an additional $8,000 as a result of the improvements, although the reasonable value of the improvements (services) was more than $16,000. Justice Byrne held that the owner was not liable for the $16,000 value of the improvements. A central reason given was that the owner had not chosen to have the improvements done; he merely acquiesced in them.[117] However, the owner was held to have been enriched by the additional $8,000 benefit which he retained as a result of the sale, as this benefit has been realised in money.

The case illustrates the principle that a defendant will generally be found to have manifested a choice of a benefit when the defendant has realised, or will realise, in money, a benefit from goods or services conferred by the plaintiff. The following, further example can be given.[118] Suppose a plaintiff improves the defendant's land without consent by adding a small separate dwelling. The defendant may legitimately argue that he has no intention of selling the cottage and had no intention of carrying out improvements himself. However, suppose the defendant then sells the land and a part of the sale price is specifically allocated to the dwelling. Because he has obtained the money value of the dwelling improvement, it is presumed that he has chosen to take the benefit of the improvements and that the additional money is a chosen benefit.

In cases of unrealised benefits it is much more difficult to establish that the defendant has manifested a choice of any benefit. Professor Birks originally argued that enrichment arose

[113] ibid [38].
[114] ibid [40].
[115] ibid [38].
[116] *Hughes v Molloy* [2005] VSC 240.
[117] ibid [20].
[118] See *Conrad v Feldbar Construction Company Ltd* [2004] OJ No 1290, (2004) 70 OR (3d) 298 [21] (Ground J).

only when a benefit is actually realised in money.[119] However, that approach would allow a defendant simply to wait until after trial to realise the benefit and deprive the plaintiff of any right to restitution. In the second edition of his book, Professor Burrows argued that the appropriate test was whether it was reasonably certain that the defendant would realise the benefit.[120] In *Cressman v Coys of Kensington (Sales) Ltd*,[121] the English Court of Appeal (Mance LJ; Wilson J and Thorpe LJ agreeing) declined to apply either approach, focusing on the difficulty in determining intention and preferring to ask instead upon whether the benefit was readily returnable. Lord Justice Mance said that the benefit 'was in practice easily returnable. If Mr McDonald chose to keep it, then I see every reason for treating him as benefited.'[122]

The editors of *Goff and Jones* argue that where a defendant receives a financial gain which is readily realisable (although not yet realised), then the benefit is an enrichment, although the appropriate remedy might be a charge over the property in dispute rather than an order for payment, which would require the property to be sold.[123] One difficulty with this approach lies in deciding what is meant by 'readily' realisable. Most benefits can be realised in money with varying degrees of difficulty. Indeed, even the term 'money' is itself very imprecise. Economists have different definitions (M0, M1, M2 and M3), depending upon the liquidity of the medium of exchange. For the purposes of enrichment, there can little doubt that if an extremely narrow meaning were taken (such as confining money to bank notes), benefits which are readily realisable in money such as bank promissory notes or credit balances in bank accounts would be benefits because of the ease in which they can be realised into banknotes.[124] Another difficulty with this approach is its normative justification. If, as we have argued, the core value preserved by the enrichment enquiry is the defendant's freedom of choice, then why should a defendant be liable, by charge or otherwise, to pay for a benefit such as an improvement to an asset which was never intended to be sold?

The best way forward is to take into account the nature of the benefit conferred, the difficulty involved in realising the benefit and the identity and individual circumstances of the defendant (and thus the likelihood that the benefit will be realised) in order to make an assessment at the date of trial whether the benefit has been chosen. For example, while it might be very difficult to characterise unsolicited and extensive work on a family home as an enrichment,[125] it would be easier to characterise as an enrichment similar improvements

[119] See now P Birks, *Unjust Enrichment*, 2nd edn (Oxford, Oxford University Press, 2005) 62, where he accepts that a 'less tender' approach seems likely to prevail.

[120] A Burrows, *The Law of Restitution*, 2nd edn (London, Butterworths, 2002) 19. See also AS Burrows, *The Law of Restitution*, 3rd edn (Oxford, Oxford University Press, 2011) 48–49.

[121] *Cressman v Coys of Kensington (Sales) Ltd* [2004] EWCA Civ 47, [2004] 1 WLR 2775.

[122] ibid [37].

[123] C Mitchell, P Mitchell and S Watterson (eds), *Goff and Jones: The Law of Unjust Enrichment*, 8th edn (London, Sweet & Maxwell, 2011) 87 [4–17].

[124] In *Miller v Race* (1758) 1 Burr 452, 457, (1758) 97 ER 398, 401, Lord Mansfield said that a cheque made out to bearer and payable on demand was currency. See also *Lipkin Gorman v Karpnale* [1991] 2 AC 548, 563 (Lord Templeman).

[125] Cf *Cooke v Dunn* (1998) 9 BPR 16,489, where the improvements were carried out to apparently abandoned premises.

to the assets of a commercial enterprise which was in the business of buying and selling those assets.[126]

iii. Free Acceptance

Lord Goff and Professor Jones first coined the phrase 'free acceptance' in 1966 to describe a scenario in which a defendant is enriched:[127]

> [The Defendant] will be held to have benefited from the services rendered if he, as a reasonable man, should have known that the claimant who rendered the services expected to be paid for them, and yet he did not take a reasonable opportunity open to him to reject the proffered services.[128]

'Free acceptance' was initially supported by Professor Birks. It is a notion which has been accepted in a number of English decisions. It is usually said that free acceptance prevents a defendant from arguing that the benefit received is not an enrichment to him because, (1) knowing it was not conferred gratuitously, (2) he did not exercise a reasonable opportunity to reject it.[129] On this approach, the defendant 'will have been exercising a voluntary choice in deciding not to reject the benefit. Consequently, the fact that the defendant freely accepted the benefit is consistent with the principle of the autonomy of the individual to decide that he or she wants the benefit which has been received'.[130]

The concept of free acceptance is controversial and cannot be applied, without qualification, in the terms expressed by Lord Goff and Professor Jones. For more than two decades, Professor Burrows has been a vociferous opponent of free acceptance. Burrows argues that a failure by the defendant to reject a benefit may signify only indifference to the proffered service, rather than a positive choice to accept.[131] This has been accepted in recent cases in Australia.[132] In a footnote to the joint judgment of Gummow, Hayne, Crennan and Kiefel JJ in *Lumbers v W Cook Builders Pty Ltd (in liq)*,[133] their Honours quoted from Professor Beatson (as his Lordship was then) and explained that '[t]he mere receipt of a benefit, when the defendant had no real option to accept or reject it, does not justify a claim' for the fair value of the benefit. As Burrows explains, the notion of free acceptance, 'undermines respect for the individuality of values' and should not be adopted as an independent test of enrichment.[134]

[126] An approach implicit in the discussion of benefit in *Anaconda Nickel Ltd v Tarmoola Australia Pty Ltd* (WASC, 24 February 1999) and *Angelopoulos v Sabatino* (1995) 65 SASR 1. Cf *McKeown v Cavalier Yachts Pty Ltd* (1988) 13 NSWLR 303.

[127] C Mitchell, P Mitchell and S Watterson (eds), *Goff and Jones: The Law of Unjust Enrichment*, 8th edn (London, Sweet & Maxwell, 2011) 92 [4-29] fn 61.

[128] ibid 453–54 [17-03].

[129] G Virgo, *The Principles of the Law of Restitution* 3rd edn (Oxford, Oxford University Press, 2015) 88; M Bryan, 'Equity and Restitution' in P Parkinson (ed), *The Principles of Equity* (Sydney, Lawbook Co, 2003) 99. See also *R (on the application of Rowe) v Vale of White Horse District Council* [2003] EWHC 388 (Admin), [2003] 1 Lloyd's Rep 418 [12] (Lightman J) and *Andrew Shelton & Co Pty Ltd v Alpha Healthcare Ltd* [2002] VSC 248, (2002) 5 VR 577 [102] (Warren J).

[130] G Virgo, *The Principles of the Law of Restitution*, 3rd edn (Oxford, Oxford University Press, 2015) 85. P Birks, *Unjust Enrichment*, 2nd edn (Oxford, Oxford University Press, 2005) 50–51; P Birks, 'In Defence of Free Acceptance' in A Burrows (ed), *Essays on the Law of Restitution* (Oxford, Clarendon Press, 1991) 128–29.

[131] See AS Burrows, *The Law of Restitution*, 3rd edn (Oxford, Oxford University Press, 2011) 56–59, 334–39.

[132] *Hughes v Molloy* [2005] VSC 240; *Fensom v Cootamundra Racecourse Reserve Trust* [2000] NSWSC 1072 [97] (Bryson J).

[133] *Lumbers v W Cook Builders Pty Ltd (in liq)* [2008] HCA 27, (2008) 232 CLR 635 [75] fn 72, [75] fn 27.

[134] AS Burrows, *The Law of Restitution*, 3rd edn (Oxford, Oxford University Press, 2011) 57.

Without more, cases of passive receipt cannot reflect a positive choice by the defendant. Nor could a passive receipt (without more) be enough to overcome the need to respect the autonomy of the individual. To succeed, 'free' acceptance would require a finding that there is a *duty* on the defendant to reject the benefit or abide by the consequences.[135] Only then could the defendant's passive receipt, and failure to reject, establish a choice. In *Andrew Shelton & Co Pty Ltd v Alpha Healthcare Ltd*,[136] Warren J found that the defendant should have refused and returned documents prepared by the plaintiff at an early stage. The failure to do so amounted to a free acceptance. However, her Honour went on to find that there were repeated requests by the defendant for the plaintiff's continued services.[137] As we have seen, these requests would have supported a finding of benefit in any event.

There are circumstances in which the law effectively recognises a duty upon a defendant to reject the benefit. In *Svenson v Payne*,[138] Svenson took a lease of a hotel for a period which was longer than the life tenant had power to grant. Svenson spent money on improvements. The remainderman knew that the improvements were being made but took no action, believing that there was nothing that she could do during the lifetime of the life tenant. After the death of the life tenant the remainderman applied for, and obtained, a declaration that the lease was void and that it be delivered up for cancellation. The High Court of Australia dismissed an appeal, and rejected an argument that Svenson was entitled to compensation. In a joint judgment, the High Court explained that if an owner is aware that another is making improvements to property as a result of a mistaken belief that the property is the improver's own, the owner will be precluded from exercising his legal rights if he remains silent.[139] But, in the case before the Court, Svenson's claims for compensation or equitable relief failed due to the lack of knowledge by the remainderman that Svenson was labouring under a mistake. The Court approved[140] the comments of Lord Cranworth in *Ramsden v Dyson*, where the Lord Chancellor said that a person, A, who sees another person building on A's land when believing the land to be that person's own, has a 'duty to be active and to state my adverse title; and that it would be dishonest in me to remain wilfully passive on such an occasion, in order afterwards to profit by the mistake which I might have prevented.'[141]

The concept of free acceptance could not be applied to contradict these principles of the law of estoppel. Nevertheless, if a plaintiff can prove that he mistakenly made improvements on the land of the defendant, and that the defendant was aware that the plaintiff was mistaken but chose to remain passive and take the benefit of the improvements, then the failure of the defendant to comply with his duty to speak might in some circumstances amount to a manifestation of a choice to accept the benefit. Hence, in *Cooke v Dunn*[142] Dunn successfully invoked the concept when his claim for adverse possession failed. Justice

[135] See *Andrew Shelton & Co Pty Ltd v Alpha Healthcare Ltd* [2002] VSC 248, (2002) 5 VR 577 [128] (Warren J) on the obligation to return a benefit. See also *Cooke v Dunn* (1998) 9 BPR 16,489.

[136] *Andrew Shelton & Co Pty Ltd v Alpha Healthcare Ltd* [2002] VSC 248, (2002) 5 VR 577 [128].

[137] ibid.

[138] *Svenson v Payne* [1945] HCA 43, (1945) 71 CLR 531.

[139] ibid 542 (Latham CJ, Rich and Williams JJ).

[140] ibid 539.

[141] *Ramsden v Dyson* (1866) LR 1 HL 129, 140–41.

[142] *Cooke v Dunn* (1998) 9 BPR 16,489.

Santow held that although Dunn was not entitled to possession of the property, he was entitled to restitution of the value of the maintenance, repair and renovation work on the property which he had undertaken throughout the 1980s and particularly from 1990 onwards. The owner was aware, from either 1983 or 1985, that someone was living in the property and making various improvements to it, and was happy to be the beneficiary of the improvements. By contrast, in *Roy v Lagona,*[143] Hansen J rejected a claim for unjust enrichment in circumstances in which the owner was not aware that the adverse possessor was labouring under any mistake, and the owner was therefore under no duty to speak. As Hansen J explained, the owners did not 'stand by knowing the defendant was expending money on improvements and letting him do so being aware that they were the true owners of the property and declining to act. They did not become aware they might be entitled to the property until … the great majority of the work was complete.'[144]

The concept of 'free acceptance' has also been accepted and applied in England.[145] Like the Australian decisions, the English courts generally insist that the mere passive receipt of a benefit, even with the opportunity of rejecting the benefit, is insufficient to show that the defendant has chosen the benefit.[146]

E. Proof of Choice in Services Cases is not Limited to Request

The discussion above has explained that there are cases where the benefit of an unrequested service is chosen if the service has been freely accepted or if it has been converted into money. We have also seen that other cases, like *Monks v Poynice* or *Anaconda Nickel,* have accepted that a service was chosen when the performance of the service discharges a defendant's necessary expense. But there have been comments in the High Court of Australia that might be read to suggest that in cases of services the only way in which a choice of the service can be proved is by express or implied request. The suggestion was made in *Stewart v Atco Controls Pty Ltd (in liq)*[147] by reference to the earlier decision in *Lumbers v W Cook Builders Pty Ltd (in liq).*[148]

In *Lumbers,* owners of land entered a contract with builders for construction of a house. The builders subcontracted to an associated company much of the work without the knowledge of the owners. The associated company brought a claim against the owners for restitution of the value of the work it had completed but for which it had not been paid by the builders. As we will see in Chapter 7, the claim failed because the owners had received the work, and were entitled to retain its benefit, under a valid contract with the builders. However, the joint judgment of Gummow, Hayne, Crennan and Kiefel JJ observed that 'the

143 *Roy v Lagona* [2010] VSC 250.

144 *Roy v Lagona* [2010] VSC 250 [339].

145 For instance *R (on the application of Rowe) v Vale of White Horse District Council* [2003] EWHC 388 (Admin), [2003] 1 Lloyd's Rep 418; *Chief Constable of the Greater Manchester Police v Wigan Athletic AFC Ltd* [2008] EWCA Civ 1449, [2009] 1 WLR 1580.

146 *Chief Constable of the Greater Manchester Police v Wigan Athletic AFC Ltd* [2008] EWCA Civ 1449, [2009] 1 WLR 1580 [118] (Arden LJ).

147 *Stewart v Atco Controls Pty Ltd (in liq)* [2014] HCA 15, (2014) 252 CLR 307.

148 *Lumbers v W Cook Builders Pty Ltd (in liq)* [2008] HCA 27, (2008) 232 CLR 635.

bare fact of conferral of the benefit or provision of the service does not suffice to establish an entitlement to recovery'.[149] Their Honours added:[150]

> The doing of work, or payment of money, for and at the request of another, are archetypal cases in which it may be said that a person receives a 'benefit' at the 'expense' of another which the recipient 'accepts' and which it would be unconscionable for the recipient to retain without payment.

Their Honours quoted from Bowen LJ in *Falcke v Scottish Imperial Insurance Co*[151] to the effect that just as liabilities must not be forced upon people, so too benefits cannot be conferred upon people against their will. Or as Pollock CB colourfully said in *Taylor v Laird*,[152] 'One cleans another's shoes; what can the other do but put them on?' However, as Bowen LJ and the joint judgment in *Lumbers* recognised, the general principle that a benefit cannot be conferred upon people against their will 'is not unqualified'.[153] Salvage in maritime law is one qualification.[154]

The possible suggestion that request might be a necessary requirement for proof of choice arose in the High Court in *Stewart v Atco Controls Pty Ltd (in liq)*.[155] In that case, the essential question was whether a secured creditor was entitled to restitution of value from a fund created by a liquidator's efforts in a winding-up. The liquidator successfully argued that he was entitled to a charge over the fund, in priority to the secured creditor's interest. In the course of a unanimous judgment of the High Court, the court held that the decisions in *Falcke* or *Lumbers* had no application to questions arising from work undertaken in realisation of assets as part of a liquidator's statutory duties. However, the court described the decisions in *Lumbers* and *Falcke* as being concerned, in claims for work or labour, 'with whether indebtedness on the part of a person receiving the benefit of the work can arise, absent a request on their part for the work'. *Falcke* was said to stand for the proposition that 'a stranger who carries out work or services, or otherwise confers a benefit on another, without a request, actual or implied, to do so, is not entitled to payment or compensation.'[156]

These obiter dicta remarks could not have been intended to state the proposition from *Falcke* in absolute terms, requiring a request in every instance in which restitution is sought of the value of work or labour. In *Falcke* itself Bowen LJ had not expressed his remarks in absolute terms, and this had also been recognised by the joint judgment in *Lumbers*. The remarks must be read in their context, and in light of the decisions in *Falcke* and *Lumbers* which are quoted, only to be a *general* proposition that request will usually be required. As we have seen, in exceptional cases it may be sufficient to show that the benefit of services has been chosen by evidence of free acceptance or by evidence that the services have been converted into money or by evidence that the service has discharged a necessary expense.

[149] ibid [80].
[150] ibid [79].
[151] *Falcke v Scottish Imperial Insurance Company* (1886) 34 Ch D 234, 248.
[152] *Taylor v Laird* (1856) 25 LJ Ex 329, 332.
[153] *Lumbers v W Cook Builders Pty Ltd (in liq)* [2008] HCA 27, (2008) 232 CLR 635 [80].
[154] See Ch 13 pp 317–18.
[155] *Stewart v Atco Controls Pty Ltd (in liq)* [2014] HCA 15, (2014) 252 CLR 307.
[156] ibid [47]–[48].

IV. The Choice must be Made by the Defendant as Principal

A. Agents

In order for a defendant to be enriched, it is not enough that he has handled goods, or acted as a mere bailee or agent in relation to them.[157] The benefit must have been chosen and obtained by the defendant personally, not in the exercise of another's power of choice. This principle applies to agents generally. In the context of discussing claims for restitution against banks, Sir Peter Millett has said:[158]

> The essential characteristic of a recipient ... is that he should have received the property for his own use and benefit. That is why neither the paying nor the collecting bank can normally be made liable as recipient. In paying or collecting money for a customer the bank acts only as his agent. It sets up no title of its own. It is otherwise, however, if the collecting bank uses the money to reduce or discharge the customer's overdraft. In doing so it receives the money for its own benefit[.]

In Chapter 15 we will see that this principle is commonly described as a defence of ministerial receipt.[159] It arises where the plaintiff can show that the defendant (often a bank) has received a benefit but the defendant bank can prove that the benefit was not chosen by the bank but was received by the choice of its customer. Therefore the defendant bank was not enriched by the principal sum. However, difficult questions might arise concerning whether the defendant bank has chosen, and is enriched by, the use value of the money.

Although the exercise of choice must be by the defendant, this does not mean that the payment or service must be received by the defendant. We have seen that if a defendant requests a plaintiff to perform a service for, or make a payment to, a third party, then the performance of that service, or the making of that payment by the plaintiff in accordance with the request is a benefit to the defendant.[160] When the contrary was argued in *Johnson v Leader Computers Pty Ltd*,[161] Blue J (Sulan and Anderson JJ agreeing) emphasised that once a request is made by a defendant, and the benefit is conferred in accordance with that request, there is no need to show any additional benefit to that defendant.[162] But, if the request is made *on behalf of a third party*, then the choice is being exercised by the third party, not by the defendant. In *Johnson*, the court ultimately rejected a submission that Mrs Johnson had a claim for restitution against her husband, Mr Johnson, because his request for a payment had been made in his capacity as director of, and on behalf of, a third party company.

[157] R Stevens, 'Why Do Agents "Drop Out"?' [2005] *Lloyd's Maritime and Commercial Law Quarterly* 101, 110–11.

[158] PJ Millett, 'Tracing the Proceeds of Fraud' (1991) 107 *Law Quarterly Review* 71, 82–83. See also *Twinsectra Ltd v Yardley* [2002] UKHL 12, [2002] 2 AC 164 [105] (Lord Millett).

[159] Ch 15 pp 381–85.

[160] *Crown Prosecution Service v Eastenders Group* [2014] UKSC 26, [2015] AC 1; *Riverwood Legion & Community Club Ltd v Repaja & Co Pty Ltd* [2015] NSWSC 383 [210] (Stevenson J).

[161] *Johnson v Leader Computers Pty Ltd* [2014] SASCFC 14, (2014) 118 SASR 408.

[162] ibid [78]–[83].

B. Trustees

The position of trustees is difficult and has been the subject of much debate.[163] Suppose a plaintiff pays money to a trustee under a mistaken belief that it is owed as rent for one of the trust properties although the rent had already been paid. The trustee should be able to be sued for unjust enrichment if he has chosen the benefit as principal, rather than as the agent for another.

Professor Stevens has suggested a different reason why the trustee is enriched. He has argued that in the example above, the second payment is not held on trust so that the trustee must be beneficially enriched. He suggests that even if the sum was paid into a trust account, it should be capable of withdrawal by the recipient if the recipient is shown proof that the money did not belong in the account.[164] This reasoning is unsatisfactory. A trustee's common duty to account extends to all receipts, even mistaken receipts. Hence, the recipient trustee would hold the mistaken payment on trust, and not for his own benefit.[165]

The real reason why the trustee is enriched is because vis-à-vis the plaintiff, the trustee has chosen the benefit. The plaintiff might have no knowledge that the trustee holds any chosen benefit on trust for a beneficiary. Those matters need not be relevant in any way to the plaintiff. Unless the trustee is also an agent and subject to the direction of another, the trustee's personal choice means that the trustee is enriched. Indeed, as Stevens argues, the trustee is enriched *at common law* because he is the legal owner of the assets and the common law ignores the existence of trust interest. In *King v Stewart*,[166] a trustee invested £1,000 of trust money on a mortgage of the plaintiff's land. The plaintiff overpaid the interest due under the mortgage over a period of five years. On becoming aware of his mistake, the plaintiff brought an action at common law against the trustee to recover the amount of the overpayment. On appeal it was held that the trustee was the appropriate defendant. Similarly, in *Port of Brisbane Corporation v ANZ Securities Ltd*,[167] ANZ Securities attempted to defeat the claim in unjust enrichment brought against it on the basis that it had only received the monies as trustee, the monies having been paid into its client trust account. As such, it had never *beneficially* received the money and was never enriched. Justice Chesterman rejected the argument:[168]

> As between plaintiff and defendant the defendant was enriched. The plaintiff's money was in its account, if not its pocket. It cannot matter that as between the defendant and a third party the defendant may not be entitled to the benefit of the money.

[163] Cf *Port of Brisbane Corporation v ANZ Securities Ltd* [2001] QSC 466; *Port of Brisbane Corporation v ANZ Securities Ltd (No 2)* [2002] QCA 158, [2003] 2 Qd R 661; *Portman Building Society v Hamlyn Taylor Neck (a firm)* [1998] 4 All ER 202; R Grantham and CEF Rickett, *Enrichment and Restitution in New Zealand* (Oxford, Hart, 2000) 61–63; P Birks, 'Property and Unjust Enrichment: Categorical Truths' [1997] *New Zealand Law Review* 623, 654; P Birks, 'On Taking Seriously the Difference Between Tracing and Claiming' (1997) 11 *Trust Law International* 2, 7–8 and R Stevens, 'Why Do Agents "Drop out"?' [2005] *Lloyd's Maritime and Commercial Law Quarterly* 101, 111.

[164] R Stevens, 'Why Do Agents "Drop out"?' [2005] *Lloyd's Maritime and Commercial Law Quarterly* 101, 111.

[165] *Bellis v Challinor* [2015] EWCA Civ 59.

[166] *King v Stewart* (1892) 66 LT 339; see also *Springfield Acres Ltd (in liq) v Abacus (Hong Kong) Ltd* [1994] 3 NZLR 502, 510–11 (Henry J), discussed by J Moore, 'Restitution from Banks' (DPhil thesis, University of Oxford, 2000) 173–74.

[167] *Port of Brisbane Corporation v ANZ Securities Ltd* [2001] QSC 466.

[168] ibid [28].

On appeal, McPherson JA (with whom Davies and Mullins JJA agreed) queried whether ANZ Securities was enriched by its receipt '[h]aving received and dealt with the money throughout, not beneficially, but as trustee for Windermere'.[169] His Honour suggested that 'because of the common law origins of the action for restitution, trusts and beneficial ownership are, despite the Judicature Act, to be disregarded here.'[170] As a matter of both principle and policy this conclusion is unassailable. In general, trustees act as *principals* in transactions with third parties.[171] Where the plaintiff has transferred property to the defendant as principal, the defendant will be a proper party in any action for recovery of that payment. Further, from a practical point of view, it will often be highly inconvenient, expensive and, in some cases, impossible[172] to join all beneficiaries to a claim in unjust enrichment. However, the opposite result was reached by the English Court of Appeal in *Bellis v Challinor*.[173] In that case, Briggs LJ (Underhill and Moore-Bick LJJ agreeing) held that money received to a client trust account was not enrichment of the trustee solicitors. However, the point had been 'effectively conceded' at trial in that case, and the Court of Appeal also justified the decision on the basis of the defence of change of position.[174]

Although this approach means that a trustee is personally liable to meet trust liabilities, the trustee also has a right of exoneration, or indemnity which permits him to discharge properly incurred trust debts from the trust property.[175] Further, if the trust fund is insufficient to meet the liability, and the beneficiaries are identified, the trustee may be able to recoup the outstanding amount directly from the beneficiaries.[176] Finally, where the money is lost, a change of position defence may be available to the trustee. Far from being in an untenable position, therefore, the trustee has an array of procedural and substantive defences which can protect him from the otherwise harsh consequences of being the legal face of the trust.

We will see in the next chapter that this approach also means that both a trustee and a beneficiary can be enriched by a single payment. Just as an order for restitution of a mistaken payment can be made against a trustee, so too can an order for restitution of trust property be sought against the beneficiaries (although the trustee, as legal owner, must be a party to the proceedings). In *Giarrantano v Smith*,[177] Mrs Giarrantano created a trust of her land for herself and her children with herself as trustee. The transaction was held to have arisen as a result of undue influence and was rescinded. The action was brought against her children as beneficiaries and the order for restitution of the land (subject to a small interest in favour of the children due to a contribution by her father in law) was made against them.

[169] *Port of Brisbane Corporation v ANZ Securities Ltd (No 2)* [2002] QCA 158, [2003] 2 Qd R 661 [10].

[170] ibid; see also R Stevens, 'Why Do Agents "Drop Out"?' [2005] *Lloyd's Maritime and Commercial Law Quarterly* 101, 111. Most recently, see *Fisher v Nemeske* [2016] HCA 11; (2016) 90 ALJR 457, 464 [16] (French CJ and Bell J)

[171] This point is also made by Dr Moore, that trustees, like liquidators, act as principals: see J Moore, 'Restitution from Banks' (DPhil thesis, University of Oxford 2000) 173.

[172] As with some discretionary trusts. See also *Dutton v Thompson* (1883) 23 Ch D 278.

[173] *Bellis v Challinor* [2015] EWCA Civ 59.

[174] ibid [111]–[120].

[175] *Eden Productions Pty Ltd v Southern Star Group Ltd* [2002] NSWSC 1166 [226].

[176] *Hardoon v Belilios* [1901] AC 118.

[177] *Giarrantano v Smith* (NSWSC, 24 October 1985) 5. See also (1985) NSW ConvR 55-267.

V. The Benefit Obtained is Valued Objectively

Once a defendant has been found to have been enriched, the next question is how the benefit that the defendant obtained is to be valued for the purposes of assessing enrichment. The dominant academic view in English law is that the benefit is valued subjectively. That is, the benefit is valued according to the particular, and possibly idiosyncratic, views of the defendant. This view is wrong. But it was the view that appears to have been set out, albeit tentatively, in obiter dicta by a majority of the Supreme Court of the United Kingdom in *Benedetti v Sawiris.*[178] That case involved a sale by Italy's largest energy company of its share capital in a subsidiary. The sale price was €3 billion. The special purpose vehicle for the acquisition was indirectly owned by Sawiris and other members of his family. Benedetti introduced the deal to Sawiris and facilitated its completion. He brought various claims against Mr Sawiris arising from the services that he provided as part of the deal. All of Benedetti's claims failed, except one. He succeeded in a claim for restitution of unjust enrichment. By the time the case reached the Supreme Court of the United Kingdom the question was how the award of restitution should be valued. There were two alternatives: (1) by reference to the market value of the services provided by Benedetti (which was €36m, although he had already been paid €67m) or (2) by reference to the subjective price placed on those services by Mr Sawiris in subsequent negotiations (which was €75m). The Supreme Court unanimously held that the relevant amount was €36m. But different approaches were taken to the issue of principle.

One judgment was given by Lord Clarke, with whom Lords Kerr and Wilson agreed. Lord Clarke began his judgment by explaining that it was not necessary for him to express a final view on the issues.[179] But his Lordship set out his preliminary views. They were as follows:[180]

(1) The starting point is that enrichment should be valued objectively: what is the value which a reasonable person in the defendant's position would pay for the service?
(2) A defendant is then entitled to prove that he or she values the goods or services at a rate less than the market value.

Step (2) has been described by commentators as 'subjective devaluation', a label which all the Lords of Appeal in *Benedetti* considered to be inapt. There are three reasons why valuation has never been subjective, and why the tentative suggestion to the contrary by Lord Clarke should be rejected. The better approach is that of Lord Reed.[181]

First, as Lord Reed explained in his separate judgment in *Benedetti*, Lord Clarke's approach is ahistorical.[182] Historically defendants did not give evidence about their personal views

[178] *Benedetti v Sawiris* [2013] UKSC 50, [2014] AC 938.
[179] ibid [1].
[180] ibid [15]–[17].
[181] *Littlewoods Retail Ltd & Ors v HM Revenue & Customs* [2014] EWHC 868 (Ch) [363]–[374] (Henderson J); *Test Claimants in the FII Group Litigation v HM Revenue & Customs* [2014] EWHC 4302 (Ch) [271] (Henderson J). Cf *Littlewoods Ltd & Ors v HM Revenue & Customs* [2015] EWCA Civ 515 [178] (the Court).
[182] *Benedetti v Sawiris* [2013] UKSC 50, [2014] AC 938 [113]–[118].

of value in a claim for a *quantum meruit* or *quantum valebat* which were forms of action that would now sometimes be brought as claims for unjust enrichment based on the value of services or goods. Nor can such evidence assist them today. For instance in *Harrison v Madejski*[183] the value of an award of restitution for the defendant's registration of the plaintiff's licence plate was conducted on a market basis. The defendant's clear evidence of his subjective view that he would only have paid £30,000 for the licence plate did not prevent the market value of £50,000 from being applied. Similarly, in *Spencer v S Franses Ltd*,[184] S Franses Ltd was entitled to an average hourly rate of £300 and a rate of £100 per hour for an assistant for the time spent by its expert inquiry into Mr Spencer's embroideries. This amount was awarded even though the parties had never discussed a price and although Mr Spencer would not have subjectively valued the work at those rates.

Secondly, there is no reason of principle which can justify subjective devaluation. In *Benedetti*, Lord Clarke suggested that subjective devaluation is concerned with the defendant's freedom of choice.[185] The problem with this is that subjective devaluation is concerned with *value*, not choice. Further, it makes no sense for the law to determine objectively whether a benefit has been chosen, but to decide subjectively what the value of that benefit should be. Full protection for the defendant's freedom of choice can be given by the objective exercise of characterising precisely what it was that was chosen by the defendant. In most cases the answer will simply be that the defendant chose the goods or services, independently of any question of value. But in some cases a defendant might manifest an objective choice for free goods or services. Or the defendant might manifest a choice for goods or services only at a particular discount from market value.

The answer to the characterisation question of what the defendant chose determines the subject matter of the objective valuation exercise. Hence, the valuation of the benefit will be zero where the object of this defendant's choice is 'free goods' or 'free services' because the defendant reasonably believes that the services are being provided gratuitously,[186] or the defendant reasonably believes that the services are to be paid for by a third party.[187] Unfortunately, borrowing from Professor Burrows, Lord Clarke elided the choice question with the valuation question by asserting that 'a person may choose something but only at a particular price or even on the basis that it is gratuitously rendered'.[188] This is correct. But, as explained above, it is not relevant to valuation. It is part of the preliminary and objective question of whether the goods have been chosen.

Ultimately, as Lord Clarke suggested, there may be few differences of substance between his approach which concerns the subjective value to the defendant, and the approach of Lord Reed which effectively requires characterisation of the benefit that has been chosen and then values that benefit (the free service, the discounted goods) objectively. But there can still be differences.

[183] *Harrison v Madejski* [2014] EWCA Civ 361. See also *Diamandis v Wills* [2015] EWHC 312 (Ch) [93]–[95] (Stephen Morris QC).

[184] *Spencer v S Franses Ltd* [2011] EWHC 1269 (QB).

[185] *Benedetti v Sawiris* [2013] UKSC 50, [2014] AC 938 [29].

[186] *R (on the application of Rowe) v Vale of White Horse District Council* [2003] EWHC 388 (Admin), [2003] 1 Lloyd's Rep 418.

[187] *Brown & Davis Ltd v Galbraith* [1972] 3 All ER 31.

[188] *Benedetti v Sawiris* [2013] UKSC 50, [2014] AC 938 [20]. See AS Burrows, *The Law of Restitution*, 3rd edn (Oxford, Oxford University Press, 2011) 61.

One obvious difference between the subjective approach of Lord Clarke and the objective approach of Lord Reed arises because defendants often choose goods or services without choosing them at a particular price, or without a reasonable basis to expect that they are provided free. In those circumstances, subjective evidence should not be permitted. The impoverished thief who steals a Rolls-Royce should not be permitted to argue that, subjectively, he would only have been prepared, and could only have afforded, to pay $10,000 for transfer of title to the car which he chose. The defendant in *Greenwood v Bennett*[189] failed for the same reasons. That case has been followed in Australia.[190] Bennett failed in his argument that he would only have been prepared to spend £85 to repair the car, and that this should be the measure of his enrichment, rather than the £226 reasonable value of the services. The additional proceeds obtained by Bennett from the sale of the car were due to Harper's labour. Bennett chose to take the value of that labour rather than returning it to Harper. It did not matter that Bennett said that he subjectively valued the repairs at only £85.

Another difference is that if the defendant's subjective views about the value of a benefit were relevant, then a plaintiff would be liable to pay a defendant for work done which vastly exceeds the objective value of the benefit if the defendant places a higher subjective value upon the work. Professor Burrows initially suggested that it is possible to argue that this higher measure should be permitted.[191] Later, Burrows suggested that the correct view is probably that such overvaluation should not be allowed.[192] Subjective overvaluation was plainly rejected by Lords Clarke, Kerr, Wilson and Reed in the Supreme Court of the United Kingdom in *Benedetti*.[193] This rejection points to the anomaly of so-called 'subjective devaluation'. If the concern were truly with the subjective value placed upon the benefit by the defendant, then why is a defendant not enriched by an amount greater than the objective value if that is the defendant's valuation? Consider the circumstance where the benefit is a unique good or service, with only one buyer and one seller. The objective value would be the price which both parties, acting reasonably, agreed upon. The effect of having only a principle of subjective devaluation is to allow the defendant to limit liability to a defendant's personal, and unreasonable, value where that value is below the objective value but to deny the claimant the ability to argue that the defendant's value was *more* than the objective value. It is hard to see how such an anomalous principle can be justified.

For these reasons, the approach of Lord Reed is superior to the tentative view of Lord Clarke. The valuation exercise, like the question of choice, concerns an objective measure of the value of the benefit chosen to a reasonable person in the position of the defendant. In other words, once the nature of the chosen benefit has been characterised the assessment is of the reasonable value of that benefit to a person in the position of the defendant. Where the benefit chosen is 'free goods' or 'free services' or 'services at a particular price', then the

[189] *Greenwood v Bennett* [1973] QB 195.

[190] *McKeown v Cavalier Yachts Pty Ltd* (1988) 13 NSWLR 303, 308 (Young J); *Johnson Matthey (Aust) Ltd v Dascorp Pty Ltd* [2003] VSC 291, (2003) 9 VR 171 [222] (Redlich J).

[191] AS Burrows, *The Law of Restitution*, 3rd edn (Oxford, Oxford University Press, 2011) 60.

[192] AS Burrows, *A Restatement of the English Law of Unjust Enrichment* (Oxford, Oxford University Press, 2012) 158.

[193] *Benedetti v Sawiris* [2013] UKSC 50, [2014] AC 938 [29] (Lord Clarke), [120]–[121] (Lord Reed), [195] (Lord Neuberger).

characterisation will dictate the valuation. In other cases, the assessment should proceed, as Lord Reed explained:

> [The circumstances] will include any relevant characteristics of the defendant, such as, in the context of borrowing, its credit rating, or whether it belongs to the public or the private sector (as in *Sempra Metals*). They will include other personal characteristics, such as the defendant's age, gender, occupation or state of health, if they bear on the price at which such a person could obtain the services in question in the market. To give one example, a film star may not have to pay the ordinary price for a designer dress, as the fashion house may allow her a discount to reflect the fact that her wearing the dress will enhance its brand image. Her being a film star is thus an objective aspect of her position which affects the cost to her (or anyone else in her position) of obtaining such a dress, and therefore affects the value of the receipt of such a dress to a person in her position. The circumstances which are relevant to determining the value of the services to a reasonable person will not however include the personal preferences of the individual defendant, or any idiosyncratic views which the defendant may hold as to the value of the services, since the preferences or views of the particular recipient do not affect the services' value to a reasonable recipient.[194]

These conclusions might require some decisions to be reconsidered. One example is a line of decisions, as early as 1904 in the Privy Council,[195] adopted and developed in a series of intermediate appellate decisions in Australia.[196] In those cases it was held that a claimant is entitled to the assessment of a *quantum meruit* (reasonable value of services) after repudiation of a contract by the defendant. The assessment proceeds on the basis of the reasonable value of the services, which can substantially exceed the contract price. In other words, the claimant might recover restitution of the value of services even though what had been chosen by the defendant was services at a particular price. These decisions have also been open to attack for other reasons. In *Sopov & Anor v Kane Constructions Pty Ltd (No 2)*,[197] the Victorian Court of Appeal said that the criticisms by commentators of these intermediate appellate decisions were very powerful and that, unconstrained by authority, the Court might have accepted that the only remedy was for the innocent party to sue for breach of contract. But their Honours regarded the cases as being too well settled, especially in light of the rejection of special leave to appeal to the High Court of Australia in one of those cases.[198] The position in England is different. In *Taylor v Motability Finance Ltd*, Cooke J held that 'there can also be no justification, even if a restitutionary claim is available, for recovery in excess of the contract limit.'[199]

The best approach is not the blanket prohibition contemplated by Cooke J, but nor should the reasonable value of services be measured above the contract price at which the services were chosen unless there are objective *non-price* benefits which formed part of the defendant's choice. In the case of a simple contract involving the performance of a service for a price, the award of restitution should never exceed the contract price because that was the objective price at which the service was chosen. Where the contract is more complex and the defendant receives other non-price benefits, then the contract price should not be a ceiling.[200]

194 *Benedetti v Sawiris* [2013] UKSC 50, [2014] AC 938 [101].
195 *Lodder v Slowey* [1904] AC 442.
196 *Renard Constructions (ME) Pty Ltd v Minister for Public Works* (1992) 26 NSWLR 234; *Iezzi Constructions Pty Ltd v Watkins Pacific (Qld) Pty Ltd* [1995] 2 Qd R 350.
197 *Sopov & Anor v Kane Constructions Pty Ltd (No 2)* [2009] VSCA 141, (2009) 24 VR 510 [11].
198 *Renard Constructions (ME) Pty Ltd v Minister for Works* (1992) 26 NSWLR 234.
199 *Taylor v Motability Finance Ltd* [2004] EWHC 2619 (Comm) [26].
200 See further Ch 11 p 276.

VI. The Value of the Benefit is Assessed at the Time it is Chosen

When the claim in unjust enrichment seeks restitution of the value of a benefit to a defendant, there is authority that the valuation takes place at the time of receipt of the benefit.[201] An example of discussion which assumed, without argument or the need to decide the point, that enrichment arises at the time of receipt is the decision of the High Court of Australia in *Australia and New Zealand Banking Group Ltd v Westpac Banking Corporation*,[202] where the court spoke of the liability for money received and the irrelevance that 'specific money or property received can no longer be identified in the hands of the recipient or traced into other specific property'.

A more refined approach is that the appropriate time is 'the time that the [provided] benefit was taken [ie chosen]'.[203] In many cases the date of receipt will coincide with the date of choice of the provided benefit. But not always. As a matter of principle, the answer should be the time of choice of the provided benefit. As explained above, no claim can be brought, and no liability arises, when money is deposited into the account of a defendant without the knowledge of the defendant. Although a benefit has been *received*, it cannot be chosen until after the defendant knows of that benefit. The enrichment should be valued only at the time the defendant is enriched. Suppose a defendant receives title to a chattel on 1 January 2016 but discovers the transfer of title and manifests a choice to keep it on 1 June 2016, by which time the value of the chattel has fallen substantially. The defendant is enriched on 1 June 2016 and the (lower) objective value of the chattel should be assessed at that date.

The question of the time when enrichment is to be valued arose in two powerful decisions in related appeals in *Perpetual Trustees Australia Ltd v Heperu Pty Ltd*[204] and *Heperu Pty Ltd v Belle*.[205] The common facts of those appeals concerned a fraudster, Mr Cincotta, who was given cheques comprising millions of dollars for investment. Mr Cincotta provided the cheques to Perpetual. He used his apparent authority to have Perpetual credit the funds to the account of his wife. Mr Cincotta subsequently transferred the funds into another account in his wife's name, at Westpac Bank. He then further misappropriated the money, most of which was never recovered.

In the *Perpetual* appeal, one issue was whether Perpetual was liable for unjust enrichment. This is considered in Chapter 6. In the *Heperu* appeal, one issue concerned the liability of Cincotta's wife, who was found to have had no knowledge of the funds in her account which Cincotta controlled until she received notice of the plaintiff's claim. The lack of knowledge of the receipt of the funds into her bank account, and the lack of relevant means of knowledge by Mrs Cincotta, was the reason for the failure of the claim against her in

201 *Baker v Courage & Co* [1910] 1 KB 56; *Kleinwort Benson Ltd v Lincoln County Council* [1998] UKHL 38, [1999] 2 AC 349, 386, 409; *Fuller v Happy Shopper Markets Ltd* [2001] EWHC 702 (Ch), [2001] 1 WLR 1681, [12]–[18] (Lightman J); *Fea v Roberts* [2005] EWHC 2186 (Ch) [61] (Hazel Williamson QC).

202 *Australia and New Zealand Banking Group Ltd v Westpac Banking Corporation* [1988] HCA 17, (1988) 164 CLR 662, 673 [11].

203 *Dowell v Custombuilt Homes Pty Ltd* [2004] WASCA 171 [98] (EM Heenan J).

204 *Perpetual Trustees Australia Ltd v Heperu Pty Ltd* [2009] NSWCA 84, (2009) 76 NSWLR 195.

205 *Heperu Pty Ltd v Belle* [2009] NSWCA 252, (2009) 76 NSWLR 230.

relation to the proceeds which were received into her bank account. But the New South Wales Court of Appeal held that Mrs Cincotta would be liable to the extent that it could be proved that she retained a traceable benefit by her interest in real estate purchased from the misappropriated funds.[206] The potential liability for this benefit was to be assessed at the time she had notice that she had obtained property with the misappropriated funds.[207]

The timing point in the decisions in *Perpetual* and *Heperu* has sometimes been understood as focusing on the date of receipt rather than, as we have suggested, the date of choice which was conflated with the date when the defendant was notified of the claim. Two decisions in the same litigation in New South Wales illustrate the contrasting approaches: *Break Fast Investments Pty Ltd v Giannopoulos (No 5)*[208] and *Break Fast Investments Pty Ltd v Giannopoulos (No 6)*.[209] In *Giannopoulos (No 5)*, Mr Giannoupolos received $317,000 in payments made to him by a director of Break Fast without authority. By the time he was notified of the claim, he only retained some of the original receipt. Justice Black, in the New South Wales Supreme Court, applied the *Perpetual* and *Heperu* decisions and held that Giannoupolos was enriched only by the value retained by him at the date he received notice of the claim.[210] But, in *Giannopoulos (No 6)*, after the parties made submissions on the point, Black J held that Mr Giannopoulos was enriched at the time of receipt of $317,000.[211] Since that money was later applied to his use (rather than dissipated) in extinguishing his liabilities, he remained enriched. Although the decision is expressed in the language of the time of receipt, the key point is that since Mr Giannopoulos knew of his receipt and did not disclaim it, the time of receipt was also the time at which he had chosen the benefit.

There are some claims for restitution where there will rarely be a difference between the date of receipt and the date of choice of the benefit received. One type of case is where the claim is for restitution of a *right*. As we saw in Chapter 3, such a claim is usually expressed as a claim that a right be held on trust or for rescission and revesting of the right.[212] Other than in rare cases where the date of election is relevant, whether the relevant time is the time of receipt of the right or the time the right is chosen will usually make no difference to the ultimate order. In *Perpetual*, Allsop P recognised this important distinction between a claim seeking restitution of the *rights* held by Mrs Cincotta and a claim seeking restitution of the *value* obtained by Mrs Cincotta. The question of timing is relevant only in relation to the *value* of the benefit. Where restitution is sought of the right, such as by imposition in equity of a constructive or resulting trust, the only relevant timing is the identification of the person entitled to the right at the date of trial. Thus, as Allsop P explained, at common law (in a claim for the value chosen) 'it might be that the plaintiff would not be entitled to any increase in value of the asset into which funds were traced, though the position in equity may be that the plaintiff is so entitled'.[213]

206 ibid [170].
207 ibid [164]. See also *Fistar v Riverwood Legion and Community Club Ltd* [2016] NSWCA 81 [64] (Leeming JA).
208 *Break Fast Investments Pty Ltd v Giannopoulos (No 5)* [2011] NSWSC 1508.
209 *Break Fast Investments Pty Ltd v Giannopoulos (No 6)* [2012] NSWSC 286. See above pp 66–67.
210 *Break Fast Investments Pty Ltd v Giannopoulos (No 5)* [2011] NSWSC 1508 [80].
211 *Break Fast Investments Pty Ltd v Giannopoulos (No 6)* [2012] NSWSC 286 [27], [31].
212 Ch 3 pp 38–42.
213 *Heperu Pty Ltd v Belle* [2009] NSWCA 252, (2009) 76 NSWLR 230 [157].

VII. Conclusion

We have seen that the issue of enrichment requires proof of three elements by a plaintiff: (1) a benefit; (2) chosen by the defendant; (3) where the benefit was provided to the defendant in his or her personal capacity. In the common case of a receipt of money by the defendant, these issues are generally straightforward. However, other cases (such as the receipt of services or chattels or the opportunity to use, possess or exchange assets) raise difficult issues. It is fundamental to an understanding of this element of a claim for unjust enrichment to appreciate the underlying principles which include characterisation of the benefit conferred and the need to respect the defendant's freedom of choice. Once these principles are appreciated, the required elements of the enrichment enquiry can be understood, as well as consequential issues such as valuation of the enrichment and the time at which the valuation is undertaken.

5

At the Expense of the Plaintiff

Contents

I. Introduction

The previous chapter focused upon the requirements for a claim for unjust enrichment which were conveniently grouped together as 'enrichment'. This chapter focuses upon the required link in a claim for unjust enrichment between the plaintiff and the enrichment of the defendant. This issue can be usefully described as the requirement that unjust enrichment be 'at the expense of' the plaintiff.

The focus upon a requirement that an enrichment be 'at the expense of' the plaintiff originated in the civilian law of unjustified enrichment. Professor Ames, one of the finest American scholars of the late nineteenth century, first suggested this language for the common law.[1] One point must be emphasised immediately. The requirement that an enrichment be 'at the expense of' a plaintiff is not a statutory phrase. It is no more than a pointer or a guidance marker that illustrates the need for a link between the plaintiff and the defendant's enrichment.

The authority in relation to the precise nature of the link between the plaintiff and the enrichment is underdeveloped. In Australia, the leading remark is in *Roxborough v Rothmans of Pall Mall Australia Ltd*, where a joint judgment of Gleeson CJ, Gaudron and Hayne JJ approved the remark by Mason CJ[2] that 'The subtraction from the plaintiff's wealth enables one to say that the defendant's unjust enrichment has been "at the expense of the plaintiff"'.[3] The word 'subtraction' came from Professor Birks.[4] An alternative is the word 'transfer',[5] which is defined in the *Oxford English Dictionary* as the 'conveyance or removal from one place, person, etc. to another'.[6] In a claim for restitution of value, both descriptions focus upon the need for a subtraction or transfer from the plaintiff's wealth. But neither description is wholly apt.

Another attempt at formulating the principle can be seen in a passage from *Kleinwort Benson Ltd v Birmingham City Council*, which has also been adopted in Australia.[7] In that case, Morritt LJ advanced the following explanation of 'at the expense of':

> the words 'at the expense of the plaintiff' on which the authority placed such reliance do not appear in a statute and should not be construed or applied as if they did. In my view they do no more than point to the requirement that the immediate source of the unjust enrichment must be the plaintiff. Were it otherwise the decision of this court in *Banque Belge pour l'Etranger v Hambrouck* would have been different.[8]

As we will see below, an important point being made by Morritt LJ in his reference to *Banque Belge* is that the words 'at the expense of the plaintiff' do not require loss. Instead, Morritt LJ was insisting only that the plaintiff be the immediate source of the enrichment. But this broad approach is also apt to cause error because of the apparent insistence that the plaintiff be the 'immediate' source of enrichment. As *Banque Belge* also illustrates, the plaintiff will be the source of enrichment if the defendant's enrichment is directly linked to the plaintiff by a transaction *or* by an *indirect* series of transactions.

Like other chapters in this book, our main focus here is on the circumstances where an enrichment will be at a plaintiff's expense in relation to claims for restitution of value.[9] The best approach to 'at the expense of' is to conclude that value received by a defendant will be at the plaintiff's expense if it is received by a transaction or a series of transactions

[1] W Schofield, 'The Principle of *Lumley v Gye*, and Its Application' (1888) 2 *Harvard Law Review* 19, 22; JB Ames, 'The History of Assumpsit: Implied Assumpsit' (1888) 2 *Harvard Law Review* 53, 64, 68. See also *Kleinwort Benson Ltd v Birmingham City Council* [1997] QB 380 (CA) 401 (Morritt LJ).

[2] *Commissioner of State Revenue (Vic) v Royal Insurance Australia Ltd* [1994] HCA 61, (1994) 182 CLR 51, 75 [41].

[3] *Roxborough v Rothmans of Pall Mall Australia Ltd* [2001] HCA 68, (2001) 208 CLR 516 [26].

[4] P Birks, *An Introduction to the Law of Restitution*, rev edn (Oxford, Oxford University Press, 1989) 23.

[5] *Pacific National Investments Ltd v Victoria (City)* [2004] 3 SCR 575, 2004 SCC 75 [25], [34] (the Court); *Roxborough v Rothmans of Pall Mall Australia Ltd* [2001] HCA 68, (2001) 208 CLR 516 [118] (Gummow J).

[6] JA Simpson and ESC Weiner, *The Oxford English Dictionary*, vol XVIII, 2nd edn (Oxford, Clarendon Press, 1989) 395.

[7] *Huntley Management Ltd v Australian Olives Ltd* [2010] FCAFC 98, (2010) 186 FCR 430 [46] (the Court).

[8] *Kleinwort Benson Ltd v Birmingham City Council* [1997] QB 380, 400 (citation omitted).

[9] See Ch 3 pp 35–37 for the other possible meanings of restitution.

that are sufficiently linked to an initial transaction with the plaintiff. The most common, and the easiest, cases are where the immediate source of the defendant's enrichment is a single transaction with the plaintiff. For instance, if A enriches B by a mistaken payment through the banking system, then B obtains value immediately from A. The value of B's bank account (B's rights against his bank) has increased by a transaction which has reduced the value of A's bank account (A's rights against her bank). A single transaction has reduced A's value and increased B's value. In contrast, in the case of multiple transactions, and in the words of the Privy Council in *The Federal Republic of Brazil v Durant International Corporation (Jersey)*,[10] '[whether value] can properly be traced into another asset depends on whether there is a sufficient transactional link'. In more concrete terms, the question is whether the occurrence or anticipation of one transaction causes the enriching transaction.

II. The Principle Concerns Transactions not Financial Loss

It is now well established that 'The concept of impoverishment as a correlative of enrichment may have some place in some fields of continental law. [But it] is foreign to our law.'[11] Although, as we will see in Chapter 15, legislation has now recognised passing on as a defence to restitutionary claims in some circumstances (usually overpayments of tax), this is a statutory response of limited application. The concern is to protect government finances rather than to reverse the well-established position that 'at the expense of' does not require financial loss. The same is true in English courts which also have rejected passing on as a common law defence, although limited statutory exceptions exist.[12]

An example which illustrates this principle that financial loss is not required is *Roxborough v Rothmans of Pall Mall Australia Ltd.*[13] Roxborough was a tobacco retailer that purchased tobacco from Rothmans. Part of the purchase price was apportioned for a tobacco licence fee payable to the New South Wales government. The imposition of that fee by the government was subsequently declared to be unconstitutional. In its appeal to the High Court of Australia, Roxborough sought restitution for unjust enrichment (based on failure of consideration) for payments of tax which it had made to Rothmans but which Rothmans were no longer required to pay to the New South Wales government. In response, Rothmans argued that Roxborough had passed on the additional cost to consumers in the form of higher prices for cigarettes and could not recover because there was no corresponding impoverishment. A majority of the High Court rejected this argument, finding that the subtraction from the plaintiff's wealth sufficed to show that the defendant's unjust

[10] *Federal Republic of Brazil v Durant International Corporation (Jersey)* [2015] UKPC 35, [2015] 3 WLR 599 [32].

[11] *Mason v New South Wales* [1959] HCA 5, (1959) 102 CLR 108, 146 [18] (Windeyer J) approved in *Commissioner of State Revenue (Vic) v Royal Insurance Australia Ltd* [1994] HCA 61, (1994) 182 CLR 51.

[12] *Kleinwort Benson Ltd v Birmingham City Council* [1997] QB 380.

[13] *Roxborough v Rothmans of Pall Mall Australia Ltd* [2001] HCA 68, (2001) 208 CLR 516.

enrichment was 'at the expense of the plaintiff', notwithstanding that the plaintiff may have recouped the loss from third parties.[14]

The irrelevance of financial loss also explains the decision in *Banque Belge pour l'Etranger v Hambrouck.*[15] Since the recognition of unjust enrichment as a category of law, this case has been explained as based on unjust enrichment.[16] An employee forged cheques on his employer's account at Banque Belge and paid the funds from his employer's account into his own account. He later paid them on to his mistress. The mistress argued that Banque Belge could not bring a claim for restitution against her because the loss had been suffered by the employer. The reason why the employer had suffered the loss was because, oddly, the employer was not objecting to the unauthorised debit of its account by Banque Belge.[17] The English Court of Appeal nevertheless allowed the claim by Banque Belge. The bank's rights were the immediate source of the payment to the employee even though the bank had suffered no loss. The unauthorised debit to the employer's account might have recouped the bank's payment but this did not bar the claim against the employee. As we explain below, the bank could proceed against the mistress as well as the employee.

The provision of services by a plaintiff is another circumstance where a claim for unjust enrichment can be allowed despite the absence of loss to a plaintiff. It is widely accepted that obtaining the plaintiff's labour is at the plaintiff's expense, whether or not the plaintiff has suffered any actual financial loss.[18] As Warren J said in *Amin v Amin,*[19] in services cases 'whilst a benefit must be obtained at the expense of the Claimant there does not have to be a corresponding loss to the Claimant in order to measure what is recoverable'. For instance, in *ABB Power Generation Ltd v Chapple,*[20] the plaintiff was employed by a subcontractor to perform various technical services. The plaintiff performed services beyond those required by the plaintiff's contract. Some of the additional work beyond the contract had been requested by the subcontractor, but some had been requested by the defendant head contractor. The plaintiff sought restitution from the head contractor of the value of the work done. The head contractor was liable to make restitution only for the reasonable value of work that it had requested. It was not (and could not have been) suggested that the plaintiff suffered a loss because it lost an opportunity to work for someone else. The absence of financial loss does not prevent the use of the plaintiff's labour being at the plaintiff's expense.

A final example of the irrelevance of a lack of financial loss involves claims for unjust enrichment which are based upon the opportunity to use the plaintiff's asset. Suppose that B hires A's car at a market rate of $10 a day for 30 days under a contract that turns out to be void. When B returns the car, he refuses to pay A, pointing out that the contract is void.

[14] *Roxborough v Rothmans of Pall Mall Australia Ltd* [2001] HCA 68, (2001) 208 CLR 516 [26] (Gleeson CJ, Dawson and Hayne JJ) citing *Commissioner of State Revenue (Vic) v Royal Insurance Australia Ltd* [1994] HCA 61, (1994) 182 CLR 51, 75 [41] (Mason CJ).

[15] *Banque Belge pour l'Etranger v Hambrouck* [1921] 1 KB 321.

[16] *Kleinwort Benson Ltd v Birmingham City Council* [1997] QB 380, 400; *Spangaro v Corporate Investment Australia Funds Management Ltd* [2003] FCA 1025, (2003) 21 ACLC 1948.

[17] *Banque Belge pour l'Etranger v Hambrouck* [1921] 1 KB 321, 323, 328 (Scrutton LJ).

[18] *Andrew Shelton & Co Pty Ltd v Alpha Healthcare Ltd* [2002] VSC 248, (2002) 5 VR 577 [129] (Warren J).

[19] *Amin v Amin* [2010] EWHC 528 [4].

[20] *ABB Power Generation Ltd v Chapple* [2001] WASCA 412, (2001) 25 WAR 158.

As we saw in the previous chapter, B has been enriched by the opportunity to use A's car.[21] The enrichment is at A's expense because B obtained the opportunity to use A's car at the expense of A. It does not matter if the car would not have been hired to anyone by A during that period, or that the use of the car did not decrease its value, or even if A would not have used it. As Lord Shaw observed:

> If A, being a liveryman, keeps his horse standing idle in the stable, and B, against his wish or without his knowledge, rides or drives it out, it is no answer to A for B to say: 'Against what loss do you want to be restored? I restore the horse. There is no loss. The horse is none the worse; it is better for the exercise.'[22]

III. A Transactional Link is Required

A. The Meaning of a Transactional Link

The concept of a transaction is sometimes thought to refer to consensual agreements between parties. In this book the concept is certainly accepted as including such an interpretation, but it is not so limited. It is used in this book in a more literal sense. A transaction in its literal meaning is any *action* between persons. The action will be between two people if they are both directly involved in some way in the action, rather than incidental beneficiaries of the action. The focus in this book upon transactions is upon identifying the persons between whom the action is taken, rather than persons who might incidentally obtain a benefit from the transaction. There is one respect in which the term 'transaction' is used in an extended sense, although still within this definition. We will see some of these in Chapter 12. This is where the defendant's action arises as a result of his or her deliberate decision, but the plaintiff has no conscious choice about participation. A simple example is where a defendant steals money from a plaintiff's wallet. The same extension is not needed in the opposite scenario, where a plaintiff deposits money into a defendant's account without the defendant's knowledge. In that scenario, as we saw in Chapter 4, there will be no enrichment unless the benefit is chosen by the defendant. The 'at the expense of' enquiry is not engaged. However, in any event, there is no transaction in this scenario. Until the defendant adopts the payment there is just a reversible credit entry in favour of the defendant.

The label 'transaction' may not be the perfect description of the required interaction between two parties, and it may include within it different types of interaction, but it captures the idea of an action in which the relevant persons are both involved. We will see in Chapter 6 that German law uses the label 'performance' (*Leistung*) to describe the required link.[23] We prefer the label 'transaction', because in German law 'performance' has had to become a term of art to describe the required link, with up to three other types of link that are sufficient.[24]

[21] Ch 4 pp 61–62.

[22] *Watson Laidlaw & Co Ltd v Pott Cassels & Williamson* 1914 SC (HL) 18, 31. In the context of unjust enrichment see *Hambly v Trott* (1776) 1 Cowp 371, 98 ER 1136.

[23] Ch 6 p 124.

[24] G Dannemann, *The German Law of Unjustified Enrichment and Restitution* (Oxford, Oxford University Press, 2009) chs 2–5.

Some of the examples given in this chapter can illustrate the meaning of a transaction. One example is that when A heats his flat, the transaction is between A and his utility provider. It is not a transaction between A and his upstairs neighbour, whose flat might benefit from the heat but who is not directly involved in the action in any way. Another example is when B steals banknotes from A and uses them to repay B's debt to his bank, secured by a mortgage from B's parents. In that example the transactions that occur are (i) between B and A, and (ii) between B and his bank. There is no transaction by any person with B's parents, who are not directly involved in the action in any way.

B. Simple Transactions Between Plaintiff and Defendant

The simplest case where a transaction between a plaintiff and a defendant is at the expense of the plaintiff is where the plaintiff makes a payment directly to the defendant. An example is *Australia and New Zealand Banking Group Ltd v Westpac Banking Corporation.*[25] In that case, the ANZ bank had mistakenly transferred $114,158 to Westpac Bank to the credit of one of Westpac's customers. The instruction from ANZ's customer had been to transfer $14,158, not $114,158. The High Court of Australia observed that it was common ground that if ANZ had demanded repayment of $100,000 immediately after Westpac had received it, then Westpac would have been liable to repay it.[26] As we have seen, the same principle applies where the transaction between the plaintiff and the defendant involves the plaintiff conferring value on the defendant by providing services or the opportunity to use money, goods, or services.

C. The Absence of a Transactional Link should be Fatal to the Claim

It is not sufficient that the plaintiff has caused the third party to be enriched if there is no transaction with the defendant, or any subsequent linked transaction. A simple example is a person who mistakenly leaves the heating on in his flat. This not only causes him a loss but it also has the consequence, which he did not desire, of providing free heating to his upstairs neighbour, who would otherwise have had to pay for the same heat.[27] The upstairs neighbour's benefit might have been caused from downstairs, but it was not the result of a transaction with the downstairs neighbour. The upstairs neighbour does not participate in the action and he can keep the benefit. Four examples from the case law can be given to illustrate the need for a transactional link.

In *Eighty-Second Vocation Pty Ltd v Parere Investments Pty Ltd*,[28] shareholders alleged that the defendant company had been unjustly enriched by goodwill 'misappropriated' by the defendant company from the company in which the shareholders held shares. Justice Weinberg held that the claim must be brought by the shareholder's company.

[25] *Australia and New Zealand Banking Group Ltd v Westpac Banking Corporation* [1988] HCA 17, (1988) 164 CLR 662.

[26] ibid [8], 671.

[27] P Birks, *Unjust Enrichment*, 2nd edn (Oxford, Oxford University Press, 2005) 158–59.

[28] *Eighty-Second Vocation Pty Ltd v Parere Investments Pty Ltd* [2005] FCA 844, (2005) 144 FCR 88 [105] (Weinberg J).

The transaction was between the two companies. The mere loss of value by the plaintiffs was not sufficient.

A second example is the decision in *Ruabon Steamship Co Ltd v London Assurance Co Ltd*.[29] In that case, insurers were liable to pay the cost of repair of a ship, including docking costs, arising from an accident. The owner used the time while the ship was being repaired in dry dock to have the ship surveyed for the purposes of a required Lloyd's classification. The insurers claimed contribution from the owner for the saved docking expenses which the owner would otherwise have incurred. The House of Lords rejected the claim. The owner was probably enriched, but the enrichment was not linked to any transaction with the insurers.

A third example is the decision in *National Australia Bank Ltd v Rusu*.[30] In that case, a bank clerk stole money from the plaintiff bank's safe and gave some of it to her partner. The partner used it to repay part of a loan to him, which was secured by a mortgage over his parents' property. The parents were not parties to any transaction. Their mortgage was discharged simply because there was no longer any debt left for it to secure. Justice Bryson held that although the parents obtained a benefit, the benefit was 'oblique' and did not equate to a receipt of money which the bank was entitled to recover.[31]

A final example is the decision in *TFL Management Ltd v Lloyds TSB Bank Plc*.[32] The facts of that case, as Floyd LJ succinctly summarised them, were that X spent money seeking a judgment for the recovery of a debt from Y. X failed to recover the debt because the court found that the debt was not owed from Y to X, but owed from Y to Z. So Z recovered the debt by relying on the judgment. X sought restitution of unjust enrichment from Z, claiming that X's claim saved Z's legal expenses that would have been incurred in recovery. There was no transaction between X and Z. Although a majority of the English Court of Appeal refused to award summary judgment, Floyd LJ in the majority described the arguments against recovery as 'powerful'.[33] The writing is on the wall for any trial.

D. Transactional Links Between Plaintiff and Defendant by Third Party Actions

The transactional link between the plaintiff and the defendant might occur as a result of the actions of a third party. The most obvious example is where a third party represents the plaintiff as an agent in the transaction with the defendant. The actions of the agent are the actions of the plaintiff. Another example is a long line of old cases in which a defendant usurped the office of a plaintiff and intercepted payments which third parties would otherwise have paid to the plaintiff to discharge the third party's debts. The plaintiffs were entitled to restitution from the defendant in these cases even though the plaintiffs had not made the payments. In these cases, the enrichment of the defendant was caused by a transaction with the plaintiff because the action of the defendant was one in which

[29] *Ruabon Steamship Co Ltd v London Assurance* [1900] AC 6.

[30] *National Australia Bank Ltd v Rusu* [2001] NSWSC 32.

[31] ibid [38] (Bryson J).

[32] *TFL Management Services Ltd v Lloyds Bank plc* [2013] EWCA Civ 1415, [2014] 1 WLR 2006.

[33] ibid [64].

the plaintiff participated through the discharge of the debts owed by the third parties to the plaintiff.[34]

Another example is the decision of the English Court of Appeal in *Re Diplock*[35] and, on appeal, the House of Lords in *Ministry of Health v Simpson*.[36] In that case, the executors of the will of Caleb Diplock mistakenly paid money from the Diplock estate to charities (under an invalid provision of the will) instead of paying the money to the next of kin. The transaction was between the executors and the charities. But it was held that, subject to defences, the next of kin were entitled to recover. The reason for this was because the transaction was treated as having been made from the assets of the next of kin, and therefore a transaction in which the next of kin participated. A complication for this explanation arises from the later decision in *Commissioner of Stamp Duties (Queensland) v Livingston*[37] in which the Privy Council said that an expectant under a will has no legal or equitable proprietary interest, merely a *spes*, or expectancy. How then could the charities' receipt come from the next of kin's assets? The simple point is that in *Re Diplock* no argument was made that the next of kin had no property rights and therefore no basis upon which to sue. The decisions of the Court of Appeal and House of Lords in *Re Diplock* were before *Livingston*.[38] The decision therefore now looks to be one which, in the words of Gummow J in *Hill v Van Erp*,[39] was not 'concerned with restoration of benefits subtracted from the wealth of the plaintiff rather … [was concerned] with provision of a means of fulfilling expectations.'

A case like *Re Diplock* (where the assumed legal entitlement of the next of kin sufficed to say that the payment to the charities was directly from their assets) contrasts with a case such as *Re BHT (UK) Ltd*.[40] In the latter case, receivers of a company considered that a charge over book debts was a fixed charge, and paid the charge holder ahead of other preferential creditors. A subsequent decision of the Privy Council held that the charge was only a floating charge.[41] The liquidator sought directions whether (1) the charge was fixed or floating; and (2) if it was a floating charge, whether the charge holder was required to repay the money to the company so that it could be distributed to the preferential creditors. Judge Garnett QC, deciding the second question as a preliminary issue, held that the charge holder was not required to repay the money because the charge holder would not have been enriched at the company's expense. Although the other preferential creditors ranked higher in the insolvency, the floating charge holder's rights over the book debts had crystallised at the time of liquidation. The company no longer had any right to the book debts and would never have been entitled to receive any part of the book debt realisations. Therefore the distribution was not from the assets of the company.

[34] *Arris and Arris v Stukely* (1677) 2 Mod 260, 86 ER 1060; *Jacob v Allen* (1703) 1 Salk 27, 91 ER 26; *Asher v Wallis* (1707) 11 Mod 146, 88 ER 956; *Boyter v Dodsworth* (1796) 6 TR 681, 101 ER 770; *King v Alston* (1848) 12 QB 971, 116 ER 1134. For further analogous cases, see A Burrows, *The Law of Restitution*, 2nd edn (London, Butterworths, 2002) 35. Cf LD Smith, 'Three-Party Restitution: A Critique of Birks's Theory of Interceptive Subtraction' (1991) 11 *Oxford Journal of Legal Studies* 481, 494.

[35] *Re Diplock; Diplock v Wintle* [1948] Ch 465.

[36] *Ministry of Health v Simpson* [1951] AC 251.

[37] *Commissioner of Stamp Duties (Queensland) v Livingston* [1965] AC 694, 717.

[38] See further Ch 12 pp 289–90.

[39] *Hill v Van Erp* [1997] HCA 9, (1997) 188 CLR 159, 226–27 (footnote omitted).

[40] *Re BHT (UK) Ltd* [2004] EWHC 201, [2004] BCC 301.

[41] *Agnew v Commissioner of Inland Revenue* [2001] UKPC 28, [2001] 2 AC 710.

E. Transactional Links to a Defendant's Subsequently Acquired Enrichment

Consider an example. P mistakenly pays $10,000 to D. Then D uses the money to buy a car from T, an innocent third party, who enters the contract of sale with D. P then brings a claim based on 'tracing' for the value of the car acquired by D. There is only one claim for unjust enrichment by P against D. If D's purchase of the car was made pursuant to a valid contract, which cannot be rescinded, then P's claim will be for the value of the immediate receipt of $10,000, The extant contract with the third party T otherwise justifies the defendant's retention of the car. If, however, the contract is liable to be rescinded, for example on the basis that the defendant was engaged in fraud, then P's unjust enrichment is not limited to the immediate receipt of the $10,000, subject to any defence such as change of position. Instead, P stands in the position of D for the purposes of a notional rescission of the transaction with T (who is not before the court). The notional rescission means that P can bring a claim against D for the value of the car purchased by D, measured at the date of purchase.[42] If D has obtained a good bargain, the car might be worth more than $10,000. Provided that the transactions are linked, D's enrichment will still be at P's expense.

An example is *Creak v James Moore & Sons Pty Ltd.*[43] In that case, Watson stole galvanised iron from his employer. Watson, through an accomplice, then sold the iron to Creak and the sale proceeds were deposited into Watson's bank account. Watson was arrested. The police withdrew the funds from his bank account and paid them to his employer. But the employer also sued Creak for conversion of the iron. A majority of the High Court of Australia dismissed the claim because, by claiming the proceeds, the employer had adopted the sale. The question of interest for this chapter is why Watson's employer was able to claim the sale proceeds that Watson received. The High Court assumed that the employer was entitled to claim the proceeds, but the basis for this assumption was simply that Watson's retention of the proceeds was 'unjustified'.[44] Since the recognition of unjust enrichment we would say that Watson's liability was based on unjust enrichment because the sale proceeds were acquired by a transaction caused by Watson's theft of the iron from his employer.[45] Watson's employer relied on that causally related transaction (which could have been rescinded for fraud) to claim the proceeds. This is effectively what the majority meant by their reference to the employer 'adopting' the sale.

One consequence of the recognition that an enrichment can be based on subsequent transactions is that an initial transaction with the plaintiff might enrich more than one person. In *Creak v James Moore & Sons Pty Ltd,* after the proceeds from the sale of the iron were paid to Watson, a claim in unjust enrichment could have been brought by the employer either against Watson (for the exchange value of the iron originally received) or, from the position of Watson, against Creak (for the exchange value of the iron received). But the case stands as clear authority that a plaintiff must elect between defendants; otherwise the plaintiff could have recovered the exchange value of the iron many times over.[46]

[42] Subsequent profits from, for example, the later increase in value of the car, would not be available as a claim for restitution, but rather would constitute a claim for disgorgement: see Ch 3 pp 34–35.

[43] *Creak v James Moore & Sons Pty Ltd* [1912] HCA 67, (1912) 15 CLR 426.

[44] ibid 432 (Griffiths CJ).

[45] We will see in Ch 12, section IIDiii that the 'unjust factor' is the employer's ignorance of the transaction.

[46] LD Smith, *The Law of Tracing* (Oxford, Clarendon Press, 1997) 380–83.

In any case where an unjust enrichment claim is brought against a defendant which is not based upon an immediate receipt, the later receipt must be the result of a subsequent transaction which is linked to the initial receipt. In contrast with *Creak*, a case where a claim for unjust enrichment was not transactionally linked to a benefit subsequently obtained by the plaintiff is the decision of the Full Federal Court of Australia in *Australian Breeders Co-Operative Society Ltd v Jones*.[47] The applicants were investors in a syndicate. The respondents had wrongfully induced them to enter into contracts and form the syndicate. The respondents purchased mares which they leased to the syndicate as breeding stock. They also made loans to the applicants, secured by mortgages over the applicants' shares in the syndicate.[48] The leases, loans and mortgages were void or unenforceable. In the Full Federal Court, the respondents argued that they were entitled to restitution for the unjust enrichment of the applicants of tax savings that the applicants made from their leases. The Full Federal Court held that the savings were not at the expense of the respondents.[49] The consequential enrichment from tax savings arose from the leases and loans but had no transactional link to the leases or loans.

F. Transactional Links with a Defendant who is a Subsequent Recipient

Consider a case where a plaintiff, P, overpays his creditor, T, by $1,000. T is entirely unsuspicious, and transfers the payment, including the overpaid $1,000, to the defendant. The defendant still has the money. If P brought a claim against the immediate recipient T, then difficult questions would arise concerning whether T has a defence of change of position arising from his payment to the defendant (for instance, has T changed his position if he might be able to obtain restitution from the defendant by a legal proceeding?).

There is a strong reason for a general rule preventing P from bringing a successful claim directly against the subsequent recipient D. That reason is the importance of transactional links between the parties to the litigation. From the perspective of the defendant, she has never engaged in any transaction with P. She would expect that any claim against her based on the payment would be brought by T. The facts in the example above assume that P had a claim against T for unjust enrichment. But T might have asserted that the payment was made under contract or some other justifying factor.[50] Why should the defendant have to defend the assertion of P's claim against T by raising T's defences? The person properly placed to do so would be T. Further, the defendant may have a right of set-off, or another defence such as bona fide purchase,[51] against T. The proper course would be for P to sue T for unjust enrichment and for P or T to join the defendant to the action as a necessary or proper party. Issues would then be raised about the nature of T's payment to the defendant.

The situation discussed above should require recognition that there are two actions involved in such a chain of transactions. In the first, P would sue T. In the second, T would sue the defendant. Although in practice, these claims would often be heard in a single

[47] *Australian Breeders Co-Operative Society Ltd v Jones* (1997) 150 ALR 488.

[48] ibid 493 (Wilcox and Lindgren JJ; Lee J agreeing).

[49] ibid 542. Cf *Hurst v Vestcorp Ltd* (1988) 12 NSWLR 394, 417 (Kirby P) 445 (McHugh JA).

[50] Ch 6 pp 130–38.

[51] *Papadimitriou v Crédit Agricole Corpn and Investment Bank* [2015] UKPC 13, [2015] 1 WLR 4265 [21] (Lord Clarke) [33] (Lord Sumption).

proceeding, this should not conceal the general principle that P's claim is against T, and T's claim is against the defendant. The underlying reality that two claims are involved can be seen in the decision of the English Court of Appeal in *Khan v Permayer*.[52] Mr Permayer thought that he was owed money by Mr Khan and another. Mr Eaves agreed to pay Mr Permayer £40,000 of this debt, and Mr Khan reimbursed Mr Eaves. In fact, no money was owed to Mr Permayer. Mr Khan sued Mr Permayer to recover the money which he had reimbursed to Mr Eaves. Strictly, there should have been two actions before the court. Mr Eaves should have sought restitution from Mr Permayer, and then Mr Khan should have sought restitution from Mr Eaves. However, Morritt LJ (with whom Staughton J agreed) held that 'a payment made by a third party under a mistaken belief which gives rise to unjust enrichment of the defendant may be recoverable by the person at whose ultimate expense it was paid if that person is also acting under the same mistake as the third party'.[53] The insistence upon two mistakes (ie two unjust factors) is only explicable on the basis that there are two claims for unjust enrichment involved in the analysis, rather than one claim against a remote recipient.

Another illustration can be used to show why claims against subsequent recipients actually involve multiple claims in unjust enrichment rather than a single claim. P mistakenly pays $10,000 to D. Then D uses the money to purchase a car from T who is a bona fide purchaser for value without notice. T then makes a gift of the $10,000 to T2. Neither at common law nor in equity is it possible to claim successfully against either T or T2. Because T was a bona fide purchaser, the claim against T is extinguished. The defence of bona fide purchase is designed to ensure the security of transactions generally. Consequently, a claim must fail against the subsequent recipient, T2.[54] In other words, although T2 is a volunteer, the claim against T2 will fail because, to use Professor Birks' colourful metaphor, P cannot 'leapfrog' T and sue T2 directly.[55]

G. Liberal Rules Permitting an Action without Joinder of Intermediaries

As we have seen, as a matter of principle the effect of permitting a claim to be brought against the defendant based upon a series of transactions emanating from those between P and T is that all the intermediate parties should be joined to the action. As we have seen, there is a series of claims with the defendant involved by the final intermediary's transaction with her. However, the law has not always required all parties to be joined in an action against the ultimate recipient. The liberal approach appears to have been allowed where the claim against the intermediary is clear and any intermediate defences, such as change of position, are concerned only with the particular interests of the intermediary rather than broader policy considerations such as the need for security of transactions (seen in the bona fide purchase defence).[56]

52 *Khan v Permayer* [2001] BPIR 95.

53 ibid [40].

54 *Lowther v Carlton* (1741) 2 Atk 242, 26 ER 549; *Wilkes v Spooner* [1911] 2 KB 473, 487–88(Farwell LJ).

55 P Birks, *Unjust Enrichment*, 2nd edn (Oxford, Oxford University Press, 2005) 94–98. See *Brown & Davis Ltd v Galbraith* [1972] 3 All ER 31.

56 See eg *Papadimitriou v Crédit Agricole Corpn and Investment Bank* [2015] UKPC 13, [2015] 1 WLR 4265 [21] (Lord Clarke) [33] (Lord Sumption).

An early example is the decision in *Harrison v Pryse*[57] in 1740. Governor Edward Harrison paid £1000 to the South Sea Company for stock. By mistake, the legal title to the stock was transferred to a different person named Edward Harrison. The other Edward Harrison transferred the stock to a broker, Round. Round sold the stock and paid the proceeds to Edward Harrison. The simplest action would have been by Governor Harrison against the South Sea Company. He paid money for stock that he did not receive. Separately, the South Sea Company had an action in unjust enrichment against Edward Harrison. Edward Harrison was enriched by the company's mistaken transfer of the stock to him. The South Sea Company could have claimed either the value of the stock or the proceeds that Edward Harrison subsequently received. But Governor Harrison (through his executors) brought his action against Edward Harrison, without joining the South Sea Company. Lord Hardwicke recognised that the claim ought to have been brought by Governor Harrison against the company. But, nevertheless, he held that Edward Harrison's estate must account to Governor Harrison for the value of the stock.

The same liberal approach was taken in *El Ajou v Dollar Land Holdings plc.*[58] The case of *El Ajou* involved a massive share fraud in which victims were defrauded into paying money for worthless shares. The money received subsequently passed through a long chain of transactions. Justice Millett explained that a claim could be brought despite the long chain of transactions by creating a 'notional' charge over the assets being traced because the fraudulent misrepresentations meant that the plaintiffs 'are entitled to rescind the transaction ... at least to the extent necessary to support an equitable tracing claim'.[59] He said that:

> [a plaintiff's] ability to trace his money in equity is dependent on the power of equity to charge a mixed fund with the repayment of trust moneys, not upon any actual exercise of that power. The charge itself is entirely notional.[60]

Although Millett J's decision was subsequently overturned (for different reasons) by the Court of Appeal,[61] in a subsequent hearing of the case, Robert Walker J approved this reasoning of Millett J.[62] The question before Robert Walker J in the second part of the trial was whether the claimant could assert a charge over a property held by the defendant into which the claimant's payments could be traced. The defendant against whom the charge was asserted pleaded that the claim *consequent upon tracing* could not be made because it would prejudice the rights of other potential third party claimants. Justice Robert Walker held that:[63]

a. There might possibly be circumstances in which a defendant could prove prejudice to third parties and therefore raise a equitable *jus tertii* defence, but there was no evidence before him that there would necessarily be prejudice to innocent third parties.
b. Further, any potential prejudice to third parties as a result of claims which arise as a result of the tracing process can be accommodated by placing the plaintiff on terms (giving the example of a requirement for an indemnity).

57 *Harrison v Pryse* (1740) Barn Ch 324, 27 ER 664; *Harrison v Harrison* (1740) 2 Atk 121, 26 ER 476.
58 *El Ajou v Dollar Land Holdings plc* [1993] 3 All ER 717.
59 ibid 734.
60 ibid 737.
61 *El Ajou v Dollar Land Holdings plc* [1994] 2 All ER 685.
62 *El Ajou v Dollar Land Holdings plc (No 2)* [1995] 2 All ER 213, 221, 223.
63 ibid 223–24.

c. Further still, the court must have a strong inclination to order that a defendant is charged with the receipt of proceeds which traceably derive from a fraud.

The intermediate parties were again ignored by a fiction that the transfer was 'direct' in *Relfo Ltd v Varsani*.[64] Relfo owed £1.4m to Her Majesty's Revenue and Customs. One of the shareholders and directors, Mr Gorecia, wrongfully paid out £500,000 from Relfo's bank account in London into a bank account in Latvia, in exchange for a debt owed to it by Mirren. From the bank's point of view, Mr Gorecia had authority to pay the money, but he did so in breach of his duties as a director. The payment caused Relfo to become insolvent. On the same day another company, Intertrade, paid the dollar equivalent (after fees) of £500,000 to Mr Varsani's bank account in Singapore. Mr Gorecia was closely associated with the Varsani family. The circuit of payments was a dishonest design to divert funds to Mr Varsani to whom Mr Gorecia had caused trading losses. Some days later, Mr Varsani paid $100,000 to Mr and Mrs Gorecia.

In the English Court of Appeal, Mr Varsani argued the rules of tracing did not permit the payment from Relfo's account to be traced into Mr Varsani's account. The Court of Appeal rejected this argument. As for the tracing rules, the Court of Appeal accepted that an inference could be drawn that the money paid from Relfo was the 'source' of the money paid to Mr Varsani and therefore was its 'substitute'.[65] Applying this to the law of unjust enrichment, Arden LJ said that '[a]s a matter of substance, or economic reality, Mr Bhimji Varsani was a direct recipient.'[66] Although the other judges did not expressly adopt this approach, it appears that what was meant by this language of Arden LJ is that the intermediaries were all part of the fraud. They could not have had any defence, still less any defence that was not peculiar to their own interests, so that it would protect the ultimate defendant.

IV. Tracing of Causally Related Transactional Links is Part of Unjust Enrichment

In a passage which has been adopted in Australia,[67] Lord Millett has pointed out:

> Tracing is ... neither a claim nor a remedy. It is merely the process by which a claimant demonstrates what has happened to his property, identifies its proceeds and the persons who have handled or received them, and justifies his claim that the proceeds can properly be regarded as representing his property. Tracing is also distinct from claiming. It identifies the traceable proceeds of the claimant's property. It enables the claimant to substitute the traceable proceeds for the original asset as the subject matter of his claim. But it does not affect or establish his claim.[68]

Not only is tracing distinct from 'claiming' but, as Lord Millett points out, it is also distinct from 'following': '[f]ollowing is the process of following the same asset as it moves from

64 *Relfo Ltd (in liq) v Varsani* [2014] EWCA Civ 360, [2015] 1 BCLC 14.
65 ibid [56]–[57] (Arden LJ; Gloster LJ and Floyd LJ agreeing).
66 ibid [97] (Arden LJ)
67 *Evans v European Bank Ltd* [2004] NSWCA 82, (2004) 61 NSWLR 75 [133] per Spigelman CJ (Handley and Santow JJA agreeing); *Westpac Banking Corporation v The Bell Group Ltd (in liq) (No 3)* [2012] WASCA 157, (2012) 270 FLR 1 [2568] (Drummond AJA).
68 *Foskett v McKeown* [2000] UKHL 29, [2001] 1 AC 102, 128; see also 113 (Lord Steyn).

hand to hand. Tracing is the process of identifying a new asset as the substitute for the old'.[69] To illustrate the point by reference to the different types of restitution discussed in Chapter 3,[70] the process of tracing can be important where a claim is brought for restitution of *value* (the focus of this book) or of a *right* that is held by a defendant following a chain of transactions. In contrast, following is important where restitution is sought of a *thing* which has been taken from the plaintiff. As we have said, this book focuses primarily upon restitution of value.

There are hundreds of cases where defendants have been held liable to make restitution of value based on transactional links. Although these cases are usually described as 'tracing' cases, 'tracing' is not a cause of action. The cause of action is unjust enrichment. The leading English case that recognised the role of tracing as part of the law of unjust enrichment is *Lipkin Gorman v Karpnale.*[71] In that case, Cass, a rogue partner of a firm of solicitors (Lipkin Gorman), withdrew £323,222 from the solicitors' client (trust) account. He gambled and lost the money at the Playboy Club (Karpnale). The solicitors succeeded in a claim against the Playboy Club for unjust enrichment based on the club's receipt of the gambled funds (subject to a defence of change of position). The House of Lords held that when Cass withdrew money from Lipkin Gorman's client account he became the legal owner of the notes.[72] Although he was not authorised to gamble with money from the client account, he was authorised to withdraw it. The rules of tracing would therefore seem to have been important to establish a transactional link between Lipkin Gorman and then Cass and the Playboy Club. The House of Lords did not explain the way in which the transactional links between Lipkin Gorman and Cass, and Cass and the Playboy Club operated to establish the liability of the Playboy Club.

One view of their Lordships' reasoning is that they saw the case as involving one transaction rather than two. In other words, the claim involved Lipkin Gorman directly asserting a claim against the Playboy Club for unjust enrichment. For instance, although their Lordships recognised that Cass obtained title to the money withdrawn, they may have been working from a model in which Cass, as a partner, obtained title to the money as a joint tenant with the other partners. For instance, Lord Goff referred to the money received as the property of the solicitors:

> There is in my opinion no reason why the solicitors should not be able to trace their property at common law in that chose in action [ie their client account], or in any part of it, into its product, i.e. cash drawn by Cass from their client account at the bank. Such a claim is consistent with their assertion that the money so obtained by Cass was their property at common law.[73]

Indeed, it had been conceded by counsel for the Playboy Club that Lipkin Gorman could have required Cass to deposit the funds into its account.[74] The answer, therefore, to the question of why the Playboy Club's enrichment was 'at the expense of' the solicitors was

[69] *Foskett v McKeown* [2000] UKHL 29, [2001] 1 AC 102, 127.
[70] Ch 2 pp 37–46.
[71] *Lipkin Gorman v Karpnale Ltd* [1991] 2 AC 548.
[72] Following *Union Bank of Australia Ltd v McClintock* [1922] 1 AC 240 and *Commercial Banking Co of Sydney Ltd v Mann* [1961] AC 1.
[73] *Lipkin Gorman v Karpnale Ltd* [1991] 2 AC 548, 574. See also 562–66 (Lord Templeman).
[74] '[Cass's] title is liable to be displaced by the solicitors' claim': *Lipkin Gorman v Karpnale Ltd* [1991] 2 AC 548 (HL) 555.

that, as Finkelstein J later explained, '[t]he House of Lords held that the club was enriched at the expense of the firm because it had received property belonging to the firm ...'.[75]

However, a better approach, consistent with the emphasis on tracing, is to understand the decision as involving two transactions: one between Lipkin Gorman and Cass and the other between Cass and the Playboy Club. The Playboy Club's transaction was liable to be rescinded; as the House of Lords held, the Playboy Club had no defence of bona fide purchase and, with Lipkin Gorman as a party, the Playboy Club should not have succeeded with a defence based on Cass's illegality.

Despite the express recognition in *Lipkin Gorman* of a claim for unjust enrichment being based on tracing, there have been a series of cases in which claims based on tracing have been described not as unjust enrichment claims but as 'property' claims. The label 'property' does not explain why D must make restitution of *value* (including in the form of personal rights such as a bank account) to P. The cause of action is rarely made explicit. The cause of action is based on unjust enrichment or, sometimes, wrongdoing.

An example where a claim based on tracing appeared to be recognised as an unjust enrichment claim is the decision in *Trustee of the Property of FC Jones & Sons v Jones*,[76] where a partner drew three cheques, totalling £11,700, on the partnership account after having committed an act of bankruptcy. After a series of transactions, the proceeds of the cheques were obtained by Mr Jones' wife, who invested the money in an account with Raphael & Sons in potato futures. The value of her investment increased to £50,760. The Official Trustee in bankruptcy demanded the return of the balance of the Raphael & Sons account, £49,860. Raphael & Sons interpleaded. Mrs Jones conceded that an act of bankruptcy had been committed prior to the withdrawal of funds by her husband. But she argued that she was entitled to keep the profits. The English Court of Appeal held that the £49,860 was to be paid to the Trustee. Lord Justice Millett said:

> If she made a profit, how could she have any claim to the profit made by the use of someone else's money? In my judgment she could not. If she were to retain the profit made by the use of the trustee's money, then, in the language of the modern law of restitution, she would be unjustly enriched at the expense of the trustee.[77]

Although this recognition by Millett LJ was consistent with *Lipkin Gorman*, and provides a strong explanation for a claim against Mrs Jones, it is very difficult as an explanation for why the Official Trustee was entitled to any more than £11,700 plus interest. The transaction between Mr and Mrs Jones conferred a benefit upon her of £11,700. Her later investments were made as a result of valid contracts with Raphael & Sons, which were never rescinded. As we explain in section VD below, unless it was possible notionally to rescind those contracts, she should have been entitled to retain the remaining money. Perhaps for this reason, Lord Millett later explained extrajudicially that he did not consider that the recovery of the profits was explicable on the basis of unjust enrichment:

> the Court of Appeal went out of its way to say that the trustee was not suing Mrs Jones for [unjust enrichment]. In fact he was not suing her at all. He was suing the bank [Raphael's] for the balance due to her on her deposit account, and his cause of action was in debt. The dispute between the

[75] *Spangaro v Corporate Investment Australia Funds Management Ltd* [2003] FCA 1025, (2003) 54 ATR 241 [50].
[76] *Trustee of the Property of FC Jones & Sons v Jones* [1996] EWCA Civ 1324, [1997] Ch 159.
[77] ibid [19]–[20], 168.

> trustee and Mrs Jones was a property dispute: who owned the disputed property, that is, the right to claim payment from the bank: a chose in action. It had nothing to do with unjust enrichment.[78]

But, Lord Millett's explanation of a right to the profits based on 'property' is also problematic. There was no 'property dispute'. The debt was owed from Raphael & Sons to Mrs Jones. They did not undertake to pay anyone else. Although their debt to her, consisting of her rights against them, was causally related to a transaction involving rights previously held by the partnership, this cannot change the fact that the common law rights against Raphael & Sons were hers and hers alone. The claim was not a 'property' claim.

An anti-unjust enrichment approach to claims based upon tracing was also taken by the House of Lords in *Foskett v McKeown*.[79] In that case, the plaintiffs' trust funds were misappropriated and used to pay premiums for a life insurance policy. The payments of the premiums was a voidable transaction in breach of fiduciary duty.[80] After the insured died, the policy was worth a multiple of the value of the misappropriated funds: around £1 million. A majority of the House of Lords held that the plaintiffs could trace the value of their misappropriated funds into the life insurance policy and claim a proportionate amount of the much greater value.[81] The majority said that the basis for this claim was not unjust enrichment but was 'property'. Again, the label 'property' does not explain why the claimants were entitled to a claim of a much greater value than their initial rights. Lord Hoffmann suggested the policy reason for this principle was that the case was akin to the Roman principle of *confusio*.[82] A confusion occurs if things that are mixed are not easily separable.[83] The mix is owned in common in proportion to the parties' contributions to the mixture. *Foskett* involved two causally related transactions, not a mixing of assets.

Unlike *Foskett* (which purported to identify a 'property' rationale for the claim) or *Lipkin Gorman* (which recognised the claim as based on unjust enrichment), most cases do not identify the cause of action upon which the claim, following tracing, is based. A very well-known Australian decision in this category is *Black v S Freedman & Company*.[84] In that case, Mr Black stole approximately €1,400 from his employer in cash. He paid the money into his bank account. Subsequently he withdrew funds from his bank account and, in several transactions, paid them to his wife's bank account. The question for the High Court of Australia was whether Black's wife held her rights against her bank on trust for Black's employer. The court unanimously upheld the trial judge's decision that the money was held by the wife on trust. As Leeming JA has explained,[85] the recognition of a trust was a 'pragmatic' way of effecting restitution of the wife's unjust enrichment.

The High Court did not explain the cause of action that gave rise to the trust. The statement most commonly quoted to explain the liability was by O'Connor J who said that 'Where money has been stolen, it is trust money in the hands of the thief, and he cannot

[78] P Millett, 'Proprietary Restitution' in S Degeling and J Edelman (eds), *Equity in Commercial Law* (Sydney, Lawbook Co, 2005) 323.

[79] *Foskett v McKeown* [2000] UKHL 29, [2001] 1 AC 102.

[80] *Futter v Her Majesty's Revenue and Customs* [2013] UKSC 26, [2013] 2 AC 108.

[81] *Foskett v McKeown* [2000] UKHL 29, [2001] 1 AC 102, 108 (Lord Browne-Wilkinson), 129 (Lord Millett, with whom Lord Hoffmann agreed).

[82] ibid, 115.

[83] *Indian Oil Corporation Ltd v Greenstone Shipping SA (Panama)* [1988] QB 345.

[84] *Black v S Freedman & Company* [1910] HCA 58, (1910) 12 CLR 105.

[85] *Fistar v Riverwood Legion and Community Club Ltd* [2016] NSWCA 81 [37].

divest it of that character.'[86] But this does not explain *why* Black's wife held her rights on trust. The simple point is that there was no dispute about whether an order for money payment (which might be the award made today)[87] would have been more appropriate than a trust. Further, the statement might not be taken literally; Black did not hold the notes and coins on trust. Although, even as a thief, Black had a right to possession of those notes because he was in actual possession of them, his employer's right of ownership was unaffected. There was no need for Black to hold his inferior right to possession on trust for his employer who had a better right to possession.[88] However, upon the deposit by Mr Black of the notes and coins with his bank, the employer's right to the money was extinguished, and this must have been when O'Connor J considered that the trust arose. As Griffith CJ explained in *Creak v James Moore & Sons Pty Ltd*,[89] the decision in *Black* concerned the 'fund representing the proceeds'.

Although the High Court did not recognise the cause of action that gave rise to the trust in *Black v S Freedman*, an unjust enrichment analysis of *Black v S Freedman & Co* was taken in the decision of Finkelstein J in *Spangaro v Corporate Investment Australia Funds Management Ltd*.[90] In that case, Mr Spangaro paid money to a Managed Investment Scheme for the development of land for cotton production. The scheme required a minimum number of subscriptions before it could proceed. Mr Spangaro made several payments to Cardinal Financial Securities Ltd for an interest in the project. Cardinal held its rights (the bank account) on express trust to pay to the defendant, CIAFM, only when the minimum subscription was reached. But Cardinal paid the money over before the minimum subscription had been reached. Justice Finkelstein held that CIAFM was liable in unjust enrichment. The unjust factor was failure of consideration.[91] In relation to whether the payment was at Mr Spangaro's expense, Finkelstein J said:

> The requirement that the defendant's enrichment be at the plaintiff's expense gives rise to an interesting legal issue. A plaintiff will usually bring a claim for money had and received against the person to whom he made the payment. Here, CIAFM received the Application Money from Cardinal, not Mr Spangaro. Is Mr Spangaro still entitled to maintain the claim? Clearly, the answer is in the affirmative.[92]

[86] *Black v S Freedman & Company* [1910] HCA 58, (1910) 12 CLR 105, 110 (O'Connor J). Quoted, with approval, in *Creak v James Moore & Sons Pty Ltd* [1912] HCA 67, (1912) 15 CLR 426, 432 (Griffith CJ); *Spedding v Spedding* (1913) 30 WN (NSW) 81, 82 (Harvey J); *Australian Postal Corporation v Lutak* (1991) 21 NSWLR 584, 589 (Bryson J); *Lipkin Gorman v Karpnale Ltd* [1991] 2 AC 548, 565 (Lord Templeman); *Zobory v Commissioner of Taxation* (1995) 64 FCR 86, 90 (Burchett J); *Cashflow Finance Pty Ltd (in liq) v Westpac Banking Corp* [1999] NSWSC 671 [464] (Einstein J); *Menzies v Perkins* [2000] NSWSC 40 [9] (Hunter J); *Lurgi (Australia) Pty Ltd v Gratz* [2000] VSC 278 [74] (Byrne J); *Australian Broadcasting Corporation v Lenah Game Meats Pty Ltd* [2001] HCA 63, (2001) 208 CLR 199 [300] (Callinan J).

[87] *Bathurst City Council v PWC Properties Pty Ltd* [1998] HCA 59, (1998) 195 CLR 566 [42] (Gaudron, McHugh, Gummow, Hayne and Callinan JJ).

[88] R Chambers, 'Trust and Theft' in E Bant and M Harding (eds), *Exploring Private Law* (Cambridge, Cambridge University Press, 2010) ch 10. Cf J Tarrant, 'Property Rights to Stolen Money' (2005) 32 *University of Western Australia Law Review* 234; J Tarrant, 'Theft Principle in Private Law' (2006) 80 *Australian Law Journal* 531; S Barkehall Thomas, 'Thieves as Trustees: The Enduring Legacy of *Black v S Freedman & Co Ltd*' (2009) 3 *Journal of Equity* 52; J Tarrant, 'Thieves as Trustees: In Defence of the Theft Principle' (2009) 3 *Journal of Equity* 170.

[89] *Creak v James Moore & Sons Pty Ltd* [1912] HCA 67, (1912) 15 CLR 426, 432 (Griffith CJ).

[90] *Spangaro v Corporate Investment Australia Funds Management Ltd* [2003] FCA 1025, (2003) 54 ATR 241.

[91] ibid [51]. See further Ch 12.

[92] ibid [50].

The central decisions relied upon by Finkelstein J in *Spangaro* were *Lipkin Gorman v Karpnale* and *Black v S Freedman*. The best way of understanding the result in *Spangaro* is that it conflated two unjust enrichment claims. Mr Spangaro had a claim against Cardinal as a beneficiary of the trust and Cardinal had a claim against CIAFM in unjust enrichment based on failure of consideration.

Another example, which can only be explained as a case of unjust enrichment by this type of rationalisation is *Banque Belge pour L'Etranger v Hambrouck*.[93] As we saw above, that case has been treated subsequently as a case of unjust enrichment. In that case, a rogue forged cheques on his employer's account with Banque Belge. Banque Belge debited the employer's account and credited the rogue's account. The funds were withdrawn and deposited into the account of the rogue's mistress at the London Joint City and Midland Bank. The London Joint City and Midland Bank paid the remaining money from her account into court and the court held that Banque Belge was entitled to it. This case could only be re-explained as a claim for the value obtained by the mistress based upon unjust enrichment on the basis that the bank could bring a claim against the rogue and, relying on a causally related transaction, a claim against the mistress. The notional rescission needed to continue the tracing process against the mistress explains the insistence by the court that Banque Belge had a common law power to revest the proceeds of the rogue's account.[94]

V. The Rationale of the Tracing Rules

A. The Governing Principles for Rules of Tracing

We have so far considered how the process of tracing permits a court to identify the transactional links necessary to prove that an enrichment is at the plaintiff's expense. As we have seen, a transactional link is necessary to show a series of unjust enrichment claims where the defendant is a subsequent recipient of funds from the plaintiff. It is also necessary to show transactions linked to the defendant where the claim is for an enrichment subsequently received by the defendant. Several examples of the rules of tracing below show that the ultimate concern is for tracing to show that one transaction is linked to another. However, the nature of the link that is required has generally only been explored in particular contexts. The best approach is to require that the necessary transactional link be that the transaction with the defendant be caused by the defective transaction which commences the unjust enrichment claim, or caused by the expectation of that defective transaction.

No court has yet identified any governing principle which consistently and coherently guides the rules of tracing. Hence, the detail of the precise rules of tracing involves many contradictory cases and substantial dispute. The rules are even said to vary according to whether the exercise of tracing is being conducted in relation to an action that would have historically been brought in Chancery as opposed to one that would have been brought in

[93] *Banque Belge pour L'Etranger v Hambrouck* [1921] 1 KB 321. See *Spangaro v Corporate Investment Australia Funds Management Ltd* [2003] FCA 1025, (2003) 54 ATR 241 1948 [50].

[94] *Banque Belge pour L'Etranger v Hambrouck* [1921] 1 KB 321, 325 (Bankes LJ), 332 (Atkin LJ).

the common law courts. Two options have been identified in the case law, namely a 'tracing value through substitutions' analysis and a 'causally linked transactions' approach. Of the two, the second accords more closely with the existing cases and provides a principled basis for its future development.

B. The Flawed 'Tracing Value Through Substitutions' Approach

There is some authority for the 'tracing value through substitutions' approach. In *Foskett v McKeown*,[95] Lord Millett adopted the analysis of Professor Lionel Smith that the law of tracing identifies the passage of value from one asset into its substitute: '[what is traced] is not the physical asset itself but the value inherent in it'. Likewise in *Southage Pty Ltd v Vescovi*,[96] Macauley J of the Victorian Supreme Court adopted Smith's following explanation of tracing:[97]

> It is *value*, not property or assets, which can be identified in different forms after each substitution. The grammatical object of 'to trace' is 'value'. When a person makes a substitution through which we trace, value is the only constant that is held by that person before, through and after the substitution.

The same analysis can be seen underpinning a number of modern applications of the law of tracing.[98] However, there are difficulties with this analysis as a sufficient basis upon which a tracing claim can succeed. First, in none of these cases was causation between the relevant links argued as an issue in any detail. Secondly, and fundamentally, the notion of a 'transfer of value' by a substitution is incorrect. In many cases in which the law of tracing is engaged, for example, there is no substitution of one right for another, through which transfer of value can be traced. Rather, there is simply a matched creation and destruction of value. Tracing through bank accounts is a classic example. In these cases, there may be a series of transactions between a variety of bank accounts and involving a significant number of intermediaries. However, at each stage, there is no exchange or substitution of one right for another. Rather, each recipient has an increase in the value of the debt owed to him by a particular bank with a corresponding (more or less) decrease in the value of the debt owed to the payer by her particular bank. What links the matched destruction and creation of value is a transaction. And it is only where there are a series of such transactions that are sufficiently linked that the law of tracing is engaged.

An example of the approach above is *Australia and New Zealand Banking Group Ltd v Westpac Banking Corporation*[99] which was discussed earlier. In that case, the High Court of Australia observed that it was common ground that if ANZ had demanded repayment of

[95] *Foskett v McKeown* [2000] UKHL 29, [2001] 1 AC 102, 128.

[96] *Southage Pty Ltd v Vescovi* [2014] VSC 141 [44]–[50]. This aspect of the trial judge's reasoning was noted without comment on appeal: *Southage Pty Ltd v Vescovi* [2015] VSCA 117, (2015) 321 ALR 383 [28] (the Court), and is consistent with the later discussion on enrichment at [84].

[97] LD Smith, *The Law of Tracing* (Oxford, Clarendon Press, 1997) 15.

[98] See eg *Russell Gould Pty Ltd v Ramangkura* [2014] NSWCA 310, (2014) 87 NSWLR 552 [31] (Barrett JA, Bathurst CJ and Ward JA concurring); *Hillig v Darkinjung Pty Ltd* [2006] NSWSC 1217 [11] (Barrett J); *Eaton v LDC Finance Ltd* [2012] NZHC 1105, [2012] BCL 241.

[99] *Australia and New Zealand Banking Group Ltd v Westpac Banking Corporation* [1988] HCA 17, (1988) 164 CLR 662.

$100,000 immediately after Westpac had received it, then Westpac would have been liable to repay it.[100] The problem is that nothing was 'paid' from ANZ to Westpac. Nothing was 'transferred' or 'substituted'. At the end of the day, when all bank transactions were netted, these amounts would have affected the digital entry made by each of ANZ and Westpac. But nothing passed from one bank to the other. In other words, the tracing metaphor invokes the idea of a movement of funds. But no funds ever 'move' between bank accounts. All that occurs is that an electronic record is made by P's bank which reduces the value of the rights that P has against his bank and another electronic record is made by D's bank which increases the value of the rights that D has against her bank. The electronic entry by D's bank is *caused* by an instruction from P's bank. It should make no difference, as a matter of principle, which account of P's is reduced by his bank.

Lord Millett's analysis of tracing as involving an exchange or substitution was also rejected by the New South Wales Court of Appeal in *Evans v European Bank Ltd*.[101] In that case, the European Bank received a deposit of the proceeds of fraud. This caused the European Bank to deposit an equivalent amount in its own name with Citibank. In the leading judgment, Spigelman CJ said:

> [I]n property law, the new 'asset' constituted by the European Bank deposit with Citibank, was not, to use Lord Millett's terminology, a 'substitute for the old [asset]', constituted by the Benford deposit with European Bank. That 'old asset' has never been transformed or 'substituted' into any thing. The funds had been employed by the bank, but the 'old asset' always existed and still exists. The Benford account was always in credit, whether as a deposit account or as a current account. There was no occasion on which the value inherent in the account, which Benford held as trust property, had become located in the value inherent in the deposit with Citibank. No process of the character referred to by Lord Millett as 'substitution' has occurred.[102]

C. The Preferable Approach: Causally Linked Transactions

This leads us to the second analysis identified in the cases, namely that tracing rules are concerned with identifying when one transaction, actual or anticipated, has *caused* another.[103] Lord Millett also noted in *Foskett v McKeown*[104] that when dealing with account transfers, 'There is simply a series of debits and credits which are causally and transactionally linked.'

To reiterate: the fundamental point about the rules of tracing is that they involve two elements: (i) transactions, and (ii) a causal link between the transactions. Neither is sufficient by itself. As for transactions, we have already seen in section IIIB above why the case law treats the absence of a transaction as fatal to a claim for unjust enrichment based on tracing.

The second requirement, causation, is more contentious. Suppose X pays $1,000 in cash by mistake to Y. Entirely innocently, Y pays the $1,000 to his son, Z. That payment had

[100] ibid [8], 671.

[101] *Evans v European Bank Ltd* [2004] NSWCA 82, (2004) 61 NSWLR 75. See also *Darkingjung Pty Ltd v Darkinjung Local Aboriginal Land Council* [2006] NSWSC 1217 [20] (Barrett J).

[102] *Evans v European Bank Ltd* [2004] NSWCA 82, (2004) 61 NSWLR 75 [139].

[103] For the first scholarly articulation of this analysis, see P Birks, *Unjust Enrichment*, 2nd edn (Oxford, Oxford University Press, 2005) 94–98.

[104] *Foskett v McKeown* [2000] UKHL 29, [2001] 1 AC 102, 128. See also *Robb Evans of Robb Evans & Associates v European Bank Limited* [2004] NSWCA 82, (2004) 61 NSWLR 75 [134]–[135] (Spigelman CJ, Handley and Santow JJA concurring).

been earlier promised from Y to Z, although Y had intended to withdraw the money from his bank account. Can X bring a claim against Z based upon the rules of tracing, due to the mere fortuity that the money paid to Z was notes paid by X rather than different notes which Y would otherwise have withdrawn from his bank account? We do not believe that this should be so. Y's subsequent transaction with Z was not caused by X's payment to Y.

A further simple example commonly given in academic work can be given. A plaintiff mistakenly pays a $1 coin to a defendant who then buys her weekly lottery ticket with the coin. The lottery ticket later proves to be the winning ticket, now worth $1 million. The transaction involving the purchase of the lottery ticket is connected to the mistaken payment transaction because it used the same $1 coin. But the lottery ticket would have been purchased by the defendant in any event. The purchase was not caused by the mistaken payment. The defendant can keep $999,999. We saw earlier that another reason why the defendant can keep the balance is that it was obtained pursuant to a valid contract that is not liable to be rescinded.

Unfortunately, many leading cases on tracing have not needed to grapple with any consideration of causal rules.[105] The remainder of this section explains the focus of the rules of tracing on providing a link between two transactions and how a causal link as an additional requirement might be the best way forward to rationalise the rules of tracing.

It suffices for present purposes, consistently with the limited case law, to focus on this link as a required causal or 'but for' link. But it is possible that the rule might be a more relaxed rule of contribution, particularly where human decision making is involved:[106] the defective transaction is 'a factor' in a decision to enter a subsequent transaction. Further, there can sometimes be difficult evaluative assessments involved in determining whether there is a causal link between two transactions. An example is the decision of the English Court of Appeal, currently on appeal to the Supreme Court in *Investment Trust Companies v Revenue and Customs*.[107] In that case, the claimants obtained services from companies described as the Managers. On a notional amount of £100, by which the reasoning was expressed, the claimants paid value added tax (VAT) to the Managers. The Managers only paid £75 to Her Majesty' Revenue and Customs, due to a set-off that they had for £25. The Court of Appeal held that the Revenue was enriched at the expense of the claimants by £75. A crucial issue was whether the £75 enrichment was at the expense of the claimants. There were difficulties with establishing a causal link between the £100 paid by the claimants to the Managers and the £75 paid by the Managers to the Revenue. The contractual obligation of the claimants to pay VAT to the Managers was quite different from the terms of the Managers' statutory liability to account for VAT to the Revenue (including with various set-offs). The Court of Appeal noted the conclusion of the trial judge that the claimants had not proved that the VAT would not have been paid but for the payments by the claimants to the Managers.[108] However, the Court of Appeal agreed with the trial judge that the causal test should be applied liberally: the 'requirement of causation was met by having regard to the economic and commercial reality'.[109] It is not clear whether the Court of Appeal was suggesting that

105 For instance, *Sinclair v Brougham* [1914] AC 398.
106 See further Ch 8 pp 192–94.
107 *Investment Trust Companies (in liq) v Revenue and Customs Commissioners* [2015] EWCA Civ 82.
108 ibid [43] (the Court).
109 ibid [69].

the 'but for' test was met on its view of the facts or whether some other test should replace the test for causation. The dearth of analysis on this point was said to be justified by a restrictive approach to recovery where there is a valid contract with an intermediate party.

D. When Causally Linked Transactions are Insufficient for a Claim

As we have explained, a defendant's enrichment might be shown to be at the expense of a plaintiff if the defendant's enrichment is causally linked to a transaction with the plaintiff that is unjust. However, since the rules of tracing are ultimately concerned to show a series of defective transactions, a break in any link will bring the tracing process to an end. The point can be illustrated by a variant of the facts in *Relfo Ltd v Varsani*.[110] We saw in that case that the director, Mr Gorecia, wrongfully paid out £500,000 from Relfo's bank account which, by a series of causally related transactions, resulted in the enrichment of Mr Varsani by the same amount. Suppose that Mr Varsani then used the £500,000 value to purchase a property in Kensington. Although there is a causally related transaction with the innocent vendor of the Kensington property, no claim can be brought against the vendor. We will see in Chapters 6 and 7 that the reason for this is because the innocent vendor can point to the contract as a juristic reason to retain the value. In contrast, none of the intermediate parties in the series of dishonest transactions could do so. This is the reason why, as we saw above, courts have insisted that the intermediate transactions be liable to be rescinded against the person from whom the tracing is continuing.

VI. The Operation of the Tracing Rules

A. The Lowest Intermediate Balance Rule

One rule of tracing is the 'lowest intermediate balance rule'. Suppose P mistakenly pays $10,000 to D, who withdraws that value from his bank account, reducing the account balance to zero, and spends it. D later deposits $10,000 into his bank account and spends that money to purchase a car. The 'lowest intermediate balance rule' means that the transaction purchasing the car is not linked to P's payment of $10,000 unless D's later deposit was intended to replace the $10,000 paid by P. As Campbell J said in *Re French Caledonia Travel Service Pty Ltd*,[111] relying on *James Roscoe (Bolton) Ltd v Winder*:

> absent any payment in of money with the intention of making good earlier depredations, tracing cannot occur through a mixed account for any larger sum than is the lowest balance in the account between the time the beneficiary's money goes in, and the time the remedy is sought. In a case where the type of tracing being attempted involves detailed analysis of what has become of the property of a particular beneficiary, and into what other assets it has been converted or mixed, the lowest intermediate balance rule is fundamental to a principled approach to tracing.[112]

110 *Relfo Ltd (in liq) v Varsani* [2014] EWCA Civ 360, [2015] 1 BCLC 14.
111 *Re French Caledonia Travel Service Pty Ltd (in liq)* [2003] NSWSC 1008, (2003) 59 NSWLR 361 [175].
112 *James Roscoe (Bolton) Ltd v Winder* [1915] 1 Ch 62.

The focus in the lowest intermediate balance rule upon D's *intention* emphasises that the underlying concern of tracing rules is to establish a causal link between two or more transactions. It requires that the latter transaction would not have occurred 'but for' the earlier defective transaction. However, as we will see below, there is one significant exception to this in cases of 'backwards tracing'. This exception is where the defective transaction occurs *after* the transaction with the defendant, but a fraudster intends to use the proceeds from the later transaction in the earlier defective transaction.

B. Tracing Through Mixed Funds

Perhaps the most difficult tracing rule to reconcile with an understanding of tracing as concerned with causally linked transactions is where the defendant against whom the tracing claim is brought receives money from an account which includes both credits that are caused by an earlier defective transaction as well as credits deriving from other transactions. For some time the tracing rule adopted in these cases of mixing of funds was 'first in first out'.[113] This rule was based on a misunderstanding of *Clayton's case,* which was not a case about tracing at all.[114] The rule was said to be 'really a rule of convenience based upon so-called presumed intention'.[115] This rule of convenience was criticised as a fiction that could work injustice.[116] It is now rejected in many cases.[117]

In the place of a 'first in first out' rule, there have been a number of alternatives applied or contemplated. One of those alternatives is pro-rata distribution amongst the contributors to the account.[118] This is, again, a rule of convenience. On occasion, cases have refused to apply it even between innocent parties.[119] In *Scott v Scott*,[120] the High Court of Australia considered the liability of a trustee of a deceased estate who mixed the trust funds with his own and purchased property with the combined fund. The High Court did not need to decide the point, but the court said that there was much to support the view that the estate could trace its money through a mixed account into the property and claim a proportionate beneficial interest in the increased value of it.

As a matter of principle, rather than convenience, the best solution should be whether the first transaction between the plaintiff and defendant was a cause of the second transaction between the defendant and the third party. If so, then the plaintiff should be entitled to claim a share of the benefit received by the defendant from the second transaction, in proportion with the contributions of the other causes. As with the lowest intermediate balance rule, this will require an assessment of the intention of the defendant in entering the

113 See the discussion in *Re French Caledonia Travel Service Pty Ltd (in liq)* [2003] NSWSC 1008, (2003) 59 NSWLR 361 [20]–[172] (Campbell J).

114 *Devaynes v Noble* (1816) 1 Mer 529, 35 ER 767. See LD Smith, *The Law of Tracing* (Oxford, Clarendon Press, 1997) 185–94.

115 *Re Diplock; Diplock v Wintle* [1948] Ch 465, 554 (the Court).

116 *Re Registered Securities Ltd* [1991] 1 NZLR 545, 553 (the Court).

117 See the discussion in *Re French Caledonia Travel Service Pty Ltd (in liq)* [2003] NSWSC 1008, (2003) 59 NSWLR 361 [168] (Campbell J).

118 *Barlow Clowes International Ltd (in liq) v Vaughan* [1991] EWCA Civ 11, [1992] 4 All ER 22; *Russell-Cooke Trust Co v Prentis* [2002] EWHC 2227 (Ch), [2003] 2 All ER 478; *Commerzbank Aktiengesellschraft v IMB Morgan plc* [2004] EWHC 2771 (Ch), [2005] 2 All ER (Comm) 564.

119 *Re Global Finance Group Pty Ltd* [2002] WASC 63, (2002) 26 WAR 385.

120 *Scott v Scott* [1963] HCA 65, (1963) 109 CLR 649.

second transaction. However, this is not the state of the law. In *Foskett v McKeown*,[121] Lord Millett explained that the orthodox view was that where money of two innocent contributors has been mixed, 'there is no basis upon which any of the claims can be subordinated to any of the others'. This would appear to apply even to a case, such as arises in a Ponzi scheme, where a wrongdoer maintains a record of intention concerning the use of particular payments from the mixed fund. Again, the refusal to take this approach appears to be a pragmatic concession to the fact that these records are often impossible to reconstruct in a genuine way.[122] One innocent party is precluded, for pragmatic reasons, from relying on an attempt to reconstruct records to obtain an advantage over another innocent party.

There is a further exception to a purely causal rule. Where the defendant is a wrongdoer, the courts will not permit the wrongdoer to rely on causal arguments for the wrongdoer's own benefit to defeat a claim for tracing. For instance, in *Re Oatway; Hertslet v Oatway*,[123] a trustee misappropriated £3,000 of trust money. The trustee paid the money into his bank account, which also contained £4,000 of his own funds. The trustee then spent the money in the account. The only asset which remained from the expenditure was shares of £2,137 value. The trial judge, Joyce J, held that the trustee was not permitted to argue that the shares were purchased with his own funds.[124] As the Vice-Chancellor said in a well-known passage in *Frith v Cartland*:

> If a man has £1000 of his own in a box on one side, and £1000 of trust property in the same box on the other side, and then takes out £500 and applies it for his own purposes, the Court will not allow him to say that that money was taken from the trust fund. The trust must have its £1000 so long as a sufficient sum remains in the box.[125]

In other words, a defendant who wrongfully receives money cannot disprove causation if the receipt *could* have been caused by the use of funds held for the plaintiff. The argument cannot be made even if a defendant maintains a ledger allocating the funds in the mixed account and demonstrating an intention to use some funds for his own purposes. This disapplication of causal rules against a wrongdoer is not unique to the law of tracing.[126]

C. Tracing into an Overdrawn or Loan Account

It has been said that it is not possible to trace into an overdrawn account.[127] As a matter of principle it is hard to see why this should be the case, for three reasons. First, suppose that a wrongdoer has an account with an overdraft limit of $100,000. The account is overdrawn to the limit. The wrongdoer pays $50,000 of funds misappropriated from his plaintiff

[121] *Foskett v McKeown* [2000] UKHL 29, [2001] 1 AC 102, 132.

[122] *Madoff Securities International Ltd (in liq) v Raven* [2013] EWHC 3147 (Comm), [2014] Lloyd's Rep FC 95 [278] (Popplewell J).

[123] *Re Oatway; Hertslet v Oatway* [1903] 2 Ch 356.

[124] See also *Scott v Scott* [1963] HCA 65, (1963) 109 CLR 649, 659 [8] (the Court).

[125] *Frith v Cartland* (1865) 2 H & M 417, 421; 71 ER 525, 527. See *Re Hallett's Estate; Knatchbull v Hallett* (1880) 13 Ch D 696 (CA) 719–20 (Jessel MR); *Parker v The Queen* [1997] HCA 15, (1997) 186 CLR 494, 502 (Brennan CJ).

[126] Eg *Kuwait Airways Corporation v Iraqi Airways Co (Nos 4 and 5)* [2002] UKHL 19, [2002] 2 AC 883. See Lord Hoffmann, 'Causation' in R Goldberg (ed), *Perspectives on Causation* (Oxford, Hart Publishing, 2011) 6–7.

[127] *Serious Fraud Office v Lexi Holdings plc* [2008] EWCA Crim 1443, [2009] QB 376 [50] (Keane LJ); *Re BA Peters Plc (in admin)* [2008] EWCA Civ 1604, [2010] 1 BCLC 142 [15] (Lord Neuberger MR).

employer into the overdrawn account and, soon after, withdraws $50,000 to purchase an asset. If the $50,000 had been paid into an account with no balance then the employer could have traced the value to the asset purchase. Why, as a matter of principle, should it be any different if the $50,000 was used to reduce an overdraft to create the same purchasing power for the later transaction? Secondly, the cases discussed in section VID below, which recognise 'backwards tracing', are premised upon the assumption that it is possible to trace into an overdrawn account. Finally, there should be no difference between accounts in debit and those in credit, if tracing rules were ultimately rationalised around principles of causation concerning related transactions.

However, this overdraft restriction has been applied in a number of cases. For instance, in *Russell Gould Pty Ltd v Ramangkura*,[128] an alleged unauthorised payment was made from the plaintiff company's bank account to the defendant's home loan account, clearing her debt. The New South Wales Court of Appeal held that the single payment concealed two transactions. The first transaction was that the company had discharged a debt owed to its director in the amount of the payment. The second transaction was that the director had instructed the company's bank to pay the money to the defendant.[129] In terms of an unjust enrichment analysis, since the director had a juristic reason for the receipt of the money, there could be no unjust enrichment claim against him and the payment could not be traced into the subsequent transaction. However, the Court of Appeal also said that it would not have been possible to trace the value to the defendant because the process of tracing was defeated by the payment into her loan account. Justice Barrett (with whom Bathurst CJ and Ward JA agreed) said that the 'money had no identifiable existence after the payment'[130] and that 'no process of following or tracing countenanced by the common law allows to be identified in the defendant's hands anything that represents that money'.[131]

D. Tracing Backwards

The effect of recognising that causal links between transactions are sufficient invites questions of the test for causation to be applied to determine whether one transaction causes another. Courts are only now beginning to grapple with this question. One of the most difficult examples of it is 'backwards tracing'. Suppose that D borrows money from a bank to buy a yacht. At the time D borrows the money, he intends to embezzle the funds from his employer to repay the loan. D, who has authority to draw from his company's account, then withdraws funds and uses them to discharge his loan. Can the company trace 'backwards' into D's purchase of the yacht?

In principle, the answer is that it should be possible. The two transactions are linked, although not in the usual way. Usually, the transactions would be linked because D would have embezzled the money before entering into the transaction to purchase the yacht. However, in this example it is the *intention* to embezzle that causes the purchase of the yacht, the later embezzlement being the fulfilment of that intention.

[128] *Russell Gould Pty Ltd v Ramangkura* [2014] NSWCA 310, (2014) 87 NSWLR 552.
[129] ibid [39] (Barrett JA; Bathurst CJ and Ward JA agreeing).
[130] ibid [36].
[131] ibid [38].

Until recently there was very little authority considering the phenomenon of tracing backwards. In *Bishopsgate Investment Management Ltd v Homan*,[132] Dillon LJ considered that backwards tracing should be possible;[133] Leggatt LJ considered that it should not.[134] Curiously, Henry LJ agreed with both judgments.[135] In other decisions, the concept of backwards tracing has been supported,[136] although there are also opposing views[137] and the phenomenon is not consistent with the principle that tracing cannot occur through an overdrawn or loan account. The best approach was that of Scott LJ in *Foskett v McKeown*,[138] who considered that tracing backwards should be possible, but only where 'it can be shown that it was always the intention to use the trust money to acquire the asset'.

The approach of Scott LJ was adopted by the Privy Council in *The Federal Republic of Brazil v Durant International Corporation (Jersey)*.[139] In that case, Mr Maluf was mayor of a Brazilian public authority. He received bribes of US$10.5 million in connection with public road building contracts. He was held to be liable for the amount of the bribes. The Jersey courts also found that British Virgin Islands companies (a parent called Durant, and its subsidiary) which he controlled were liable as constructive trustees. In the Privy Council, Durant argued that only $7.7 million of the bribes could be traced to it because (i) the amount of the bribes were paid to Durant *before* they had been paid to Mr Maluf, (ii) Mr Maluf made the payment to Durant from a bank account which was mixed with other money, and (iii) the lowest intermediate balance rule prevented recovery of the amount of the later bribe payments. The Privy Council rejected both submissions, essentially for pragmatic reasons. One reason was that without backwards tracing, any sophisticated fraudster would be able to defeat an otherwise effective tracing claim simply by manipulating the sequence in which credits and debits were made to his account.[140] Another reason, quoting from Professor Burrows, was that even in the most common tracing cases, banks often credit the account of a recipient before the account of the payer is debited.[141] Hence, the Board effectively accepted that where payments are made in *anticipation* of the receipt from a later transaction, then the earlier receipt can be traced from the later payment. This can constitute an exception to the lowest intermediate balance rule, or the rule preventing tracing through mixed funds.

VII. Transactional and Causal Links by Subrogation

Apart from tracing claims, another way in which a plaintiff can bring a claim against a third party based upon transactional links is by a technique described by Professor Mitchell as

[132] *Bishopsgate Investment Management Ltd (in liq) v Homan* [1995] Ch 211.
[133] ibid 217.
[134] ibid 221.
[135] ibid 222.
[136] *Shalson v Russo* [2003] EWHC 1637, [2005] Ch 281 [141] (Rimer J); *Foskett v McKeown* [1998] Ch 265 (CA) 284 (Scott LJ).
[137] *Foskett v McKeown* [1998] Ch 265, 289 (Hobhouse LJ).
[138] ibid 284.
[139] *Federal Republic of Brazil v Durant International Corporation (Jersey)* [2015] UKPC 35, [2015] 3 WLR 599.
[140] ibid [13].
[141] ibid [14].

reviving subrogation.[142] We saw in Chapter 3 that equity sometimes also uses the label 'subrogation' to describe restitutionary remedies.[143] 'Subrogation' simply means 'substitution'. When an award of non-contractual substitution or 'subrogation' is made, the reality is that the court is simply recognising that the plaintiff has restitutionary rights. For instance, the House of Lords made an award of restitution described as subrogation in *Banque Financière de la Cité v Parc (Battersea) Ltd.*[144] In the leading speech, Lord Hoffmann said:

> one is here concerned with a restitutionary remedy and that the appropriate questions are therefore, first, whether the defendant would be enriched at the plaintiff's expense; secondly, whether such enrichment would be unjust; and thirdly, whether there are nevertheless reasons of policy for denying a remedy.[145]

Like 'tracing', the label 'subrogation' in these non-contractual cases says nothing about the reason for the right to restitution. We saw in Chapter 3 that in *Banque Financière* the House of Lords explained that the reason that the enrichment was unjust was because of the plaintiff's mistake in discharging the debt (which enriched the defendant by increasing its priority). However, there might be many other reasons why restitution in this form of subrogation or substitution is awarded. In *Boscawen v Bajwa*[146] Millett LJ, referring to subrogation, said: that 'It is available in a wide variety of different factual situations in which it is required in order to reverse the defendant's unjust enrichment.' For a time there was growing recognition of this view in Australia.[147] But, although this is the better view, we saw in Chapter 3 that Australian law no longer accepts that subrogation is part of the law of unjust enrichment.[148]

The operation of 'reviving subrogation' as a method of conflating linked transactions can be seen in a typical scenario. The scenario involves a mistaken payment from A to B which B then uses to discharge debts that B owes to C.[149] A can bring an action for restitution against B by seeking to be put into C's former position. The courts treat B's debt to C as if it were revived and then allow A to sue B based upon that revived debt. Hence, subrogation has a distinct advantage over tracing. It does not remove the intermediary, B, but instead allows the plaintiff to bring an action against the intermediary by subrogation to the position of the third party, C. The transactional link between A and B is preserved, and all parties are before the court. For example, in *Butler v Rice*,[150] B made a loan to R. B mistakenly thought that he was lending to allow R to discharge his mortgage. But R had no mortgage. He had fraudulently misrepresented to B that he had a mortgage and, instead, used the money to

[142] C Mitchell, *The Law of Subrogation* (Oxford, Clarendon Press, 1994) ch 9, esp 124–29, 133–35.

[143] Cf *Challenger Managed Investments Ltd v Direct Money Corporation Pty Ltd* [2003] NSWSC 1072, (2003) 59 NSWLR 452, (2003) 12 BPR 22,257 [50] (Barrett J).

[144] *Banque Financière de la Cité v Parc (Battersea) Ltd* [1998] UKHL 7, [1999] 1 AC 221.

[145] ibid 234 (Lord Griffiths concurring).

[146] *Boscawen v Bajwa* [1996] 1 WLR 328, 335. See also *Banque Financière de la Cité v Parc (Battersea) Ltd* [1998] UKHL 7, [1999] 1 AC 221, 236 (Lord Hoffmann; Lord Griffiths agreeing).

[147] *Clout v Klein* [2003] QSC 152 [17] (Holmes J); *Prosser v Eagle* [2002] NSWSC 787 [14] (Dunford J). This is described by Young J as an 'avant garde' view: *National Australia Bank Ltd v Market Holdings Pty Ltd (in liq)* [2001] NSWSC 253, (2001) 161 FLR 1 [162].

[148] Ch 3 pp 42–45.

[149] *Bannatyne v D & C MacIver* [1906] 1 KB 103; *Reid v Rigby & Co* [1894] 2 QB 40; *B Liggett (Liverpool) Ltd v Barclays Bank Ltd* [1928] 1 KB 48; *Re Cleadon Trust Ltd* [1939] Ch 286.

[150] *Butler v Rice* [1910] 2 Ch 277. Referred to with approval by the House of Lords in *Banque Financière de la Cité v Parc (Battersea) Ltd* [1998] UKHL 7, [1999] 1 AC 221, 233 (Lord Hoffmann; Lord Griffiths concurring).

discharge his wife's mortgage. B succeeded in recovering the payment from R's wife by being subrogated to the (fictionally revived) rights of her mortgagee. Although the reasoning in *Butler v Rice* proceeded on the fiction that B intended to keep the mortgage alive for his own benefit,[151] the House of Lords has said (but the High Court of Australia has denied)[152] that this fiction should be replaced by recognition that such rights are restitutionary and generated by unjust enrichment.[153] As we saw in Chapter 3, the reasoning of the House of Lords is compelling. B had a claim against R and R had a claim against his wife. The two claims were able to be conflated in the proceeding by subrogation.

There are two leading English cases which recognise reviving subrogation as based upon a principle of preventing unjust enrichment. The first is *Banque Financière de la Cité v Parc (Battersea) Ltd*.[154] In that case, the plaintiff, mistakenly thinking that it held a valid letter of postponement, paid money which was used to discharge a debt of its subsidiary. The subsidiary's creditor had secured the debt by a first charge over a property owned by the subsidiary. The first charge was discharged when the debt was paid. The claim was not brought against the subsidiary even though the subsidiary was enriched by the discharge of its debt. Instead, the claim was brought against a company that held a second charge over the property of the subsidiary. The House of Lords held that the mistaken discharge of the first charge had enriched the defendant company by increasing the priority of its second charge. The plaintiff was entitled to be subrogated to the ('revived') first charge against its subsidiary to obtain priority over the second chargee.[155]

The second English case is *Bank of Cyprus UK Ltd v Menelaou*.[156] In that case, the parents of the appellant, Melissa, purchased a property called Great Oak Court in her name, to be used as the family home and held on trust for her and her siblings. Melissa was only able to pay the vendor because her parents sold the previous family home, called Rush Green Hall, which was owned by them. The Rush Green Hall property had been mortgaged to the Bank of Cyprus. The proceeds from the sale were used to buy Great Oak Court in Melissa's name. If the proceeds from Rush Green Hall had not been used, the vendor of Melissa's property would have had an unpaid vendor's lien over it. The Bank of Cyprus expected to obtain a charge from Melissa over Great Oak Court, but the charge over Melissa's property was invalid because her signature had been forged. One argument by the Bank of Cyprus was that Melissa would be unjustly enriched from the use of the proceeds which it paid to her parents unless it were subrogated to the unpaid vendor's lien that would otherwise have existed. The Court of Appeal granted this relief. The Supreme Court upheld this conclusion, with a majority of the court expressing the conclusion on the basis of unjust enrichment.[157]

The principles of subrogation are the same as those underlying tracing. There is a need for causally related transactions. The decision of the English Court of Appeal in *Swynson*

[151] *Butler v Rice* [1910] 2 Ch 277, 282 (Warrington J).

[152] *Bofinger v Kingsway Group Ltd* [2009] HCA 44, (2009) 239 CLR 269 [97] (the Court).

[153] *Banque Financière de la Cité v Parc (Battersea) Ltd* [1998] UKHL 7, [1999] 1 AC 221.

[154] ibid.

[155] In *Challenger Managed Investments Ltd v Direct Money Corp Pty Ltd* [2003] NSWSC 1072, (2003) 59 NSWLR 452, (2003) 12 BPR 22,257 [50], Bryson J accepted that the second chargee was enriched although his Honour denied that subrogation should have given a restitutionary remedy in the form of a *right* rather than merely value. See further, Ch 3 pp 42–45.

[156] *Bank of Cyprus UK Ltd v Menelaou* [2015] UKSC 66.

[157] *Swynson Ltd v Lowick Rose LLP* [2015] UKSC 66 [18] (Lord Clarke) [77] (Lord Neuberger; Lord Kerr and Lord Wilson agreeing).

Ltd v Lowick Rose LLP[158] illustrates the need for a causally related *transaction* in the context of subrogation. A firm of accountants negligently failed to exercise care in a due diligence report into a prospective borrower. The lending company lent money in 2006 and 2007 to the borrower in reliance upon this report. The owner of the lending company lent money to the borrower in 2008. When the borrower was in severe financial distress, the owner of the lending company, through a different company, repaid the 2006 and 2007 loans for various commercial reasons. The repayment was not a matter brought into account in the assessment of damages, so the lending company's alternative argument concerning unjust enrichment did not need to be considered. However, a majority of the Court of Appeal would have rejected the subrogation argument. That argument was that if the lending company had lost its right to damages, then the accountants were effectively benefited by the owner's payment by reduction in their damages which the owner's payment, via another company, would have mistakenly caused. Lord Justice Longmore, with whom Davis LJ agreed on this point, said that there were two reasons this claim would fail. One was that there was no relevant transaction to be revived or otherwise to which the owner was a party.[159] The relevant transaction was the company's repayment of the 2006 and 2007 loans which (if the damages claim had failed) would have reduced the accountants' liability. The owner was not a party to this transaction. The other reason was that there was no unjust factor, no finding of mistake, to support the claim.[160]

The need for a *causal* connection can also be seen in *Menelaou v Bank of Cyprus UK Ltd.*[161] In the English Court of Appeal in that case, the court observed that the unusual feature was that the bank had benefited the parents by releasing a security rather than by advancing funds. In the leading judgment, Floyd LJ accepted that the bank was 'the source of the moneys used as a matter of economic reality'.[162] In other words, there was a transactional link. There was one complication in relation to causation. The purchase of Melissa's property had occurred *before* the charge had been released. However, as Moses LJ explained, everyone knew that the bank's security would be released. The transaction that released the bank's charge was causally related to the earlier transaction involving the purchase of the property in Melissa's name because it was intended that the earlier transaction would not occur without the latter. The situation was materially identical to the causation question in a case of backwards tracing. When that case came before the United Kingdom Supreme Court, the issue was avoided because the two transactions were treated as 'one scheme'.[163]

VIII. Conclusion

The two essential lessons of this chapter can be summarised briefly. The first is that the concept that an enrichment be 'at the expense of the plaintiff' is not concerned with any financial loss to the plaintiff. Instead, it directs attention to the particular transaction which

158 *Swynson Ltd v Lowick Rose LLP (in liq)* [2015] EWCA Civ 629, [2015] PNLR 28.
159 ibid [23]–[24].
160 ibid [25].
161 *Menelaou v Bank of Cyprus UK Ltd* [2013] EWCA Civ 1960, [2014] 1 WLR 854.
162 ibid [48].
163 *Swynson Ltd v Lowick Rose LLP* [2015] UKSC 66 [67] (Lord Neuberger).

is the subject of the claim for unjust enrichment. Secondly, in an unjust enrichment claim seeking restitution of value obtained by a defendant, the source of the defendant's enrichment need not be a transaction directly with the plaintiff, but it must be a transaction *linked* to the plaintiff. The rules of tracing and subrogation establish when a link will be sufficient. Where there is a single transaction, the question is whether the immediate source of the defendant's enrichment is that transaction with the plaintiff. Where there are subsequent transactions with a third party defendant after the enrichment of an initial party, the question is whether the existence or anticipation of the defective transaction causes the transaction that directly enriches the defendant.

6

The Unjust Enquiry

Contents

I. Introduction

The previous two chapters explained the first two elements for a prima facie claim for unjust enrichment: (1) that the defendant was enriched; and (2) that the enrichment came at the expense of the plaintiff. This chapter is concerned with the meaning of the third requirement, namely that the enrichment must be 'unjust'.

There are a number of different approaches to the question of whether an enrichment at the plaintiff's expense is 'unjust'. Different legal systems appear to adopt different techniques. Ultimately, however, similar questions are asked by each legal system.

The lessons from this chapter are simple. An enquiry into whether an enrichment is unjust does *not* ask whether there is injustice in an idiosyncratic sense. Instead, the enquiry concerns (1) whether the plaintiff can prove an established legal ground or 'unjust factor' which permits restitution, and, if so, (2) whether the plaintiff can negate any right that the defendant asserts to retain the enrichment. Some legal systems focus on the latter element while others focus on the former. But, in truth, all legal systems must ultimately ask both questions.

II. The Unjust Enquiry is not the Exercise of Idiosyncratic Discretion

In one respect the word 'unjust' might not have been the best description for Australian and English law to have settled upon. A better description of the subject might have been 'unjustified' enrichment. The word 'unjust' carries connotations of idiosyncratic discretion and an individual's malleable sense of fairness. This chapter therefore begins by sounding a strong note of caution. On this matter, all courts and commentators speak with a single voice. Whichever approach is adopted, the 'unjust' element in unjust enrichment is '*not* to assert a judicial discretion to do whatever idiosyncratic notions of what is fair and just might dictate'.[1]

III. The Plaintiff must Prove the Existence of an Unjust Factor

A. The Meaning of an Unjust Factor

The requirement for an unjust factor was articulated most clearly in the ground-breaking work of Professor Birks in 1985.[2] Although Birks changed his mind in 2003, his original work was, and is, extremely influential. Drawing from three extraordinary eighteenth-century English jurists, Lord Mansfield,[3] Sir William Blackstone,[4] and Sir William Evans,[5] Birks explained that the unjust factors approach enquires into whether there is any established 'unjust factor' that entitles the plaintiff to restitution. Birks used the term 'unjust factor' to describe those recognised legal principles that give rise to the conclusion that an enrichment is unjust. As Mason P explained, the term 'unjust factor' therefore 'expresses the common quality of those factors which, when present in conjunction with 'enrichment', have been held to call for restitution'.[6] In *Moses v Macferlan*, Lord Mansfield gave examples of common law unjust factors permitting restitution of money paid which have hardly been expanded upon in the subsequent three centuries: '[M]oney paid by mistake; or upon a consideration which happens to fail; or for money got through imposition, (express, or implied;) or extortion; or oppression…'.[7]

[1] *Pavey & Matthews Pty Ltd v Paul* [1987] HCA 5, (1987) 162 CLR 221, 256 [14] (Deane J) (emphasis added). A recent example is *Mega-top Cargo Pty Ltd v Moneytech Services Pty Ltd* [2015] NSWCA 402 [50] (Leeming JA).
[2] P Birks, *An Introduction to the Law of Restitution* (Oxford, Clarendon Press, 1985).
[3] See *Moses v Macferlan* (1760) 2 Burr 1005, 97 ER 676.
[4] See W Blackstone, *Commentaries on the Laws of England*, bk III (Oxford, Clarendon Press, 1768) 62, reproduced in W Blackstone, *Commentaries on the Laws of England* (first published 1765–1769, Chicago, The University of Chicago Press, 1979).
[5] See W Evans, 'An Essay on the Action for Money Had and Received' in W Evans, *Essays: On the Action for Money Had and Received, on the Law of Insurances and on the Law of Bills of Exchange and Promissory Notes* (Liverpool, Merrit & Wright, 1802, reprinted in [1998] RLR 1).
[6] *Concrete Constructions Group v Litevale Pty Ltd (No 2)* [2003] NSWSC 411, [11] (Mason P).
[7] *Moses v Macferlan* (1760) 2 Burr 1005, 1012, 97 ER 676, 681.

B. The Requirement for an Unjust Factor as a Matter of Authority

The requirement for an established unjust factor has not always been explicit. As we saw in Chapter 2, for hundreds of years the corpus of case law in unjust enrichment was concealed within forms of action. Cases at common law where a plaintiff sought restitution of unjust enrichment would be pleaded in forms which involved counts of *indebitatus assumpsit.* These counts included money had and received, money paid, goods sold and delivered, and (later) *quantum meruit*, and *quantum valebat.* But these formal pleadings said nothing about the basis for the restitutionary claim. Nor did the judgments of the time explain the basis for restitution. For instance, in a case where a defendant defrauded a plaintiff into mistakenly paying money to the defendant, the judgment might say that the plaintiff was entitled to repayment of money as 'money had and received'. Was this recognising a claim for restitution for unjust enrichment? Or was it a claim for restitution for wrongdoing? Or was it a claim for restitution for some other reason? If it was a claim for unjust enrichment, what was the 'unjust factor'? In the pre-1832 age of forms of action the answers to these questions were not important. Now they are essential. It is no longer adequate to plead a case of unjust enrichment by reference to one of the forms of action. A defendant must know the case which he or she is called upon to answer.

In Australia the unjust factor approach was adopted in a joint judgment of five justices of the High Court of Australia in *David Securities Pty Ltd v Commonwealth Bank of Australia.*[8] Five justices said that restitution for unjust enrichment required proof of 'a qualifying or vitiating factor such as mistake, duress or illegality'.[9] It was reiterated by the High Court of Australia in *Farah Constructions Pty Ltd v Say-Dee Pty Ltd*:[10] '[R]ecovery rather depends on the existence of a qualifying or vitiating factor falling into some particular category'. Since *David Securities* many Australian cases have insisted that a plaintiff plead and prove an unjust factor.[11] For instance, in *Wasada Pty Ltd v State Rail Authority of New South Wales (No 2)* Campbell J said:

> But to the extent that [legal principles governing injustice] have been developed they may be termed 'unjust factors'. 'Unjust' is the 'generalisation of all the factors which the law recognises as calling for restitution'. Because we need to search for *recognised* factors, examination of which involves an analysis of case law, the reference to 'injustice' as an element of unjust enrichment, is not a reference to judicial discretion. Normal judicial processes are involved and it is only in cases where there is no recognised basis for saying that injustice has arisen that problems can arise.[12]

[8] *David Securities Pty Ltd v Commonwealth Bank of Australia* [1992] HCA 48, (1992) 175 CLR 353.

[9] ibid [46], 379 (Mason CJ, Deane, Toohey, Gaudron, and McHugh JJ).

[10] *Farah Constructions Pty Ltd v Say-Dee Pty Ltd* [2007] HCA 22, (2007) 230 CLR 89 [150] (the Court).

[11] *QMT Constructions Pty Ltd v Carringbush Corporation Pty Ltd* [2000] NSWSC 577 [42] (Einstein J); *Hollis v Atherton Shire Council* [2003] QSC 147, (2003) 128 LGERA 348 [9], [10] (Jones J); *Wasada Pty Ltd v State Rail Authority of New South Wales (No 2)* [2003] NSWSC 987 [16] (Campbell J); *Australian Fast Foods Pty Ltd v Hethersett Pty Ltd* (WASC, 23 February 1993); *National Australia Bank Ltd v Budget Stationery Supplies Pty Ltd* (1997) 217 ALR 365, 371 (Mason P); *Roxborough v Rothmans of Pall Mall Australia Ltd* [2001] HCA 68, (2001) 208 CLR 516, 257 [139] n 229,; *Spangaro v Corporate Investment Australia Funds Management Ltd* [2003] FCA 1025, (2003) 21 ACLC 1948, 1961 [48] (Finkelstein J); *Karl Suleman Enterprizes Pty Ltd (in liq) v Babanour* [2004] NSWCA 214, (2004) 49 ACSR 612 [71] (Beazley JA; Spigelman CJ and Santow JA agreeing).

[12] *Wasada Pty Ltd v State Rail Authority of New South Wales (No 2)* [2003] NSWSC 987 [16] citing K Mason and J Carter, *Restitution Law in Australia* (Sydney, Butterworths, 1995) 59–60. Quoted in part with approval in *Australian Financial Services and Leasing Pty Ltd v Hills Industries Ltd* [2014] HCA 14, (2014) 307 ALR 512 [141] (Gageler J).

The restitutionary claim in that case failed because 'the pleading … did not plead any of the recognised categories of injustice which leads to a restitutionary claim, such as mistake or duress'.[13]

Another strong example of the essential need to plead and prove an unjust factor is the decision in *Electric Life Pty Ltd v Unison Finance Group Pty Ltd*.[14] In that case, the New South Wales Court of Appeal concluded that the applicant had made rental payments after 10 November 2003 without any obligation to do so. However, the renter's evidence was simply that he had left the payments of rent to a bookkeeper. Giving the leading judgment, Emmett AJA noted that there was no allegation of mistake in the plaintiff's pleadings.[15] Further, while it may have been that the renter could have proved a mistake, no sufficient evidence was led to that effect.[16] English law has also insisted on the need to plead and prove an unjust factor. In *Woolwich Equitable Building Society v Inland Revenue Commissioners*,[17] Lord Goff emphasised the need for an unjust factor, in a passage repeated by Lord Hoffmann a decade later. In *Deutsche Morgan Grenfell plc v Inland Revenue Commissioners*, Lord Hoffmann said:

> [A]t any rate for the moment, … unlike civilian systems, English law has no general principle that to retain money paid without any legal basis (such as debt, gift, compromise, etc) is unjust enrichment. In the *Woolwich* case … Lord Goff said that English law might have developed so as to recognise such a general principle—the condictio indebiti of civilian law—but had not done so. In England, the claimant has to prove that the circumstances in which the payment was made come within one of the categories which the law recognizes as sufficient to make retention by the recipient unjust.[18]

So too, in *Kleinwort Benson Ltd v Lincoln City Council*,[19] Lord Hope stressed that '[t]he approach of the common law is to look for an unjust factor, something which makes it unjust to allow the payee to retain the benefit … It is the mistake by the payer which, as in the case of failure of consideration and compulsion, renders the enrichment of the payee unjust.' First instance and Court of Appeal decisions in England have emphasised this need for an unjust factor.[20]

[13] *Wasada Pty Ltd v State Rail Authority of New South Wales (No 2)* [2003] NSWSC 987 [31]. See also *Alexiadis v Zirpiadis* [2013] SASCFC 64, (2013) 302 ALR 148 [27] (Kourakis CJ) [116]-117] (Gray J); *Matland Holdings Pty Ltd v NTZ Pty Ltd* [2004] FCA 710 [171] (Kenny J); *Ideas Plus Investments Ltd v National Australia Bank Ltd* [2005] WASC 51 [81] (Commissioner Siopis SC); *Ideas Plus Investments Ltd v National Australia Bank* Ltd [2006] WASCA 215, (2006) 32 WAR 467 [64]-[66] (the Court); *SCI Operations Pty Ltd v Commonwealth* (1996) 69 FCR 346, 397 (Sackville J).

[14] [2015] NSWCA 394.

[15] ibid [15], [57] (Emmett AJA; Gleeson JA and Tobias AJA agreeing).

[16] ibid [70].

[17] *Woolwich Equitable Building Society v Inland Revenue Commissioners* [1993] AC 70, 172 (HL).

[18] *Deutsche Morgan Grenfell Plc v Inland Revenue Commissioners* [2006] UKHL 49, [2007] 1 AC 558 [21].

[19] *Kleinwort Benson Ltd v Lincoln City Council* [1998] UKHL 38, [1999] 2 AC 349, 409.

[20] *Uren v First National Home Finance Ltd* [2005] EWHC 2529 [13] (Mann J); *Chief Constable of the Greater Manchester Police v Wigan Athletic AFC Ltd* [2008] EWCA Civ 1449, [2009] 1 WLR 1580 [50] (Morritt C; Smith LJ agreeing); *Investment Trust Companies (in liq) v Revenue and Customs Commissioners* [2012] EWHC 458, [2012] STC 1150 [74] (Henderson J); *Brennan v Brighton Borough Council, The Times*, 15 May 1997 (Sir Christopher Slade); *Portman Building Society v Hamlyn Taylor Neck (a firm)* [1998] 4 All ER 202, 206 (Millett LJ); *Banque Financière de la Cité v Parc (Battersea) Ltd* [1998] UKHL 7, [1999] 1 AC 221, 227 (Lord Steyn) 234 (Lord Hoffmann); *Lloyds Bank Plc v Independent Insurance Co Ltd* [2000] 1 QB 110, 123 (Waller LJ); *Cressman v Coys of Kensington (Sales) Ltd* [2004] EWCA Civ 47, [2004] 1 WLR 2775 [22] (Mance LJ); *Niru Battery Manufacturing Co v Milestone Trading Ltd (No 2)* [2004] EWCA Civ 487, [2004] 2 All ER (Comm) 289 [28], [41] (Clarke LJ); *Filby v Mortgage Express (No 2) Ltd* [2004] EWCA Civ 759 [44]–[62] (May LJ).

However, in 2003, Professor Birks, the pioneer of the language of 'unjust factors' changed his mind, relying in part upon the arguments of the civilian scholar Sonja Meier.[21] Birks said that English law had changed direction and had adopted the juristic reasons approach (which he described as a 'no basis' approach).[22] On this 'no basis' approach, he said that it was not necessary to ask whether there was any unjust factor involving an imperfection in the plaintiff's intention. Instead, the question was simply whether there was any juristic reason for the defendant to retain the enrichment. Examples of juristic reasons would be if the defendant obtained the enrichment by a contract, or a gift or a transfer on trust.

Against the heavy weight of obiter dicta, Professor Birks' argument relied upon *ultra vires* closed interest rate swap cases in which courts had justified restitution simply upon the ground of the invalidity of the obligation rather than any unjust factor.[23] He argued that this approach had not been explicitly rejected by the House of Lords in *Kleinwort Benson Ltd v Lincoln City Council*.[24]

Birks' view was not adopted by the courts. The closest that courts came to adopting this view was a tentative consideration by Lord Walker in the House of Lords, who concluded that 'it is in the nature of the common law to develop slowly' and said:

> I doubt whether this is the right time for your Lordships to decide whether to rebase the whole law of unjust enrichment on a highly abstract principle which ... would represent a distinct departure from established doctrine. ... my tentative inclination is to welcome any tendency of the English law of unjust enrichment to align itself more closely with Scottish law, and so to civilian roots. I see attractions in the suggestion made by Professor Birks in *Unjust Enrichment*, 2nd ed, p 116, under the heading 'The Pyramid: A Limited Reconciliation'.[25]

More recently, in *Crown Prosecution Service v Eastenders Group*,[26] Lord Toulson (with whom Lady Hale, and Lords Kerr, Wilson and Hughes agreed) approved the statement from the Australian decision (quoted above) in *Wasada* that the unjust element in unjust enrichment is simply a 'generalisation of all the factors which the law recognises as calling for restitution'. There would seem to be little prospect of an abolition of unjust factors in Australia or England.

We will see below the difficulty of abandoning unjust factors as a matter of principle. But an instructive comparison of what can happen if they were abolished is the recent change of direction in Canadian law. In 2004 the Supreme Court of Canada purported to abolish unjust factors, in a decision described by Professor McInnes as a 're-map[ping of] virtually the whole of the restitutionary seascape'.[27] Prior to the decision of the Supreme Court,

[21] S Meier, 'Restitution After Executed Void Contracts' in P Birks and F Rose (eds), *Lessons of the Swaps Litigation* (London, Mansfield Press, 2000). See also R Zimmermann 'Unjustified Enrichment: The Modern Civilian Approach' (1995) 15 *Oxford Journal of Legal Studies* 403, 416: '[I]t is hardly conceivable that a legal system engaged with the task of rationally reorganizing its law of unjustified enrichment should take its lead from English jurisprudence.'

[22] P Birks, *Unjust Enrichment* (Oxford, Oxford University Press, 2003).

[23] *Kleinwort Benson Ltd v Sandwell Borough Council* [1994] 4 All ER 890; *Guinness Mahon & Co Ltd v Kensington & Chelsea Royal London Borough Council* [1999] QB 215.

[24] *Kleinwort Benson Ltd v Lincoln City Council* [1998] UKHL 38, [1999] 2 AC 349. See now P Birks, *Unjust Enrichment*, 2nd edn (Oxford, Oxford University Press, 2005) 110, 112.

[25] *Deutsche Morgan Grenfell Plc v Inland Revenue Commissioners* [2006] UKHL 49, [2007] 1 AC 558 [155], [158].

[26] *Crown Prosecution Service v Eastenders Group* [2014] UKSC 26, [2015] AC 1 [102].

[27] M McInnes, 'Juristic Reasons and Unjust Factors in the Supreme Court of Canada' (2004) 120 *Law Quarterly Review* 554, 558.

lower courts had oscillated between the new approach and an unjust factors approach. The revolutionary decision was *Garland v Consumers' Gas Co.*[28] In that case, a class action was brought for the recovery of penalties paid by consumers to an electricity utility, Consumers' Gas Company. The gas company thought that the penalties were valid because they were made pursuant to orders of the Ontario Energy Board, a statutory body. However, the penalties were illegal interest charges which violated the Criminal Code, and the orders were therefore inoperative.[29] The question for the Supreme Court was whether an action in unjust enrichment could be brought to recover the payments. In the Ontario Court of Appeal an unjust factors approach had been taken, but Borins JA (referring to an article by Professor Smith)[30] observed that Canadian courts had oscillated between requiring unjust factors and abolishing them.[31]

The Supreme Court abolished them. The Supreme Court held that the gas company was unjustly enriched because there was 'no juristic reason' for the payments. Instead of asking whether there was an unjust factor entitling the consumers to recover, the Supreme Court asked whether there was a juristic reason entitling the gas company to retain the payments. The payments were not made pursuant to a contract, a disposition of law (because the orders were contrary to the Criminal Code and inoperative), a donative intent or any other valid common law, equitable or statutory obligation.[32] For the period from when the action was commenced (when the defendant had notice that the orders were possibly inoperative) the gas company could not show any juristic reason to rebut this prima facie case. The Supreme Court even added to the list of juristic matters or 'reasons' which form a different category from general legal categories: the reasonable expectations of the parties, and reasons of public policy.[33]

C. The Requirement for an Unjust Factor as a Matter of Principle

The requirement that a plaintiff prove the existence of an unjust factor is necessary as a matter of principle. It is an implicit requirement even in civilian legal systems that do not expressly recognise a requirement for an unjust factor. For instance, in German, French and (now) Canadian law, the express focus is often said to be only upon whether there is a juristic reason or basis for retention of the enrichment. Common examples of juristic reasons would be a statutory right to retain the enrichment or a contract. But this approach merely conceals the presence of unjust factors. Consider a simple case where a shopkeeper at the checkout makes an over-payment of change to a customer. Under the juristic reasons approach, the shopkeeper is said to be entitled to restitution of the overpayment because there is no juristic reason for the payment: no contract in relation to that payment exists and there is no other juristic reason for the customer to retain the money (eg gift, trust or other basis). Section 812(1) of the German Civil Code (*Bürgerliches Gesetzbuch*), which

28 *Garland v Consumers' Gas Co* [2004] 1 SCR 629, 2004 SCC 25. See also *Pacific National Investments Ltd v Victoria (City)* [2004] 3 SCR 575, 2004 SCC 75.

29 Criminal Code, RSC 1985, c C-46.

30 L Smith, 'The Mystery of "Juristic Reason"' (2000) 12 *Supreme Court Law Review* 211.

31 *Garland v Consumers' Gas Co Ltd* (2001) 208 DLR (4th) 494 [126].

32 *Garland v Consumers' Gas Co* [2004] 1 SCR 629, 2004 SCC 25 [53].

33 *Garland v Consumers' Gas Co* [2004] 1 SCR 629, 2004 SCC 25 [55]–[61].

takes a similar approach to French,[34] and now Canadian,[35] law is a typical example of this juristic reasons approach. German law provides:

> He who obtains something through someone else's performance or in another way at his expense without a legal cause, is obliged to make restitution to the other. This obligation arises also where the legal cause later disappears or where the result contemplated by the legal transaction is not attained.[36]

In these jurisdictions, the 'golden thread'[37] apparently binding together every case of unjust enrichment is said to be that there is no juristic reason or basis to retain the enrichment. But as soon as more facts are added to the shopkeeper scenario, the thread unravels. It becomes clear that the juristic reasons approach cannot survive without unjust factors. Suppose, in the simplest of mistake cases, the shopkeeper says 'Here's your change' when making the overpayment. Why doesn't this amount to a gift of the overpayment, and therefore a juristic reason for the customer to retain the enrichment? The only way that the shopkeeper can establish that the overpayment was not a gift is to say that it was not intended as a gift. But the reason why it was not intended as a gift is because it was made by *mistake*. Even on a juristic reasons approach, the unjust factor operates implicitly.

In Canada, the first Supreme Court case which formally recognised the juristic reasons approach immediately recognised problems with it. The Supreme Court saw a need to create an exception to recovery even where there was no juristic reason to retain the enrichment. That exception was based on 'reasonable expectations'. So in *Garland v Consumers' Gas Co*[38] the Supreme Court recognised that the claim for restitution of interest payments which had been made under the inoperative Order could be (and was) met by a defence where the defendant had a reasonable expectation that it would be able to keep the interest payments. Until the filing of the writ, which alleged that the Order was invalid, the defendant had a reasonable expectation of entitlement to the money. So too, if neighbour A improved his land, unwittingly also increasing the value of neighbour B's land, then neighbour B would have a reasonable expectation that he would be entitled to keep the benefit of the increase in the value of his land.

The defence of reasonable expectations is blunt and uncertain.[39] And the existence of a reasonable expectation might depend upon whether the plaintiff is mistaken, or whether the defendant could reasonably have known that the plaintiff was, or might be mistaken. Again, mistake will play an important role. The example of adjoining neighbours is based on a case where it was held that there was *no* reasonable expectation of retaining the enrichment because the parties had a shared understanding that the defendant would pay for the

[34] Art 1235 of the French *Code civil*, *repetition de l'indu* ('recovery of what is not due').

[35] *Garland v Consumers' Gas Co* [2004] 1 SCR 629, 2004 SCC 25; *Pacific National Investments Ltd v Victoria (City)* [2004] 3 SCR 575, 2004 SCC 75—cases which reinterpreted remarks from *Rathwell v Rathwell* [1978] 2 SCR 436 and *Pettkus v Becker* [1980] 2 SCR 834.

[36] This is Dr Krebs' translation. For a detailed discussion of this provision see T Krebs, *Restitution at the Crossroads: A Comparative Study* (London, Cavendish, 2001) ch 11.

[37] R Stevens, 'Is there a Law of Unjust Enrichment?' in S Degeling and J Edelman (eds), *Unjust Enrichment in Commercial Law* (Sydney, Lawbook Co, 2008) 16.

[38] *Garland v Consumers' Gas Co* [2004] 1 SCR 629, 2004 SCC 25. See also *Pacific National Investments Ltd v Victoria (City)* [2004] 3 SCR 575, 2004 SCC 75.

[39] Compare, for example, the majority and minority approaches in *Canadian-Automatic Data Processing Services Ltd v Bentley* [2004] BCCA 408, (2004) 242 DLR (4th) 250.

work. But the judge in that case rightly considered this to be an 'unjust factor'.[40] The failure of the shared understanding is an example of the unjust factor of failure of consideration. Once again, the unjust factors approach brings the reason for recovery (such as mistake, duress or illegitimate pressure, undue influence or failure of consideration) to the surface. In the words of Lord President Rodger (as the late Lord Rodger was then) the 'underlying realities' become apparent.[41]

The argument in this book is that the law of unjust enrichment does have a unifying theme: it is concerned with transactions arising by imperfect intention. As between a plaintiff and a defendant, an enrichment may be unjust if the plaintiff does not intend to enter the transaction that enriches the defendant, or the plaintiff's intention is vitiated or subject to a condition or qualification which fails. Juristic reasons are a separate matter. There may still be juristic reasons why a claim for unjust enrichment in these circumstances will not be unjust. But these juristic reasons are concerned with the coherence of the law. For instance if a transaction with a defendant, which was imperfectly intended (say, by mistake), was by gift, contract, deed or court order, then coherence in the law will usually require that the gift, contract, deed, or court order be rescinded before restitution will be ordered. Otherwise the order for restitution of unjust enrichment would contradict another branch of the law which determines that a defendant has a right to retain the enrichment.

We will see in Chapter 7 that there are additional rules which govern when, in the example above, the contract, deed, or gift can be rescinded. For instance, although there is a prima facie right to restitution of a mistaken payment made without obligation, a *contract* to pay money can generally only be avoided if the mistake is sufficiently fundamental,[42] induced by a misrepresentation of the defendant[43] or known to the defendant in circumstances in which the defendant took steps to ensure that the plaintiff did not become aware of the mistake.[44] A voluntary deed is subject to different rules again.[45] In Continental European jurisdictions the juristic reasons approach purports to avoid all these difficult rules by pushing them into other areas of the law. So in Germany, rules relating to when a contract can be avoided (so that it can be said that there is no juristic reason for the defendant's enrichment) are treated as part of the law of contract.[46] It is thought that issues of unjust enrichment can only arise once the obligation has been extinguished. So in Germany, only once the contract is avoided do issues of unjust enrichment arise in relation to the value of assets transferred.

The problem with this continental European approach is that it conceals the operation of unjust factors in the law of unjust enrichment and makes it appear as if the law of unjust

[40] *Conrad v Feldbar Construction Co Ltd* [2004] OJ No 1290, (2004) 70 OR (3d) 298 [18] (Ground J).

[41] *Shilliday v Smith* [1998] SC 725, 727 (Lord President Rodger).

[42] *Cundy v Lindsay* (1878) 3 App Cas 459; *Smith v Hughes* (1871) LR 6 QB 597; *Bell v Lever Brothers Ltd* [1932] AC 161; *Great Peace Shipping Ltd v Tsavliris Salvage (International) Ltd* [2002] EWCA Civ 1407, [2003] QB 679.

[43] *Redgrave v Hurd* (1881) 20 Ch D 1; *Marks v GIO Australia Holdings Ltd* [1998] HCA 69, (1998) 196 CLR 494 [117] (Kirby J).

[44] *Taylor v Johnson* [1983] HCA 5, (1983) 151 CLR 422, 432 [14]; *Smith v Smith* [2004] NSWSC 663, (2004) 12 BPR 23,051.

[45] See Ch 7 pp 151–52. See also *Walker v Armstrong* (1856) 8 De GM & G 531, 44 ER 495; *Ogilvie v Littleboy* (1897) 13 TLR 399; *Re Walton's Settlement; Walton v Peirson* [1922] 2 Ch 509; *Meadows v Meadows* (1853) 16 Beav 401, 51 ER 833; *Ellis v Ellis* (1909) 26 TLR 166; *Phillipson v Kerry* (1863) 32 Beav 628, 55 ER 247; *Gibbon v Mitchell* [1990] 3 All ER 338; *Pitt v Holt* [2011] EWCA Civ 197, [2012] Ch 132; *Franknelly Nominees Pty Ltd v Abrugiato* [2013] WASCA 285, (2013) 10 ASTLR 558 [179] (Buss JA).

[46] Principles of rescission (*Anfechtungserklärung*) are found in a separate part of the *Bürgerliches Gesetzbuch*, in ss 142–44.

enrichment is concerned only with the defendant's juristic reason to retain the enrichment. Consider, for example, a claim for restitution of money transferred under a contract entered into by the defendant's undue influence. The undue influence operates in two ways. First, it operates to avoid the contract and to remove any juristic reason for the defendant to retain the money. Secondly, it provides the plaintiff with a positive reason for restitution. In neither case is the undue influence part of the law of contract. As Birks said, a power to avoid a contract is 'not granted by contract and cannot be said to arise from [its] own effect'.[47] The juristic reasons approach simply pushes the difficult issues arising as a result of the unjust factor into other areas of law where they do not belong.

D. Recognised Unjust Factors and the Common Feature of Unjust Factors

Part III (comprising Chapters 8 to 12) considers the established unjust factors. These are unjust factors 'concerned with recovery of benefits which are conferred not voluntarily and by virtue of mistake [Chapter 8], compulsion [Chapter 9] and total failure of consideration [Chapter 11]'.[48] To this list can be added the unjust factor of undue influence (Chapter 10). Undue influence is like duress or illegitimate pressure, because '[u]ndue influence [in equity], like common law duress, looks to the quality of the consent or assent of the weaker party'.[49] In *David Securities*, the joint judgment referred to 'compulsion' and 'undue influence' interchangeably when speaking of liability in unjust enrichment.[50] In England, undue influence has expressly been recognised as part of the law of unjust enrichment.[51]

There are other potential unjust factors. For instance, suppose a thief steals your wallet containing $500. You have not made any mistake. Nor is there any illegitimate pressure or undue influence involved in the transfer of the notes to the thief. It would be bizarre if the law recognised a claim for restitution of the $500 for unjust enrichment against a defendant who had been mistakenly paid $500 but did not recognise a claim for unjust enrichment against a thief who stole $500. Whatever other claims might be available against the thief, in both cases the thief has obtained value from you without your consent. Arguments that you might still have title to the $500 of notes in the case of theft will not assist you when you try to use that title to the notes you do not have to purchase a bicycle. Chapter 12 considers potential unjust factors in cases such as theft, where a plaintiff has no intention to enter the transaction that enriches the defendant.

All of the unjust factors that we have described so far are unjust factors that involve an imperfect intention in the transfer of value from a plaintiff to a defendant. Either (i) the plaintiff did not intend to enter the transaction that enriched the defendant, or (ii) the plaintiff's intention was vitiated by mistake, illegitimate pressure, or undue influence, or

[47] P Birks, *Unjust Enrichment*, 2nd edn (Oxford, Oxford University Press, 2005) 126.

[48] *Winterton Constructions Pty Ltd v Hambros Australia Ltd* [1991] FCA 171, (1991) 101 ALR 363, 374 [53] (Gummow J).

[49] *Commercial Bank of Australia Ltd v Amadio* [1983] HCA 14, (1983) 151 CLR 447, 474 [13] (Deane J); *Bridgewater v Leahy* [1998] HCA 66, (1998) 194 CLR 457; A Mason, 'The Impact of Equitable Doctrine on the Law of Contract' (1998) 27 *Anglo-American Law Review* 1, 6–8.

[50] *David Securities Pty Ltd v Commonwealth Bank of Australia* [1992] HCA 48, (1992) 175 CLR 353, 374 [36] (Mason CJ, Deane, Toohey, Gaudron and McHugh JJ).

[51] *Benedetti v Sawiris & Ors* [2013] UKSC 50, [2014] AC 938 [175] (Lord Neuberger). See also *Hart v Burbidge* [2014] EWCA Civ 992 [43] (Vos LJ; Richards and Black LJJ agreeing).

(iii) the plaintiff did intend to enter the transaction that enriched the defendant, but subject to a condition or on a basis that failed. In all of these situations the plaintiff does not have a perfected intention to enter the transaction by which the defendant was enriched.

E. There may be More than One Unjust Factor in a Single Case

The decision of the High Court of Australia in *David Securities Pty Ltd v Commonwealth Bank of Australia*[52] shows the possibility that several different unjust factors may be available on one set of facts. David Securities entered into a contract of mortgage with the Commonwealth Bank (the contracting branch of which was in Singapore, and subject to withholding tax). One clause of that contract required David Securities to make payments to the bank to cover withholding tax imposed upon the bank's receipt of interest. Legislation provided that such a term was 'absolutely void'. David Securities sought restitution of the amounts paid pursuant to the clause, relying upon the unjust factor of mistake. The High Court accepted that restitution would follow if David Securities had been mistaken, and referred the case back to trial to determine whether the mistake had caused the payment, as 'it [was] arguable that [David Securities] may have wished to ensure that there was a roll-over, whatever their belief as to the existence of an obligation to do so'.[53]

Another possible unjust factor on the facts of *David Securities* was failure of consideration. As will be seen in Chapter 11, 'consideration' in this context is not used in its contractual sense (commonly, a promise for a promise), but instead means the 'state of affairs, which was within the contemplation of the parties as the basis of their dealings'.[54] David Securities could have argued that the money was paid on the basis, assumed by both parties, that the contractual provision was valid. When it turned out that this 'basis' did not exist, they were entitled to restitution.

F. Policy Reasons for Restitution and Instances of Wrongdoing are not Unjust Factors

If no unjust factor exists in a particular case then the plaintiff's intention in relation to the defendant's enrichment is not imperfect. Any reason for restitution of value obtained by the defendant cannot be part of the law of unjust enrichment. As between plaintiff and defendant, there is no defect or qualification to the plaintiff's intention to enter the impugned transaction. There is no injustice, between the parties, in refusing restitution.

Although there is no action based on unjust enrichment, there might still be other reasons for restitution. One category of reasons for restitution, independent of unjust enrichment, was seen in Chapter 2 (section IIID). That is the category of wrongdoing (including torts and equitable wrongs). Another reason why restitution might be made, independently of unjust enrichment, is reasons of policy. Policy reasons are external to issues of interpersonal

[52] *David Securities Pty Ltd v Commonwealth Bank of Australia* [1992] HCA 48, (1992) 175 CLR 353.

[53] ibid 368 [25] (Mason CJ, Deane, Toohey, Gaudron and McHugh JJ); see also ibid 403 [4] (Dawson J). See also *Leisure Resort Holdings Pty Ltd v Leisure Resort Group Pty Ltd* [1996] QCA 518.

[54] *Roxborough v Rothmans of Pall Mall Australia Ltd* [2001] HCA 68, (2001) 208 CLR 516 [17] (Gleeson CJ, Gaudron and Hayne JJ).

justice between the parties. They are reasons why restitution should be allowed but they are not part of the law of unjust enrichment.

The possibility of an independent basis for restitution based on reasons of policy was recognised in *David Securities*. The purpose of the applicable tax statute was to ensure that the party that derived the income from an overseas transaction paid withholding tax. The joint judgment said this:

> The respondent knew of the existence of s 261 and understood its potential reach even if it was not aware that it invalidated cl 8(b). It acknowledged drafting cl 8(b) with s 261 in mind. In circumstances where the party in the best position to order its affairs in the light of specialist advice has deliberately chosen to charge a particular interest rate and seek additional amounts by virtue of separate provision in the loan agreement, there is no injustice to that party in ordering recovery. Otherwise the policy of s 261 would be defeated.[55]

Another example of a statutory policy requiring restitution, as we will see in Chapter 13, is where a landlord unlawfully demands key money from a tenant as a condition for entry into a lease.[56] The tenant might not be mistaken, nor be under any illegitimate pressure or undue influence, in making the payment. But the policy of the legislation requires restitution even though the tenant perfectly intends the landlord to receive the benefit.

A number of cases have adopted and developed the suggestion from *David Securities* that restitution might be allowed for reasons of policy.[57] In *Australian Breeders Co-Operative Society Ltd v Jones*,[58] the respondents misled the applicants into participating in a breeding syndicate. The syndicate leased 14 mares for breeding and purchased four foals. The respondent also made loans to all except one of the syndicate members, and secured the loans by mortgages over each member's ownership share in the syndicate. The syndicate members eventually terminated their contracts with the respondent and argued that the leases, loans and mortgages were unenforceable. The respondent argued that even if its leases, loans and mortgages were unenforceable, it was entitled to restitution of its costs in purchasing the mares, the savings made by the applicants on their leases, and the money lent to the investors. The Full Court cited the decision of the New South Wales Court of Appeal in *Hurst v Vestcorp Ltd*,[59] in which McHugh JA held that 'If appellants are not required to refund the moneys which they borrowed, they will reap an unmerited benefit. That, of course, is often the result of the illegality doctrine.' Justices Wilcox and Lindgren described the recovery as based on 'an illegal contract where there would otherwise be unjust enrichment'.[60] A better approach might have been for recovery to be based on the unjust factor of failure of consideration.[61] But, if illegality were to be relied upon as the reason for recovery,

[55] *David Securities Pty Ltd v Commonwealth Bank of Australia* [1992] HCA 48, (1992) 175 CLR 353, 384 [57] (Mason CJ, Deane, Toohey, Gaudron and McHugh JJ).

[56] Ch 13 p 305.

[57] *O'Brien v Melbank Corporation Ltd* (1991) 7 ACSR 19; *Stammer v Akron Securities Ltd* (1997) 140 FLR 146, 156; (1997) 24 ACSR 498, 507–08 (Mason P); *Davis v Mortgage Acceptance Nominees Ltd* (NSWSC, 20 April 1994); *Hurst v Vestcorp Ltd* (1988) 12 NSWLR 394; *Australian Breeders Co-Operative Society Ltd v Jones* (1997) 150 ALR 488.

[58] *Australian Breeders Co-Operative Society Ltd v Jones* (1997) 150 ALR 488.

[59] *Hurst v Vestcorp Ltd* (1988) 12 NSWLR 394, 445–46. See also *Fitzgerald v FJ Leonhardt Pty Ltd* [1997] HCA 17, (1997) 189 CLR 215, 231–32 (Kirby J).

[60] *Australian Breeders Co-Operative Society Ltd v Jones* (1997) 150 ALR 488, 541.

[61] *Equuscorp Pty Ltd v Haxton; Equuscorp Pty Ltd v Bassat; Equuscorp Pty Ltd v Cunningham's Warehouse Sales Pty Ltd* [2012] HCA 7, (2012) 246 CLR 498.

in the absence of some defect in intention as between the plaintiff and defendant, then restitution would have been awarded for reasons of policy, independently of any *inter partes* claim for unjust enrichment.

The policy reason might also be constitutional. In *British American Tobacco Australia Ltd v Western Australia*,[62] McHugh, Gummow and Hayne JJ said that a claim for restitution of money transferred from BAT to the government relied on the ground (unjust factor) that it had 'unlawfully been demanded by the defendant colore officii and paid involuntarily'.[63] However, their Honours alternatively referred to the unconstitutional nature of the statute that 'render[ed] the retention of the moneys against conscience'.[64] As we will explain in Chapter 13, these circumstances of statutory or constitutional policy are sometimes broadly described as 'illegality'.

There are also controversial examples where restitution has been allowed for reasons between the parties and not concerned with general policy. These examples are controversial because restitution is allowed even if the plaintiff had an unimpaired intention to enter the transaction that enriched the defendant. An example of such a controversial unjust factor is 'free acceptance'. In Chapter 13, we argue that this should not be a ground for restitution. But if it is recognised as such then the basis for restitution must lie in some policy that requires restitution despite the plaintiff's perfect intention enter the transaction that enriched the defendant.

The unjust factor of free acceptance was originally proposed by Lord Goff and Professor Jones[65] to explain a number of older cases where awards of restitution were made. Building on the work of Lord Goff and Professor Jones, Professor Birks argued that free acceptance was an unjust factor as well as a test for enrichment.[66] Birks argued that free acceptance will be satisfied if a defendant

(i) with an opportunity to reject a benefit conferred by the plaintiff,
(ii) knowing it that the benefit is not conferred gratuitously,
(iii) elects to accept it.

As a matter of authority, there is also some support for it in Australia[67] and England.[68] But the authority is not strong. Many of the older authorities on free acceptance reached the conclusion that restitution must be made by reasoning that there was an 'implied contract'. Such a fiction of 'implied contract' is no longer accepted. The unjust factor of free

[62] *British American Tobacco Australia Ltd v Western Australia* [2003] HCA 47, (2003) 217 CLR 30.

[63] ibid [43], approving *Antill Ranger & Co Pty Ltd v Commissioner for Motor Transport* (1955) 93 CLR 83, 102–03 (Fullagar J).

[64] *British American Tobacco Australia Ltd v Western Australia* [2003] HCA 47, (2003) 217 CLR 30 [41].

[65] R Goff and G Jones, *The Law of Restitution* (London, Sweet & Maxwell, 1966).

[66] P Birks, *An Introduction to the Law of Restitution*, rev edn (Oxford, Oxford University Press, 1989) 265–93. See also K Mason and J Carter, *Restitution Law in Australia* (Sydney, Butterworths, 1995) 341–42.

[67] Discussion in *Lampson (Australia) Pty Ltd v Fortescue Metals Group Ltd (No 3)* [2014] WASC 162 [56]–[76] (Edelman J). Compare *Stewart v Atco Controls Pty Ltd (in liq)* [2014] HCA 15, (2014) 252 CLR 307 [47] (the Court).

[68] *Leigh v Dickeson* (1884) 15 QBD 60, 64–65 (Brett MR); *Lamb v Bunce* (1815) 4 M & S 275, 105 ER 836; *Chief Constable of the Greater Manchester Police v Wigan Athletic AFC Ltd* [2008] EWCA Civ 1449, [2009] 1 WLR 1580; *Benedetti v Sawiris* [2010] EWCA Civ 1427 (not considered on appeal: *Benedetti v Sawiris* [2013] UKSC 50, [2014] 1 AC 938). See also C Mitchell, P Mitchell and S Watterson (eds), *Goff and Jones: The Law of Unjust Enrichment*, 8th edn (London, Sweet & Maxwell, 2011) ch 17.

acceptance has also been powerfully attacked, particularly by Professor Burrows[69] and Mr Mead.[70] Professor Birks, who was initially one of its strongest proponents, later rejected it.[71] He accepted Professor Burrows' view that the cases which he thought had supported it are better analysed as based on the unjust factor of failure of consideration.[72] In Chapter 13, we will see why this approach to those cases may be preferable in terms of principle, and not inconsistent with High Court of Australia authority.[73] It is shown in that chapter that policy reasons cannot support an unjust factor of free acceptance, which implicitly rewards risk-taking. Even one of its key Australian judicial supporters, Mason P, conceded that 'The validity of the principle is not beyond dispute.'[74]

IV. The Plaintiff must Negate Any Alleged Juristic Reason to Retain the Enrichment

A. The Recognition of a Lack of Juristic Reason to Retain an Enrichment

Apart from the existence of an unjust factor, the law of unjust enrichment also requires that there be no juristic reason entitling the defendant to retain the enrichment. This requires the plaintiff to negate any juristic reason raised by the defendant as a reason why the defendant can retain the enrichment. The requirement that an enrichment be 'unjust' therefore requires (i) an unjust factor that causes the enrichment, and (ii) that the defendant has no juristic reason entitling her to retain the enrichment. As Gleeson CJ, Gaudron and Hayne JJ said in *Roxborough v Rothmans of Pall Mall Australia Ltd*:

> there are two questions. The first is whether there has been a failure of a severable part of the consideration [the unjust factor in that case: failure of consideration]. The second is whether, in the absence of restitution, the respondent will retain money at the expense of the appellants.[75]

In that case, as their Honours later explained, restitution was allowed because the answers to the two questions were that 'there has been a payment of moneys by the appellants to the respondent for a consideration which has failed [ie the unjust factor], *and* the respondent has no title to retain the moneys'.[76] This was not a novel approach. As we have seen, the unjust factors approach was most clearly enunciated by Lord Mansfield in *Moses v Macferlan*,[77] where unjust factors were listed including mistake, failure of consideration,

[69] AS Burrows, 'Free Acceptance and the Law of Restitution' (1988) 104 *Law Quarterly Review* 576. See now A Burrows, *The Law of Restitution*, 2nd edn (London, Butterworths, 2002) 20–23, 402–07.

[70] G Mead, 'Free Acceptance: Some Further Considerations' (1989) 105 *Law Quarterly Review* 460.

[71] Birks' initial partial retreat from free acceptance was in P Birks, 'In Defence of Free Acceptance' in A Burrows (ed), *Essays on the Law of Restitution* (Oxford, Clarendon Press, 1991) 105–06, 109. Free acceptance as an unjust factor was abandoned by Birks in P Birks and C Mitchell, 'Unjust Enrichment' in P Birks (ed), *English Private Law*, vol II (Oxford, Oxford University Press, 2000) ch 15.

[72] AS Burrows, *The Law of Restitution* (London, Butterworths, 1993) 301–02.

[73] Ch 13 pp 323–28.

[74] *Concrete Constructions Group v Litevale Pty Ltd (No 2)* [2003] NSWSC 411 [15].

[75] *Roxborough v Rothmans of Pall Mall Australia Ltd* [2001] HCA 68, (2001) 208 CLR 516 [20]. See also *Australian Breeders Co-Operative Society Ltd v Jones* (1997) 150 ALR 488, 541 (Wilcox and Lindgren JJ).

[76] *Roxborough v Rothmans of Pall Mall Australia Ltd* [2001] HCA 68, (2001) 208 CLR 516 [27] (emphasis added).

[77] *Moses v Macferlan* (1760) 2 Burr 1005, 1012; 97 ER 676, 681.

compulsion, and undue influence. However, as Dr Kremer has explained,[78] in many of Lord Mansfield's judgments which considered awards of restitution, there are also references to whether a *defendant* has any 'right to retain' an enrichment.[79]

Understood in this manner, the statements in Australian and English authorities concerning a requirement for an absence of juristic reason to retain an enrichment are *not* suggestions that an unjust factors approach should be abandoned. They are simply statements that an action for unjust enrichment, based on an unjust factor, can only succeed if there is also no juristic reason for the defendant to retain the enrichment. Statements in the modern authorities to this effect are prolific. A few of the many examples in Australia and England can be given. In *Portman Building Society v Hamlyn Taylor and Neck*, Millett LJ contended that 'The obligation to make restitution must flow from the ineffectiveness of the transaction under which the money was paid and not from a mistake or misrepresentation which induced it.'[80] In *Kleinwort Benson Ltd v Birmingham City Council*, Saville LJ held that the 'obligation to return the money is ... [based on] the simple ground that it is unjust that he should keep something to which he has no right'.[81] Similarly, in *Baumgartner v Baumgartner*,[82] Toohey J asked whether there is a 'juristic reason' which can support the transfer to the defendant. And, as we have seen, in *Roxborough v Rothmans of Pall Mall Australia Ltd*,[83] Gleeson CJ, Gaudron and Hayne JJ identified the requirement that 'in the absence of restitution, the respondent will retain money at the expense of the appellants'.

In *David Securities Pty Ltd v Commonwealth Bank of Australia* (not dissenting on this point), Brennan J spoke of the requirements for restitution when 'a defendant receives a payment which he has no right to receive *and* which the plaintiff has paid to him by mistake'.[84] In *Kleinwort Benson Ltd v Lincoln City Council*,[85] Lord Hope quoted this passage and later added that although an unjust factor was required 'The purpose of the principle is to provide a remedy for recovery of the enrichment where no legal ground exists to justify its retention'.[86] And in *Deutsche Morgan Grenfell Group plc v Inland Revenue Commissioners*, Lord Walker said that

> The recognition of 'no basis' [ie no juristic reason] as a single unifying principle would preserve what Lord Hope refers to as the purity of the principle on which unjust enrichment is founded, without in any way removing (as this case illustrates) the need for careful analysis of the content of particular 'unjust factors' such as mistake.[87]

[78] B Kremer, 'The Action for Money Had and Received' (2001) 17 *Journal of Contract Law* 93, 109.

[79] Eg *Price v Neal* (1762) 3 Burr 1354, 1357; 97 ER 871, 872 (Lord Mansfield); *Sadler v Evans* (1766) 4 Burr 1984, 1986; 98 ER 34, 35 (Lord Mansfield); *Dale v Sollet* (1767) 4 Burr 2133, 2134; 98 ER 112, 113 (Lord Mansfield).

[80] *Portman Building Society v Hamlyn Taylor Neck (a firm)* [1998] 4 All ER 202, 208. See also *Criterion Properties Plc v Stratford UK Properties LLC* [2004] UKHL 28, [2004] 1 WLR 1846 [3]–[4] (Lord Nicholls; Lord Walker agreeing).

[81] *Kleinwort Benson v Birmingham City Council* [1997] QB 380, 394.

[82] *Baumgartner v Baumgartner* [1987] HCA 59, (1987) 164 CLR 137, 153 [7].

[83] *Roxborough v Rothmans of Pall Mall Australia Ltd* [2001] HCA 68, (2001) 208 CLR 516 [20].

[84] *David Securities Pty Ltd v Commonwealth Bank of Australia* [1992] HCA 48, (1992) 175 CLR 353, 393 [7] (emphasis added).

[85] *Kleinwort Benson Ltd v Lincoln City Council* [1998] UKHL 38, [1999] 2 AC 349, 407.

[86] ibid 409.

[87] *Deutsche Morgan Grenfell Group Plc v Inland Revenue Commissioners* [2006] UKHL 49, [2007] 1 AC 558 [158].

The approach was also applied in *Perpetual Trustees Australia Ltd v Heperu Pty Ltd*[88] and *Heperu Pty Ltd v Belle*.[89] The common facts of those appeals concerned a fraudster, Mr Cincotta, who was given cheques comprising millions of dollars for investment. Mr Cincotta provided the cheques to Perpetual. He used his apparent authority to have Perpetual credit the funds to the account of his wife. Mr Cincotta subsequently transferred the funds into another account in his wife's name at Westpac Bank. He then further misappropriated the money, most of which was never recovered. In the *Perpetual* appeal, one issue was whether Perpetual was liable for unjust enrichment. President Allsop and Handley JA (with whom Campbell JA agreed) proceeded on the basis that Perpetual had been unjustly enriched by the receipt of the cheques but that Perpetual had a defence of change of position. However, describing the claim for unjust enrichment, their Honours said that the inequitable retention of money or benefit lies at the root of both the injustice of the enrichment and the related concept of change of position.[90]

A similar approach has been taken in Canada in cases where it has been held that at 'the heart of the doctrine of unjust enrichment, whether expressed in terms of the traditional categories of recovery or general principle, lies the notion of restoration of a benefit which justice does not permit one to retain'.[91] On many occasions the Supreme Court of Canada has emphasised that unjust enrichment requires an absence of juristic reason.[92] As we explained above, although unjust factors are not often made explicit, an unjust factor implicitly, and sometimes even explicitly,[93] remains part of the Canadian assessment of unjust enrichment.

B. Matters that will be Juristic Reasons

The category of matters that can amount to a juristic reason are not closed. Some juristic reasons are obvious. The receipt of a benefit under an extant contract is a good juristic reason to retain the enrichment. Another is the receipt of an enrichment by a deed of gift which is not rescinded. Another is a statutory right to receive and retain the enrichment. Other juristic reasons are simply described as based upon 'natural justice' or 'natural reason'. For instance, we will see in Chapter 12 the example of a guarantor who is called upon by a creditor to pay, and is powerless to prevent the discharge of the principal debtor's debt. The guarantor can recover from the principal debtor the value of the debt discharged. But if the principal debtor is called upon by the creditor and discharges the guarantor's liability, the guarantor has a right to retain that enrichment.

The requirement that a plaintiff negate a juristic reason does not mean that the plaintiff must plead and prove the absence of an infinite number of possible juristic reasons. There

88 *Perpetual Trustees Australia Ltd v Heperu Pty Ltd* [2009] NSWCA 84, (2009) 76 NSWLR 195.

89 *Heperu Pty Ltd v Belle* [2009] NSWCA 252, (2009) 76 NSWLR 230.

90 *Perpetual Trustees Australia Ltd v Heperu Pty Ltd* [2009] NSWCA 84, (2009) 76 NSWLR 195 [128] citing *Lipkin Gorman v Karpnale Ltd* [1991] 2 AC 548, 578–80 (Lord Goff; Lord Bridge of Harwich, Lord Griffiths, and Lord Ackner agreeing).

91 *Peel (Regional Municipality) v Canada* [1992] 3 SCR 762, 788 (McLachlin J); *Bhasin v Hrynew* [2014] 3 SCR 494, 2014 SCC 71 [68] (the Court).

92 *Pettkus v Becker* [1980] 2 SCR 834, 848 (Laskin CJ and Dickson, Estey, McIntyre, Chouinard and Lamer JJ); *Peel (Regional Municipality) v Canada* [1992] 3 SCR 762, 784 (McLauchlin J); *Garland v Consumers' Gas Co* [2004] 1 SCR 629, 2004 SCC 25 [30] (the Court).

93 For instance, *BMP Global Distribution Inc v Bank of Nova* Scotia [2009] 1 SCR 504, 2009 SCC 15.

must be an evidentiary onus on the defendant to raise, in the defence, a juristic reason (based on some evidence) before the plaintiff could be required to negate it. However, the substantive disproof of the juristic reason falls on the plaintiff, who will plead in reply the reasons why the alleged juristic reason does not apply. In that sense the disproof of juristic reasons is properly treated in all the cases as part of the prima facie assessment of unjust enrichment at trial before independent defences are considered. But, putting aside the defendant's evidentiary onus, as we will see below both authority and principle require that the plaintiff must negate the existence of a juristic reason asserted (based on some evidence) by the defendant.

C. Juristic Reasons and Unjust Factors

The two matters of (i) an unjust factor, and (ii) a lack of juristic reason to retain the enrichment, are not two sides of the same coin. For instance, suppose a person pays tax on his income, mistakenly believing that the tax could not have been avoided by the creation of a trust. Although mistake is an unjust factor, he cannot claim restitution of the money paid due to his mistake. The reason is that the taxation legislation provides a juristic reason for the payment. A second example, which we will see in Chapter 12, is where a company officer pays company money to a third party. Even if there is an unjust factor, such as a mistake by the company or its ignorance of the transaction, if the company officer has actual or ostensible authority to make the payment then the defendant will have a juristic reason to retain the enrichment. That juristic reason arises in the application of company law rules which determine the circumstances in which a recipient is entitled to retain an enrichment transferred with authority. A third example might be where a person has two contractual creditors but limited funds. He pays one creditor by mistake. The debt is discharged. Again, the payer cannot obtain restitution because the payee has a juristic reason for the receipt of the payment. In his judgment in *David Securities* (not dissenting on this point), Brennan J said:

> In essence, to say that a defendant has been unjustly enriched by the receipt of a payment is to say that the defendant has no right to receive it. ... If a defendant has a right to receive a payment, whether under a statute, in discharge of a liability owing to him or pursuant to a contract, a mistake by the plaintiff in making the payment does not convert the receipt into an unjust enrichment.[94]

This approach was applied in *CSR Ltd v Hornsby Shire Council*.[95] CSR was the registered proprietor of land compulsorily acquired by the defendant council. The Valuer-General determined the value of the land at $25,099,500. The Council argued that this included GST and deducted $2,300,000. To a claim that it had no power to withhold amounts of the determined compensation, the Council argued that if the full amount were paid, CSR would be unjustly enriched by the amount of GST. Justice Gzell held that there was nothing 'unjust' about the payment to CSR that entitled the Council to restitution. The payment was pursuant to a statutory obligation. Justice Gzell J focused on this juristic reason, saying

[94] *David Securities Pty Ltd v Commonwealth Bank of Australia* [1992] HCA 48, (1992) 175 CLR 353, 392 [6] (footnotes omitted).

[95] *CSR Ltd v Hornsby Shire Council* [2004] NSWSC 946, (2004) 57 ATR 201.

'the notion that an enrichment be unjust requires that it not be one conferred pursuant to an effective transaction or valid legal obligation'.[96]

As we explain below, there is one qualification that must be added to this reasoning. Although a lack of a juristic reason to *receive* an enrichment will almost always mean that there is no juristic reason to *retain* the enrichment, the opposite is not always true. In other words, there can be some situations in which there is a juristic reason to *receive* an enrichment but, by the time of trial, there is no longer a juristic reason to *retain* it. The emphasis on *retention* rather than *receipt* was made in a joint judgment of the High Court in 1957,[97] where the High Court said that the 'unconscientious retention' by the defendant of the sum claimed by the plaintiff was 'the reason of the rule under which an action of money had received lies in cases of payment by mistake'. This passage was quoted by Gummow J with approval in *Roxborough v Rothmans of Pall Mall Australia Ltd*,[98] after unjust enrichment had been recognised as a body of law in Australia.

The short point is that an unjust factor is not sufficient for restitution if the defendant can point to a juristic reason to retain the benefit. It is for this reason that cases both before and after *David Securities* speak of the requirements of *both* unjust factors and lack of entitlement of the defendant to retain an enrichment.[99] A conclusion that a defendant has been unjustly enriched by the receipt of a payment cannot be reached unless it is also concluded that the defendant has no right to retain it.[100]

D. The Requirement in Principle for no Juristic Reason to Retain

There is a simple reason in principle why the law requires, in addition to an unjust factor, a lack of juristic reason for a plaintiff to retain an enrichment. That reason is the coherence of the law. Courts, particularly in Australia, have emphasised and re-emphasised the importance of coherence in private law.[101] A law of unjust enrichment would be incoherent if it were based on notions that

(i) a defendant has a subsisting right to an enrichment due to a juristic reason such as contract, or gift, or order of a court, *but*
(ii) the defendant must nevertheless make restitution of that enrichment to the plaintiff.

In other words, the law would be internally contradictory if one branch of the law held that a defendant had a right to an enrichment and another held that the defendant must give back the enrichment.

[96] ibid [14].

[97] *South Australian Cold Stores Ltd v Electricity Trust of South Australia* [1957] HCA 69, (1957) 98 CLR 65, 75 [14].

[98] *Roxborough v Rothmans of Pall Mall Australia Ltd* [2001] HCA 68, (2001) 208 CLR 516 [89].

[99] See *South Australian Cold Stores Ltd v Electricity Trust of South Australia* [1957] HCA 69, (1957) 98 CLR 65, 75 [14] (the Court); *McDonald v Dennys Lascelles Ltd* [1933] HCA 25, (1933) 48 CLR 457, 477 (Dixon J); *Mason v New South Wales* [1959] HCA 5, (1959) 102 CLR 108, 146 [18] (Windeyer J); *David Securities Pty Ltd v Commonwealth Bank of Australia* [1992] HCA 48, (1992) 175 CLR 353, 379 [46] (Mason CJ, Deane, Toohey, Gaudron and McHugh JJ); *Roxborough v Rothmans of Pall Mall Australia Ltd* [2001] HCA 68, (2001) 208 CLR 516 [27] (Gleeson CJ, Gaudron and Hayne JJ).

[100] See also *Issitch v Worrell* [2000] FCA 477, (2000) 172 ALR 586 [41] (Drummond J; Spender and Katz JJ concurring); *David Securities Pty Ltd v Commonwealth Bank of Australia* [1992] HCA 48, (1992) 175 CLR 353, 392 [6] (Brennan J).

[101] *Miller v Miller* [2011] HCA 9, (2011) 242 CLR 446 [15] (the Court); *Sullivan v Moody* [2001] HCA 59, (2001) 207 CLR 562 [42], [53]–[55] (the Court); *Agricultural and Rural Finance Pty Ltd v Gardiner* [2008] HCA

E. A Difference from a Juristic Reason to *Receive* an Enrichment

We have seen that, in most cases, a juristic reason for the *receipt* of an enrichment will mean that the defendant has a juristic reason to *retain* the enrichment. But not always. There are a number of situations in which a defendant has a juristic reason for receipt, but no juristic reason to retain an enrichment. The most common situation in which this arises is cases where the unjust factor is failure of consideration.

Consider the facts of the famous English case of *Fibrosa Spolka Akcyjna v Fairbairn Lawson Combe Barbour Ltd.*[102] That case is considered in more detail in Chapter 11, but it is a useful illustration of a group of cases which allow restitution despite the existence of a juristic reason for a defendant to receive an enrichment. By contract dated 12 July 1939, an English company agreed to supply textile machinery to a company in Poland. The Polish company agreed to pay £4,800. One-third of the price (£1,600) was payable with the order and the remainder was payable when the shipping documents were presented. The order was placed and £1,000 of the price due was paid on 18 July 1939. On 1 September 1939 Germany invaded Poland and two days later Great Britain declared war on Germany. The contract was frustrated.

The contract 'on its true construction' did not provide what was to happen to money already paid in the event of frustration.[103] It provided only that the money had fallen due at the date of the order. Counsel for the English company objected that since the effect of frustration was not to discharge obligations which had already accrued, the contract could not provide *both* that the money had fallen due *and* that it must be repaid. The answer given by the House of Lords was simple. The claim for the return of the money was not based on the contract. As Viscount Simon said, 'The claim arises not because the right to be repaid is one of the stipulated conditions of the contract, but because, in the circumstances that have happened, the law gives the remedy.'[104] In other words, the contract provided a juristic reason for the receipt of the money, but once the contract had been terminated without the counter-performance upon which the payment depended, there was no accrued right to *retain* the payment. This is why Lord Wright said that the payment was conditional and the right to retain it fell away when the condition failed.[105]

A more controversial example is *Deutsche Morgan Grenfell plc v Inland Revenue Commissioners.*[106] In that case, a section of the Income and Corporation Taxes Act 1988 allowed subsidiaries of UK companies to apply to make a group income election to defer payment of tax. DMG was a subsidiary of a German parent. According to the Act, therefore, DMG could not apply to defer payment. So DMG paid its tax within the time required by the

57, (2008) 238 CLR 570 [100] (Gummow, Hayne and Kiefel JJ); *CAL No 14 Pty Ltd v Motor Accidents Insurance Board* [2009] HCA 47, (2009) 239 CLR 390 [39]–[42] (Gummow, Heydon and Crennan JJ); *Equuscorp Pty Ltd v Haxton; Equuscorp Pty Ltd v Bassat; Equuscorp Pty Ltd v Cunningham's Warehouse Sales Pty Ltd* [2012] HCA 7, (2012) 246 CLR 498.

102 *Fibrosa Spolka Akcyjna v Fairbairn Lawson Combe Barbour Ltd* [1942] UKHL 4, [1943] AC 32.

103 *Fibrosa Spolka Akcyjna v Fairbairn Lawson Combe Barbour Ltd* [1942] UKHL 4, [1943] AC 32, 42–43 [3] (Viscount Simon).

104 ibid 47 [6] (Viscount Simon). See also Lord Atkin ibid 55 [11] ('a general doctrine which is independent of the special contract'); Lord Macmillan ibid 59 [15] ('restitution is regarded as a separate principle of the law independent of contract'); Lord Wright ibid 61 [17] ('remedies for cases of what has been called unjust enrichment ... are generically different from remedies in contract').

105 ibid 65 [19].

106 *Deutsche Morgan Grenfell Plc v Inland Revenue Commissioners* [2006] UKHL 49, [2007] 1 AC 558.

Act. In March 2001 the European Court of Justice held that the failure to allow DMG this opportunity to defer its tax unlawfully discriminated between parents of companies resident in the United Kingdom, and those of other member states, contrary to freedom of establishment provisions in the EC Treaty. DMG claimed restitution of the value of the opportunity to use its money (interest) over the period for which it could have been entitled to defer the payment. The trial judge held that although DMG was legally required to make the tax payment when it did, DMG was nevertheless entitled to restitution because it was mistaken about its European rights in relation to the group income election.[107] Professor Birks condemned this decision[108] saying that it could not stand with an absence of juristic reasons approach because it involved restitution despite the existence of a valid domestic obligation and '[a] payment made to discharge a valid obligation cannot be said to lack a sufficient legal basis'.[109] When the case reached the House of Lords, Lord Scott dissented for this reason.[110] But there are possible answers to the objection of Professor Birks and Lord Scott. One answer given by two of their Lordships in the majority is that the ECJ decision had 'invalidated' the tax obligation.[111] To similar effect, in a different context, Lady Hale (speaking for four other Supreme Court judges) has described a domestic law obligation being 'disapplied' by European law.[112] More radically, in *DMG*, Lords Walker and Hope agreed with the approach of the trial judge but considered that the existence of a valid legal basis was not a fatal obstacle to an action for restitution of unjust enrichment.[113] Her Majesty's Revenue Commissioners had a right to demand the tax and a juristic reason to receive it, but the disapplication or invalidity of the domestic legislation considered to be required by section 2 of the European Communities Act 1972 meant that they did not have a juristic reason to *retain* it.

A similar approach was taken by the Court of Appeal in *Investment Trust Companies (In Liquidation) v Revenue and Customs Commissioners*.[114] Relevantly for present purposes, managers had provided services to the plaintiff investment trust companies pursuant to various service contracts. The contracts provided for payment of their fees, which included any VAT payable by the managers on the services rendered. The managers paid VAT for many years and recouped the applicable tax from the plaintiffs under the service contracts. The VAT legislation provided that the managers were entitled to deduct from the VAT payments received from the plaintiffs a portion of the tax (set, for the purposes of the judgment discussion, at a notional amount of £25 out of every £100 paid by the plaintiffs). This sum represented a taxation set-off or allowance to which the plaintiffs were entitled under the

[107] *Deutsche Morgan Grenfell Plc v Inland Revenue Commissioners* [2003] EWHC 1779, [2003] 4 All ER 645 [25] (Park J). A complicating factor, ignored in the decisions in this case, was that 'but for' the plaintiff's mistake the Revenue would still have had the use of the money because any application for deferral would have been refused: see R Chambers, 'Deutsche Morgan Grenfell Group plc v IRC' (2006) 6 *Oxford University Commonwealth Law Journal* 227. The obvious answer to this objection, which we will see in Ch 8, is that it applies the wrong test for causation.

[108] P Birks, *Unjust Enrichment*, 2nd edn (Oxford, Oxford University Press, 2005) 138.

[109] ibid 139.

[110] *Deutsche Morgan Grenfell plc v Inland Revenue Commissioners* [2006] UKHL 49, [2007] 1 AC 558 [85].

[111] ibid [32] (Lord Hoffmann), [172] (Lord Brown). See also *Evans v Information Commissioner* [2015] UKSC 21 [108] (Lord Neuberger), [147]–[149] (Lord Mance).

[112] *North v Dumfries and Galloway Council (Scotland)* [2013] UKSC 45, [2013] 4 All ER 413 [2].

[113] *Deutsche Morgan Grenfell plc v Inland Revenue Commissioners* [2006] UKHL 49, [2007] 1 AC 558 [143] (Lord Walker), [62] (Lord Hope).

[114] *Investment Trust Companies (in liq) v Revenue and Customs Commissioners* [2015] EWCA Civ 82.

legislation. Eventually it was determined in another action that the plaintiffs should have been exempted from VAT under EU law, and that the domestic legislation had failed to comply with that law. The legislation was therefore 'disapplied' to the extent of the inconsistency. As the Court explained,[115] this did not mean that the domestic legislation was a nullity. So the managers were, at the time they deducted the £25, entitled to that amount pursuant to the legislation. However, the disapplication of the legislation meant that the managers were no longer entitled to retain the benefit.

F. Onus of Proof on the Plaintiff to Disprove a Juristic Reason for Retention

We commenced this section with the assertion that the requirement of a lack of juristic reason is an onus on a plaintiff to negate any juristic reason raised by the defendant as a reason why the defendant can retain the benefit. As a matter of principle this must be the case. The alternative would create an inconsistency between exactly the same allegation of a contract in two similar situations. The first situation is where A alleges that B owes him money under a contract. If B denies the contract, then the onus is on A to prove the contract. It is not sufficient simply for A to point to a payment that he made to B. The second situation is where A alleges that he is entitled to restitution of a mistaken payment made to B. If B alleges that the payment was made under a contract, then the onus lies upon A to negate it. In the first case there is no presumption of the alleged contract that would entitle A to payment. In the second case there is no presumption of a *lack* of the alleged contract so that A would be entitled to restitution. In both cases, the party asserting liability must prove the necessary presence or absence of the contract.

In *Big Island Construction (HK) Ltd v Wu Yi Development Company Ltd*,[116] this issue was confronted by the Hong Kong Final Court of Appeal. In that case, Big Island claimed that it had entered an oral agreement with the two respondents, pursuant to which it provided a massive loan to them. Alternatively, Big Island claimed restitution of the amount provided in unjust enrichment based on an alleged failure of consideration. The respondents pleaded that the money had been paid to them in discharge of obligations owed by Big Island to them under exchange agreements. The Court of Final Appeal accepted this defence, but Sir Anthony Mason NPJ (with whom Ribeiro, and Fok PJJ and Chan NPJ agreed) also considered the situation that would arise if, as the courts below had held, the allegations of both loan agreement (Big Island) and exchange agreements (the respondents) were rejected. As a matter of principle, Sir Anthony Mason NPJ explained that 'the making of a bare payment to another may in the nature of things be explicable by reference to a wide variety of possibilities'. Hence 'the probability that there is an obligation to repay the amount is not so strong that it should become the subject of a presumption'.[117]

In the course of reaching this decision, Sir Anthony Mason rejected the contrary English approach in *Seldon v Davidson*.[118] In that case, Ms Seldon paid her chauffeur £1,550 by

[115] ibid [34]–[36] (the Court).
[116] *Big Island Construction (HK) Ltd v Wu Yi Development Company Ltd* [2015] HKCFA 47.
[117] ibid [106].
[118] *Seldon v Davidson* [1968] 1 WLR 1083.

two cheques. He used the money to buy a house. Ms Seldon later sought restitution of the money. The chauffeur said that they were either a gift or a loan which was not repayable until he was in a position to repay. The Court of Appeal (Willmer and Edmund Davies LJJ) in *ex tempore* judgments held that the onus was on the chauffeur to prove the facts of the loan or the gift. Lord Justice Willmer reached this conclusion on the basis that in the absence of a presumption of advancement (which arises in cases involving resulting trusts), the mere fact of payment 'imported an obligation to repay'.[119] Lord Justice Edmund Davies described the mere fact of payment as giving rise to a 'prima facie obligation to repay'.[120] The analogy drawn by their Lordships with a resulting trust was inapt. The onus of proof in a case of a resulting trust is difficult to justify today and certainly should not be expanded into cases involving personal claims. The 'presumption' of resulting trust originated in circumstances in which almost all land in England was conveyed to uses and it was not usual to include words of trust on the conveyance.[121] Although *Seldon* was followed uncritically in a number of later English decisions, it is inconsistent with earlier English cases (which were not cited in *Seldon*)[122] and also with a line of Australian cases.[123]

V. Conclusion

There has been considerable debate in academic circles concerning the proper approach to determine whether an enrichment is unjust. Some argue that the proper approach is based on unjust factors. Others argue that the proper approach is based on whether there is a right to retain an enrichment or juristic reason for it. Properly understood, however, both are partly correct. The requirement that an enrichment be unjust is a requirement *both* that there is an unjust factor *and* that the defendant should have no juristic reason to retain the enrichment.

The need for an unjust factor requires that the plaintiff plead and prove a reason for restitution arising from some imperfection or defect in the plaintiff's decision to enter the transaction that enriches the defendant. Common examples of such reasons are mistake, illegitimate pressure, failure of consideration or undue influence. Others involve a complete lack of intention to enter the impugned transaction that enriches the defendant. This requirement of an unjust factor is essential for the transparency of this area of law as well as to permit a defendant to know the case which he or she is called upon to meet: 'it both highlights, rather than suppresses, the need for normative justification'.[124] Unjust factors are all the possible matters between the plaintiff and the defendant by which the *plaintiff's* intention to make a transfer is imperfect. If the plaintiff has a perfect intention to enter the transaction that enriches a defendant then there can be no claim for restitution based on

[119] ibid 1088.

[120] ibid 1090.

[121] See the discussion in *Anderson v McPherson (No 2)* [2012] WASC 19 [106]–[116] (Edelman J).

[122] *Cary v Gerrish* (1801) 4 Esp 10, 170 ER 624; *Welch v Seaborn* (1816) 1 Stark 474, 171 ER 534; *Aubert v Walsh* (1810) 4 Taunt 294, 128 ER 110.

[123] *Heydon v The Perpetual Executors, Trustees & Agency Co (WA) Ltd* (1930) 45 CLR 111, 113 (Dixon J); *Joaquin v Hall* [1976] VR 788, 789 (Jenkinson J).

[124] H Dagan, *The Law and Ethics of Restitution* (Cambridge, Cambridge University Press, 2004) 31.

unjust enrichment. If restitution is to be ordered in such a case it must be based on some legal wrongdoing, or based upon reasons of policy, external to the parties.

Chapters 8 to 12 are all concerned with different unjust factors based upon imperfect intention. Chapter 13 then considers restitution for reasons of policy and explains why these instances of restitution are not part of the law of unjust enrichment even though these cases, like restitution for wrongdoing, are sometimes loosely described as based upon unjust enrichment.

The second requirement to show that an enrichment is 'unjust' focuses not upon the plaintiff, but upon the defendant. It preserves the coherence or integrity of the law. It requires that restitution be refused if, despite the existence of an unjust factor, a defendant has the right to retain an enrichment for some other juristic reason such as because it was a gift that has not been rescinded, or conferred under contract or other legal obligation. Once a defendant pleads some juristic reason, the onus is upon the plaintiff to disprove the existence of, avoid, or prove reason to disregard it.

These two requirements have long been elements of unjust enrichment. They can be illustrated by reference to the facts of *Kelly v Solari*.[125] An insurance company paid money to a widow upon her deceased husband's life insurance policy. However, the policy had lapsed. The insurance company had paid when it was not liable to pay. The widow was enriched and the enrichment was at the expense of the insurance company. But was the enrichment 'unjust'? A requirement for an unjust factor means that the insurance company was required to prove the unjust factor that it alleged, namely that it was mistaken in making the payment. A requirement for an absence of juristic reason to retain the enrichment means that the insurance company was required to negate the juristic reason alleged by the widow, namely that it made a gift to her. Proof of a mistake could serve both purposes. It could operate to negate the allegation of gift. And it could operate to provide the positive reason for restitution of the value transferred. In the words of the High Court of Australia, the insurance company would need to prove that the money 'would not have come to [Mrs Solari's] hands if it had not been for a false supposition of fact on the part of the payer causing [him] to believe that he was compellable to make the payment or at all events that he ought to make it'.[126] In that case, Parke B made it clear that each element (unjust factor and right to retain) is a requirement of unjust enrichment. The insurance company was required to prove that 'the receiver was not entitled to it, nor intended to have it.'[127] The next chapter illustrates how a plaintiff may negate a juristic reason so as to obtain restitution for unjust enrichment.

[125] *Kelly v Solari* (1841) 9 M & W 54, 152 ER 24. For Professor Birks this is 'a core case': P Birks, *Unjust Enrichment*, 2nd edn (Oxford, Oxford University Press, 2005) ch 1.

[126] *South Australian Cold Stores Ltd v Electricity Trust of South Australia* [1957] HCA 69, (1957) 98 CLR 65, 75 [14] (the Court); *Roxborough v Rothmans of Pall Mall Australia Ltd* [2001] HCA 68, (2001) 208 CLR 516 [89] (Gummow J).

[127] *Kelly v Solari* (1841) 9 M & W 54, 59; 152 ER 24, 26.

7

Negating Juristic Reasons

Contents

I. Introduction

In the previous chapter we considered the requirement that an enrichment be 'unjust'. This requirement embodies two elements. First, the plaintiff must plead and prove an unjust factor. Secondly, the plaintiff must negate any juristic reason raised by the defendant. This chapter focuses on the common juristic reasons and, when they are raised in a defence, the ways in which they are negated in the plaintiff's pleaded reply.

As we saw in the previous chapter, the need for coherence in the law is the underlying reason why a plaintiff must negate a juristic reason before an enrichment will be unjust. When confronted with the question of whether restitution should be made of value received, the law of unjust enrichment should not contradict other branches of the law. For instance, it would be intolerable if the rules of contract law entitled a plaintiff to keep an enrichment but the law of unjust enrichment required the plaintiff to make restitution of it. As Lord

Hope observed in *Kleinwort Benson Ltd v Lincoln City Council* in the context of the unjust factor of mistake:

> the payee cannot be said to have been unjustly enriched if he was entitled to receive the sum paid to him. The payer may have been mistaken as to the grounds on which the sum was due to the payee, but his mistake will not provide a ground for its recovery if the payee can show that he was entitled to it on some other ground.[1]

This chapter considers seven broad categories of juristic reason and various manners in which each can be negated by a plaintiff. Each category identifies circumstances where the defendant has an overriding entitlement or juristic reason to retain the enrichment. These categories of justifying grounds are not closed. They may overlap. Some of the most common examples, which are considered in this chapter, include: (1) contract; (2) gifts and deeds of gift; (3) deeds where consideration moves to a third party; (4) receipt in satisfaction of right; (5) statute; (6) incapacity; and (7) court orders. The final section reiterates a point made in the previous chapter. In some cases, restitution will be allowed despite the presence of a juristic reason because although the defendant had a right to receive the enrichment, the defendant is not entitled to retain it. The juristic reason must be a reason to *retain* the enrichment, not merely a reason to receive it.

Although the process of negating a juristic reason is treated as part of the 'unjust' enquiry, in many cases the process could be understood as itself being an action for unjust enrichment. As we saw in Chapter 3, if the remedy of restitution is understood in a broad sense, it could include the process of rescission of those rights that form the juristic reason relied upon by a defendant.

II. A Contractual Bargain as a Juristic Reason

Where a defendant is enriched by a benefit conferred by contract, the contract will usually justify the defendant's retention of the enrichment. If restitution were allowed, it would generally contradict the contract and operate to redistribute the contractual allocation of risk.[2]

In *Lumbers v W Cook Builders Pty Ltd (in liq)*[3] the High Court emphasised the need for unjust enrichment claims to respect existing contractual regimes, and the allocations of risk made under contracts. In that case, builders completed work on the Lumbers' house. The work had been commenced pursuant to a contract between the Lumbers and a related building company (Sons). The builders' claim for restitution of the reasonable value of their services failed. The terms of the contract between Lumbers and Sons governed the

[1] *Kleinwort Benson Ltd v Lincoln City Council* [1998] UKHL 38, [1999] 2 AC 349, 408.

[2] *Lumbers v W Cook Builders Pty Ltd (in liq)* [2008] HCA 27, (2008) 232 CLR 635 [51] (Gleeson CJ), [78] (Gummow, Hayne, Crennan and Kiefel JJ); *Perum Building & Construction Pty Ltd v Tallenford Pty Ltd* [2007] WASCA 245 [20]–[25] (the Court); *Anderson v McPherson (No 2)* [2012] WASC 19 [239] (Edelman J).

[3] *Lumbers v W Cook Builders Pty Ltd (in liq)* [2008] HCA 27, (2008) 232 CLR 635.

Lumbers' rights to receive any benefits. There was no room left for a claim for unjust enrichment. The same principle has been applied in the Court of Appeal in England.[4]

Another example is *Brady Contracting Pty Ltd v Kellyville Christmas Tree Farm Pty Ltd*.[5] In that case, a demolition company contracted to deliver timber taken from demolition of wharves to a firewood company. The demolition company mistakenly selected timber that was of more commercial value than it intended to provide under the contract. The New South Wales Court of Appeal held that no claim for unjust enrichment was available. Justice Santow emphasised that the contract governed the allocation of risks, and the risk of mistake was borne by the demolition company.[6]

Since a contract will provide a plaintiff with a right to retain an enrichment, the plaintiff must demonstrate that the express or implied terms of the contract do not constitute a juristic reason for the defendant to retain the enrichment. The plaintiff can do this in a variety of ways. These include proving that the putative contract is void or non-existent; rescinding the contract based on some vitiating factor; or proving that the basis upon which the rights which were conferred by the contract has wholly failed. We consider each of these possibilities below before turning to the possibility that the contract might provide a right to receive an enrichment, but not a right to retain it.

A. No Juristic Reason if the Contract is Void

A plaintiff may be able to challenge the validity of a contract on a number of grounds. Particular statutory provisions that invalidate the contract are the most common ground of challenge. Whether the contract is rendered void, voidable or unenforceable is 'a question of construction turning on the particular provisions, the scope and purpose of the statute'.[7] We return to this question below when we consider the juristic reason of statutory terms and statutory policy.

A putative contract can be void at common law for different reasons. These reasons usually entail that the consent of one or both parties to a contract is so fundamentally impaired as to render the contract void *ab initio*: a nullity from the beginning. Where a contract is a nullity, the contractual right to retain an enrichment ceases to be a juristic reason entitling the defendant to retain the benefit.

The first category at common law is the rule of *non est factum*.[8] This doctrine applies where a plaintiff who, through blindness, illiteracy, mental infirmity[9] or other reasons

[4] Costello v MacDonald [2011] EWCA Civ 930, [2012] QB 244 [21]-[30] (Etherton LJ; Patten and Pill L:JJ concurring).

[5] *Brady Contracting Pty Ltd v Kellyville Christmas Tree Farm Pty Ltd* [2005] NSWCA 22.

[6] ibid [3], [5] (Santow JA).

[7] *Yango Pastoral Company Pty Ltd v First Chicago Australia Ltd* [1978] HCA 42, (1978) 139 CLR 410, 425 [17] (Mason J; Aickin J concurring), see also 423 (Mason J) and 413 (Gibbs ACJ); *Nelson v Nelson* [1995] HCA 25, (1995) 184 CLR 538, 551–52 [45] (Deane and Gummow JJ); *Equuscorp Pty Ltd v Haxton; Equuscorp Pty Ltd v Bassat; Equuscorp Pty Ltd v Cunningham's Warehouse Sales Pty Ltd* [2012] HCA 7, (2012) 246 CLR 498 [23] (French CJ, Crennan and Kiefel JJ); *Barker v Midstyle Nominees Pty Ltd* [2014] WASCA 75 [36]–[50] (Buss JA; Newnes JA concurring).

[8] 'It is not my deed'.

[9] *PT Ltd v Maradona Pty Ltd* (1992) 25 NSWLR 643; *Ford v Perpetual Trustees Victoria Ltd* [2009] NSWCA 186, (2009) 75 NSWLR 42.

including lack of understanding of the language in which the document is written, is incapable of having any understanding of the document that he signed.[10] It does not matter whether he has signed a contract or deed: the plaintiff's mind did not go with his deed.[11] The consequence is that the contract is void *ab initio*. Thus in *Ford v Perpetual Trustees Victoria Ltd*, Mr Ford was manipulated by his son into signing loan documents to finance the purchase of a cleaning business. Mr Ford had the mental capacity of a young child and could not write, although he could 'draw' a signature. The loan documents were held to be *void ab initio*.[12]

Although the doctrine of *non est factum* usually concerns cases of 'fundamental' mistakes, the same principle informs cases of extreme duress or illegitimate pressure, such as where a defendant physically forces the plaintiff to sign a document. In this case, the plaintiff's consent is so profoundly impaired as to negate consent entirely. An equivalent principle applies in equity in cases of extreme undue influence. Where the plaintiff is so wholly submissive to the defendant's will that he entirely lacks any independent judgement, the plaintiff is later entitled to say 'that is not my deed'. Examples often arise when courts are considering dispositions of property made by the elderly in circumstances of undue influence, often (but not exclusively) in the context of wills. A recent example is *Veall v Veall*,[13] where the deceased changed his will radically in what were alleged to constitute 'suspicious circumstances' sufficient that probate should be denied. Justice Santamaria of the Victorian Supreme Court of Appeal, with whom Beach and Kyrou JJA agreed, examined the history of familial dealings leading up to execution of the final will. His Honour found that the testator lacked testamentary capacity.[14] There was no evidence of coercion in this case. Rather, it was a case of overwhelming influence. The deceased would sign whatever documents Rowland put in front of him. Sometimes, when out of Rowland's presence, he would then deny that the documents had been signed by him.[15] The case therefore involved an extended course of dealings in which the deceased had repeatedly said that documents physically signed by him under extreme undue influence were 'not his deeds'.

The second category is, 'common mistake' at common law. This is usually described as a circumstance where the parties make a common mistake at common law that relates to the essence of the contract. Although this doctrine is usually described as one of 'common mistake', it is really a doctrine of 'failure of consideration'.[16] A claim based on common 'mistake' requires a 'common assumption as to the existence of a state of affairs' which concerns the existence of a vital attribute of the consideration, and that matter must not be governed by contract terms.[17]

[10] *Petelin v Cullen* [1975] HCA 24, (1975) 132 CLR 355.

[11] Discussed in *Perpetual Trustees Victoria Ltd v Ford* [2008] NSWSC 29, (2008) 70 NSWLR 611 [61]–[84] (Harrison J), and on appeal in *Ford v Perpetual Trustees Victoria Ltd* [2009] NSWCA 186, (2009) 75 NSWLR 42 [36]–[90] (Allsop P and Young JA).

[12] Perpetual Trustees' counterclaim for restitution of benefits transferred pursuant to the contract failed, discussed in Chs 4 and 15.

[13] *Veall v Veall* [2015] VSCA 60. Cf *Anderson v Anderson* [2013] QSC 8 [64] (Dalton J).

[14] *Veall v Veall* [2015] VSCA 60 [204].

[15] ibid [207].

[16] Compare, for example, the description of failure of consideration in *Crown Prosecution Service v Eastenders Group* [2014] UKSC 26, [2015] AC 1 [115] (Lord Toulson; Lady Hale, and Lords Kerr, Wilson and Hughes agreeing).

[17] *Great Peace Shipping Ltd v Tsavliris Salvage (International) Ltd* [2002] EWCA Civ 1407, [2003] QB 679 [76] (the Court).

A decision of the High Court of Australia which makes explicit the connection between claims of common mistake and failure of consideration is *Svanosio v McNamara*.[18] In that case, the plaintiff alleged that the parties entered into a contract for the purchase of a hotel under a 'common mistake as to the existence of a fact accepted by all parties as a basis or condition fundamental to [these] transactions, namely that the defendants were the owners of the whole of the land upon which the [hotel] was erected'.[19] The plaintiff's claim failed because it was inconsistent with the express terms of the contract relating to the effect of misdescription on the parties' rights.[20] However, an additional reason was that the consideration for the purchase price had not wholly failed. As Dixon CJ and Fullagar J noted, the apportionment of the purchase price pursuant to the contract showed that the main consideration for the agreement was conveyance of the hotel licence. As there was a valid licence and it had been transferred, there was no total failure of consideration.[21] In reaching the same conclusion, McTiernan, Williams and Webb JJ explained that 'common mistake' cases such as *Bingham v Bingham*[22] were ones where the basis for the contract had wholly failed. In that case, the plaintiff had contracted to purchase land under the mistaken belief that the vendor held title to it, when in truth the title was already held by the purchaser.

The third category of case where a putative contract will be void at common law is where the parties are at cross-purposes concerning a fundamental aspect of the contract (a so-called 'mutual mistake'). Provided that there is a latent ambiguity in one of the fundamental contract terms, the contract will be void for uncertainty. The classic example of this category of case is *Raffles v Wichelhaus*.[23] The defendant agreed to purchase cotton 'to arrive ex "Peerless" from Bombay'.[24] But there were two ships of that name; one of which sailed from Bombay in October and the other in December. The defendant successfully argued, by way of demurrer, that there was no means of determining, from the objective facts available, which ship was the intended subject of the agreement. The consequence was that no contract was formed.

The fourth category of case where a contract will be found void for fundamental mistake, in English law, is where the plaintiff was under a fundamental but unilateral error and the defendant was aware of, or contributed to, that mistake. We will see below that the Australian position may have become that the contract is *voidable* in these cases. Common examples of this category of case involve fundamental mistakes as to (i) the identity of the other contracting party,[25] (ii) the terms of the contract[26] or (iii) the subject matter of the contract.[27] Many cases involving fundamental mistakes relating to the identity of the other contracting party arise from the other party's deception. But the discussion in those

[18] *Svanosio v McNamara* [1956] HCA 55, (1956) 96 CLR 186.

[19] ibid 189–90 (Dixon and Fullagar J).

[20] *Svanosio v McNamara* [1956] HCA 55, (1956) 96 CLR 186, 199–200 (Dixon CJ and Fullagar J) 204–05 (McTiernan, Williams and Webb JJ).

[21] ibid 200; see also 211 (McTiernan, Williams and Webb JJ).

[22] *Bingham v Bingham* (1748) 1 Ves Sen 126, 27 ER 934.

[23] *Raffles v Wichelhaus* (1864) 2 H & C 906, 159 ER 375.

[24] Ibid 906; 375.

[25] *Cundy v Lindsay* (1878) 3 App Cas 459.

[26] *Hartog v Colin & Shields* [1939] 3 All ER 566.

[27] *Falck v Williams* [1900] AC 176.

authorities generally does not insist upon the mistake being one which is induced by the other party.[28] It is enough that the defendant was aware of the fundamental mistake. An example is *Smith v Hughes*,[29] where a buyer purchased oats believing them to be old when, in fact, they were new. He sought to return the oats and recover the purchase price. The trial judge told the jury to find for the buyer if (1) the seller had expressly described the oats as old or (2) that the seller knew that the buyer believed he was contracting for the purchase of old oats. The jury found for the purchaser. On appeal, the court accepted that either inducement or knowledge on the part of the vendor of a fundamental mistake by the purchaser rendered the contract void.[30]

The traditional position is that mistakes as to the *quality* or *value* of the subject matter of the contract, or the *attributes* of the other contracting party (as opposed to his identity), are not fundamental and therefore will not render a contract void, no matter how important that issue may have been to the contracting parties.[31] Thus in *Smith v Hughes*, both Blackburn J and Hannen J separately emphasised that it was not enough for the seller to have believed that the buyer was mistaken as to the quality of the oats. It was necessary that the buyer believed (incorrectly) that they had been *warranted* as old and that the seller knew this. As the trial judge's direction to the jury did not clearly draw the distinction between a known mistake as to the terms of the contract (a fundamental mistake), as opposed to the quality of the oats (a non-fundamental mistake), the court ordered a new trial.

The reason for the distinction between fundamental and non-fundamental errors in cases of common and unilateral mistake is that it would undermine effective pursuit of commerce if mistakes as to quality or character were sufficient to negate a commercial contract.[32] Those mistakes of quality or character commonly require an exercise of judgement and hence an increased risk of error. *Bell v Lever Brothers Ltd*[33] is another good example. Bell and Snelling were executives of Lever Brothers. Lever Brothers wanted to terminate their contracts of employment so that its business could be reorganised. They contracted to pay £30,000 compensation to Bell and £20,000 to Snelling in consideration of termination of their employment contracts. Lever Brothers later discovered it could have terminated their employment summarily because of serious breaches. In today's money, Lever Brothers therefore made a mistake running into many millions of pounds. At trial, the professional jury accepted that when they entered into their compensation agreements, Bell and Snelling had forgotten about these breaches and were also mistaken about the need to make a compensation agreement to terminate their employment. Lever Brothers sought restitution of the payments on the ground of common mistake. A majority of the House of Lords held that a common mistake would only make a contract void and allow restitution if the subject

[28] *Shogun Finance Ltd v Hudson* [2003] UKHL 62, [2004] 1 AC 919; *Cundy v Lindsay* (1878) 3 App Cas 459; *Ingram v Little* [1961] 1 QB 31.

[29] *Smith v Hughes* (1871) LR 6 QB 597.

[30] ibid 609; see also 610–11 (Hannen J).

[31] *Psaltis v Schultz* [1948] HCA 31, (1948) 76 CLR 547, 561 [12] (Dixon J).

[32] *Deputy Commissioner of Taxation v Chamberlain* [1990] FCA 71, (1990) 26 FCR 221, 233 [36] (Wilcox J); *George Wimpey UK Ltd v VI Construction Ltd* [2005] EWCA Civ 77, [2005] BLR 135 [62] (Sedley LJ). See also AJ Duggan, 'Is Equity Efficient?' (1997) 113 *Law Quarterly Review* 601, 609–11.

[33] *Bell v Lever Brothers Ltd* [1932] AC 161.

matter of the contract had ceased to exist or if the quality of the subject matter was essentially different from the quality it was supposed to be. As Lord Atkin said, Lever Brothers '[got] exactly what [they] bargain[ed] for.'[34]

B. No Juristic Reason if the Contract is Voidable and is Rescinded

Under the general law, a contract should be voidable and potentially able to be rescinded, when the defendant induces the plaintiff's impaired consent, or when the defendant knows that the plaintiff's consent is impaired when entering into the contract. An example is *Edgington v Fitzmaurice*[35] where the plaintiff was able to rescind a contract for subscription of shares in a company on the grounds of fraudulent misrepresentations contained in the company prospectus. The defendant cannot rely upon a contractual allocation of risk to avoid restitution when the mistake, illegitimate pressure or undue influence is attributable to him, or he is aware that the plaintiff entered the contract pursuant to a mistake, or while subject to illegitimate pressure[36] or undue influence.[37] However, the effect of the contract being voidable, not void, means that it must first be rescinded before the juristic basis for any benefits conferred under the contract is negated.[38] At common law this requires an election by the plaintiff, which generally involves giving notice of rescission to the defendant.[39]

There is an apparent inconsistency between the voidable nature of contracts in these circumstances and the *void* nature of contracts under English law where the defendant is aware of the plaintiff's fundamental unilateral mistake. This conflict can be seen in the majority and minority judgments in *Shogun Finance Ltd v Hudson.*[40] A fraudster induced the plaintiff finance company to enter into a hire-purchase arrangement with him by assuming a third party's identity (Mr Patel). The fraudster on-sold the car to the defendant, who was a bona fide purchaser for value. A critical issue was whether the plaintiff's unilateral mistake rendered the contract void, in which case the plaintiff's claim for damages for conversion against the defendant would succeed. On the other hand, if the contract was merely voidable, the defendant was protected from the claim under statute. The majority (Lords Hobhouse, Phillips and Walker) considered that since the agreement had been concluded in writing, the proper approach to its construction was to identify the parties to the agreement by reference to its terms.[41] On that basis, the contracting party was Mr Patel whose identity

[34] ibid 223–24.

[35] *Edgington v Fitzmaurice* (1885) 29 Ch D 459.

[36] *Talbot v Von Boris* [1911] 1 KB 854; *Halpern v Halpern* [2006] EWHC 603, [2006] 2 All ER 251 [96] (Christopher Clarke J); *Tsarouhi v Tsarouhi* [2009] FMCAfam 126 [19]–[43] (Riley FM).

[37] *Cobbett v Brock* (1855) 20 Beav 524, 528, 531; 52 ER 706, 707–08 (Romilly MR); *Kempson v Ashbee* (1874) LR 10 Ch App 15, 21 (James LJ); *Bainbrigge v Browne* (1881) 18 Ch D 188, 197 (Fry J); *Bank of New South Wales v Rogers* [1941] HCA 9, (1941) 65 CLR 42, 51–52, 55 (Starke J); *Royal Bank of Scotland plc v Etridge (No 2)* [2001] UKHL 44, [2002] 2 AC 773 [38]–[41] (Lord Nicholls). 'I see no reason why the position should be different [from cases of volunteers] … if the other party to the instrument had notice of the undue influence': *O'Sullivan v Management Agency and Music Ltd* [1985] QB 428, 464 (Fox LJ).

[38] *Fysh v Page* [1956] HCA 13, (1956) 96 CLR 233, 243–44 [5] (Dixon CJ, Webb and Kitto JJ); *Universe Tankships Inc of Monrovia v International Transport Workers Federation* [1983] 1 AC 366, 384 (Lord Diplock); *Crescendo Management Pty Ltd v Westpac Banking Corporation* (1988) 19 NSWLR 40, 45 (McHugh J).

[39] *Car & Universal Finance Co Ltd v Caldwell* [1965] 1 QB 525.

[40] *Shogun Finance Ltd v Hudson* [2003] UKHL 62, [2004] 1 AC 919.

[41] ibid [49] (Lord Hobhouse), [167], [179] (Lord Phillips), [180], [191]–[193] (Lord Walker).

had been assumed and who had not consented to enter into any agreement with the company. Unfortunately, the majority considered that another way of reaching this conclusion was to say that the contract was formed between the plaintiff and the rogue, but the plaintiff was operating under a fundamental mistake as to the identity of the other party. On either analysis, according to the majority, there was no 'consensus ad idem' between the parties, and the contract was void.[42] The first approach of the majority is consistent with the objective theory of contract. The second is not. Nevertheless, English courts have subsequently held that a contract is either void for mistake or it is valid; in English law there is no separate doctrine of voidability for mistake at common law or in equity.[43]

In the minority in *Shogun*, Lords Nicholls and Millett separately emphasised that a unilateral mistake should render any contract objectively established on the facts voidable, not void.[44] On their analysis, the contract was formed between the company and the fraudster. The minority approach suffers from the problem that it means that a contract was formed between the company and a person who was not a party to the written contract. But if the written parties to the contract could be ignored, the benefit of the approach of the minority is that the company (by its officers) mistakenly thought that it had been dealing with a creditable party.[45] As this mistake was known of and induced by that party, the contract should have been voidable for mistake.

From time to time, Australian courts have similarly questioned how common mistake cases and known unilateral mistake cases fit with the objective approach to construction of contracts.[46] Some Australian courts have adopted the prevailing English approach, which treats the contract as void.[47] The better view, however, is that, in accordance with the High Court's adoption of an objective approach to construction of contracts, an actionable unilateral or common mistake renders a contract voidable in equity, not void. The leading case is *Taylor v Johnson*.[48] Mrs Johnson gave Mr Taylor an option to purchase two lots of land for $15,000. Mr Taylor exercised the option and entered into a contract, but Mrs Johnson later refused to complete the purchase. She sought rescission or rectification of the option and contract because of her mistake in considering that the agreed price was $15,000 *per acre*, which represented a total price of about $150,000. The value of the subject land under the current zoning was about $50,000 but it would have increased to around $195,000 if a proposed rezoning of the land had become effective. The evidence was that Mr Taylor 'deliberately set out to ensure that Mrs Johnson was not disabused of the mistake or misapprehension under which he believed her to be acting.'[49] A majority of the High Court of

[42] ibid [50] (Lord Hobhouse), [123], [167], [179] (Lord Phillips), [180], [191]–[193] (Lord Walker).

[43] *Statoil ASA v Louis Dreyfus Energy Services LP* [2008] EWHC 2257.

[44] *Shogun Finance Ltd v Hudson* [2003] UKHL 62, [2004] 1 AC 919 [6]–[9] (Lord Nicholls), [76], [78]–[82] (Lord Millett).

[45] ibid [30], [39] (Lord Nicholls).

[46] *Errichetti Nominees Pty Ltd v Paterson Group Architects Pty Ltd* [2007] WASC 77 [61]–[63] (Master Newnes); *Zhang and Wu v South Sky Investments Pty Ltd* [2011] QSC 367 [28] (Fryberg J) discussing but not applying *Australia Estates Pty Ltd v Cairns City Council* [2005] QCA 328, and citing N Seddon, 'Contract: Mistake Mistake' (2006) 80 *Australian Law Journal* 95.

[47] *Australia Estates Pty Ltd v Cairns City Council* [2005] QCA 328 [45] (Atkinson J), a case of common mistake; see also *Manna v Manna* [2008] ACTSC 10.

[48] *Taylor v Johnson* [1983] HCA 5, (1983) 151 CLR 422. See also *Hawcroft v Hawcroft General Trading Co Pty Ltd* [2016] NSW SC 555.

[49] *Taylor v Johnson* [1983] HCA 5, (1983) 151 CLR 422, 428 [5] (Mason ACJ, Murphy and Deane JJ).

Australia held that the contract should be rescinded. Their Honours relied upon English and American authorities that suggested that a contract is voidable where the mistake is induced by or known to the other party.[50] The joint judgment concluded that it was sufficient to say that a contract will be voidable when 'the other party is aware that circumstances exist which indicate that the first party is entering the contract under some serious mistake or misapprehension … and deliberately sets out to ensure that the first party does not become aware of the existence of his mistake or misapprehension.'[51]

In the course of their reasoning, Mason ACJ, Murphy and Deane JJ observed that the approach adopted by Blackburn and Hannen JJ in *Smith v Hughes* was consistent with a subjective approach to contract formation whereby the true consent of the parties is required to form a contract. They considered, however, that the objective approach had 'command of the field',[52] a view which has been subsequently iterated and reiterated by the High Court.[53] On this approach, the law is concerned, not with the real intentions of the parties, but with the outward manifestations of those intentions.[54] It follows that where there is objective agreement and all other formation requirements are met, the contract will be valid. On this approach, a contract entered into as a result of the plaintiff's unilateral mistake that is known of or induced by the defendant will at most be voidable, not void.

This objective focus on a contract does not contradict a contract being void for mutual mistake. Cases such as *Raffles v Wichelhaus* support the underlying reason for mutual mistake as being the uncertainty arising from a latent ambiguity in a fundamental term. The term is still construed objectively; the issue is simply that there is fundamental uncertainty. Nor is the reasoning in *Taylor v Johnson* inconsistent with the continued existence of a doctrine of common mistake that renders a contract void. As we explained, cases of common mistake are better understood as involving a failure of the consideration (which, here, means an objective basis) of the contract. The basis or purpose of a contract is determined objectively, in the same manner as for construction of contracts.

Under both English and Australian law, contracts induced by the misrepresentation, illegitimate pressure or undue influence of a third party will similarly be set aside where the defendant knew of the vitiating factor at the time of entering into the contract.[55] In *Halpern v Halpern*[56] the defendants alleged a settlement agreement was induced by the illegitimate pressure of a third party (a rabbi involved in the compromise negotiations). In interlocutory proceedings, the plaintiff sought summary judgment against the defendants to enforce

[50] ibid 431, 432, [12], [13], including *Solle v Butcher* [1950] 1 KB 671, 692 (Denning LJ); *Riverlate Properties Ltd v Paul* [1975] Ch 133, 145 (the Court).

[51] *Taylor v Johnson* [1983] HCA 5, (1983) 151 CLR 422, 432 [14] (Mason ACJ, Murphy and Deane JJ).

[52] ibid 428–29, [8]–[9].

[53] Eg *Codelfa Construction Pty Ltd v State Rail Authority of NSW* [1982] HCA 24, (1982) 149 CLR 337, 348–53 [12]–[25] (Mason J); *Ermogenous v Greek Orthodox Community of SA Inc* [2002] HCA 8, (2002) 209 CLR 95 [25] (Gaudron, McHugh, Hayne and Callinan JJ); *Pacific Carriers Ltd v BNP Paribas* (2004) 218 CLR 451 [22] (the Court); *Toll (FGCT) Pty Ltd v Alphapharm Pty Ltd* [2004] HCA 52, (2004) 219 CLR 165 [38]–[41] (the Court); *Equuscorp Pty Ltd v Glengallan Investments Pty Ltd* [2004] HCA 55, (2004) 218 CLR 471 [34] (the Court).

[54] *Taylor v Johnson* [1983] HCA 5, (1983) 151 CLR 422, 428 [7] (Mason ACJ, Murphy and Deane JJ).

[55] On misrepresentation, see *Stone v Compton* (1838) 5 Bing NC 142, 156–57; 132 ER 1059, 1064–65; 132 ER 1059, 1065 and *Spencer v Handley* (1842) 4 Man & G 414, 134 ER 169, cited in *Commercial Bank of Australia Ltd v Amadio* [1983] HCA 14, (1983) 151 CLR 447, 458 [17] (Gibbs CJ).

[56] *Halpern v Halpern* [2006] EWHC 603, [2006] 2 All ER (Comm) 251, discussed Ch 9 p 200. *Tsarouhi v Tsarouhi* [2009] FMCAfam 126 [19]–[43].

the agreement on the basis, inter alia, that the illegitimate pressure had not come from the plaintiffs. In rejecting this argument, Christopher Clarke J stated that 'the fact that Rabbi Schmerler was the person who exercised the alleged duress does not automatically exonerate the claimants. But it would have, at the least, to be established that [the claimants] knew that Rabbi Schmerler was exerting illegitimate pressure on [the defendants] and took the benefit of it.'[57]

Halpern was a case of duress or illegitimate pressure. An example in the context of undue influence is *Khan v Khan*.[58] The defendants were a mother and son who had orally agreed to enter into a contract for sale of a residential property to the plaintiffs. The mother subsequently changed her mind and decided not to go through with the sale. Her son arranged for the Imam of the local mosque to attend a meeting between the parties and to act as their religious adviser. The Imam, acting entirely in good faith, advised the mother of her religious obligation to keep her word and instructed her to sign the memorandum of sale. The mother duly signed. The next day, her son brought the memorandum to her to initial a minor amendment and she tore it up. The plaintiffs sought specific performance of the contract of sale. The mother responded by pleading that she had entered into the contract as a result of undue influence. Justice Barrett said that the memorandum could only be set aside if the plaintiffs were aware that the transaction was a result of the Imam's influence. This requirement was satisfied because the plaintiffs had witnessed the mother submitting to the Imam's direction to sign.

C. No Juristic Reason if the Basis of the Entitlement Wholly Failed

The previous section has shown that if a defendant enriches a plaintiff due to a contractual obligation to do so, it will usually be necessary, before restitution is awarded, for the plaintiff to show that the contract was void, or was voidable and has been rescinded.

There are, however, some circumstances where restitution of a contractual payment can be awarded despite the contract not being void or rescinded or even terminated. In *Thomas v Brown*,[59] the plaintiff brought an action to recover a deposit paid under a contract for purchase of a shop for failure of consideration. One reason why the action failed was that the time for performance had not yet arrived. Justice Quain explained that the consideration for a transaction has not failed if the defendant might still be ready and willing to perform.[60] In other words, until it is known that the defendant cannot and will not perform, it cannot be said that the basis for the plaintiff's performance has failed. This is not a requirement that the contract be void, or rescinded, or terminated. It is a requirement only that a fundamental basis for the contract has wholly failed.[61]

[57] *Halpern v Halpern* [2006] EWHC 603, [2006] 2 All ER (Comm) 251 [96].

[58] *Khan v Khan* [2004] NSWSC 1189, (2004) 62 NSWLR 229.

[59] *Thomas v Brown* (1876) 1 QBD 714.

[60] ibid 723. See also *Weston v Downes* (1778) 1 Dougl 23, 24-25; 99 ER 19, 20 (Ashurst, Willes JJ); *Baltic Shipping Co v Dillon Baltic Shipping Co v Dillon* [1993] HCA 4, (1993) 176 CLR 344, 385 [6] (Gaudron J).

[61] *Crown Prosecution Services v Eastenders Group* [2014] UKSC 26, [2015] AC 1 [115] (Lord Toulson; Lady Hale, and Lords Kerr, Wilson and Hughes agreeing).

This same requirement can be seen in *Roxborough v Rothmans of Pall Mall Ltd*.[62] In that case, a majority of the High Court of Australia allowed a claim for restitution of a severable portion of the contract price, despite the existence of an enforceable contract that had previously required its payment. Tobacco retailers had purchased cigarettes from wholesalers for a price that included a distinct payment representing the tax due from the wholesalers to the government. It was later discovered that the tax was unconstitutional. This meant the wholesaler was not required to pay the tax to the government. But the unconstitutional tax did not invalidate the agreement between the retailer and the wholesaler. The wholesaler argued that restitution for unjust enrichment should not be ordered, because there remained a valid juristic reason.[63] The majority simply treated the question as one of whether the basis for the plaintiff's performance of the distinct payment obligation was still open. The only judge in the majority who considered that termination was necessary was Callinan J, who quoted from the trial judge:

> The contract [here] has been executed in all respects save for payment of the licence fee by the respondent. The licence fee is no longer payable. It cannot and will not be paid by the respondent. That is the end of the matter. Performance is no longer possible. If formal termination by the appellants is necessary, then bringing these proceedings is sufficient.[64]

The effect of the decision in *Roxborough* is that there can be cases where restitution will be allowed, despite the existence of a valid contractual obligation. However, such claims should only be permitted where the basis for that contractual obligation has itself wholly failed. Otherwise the order for restitution will contradict the allocation of risk under the contract.[65] That risk allocation was premised upon a particular basis: only if the basis does not exist from the outset, or was conditioned on some fact or matter that subsequently failed, can the risk allocation be disregarded. In *Roxborough*, even if the contract had not been terminated, the basis for the severable portion of the payment by the appellants was that the licence fee was due and payable as tax to the New South Wales government: as the tax was void, that basis failed. In their joint judgment in *Roxborough*, Gleeson CJ, Gaudron and Hayne JJ were careful to say that allowing restitution for failure of that basis would not subvert contractual risk, because the tax was externally imposed, and was not the subject of negotiation.[66]

In cases where the fundamental basis for the risk allocation under a contractual term fails, there will be an unjust factor to support a claim for restitution of any enrichment transferred under that term. An early example is *Clifton v Coffey*.[67] Mr Coffey paid £300 as a deposit for the purchase of the lease, licence, goodwill and furniture of a hotel from Mr Clifton. The contract provided that part of the purchase price was to be financed by a loan to Mr Coffey from a brewery. A majority of the High Court of Australia (Isaacs ACJ

[62] *Roxborough v Rothmans of Pall Mall Australia Ltd* [2001] HCA 68, (2001) 208 CLR 516.

[63] *Roxborough v Rothmans of Pall Mall Australia Ltd* [2001] HCA 68, (2001) 208 CLR 516 [197] (Callinan J) quoting *Roxborough v Rothmans of Pall Mall Ltd* [1999] FCA 1535, (1999) 95 FCR 185 [106] (Gyles J).

[64] *Roxborough v Rothmans of Pall Mall Australia Ltd* [2001] HCA 68, (2001) 208 CLR 516 [197].

[65] See also *Equuscorp Pty Ltd v Haxton; Equuscorp Pty Ltd v Bassat; Equuscorp Pty Ltd v Cunningham's Warehouse Sales Pty Ltd* [2012] HCA 7, (2012) 246 CLR 498 [26] fn 37, where French CJ, Crennan and Kiefel JJ noted, citing *Roxborough* and *Lumbers*, that: 'Relief may be granted in respect of benefits provided under an existing contract depending upon how the claim fits with the contract.' See also *Crown Prosecution Service v Eastenders Group* [2014] UKSC 26, [2015] AC 1 [115] (Lord Toulson; Lady Hale, and Lords Kerr, Wilson and Hughes agreeing).

[66] *Roxborough v Rothmans of Pall Mall Australia Ltd* [2001] HCA 68, (2001) 208 CLR 516 [22]–[23].

[67] *Clifton v Coffey* [1924] HCA 35, (1924) 34 CLR 434.

and Gavan Duffy J, Starke J dissenting) held that this was 'an essential circumstance on the faith of which as a fundamental term and condition the purchaser entered into the bargain. This fundamental term and condition having failed ... justice requires the return of what the vendor has in the meantime received.'[68]

III. Deeds of Gift as a Juristic Reason

A. No Juristic Reason if the Deed is Rescinded (Undue Influence or Illegitimate Pressure)

Where enrichments are transferred by a valid deed of gift (including a deed of trust) rather than a contract, then an award of restitution generally requires that the deed must be rescinded or be shown to have been made on a basis that totally failed. A deed of gift constitutes a juristic reason to retain the enrichment. A common basis for avoiding a deed of gift is that it was the product of illegitimate pressure or undue influence. As with gifts that are made without a deed, there is no requirement (such as that found in cases of contract) that the defendant have involvement or knowledge of the undue influence or illegitimate pressure. In *Giarrantano v Smith*,[69] for example, Mrs Giarrantano created a trust of her land for herself and her children, with herself as trustee. The New South Wales Supreme Court held that she was entitled to restitution in circumstances where the undue influence had come from a third party (her father-in-law). No evidence was brought, nor was it suggested as relevant to the case, that her children were aware of their grandfather's influence or that they were responsible for bringing about the transaction.

B. No Juristic Reason if the Deed of Gift is Rescinded (Mistake)

Unlike cases of illegitimate pressure or undue influence, a mistake which induces the plaintiff to enter a deed of gift has not always been treated as sufficient to rescind the deed. It would otherwise be too easy for plaintiffs to undo transactions, thereby damaging an innocent defendant's interest in the security of his receipt under a deed. However, the restrictions on rescission of deeds for mistake are not as onerous as those involving bilateral contractual bargains. For some time, the approach taken by the courts, following the test developed in *Gibbon v Mitchell*,[70] was to distinguish between a mistake as to the 'legal effects' of a transaction (which was sufficient) and a mistake as to the 'consequences' of a transaction (which was not). That approach has been followed in Australia,[71] although in one case apparently

[68] *Clifton v Coffey* [1924] HCA 35, (1924) 34 CLR 434, 440 (Issacs ACJ and Gavan Duffy J).

[69] *Giarratano v Smith* (NSWSC, 24 October 1985). See also *Giarrantano v Smith* (1985) NSW ConvR 55-267.

[70] *Gibbon v Mitchell* [1990] 3 All ER 338, 343 (Millett J).

[71] *Commissioner of Stamp Duties (NSW) v Carlenka Pty Ltd* (1995) 41 NSWLR 329, 343–44 (Sheller JA, Mahoney A-P agreeing); *Baird v BCE Holdings Pty Ltd* (1996) 40 NSWLR 374, 384–85 (Young J); *Club Cape Schanck Resort Co Ltd v Cape Country Club Pty Ltd* [2001] VSCA 2, (2001) 3 VR 526 [44]–[45] (Chernov JA); *Baxter v Federal Commissioner of Taxation* [2002] FCA 1256, (2002) 196 ALR 519 [26] (Gyles J).

without the knowledge that *Gibbon* had been overturned in *Pitt v Holt*.[72] As we will see in Chapter 8, in substance this approach is similar to that taken in cases of simple mistaken transfers in England.

In *Pitt v Holt*,[73] Lord Walker (delivering the judgment of the court) rejected the Revenue's 'heterodox submission' that deeds of gift may only be negated for mistake on the same grounds as contract. However, his Lordship said that since a unilateral mistake may be sufficient to found relief, this 'is arguably a good reason for the court to apply a more stringent test as to the seriousness of the mistake before granting relief.'[74] In that case, Mr Pitt was the victim of a serious accident that rendered him incapable of looking after his own affairs. As his court-appointed receiver, his wife, Mrs Pitt, settled on trust for his benefit the amounts Mr Pitt had received by way of compromise of his claim for compensation. She had obtained extensive advice about the tax consequences of the settlement. But, unknown to her, inheritance tax applied to the settlement. The Supreme Court held that rescission should be ordered. But the court rejected the test developed in *Gibbon v Mitchell*[75] as being too uncertain. The Court considered that a better test was to ask whether there had been a 'causative mistake of sufficient gravity' such that it would be 'unconscionable' for the defendant to retain the benefit of the deed.[76] We will see in Chapter 8 that this reformulation might be interpreted as reviving the sorts of limitations on the unjust factor of mistake that have been expressly rejected by the High Court of Australia and which is capable of causing great uncertainty. However, a better interpretation is that Lord Walker's reasoning is consistent with adoption of a requirement that the plaintiff must not have accepted the risk of error in order to obtain restitution for mistake.[77]

IV. Deeds where Consideration is Given to a Third Party as a Juristic Reason

There are additional restrictions upon rescission where the deed embodies a contractual bargain (making the case similar to a bilateral contract scenario) *but* the plaintiff is a volunteer (making the case similar in this respect to a unilateral deed). This category was first recognised in cases where a wife entered into a deed of mortgage or guarantee to secure her husband's debt as a result of some mistake as to its purport or effect, illegitimate pressure or undue influence.[78] As in the case of the deed of gift, the wife often receives no benefit and does not bargain for any benefit in exchange. But, unlike the deed of gift, the defendant financier gives consideration in exchange: the loan to the husband. The financier's legitimate interest in security of receipt lies somewhere between the deed of gift and the contract for value. The interest is stronger than in the case of a deed of gift because the financier

[72] *Franknelly Nominees Pty Ltd v Abrugiato* [2013] WASCA 285, (2013) 10 ASTLR 558 [179] (Buss JA).
[73] *Pitt v Holt* [2013] UKSC 26, [2013] 2 AC 108 [115].
[74] ibid [114].
[75] *Gibbon v Mitchell* [1990] 3 All ER 338, 343 (Millett J).
[76] *Pitt v Holt* [2013] UKSC 26, [2013] 2 AC 108 [122], [124].
[77] Ch 8 pp 176, 184–85.
[78] *Yerkey v Jones* [1939] HCA 3, (1939) 63 CLR 649.

has given consideration in exchange to a third party. But the interest is weaker than that of a contractual bargain because the defendant wife receives no benefit. The additional restriction imposed upon rescission and restitution in these cases therefore falls between the restrictions in cases of contractual bargains and those in the case of deeds of gift.

The broader principle that has developed from these cases is that a deed under which consideration moves to a third party will be set aside where (1) the plaintiff entered into the transaction as a result of an impaired intention; (2) the plaintiff received no benefit from it; and (3) the defendant was aware that the plaintiff was in a relationship (or, potentially, aware of other facts or matters) which gave rise to a risk of the plaintiff's intention being impaired.[79] In those circumstances, the defendant will only be entitled to retain the benefit if it shows that it took steps to eliminate the risk of impairment to a level that made it reasonable to proceed. The following sections consider this broader principle in the context of the domestic suretyship cases in which it has largely developed.

A. No Juristic Reason where the Deed is Rescinded for Mistake

In *Garcia v National Australia Bank Ltd*,[80] the High Court of Australia held that a deed of surety may be rescinded on the ground of mistake where (i) the financier knows the surety is the principal debtor's wife, (ii) the transaction is not for the benefit of the wife and that, accordingly, (iii) there is an objective risk that she is labouring under a mistake about the nature or effect of the deed. In that case, the bank knew that the relationship between guarantor and primary debtor was one of wife and husband. The High Court explained that a reasonable person in the position of the bank would therefore realise that the relationship was one of trust and confidence in which there was a real possibility that explanations of commercial matters might not be full or effective. This in turn meant there was a real risk that the husband's explanation of the instant transaction had not been full or effective. This possibility was sufficient to shift the risk of the mistake by the wife to the financier, and the High Court held that the wife's guarantee should be set aside.

Although *Garcia* applied this approach in the context of a mistaken wife, the principle extends to other cases involving analogous relationships of trust and confidence. Not only should a husband be treated in exactly the same way, but a marital relationship is only one instance of a relationship of trust and confidence. In the New South Wales Supreme Court case of *Liu v Adamson*,[81] the principle was applied where a bank officer knew that the woman giving the security was the long-term de facto partner of the primary debtor. He was clearly aware of the relationship of trust and confidence and there was no great difficulty in extending the operation of the principle to that relationship.[82] The Supreme

[79] See *National Australia Bank Ltd v Starbronze Ltd* [2000] VSC 325, (2001) V ConvR 54–640 [84] (Coldrey J); *Multi-Span Constructions No 1 Pty Ltd v 14 Portland Street Pty Ltd* [2001] NSWSC 696, (2001) 10 BPR 19,253 [58] (Barrett J); *Watt v State Bank of New South Wales* [2003] ACTCA 7 [21] (Higgins CJ and Crispin P); *Amtel Pty Ltd v Ah Chee* [2015] WASC 341 [258] (Pritchard J).

[80] *Garcia v National Australia Bank Ltd* [1998] HCA 48, (1998) 194 CLR 395.

[81] *Liu v Adamson* [2003] NSWSC 74, (2003) 12 BPR 22,205 [22]–[23] (Macready M). See also *Kranz v National Australia Bank Ltd* [2003] VSCA 92, (2003) 8 VR 310 [23]–[31] (Charles JA).

[82] See also *Royal Bank of Scotland plc v Etridge (No 2)* [2001] UKHL 44, [2002] 2 AC 773 [82] (Lord Nicholls): 'What is appropriate for sexual relationships ought, in principle, to be appropriate also for other relationships where trust and confidence are likely to exist.'

Court of New South Wales has also applied the *Garcia* approach to a relationship between parents and their son.[83] In that case, the guarantors, who were parents of the principal debtor, reposed significant trust and confidence in their son due to the cultural background of their family, a fact of which the financier bank was aware through 'previous experience'.[84]

B. No Juristic Reason where the Deed is Rescinded for Illegitimate Pressure or Undue Influence

This same principle applies to cases of illegitimate pressure or undue influence.[85] However, it is often difficult for a plaintiff to establish that the financier had sufficient knowledge of the circumstances that gave rise to a risk that the deed had been procured by illegitimate pressure. The decision of the English Court of Appeal in *Bank of Scotland v Bennett*[86] illustrates the challenge. Mrs Bennett was threatened with divorce unless she agreed to enter into a guarantee agreement and charge over the family home[87] in favour of the appellant bank to secure her husband's[88] company's debts. The trial judge found, and the Court of Appeal accepted, that the transactions were obtained by the exercise of illegitimate pressure. But the focus in the Court of Appeal was on 'whether *the bank* is able to rely on the guarantee and the charge in those circumstances.'[89] The Court of Appeal held that insufficient facts were known by the bank to alert it to the risk of the wife's intention to make the transaction being impaired. The bank was 'providing new money, against security, in connection with a venture which must have been seen to have real prospects of success.'[90] There was nothing in Mrs Bennett agreeing to provide security over her property which could have reasonably suggested to the bank that her intention might have been obtained by the exertion of illegitimate pressure from her husband. To the contrary, she and her family were the obvious beneficiaries of the company's potential success. Further, the bank knew Mrs Bennett was receiving advice from a solicitor in relation to the charge over the family home. It was irrelevant, from the bank's perspective, that the solicitor's advice was not full or effective.[91]

[83] *State Bank of New South Wales v Layoun* [2001] NSWSC 113, [2001] NSW ConvR 55-984.

[84] ibid [51] (Levine J).

[85] See, eg, *Bank of Scotland v Bennett* [1999] 1 FLR 1115; *First National Bank plc v Achampong* [2003] EWCA Civ 487, [2004] 1 FCR 18; *Barbaro v Millington* [2004] ACTSC 7 may also come within this category.

[86] *Bank of Scotland v Bennett* [1999] 1 FLR 1115.

[87] The house had been transferred into her sole name prior to executing the charge, a fact of which the bank arguably was not aware: ibid 1137–38 (Chadwick LJ; Sir Christopher Staughton and Auld LJ agreeing).

[88] The vast majority of shares in the company were held by her husband: ibid 1121, 1137 (Chadwick LJ; Sir Christopher Staughton and Auld LJ agreeing).

[89] ibid 1135 (Chadwick LJ; Sir Christopher Staughton and Auld LJ agreeing) (emphasis added).

[90] ibid 1141 (Chadwick LJ; Sir Christopher Staughton and Auld LJ agreeing).

[91] Although the bank appealed this issue to the House of Lords, the House decided the case on another ground, namely that the bank ought to have disclosed to Mrs Bennett the existence of a ranking agreement, the consequence of which was that Mrs Bennett's right of subrogation arising out of the guarantee was subordinated to those of a third party: see *Royal Bank of Scotland plc v Etridge (No 2)* [2001] UKHL 44, [2002] 2 AC 773 [346]–[350] (Lord Scott).

By contrast, cases involving domestic sureties who are the subject of undue influence seem to succeed more often.[92] This is because where a wife receives no real benefit from the transaction, and the bank knows she is married to the principal debtor, the bank is taken to know that there is a real risk that the wife may have entered into the transaction as a result of undue influence. In Australia, this is described as the first limb of the principle in *Yerkey v Jones*.[93] While the principle in *Yerkey v Jones* was expressed only in terms of wives securing their husbands' debts, its underlying rationale extends far beyond the marital relationship, to any relationship of trust and confidence which carries with it a real risk of the plaintiff's intention being impaired through undue influence.[94] Thus, surety transactions have been set aside against banks where the bank knew the debtor stood, or recently stood, in a position of guardian or *in loco parentis*, to the surety.[95] Moreover, the circumstances which may raise the risk of excessive influence are not limited to those analogous to the classes of relationship in which influence is presumed. A relationship of elderly parent to son, for example where the son is a businessman in whose favour a guarantee is being executed by the parent, may be one where a bank should see a risk of undue influence as well as mistake.[96] Nor is it necessary that the bank suspect the precise nature of the relationship of influence that is found to exist. In *Bank of New South Wales v Rogers*,[97] the bank was aware that the surety lived with the debtor, was not a boarder or guest, and was most likely in a 'near relationship' with the debtor. This was enough to 'put the bank on enquiry' as to whether the surety was in a relationship of influence that caused her to enter into the transactions.[98] The fact that the bank may not have known of the precise nature of the relationship giving rise to the risk of influence—the debtor standing *in loco parentis* to his niece—was irrelevant.

In England, the same principle extends to all cases where the surety stands in a non-commercial relationship with the primary debtor.[99] An example is *Credit Lyonnais Bank Nederland NV v Burch*[100] where the bank was aware that the guarantor was a junior

[92] *Royal Bank of Scotland plc v Etridge (No 2)* [2001] UKHL 44, [2002] 2 AC 773 [44]–[49] (Lord Nicholls, expressly noting at [48] that the position may well be different where the loan is made jointly to husband and wife); see also *UCB Group Ltd v Hedworth* [2003] EWCA Civ 1717, [2003] 3 FCR 739 (loan made jointly to husband and wife to refinance their existing borrowing) and *Chater v Mortgage Agency Services Number Two Ltd* [2003] EWCA Civ 490, [2003] HLR 61 (loan made jointly to mother and son).

[93] *Yerkey v Jones* [1939] HCA 3, (1939) 63 CLR 649; *Amtel Pty Ltd v Ah Chee* [2015] WASC 341 [242]–[243] (Pritchard J); *Annulment Funding Co Ltd v Cowey* [2010] EWCA Civ 711, [2010] BPIR 1304 [61]–[64] (Morgan J; Arden and Jackson LJJ concurring).

[94] *Kranz v National Australia Bank Ltd* [2003] VSCA 92, (2003) 8 VR 310 [24] (Charles JA; Winneke P and Eames JA concurring); *ANZ Banking Group Ltd v Alirezai* [2004] QCA 6, (2004) Q ConvR 54-601 [115]–[116] (Wilson J) followed *McIvor v Westpac Banking Corporation* [2012] QSC 404 [104] (Applegarth J); see J Edelman and E Bant, 'Setting Aside Contracts of Suretyship: The Theory and Practice of Both Limbs of *Yerkey v Jones*' (2004) 15 *Journal of Banking and Finance Law and Practice* 5.

[95] *Maitland v Irving* (1846) 15 Sim 437, 441; 60 ER 688, 690 (Shadwell VC); *Maitland v Backhouse* (1847) 16 Sim 58, 60 ER 794; *Espey v Lake* (1852) 10 Hare 260, 262; 68 ER 923, 925 (Turner VC).

[96] *State Bank of New South Wales v Layoun* [2001] NSWSC 113, [2001] NSW ConvR 55-984.

[97] *Bank of New South Wales v Rogers* [1941] HCA 9, (1941) 65 CLR 42, 71 (McTiernan J).

[98] ibid 70–72 (McTiernan J); see also McTiernan J's express reliance on the principle in *Yerkey v Jones* at 61.

[99] *Royal Bank of Scotland plc v Etridge (No 2)* [2001] UKHL 44, [2002] 2 AC 773 [42]–[49], [82]–[89] (Lord Nicholls); *Annulment Funding Co Ltd v Cowey* [2010] EWCA Civ 711, [2010] BPIR 1304 [61]–[64] (Morgan J; Arden and Jackson LJJ concurring).

[100] *Credit Lyonnais Bank Nederland NV v Burch* [1997] 1 All ER 144, approved in *Royal Bank of Scotland plc v Etridge (No 2)* [2001] UKHL 44, [2002] 2 AC 773 [83] (Lord Nicholls). For a post-*Etridge* example, see *Burbank Securities Ltd v Wong* [2008] EWHC 552.

employee of the debtor company, who had no interest in the company as a shareholder or director, and was taking on an obligation unlimited both in terms of amount and duration.

A financier can take steps to protect itself from a finding that it had sufficient knowledge of the circumstances of mistake, illegitimate pressure or undue influence, such that it assumed the risk of the guarantor's impaired consent. To avoid the conclusion that the financier took the risk of the plaintiff's impaired intention, the financier should take steps to satisfy itself that the surety's intention is the fully informed 'expression of [that] person's free will'.[101] In the leading speech in *Royal Bank of Scotland v Etridge (No 2),* Lord Nicholls said that '[o]rdinarily it will be reasonable that a bank should be able to rely upon confirmation from a solicitor, acting for the wife, that he has advised the wife appropriately'.[102] However, the position will be different if 'the bank knows that the solicitor has not duly advised the wife or ... if the bank knows facts from which it ought to have realised that the wife has not received the appropriate advice'.

V. Receipt in Satisfaction of Right as a Juristic Reason

In *Barclays Bank Ltd v WJ Simms Son & Cooke (Southern) Ltd,*[103] Robert Goff J said that a claim to recover a mistaken payment may fail where a

> payment is made for good consideration, in particular if the money is paid to discharge, and does discharge, a debt owed to the payee (or a principal on whose behalf he is authorised to receive the payment) by the payor or by a third party by whom he is authorised to discharge the debt.[104]

There has been considerable debate about what Robert Goff J meant by 'good consideration'. The difficulty is that there are at least five[105] different principles that are commonly brought under the umbrella label of 'good consideration'.

The first is the concept of 'receipt in satisfaction of a right'. The second is a counterclaim by way of set-off for failure of consideration.[106] Very recently, a third principle has been proposed: a defence of 'bona fide discharge of debt'.[107] A fourth possibility considered by some cases is that 'good consideration' is the defence of change of position.[108] A fifth possibility

[101] *Royal Bank of Scotland plc v Etridge (No 2)* [2001] UKHL 44, [2002] 2 AC 773 [7] (Lord Nicholls).

[102] ibid [56]; see also [57] (Lord Nicholls). For an early example, see *Cobbett v Brock* (1855) 20 Beav 524, 52 ER 706.

[103] *Barclays Bank Ltd v WJ Simms Son & Cooke (Southern) Ltd* [1980] QB 677.

[104] ibid 695.

[105] Cf American Law Institute, *Restatement of the Law (Third) Restitution and Unjust Enrichment*, 2 vols (St Paul, Minn, American Law Institute Publishers, 2011): §62, approximating the defence of receipt in satisfaction of right; §67, incorporating discharge of debt; and, §27 and §63(d), which together address counterclaims for failure of consideration.

[106] Eg *Ovidio Carrideo Nominees Pty Ltd v The Dog Depot Pty Ltd* [2006] VSCA 6, (2006) V ConvR 54-713 [21]–[22] (Chernov JA), [32]–[50] (Nettle JA).

[107] *Hills Industries Ltd v Australian Financial Services and Leasing Pty Ltd* [2012] NSWCA 380, (2012) 295 ALR 147 [83] (Allsop P).

[108] *Lloyds Bank plc v Independent Insurance Co Ltd* [2000] QB 110 (CA) 125–26 (Waller LJ). See also *K & S Corp Ltd v Sportingbet Australia* [2003] SASC 96, (2003) 86 SASR 312 [161] (Besanko J) (defence of good consideration considered as part of change of position defence rejected because credit entry was reversible).

sees the label as describing the defence of payment in satisfaction of a legal claim.[109] These five options constitute alternative analyses that may be available on the particular facts of any case to sustain a claim of 'good consideration'. The second to fifth analyses constitute independent defences, and are considered separately in Chapters 14 and 15. A plea from a defendant that he was entitled to his receipt in satisfaction of an existing right, however, falls within the category of an assertion of a juristic reason to retain the benefit. It remains an independent principle that may operate to defeat a claim of restitution for unjust enrichment, notwithstanding the possible presence of other, alternative interpretations of the concept of 'good consideration'.[110] It is only that plea with which this section is concerned.

The principle of receipt in satisfaction of right is applicable to all claims in unjust enrichment, not just mistaken payments.[111] But the most common instance of this principle is where a payment of money by mistake discharges a debt. Suppose a defendant receives a mistaken payment from the plaintiff which discharges rights that the defendant had against the plaintiff under a contract or statute.[112] The plaintiff cannot recover the value of that benefit unless the defendant's right is negated.[113] In *Lloyds Bank plc v Independent Insurance Co Ltd*,[114] the plaintiff bank made a payment to its client's creditor to discharge a debt owing from the client to the creditor. The payment was made after the client's instructions, but the bank had a mistaken belief that the client had sufficient funds in its account to cover the payment. The English Court of Appeal refused the bank restitution because the creditor had given 'good consideration' for the payment, by discharging the debt owed to it. The same point was made in the joint judgment in *David Securities Pty Ltd v Commonwealth Bank of Australia* where their Honours said that mistake of law[115] 'would not, for example, extend to a case where the moneys were paid under a mistaken belief that they were legally due and owing under a particular clause of a particular contract when in fact they were legally due and owing to the recipient under another clause or contract'.

These cases concern situations where there was a juristic reason to retain the benefit, namely that a defendant was entitled to the receipt of the benefit because it discharged a debt.

[109] *Hookway v Racing Victoria Ltd* [2005] VSCA 310, (2005) 13 VR 444 [39] (Ormiston J).

[110] *Australian Financial Services and Leasing Pty Ltd v Hills Industries Ltd* [2014] HCA 14, (2014) 253 CLR 560 [101] (Crennan, Kiefel, Bell and Keane JJ).

[111] *Public Service Employees Credit Union Co-operative Ltd v Campion* (1984) 75 FLR 131, 138–39 (Kelly J); *Scolio Pty Ltd v Cote* (1992) 6 WAR 475, 479 (Rowland J), 484 (Ipp J); *Flower v Sadler* (1882) 10 QBD 572; *Ward v Lloyd* (1843) 6 Man & G 785, 134 ER 1109. *Fistar v Riverwood Legion and Community Club Ltd* [2016] NSWCA 81 [79]–[81] (Leeming JA; Bathurst CJ and Sackville AJA concurring).

[112] An enrichment paid in satisfaction of a right that is unenforceable or statute barred raises a different defence of 'natural obligation'. See *Platemaster Pty Ltd v M & T Investments Pty Ltd* [1973] VR 93.

[113] *Barclays Bank Ltd v WJ Simms Son & Cooke (Southern) Ltd* [1980] QB 677, 695 (Robert Goff J); *Pan Ocean Shipping Co Ltd v Creditcorp Ltd (The Trident Beauty)* [1993] 1 Lloyd's Rep 443, 454 (Beldam LJ); *Gulf International Bank BSC v Albaraka Islamic Bank BSC* [2004] EWCA Civ 416; *Deutsche Morgan Grenfell Group plc v Inland Revenue Commissioners* [2006] UKHL 49, [2007] 1 AC 558 [84]–[86] (Lord Scott); *Test Claimants in the FII Group Litigation v Revenue and Customs Commissioners* [2010] EWCA Civ 103 [181] (Arden LJ, delivering the judgment of the Court); *National Mutual Life Association of Australasia Ltd v Walsh* (1987) 8 NSWLR 585, 592 (Clarke J); *Griffiths v Commonwealth Bank of Australia* (1994) 123 ALR 111, 123–24 (Lee J); *Re Magarey Farlam Lawyers Trust Accounts (No 3)* [2007] SASC 9, (2007) 96 SASR 337 [168], [177]–[183] (Debelle J); *Clarke v Abou-Samra* [2010] SASC 205 [69]–[72], [103]–[106] (Kourakis J); *Commissioner of Inland Revenue v Stiassny* [2012] NZCA 93, [2013] 1 NZLR 140 [94] (Randerson J, giving the judgment of the Court).

[114] *Lloyds Bank plc v Independent Insurance Co Ltd* [2000] QB 110.

[115] *David Securities Pty Ltd v Commonwealth Bank of Australia* [1992] HCA 48, (1992) 175 CLR 353, 376 [40] (Mason CJ, Deane, Toohey, Gaudron and HcHugh JJ).

As with other juristic reasons, the onus lies on the defendant to show that the juristic reason exists by proving that he received the benefit by way of satisfaction of an existing right.[116] The plaintiff must then, by reply, negate the juristic reason by attacking the basis of the right, as where the contract on which the right depends is void or voidable (and rescinded).[117] Alternatively, the plaintiff can dispute the satisfaction of the right by proving that the payment was not effective to discharge the debt held by the defendant or, as we have seen above, argue that the right was not presently exercisable. A good example is *Barclays Bank Ltd v WJ Simms Son & Cooke (Southern) Ltd.*[118] In that case, the defendant presented a cheque for payment to the plaintiff bank. The bank paid out, having overlooked a stop order that had been placed on the cheque. Justice Robert Goff found that this causative mistake gave rise to a right to restitution of the payment from the defendant. Further, the defence of good consideration (receipt in satisfaction of a right) was not satisfied because the plaintiff bank's payment to the defendant was not authorised by the client and was not effective to discharge the debt.

VI. Statutory Terms, Public Policy and Statutory Policy as a Juristic Reason

Another juristic basis which a defendant can assert to retain an enrichment is where restitution would contravene another legal rule, including a rule of public policy. The other legal rule is a juristic reason to retain the benefit. An example where a claim for restitution failed because of public policy is *Parkinson v College of Ambulance Ltd.*[119] In that case, Colonel Parkinson paid £10,000 to the defendant charity in reliance on a fraudulent misrepresentation made by the charity's secretary. The representation was that the secretary or the charity was in a position to secure Colonel Parkinson a knighthood if the sum was paid. When the plaintiff realised that he had been fooled, he sought restitution in an action for money had and received. Justice Lush denied the claim, noting that it was:

> derogatory to the dignity of the Sovereign who bestows the honour … [Further] it would produce, or might produce, most mischievous consequences. It would tend to induce the person who was to procure the title to use improper means to obtain it, because he had his own interests to consider. It would tend to make him conceal facts as to the fitness of the proposed recipient.[120]

The most common circumstance where a defendant relies upon a juristic reason concerning another rule of law arises where a defendant alleges that an order for restitution would

[116] *Cook's Construction Pty Ltd v SFS 007.298.633 Pty Ltd* [2009] QCA 75, (2009) 254 ALR 661 [65]–[67] (Keane JA), [133]–[135] (Fraser JA), (Daubney JA concurring in both judgments).

[117] *Barclays Bank Ltd v WJ Simms Son & Cooke (Southern) Ltd* [1980] QB 677, 695 (Robert Goff J); *Ward & Co v Wallis* [1900] 1 QB 675, 679 (Kennedy J).

[118] *Barclays Bank Ltd v WJ Simms Son & Cooke (Southern) Ltd* [1980] QB 677. See also *Crantrave Ltd (in liq) v Lloyds Bank plc* [2000] QB 917, 923–24 (Pill LJ; May LJ concurring in a separate judgment); *Customs and Excise Commissioners v National Westminster Bank plc* [2002] EWHC 2204 [15] (Judge Rich QC); *Gulf International Bank BSC v Albaraka Islamic Bank BSC* [2004] EWCA Civ 416 [24] (Clarke LJ, Sedley LJ and Butler-Sloss P agreeing); *Jones v Churcher* [2009] EWHC 722 [50]–[55] (Judge Havelock-Allan QC).

[119] *Parkinson v College of Ambulance Ltd* [1925] 2 KB 1.

[120] ibid 13.

be inconsistent with the express or implied terms of legislation or the policy of particular legislation. In England, the rules of 'illegality' can only be described as a mess. Different tests have been proposed. These include a causal test,[121] an 'inextricable link' test,[122] a test that asks whether the plaintiff needs to plead his or her illegality[123] and an analysis that weighs the competing policy considerations.[124] In general, a dominant approach has been the highly technical and sometimes arbitrary ground[125] of asking whether the plaintiff is forced to *plead* the illegality in order to obtain relief (the '*Bowmakers* rule').[126] Lord Neuberger has suggested that 'the proper approach to the defence of illegality needs to be addressed by this court (certainly with a panel of seven and conceivably with a panel of nine Justices) as soon as appropriately possible'.[127]

In the most recent case of *Jetivia SA v Bilta (UK) Ltd*,[128] the UK Supreme Court considered whether the 'defence' of illegality operated to defeat an action by a company against the directors who caused it to act dishonestly, for damages representing the losses flowing from that dishonesty. The Court decided that it did not. However, a majority of the Court reached that conclusion on the restricted ground that the directors' dishonest acts could not be attributed (as a matter of agency law) to the company. Given that it was, therefore, strictly unnecessary to apply the illegality defence, and given what it perceived as a lack of full argument on the point, a majority of the Court refused to reconsider the *Bowmakers* rule.[129]

In Australia, by contrast, the *Bowmakers* rule has been discarded in favour of a fresh approach to illegality, which identifies the defence in terms of the overriding principle of coherence. The clarity of this approach may be a good reason for it to be adopted in England, as it appears to be one possible direction based on a number of more recent English decisions.[130] Under this approach, a plaintiff will be denied recovery only where

[121] *Gray v Thames Trains Ltd* [2009] UKHL 33, [2009] 1 AC 1339.

[122] *Cross v Kirkby* (CA, 18 February 2000).

[123] *Tinsley v Milligan* [1994] 1 AC 340.

[124] *Hounga v Allen* [2014] UKSC 47, [2014] 1 WLR 2889.

[125] The rule has now come under sustained judicial criticism and confinement in England in the context of torts: see *Gray v Thames Trains Ltd* [2008] EWCA Civ 713, [2009] 2 WLR 351 [13]–[20] (the Court); *Gray v Thames Trains Ltd* [2009] UKHL 33, [2009] 1 AC 1339 [30]–[31] (Lord Hoffmann), [61]–[69] (Lord Rodger), (Lord Scott concurring with both judgments); *Stone & Rolls Ltd (in liq) v Moore Stephens (A Firm)* [2009] UKHL 39, [2009] 1 AC 1391; *Safeway Stores Ltd v Twigger* [2010] EWCA Civ 1472, [2011] 2 All ER 841; *Hounga v Allen* [2014] UKSC 47, [2014] 1 WLR 2889 [42]–[52] (Lord Wilson JSC). Cf *Les Laboratoires Servier v Apotex Inc* [2014] UKSC 55, [2015] AC 430, which did not cite *Hounga v Allen*. See also the criticisms of McHugh J in *Nelson v Nelson* [1995] HCA 25, (1995) 184 CLR 538, 609 [26].

[126] Named after *Bowmakers Ltd v Barnet Instruments Ltd* [1945] KB 65, although the rule rested on a misunderstanding of an obiter dictum of Lord Mansfield in *Holman v Johnson* (1775) 1 Cowp 341, 98 ER 1120. See also *Tinsley v Milligan* [1994] 1 AC 340; *Tribe v Tribe* [1996] Ch 107.

[127] *Bilta (UK) Ltd (in liq) v Nazir (No 2)* [2015] UKSC 23, [2015] 2 WLR 1168 [15].

[128] ibid; *Patel v Mirza* [2014] EWCA Civ 1047, [2015] Ch 271 [22] (Rimer LJ), [102] (Vos LJ). Cf the approach by Gloster LJ, [65], adopting the stultification approach to illegality.

[129] *Bilta (UK) Ltd (in liq) v Nazir (No 2)* [2015] UKSC 23, [2015] 2 WLR 1168 [15]–[16] (Lord Neuberger PSC; Lord Clarke and Lord Carnwath JJSC agreeing), [34] (Lord Mance JSC), [105] (Lord Sumption).

[130] *Haugesund Kommune v Depfa ACS Bank* [2010] EWCA Civ 579, [2012] QB 549; *Langsam v Beachcroft LLP* [2011] EWHC 1451 [253] (Roth J); *Patel v Mirza* [2014] EWCA Civ 1047, [2015] Ch 271 [65] (Gloster LJ); *Hounga v Allen* [2014] UKSC 47, [2014] WLR 2889 [42]–[52] (Lord Wilson JSC), discussed at length by Lords Toulson and Hodge JJSC in *Bilta (UK) Ltd (in liq) v Nazir (No 2)* [2015] UKSC 23, [2015] 2 WLR 1168 [171]–[174], see also at [129] and adopted by Sales LJ, with whom McCombe LJ agreed, in *R (on the application of Best) v Chief Land Registrar* [2015] EWCA Civ 17 [70].

that result is required by the terms or policy of the statute or the common law principle that has been infringed.[131] In other words, the only rational objection to allowing recovery in respect of an illegal transaction is that it would stultify, or make nonsense of, the law's prohibition.[132] Where recovery would not result in stultification of the law, it should be permitted. In *Nelson v Nelson*, McHugh J expressed the circumstances in which a claim would be refused in the following terms:

> (a) the statute discloses an intention that those rights should be unenforceable in all circumstances; or (b)(i) the sanction of refusing to enforce those rights is not disproportionate to the seriousness of the unlawful conduct; (ii) the imposition of the sanction is necessary, having regard to the terms of the statute, to protect its objects or policies; and (iii) the statute does not disclose an intention that the sanctions and remedies contained in the statute are to be the only legal consequences of a breach of the statute or the frustration of its policies.[133]

These categories are not exhaustive or self-exclusive. In particular, as French CJ, Crennan, Kiefel and Bell JJ recently emphasised in *Gnych v Polish Club Ltd*,[134] 'the consequence of illegality is a matter of statutory construction whatever category of illegality is involved'. Close attention must therefore be paid to the terms and purpose of the statute in every case. An example of the first category of claim (category (a)) is *Sevastopoulos v Spanos*.[135] In that case, a builder brought an action for restitution of the reasonable value of work performed pursuant to an oral variation to a contract. Section 19 of the House Contract Guarantee Act 1987 (Vic) provided that 'the builder is not entitled to recover in any court the cost of any work performed or material supplied under the variation unless the variation is in writing and signed' by each of the parties. Justice Beach of the Supreme Court of Victoria concluded that the statute in its terms expressly excluded a claim for recovery whether based in contract, unjust enrichment (*indebitatus assumpsit*) or otherwise. His Honour distinguished

[131] *Nelson v Nelson* [1995] HCA 25, (1995) 184 CLR 538; *Miller v Miller* [2011] HCA 9, (2011) 242 CLR 446; *Equuscorp Pty Ltd v Haxton; Equuscorp Pty Ltd v Bassat; Equuscorp Pty Ltd v Cunningham's Warehouse Sales Pty Ltd* [2012] HCA 7, (2012) 246 CLR 498, applied in *Redwood Anti-Ageing Pty Ltd v Knowles* [2013] NSWSC 508, (2013) 101 IPR 358 [119] (White J); *Gnych v Polish Club Ltd* [2015] HCA 23, (2015) 89 ALJR 658. The precise scope of the principle and, in particular, the extent to which it is controlled by the language of the statute is discussed in *Plan B Trustees Ltd v Parker (No 2)* [2013] WASC 216, (2013) 11 ASTLR 242 [92]–[96] (Edelman J) and further below at pp 161–62. For a recent example, using the equitable language of the 'clean hands' bar, see *Nu Line Construction Group Pty Ltd v Fowler* [2012] NSWSC 587, (2012) 16 BPR 31,011 [299]–[309] (Ward J). Cf *Alexiadis v Zirpiadis* [2013] SASCFC 64, (2013) 302 ALR 148, where the parties' elaborate evasions during the trial regarding the purpose of an impugned transaction (suspected by the courts at first instance and on appeal to hide an illegal transaction) undermined the plaintiff's ability to establish the basis of his claim for restitution.

[132] *Boissevain v Weil* [1950] AC 327, 341 (Lord Radcliffe), discussed by P Birks, 'Recovering Value Transferred under an Illegal Contract' (2000) 1 *Theoretical Inquiries in Law* 155, 169.

[133] *Nelson v Nelson* [1995] HCA 25, (1995) 184 CLR 538, 613 [38] (McHugh J), following *Yango Pastoral Company Pty Ltd v First Chicago Australia Ltd* [1978] HCA 42, (1978) 139 CLR 410, 429 [27] (Mason J) and *St John Shipping Corporation v Joseph Rank Ltd* [1957] 1 QB 267. See also *Equuscorp Pty Ltd v Haxton; Equuscorp Pty Ltd v Bassat; Equuscorp Pty Ltd v Cunningham's Warehouse Sales Pty Ltd* [2012] HCA 7, (2012) 246 CLR 498 [23] (French CJ, Crennan and Kiefel JJ) and *Fitzgerald v FJ Leonhardt Pty Ltd* [1997] HCA 17, (1997) 189 CLR 215, 229–31 (McHugh and Gummow JJ).

[134] *Gnych v Polish Club Ltd* [2015] HCA 23, (2015) 89 ALJR 658 [36].

[135] *Sevastopoulos v Spanos* [1991] 2 VR 194; see also *Kasumu v Baba-Egbe* [1956] AC 539; *Marshall v Marshall* [1999] 1 Qd R 173, 176 (McPherson J); *Sutton v Zullo Enterprises Pty Ltd* [1998] QCA 417, [2000] 2 Qd R 196; *Cook's Construction Pty Ltd v SFS 007.298.633 Pty Ltd* [2009] QCA 75, (2009) 254 ALR 661.

the case from *Pavey & Matthews Pty Ltd v Paul*.[136] In that case, the High Court allowed a builder to recover restitution of the reasonable value of work done under an oral building agreement that was unenforceable by the builder pursuant to section 45 of the Building Licence Act 1971 (NSW). The basis for distinguishing *Pavey* was that section 45 did not disclose any legislative intent to penalise the builder, beyond making the agreement itself unenforceable by him against any other party.[137] It followed that the builder was entitled to maintain his claim for restitution of the value of the benefits conferred pursuant to the contract because this would not stultify the legislative intent.[138] Because of the language of the legislation, Beach J held that the opposite was true in *Sevastopoulos v Spanos*.[139]

As for category (b), much will depend on a close analysis of the precise terms of the statute and its underlying policy. Courts should be slow to conclude that a statutory regime precludes a claim in unjust enrichment in the absence of clear expression to that effect in its terms. Further, as Gageler J recently emphasised in *Gnych v Polish Club Ltd*[140] the extent to which the statute imposing the prohibition expressly addresses the consequences of its breach is of particular significance, and is often decisive, in this enquiry. Where the statute makes elaborate provision for the consequences of breach, courts should be slow to add to those consequences additional outcomes, such as the denial of a claim in unjust enrichment that the contravenor would otherwise have. Where, unusually, further consequences of breach appear to be demanded, the court must be satisfied that the consequence of withholding the remedy is both proportionate to the seriousness of the illegality and not incongruous with the statutory scheme.[141]

The potential for different views to be reached about statutory policy is exemplified by the division of the High Court in *Equuscorp Pty Ltd v Haxton*.[142] The appellant (Equuscorp) was the assignee of loans made to the respondent investors. However, contrary to the relevant provisions of the Companies Code of each investor's home state, no prospectus or valid prospectus had been registered when the investors were offered what was a 'prescribed interest' within the terms of that section. Because the relevant loan agreements had been made solely to facilitate entry into the investment schemes they were unenforceable against the investors. This meant that the basis of the loans failed and the investors had a right to restitution. The critical question then became whether permitting restitution

[136] *Pavey & Matthews Pty Ltd v Paul* [1987] HCA 5, (1987) 162 CLR 221. See also *Gino D'Alessandro Constructions Pty Ltd v Powis* [1987] 2 Qd R 40, 54–56 (McPherson J; Connolly J and Derrington J concurring in separate judgments); *Mostia Constructions Pty Ltd v Cox* [1994] 2 Qd R 55.

[137] *Pavey & Matthews Pty Ltd v Paul* [1987] HCA 5 [23], (1987) 162 CLR 221, 262 (Deane J).

[138] See also *Tea Tree Gully Builders Co Pty Ltd v Martin* (1992) 59 SASR 344; *Australian Breeders Co-operative Society Ltd v Jones* (1997) 150 ALR 488; *Hurst v Vestcorp Ltd* (1988) 12 NSWLR 394; *Riley v Melrose Advertisers* (1915) 17 WALR 127.

[139] The dance that may follow between court and legislature on this approach to illegality is nicely described in *Cook's Construction Pty Ltd v SFS 007.298.633 Pty Ltd* [2009] QCA 75, (2009) 254 ALR 661 [53]–[59] (Keane JA; Daubney JA concurring); see also at [116]–[120] (Fraser JA). For a recent reconsideration of the issue consistent with this discussion, see *CMF Projects Pty Ltd v Riggall* [2014] QCA 318 [28]–[46] (Gotterson JA; Holmes and Morrison JJA concurring).

[140] *Gnych v Polish Club Ltd* [2015] HCA 23, (2015) 89 ALJR 658 [68]–[69], [73]. See also *Yango Pastoral Company Pty Ltd v First Chicago Australia Ltd* [1978] HCA 42, (1978) 139 CLR 410, 429 [27] (Mason J).

[141] *Gnych v Polish Club Ltd* [2015] HCA 23, (2015) 89 ALJR 658 [75] (Gageler J) citing *Nelson v Nelson* [1995] HCA 25, (1995) 184 CLR 538, 612–13 [36] (Deane and Gummow JJ); *Fitzgerald v FJ Leonhardt Pty Ltd* [1997] HCA 17, (1997) 189 CLR 215, 229–30, 249–50 (McHugh and Gummow JJ).

[142] *Equuscorp Pty Ltd v Haxton; Equuscorp Pty Ltd v Bassat; Equuscorp Pty Ltd v Cunningham's Warehouse Sales Pty Ltd* [2012] HCA 7, (2012) 246 CLR 498.

would undermine or stultify the policy or purpose of the law. A majority of the High Court (French CJ, Crennan and Keifel JJ in one joint judgment, Gummow and Bell JJ in another), held that the appellant's claim to restitution was defeated on the ground of illegality. This was because to allow restitution would undermine the protective purpose of the statute, the object of which was to protect investors entering such investment schemes.[143] By contrast, Heydon J found that the policy of the statute did not exclude the appellant's restitutionary claim. Of key importance in this analysis were that the statutory scheme provided a full range of onerous sanctions for breach[144] and that it rendered the particular loan agreements unenforceable by the appellants.[145] Taken together, and in the absence of express exclusion of claims in unjust enrichment, the provisions constituted a statutory indication that the sanctions provided were sufficient to deal with any breach. Whilst Heydon J accepted that the statutory scheme could have as its aim protection of an identified class, it effected that protection by imposing criminal sanctions and rendering the contracts of loan unenforceable.[146] There was no call, therefore, for removing the appellant's claim in unjust enrichment which was independent of the impugned contracts.

Another example of category (b) concerning the policy of the statute concerns the effect of registration under the Torrens system of land title registration on any claim in unjust enrichment.[147] Again, this is a complex issue that requires close consideration of the relevant provisions in light of the purpose of the particular Torrens statute as revealed by its terms. In general, registration will not defeat many claims in unjust enrichment in England because, as a matter of statutory interpretation, the Land Registration Act 2002 introduces a very weak and qualified form of immediate indefeasibility. This permits challenge to registrations that have occurred as a result of mistake, undue influence or illegitimate pressure.[148] By contrast, where the purchaser is one step removed from the impugned transaction, the legislation operates to confer a 'deferred indefeasibility' in a far greater range of cases, so as to defeat any claim in unjust enrichment. This position stands in contrast to the position in Australia, where registration is much more likely to constitute a bar to unjust enrichment claims. This is because of the emphasis in the various state statutes of the principle of immediate indefeasibility, designed to protect registering proprietors not only from defects in prior title, but defects in the transaction leading to registration. This principle has only very limited exceptions, which will not generally apply to cases of unjust enrichment. After a slow start, Australian courts are starting more consistently to recognise the relevance of registration in defeating claims in unjust enrichment for restitution of rights pursuant to a constructive trust.[149] Unfortunately, it has not been appreciated that the principle of coherence demands that personal claims for restitution of value should likewise be subject to

143 ibid [45] (Black CJ, Crennan and Keifel JJ), [109]–[111] (Gummow and Bell JJ).

144 ibid [130].

145 ibid [123], [130].

146 ibid [130], [133].

147 Examined in detail in E Bant, 'Registration as a Defence to Claims in Unjust Enrichment: Australia and England Compared' [2011] (4) *The Conveyancer and Property Lawyer* 309.

148 Ss 28 and 29 are key to the scheme.

149 Following *Farah Constructions Pty Ltd v Say-Dee Pty Ltd* [2007] HCA 22, (2007) 230 CLR 89 [131]–[158] (the Court). See eg *Sze Tu v Lowe* [2014] NSWCA 462 [224]–[244] (Gleeson JA; Meagher and Barrett JJA concurring).

defeat on registration.[150] Allowing the claim for value thoroughly undermines the protection otherwise given on the defendant's registration and thereby the policy of the statute.

VII. Incapacity as a Juristic Reason

Incapacity is usually considered to be an independent defence. However, it is better understood as a collection of instances in which the courts refuse restitution because to allow a defendant to retain an enrichment would stultify some overriding public or legislative policy. There are four main types of legal incapacity: the doctrine of *ultra vires*, minority, mental incapacity, and intoxication. The particular public or legislative policy underpinning each category of incapacity constitutes a juristic reason to retain an enrichment. It follows that incapacity in and of itself will not always constitute a juristic reason to retain an enrichment. The overriding question is whether the particular policy of the law concerning capacity requires, in the interests of maintaining coherence in the law, that the defendant be entitled to retain the enrichment.

Westdeutsche Landesbank Girozentrale v Islington London Borough Council[151] demonstrates the distinction between the issues of incapacity and the presence of a juristic reason to retain an enrichment. This was one of a line of English cases[152] in which local authorities entered into interest rate swap contracts with financial institutions that were *ultra vires* the authorities.[153] In none of those cases did the incapacity of the authority operate to defeat its claim for restitution. Focus on the overriding question identified above explains why. In the context of investment transactions by public authorities, the doctrine of *ultra vires* is concerned to protect the public funds of the ratepayers. That policy is not undermined, but is rather promoted, by allowing restitution to a local authority that was a net loser in a swap contract. Allowing restitution protects the funds of the ratepayers. Even if the financial institution is the loser, the ratepayer's funds are not at risk by requiring the local authority to make restitution of the enrichment obtained at the expense of the *financial institution*. Consistently with this analysis, in *Westdeutsche*,[154] Lord Browne-Wilkinson (with whom Lords Slynn and Lloyd agreed) expressly overruled previous authority to the contrary,[155] and held that *ultra vires* was not a defence to the claim in unjust enrichment in that case.

The same analysis applies to other forms of incapacity. The policy behind denying contractual capacity to minors is to protect them from exploitation, their assumed youthful proclivity to act impulsively and without mature consideration and from the potentially crushing effects of significant long-term personal liability. The minority of the defendant will therefore operate as a juristic reason to retain an enrichment where, and to the extent

[150] *Riverwood Legion & Community Club Ltd v Repaja & Co Pty Ltd* [2015] NSWSC 383 [215]–[223] (Stevenson J); *Fistar v Riverwood Legion and Community Club Ltd* [2016] NSWCA 81 [82] (Leeming JA; Bathurst CJ and Sackville AJA concurring).

[151] *Westdeutsche Landesbank Girozentrale v Islington London Borough Council* [1996] UKHL 12, [1996] AC 669.

[152] See also *Kleinwort Benson Ltd v Lincoln City Council* [1998] UKHL 38, [1999] 2 AC 349 considered in Ch 8 pp 186–87.

[153] *Hazell v Hammersmith and Fulham London Borough Council* [1992] 2 AC 1.

[154] *Westdeutsche Landesbank Girozentrale v Islington London Borough Council* [1996] UKHL 12, [1996] AC 669, 710 (Lord Browne-Wilkinson), 718 (Lord Slynn), 738 (Lord Lloyd).

[155] *Sinclair v Brougham* [1914] AC 398.

that, those policies would be undermined by an order for restitution. Consistently with this approach, claims against minors for restitution of enrichment have generally been restricted by the courts in two ways. First, any personal claim against a minor for benefits received under an unenforceable contract is limited to the reasonable value of such benefits as the law deems are 'necessaries', or can be shown were used to purchase necessaries.[156] The protective policies of the law are not stultified where the claim is for restitution of the reasonable value of a 'necessary' enrichment received by the infant defendant. The second method of protecting minors from excessive personal liability is to restrict the plaintiff to a claim for restitution of the rights held or, perhaps better, restitution of the remaining value. On this approach, a creditor could bring an action to recover the amount of a loan against a bankrupt minor, but only on the ground that the creditor 'had a claim on his assets, not against him personally'.[157] As Lord Sumner stated in *R Leslie Ltd v Sheill*:[158] 'Restitution stopped where repayment began.' Restricting the plaintiff's remedy in this way ensures that the minor is protected from the personal consequences of his poor judgement while allowing recovery where the enrichment can still be identified. There are many examples of both methods being applied in cases of loans to minors: the minor will only be liable to make restitution of the amount of the loan to the extent that he retains the money or it was used to obtain necessaries.[159] A similarly protective approach is taken with cases of mental incapacity (including severe intoxication), which have similar underlying policies to cases of minority.[160]

VIII. Court Orders as a Juristic Reason

A defendant is prima facie entitled to any benefit conferred on him by a court order. In *Crown Prosecution Service v Eastenders Group*,[161] a receiver was appointed to protect and preserve assets of companies the subject of criminal proceedings and was given a right of remuneration against the company assets. The appointment was set aside by the English Court of Appeal. The receiver sought remuneration for his services during the period of his appointment. The Supreme Court approved the view of Laws LJ that the 'setting aside

[156] That is, articles and services 'fit to maintain the [defendant] in the state, station, and degree in life' in which he moves: *Peters v Fleming* (1840) 6 M & W 42, 47; 151 ER 314, 315 (Parke B); see also 48; 316 (Alderson B), 49; 316 (Rolfe B).

[157] *R Leslie Ltd v Sheill* [1914] 3 KB 607, 616 (Lord Sumner). See also *Re King, ex p The Unity Joint Stock Mutual Banking Association* (1858) 3 De G & J 63, 44 ER 1192.

[158] *R Leslie Ltd v Sheill* [1914] 3 KB 607, 618. See also 623–24 (Kennedy LJ), 627 (Lawrence J).

[159] *Ellis v Ellis* (1703) Comb 482, 90 ER 605; *Earle v Peale* (1711) 1 Salk 386, 91 ER 336; *R Leslie Ltd v Sheill* [1914] 3 KB 607; *Marlow v Pitfeild* (1719) 1 P Wms 558, 559; 24 ER 516, 517 affirmed in *Re National Permanent Benefit Building Society, ex p Williamson* (1869) LR 5 Ch App 309, 313 (Giffard LJ). See also *Martin v Gale* (1876) 4 Ch D 428, 431–32 (Jessel MR).

[160] On necessaries, see *Re Rhodes; Rhodes v Rhodes* (1890) 44 Ch D 94, 105 (Cotton LJ); *Re Brooks* (1903) 21 WN (NSW) 4, 5 (Simpson CJ in Eq); *McLaughlin v Freehill* [1908] HCA 15, (1908) 5 CLR 858, 861–62 (Griffith CJ), 864 (Isaacs J). On restricting a plaintiff to a proprietary claim, see *Re Beavan; Davies Banks & Co v Beavan* [1912] 1 Ch 196, 201–02 (Neville J); *Harris v Lee* (1718) 1 P Wms 482, 483; 24 ER 482, 482; *Jenner v Morris* (1861) 3 De G F & J 45, 51–52; 45 ER 795, 797–98 (Lord Campbell LC), 55–56; 779 (Turner LJ); *Re Wood's Estate; Davidson v Wood* (1863) 1 De G J & S 465, 467; 46 ER 185, 186 (Bruce LJ).

[161] *Crown Prosecution Service v Eastenders Group* [2014] UKSC 26, [2015] AC 1.

of the receivership order by the Court of Appeal did not render the order under which the receiver was appointed a nullity *ab initio*. The Crown Court order had the force of law until it was set aside and the setting aside of the order did not retrospectively deprive the receiver of his right to remuneration under it.'[162] This reasoning must be applied carefully. The obvious reason why the setting aside of the receivership order did not deprive the receiver of his right to remuneration was because that right to remuneration was not dependent upon the receivership order. The right to remuneration arose because the receiver had made payments and provided services on a basis which failed.[163] Failure of basis is an unjust factor that is considered in Chapter 11. In contrast, where an enrichment is provided because of a court order then the quashed court order will *not* usually be a sufficient reason to retain the benefit. We will see in Chapter 13 that the unjust factor requiring restitution of money paid under a court order that is later reversed has been founded in mistake in some cases, in others on failure of consideration and in yet others on a basis outside the unjust enrichment considerations between the parties, founded on the policy imperative to uphold the integrity of the appeal process.

Although the quashing of a court order will usually require restitution of enrichment provided under that court order, the juristic reason provided by the court order might sometimes justify retention of an enrichment. In *State of New South Wales v Kable*,[164] the High Court emphasised that in the Australian constitutional context the decision of a superior court constitutes a valid and justifying ground for some actions taken during the period the decision is in force, even if it is later overturned.[165] For this reason the State of New South Wales was found not liable to compensate Mr Kable for false imprisonment, when he had been jailed by order of the New South Wales Supreme Court pursuant to legislation that was subsequently found to be void. Although the legislation was void, the High Court found that, during the relevant period, the imprisonment was nonetheless lawful because it was carried out pursuant to orders of a Supreme Court of Record.[166] The fact that those orders could be set aside (as the High Court proceeded to do) did not mean that they ceased being a valid reason for the act of imprisonment at the time it occurred.[167] It followed that no tort had been committed, and there was no right to compensation.

However, two points need to be made. The first is that it will be very rare that a defendant could point to any basis during the period in which the order was in force as a reason to retain money, particularly if an appeal has been brought so that the defendant knows that her right to retain the value of the payment is insecure. Secondly, the relevant enrichment is not the actual use to which a defendant puts a judgment sum where the judgment is later reversed. The actionable enrichment is the *opportunity* to use the money, not the *actual* use made by the defendant of the sum.[168] As we saw in Chapter 44, the opportunity to use the money is measured by its value to a reasonable person in the position of the defendant.

[162] ibid [73], [84] (Lord Toulson; Lady Hale, and Lords Kerr, Wilson and Hughes agreeing).
[163] ibid [108] (Lord Toulson; Lady Hale, and Lords Kerr, Wilson and Hughes agreeing).
[164] *State of New South Wales v Kable* [2013] HCA 26, (2013) 252 CLR 118.
[165] ibid [32]–[36] (French CJ, Hayne, Crennan, Kiefel, Bell and Keane JJ), [46]–[47] (Gageler J).
[166] ibid [40]–[43] (French CJ, Hayne, Crennan, Kiefel, Bell and Keane JJ), [46]–[47] (Gageler J).
[167] See also *Crown Prosecution Service v Eastenders Group* [2014] UKSC 26, [2015] AC 1 [73], [84] (Lord Toulson; Lady Hale, and Lords Kerr, Wilson and Hughes agreeing).
[168] See Ch 4 pp 59–61.

It follows that the fact that a defendant may be entitled to make a profit from the judgment sum does not say anything about his restitutionary liability.

IX. A Juristic Reason Must Confer a Right to Retain the Enrichment

We commenced this chapter by noting that the need for coherence in the law is the underlying reason why a plaintiff must negate a juristic reason before an enrichment will be unjust. When confronted with the question of whether restitution should be made, the law of unjust enrichment should not contradict other branches of the law. Exceptionally, however, a valid juristic reason to receive an enrichment may not entitle a defendant to retain the enrichment.[169] We saw an example earlier in this chapter when discussing the case of *Roxborough v Rothmans of Pall Mall Ltd*.[170] As that and other cases demonstrated, a plaintiff may be entitled to restitution of a benefit conferred pursuant to an otherwise valid contractual obligation, where the basis for that contractual obligation has itself wholly failed. The contractual obligation provided a right to receive the enrichment but when the basis for that obligation failed, there was no right to retain the enrichment.

The same analysis applies in cases involving frustration. It was explained in Chapter 3 that a defendant's future rights will be discharged when a plaintiff establishes that the basis of those rights has wholly failed due to a frustrating event. The plaintiff obtains a discharge of those future rights. In substance, the consequence of frustration is that the contract is void *in futuro*. However, if the plaintiff has already transferred a benefit pursuant to the contract then although there was a right to receive that enrichment there will no longer be a right to retain it after the frustrating event. This was the effect of the decision in *Fibrosa Spolka Akcyjna v Fairbairn Lawson Combe Barbour Ltd*.[171]

Further examples where a right to receive a payment does not equate to a right to retain the payment are seen in the context of contribution and recoupment, addressed in Chapter 12.

In cases of recoupment, the plaintiff's liability to a third party to pay the defendant's debt (such as arises under a contract of suretyship) is secondary to the primary liability of the defendant. The contract obliges the defendant to repay the plaintiff, and in that sense gives the third party a right to the benefit of having its obligation to the plaintiff discharged. But between the third party and the defendant, the third party has no right to retain that benefit to the extent that it exceeds the 'proper share' or 'burden' to be borne by the defendant, consistently with the nature of the joint obligation.

The same principle applies in statutory contexts to permit restitution in some cases, notwithstanding the existence of a valid, justifying statute. In the last chapter, we considered

[169] See discussion of Lord Mance (with whom Lords Clarke, Carnwath and Hodge agreed) in *International Energy Group Ltd v Zurich Insurance plc UK Branch* [2015] UKSC 33, [2015] 2 WLR 1471 [68]–[72].

[170] *Roxborough v Rothmans of Pall Mall Australia Ltd* [2001] HCA 68, (2001) 208 CLR 516.

[171] *Fibrosa Spolka Akcyjna v Fairbairn Lawson Combe Barbour Ltd* [1942] UKHL 4, [1943] AC 32, discussed in Ch 6 p 135 and Ch 11 p 256.

Deutsche Morgan Grenfell plc v Inland Revenue Commissioners[172] and *Investment Trust Companies (In Liquidation) v Revenue and Customs Commissioners*[173] in which the defendant was entitled to receive taxation benefits under domestic UK legislation. However, in both cases, restitution was permitted: although Her Majesty's Revenue Commissioners had a juristic reason to receive the taxation payments, a European obligation required that they did not have a juristic reason to *retain* it.

The lesson of this section is that although a valid juristic reason will often operate to defeat a plaintiff's claim to restitution for unjust enrichment, it must not be forgotten that the reason behind the general rule is one of coherence. It follows that restitution will be permitted notwithstanding the existence of a juristic reason to receive the benefit if considerations of coherence of the law have the effect that the juristic reason is not one which continues to permit the retention of the benefit.

X. Conclusion

This chapter has been devoted to exploring the main categories of juristic reasons that must be negated in order for any claim in unjust enrichment to succeed. We have seen that these reasons include contract, deeds of gift, deeds where the consideration moves to a third party, where the receipt is in satisfaction of right, where statute justifies the retention of the enrichment, cases of incapacity and the justifying effect of court orders. These are just some of the main, and well recognised, examples of juristic reasons which justify retention of an enrichment. There are other categories which are more controversial. Suppose a plaintiff unilaterally promises, without consideration, to pay a defendant $100 but never intends to honour that promise. If the plaintiff later pays the defendant by mistake, can the defendant point to the promise as a juristic reason to retain the benefit even though the promise is not binding in law? Much will depend upon whether the institution of promising is regarded as a basic principle of the law independently of the institution of contract.

There are ways in which a plaintiff may be able to negate a juristic reason raised by the defendant, such as by impugning its existence or ongoing validity. But unless a plaintiff negates one of these juristic reasons, a defendant will be entitled to retain the enrichment. The single most important lesson is that the underlying question when any juristic reason is asserted is whether the claim in unjust enrichment would undermine or stultify some overriding principle or prohibition of the law.

[172] *Deutsche Morgan Grenfell Group plc v Inland Revenue Commissioners* [2006] UKHL 49; [2007] 1 AC 558.
[173] *Investment Trust Companies (in liq) v Revenue and Customs Commissioners* [2015] EWCA Civ 82.

Part III

The Unjust Factors

8

Mistake

Contents

I. Introduction

The first unjust factor we will consider is mistake. Claims for restitution of money paid by mistake are the most common claims in unjust enrichment. In *Fibrosa Spolka Akcyjna v Fairbairn Lawson Combe Barbour Ltd*[1] Lord Wright said that 'It is clear that any civilized system of law is bound to provide remedies for cases of what has been called unjust enrichment … a particular species of the category [is] money paid under a mistake of fact'. In the sixth century, in Justinian's *Digest*, Paul gave the example that a payment to a person mistakenly believed to have assisted with the payer's business affairs can be recovered.[2]

Mistake is now extremely well established as an unjust factor in unjust enrichment. This chapter focuses upon the operation of mistake as an unjust factor which vitiates a transaction (and may also permit a claim based on tracing into causally related transactions). The unjust factor of mistake consists of the following elements: (1) a mistake of fact or law; and (2) the mistake having caused or contributed (as a factor) to the plaintiff's decision to enter

[1] *Fibrosa Spolka Akcyjna v Fairbairn Lawson Combe Barbour Ltd* [1942] UKHL 4, [1943] AC 32, 61 [17].
[2] CH Monro (tr), *The Digest of Justinian*, vol II (Cambridge, Cambridge University Press, 1909) 12.6.65.2.

the transaction that enriched the defendant.[3] Beneath this simple test there lurk some extremely difficult conceptual issues. When is a plaintiff mistaken? Does ignorance of a relevant fact or law count as a mistake? What is the difference between a mistake and a misprediction? Is risk-taking behaviour by the plaintiff relevant in mistake cases? If it is, what are the substantive reasons that support the legal conclusion that a plaintiff took an undue risk? Section II in this chapter addresses these questions in considering what is meant by a mistake. Section III considers the evolution of the law to the modern approach, in which all types of mistake (common law or equitable, mistaken payments, provision of goods or services, or mistakes of fact or law) are treated alike but the defendant is protected through the defence of change of position. And section IV examines the second requirement of the unjust factor, which is that the mistake must cause or contribute to the plaintiff's decision to enter the transaction that enriched the defendant.

Although this chapter focuses on mistake as an unjust factor or reason for restitution, it should not be forgotten that a successful action for unjust enrichment also requires a plaintiff to negate any juristic reason that entitles the defendant to retain the enrichment. Mistake can also be a way to negate a juristic reason to retain an enrichment. This was addressed in Chapter 7.

II. The Meaning of Mistake

A. The Definition of Mistake

Although it is unusual to encounter a comprehensive definition of mistake,[4] the best definition is that a mistake is made when a person's decision is based on incorrect data.[5] Although this concept of mistake assumes that it is possible to know the 'true' state of affairs at any particular moment in time, courts have not generally entertained epistemological objections of this nature.[6] A narrower definition, which would meet the criticism of an inability to know a true state of affairs, is advanced by Dr Sheehan. He argues that a mistake involves 'a belief in something that can, at the time it is acted upon, be proven not to be the case.'[7]

[3] *David Securities Pty Ltd v Commonwealth Bank of Australia* [1992] HCA 48, (1992) 175 CLR 353; *Barclays Bank Ltd v WJ Simms Son & Cooke (Southern) Ltd* [1980] QB 677; *Deutsche Morgan Grenfell Group plc v Inland Revenue Commissioners* [2006] UKHL 49, [2007] 1 AC 558.

[4] *Barrow v Isaacs & Son* [1891] 1 QB 417 425, (Kay LJ): 'Very wisely, as I presume to think, the Courts have abstained from giving any general definition of what amounts to mistake.'

[5] *Great Peace Shipping Ltd v Tsavliris Salvage (International) Ltd* [2002] EWCA Civ 1407, [2003] QB 679 [28] (Lord Phillips MR): 'an erroneous belief'; *Roles v Pascall & Sons* [1911] 1 KB 982, 987 (Buckley LJ): '[a] mistake exists when a person erroneously thinks that one state of facts exists when, in reality, another state of facts exists'; *Barrow v Isaacs & Son* [1891] 1 QB 417. 420 (Lord Esher MR): '[thinking] that one thing was in existence, whereas something else was in existence'; *Westpac Banking Corporation v Hilliard* [2006] VSC 470 [211] (Hansen J): 'a positive belief in the existence of something which does not exist but also may include sheer ignorance of something relevant to the transaction in hand', approved on appeal in *Hilliard v Westpac Banking Corporation* [2009] VSCA 211, (2009) 25 VR 139 [68] (Maxwell P, Dodds-Streeton JA and Osborn AJA).

[6] An exception is the reference by Lord Hoffmann to Schrödinger's cat in *Kleinwort Benson Ltd v Lincoln City Council* [1998] UKHL 38, [1999] 2 AC 349, 399.

[7] D Sheehan, 'What Is a Mistake?' (2000) 20 *Legal Studies* 538, 538; a definition repeated at 539, and developed at 540–41 and 545–49.

This definition is too narrow for two reasons. First, it is irrelevant that it might have been impossible for a plaintiff to access sufficient information to prove her mistake at the time she made it. A plaintiff's decision will be impaired if it is based upon incorrect data even if that data could not be obtained at the time of the mistake. Of course, the plaintiff must be able to prove at the time of trial that the data upon which she based her decision was incorrect at the earlier date. However, there is nothing in the concept of mistake itself which requires that the necessary dissonance between the plaintiff's state of belief and objective reality must have been provable at the time it operated. Second, the restriction is contrary to the common understanding of what constitutes a mistake. Suppose, prior to the advent of DNA testing, I pay you money because you and I both believe that you are my lost brother. There are no family members alive, and no documentary or other evidence in existence that would indicate the contrary. Several years later, the advent of DNA testing technology reveals that you are not my brother. I was mistaken when I made the payment, notwithstanding that the mistake could not have been proved at that time.[8]

B. Ignorance of a Relevant Fact

Mistakes are not restricted to decisions based on consciously identified, incorrect data. As the High Court of Australia noted in *David Securities Pty Ltd v Commonwealth Bank of Australia*, mistakes can also include 'sheer ignorance' of a fact or matter relevant to the transaction.[9] Thus, in *David Securities*, the plaintiff alleged that the impugned payments were made in ignorance of a legislative provision that rendered void the contractual covenant pursuant to which the payments were made. The High Court held that, in principle, this qualified as an actionable mistake. The High Court remitted the case back to the trial judge to decide whether the mistake had caused the payments.[10] The same approach was taken by the UK Supreme Court in *Pitt v Holt*, which considered that ignorance could constitute a relevant mistake where it informed a tacit but incorrect assumption upon which a decision was based.[11] This definition of mistake includes cases where the plaintiff once knew of the fact but was later ignorant of it because it had been forgotten. An example of this kind of mistake is *Lady Hood of Avalon v MacKinnon*,[12] where the plaintiff made an appointment to her elder daughter by deed poll, forgetting that she had already provided for her.[13]

[8] This is based on an example given in A Burrows, *The Law of Restitution*, 2nd edn (London, Butterworths, 2002) 156; see now 3rd edn (Oxford, Oxford University Press, 2011) 228.

[9] *David Securities Pty Ltd v Commonwealth Bank of Australia* [1992] HCA 48, (1992) 175 CLR 353, 369 [27] (Mason CJ, Deane, Toohey, Gaudron and McHugh JJ), citing PH Winfield, 'Mistake of Law' (1943) 59 *Law Quarterly Review* 327, 327; see also *Commissioner of State Revenue (Vic) v Royal Insurance Australia Ltd* [1994] HCA 61, (1994) 182 CLR 51; *Mercantile Mutual Health Ltd v Commissioner of Stamp Duties* [2002] QCA 356, [2003] 2 Qd R 515; *Hilliard v Westpac Banking Corporation* [2009] VSCA 211, (2009) 25 VR 139. Cf *Commonwealth v Davis Samuel Pty Ltd (No 7)* [2013] ACTSC 146, (2013) 282 FLR 1 [1690]–[1707] (Refshauge J), perhaps better understood as involving the unjust factor of 'no intention to benefit'; see Ch 12 p 282.

[10] *David Securities Pty Ltd v Commonwealth Bank of Australia* [1992] HCA 48, (1992) 175 CLR 353, 386 [62] (Mason CJ, Deane, Toohey, Gaudron and McHugh JJ).

[11] *Pitt v Holt* [2013] UKSC 26, [2013] 2 AC 108 [105]–[108] (Lord Walker, delivering the judgment of the Court).

[12] *Lady Hood of Avalon v MacKinnon* [1909] 1 Ch 476, discussed in *Pitt v Holt* [2013] UKSC 26, [2013] 2 AC 108 [106].

[13] See also *Kelly v Solari* (1841) 9 M & W 54, 152 ER 24; *Barclays Bank Ltd v WJ Simms Son & Cooke (Southern) Ltd* [1980] QB 677; *Simos v National Bank of Australasia Ltd* (1976) 10 ACTR 4, (1976) 45 FLR 97.

It may be objected that by including cases of ignorance, the concept of mistake becomes too broad. In particular, the objection might be that it is extremely common to be ignorant of, or to have forgotten, facts that might have changed a plaintiff's decision. For this reason, in *Pitt v Holt*, the Supreme Court excluded cases of 'mere causative ignorance' from the definition of an actionable mistake and also insisted that the mistake be sufficiently serious.[14] The exclusion of cases of 'mere' ignorance still permits the examples described above where the matter forgotten informed the positive assumptions on which a plaintiff based her decision. However, the Supreme Court's insistence upon sufficient seriousness invites arbitrary distinctions based upon some external judgment concerning the seriousness of the plaintiff's mistake. As we will see below, this aspect of the test can be very problematic. A better approach, which is adopted in some Australian decisions, is to require only that any mistake is sufficient provided that it was a factor which contributed to the decision to enter the transaction that enriched the defendant. To the extent that unexpressed, tacit assumptions contribute to a decision then any concerns about excessive restitution can be mitigated through the operation of the defence of change of position.

C. Mistakes and Mispredictions

Mistakes are commonly contrasted with mispredictions. Mispredictions occur when a person is in possession of all the correct, current data, but he predicts (incorrectly) what will happen in the future. His decision is not impaired at the time of transaction, as it is in the case of mistake. Rather, he acts on the basis of an assessment of what might happen in the future, thereby taking a risk that his prediction will turn out to be incorrect. As Professor Birks said, 'To act on the basis of a prediction is to accept the risk of disappointment.'[15] Hence, Birks argued that a misprediction is not a basis for restitution.[16]

Although the distinction between mistakes and mispredictions appears clear in theory, it can be difficult to separate the two concepts in practice. In *Dextra Bank & Trust Co Ltd v Bank of Jamaica*,[17] the plaintiff ('Dextra') was induced by fraudsters to pay nearly US$3 million to the defendant ('BOJ'). Dextra relied on two mistakes. The first was that Dextra believed that the BOJ had previously agreed to take a loan from Dextra. The Privy Council accepted that this was a mistake of fact, but held that it was not causative of the payment, and so it was not a basis for restitution.[18] The second mistake was that Dextra believed that its payment was made as part of a loan transaction. But in delivering the advice to the Privy Council, Lords Bingham and Goff held that this was not a mistake of fact. They considered that it was a misprediction about a future transaction, because at the time Dextra handed its cheque to its agent, no loan transaction was in place.[19] This analysis shows the fine line

[14] *Pitt v Holt* [2013] UKSC 26, [2013] 2 AC 108 [105]–[108], [114] (Lord Walker, delivering the judgment of the Court).

[15] P Birks, *An Introduction to the Law of Restitution* (Oxford, Clarendon Press, 1985) 147.

[16] *Cadorange Pty Ltd (in liq) v Tanga Holdings Pty Ltd* (1990) 20 NSWLR 26, 32 (Young J); *Sunstar Fruit Pty Ltd v Cosmo* [1995] 2 Qd R 214, 225–27 (Derrington J); *Hookway v Racing Victoria Ltd* [2005] VSCA 310, (2005) 13 VR 444 [61]–[62] (Ormiston JA); *Re Magarey Farlam Lawyers Trust Accounts (No 3)* [2007] SASC 9, (2007) 96 SASR 337 [171] (Debelle J); *Lahoud v Lahoud* [2010] NSWSC 1297 [180] (Ward J); *Re Griffiths* [2008] EWHC 118 (Ch), [2009] Ch 162 [23]–[24] (Lewison J).

[17] *Dextra Bank & Trust Co Ltd v Bank of Jamaica* [2001] UKPC 50, [2002] 1 All ER (Comm) 193.

[18] ibid [30]. We discuss the issue of causation in section IV below.

[19] ibid [29].

between misprediction and mistake. For instance, if the time of the enrichment of BOJ was the moment when Dextra's agent handed the cheque to BOJ,[20] why was there not a mistake about the trustworthiness of the agent or the type of transaction in which Dextra was currently participating through its agent (in particular, whether Dextra held a valid promissory note which it required before its agent could pay over the cheque)?

Another reason for the difficulty in legally separating mispredictions and mistakes is that many mispredictions involve an exercise of judgement based on a mistake.[21] Further, whether a mistake was made can turn on the nicest point of timing as to when the facts upon which a decision was made changed, and hence became falsified. Both points are illustrated in the case of *Re Griffiths*.[22] In that case, Mr Griffiths entered a series of transactions designed to minimise his tax liability. This objective was dependent upon him surviving seven years after execution of the instruments. The object was defeated by his premature death from cancer. His executors sought to have all the transactions set aside for mistake.

Justice Lewison accepted the distinction between mistake and misprediction[23] and found that, at the time of entering into the first two transactions in 2003, the deceased had not yet developed lung cancer. Hence, there was no underlying mistake as to the state of his health that had contributed to him entering into the transaction. Rather, the deceased was merely labouring under a misprediction that he would live for the required period. By the time of the final transaction in 2004, his condition had changed and hence an operative mistake was present.[24] The result of the case therefore ultimately rested on a 'hair's breadth finding'[25] of the precise timing of the onset of the cancerous changes to Mr Griffith's cells.[26] This is unsatisfactory (especially because of the paucity of the evidence on which it was based).[27] It is also problematic when we consider that Mr Griffiths probably entered *all* the transactions on the basis of his assessment of *both* his present and future state of health. It is highly unlikely that Mr Griffiths had not assumed some baseline of current health when entering into the earlier transactions, albeit a baseline that (given his age) was liable to change at any moment.

As we will see in Chapter 11, relief from the consequences of a misprediction is not always denied in the law of unjust enrichment. Failure of the objective basis of the transaction that enriched the defendant is a ground upon which restitution can be awarded. The objective basis may involve a mistake or a misprediction. It is not enough, however, that any misprediction was the subjective basis on which a plaintiff proceeded. This restriction is necessary to prevent plaintiffs from recovering in cases where they have run the risk of error. This suggests that the better distinction is, therefore, not between mistakes and mispredictions, but a distinction between cases where the plaintiff has assumed the risk of being mistaken and those where the plaintiff has not. On this approach, the correctness of the result in *Re Griffiths* must be considered doubtful: as Lloyd LJ noted in the Court of Appeal in *Pitt v Holt*,[28] had the case been the subject of full adversarial argument,

[20] *Westpac Banking Corporation v ATL Pty Ltd* [1985] 2 Qd R 577.
[21] W Seah, 'Mispredictions, Mistakes and the Law of Unjust Enrichment' [2007] *Restitution Law Review* 93.
[22] *Re Griffiths* [2008] EWHC 118, [2009] Ch 162.
[23] ibid [23].
[24] *Pitt v Holt* [2013] UKSC 26, [2013] 2 AC 108 [98].
[25] ibid [113].
[26] Cf *Alcan Gove Pty Ltd v Zabic* [2015] HCA 33, (2015) 89 ALJR 845 [20] (the Court).
[27] *Pitt v Holt* [2013] UKSC 26, [2013] 2 AC 108 [112]–[113].
[28] *Pitt v Holt* [2011] EWCA Civ 197, [2012] Ch 132 [198].

'there would have been a strong argument for saying that, having declined to follow the recommendation that he should take out term insurance, Mr Griffith was taking the risk that his health was, or would come to be, such that he did not survive.' This assessment of the case was expressly endorsed on appeal by the Supreme Court in *Pitt v Holt*.[29]

Re Griffiths presents a strong contrast on the issue of risk with the facts of *Pitt v Holt*. In that case, there was once again a very fine line between mistake and misprediction. On one view, Mrs Pitt was labouring under a misprediction as to the tax consequences of the deed of settlement into which she entered.[30] On the contrary view adopted in the Supreme Court, Mrs Pitt was suffering from a serious mistake as to the inherent taxation incidents of the transaction.[31] In the Supreme Court, Lord Walker, delivering the leading judgment,[32] rightly cast doubt on the value of the mistake–misprediction distinction and noted that the conclusion that a plaintiff assumed the risk of mistake should bar relief.[33] As Lord Walker also noted,[34] Mrs Pitt had sought taxation advice from two different professional firms, and the deed had been approved by the Court of Protection. In those circumstances, Mrs Pitt could hardly be regarded as having assumed the risk of mistake. This test for assumption of risk is a sharper and better approach than an attempt to distinguish between mistakes and mispredictions. However, Lord Walker also went on to propose a test that required identification of 'a causative mistake of sufficient gravity'[35] that it would be 'unconscionable'[36] for the defendant to retain the enrichment. As we will see below, this new test is highly ambiguous. The better approach is to ask only whether the plaintiff assumed the risk of error.

D. Fault, Doubt and Risk-Taking on the Part of the Plaintiff

A test for mistake which also requires a determination of whether the plaintiff assumed the risk of the mistake requires further consideration of the roles of and interaction between the concepts of fault, doubt and risk. Early common law cases insisted that payments made under a mistake of fact had to be made without any negligence on the plaintiff's part, if restitution was to be ordered.[37] But equity allowed restitution even where the plaintiff was at fault. In *Pusey v Desbouvrie*,[38] a father left his adult daughter £10,000 in his will, on the condition that she release any other claim she had to his personal estate and also that she release her part ownership of an orphanage. Being mistaken as to the value of her share in the orphanage (which was far more than £10,000) she released her interest in it to the estate. The Lord Chancellor held that the executor (her brother) had acted 'without the least appearance of fraud'.[39] He had told her that he would prepare a full account of

[29] *Pitt v Holt* [2013] UKSC 26, [2013] 2 AC 108 [113].
[30] *Pitt v Holt* [2010] EWHC 45 (Ch), [2010] 1 WLR 1199 [51]–[53] (Justice Robert Englehart QC); *Pitt v Holt* [2011] EWCA Civ 197, [2012] Ch 132 [216]–[219].
[31] *Pitt v Holt* [2013] UKSC 26, [2013] 2 AC 108 [133].
[32] Lord Neuberger, Baroness Hale, Lord Mance, Lord Clarke, Lord Sumption and Lord Carnwath agreeing.
[33] *Pitt v Holt* [2013] UKSC 26, [2013] 2 AC 108 [109]–[113].
[34] ibid [133].
[35] ibid [122].
[36] ibid [124]–[126].
[37] *Milnes v Duncan* (1827) 6 B & C 671, 677; 108 ER 598, 600 (Bayley J, Holroyd and Littledale JJ concurring).
[38] *Pusey v Desbouvrie* (1734) 3 P Wms 315, 24 ER 1081.
[39] ibid 320, 1082.

the value of the estate if she wished. The Lord Chancellor nevertheless found that she was entitled to set aside this release because of her mistake, even though she could have avoided the mistake by taking up her brother's offer (and to that extent, could be regarded as at fault). Another example of restitution for mistake in equity is *Bingham v Bingham.*[40] In that case, the defendant purported to sell an estate to the plaintiff. Neither party realised that the plaintiff already owned the estate. The plaintiff's claim in equity for restitution of the purported purchase price was successful. Although the defendant argued that the mistake was the fault of the plaintiff, the Lord Chancellor held that the contract was void and it was enough that 'there was a plain mistake, such as the court was warranted to relieve against, and not to suffer the defendant to run away with the money in consideration of the sale of an estate, to which he had no right.'[41] These are not isolated older cases. They are part of a long line of authority.[42]

In *Kelly v Solari*,[43] the common law adopted the equitable approach. Directors of the plaintiff insurance company claimed they had paid the benefit of a life insurance policy to the widow of the insured, forgetting that the deceased man had failed to pay his last premium. In turn, this led them to believe that the contract remained on foot, and that they were thus liable to pay. On appeal from a finding of liability, it was held that the insurance company was entitled to restitution provided that, as would be determined at a new trial, the mistake caused the payment. There are now a number of cases that have accepted that a plaintiff who negligently but mistakenly pays a defendant is entitled to restitution, provided that he paid as a result of the mistake.[44] In *Pitt v Holt*, the Supreme Court said that this was 'uncontroversial'.[45]

We have seen that in *Pitt v Holt*, Lord Walker also observed that courts will deny a plaintiff relief from the consequences of a mistake where the plaintiff was mistaken but had nevertheless assumed the risk of error. By itself, the concept of a party bearing the risk of error asserts as a conclusion the very thing that is to be proved. However, Lord Walker seemed to contemplate a case where the plaintiff held doubts regarding the fact or matter about which they were mistaken, but chose to proceed nonetheless.[46] This is what is meant by the label 'assumption of risk'. The denial of recovery in such a case has been explained on the grounds of personal autonomy: a plaintiff is required to bear responsibility for knowingly accepted risks.[47] It is necessary, of course, to draw a line between those doubts that

[40] *Bingham v Bingham* (1748) 1 Ves Sen 126, 27 ER 934.

[41] ibid 127; 934 (reference omitted).

[42] *Meadows v Meadows* (1853) 16 Beav 401, 51 ER 833; *Walker v Armstrong* (1856) 8 De GM & G 531, 44 ER 495; *Phillipson v Kerry* (1863) 32 Beav 628, 55 ER 247; *Ellis v Ellis* [1909] 1 Ch 618; *Re Walton's Settlement, Walton v Peirson* [1922] 2 Ch 509; *Gibbon v Mitchell* [1990] 3 All ER 338, 343 (Millett J); *Dent v Dent* [1996] 1 All ER 659; *Re Griffiths* [2008] EWHC 118, [2009] Ch 162; *Pitt v Holt* [2013] UKSC 26, [2013] 2 AC 108.

[43] *Kelly v Solari* (1841) 9 M & W 54, 152 ER 24.

[44] The leading cases are *David Securities Pty Ltd v Commonwealth Bank of Australia* [1992] HCA 48, (1992) 175 CLR 353; *Dextra Bank & Trust Co Ltd v Bank of Jamaica* [2001] UKPC 50, [2002] 1 All ER (Comm) 193 [45].

[45] *Pitt v Holt* [2013] UKSC 26, [2013] 2 AC 108 [114] (Lord Walker, delivering the judgment of the Court).

[46] *Kleinwort Benson Ltd v Lincoln City Council* [1998] UKHL 38, [1999] 2 AC 349, 410 (Lord Hope): 'A person who pays when in doubt takes the risk that he may be wrong'. Cf American Law Institute, *Restatement of the Law (Third) Restitution and Unjust Enrichment*, vol 1 (St Paul, Minn, American Law Institute Publishers, 2011) §5(3): 'A claimant bears the risk of a mistake when … (b) the claimant has consciously assumed the risk by deciding to act in the face of a recognized uncertainty'. *Maskell v Horner* [1915] 3 KB 106, 117 (Lord Reading CJ), 123 (Buckley LJ), 126 (Pickford LJ). Cf failure of basis, ch 11 pp 253–54.

[47] M McInnes, *The Canadian Law of Unjust Enrichment and Restitution* (Markham, Ontario, LexisNexis, 2014) 398.

are sufficient to merit the conclusion of bearing the risk and those which are not. Several examples can be given to highlight how this evaluative exercise is undertaken.

In *Brennan v Bolt Burdon*,[48] Miss Brennan brought claims for negligence out of time. Her claims were struck out by the Recorder. She was advised by her solicitors that she had little prospect of a successful appeal, because of case law that supported the decision of the Recorder. Leading counsel thought that the case law was wrong, but he advised there was little prospect of persuading the Court of Appeal of this. Miss Brennan subsequently compromised her proceedings, and her solicitors made no enquiry about any possible appeal. When the case law was later reversed she sought to set aside her compromise on the grounds that it had been entered into by mistake. The Court of Appeal refused to set aside her compromise. One reason given[49] was that she was not mistaken, but merely in a state of doubt.[50] A better way of expressing this is to say that she had assumed the risk of a mistake.

A recent Australian example is *Lahoud v Lahoud*,[51] where a settlement agreement entered into by two brothers contained an audit clause included at the instigation of the plaintiff. A subsequent audit revealed that the amount paid by the plaintiff under the settlement agreement was incorrect. The plaintiff sought, amongst other relief, repayment of the use value (interest) of the overpaid principal. While Ward J of the New South Wales Supreme Court accepted that, in principle, the opportunity to use the amount of the overpayment (ie interest) constituted an actionable enrichment, relief was ultimately denied. One reason given was that the plaintiff had doubts about the accuracy of the settlement figure, and in that context had assumed the risk of error.[52] Justice Ward considered that the so-called 'mistake' was actually a misprediction which could not justify recovery.

These cases demonstrate that a plaintiff who continues with a transaction despite doubts about a particular matter may have accepted the risk of being mistaken on that matter when the doubts are sufficiently substantial. A small amount of doubt will not be sufficient. Many actionable mistakes involve some degree of doubt, even if the doubt is very small. The question will be the extent of the doubt that was harboured. An assessment of the extent of that doubt may depend upon evidence given by the plaintiff about his or her state of mind. But, more commonly, the assessment of the extent of doubt in the plaintiff's mind will proceed by drawing an inference from all the known circumstances, including the extent to which the circumstances could reasonably have been known by the plaintiff. In *Deutsche Morgan Grenfell Group plc v Commissioner of Inland Revenue*[53] the plaintiff paid advanced

[48] *Brennan v Bolt Burdon* [2004] EWCA Civ 1017, [2005] QB 303. See also *Hayward v Zurich Insurance Company plc* [2015] EWCA Civ 327, [2015] CP Rep 30, [16] and [19], [25] (Underhill LJ), [32]–[33] (Beatson LJ), [37] (King LJ, agreeing with both judgments) currently on appeal to the Supreme Court and distinguished in *Gohil v Gohil* [2015] UKSC 61, [2015] 3 WLR 1085 [21]–[22] (Lord Wilson: duty to disclose on the part of the defendant meant no assumption of risk by plaintiff) (with whom Lord Neuberger, Lady Hale, Lord Clarke, Lord Sumption, Lord Reed and Lord Hodge agreed). See further *TFL Management Services Ltd v Lloyds Bank plc* [2013] EWCA Civ 1415, [2014] 1 WLR 2006 [66]–[67] (Floyd LJ), [88]–[89] (Beatson LJ); *HSH Nordbank AG v Intesa Sanpaolo SpA* [2014] EWHC 142 [50]–[51] (Mr Justice Burton); *Southern Cross Employment Agency Ltd v Revenue and Customs Commissioners* [2015] UKUT 122 [58] (Newey J).

[49] For other reasons, see Ch 15 p 400 (defence of dispute resolved), and Ch 7, section II (mistake in contracts).

[50] *Brennan v Bolt Burdon* [2004] EWCA Civ 1017, [2005] QB 303 [23] (Maurice Kay LJ), [35] (Bodey LJ). See also *Qld Alumina Ltd v Alinta DQP Pty Ltd* [2007] QCA 387 [70]–[72] (Holmes JA); *Re Magarey Farlam Lawyers Trust Accounts (No 3)* [2007] SASC 9, (2007) 96 SASR 337 [172] (Debelle J).

[51] *Lahoud v Lahoud* [2010] NSWSC 1297. See also *Salib v Gakas* [2010] NSWSC 505, especially [333] (Ward J).

[52] *Lahoud v Lahoud* [2010] NSWSC 1297 [180]. Another was that the mistake was not 'a factor' in the plaintiff's decision to enter the transaction that enriched the defendant: see [176]. On causation, see section IV below.

[53] *Deutsche Morgan Grenfell Group plc v Inland Revenue Commissioners* [2006] UKHL 49, [2007] 1 AC 558 [27].

corporation tax after it became aware that the validity of the applicable taxing act had been challenged. The challenge proved successful. The Revenue argued the payment was made in a state of doubt and hence was not recoverable. Lord Hoffmann said:

> I would not regard the fact that the person making the payment had doubts about his liability as conclusive of the question of whether he took the risk, particularly if the existence of these doubts was unknown to the receiving party. … It would be more rational if the question of whether a party should be treated as having taken the risk depended upon the objective circumstances surrounding the payment as they could reasonably have been known to both parties, including of course the extent to which the law was known to be in doubt.[54]

Pitt v Holt is itself a good example. As Lord Walker emphasised,[55] the particular transaction in *Pitt v Holt* had been the subject of taxation advice from two different professional firms and had been approved by the Court of Protection. In those circumstances, Mrs Pitt could hardly be regarded as having assumed the risk of mistake. The objective circumstances of the transaction revealed no risk of error. The Canadian case of *Re Pallen Trust*[56] follows a similar pattern of reasoning. Mr Pallen engaged in a complicated series of corporate restructures and trust arrangements with a view to 'asset protection' for the family business, but with a strong emphasis on obtaining valuable taxation advantages. Key to the scheme was that the newly created Pallen Trust should receive corporate dividends that would be tax-free. This conclusion was based on a certain understanding of the operation of section 75(2) of the Income Tax Act 1985,[57] a view shared by income tax professionals as well as the Canada Tax Agency. This understanding was however shown to be mistaken by a subsequent decision of the Tax Court of Canada, affirmed by the Federal Court of Canada. The result was that the Trust was liable to taxation at the highest possible rate on the dividends. The Trust accordingly sought rescission of the dividends. Justice Masuhara adopted the analysis in *Pitt v Holt* to hold that the dividends should be set aside on the grounds of mistake. His Honour identified as a key factor in his decision that the widespread understanding of section 75(2) showed that there was not an undue assumption of risk sufficient to refuse relief. The result might however have been different had the understanding been less certain.[58]

III. The Operation of the Unjust Factor of Mistake

A. Mistake in Equity

Although most cases focus on the historical award of restitution for mistake at common law, we have seen that courts of equity also exercised jurisdiction to grant restitution for mistake. There is no rational reason for treating cases of mistake in equity differently from

[54] ibid [27]; cited with approval in *Stiassny v Commissioner of Inland Revenue* [2010] NZHC 2351 [118]–[119] (Allan J); see also American Law Institute, *Restatement of the Law of Restitution: Quasi Contracts and Constructive Trusts* (St Paul, Minn, American Law Institute, 1937) §10(1).

[55] *Pitt v Holt* [2013] UKSC 26, [2013] 2 AC 108 [133].

[56] *Re Pallen Trust* [2014] BCSC 305.

[57] Income Tax Act, RSC 1985, c 1 (5th Supp).

[58] *Re Pallen Trust* [2014] BCSC 305 [57].

their treatment at common law. Indeed the jurisdictions evolved in a similar way. For example, we have seen that the plaintiffs in both *Pusey v Desbouvrie*[59] and *Bingham v Bingham*[60] were entitled to restitution even though their mistake was partly caused by their own carelessness. The same approach to fault was adopted at common law following *Kelly v Solari*.[61] Further, equity's definition of mistake was similar to that at common law. A decision to proceed despite having substantial doubts meant that the plaintiff assumed the risk of error. For instance, a leading decision concerning mistake in the context of equitable estoppel in 1866 held that a tenant who improved land with only an uncertain hope that a further term would be granted, or the expenditure reimbursed, was not able to recover restitution for his disappointed expectations.[62] A recent example is *Roy v Lagona*,[63] where a squatter improved and paid council rates on a residential property in Melbourne. In subsequent proceedings for possession brought by the registered proprietors, the squatter cross-claimed for restitution of the amount of the enrichment said to have been conferred through his services. He claimed to have conferred the enrichment under the mistaken belief that no one claimed the property or intended to claim the property and that (hence) he was entitled to enjoy the fruits of his labour. In rejecting the claim, Hansen J said:

> I find that the defendant took a knowing risk that the person truly entitled to the property may one day appear and claim it, and that he may have to give up possession. He did so adventitiously, with no encouragement from any person, hoping that one day, if he were there long enough, the property would become his, but aware it may not.[64]

One area where there potentially exist differences between the treatment of mistake cases at common law and in equity is in the sphere of restitution of rights pursuant to a constructive trust. In *Westdeutche Landesbank Girozentrale v Islington LBC*,[65] Lord Browne-Wilkinson suggested in obiter dicta that a constructive trust may be awarded in circumstances of mistaken payment, where the defendant had sufficient knowledge of the mistake. Although this 'tentative'[66] view has been doubted in England,[67] there is now a line of Australian cases that have adopted the analysis.[68] It is unclear why knowledge is considered an additional

[59] *Pusey v Desbouvrie* (1734) 3 P Wms 315, 24 ER 1081.

[60] *Bingham v Bingham* (1748) 1 Ves Sen 126, 27 ER 934.

[61] *Kelly v Solari* (1841) 9 M & W 54, 152 ER 24.

[62] *Ramsden v Dyson* (1866) LR 1 HL 129, 171.

[63] *Roy v Lagona* [2010] VSC 250.

[64] ibid [328].

[65] *Westdeutche Landesbank Girozentrale v Islington London Borough Council* [1996] UKHL 12, [1996] AC 669, 704–06; concurring at 718 (Lord Slynn), 720 (Lord Woolf), 738 (Lord Lloyd). See also *Kaupthing Singer & Friedlander Ltd (In Administration) v UBS AG* [2014] EWHC 2450; *Deutche Bank AG v Vik* [2010] EWHC 551 [4] (Burton J); *Re Farepak Food and Gifts Ltd (In Administration)* [2006] EWHC 3272, [2008] BCC 22 [40] (Mann J); *Papamichael v National Westminster Bank plc (No 2)* [2003] EWHC 164, [2003] 1 Lloyd's Rep 341 [221]–[229] (Judge Chambers QC).

[66] *Maqsood v Mahmood* [2012] EWCA Civ 251 [37] (Ward LJ, Lloyd and Jackson LJJ concurring); *Wuhan Guoyu Logistics Group Co Ltd v Emporiki Bank of Greece SA* [2013] EWCA Civ 1679, [2014] 1 All ER (Comm) 870 [19] (Tomlinson LJ; Rimer and Longmore LJJ concurring); see also *Ashworth v Newnote Ltd* [2007] EWCA Civ 793, [2007] BPIR 1012 [56] (Lawrence Collins LJ [Buxton LJ concurring).

[67] *Fitzalan-Howard v Hibbert* [2009] EWHC 2855, [2010] PNLR 11 [49] (Tomlinson J); *Wuhan Guoyu Logistics Group Co Ltd v Emporiki Bank of Greece SA* [2013] EWCA Civ 1679, [2014] 1 All ER (Comm) 870 [19] (Tomlinson LJ; Rimer and Longmore LJJ concurring); *London Allied Holdings Ltd v Lee* [2007] EWHC 2061 [271]–[273] (Etherton J).

[68] *Wambo Coal Pty Ltd v Ariff* [2007] NSWSC 589, (2007) 63 ACSR 429, building on the dictum of Lord Browne-Wilkinson in *Westdeutsche Landesbank Girozentrale v Islington London Borough Council* [1996] UKHL 12,

requirement where the order sought is for restitution of rights by a constructive trust, rather than a mere order for payment of money as restitution of value. The reason for insistence upon knowledge in the equity cases concerning restitution of rights transferred by mistake cannot be because the defendant is subject to express trust-like duties and therefore knowledge is required: the 'trust' in these cases is akin to a simple order for conveyance and carries no other substantive obligations.[69] It is also unclear why an order for restitution of value is not an adequate remedy, given that the impugned transactions in these cases involve simple transfers of value. While as a matter of practical outcome, a constructive trust may yield more fulsome relief in cases of insolvency, the weight of Australian authority suggests that insolvency is a reason against awarding the trust not in favour of it.[70] It remains to be seen whether, on full argument, this line of cases will continue to evolve and, if so, on what basis.

B. Mistaken Provision of Goods and Services

Although the mistaken payment is the most common example of restitution arising from the unjust factor of mistake, we saw in Chapter 4 that a defendant can also be enriched as a result of the receipt of goods or services, although proof of enrichment in such cases is not as simple.[71] Perhaps for this reason, cases of mistaken provision of goods or services are not as commonly recognised by courts as being part of the law of unjust enrichment. However, provided enrichment can be satisfied, the unjust factor of mistake applies in cases involving mistaken performance of goods or services just as it does in cases of mistaken payment.

The case of *Weatherby v Banham*[72] is a good example.[73] In that case a publisher sent copies of a magazine to a gentleman for many years. After the gentleman died, the publisher, mistakenly continued to send the magazine to the address where the defendant now resided. The defendant received the magazine for two years but did not return it or notify the publisher that the gentleman had died. Lord Tenterden CJ held that the common law action for goods sold and delivered could be brought for restitution of the value of the magazines mistakenly delivered to the defendant.

The same approach taken to mistaken provision of goods also applies to cases involving mistaken provision of services. In *Earl of Cawdor v Lewis*,[74] the plaintiff made improvements to buildings under a mistaken impression that the land was his own. The Court of

[1996] AC 669, 705 (Lord Browne-Wilkinson; Lords Slynn and Loyd agreeing); *Shields v Westpac Banking Corporation* [2008] NSWCA 268; *Credit Union Australia Ltd v Lyons* [2009] NSWSC 1188; *Focus Metals Pty Ltd v Babicci* [2014] VSC 380.

[69] *Giumelli v Giumelli* [1999] HCA 10, (1999) 196 CLR 101 [5] (Gleeson CJ, McHugh, Gummow & Callinan JJ).

[70] *Bathurst City Council v PWC Properties Pty Ltd* [1998] HCA 59, (1998) 195 CLR 566 [42] (Gaudron, McHugh, Hayne and Callinan JJ); *Giumelli v Giumelli* [1999] HCA 10, (1999) 196 CLR 101 [10], [49]–[50] (Gleeson CJ, McHugh, Gummow and Callinan JJ); *John Alexander's Clubs Pty Ltd v White City Tennis Club Ltd* [2010] HCA 19, (2010) 241 CLR 1 [126]–[129] (the Court); *Grimaldi v Chameleon Mining NL (No 2)* [2012] FCAFC 6, (2012) 200 FCR 296 [503]–[508] (the Court).

[71] Ch 4, section III.

[72] *Weatherby v Banham* (1832) 5 Car & P 228, 172 ER 950. The enrichment requirement in this case is discussed in Ch 4 p 71.

[73] Ch 4 pp 58 and 71.

[74] *Lord Cawdor v Lewis* (1835) 1 Y & C Ex 427, 160 ER 174. A common law equivalent is *Greenwood v Bennett* [1973] QB 195.

Chancery held that he was entitled to bring a claim—for set-off, in separate proceedings—for the value of the improvements. Although the decision might be flawed in relation to the issue of enrichment,[75] it cannot be faulted for treating a mistaken provision of services in the same way as a mistaken payment. The underlying rationale applies equally to both.

Professor Tang has noted that the consequences of being found liable to make restitution for improvements to land potentially leaves defendants in a position where they are required to sell the land to meet the claim, thereby undermining their autonomy.[76] Such concerns may underpin recent statements by both Australian and English courts that, in cases of land, the plaintiff must prove an additional requirement of unconscionable conduct (such as standing by with knowledge of the mistake) on the part of the defendant.[77] This requirement was probably borrowed from the law of proprietary estoppel.[78] However, as we saw earlier, a defendant's knowledge of the plaintiff's mistake is not a requirement of the unjust factor of mistake where the defendant's enrichment is the retention of money or goods. It should not be a requirement for cases involving land. The real role for knowledge of a plaintiff's mistake is twofold. First, if a *defendant* has knowledge that a plaintiff is mistakenly improving the defendant's land, then as we saw in Chapter 4, that enrichment will be easier to prove. Secondly, if a *plaintiff* has knowledge, or a high level of suspicion, that he is mistaken then the plaintiff might be found to have assumed the risk of his mistake.

Blue Haven Enterprises v Tully is an example of a case where better appreciation of the nature of the enrichment requirement and the role of assumption of risk would have led to a more principled approach.[79] The plaintiff commenced improvements to land on an erroneous assumption that he held good title to it. Subsequently, he was advised of an adverse claim by the defendant, who was the true titleholder. The plaintiff's claim for restitution with respect to his services and improvements to the land was denied because, it was said, the defendant had neither known of nor encouraged the services.[80] We saw in Chapter 4 that encouragement may be evidence that the defendant chose the services and so was enriched by their receipt. However, in *Blue Haven*, notwithstanding the lack of encouragement on the part of the defendant, the services arguably enriched the defendant because he accepted that he would have had to undertake similar improvements himself. The plaintiff had therefore saved him a necessary expense. On this basis, the plaintiff should have been entitled to restitution—but only in respect of those enrichments conferred prior to receiving notification of the adverse claim. From that moment, the plaintiff entertained serious doubts as to his title, with the consequence that expenditure after that point should have been at his risk. Close focus on the issues of enrichment and assumption of risk would have

[75] See Ch 4 p 63.

[76] HW Tang, 'An Unjust Enrichment Claim for the Mistaken Improver of Land' [2011] *The Conveyancer and Property Lawyer* 8, 28.

[77] *Blue Haven Enterprises v Tully* [2006] UKPC 17 [20]; *JS Bloor Ltd v Pavillion Developments Ltd* [2008] EWHC 724, [2008] 2 EGLR 85 [48] (Judge Frances Kirkham); *Roy v Lagona* [2010] VSC 250. See HW Tang, 'An Unjust Enrichment Claim for the Mistaken Improver of Land' [2011] *The Conveyancer and Property Lawyer* 8.

[78] K Low, 'Unjust Enrichment and Proprietary Estoppel: Two Sides of the Same Coin?' [2007] *Lloyd's Maritime and Commercial Law Quarterly* 14, and B McFarlane, 'Case Note: *Blue Haven Enterprises Ltd v Tully*' (2006) 1 *Journal of Equity* 156.

[79] *Blue Haven Enterprises v Tully* [2006] UKPC 17.

[80] ibid [25]–[26].

sufficed to avoid excessive restitution, without introducing any additional requirements to the unjust factor of mistake, such as knowledge or unconscionability.

C. The Nature of the Mistake is Irrelevant

We have seen that courts have traditionally been, and continue to be, concerned with how to balance recoverability of enrichments caused or contributed to by mistake and allowing restitution too readily. Mistakes are endemic to everyday life. Further, it is relatively difficult as a defendant to know when a person is making a mistake, at least where those mistakes are 'spontaneous' or internal to the plaintiff, or arise from the acts of a third party, rather than being induced by the defendant.[81] People must be entitled to order their affairs on the basis of their apparent wealth. The recognition of mistake as a strict liability unjust factor means that a defendant's receipt of value, whether as money, goods or services, can become insecure. Apart from restraints discussed above concerning the assumption of the risk of a mistake and restrictions concerning enrichment, there are two main ways of reducing the threat to the security of a defendant's receipts. One is to restrict the types of mistake that found a claim in unjust enrichment. The other is to make available a defence or defences the effect of which is to protect that security of receipt in appropriate circumstances.

The first approach was taken in *Kelly v Solari*, which restricted the mistakes for which recovery were permitted to 'liability mistakes'. As Baron Parke said:

> I think that where money is paid to another under the influence of a mistake, that is, upon the supposition that a specific fact is true, which would entitle the other to the money, but which fact is untrue, and the money would not have been paid if it had been known to the payer that the fact was untrue, an action will lie to recover it back ...[82]

While the liability mistake test captured many meritorious mistake claims, it also excluded a number of equally worthy cases. For example, a person who made a gift twice, forgetting she had already made a gift to the defendant, was not entitled to restitution on the liability mistake test.[83] Thus, other bases for distinguishing between actionable and non-actionable mistakes were required. In Australia, a different restriction developed. Instead of a 'liability mistake', the mistake needed to be 'fundamental'.[84] An example of a fundamental mistake was a mistake as to the nature of the transaction into which a plaintiff was entering. In contrast, a mistake affecting the plaintiff's motivation for entering into the transaction was not, in general, sufficiently fundamental. As the High Court noted in *David Securities*, however, '[t]he notion of fundamentality is ... extremely vague',[85] with the consequence that it was often difficult to determine whether a mistake satisfied the requirements of the test.

[81] See ch 7 p 148.

[82] *Kelly v Solari* (1841) 9 M & W 54, 58; 152 ER 24, 26.

[83] The example given by Robert Goff J in *Barclays Bank Ltd v WJ Simms Son & Cooke (Southern) Ltd* [1980] QB 677, 696–97.

[84] *Porter v Latec Finance (Qld) Pty Ltd* [1964] HCA 49, (1964) 111 CLR 177, 187 (Barwick CJ), 190 (Kitto J), 204 (Windeyer J); *Commercial Bank of Australia Ltd v Younis* [1979] 1 NSWLR 444.

[85] *David Securities Pty Ltd v Commonwealth Bank of Australia* [1992] HCA 48, (1992) 175 CLR 353, 377–78 [43] (Mason CJ, Deane, Toohey, Gaudron and McHugh JJ).

In *Barclays Bank Ltd v WJ Simms Son & Cooke (Southern) Ltd*,[86] Robert Goff J rejected the liability and the fundamental mistake approaches. His Honour preferred instead a simple 'causative mistake' test: did the mistake cause the plaintiff to enter the transaction that enriched the defendant?[87] This wider basis for recovery was counterbalanced, inter alia, by a change of position defence, which, where it applies, had the consequence of rendering defendants' receipts more secure.[88] This approach has gradually become dominant in England.[89] It was authoritatively adopted by the High Court of Australia in *David Securities Pty Ltd v Commonwealth Bank of Australia*.[90] As the joint judgment of Mason CJ, Deane, Toohey, Gaudron and McHugh JJ explained:

> If the payer has made the payment because of a mistake, his or her intention to transfer the money is vitiated and the recipient has been enriched. There is therefore no place for a further requirement that the causative mistake be fundamental; insistence upon that factor would only serve to focus attention in a non-specific way on the nature of the mistake, rather than the fact of enrichment.[91]

In the course of their reasoning the plurality also expressly rejected the submission that the appellant must separately prove any 'injustice' to restrict further recovery based upon the mistake.[92] However, the recent Supreme Court decision of *Pitt v Holt*[93] saw a return to a test which restricted the types of mistake which could ground recovery. In that case, Lord Walker (with whom all other members agreed) considered the fact that 'a purely unilateral mistake may be sufficient to found relief is arguably a good reason for the court to apply a more stringent test as to the seriousness of the mistake before granting relief.'[94] Although that case concerned rescission of deeds of gift, Lord Walker's statements appear to have been intended to be of general application.[95] In the context of rescission of deeds of gift, the Supreme Court held that the test to be applied should be whether the mistake was a 'causative mistake of sufficient gravity' such that it would be 'unconscionable' for the defendant to retain the enrichment.[96] At first sight, this seems to revive the very difficult qualifications on actionable mistake of the sort expressly rejected by the High Court of Australia. However, we saw earlier that Lord Walker's reasoning is consistent with adoption of a requirement that the plaintiff must not have accepted the risk of error in order to

[86] *Barclays Bank Ltd v WJ Simms Son & Cooke (Southern) Ltd* [1980] QB 677.

[87] ibid 695.

[88] *Australian Financial Services and Leasing Pty Ltd v Hills Industries Ltd* [2014] HCA 14, (2014) 253 CLR 560 [92] (Hayne, Crennan, Kiefel, Bell and Keane JJ). The other defences nominated by Robert Goff J are considered in Ch 7 pp 156–58 and Ch 15 pp 364–68.

[89] *Lloyds Bank plc v Independent Insurance Co Ltd* [2000] QB 110, 129 (Peter Gibson LJ); *Deutsche Morgan Grenfell Group plc v Inland Revenue Commissioners* [2006] UKHL 49, [2007] 1 AC 558 [59]–[62] (Lord Hope), [84] (Lord Scott), [143] (Lord Walker).

[90] *David Securities Pty Ltd v Commonwealth Bank of Australia* [1992] HCA 48, (1992) 175 CLR 353, 376–78 [41]–[43] (Mason CJ, Deane, Toohey, Gaudron and McHugh JJ).

[91] ibid 378 [43].

[92] ibid 378–79 [44]–[47]. On the meaning of 'unconscionable retention of benefit', see Ch 6 pp 130–34.

[93] *Pitt v Holt* [2013] UKSC 26, [2013] 2 AC 108. See also the reservations of Lord Scott in *Deutsche Morgan Grenfell Group plc v Inland Revenue Commissioners* [2006] UKHL 49, [2007] 1 AC 558 [84]–[87], suggesting that a serious mistake may be required in the case of gifts.

[94] *Pitt v Holt* [2013] UKSC 26, [2013] 2 AC 108 [114].

[95] The approach has since been applied in a case of rectification: see *Lobler v Revenue and Customs Commissioners* [2015] UKUT 152, [2015] STC 1893. Cf *Kennedy v Kennedy* [2014] EWHC 4129, [2015] BTC 2 [45] (Sir Terence Etherton C).

[96] *Pitt v Holt* [2013] UKSC 26, [2013] 2 AC 108 [122], [124].

obtain restitution for mistake. This restriction, together with (i) restrictions which are part of the test of enrichment, and (ii) the role of defences together operate to reduce the danger of too much restitution.

D. Mistakes of Law

Another traditional limitation on the actionability of causative mistakes came in the form of the so-called mistake of law bar. In *Bilbie v Lumley*,[97] an insurance company made a payment to a customer believing that it was legally liable to do so. In refusing relief, Lord Ellenborough held that, since a plaintiff could not be heard to be ignorant of the law, it followed that recovery of enrichment conferred by mistake of law must be denied. This decision was the basis for a rule that persisted for almost two centuries: that a payment as a result of a mistake of law was irrecoverable at common law.

There were several powerful criticisms of this decision. First, on the ground of authority, *Bilbie v Lumley* was inconsistent with cases in which recovery for mistaken payments had been held to be available whether the mistake was one of law or fact.[98] The decision in *Bilbie v Lumley* was therefore, ironically, based upon a legal error. Second, as a matter of principle, it was arbitrary to maintain the distinction between mistakes of fact and mistakes of law when both produced the same effect on the payer's mind. If a mistaken payment was recoverable because the plaintiff's decision was vitiated by the mistake, why should it matter what type of mistake it was? Third, it was often difficult to work out whether a mistake was a mistake of law or a mistake of fact. This ambiguity, together with a desire to escape the confines of the 'mistake of law' bar, often led courts to treat as a mistake of fact what clearly was a mistake of law.[99] The same desire also led to a proliferation of *ad hoc* exceptions to the bar.[100] Finally, as was observed in the joint judgment in *David Securities Pty Ltd v Commonwealth Bank of Australia*, Lord Ellenborough misapplied the maxim that ignorance is no excuse.[101] As Dawson J explained, the maxim applies where a person is seeking to escape the consequences of breaking the law by pleading ignorance of it. It was never intended to apply to cases where a person sought to invoke the aid of the law, as where the plaintiff sought recovery of a mistaken payment.[102] The decisions of the High Court of Australia in *David Securities* and the House of Lords in England in *Kleinwort Benson*

[97] *Bilbie v Lumley* (1802) 2 East 469, 102 ER 448.

[98] E McKendrick, 'Mistake of Law—Time for a Change?' in W Swadling (ed), *The Limits of Restitutionary Claims: A Comparative Analysis* (London, United Kingdom National Committee of Comparative Law, 1997) 214; *Kleinwort Benson Ltd v Lincoln City Council* [1998] UKHL 38, [1999] 2 AC 349, 386 (Lord Goff).

[99] A prime example was the rule that a mistake as to private rights was a mistake of fact: *Cooper v Phibbs* (1867) LR 2 HL 149, 170 (Lord Westbury); *Solle v Butcher* [1950] 1 KB 671. See also *Rover International Ltd v Cannon Film Sales Ltd* [1989] 1 WLR 912.

[100] See, eg, the jurisdiction to relieve against mistakes of law by administrators, receivers and liquidators: *Ex p James, Re Condon* (1874) LR 9 Ch App 609; *Hartogen Energy Limited (in liq) v Australian Gas Light Company* [1992] FCA 322, (1992) 36 FCR 557, 574 [61]–[63] (Gummow J); *Young v ACN 081 162 512 (formerly Dallen Design Pty Ltd)* [2005] NSWSC 139, (2005) 218 ALR 449.

[101] *David Securities Pty Ltd v Commonwealth Bank of Australia* [1992] HCA 48, (1992) 175 CLR 353, 370 [30] (Mason CJ, Deane, Toohey, Gaudron and McHugh JJ).

[102] *David Securities Pty Ltd v Commonwealth Bank of Australia* [1992] HCA 48, (1992) 175 CLR 353, 401–02 [2] (Dawson J).

Ltd v Lincoln City Council[103] to abolish the mistake of law bar to restitution were widely applauded as a matter of precedent, principle and practice.

However, although anomalies in the law have been removed by the recognition that restitution is available for mistakes of law, new difficulties have arisen. The most significant difficulty lies in the retroactivity of judicial decision-making. Has a plaintiff made a mistake of law if his payment was valid according to the common law at the time of his payment, but the law is later overruled? The difficulty with the retroactive nature of decision-making does not usually arise where the mistake relates to the existence or clear effect of legislation. In such cases, the mistake is very close to a mistake of fact. It will be recalled that in the leading decision of *David Securities*, the plaintiff's mistaken payment arose because of an erroneous assumption that a contractual term was valid. The High Court held that the plain effect of legislation was that the term was invalid and that David Securities had made an error of law. The error of law was itself a matter of fact (the existence of a legislative provision) and caused no real theoretical problems. The English case of *Pitt v Holt*[104] is another case in the same mould. In contrast, in *Torrens Aloha Pty Ltd v Citibank NA*,[105] the same issue led to consideration of the retroactive nature of judicial decision making. Torrens made payments to Citibank mistakenly thinking that a contractual term meant that it was required to pay withholding tax. The difficulty for Torrens was that it brought its claim nine years after the mistaken payments, so a claim for restitution was statute-barred. However, the payments were made only three years after the decision in *David Securities,* so Torrens argued that it was only from that date that its action based on mistake of law accrued, and that the limitation period only ran from that date.[106] Justice Sackville (with whom Foster and Lehane JJ agreed) held that the cause of action arose when all the facts necessary to establish it had occurred, rather than when the action was itself recognised by the law.[107] An application for special leave to appeal to the High Court was dismissed on the basis that the case was not a suitable vehicle to examine the issue.[108]

Subsequently, the issue was raised before the House of Lords in *Kleinwort Benson Ltd v Lincoln City Council.*[109] In that case, the plaintiff bank entered interest rate swap transactions with four local authorities. Each transaction was fully completed and resulted in the bank making net payments of £811,208 to the local authorities. After the transactions were completed, the House of Lords delivered its decision in *Hazell v Hammersmith and Fulham London Borough Council*,[110] which held that the transactions were *ultra vires* and void. The retroactive nature of the decision in *Hazell* meant that the transactions pursuant to which the bank had made its payments were void. The bank argued that it had made the payments under the mistaken belief that it was legally obliged to do so, when that was, as it turned

[103] *Kleinwort Benson Ltd v Lincoln City Council* [1998] UKHL 38, [1999] 2 AC 349.

[104] *Pitt v Holt* [2013] UKSC 26, [2013] 2 AC 108.

[105] *Torrens Aloha Pty Ltd v Citibank NA* [1997] FCA 77 (1997) 72 FCR 581.

[106] A separate argument based on discoverability also failed because the discoverability extension for limitation purposes runs from the date the mistake can be discovered, not the actionability of the mistake: See s 56(1) of the Limitation Act 1969 (NSW).

[107] Citing *Cooke v Gill* (1873) LR 8 CP 107, 116 (Brett MR); *Do Carmo v Ford Excavations Pty Ltd* [1984] HCA 17, (1984) 154 CLR 234, 245 [13] (Wilson J).

[108] *Torrens Aloha Pty Ltd v Citibank NA* [1997] FCA 77, (1997) 72 FCR 581.

[109] *Kleinwort Benson Ltd v Lincoln City Council* [1998] UKHL 38, [1999] 2 AC 349.

[110] *Hazell v Hammersmith and Fulham London Borough Council* [1992] 2 AC 1.

out, incorrect. This was accepted by a majority of the House of Lords.[111] The foundation of the reasoning of the majority was the retroactive nature of judicial decision-making. As Lord Goff rhetorically asked: 'what can our judges do but make new law and how can they prevent it from having retrospective effect?'[112] Indeed, whenever a judicial decision changes the law, it must apply retroactively to the parties before it, because the litigated facts occurred some time in the past. A similar, recent example from Canada is *Re Pallen Trust.*[113] It will be recalled that Mr Pallen pursued a complex taxation plan founded on a widespread understanding of the operation of a provision of an income tax act. Subsequent decisions of Canadian taxation and federal courts revealed the common understanding to be incorrect. Justice Masuhara held that dividends received by the Pallen Trust on the basis of the earlier, common understanding were liable to be rescinded for mistake.

Professor Dworkin provided a jurisprudential theory of adjudication that supported these conclusions.[114] On Dworkin's theory of adjudication, judges (unlike legislators) are interpreters of the law and are heavily constrained by the framework of legal adjudication. In contrast, legislators create law in a normative fashion, free from the constraints that limit legal decision-making. Dworkin's theory has support in the refusal of Australian courts to recognise the notion of prospective overruling: 'The adjudication of existing rights and obligations as distinct from the creation of rights and obligations distinguishes the judicial power from non-judicial power';[115] or, put another way, prospective overruling turns judges into 'undisguised legislators'.[116] Dworkin's thesis argues for a very strong version of the interpretative role of judges: even in hard cases, there is a 'right answer'.[117] His theory explains why a mistake as to the common law (however undiscoverable at the time) is a genuine mistake of law. It is consistent with the recognition that legislation that is expressed to operate retrospectively does not render mistaken an earlier payment made on the basis of the law as it stood prior to the change.[118] The theory does raise very difficult questions concerning identification by judges of what the law was at the point in time of the defendant's enrichment.[119] But on Dworkin's theory, the state of the law at a point in time is a matter of fact; judges find many other facts difficult to determine, and this should be no different. Ascertaining the law at a particular point in time is not a precise exercise, but the same can be true of the epistemology of determining facts. Even if Dworkin's right answer thesis were

[111] Lords Goff, Hoffmann and Hope; Lords Browne-Wilkinson and Lloyd dissenting.

[112] *Kleinwort Benson Ltd v Lincoln City Council* [1998] UKHL 38, [1999] 2 AC 349, 379.

[113] *Re Pallen Trust* [2014] BCSC 305.

[114] R Dworkin, *Law's Empire* (Cambridge, Mass, Harvard University Press, 1986). See D Sheehan, 'What Is a Mistake?' (2000) 20 *Legal Studies* 538.

[115] *Ha v New South Wales* [1997] HCA 34, (1997) 189 CLR 465, 503–04 (Brennan CJ, McHugh, Gummow and Kirby JJ), 515 (Dawon, Toohey and Gaudron JJ). Cf *National Westminster Bank Plc v Spectrum Plus Ltd (in liq)* [2005] UKHL 41, [2005] 2 AC 680.

[116] *Babaniaris v Lutony Fashions Pty Ltd* [1987] HCA 19, (1987) 163 CLR 1, 15 [13], citing Devlin, 'Judges and Law Makers' (1976) 39 *The Modern Law Review* 1, 11; see also *Torrens Aloha Pty Ltd v Citibank NA* [1997] FCA 77, (1997) 72 FCR 581, 594 (Sackville J; Foster and Lehane J concurring).

[117] R Dworkin, *Law's Empire* (Cambridge, Mass, Harvard University Press, 1986) 239.

[118] *Commissioner of State Revenue (Vic) v Royal Insurance Australia Ltd* [1994] HCA 61, (1994) 182 CLR 51, 89–90 (Brennan J; Toohey and McHugh JJ concurring), 100–01 (Dawson J), 67 (Mason CJ dissenting); *University of Wollongong v Metwally* [1984] HCA 74 [5], (1984) 158 CLR 447, 478 (Deane J); *Kleinwort Benson Ltd v Lincoln City Council* [1998] UKHL 38, [1999] 2 AC 349, 359 (Lord Browne-Wilkinson), 381 (Lord Goff), 394(Lord Lloyd), cf 400 (Lord Hoffmann).

[119] In the majority only Lord Hope focused upon the state of the law at the time of the payments: see *Kleinwort Benson Ltd v Lincoln City Council* [1998] UKHL 38, [1999] 2 AC 349, 411 (Lord Hope).

rejected, a later judge could strive to determine the best construction of the state of the law at a point in time, just as the judge does so by reference to the state of facts (based only on the usually limited evidence in court).

On the other hand, the minority in *Kleinwort Benson* argued not only that judges create new rights and obligations but also that a pretension otherwise, by recognition of a mistake of law where the common law had been changed, is to 'restrospecti[vely] ... falsify history'.[120] The theory of law that provides the most powerful support for this view is the school of American realism associated with Justice Holmes' predictive theory of law. For Holmes, the study of the law was nothing more than a means to predict the result that a judge may prefer in any case.[121] Weaker support can be derived from theories of law such as that of Professor Hart, who argued that in hard cases, judges have judicial discretion, and there is no right answer.[122] Hart's thesis requires differentiation between cases where the mistake of law cannot relate to existing data (however undiscoverable) and weak cases where the legal answer is clear and there is a true mistake.[123] Although the minority in *Kleinwort Benson* did not engage in discussion of these theories of law, the legal issue concerning the validity of the swaps agreements was undoubtedly a 'hard case' (the House of Lords in *Hazell* having overruled the Court of Appeal) so either theory—Holmes or Hart—supports the minority's conclusion that there was no mistake.

In addition to issues arising out of the retroactivity of mistakes of law, the removal of the mistake of law bar has also given rise to apparent logical conundrums. Suppose a plaintiff, suspecting a payment is not due, makes it anyway because of legal advice that if it is not due, the payment is recoverable. If the legal advice is correct, there is no mistake of law and so the payment is irrecoverable for mistake of law. But this means that the legal advice is then incorrect and so the payment must be recoverable for mistake of law.[124] We will see below that when faced with this issue in *Nurdin & Peacock plc v DB Ramsden & Co Ltd*, Neuberger J used the causation requirement to 'cut the vicious circle'.[125] However, a better way may be to characterise the plaintiff's mistake as being that the money was recoverable as a matter of law, independently of his mistake, if it was paid with the uncommunicated belief that it must always be returned if not due. Although Neuberger J did not analyse the problem in this way, the plaintiff in that case would have been mistaken because the money could *not* be recovered for a failure of basis that was not communicated to the other party.

The final point to be made in relation to mistakes of law is to recall that restitution may be denied where the plaintiff has assumed the risk of a mistake. It is notorious that law is less certain than fact, hence the need for lawyers and appellate courts. Parties frequently

[120] *Kleinwort Benson Ltd v Lincoln City Council* [1998] UKHL 38, [1999] 2 AC 349, 358 (Lord Browne-Wilkinson); see also 396 (Lord Lloyd).

[121] OW Holmes, 'The Path of the Law' in SM Novick (ed), *The Collected Works of Justice Holmes: Complete Public Writings and Selected Judicial Opinions of Oliver Wendell Holmes*, vol 3 (Chicago, University of Chicago Press, 1994) 393.

[122] HLA Hart, *The Concept of Law*, 2nd edn (Oxford, Clarendon Press, 1994) 141–47.

[123] The Property Law Act 1969 (WA) s 124(2) takes the opposite stance by refusing mistake claims where there is a settled understanding of the law ('easy cases' of mistake): see *Bell Bros Pty Ltd v Shire of Serpentine-Jarrahdale* [1969] WAR 155.

[124] *Nurdin & Peacock plc v DB Ramsden & Co Ltd* [1999] 1 WLR 1249, 1271 (Neuberger J), discussed further below p 190.

[125] ibid 1274.

settle disputes precisely in order to obtain some measure of certainty, a point which of itself has promoted a very cautious approach to rescission of settlement agreements.[126] In many cases where mistakes of law are made, the unjust enrichment plaintiff will know that the law is uncertain at the time of the transaction. The question in that context is whether the plaintiff assumed the risk of mistake when making the transaction.

IV. Causation and Contribution

A. The Concepts of Causation and Contribution

It is not enough for a plaintiff to prove that she was mistaken in order to recover the value of the enrichment conferred on the defendant by the impugned transaction. There must also be a link between the mistake and the transaction by which the defendant was enriched. The difficult issue in this second requirement is to determine the test to be applied.

The cases reveal three possibilities for the requisite test for the link between mistake and transaction: (1) 'but for' causation; (2) that the mistake is a 'significant reason' or 'material contribution' to the transaction that enriches the defendant; or (3) that the mistake is 'a factor' in the decision-making process which leads to the transaction that enriches the defendant. It must be recognised at the outset, however, that these tests undertake quite different inquiries. The 'but for' test is a philosophical investigation into a counterfactual world where the putative event (in the context of claims in unjust enrichment, events such as mistake, undue influence or illegitimate pressure) did not exist. The aim of this enquiry is to determine whether it is more likely than not that the event was necessary for the particular outcome the subject of the claim. If, in the hypothetical world, the absence of the event would have led to a different outcome, then the event was necessary for the outcome. Causation is established. In the context of claims based on the unjust factor of mistake, this counterfactual enquiry is expressed as whether, *but for* the mistake, the plaintiff would not have entered the transaction that enriched the defendant. This is not a factual question, but a counterfactual question, and therefore metaphysical.

The second and third tests, on the other hand, investigate whether, as a matter of fact, a certain event played some role (which, on the second test, must be significant or material) in the historical process that led to the result that in fact occurred. The third test is really a subset of the second. On this approach an event that made a positive contribution, as 'a factor' in the decision-making process, will still be sufficient even if it was unnecessary for the result that occurred.[127] In the context of the unjust factor of mistake, the enquiry on this approach is whether, as a matter of historical fact, the mistake played some role (which would need to be not insignificant or trivial) in the decision-making process of the plaintiff to enter into the transaction that enriched the defendant. This is a factual enquiry as to the mechanics of the transaction.

[126] Discussed in Ch 15 pp 398–400.
[127] J Stapleton, 'Unnecessary Causes' (2013) 129 *Law Quarterly Review* 39.

B. The Test for Causation or Contribution in Mistake

In England, after an uncertain start, the authorities on causation in cases of the unjust factor of mistake have gradually settled in favour of the 'but for' test.[128] However, in all of them, the 'a factor' test would also have been satisfied. The first modern case to consider causation in mistake is *Dextra Bank and Trust Co Ltd v Bank of Jamaica.*[129] It will be recalled that the plaintiff had paid money to the defendant mistakenly believing that the defendant had agreed to take a loan from the plaintiff. The Privy Council held that this mistake did not cause the transaction because the plaintiff subsequently instructed its agent not to make the payment unless he received a promissory note as evidence of the loan and its terms. The agent, a fraudster, ignored the instructions, and it was this duplicity, rather than the plaintiff's mistaken belief that a loan had been previously agreed, that caused entry into the transaction.[130] However, the error clearly constituted a 'but for' cause because but for the mistake, the cheque would not have been given to the agent and the transaction would not have proceeded. The mistake was also 'a' factor that influenced the decision-making process that led to the payment being made. The only conclusion can be that restitution was denied for other (scope of liability) reasons, possibly because it was considered unjust to lay the consequences of the fraud of the plaintiff's agent at the feet of the defendant.[131] However, there is little reason why the intervening act of a fraudulent agent should be treated any differently than it is in cases where the mistaken payment was induced by the fraud of a third party, where recovery is commonly allowed. The scope of liability concerns in this case are better met through responses such as change of position, which the Privy Council also considered and applied.

In *Nurdin & Peacock plc v DB Ramsden & Co Ltd,*[132] the issue of causation was discussed in the context of considering whether restitution could be awarded where payments were made by the plaintiff under the mistaken belief that they were recoverable. Justice Neuberger relied upon the 'but for' test as a way to break the vicious logical circle between whether the belief was mistaken—in which case the payments were recoverable and so there was no mistake—or correct—in which case the payments were not recoverable, which meant that the belief was mistaken.[133] However, his Lordship could equally have applied a test of 'a factor' to break the logical conundrum. And, as we saw earlier, in any event it was possible to find an actionable mistake that did not trigger the apparent logical conundrum. The strength of this English authority is further weakened by the fact that Neuberger J also said that there were additional requirements for causation: a close and direct connection between the mistake and the payment transaction or a requirement that

[128] See, for example, *Kleinwort Benson Ltd v Lincoln City Council* [1998] UKHL 38, [1999] 2 AC 349, 372 (Lord Goff), 399 (Lord Hoffman), 407–08 (Lord Hope); *Nurdin & Peacock plc v DB Ramsden & Co Ltd* [1999] 1 WLR 1249, 1273 (Neuberger J); *Dextra Bank & Trust Co Ltd v Bank of Jamaica* [2001] UKPC 50, [2002] 1 All ER (Comm) 193; *Saunders & Co v Hague* [2004] 2 NZLR 475, 490–91 (Chisholm J); *Test Claimants in the FII Group Litigation v Revenue and Customs Commissioners* [2008] EWHC 2893, [2009] STC 254 [264] (Henderson J); *Re Griffiths* [2008] EWHC 118, [2009] Ch 162; *Pitt v Holt* [2011] EWCA Civ 197, [2012] Ch 132.

[129] *Dextra Bank & Trust Co Ltd v Bank of Jamaica* [2001] UKPC 50, [2002] 1 All ER (Comm) 193.

[130] ibid.

[131] *McKew v Holland & Hannen & Cubitts (Scotland) Ltd* [1969] 3 All ER 1621; *March v E & MH Stramare Pty Ltd* [1991] HCA 12, (1991) 171 CLR 506, 517 [24] (Mason CJ).

[132] *Nurdin & Peacock plc v DB Ramsden & Co Ltd* [1999] 1 WLR 1249, 1273.

[133] ibid.

the mistake impinges on the relationship between payer and payee—which have no support in the authorities and are inconsistent with many cases allowing recovery for mistake, where the mistake was not one as between payer and payee.[134] Again, the legitimate scope of restitutionary liability concerns informing these additional elements are best addressed transparently through mechanisms specifically adapted for the purpose, such as the change of position defence.

We have already considered the cases of *Re Griffiths*[135] and *Pitt v Holt*,[136] both of which were cases where the plaintiff's ignorance of a fact relevant to the transaction contributed to the assumptions on which they acted (in *Re Griffiths*, the deceased's good health; and in *Pitt*, the taxation implications of the settlement). In those cases, assuming a relevant mistake was made, it was clearly 'a factor' informing the plaintiffs' assumptions on which they based their decision to enter the impugned transaction. A link based on an 'a factor' approach was therefore satisfied. The courts' application of the 'but for' test as the relevant criterion for causation led to the same conclusion. However, the 'but for' test will generally be overly inclusive of putative causes in ignorance cases. It is all too often the case that, had plaintiffs been aware of some fact or matter of which they were ignorant, they might have acted differently.[137] This is so even where the particular plaintiff never turned her mind to the matters informed by the 'missing' fact, and therefore had not based her decision to enter the transaction that enriched the defendant on any assumption informed by her ignorance. This over-inclusiveness led the Supreme Court to narrow the definition of mistake to exclude cases of 'mere causative ignorance'.[138] By contrast, on the 'a factor' approach, this further step is unnecessary, because such cases do not satisfy the 'a factor' approach. For instance, Professor Tettenborn's example of a donor who gives £1000 to his niece in ignorance of the fact that she has married his despised enemy[139] does not satisfy the 'a factor' approach, because the donor had no belief, and made no assumption, about his niece's marital status in making his gift. It did not influence the decision-making process by which he entered the transaction that enriched the defendant.

In Australia, courts directly considering the question of causation for the unjust factor of mistake and drawing an analogy with the approach taken in cases of misrepresentation have adopted the 'a factor' test.[140] Although there are some suggestions in those cases that a contributory reason must be a 'significant' factor to count (the second test), this would run contrary to the tenor of the High Court's decision in *David Securities*. In that case, the High Court did not expressly consider the appropriate test for causation or the required contributing link.[141] Instead, the case was remitted to the trial judge to determine whether the payments were made 'because of their mistaken belief'.[142] However, given the unanimous

[134] See for example *Lloyds Bank plc v Independent Insurance Co Ltd* [2000] QB 110, where the plaintiff's mistake was as to the state of its customer's account, rather than anything pertaining to the defendant. See also *Barclays Bank Ltd v WJ Simms Son & Cooke (Southern) Ltd* [1980] QB 677, 689–96 (Goff J).

[135] *Re Griffiths* [2008] EWHC 118, [2009] Ch 162.

[136] *Pitt v Holt* [2013] UKSC 26, [2013] 2 AC 108.

[137] *Pitt v Holt* [2010] EWHC 45, [2010] 1 WLR 1199 [50] (Justice Robert Englehart QC).

[138] *Pitt v Holt* [2013] UKSC 26, [2013] 2 AC 108 [108] (Lord Walker, giving the judgment of the Court).

[139] A Tettenborn, *Law of Restitution in England and Ireland*, 3rd edn (London, Cavendish 2002) 76.

[140] *Salib v Gakas* [2010] NSWSC 505 [328] (Ward J); *Lahoud v Lahoud* [2010] NSWSC 1297 [176] (Ward J).

[141] *David Securities Pty Ltd v Commonwealth Bank of Australia* [1992] HCA 48, (1992) 175 CLR 353, 378 [43] (Mason CJ, Deane, Toohey, Gaudron and McHugh JJ).

[142] *David Securities Pty Ltd v Commonwealth Bank of Australia* [1992] HCA 48, (1992) 175 CLR 353, 386 [62] (Mason CJ, Deane, Toohey, Gaudron and McHugh JJ), 407 [18] (Dawson J).

rejection of a test for 'fundamental' mistake, a test for 'fundamental' cause or 'significant' cause is unlikely to have been favoured by the High Court. Consistently with that view, it is suggested that the reference to 'significant' cause or 'material' contribution in recent decisions is best understood as excluding factors that clearly had a negligible effect on the decision in question, rather than introducing a new substantive standard for the link required between the mistake and the enrichment.[143]

Although an 'a factor' approach might seem unduly generous to plaintiffs, it still constitutes a real limitation on liability, as the Tettenborn example above shows. Further, 'a factor' causation will not be satisfied if the plaintiff considers a matter but decides to make the payment irrespective of whether it is true or not.[144] For instance, in *Euphoric Pty Ltd v Ryledar Pty Ltd*,[145] the plaintiff, a petroleum supplier, pleaded that it had allowed rebates to the defendant, a reseller of petroleum products, in the mistaken belief that the rebates were required under a supply agreement with the defendant. On the seventh day of the trial, counsel for the plaintiff conceded that the mistake claim must fail. The plaintiff's general manager had testified that the rebates were allowed because they made commercial good sense, not because of a mistake that they were required under the terms of the supply agreement. As Palmer J concluded, the manager's evidence made it clear that the plaintiff's allowance of rebates 'was not the result of any mistaken understanding that Ryledar was contractually entitled to such rebates; it was a result of Mr Hobbs' commercial decision, which was made regardless of the terms of the Supply Agreement'.[146] Even if the plaintiff were labouring under a mistake (which was doubtful on the evidence), that mistake was not 'a factor' that influenced its decision to allow the rebates. A more recent example is *Salib v Gakas*.[147] The plaintiff in that case made a payment to the defendant, which he suspected did not reflect the defendant's proper entitlement. In addressing the question of the causative or contributing link required, Ward J adopted an 'a factor' test. The payments were made to settle claims made by the defendant, whether or not the amounts of those claims were accurate.

C. Why 'A Factor' Instead of 'But For'?

On one view, the 'but-for' test is the only true test of causation and tests such as whether something is 'a factor' in the decision making process are instead concerned with non-causal contributions. If this is correct,[148] it is important to be very clear about the reasons for departing from a 'but for' test where the imposition of responsibility flows more comfortably from the conclusion that the mistake was necessary for the plaintiff's decision to enter the transaction that enriched the defendant. A departure from this rule of necessity without fully considered and justified reasons may lead the law to develop in an incoherent

[143] *Como Investments Pty Ltd (in liq) v Yenald Nominees Pty Ltd* (1997) 19 ATPR 41-550, 43,619, quoted with approval in *Henville v Walker* [2001] HCA 52, (2001) 206 CLR 459 [109] (McHugh J).

[144] *Barclays Bank Ltd v WJ Simms, Son and Cooke (Southern) Ltd* [1980] QB 677, 695 (Robert Goff J).

[145] *Euphoric Pty Ltd v Ryledar Pty Ltd* [2006] NSWSC 2.

[146] ibid [14].

[147] *Salib v Gakas* [2010] NSWSC 505 [328]–[334]; see also *Lahoud v Lahoud* [2010] NSWSC 1297 [176]–[179] (Ward J).

[148] Cf J Stapleton, 'Unnecessary Causes' (2013) 129 *Law Quarterly Review* 39.

and unprincipled manner. As Lord Hodge recently noted, 'courts continue to grapple with the consequences of departing from the "but for" test of causation in order to provide a remedy to those who have contracted mesothelioma as a result of wrongful exposure to asbestos fibres'.[149] He later commented that the 'law has tampered with the "but for" test of causation at its peril.'[150]

There are a number of possible reasons why an 'a factor' test is preferred by Australian courts in cases involving questions of decision-making.[151] The first is that it reflects a desire to award restitution in cases of 'over- and under-determination', notwithstanding that these cases do not satisfy 'but for' causation. Over-determination occurs where there is more than one independently sufficient reason to produce the result that in fact occurred. For instance, five people push the plaintiff's car off a cliff when any four would have been sufficient to push it. A related scenario is where there are multiple reasons that taken singly are insufficient, but when combined in one or more ways are sufficient, to produce the result that occurred ('under-determination'). Whilst instances of over- and under-determination are comparatively rare in cases of involuntary events, they are rife in cases involving decision-making. Courts (both in England and in Australia) have repeatedly refused to adopt the 'but for' test in these circumstances and have, instead favoured an 'a factor' approach.

The second reason is consistency with other areas involving decision-making where this approach is well established. We will see later in this book that in cases involving other types of impairments in plaintiffs' decisions, such as the unjust factors of illegitimate pressure or undue influence, the same contributory test of causation applies.[152] It is also well-established in claims of fraudulently induced mistake and estoppel.[153] An example is a leading authority on misrepresentation, *Edgington v Fitzmaurice*.[154] There, the plaintiff admitted that but for the defendant's misrepresentation in a company circular, he would likely have purchased the company shares anyway because of his own, independent mistake. This was, therefore, a case of over-determination. However, he argued (and it was accepted by the court) that the defendant's misstatement was also a factor that he took into account when making his decision. Lord Justice Bowen explained that the relevant question of causation in such cases is 'if his mind was disturbed by the misstatement of the Defendants, and such disturbance was in part the cause of what he did'.[155] This test is now well established as the relevant test of causation for misrepresentation.[156] The same test should

[149] *International Energy Group Ltd v Zurich Insurance plc UK Branch* [2015] UKSC 33, [2015] 2 WLR 1471 [98] (with whom Lord Mance, Lord Clarke and Lord Carnwath agreed).

[150] ibid [102], citing *Sienkiewicz v Greif (UK) Ltd* [2011] UKSC 10, [2011] 2 AC 229 [186] (Lord Brown).

[151] E Bant, 'Causation and Scope of Liability in Unjust Enrichment' [2009] *Restitution Law Review* 60. See also HW Tang, 'Restitution for Mistaken Gifts' (2004) 20 *Journal Contract Law* 1, 25, discussing T Honoré, 'Necessary and Sufficient Conditions in Tort Law' in DG Owen (ed), *Philosophical Foundations of Tort Law* (Oxford, Clarendon Press, 1995) 363–85.

[152] See Ch 9 pp 219–24; Ch 10 pp 235–42.

[153] In estoppel, see eg *Amalgamated Investment & Property Co Ltd (in liq) v Texas Commerce International Bank Ltd* [1982] QB 84, 104–05 (Robert Goff J), affirmed on appeal; *Sidhu v Van Dyke* [2014] HCA 19, (2014) 251 CLR 505 [71]–[74] (French CJ, Kiefel, Bell and Keane JJ; Gageler J dissenting on this point).

[154] *Edgington v Fitzmaurice* (1885) 29 Ch D 459.

[155] ibid 483; see also 481 (Cotton LJ), 485 (Fry LJ). See also *Nicholas v Thompson* [1924] VLR 554; *Wilcher v Steain* [1962] NSWR 1136.

[156] *Gould v Vaggelas* [1985] HCA 75, (1985) 157 CLR 215, 216 (Wilson J), 250–51 (Brennan J); *San Sebastian Pty Ltd v Minister Administering the Environmental Planning and Assessment Act 1979 (NSW)* [1986] HCA 68, (1986) 162 CLR 340, 370 (Brennan J); *Henville v Walker* [2001] HCA 52, (2001) 206 CLR 459 [106] (McHugh J).

logically be adopted in cases of spontaneous mistake as for induced mistake, given that both are instances of the law's response to the plaintiff's impaired decision to enter the transaction that enriched the defendant.

The third reason potentially favouring application by courts of an 'a factor' test relates to the uncertain aetiology of decision-making. Unlike chains of involuntary events, the sequencing of which generally[157] can be identified and tested in a counterfactual enquiry, the identity, relative weight and influence of one factor amongst many (both conscious and subconscious) in a party's decision-making is not something that can be readily determined and hence replicated. This is a significant reason in support of a test which only asks whether or not the factor played some part rather than to contrive a metaphysical consideration of the situation without that factor.[158] As Professor Birks put it:

> mental processes cannot be weighed and measured. Will-power has no voltage. So, if we ask, in relation to the mental process which goes into a decision to transfer wealth, how much disturbance shall count as an operative, restitution-yielding vitiation ... the truth is that there can be no exact answer.[159]

In these circumstances, courts revert to a process-based enquiry into whether, as a matter of historical fact, the putative cause was more likely than not one of the factors that contributed to the plaintiff's decision to act:

> Acknowledging that people are often swayed by several considerations, influencing them to varying extents, the law attributes causality to a single one of those considerations, provided it had some substantial rather than negligible effect.[160]

V. Conclusion

Although the unjust factor of mistake raises difficult issues when it is examined closely, the essential requirements are that the plaintiff is mistaken and that the mistake causes or contributes to the plaintiff's decision to enter the transaction that enriched the defendant. The mistake can be either a mistake of fact or of law. It can relate to transactions involving a defendant's enrichment by the receipt of value including provision of money, goods or services. It should operate identically at common law and in equity. The plaintiff will not have an actionable mistake if she assumed the risk of error, which will be found to have occurred where the plaintiff has sufficient doubts about the matter upon which she is said

[157] The mesothelioma cases that led to such decisions as *Fairchild v Glenhaven Funeral Services Ltd* [2002] UKHL 22, [2003] 1 AC 32, demonstrate the difficulties courts experience in applying a 'but for' test when the mechanism by which a particular outcome is produced is unknown.

[158] *Reynell v Sprye* (1852) 1 De GM & G 660, 708–09; (1852) 42 ER 710, 728–29 (Lord Cranworth); *Smith v Kay* (1859) 7 HLC 750, 759; (1859) 11 ER 299, 303 (Lord Chelmsford LC); *Arnison v Smith* (1875) 41 Ch D 348, 369 (Lord Halsbury LC). But cf *Mills v Mills* [1938] HCA 4; (1938) 60 CLR 150, 185–86 (Dixon J); *Eclairs Group Ltd and Glengary Overseas Ltd v JKX Oil & Gas plc* [2015] UKSC 71 [20]–[21] (Lord Sumption), [54] (Lord Mance); *Brosnan v Katke* [2016] FCAFC 1 [123] (the Court).

[159] P Birks, *An Introduction to the Law of Restitution*, rev edn (Oxford, Oxford University Press, 1989) 157.

[160] *Como Investments Pty Ltd (in liq) v Yenald Nominees Pty Ltd* [1997] FCA 12, (1997) 19 ATPR 41-550, 43,619, quoted with approval in *Henville v Walker* [2001] HCA 52, (2001) 206 CLR 459 [109] (McHugh J).

to be mistaken. As we have seen, the extent of doubt which will be sufficient is ultimately an evaluative exercise having regard to similar cases. Once a plaintiff is shown to be mistaken, the plaintiff must demonstrate that the mistake caused or contributed to the plaintiff's decision to enter the transaction that enriched the defendant. Australian courts favour 'a factor' over the 'but for' test applied in English courts. The innocent defendant's security of his receipt is further protected through defences, particularly the change of position defence. Finally, as explained in Chapter 7, the plaintiff must negate any juristic reason to retain the enrichment raised by the defendant as a condition of obtaining restitution.

We began our consideration of the different unjust factors with mistake because it is the most widely recognised and acknowledged unjust factor in the law of unjust enrichment. We have seen that restitution is available where a plaintiff's decision to enter a transaction that enriched a defendant is impaired by a mistake and where there is no juristic reason to retain the enrichment. The next two chapters consider two other types of impairment of a plaintiff's intention to enrich the defendant: duress or illegitimate pressure; and undue influence. We will then turn to consider cases in which the plaintiff's intention to enter the transaction that enriched the defendant was conditional, and cases in which a transaction occurs by which the defendant is enriched without the plaintiff's intention at all.

9

Duress or Illegitimate Pressure

Contents

I. Introduction

We move now from the unjust factor of mistake to the unjust factor of illegitimate pressure. Illegitimate pressure is sometimes described as 'compulsion' or 'duress'. It is commonly recognised as a central example of a vitiating factor within the law of unjust enrichment.[1] This chapter is entitled 'duress or illegitimate pressure' because the label 'duress' has an historic association with common law. We prefer the terminology in this chapter of 'illegitimate pressure' because that label is neutral between common law and equity where pressure is also an unjust factor which permits restitution.

As we saw in Chapter 7, in order to succeed in a claim of illegitimate pressure, the plaintiff must prove (i) an unjust factor or reason for restitution, and (ii) negate any juristic reason that entitles the defendant to retain the enrichment. Like other unjust factors, duress or illegitimate pressure can provide a reason for restitution and can also negate a juristic reason asserted by a defendant as a reason to retain an enrichment. In relation to negating a juristic reason, in Chapter 7 we saw that duress or illegitimate pressure can negate a juristic reason such as a contract or deed.[2] In those circumstances, the same facts of illegitimate pressure will usually permit restitution of the defendant's enrichment.

This chapter first explains the nature of an action for unjust enrichment based on illegitimate pressure which vitiates a transaction (and can also permit tracing through causally related transactions, as we saw in Chapter 5). We will see that the unjust factor of illegitimate pressure has two elements:[3]

(1) an illegitimate exertion of pressure upon the plaintiff that
(2) caused or contributed to (is a factor in) the plaintiff's decision to enter a transaction that enriches the defendant.

As to the first element, cases of illegitimate pressure divide into unlawful and lawful pressures. If the pressure involves a threat to commit an unlawful act or (more rarely) is pressure which derives from unlawful conduct, it is prima facie illegitimate. If the pressure is

[1] *Woolwich Equitable Building Society v Inland Revenue Commissioners* [1993] AC 70 164–65 (Lord Goff), see also 157 (Lord Keith), 160–61, 178–79 (Lord Jauncey), 197–98 (Lord Browne-Wilkinson), 205 (Lord Slynn); *Test Claimants in the FII Group Litigation v Revenue and Customs Commissioners* [2010] EWCA Civ 103, [2010] STC 1251 [156] (the Court); *Halpern v Halpern* [2007] EWCA Civ 291, [2008] QB 195; *David Securities Pty Ltd v Commonwealth Bank of Australia* [1992] HCA 48, (1992) 175 CLR 353, 379 [46] (Mason CJ, Deane, Toohey, Gaudron and McHugh JJ).

[2] As Ch 7 shows, other requirements may also be necessary, such as the defendant being responsible for or aware of the illegitimate pressure in cases of contract: see p 146.

[3] *Crescendo Management Pty Ltd v Westpac Banking Corporation* (1988) 19 NSWLR 40, 45–46 (McHugh JA); *Bloomingdale Holdings Pty Ltd v 63 Buckley Street Pty Ltd* [2008] VSC 168 [427] (Hargrave J); *Electricity Generation Corporation t/as Verve Energy v Woodside Energy Ltd* [2013] WASCA 36 [24] (McLure P; Newnes JA concurring); *Universe Tankships Inc of Monrovia v International Transport Workers Federation (The Universe Sentinel)* [1983] 1 AC 366, 400 (Lord Scarman); *Dimskal Shipping Co SA v International Transport Workers Federation (The Evia Luck) (No 2)* [1992] 2 AC 152, 165 (Lord Goff). More recent English courts show a tendency formally to separate pressure and illegitimacy into discrete elements, but their substantive analysis then consistently focuses on the illegitimacy of any pressure and its causative effect: see, eg, *DSND Subsea Ltd v Petroleum Geo-Services ASA* [2000] BLR 530 [131] (Dyson J); *Adam Opel GmbH v Mitras Automotive UK Ltd* [2007] EWHC 3205, [2008] Bus LR D55 [25]–[26] (David Donaldson QC); *Kolmar Group AG v Traxpo Enterprises PVT Ltd* [2010] EWHC 113, [2011] 1 All ER (Comm) 46 [92] (Christopher Clarke J). On the role of 'no reasonable alternative' as a suggested third element, see below pp 205–07.

lawful, it may still be illegitimate if there is no reasonable connection between, on the one hand, the nature and extent of the threats being made and, on the other hand, the subject matter which is demanded and any legitimate interest that the defendant has in that subject matter (a test of 'disproportionality'). The good faith of the defendant may inform this enquiry, but good faith is not an independent element.

The second element requires that any illegitimate pressure caused or contributed to the plaintiff's decision to enter the transaction. Enquiries into whether there was 'no reasonable alternative' open to the plaintiff, the bona fides of the defendant, and evidence of any 'protest' are matters relevant to this enquiry.

The final section of this chapter returns to a point made in Chapters 2 and 6. It explains that illegitimate pressure is an unjust factor and is not an action based upon wrongdoing. However, although illegitimate pressure does not necessarily involve a civil wrong, in some cases there may be a concurrent action for wrongdoing against the party that exerts the illegitimate pressure.

II. The Nature of Illegitimate Pressure

A. The Rationale of Illegitimate Pressure

It is often said that illegitimate pressure must amount to 'a coercion of [the] will so as to vitiate … consent'.[4] This suggests that the rationale for illegitimate pressure is the coercion or overbearing of the plaintiff's will. But the overborne will rationale is inconsistent with the main body of authority.[5] It also obscures the fact that illegitimate pressure generally involves a conscious choice by most victims of the pressure to submit to the demand rather than take an alternative course of action.[6]

The usual cases of illegitimate pressure therefore concern circumstances where the plaintiff's consent was valid but impaired by illegitimate pressure. In *Crescendo Management Pty Ltd v Westpac Banking Corporation*,[7] McHugh JA rejected the overborne will theory of illegitimate pressure and held that the 'proper approach … is to ask whether any applied

[4] *Occidental Worldwide Investment Corporation v Skibs A/S Avanti (The Siboen and The Sibotre)* [1976] 1 Lloyd's Rep 293, 336 (Kerr J); see also *North Ocean Shipping Co Ltd v Hyundai Construction Co Ltd* [1979] QB 705; *Pao On v Lau Yiu Long* [1980] AC 614, 635 (Lord Scarman); *Padilla Chien Mateo v Madam Chan Choi Hing* [1997] HKCFI 410, [1997] HKLRD 539; *Jones v Morgan* [2001] EWCA Civ 995, [2002] 1 EGLR 125, 130 [43] (Chadwick LJ; Lord Phillips MR and Pill LJ agreeing); *Capital Structures plc v Time and Tide Construction Ltd* [2006] EWHC 591, [2006] BLR 226 [17] (David Willcox J). In New Zealand, the overbearing of the will approach was adopted in *Shivas v Bank of New Zealand* [1990] 2 NZLR 327, 345 (Tipping J) and *Pharmacy Care Systems Ltd v Attorney-General* [2004] NZCA 187, (2004) NZCCLR 187 [89] (Hammond J) (delivering judgment of the court) but subsequently unanimously rejected in *McIntyre v Nemesis DBK Ltd* [2009] NZCA 329, [2010] 1 NZLR 463 [63]–[67] (the Court).

[5] *Director of Public Prosecutions for Northern Ireland v Lynch* [1975] AC 653 (rejecting the 'overborne will' approach in the context of criminal duress) and *Barton v Armstrong* [1976] AC 104.

[6] P Atiyah, 'Economic Duress and the "Overborne Will"' (1982) 98 *Law Quarterly Review* 197, 200; *Director of Public Prosecutions for Northern Ireland v Lynch* [1975] AC 653; endorsed by McHugh JA in *Crescendo Management Pty Ltd v Westpac Banking Corporation* (1988) 19 NSWLR 40, 45–46; in turn endorsed in *Dimskal Shipping Co SA v International Transport Workers Federation (The Evia Luck) (No 2)* [1992] 2 AC 152, 165–66 (Lord Goff).

[7] *Crescendo Management Pty Ltd v Westpac Banking Corporation* (1988) 19 NSWLR 40.

pressure induced the victim to enter the contract and then ask whether that pressure went beyond what the law is prepared to countenance as legitimate'.[8] This must be the true rationale because, as McHugh JA observed, if a plaintiff's intention were required to be entirely overcome then any transaction (such as a juristic reason of contract, or a will, or a trust) brought about through the operation of illegitimate pressure would be void rather than, as the cases recognise, voidable. As Lord Diplock said in *Universe Tankships Inc of Monrovia v International Transport Workers Federation*:

> The rationale is that his apparent consent was induced by pressure exercised upon him by that other party which the law does not regard as legitimate, with the consequence that the consent is treated in law as revocable unless approbated either expressly or by implication after the illegitimate pressure has ceased to operate on his mind.[9]

With its rationale as the application of illegitimate pressure it is immediately apparent that illegitimate pressure shares with mistake a concern to protect the plaintiff's autonomous decision-making ability. However, like cases of extreme mistake[10] or undue influence,[11] it is possible in very rare cases for illegitimate pressure to be so overwhelming as to negate consent entirely. In those exceptional cases, where the plaintiff made no real choice, the juristic basis for a transaction might be void.

B. Illegitimate Pressure in Equity

In *Barton v Armstrong*[12] Lord Cross explained that because the scope of common law duress was historically very limited, equity developed a jurisdiction to give relief in cases where 'the disposition in question had been procured by the exercise of pressure which the Chancellor considered to be illegitimate—although it did not amount to common law duress'. Illegitimate pressure at common law was originally limited to duress to the person and (later) duress to goods. Other types of pressure did not count. Courts of equity recognised that other forms of pressure could be equally illegitimate, although not involving threats to life and limb. In particular, equity intervened to grant relief in a number of cases of lawful, but illegitimate, pressure which we will discuss below.

Although the historical restrictions on common law duress explain the separate treatment of illegitimate pressure at common law and in equity, modern courts no longer emphasise that distinction. This is because both jurisdictions now recognise a wide variety of forms of illegitimate pressure. It follows that there is no reason to continue to distinguish between common law and equitable doctrines of illegitimate pressure. In *R v Attorney-General for England and Wales*,[13] a claim for common law duress was brought to avoid a contract which had been induced by a threat to 'return a soldier to unit' unless he signed the contract. While the soldier failed to make his case in duress, the Privy Council assumed

[8] ibid 46.

[9] *Universe Tankships Inc of Monrovia v International Transport Workers Federation (The Universe Sentinel)* [1983] 1 AC 366, 384 (emphasis added).

[10] As in cases of *non est factum*: *PT Ltd v Maradona Pty Ltd* (1992) 25 NSWLR 643; *Ford v Perpetual Trustees Victoria Ltd* [2009] NSWCA 186, (2009) 75 NSWLR 42, discussed in Ch 7 pp 142–43.

[11] Eg *Veall v Veall* [2015] VSCA 60, discussed in Ch 7 p 143.

[12] *Barton v Armstrong* [1976] AC 104, 118.

[13] *R v Attorney-General for England and Wales* [2003] UKPC 22, [2003] EMLR 24.

that common law duress could extend to such circumstances. The jurisdictional origin of the doctrine was simply ignored. A similarly broad view was taken in *Halpern v Halpern (Nos 1 & 2)*.[14] In that case, the pleaded pressure consisted of a rabbi's threats to require certain of the defendants to swear a ritual oath or pay a penalty of £250,000 if their inheritance dispute with the plaintiffs was not settled. The defendants asserted that the rabbi knew that the oath would not be sworn by an observant Jew. Justice Christopher Clarke held that the threat was capable of supporting a finding of duress.[15] Therefore the summary judgment application was dismissed. Before the English Court of Appeal, this ruling was not challenged.[16] Again, the jurisdictional origin of the doctrine played no role in the Court's consideration of its operation on the facts of the case. Similarly in an Australian family law decision,[17] the umbrella term 'equitable duress' was used to signify all forms of illegitimate pressure, whatever their jurisdictional source. The irresistible conclusion is that illegitimate pressure at common law and in equity has the same structure and effect.[18] For this reason this chapter refers interchangeably to 'duress or illegitimate pressure' to emphasise that illegitimate pressure is actionable in equity just as it is at common law where it is usually entitled 'duress'.

Unfortunately, cases in equity involving pressure have sometimes been labelled 'undue influence'. This has probably occurred because 'duress' is associated with common law, but undue influence is a very well recognised head of equity.[19] Also, as Carnwath LJ (Waller and Sedley LJJ concurring) noted in *Halpern v Halpern*, 'duress and undue influence have much in common'.[20] Both are vitiating factors that may impair a plaintiff's consent to enter a transaction that enriches the defendant so as to give rise to a right to restitution.[21] But notwithstanding their similarities, the unjust factors are distinct. We will see in Chapter 10 that the central distinction between undue influence and illegitimate pressure is that undue influence typically arises in cases where the plaintiff's intention to enrich the defendant is impaired by his excessive dependence on, or lack of emancipation from, another person. Pressure is not required. Indeed, undue influence cases often involve no application of pressure by the dominant party. The influence over the plaintiff may have arisen for innocuous reasons, such as mutual affection or the defendant's status as a spiritual or legal adviser. Plaintiffs in undue influence cases are typically over-eager and willing to enter the

[14] *Halpern v Halpern (Nos 1 & 2)* [2007] EWCA Civ 291, [2008] QB 195.

[15] *Halpern v Halpern* [2006] EWHC 603, [2006] 2 All ER (Comm) 251 [85]. The plaintiff's argument that the claim of duress must fail because it came from a third party was also rejected (at [96]), and rightly so: see Ch 7 pp 148–49.

[16] ibid [69] (Carnwath LJ; Waller and Sedley LJJ concurring).

[17] *SH v DH (No 1)* (2003) 31 Fam LR 102; see also *Wagner v Wagner* [2009] FamCAFC 16.

[18] *Royal Bank of Scotland plc v Etridge (No 2)* [2001] UKHL 44, [2002] 2 AC 773 [8] (Lord Nicholls, distinguishing within the broad label of undue influence 'acts of improper pressure or coercion such as unlawful threats' from cases of 'influence' or 'ascendancy'); *Halpern v Halpern (Nos 1 & 2)* [2007] EWCA Civ 291, [2008] QB 195 [69], [70] (Carnwath LJ; Waller and Sedley LJJ concurring).

[19] See, eg, *Williams v Bayley* (1866) LR 1 HL 200 where all the Lords recognised that recovery was based on pressure and coercion and only Lord Chelmsford referred to 'undue influence'. See also *Collins v Hare* (1828) 1 Dow & Cl 139, 6 ER 476; *Mutual Finance Ltd v John Wetton & Sons Ltd* [1937] 2 KB 389; WHD Winder, 'Undue Influence and Coercion' (1939) 3 *The Modern Law Review* 97, 111.

[20] *Halpern v Halpern (Nos 1 & 2)* [2007] EWCA Civ 291, [2008] QB 195 [70], [71] (Waller and Sedley LJJ concurring). See also *Electricity Generation Corporation t/as Verve Energy v Woodside Energy Ltd* [2013] WASCA 36 [23] (McLure P; Newnes JA concurring), describing illegitimate pressure as a 'close cousin' of undue influence, see also [175] (Murphy JA).

[21] *Halpern v Halpern (Nos 1 & 2)* [2007] EWCA Civ 291, [2008] QB 195 [75], [76] (Carnwath LJ; Waller and Sedley LJJ concurring).

transaction, without considering their own interests. By contrast, plaintiffs in illegitimate pressure cases typically are only too aware of their own interests and are loathe to succumb to 'some coercion from outside, some overreaching, some form of cheating'.[22]

An example of an equitable pressure case pleaded as a case of undue influence is *Bank of Scotland v Bennett*.[23] Mrs Bennett claimed that she had entered the impugned contract as a result of the undue influence of her husband. Lord Justice Chadwick (with whom Sir Christopher Staunton and Auld LJ agreed) observed that the plea of 'actual undue influence' was really a plea of undue pressure (the equitable equivalent of duress). His Lordship observed that a claim based on pressure was irreconcilable with one based on influence. It was found that Mrs Bennett had entered the transaction unwillingly and as a result of her husband's illegitimate pressure: her 'husband had succeeded in overcoming her will without convincing her reason'.[24] This finding in her favour on illegitimate pressure defeated her case of undue influence because her unwillingness indicated that she retained a fully independent or emancipated judgment with respect to her husband.[25]

The error of labelling pressure cases as 'undue influence' has not been confined to equity. Some common law pressure cases have also been described as undue influence. For example, in *National Australia Bank Ltd v Satchithanantham*[26] a wife consented to enter a loan agreement secured against her home. She did so in fear of her husband's physical violence. The case involved a straightforward common law claim for duress 'to the person', but counsel and the courts at first instance and on appeal characterised the pressure as 'actual undue influence'.

There is similar inaccurate labelling in testamentary undue influence cases. The common law probate doctrine allowed a will to be set aside because of what Sir James Wilde (later Lord Penzance) described as overpowering pressure[27] and what the High Court of Australia has described as 'coercion'.[28] As early as 1939, Professor Winder suggested that the common law doctrine should not be described as 'undue influence' but should be called 'coercion'.[29] Unfortunately, although common law illegitimate pressure could vitiate a will or testamentary gift, a true unjust factor of undue influence was never applied to testamentary gifts, creating an anomaly between gifts *inter vivos* (to which undue influence applied) and testamentary gifts (to which it did not).[30] In the High Court, Gaudron, Gummow and Kirby JJ have hinted at abolition of this anomaly.[31]

[22] *Allcard v Skinner* (1887) 36 Ch D 145, 181 (Lindley LJ).

[23] *Bank of Scotland v Bennett* [1999] 1 FLR 1115; appeal conjoined and allowed on another ground in *Royal Bank of Scotland plc v Etridge (No 2)* [2001] UKHL 44, [2002] 2 AC 773. Cf *Tabtill Pty Ltd v Creswick; Creswick v Creswick* [2011] QCA 381.

[24] *Bank of Scotland v Bennett* [1999] 1 FLR 1115, 1127, 1131.

[25] Cf K Mason, JW Carter and GJ Tolhurst, *Mason and Carter's Restitution Law in Australia*, 2nd edn (Chatswood, NSW, LexisNexis Butterworths, 2008) [518] fn 203, who cite this case as a paradigm example of undue influence; see further below at p 218.

[26] *National Australia Bank Ltd v Satchithanantham* [2009] NSWSC 21, upheld [2009] NSWCA 268.

[27] *Hall v Hall* (1868) LR 1 P & D 481, 481. See also *Barry v Butlin* (1838) 2 Moo PC 480, 491; 12 ER 1089, 1093 (Parke B): 'The undue influence ... must be of the nature of fraud or duress'. For a recent exposition of the doctrine in consistent terms, see *Edwards v Edwards* [2007] EWHC 1119, [2007] WTLR 1387 [47] (Lewison J).

[28] *Bridgewater v Leahy* [1998] HCA 66, (1998) 194 CLR 457 [62].

[29] WHD Winder, 'Undue Influence and Coercion' (1939) 3 *The Modern Law Review* 97, 108.

[30] The anomaly is powerfully criticised in P Ridge, 'Equitable Undue Influence and Wills' (2004) 120 *Law Quarterly Review* 617. For recent judicial acknowledgement of the need for review, and moving away from a conception of coercion, see *Nicholson v Knaggs* [2009] VSC 64.

[31] *Bridgewater v Leahy* [1998] HCA 66, (1998) 194 CLR 457 [63].

III. An Exertion of Illegitimate Pressure

We have seen that the two elements of the unjust factor of illegitimate pressure are (1) that the plaintiff be subject to an exertion of illegitimate pressure and (2) that this pressure must contribute to the plaintiff's decision to enter the transaction that enriches the defendant. The fundamental point relating to the first requirement is that it focuses upon the nature of the pressure rather than its extent. As Lords Wilberforce and Simon observed in *Barton v Armstrong*, 'in life, including the life of commerce and finance, many acts are done under pressure, sometimes overwhelming pressure ... [but] the pressure must be one of a kind which the law does not regard as legitimate'.[32]

A. Threats Distinguished from Warnings, Requests and Offers

The first element of illegitimate pressure is that the plaintiff was subject to pressure of such a nature that the law regards it as illegitimate. The pressure will usually take the form of an explicit or implicit threat made to the plaintiff that undesirable consequences will follow unless the plaintiff enters a transaction that enriches the defendant or a third party. Pressure that arises from an existing or past breach of duty (for example, where the defendant detains the plaintiff's asset in breach of duty to the plaintiff in order to extract some benefit from the plaintiff)[33] almost invariably involves an implicit threat of ongoing or future breaches. A past breach of duty which involves no likelihood of repetition will rarely, by itself, be sufficient pressure to cause a plaintiff to act.

The types of threat of unlawful action which are sufficient are wide ranging. It does not matter if the threat is implicit rather than explicit: the surrounding circumstances are judged 'as a matter of substance and reality, and not mere form'.[34] However, a threat of unlawful action, which is often illegitimate, needs to be distinguished from a warning, which is not illegitimate. In general, a person issuing a warning has little or no control over the predicted consequences.[35] An example is *Williams v Roffey Brothers & Nicholls (Contractors) Ltd.*[36] A carpenter (Williams) entered a contract with the defendant contractor to refurbish a number of London flats. Williams won the job on the basis of a tender that was unrealistically low. As the job progressed, it became increasingly clear that Williams would not be able to complete the job unless he was paid an additional amount. The unwelcome news of Williams' position was conveyed to the contractor by a third party. But as Professor

[32] *Barton v Armstrong* [1976] AC 104, 121.

[33] *Astley v Reynolds* (1731) 2 Str 915, 93 ER 939, discussed below at p 204.

[34] *Electricity Generation Corporation t/as Verve Energy v Woodside Energy Ltd* [2013] WASCA 36 [180] (Murphy JA; McLure P and Newnes JA concurring on this point); see also *B & S Contracts and Design Ltd v Victor Green Publications Ltd* [1984] ICR 419. An obvious example is where a gunman simply points a gun to another's head and demands money. The possibility of 'unilateral illegitimate pressure' is considered below at pp 218–19.

[35] J Beatson, *The Use and Abuse of Unjust Enrichment: Essays on the Law of Restitution* (Oxford, Clarendon Press, 1991) 118; SA Smith, 'Contracting under Pressure: A Theory of Duress' (1997) 56 *Cambridge Law Journal* 343, 346. For a perceptive discussion of the difference between warnings, requests and threats in the context of the tort of intimidation, see *Berezovsky v Abramovich* [2010] EWHC 647 [79]–[80], [85]–[86] (Sir Anthony Coleman).

[36] *Williams v Roffey Brothers & Nicholls (Contractors) Ltd* [1991] 1 QB 1.

(now Lord Justice) Beatson[37] observed, Williams could have conveyed the information himself. Had Williams done so, it would have been a warning not a threat. It would only have been a threat if Williams had been able to complete the job, but threatened its non-completion in order to extract further moneys from the defendant.[38] Threats must also be distinguished from requests (where no unwelcome consequence is proposed or consequential upon the request) and offers (in which the proposed consequence is usually welcome).[39]

Once pressure has been established, the issue of whether the pressure is illegitimate can involve fine exercises of judgement. Particularly in the context of commercial transactions, the line between 'impermissible economic duress (on the one hand) [and] the permissible (even necessary) operation of the market economy (on the other)'[40] can be very fine. A starting point is to divide pressure into the categories of threatened conduct that is *unlawful* (and usually illegitimate)[41] and threatened conduct that is *lawful* (and usually legitimate).[42]

B. Exertion of Pressure by Unlawful Threats

An unlawful threat is a threatened breach of statutory or general law duty, whether criminal or civil. Like unlawful conduct, the examples of unlawful threat are protean. We will focus on five types of threat:

(i) violence (a tort and usually a crime);
(ii) unlawful interference with chattels or property rights;
(iii) breaches of contract and interference with contractual relations;
(iv) refusal by public officers to perform a duty required by statute; and
(v) breaches of equitable duties.

i. Threats of Violence

Threats of physical violence are almost invariably unlawful. Therefore, a threat of physical violence to a plaintiff or a plaintiff's family in order to exact a benefit is also illegitimate. This category of case was traditionally labelled as 'duress to the person'. We have already seen an example in *Barton v Armstrong*,[43] where the plaintiff was threatened with death unless he entered the contract. A majority of the Privy Council held that the contract was voidable for illegitimate pressure.[44] Another is *Toman v Toman*[45] in which a mother sold her

[37] J Beatson, *The Use and Abuse of Unjust Enrichment: Essays on the Law of Restitution* (Oxford, Clarendon Press, 1991) 120.

[38] See further discussion below at p 207.

[39] SA Smith, 'Contracting under Pressure: A Theory of Duress' (1997) 56 *Cambridge Law Journal* 343, 346–49.

[40] *Equiticorp Finance Ltd (in liq) v Bank of New Zealand* (1993) 32 NSWLR 50, 106 (Kirby P).

[41] *Universe Tankships Inc of Monrovia v International Transport Workers Federation (The Universe Sentinel)* [1983] 1 AC 366, 401 (Lord Scarman); *Australia and New Zealand Banking Group Ltd v Karam* [2005] NSWCA 344, (2005) 64 NSWLR 149 [66] (the Court).

[42] *Electricity Generation Corporation t/as Verve Energy v Woodside Energy Ltd* [2013] WASCA 36 [25] (McLure P; Newnes JA concurring). Opposed to this division is K Mason, JW Carter and GJ Tolhurst, *Mason and Carter's Restitution Law in Australia*, 2nd edn (Chatswood, NSW, LexisNexis Butterworths, 2008) [518], [529].

[43] *Barton v Armstrong* [1976] AC 104.

[44] The minority dissented on the ground that the pressure did not cause entry into the contract, discussed below at p 221.

[45] *Toman v Toman* [2009] NZHC 1000 [15]–[16].

house to her son at a gross undervalue because he demanded it and she was afraid of him. Justice MacKenzie of the New Zealand High Court held that she entered the contract under illegitimate pressure and that the son must make restitution of the title to the property by an order for a constructive trust.

ii. Threats of Unlawful Interference with Goods and Land

Like illegitimate pressure involving threats of violence, the category of illegitimate pressure traditionally known as 'duress to goods' usually involves threats of unlawful conduct.[46] A typical example of the unlawful conduct would involve the tort of conversion. For example, in *Astley v Reynolds*,[47] the plaintiff pawned silver plate to the defendant. When he came to redeem the plate, the defendant refused to return it, and threatened to continue to retain it indefinitely unless the plaintiff paid him an unlawful penalty interest rate. Eventually the plaintiff succumbed to the defendant's demand in order to obtain the return of his plate. The court ordered restitution of the amount of interest in excess of the legal rate.

The same principle applies in cases involving rights to land. In *Criterion Theatres Ltd v Melbourne & Metropolitan Board of Works*,[48] the plaintiffs were the owners of the Ascot racecourse, which had been possessed by the Commonwealth of Australia for a period during the Second World War. The defendant Board of Works levied rates upon the plaintiffs in respect of the racecourse. The rates were paid after the Board of Works threatened that the water supply would be cut off if the payments were not made. The court found that the occupier of the property, the Commonwealth, was liable for the rates. The plaintiffs claimed restitution of their payments on the basis that they had been made as a result of duress by the Board of Works. In response, the Board of Works argued that its threat to cut off the water supply was made to the state trotting association, not to the plaintiffs. This was rejected by Lowe J, who observed that the threat concerned the land owned by the plaintiffs and, if carried out, would have destroyed their racing track.

iii. Threats of Breach of Contract and Interference with Contractual Relations

A difficult question is whether a threatened breach of contract is always illegitimate. On the one hand, a breach of contract is a breach of duty and therefore unlawful. The contrary view of Holmes was that there is no duty to perform a contract, only one to choose whether to perform or pay damages.[49] But this has been rejected in England and Australia.[50]

[46] Cf *Denmeade v Stingray Boats* [2003] FCAFC 215 [16] (the Court) where the respondent's retention of the appellant's boat was found to be justified by a possessory lien and so the appellant's claim of 'economic duress' failed. On the protean nature of 'economic duress' see below at p 215.

[47] *Astley v Reynolds* (1731) 2 Str 915, 93 ER 939; for an example in a modern context, see *Hawker Pacific Pty Ltd v Helicopter Charter Pty Ltd* (1991) 22 NSWLR 298.

[48] *Criterion Theatres Ltd v Melbourne and Metropolitan Board of Works* [1945] VLR 267; see also *Close v Phipps* (1844) 7 Man & G 586, 590; 135 ER 236, 238; *Fraser v Pendlebury* (1861) 31 LJCP 1, 2–3 (Erle CJ), 3 (Williams J), 3–4 (Byles J); *Nixon v Furphy* (1925) 25 SR (NSW) 151, 158 (Tindal CJ); *Re Hooper & Grass' Contract* [1949] VLR 269; *J & S Holdings Pty Ltd v NRMA Insurance Ltd* (1982) 41 ALR 539, 555 (Blackburn, Deane and Ellicott JJ).

[49] OW Holmes, *The Common Law* (Boston, Little, Brown & Company, 1881) 301; OW Holmes, 'The Path of the Law' (1897) 10 *Harvard Law Review* 457, 462; *Globe Refining Company v Landa Cotton Oil Company* 190 US 540 (1903) 544.

[50] *Beswick v Beswick* [1968] AC 58, 91 (Lord Pearce); *Coulls v Bagot's Executor and Trustee Co Ltd* [1967] HCA 3, (1967) 119 CLR 460, 504 [33] (Windeyer J); *Tabcorp Holdings Ltd v Bowen Investments Pty Ltd* [2009] HCA 8, (2009) 236 CLR 272 [13] (the Court).

Consistently with the treatment of breach of contract as unlawful, there are numerous authorities in which it has been accepted that threatened breach of a contract can be illegitimate pressure.[51]

However, some judges have suggested that a threatened breach of contract is not always illegitimate. In the Privy Council decision in *Pao On v Lau Yiu Long*[52] the defendant's threat to breach a contract (a refusal to complete a purchase of shares) caused the plaintiff to agree to guarantee that they would purchase the shares at the end of the year at a fixed price. The plaintiff's action to avoid the guarantee for illegitimate pressure failed. Delivering the advice of the Board, Lord Scarman said that

> in a contractual situation commercial pressure is not enough … it is material to inquire whether the person alleged to have been coerced did or did not protest; whether, at the time he was allegedly coerced into making the contract, he did or did not have an alternative course open to him such as an adequate legal remedy; whether he was independently advised; and whether after entering the contract he took steps to avoid it.[53]

It is difficult to know what Lord Scarman meant. Were the factors of (i) protest, (ii) alternative courses open, and (iii) independent legal advice relevant to the question of the illegitimacy of the threat, or to causation or contribution, or were they suggested as additional and independent requirements? Lord Scarman spoke of their relevance to the 'voluntariness' of the plaintiff's conduct, which suggests a link to causation or contribution to the plaintiff's decision. We return to their role in that context below. But he also said that they were essential elements for the threat to amount to illegitimate pressure, which suggests that they are relevant to the legitimacy of the threat.[54] On this approach, not all threatened breaches of contract will be illegitimate, despite being unlawful. Similar arguments have sometimes been made with respect to so-called 'good faith' actual or threatened breaches of contract, made in response to unforeseen changes that render the original contract highly unprofitable for the defendant.[55]

A line of English cases has subsequently identified the 'no reasonable alternative' requirement as an independent element of illegitimate pressure.[56] Australian courts have not followed this lead. They have been right not to do so, for at least three reasons. First, if adopted, the 'no reasonable alternative' requirement would operate as an objective standard of moral

[51] Eg *Atlas Express Ltd v Kafco (Importers and Distributors) Ltd* [1989] QB 833; *Adam Opel GmbH v Mitras Automotive UK Ltd* [2007] EWHC 3205, [2008] Bus LR D55 [27] (David Donaldson QC); *Kolmar Group AG v Traxpo Enterprises PVT Ltd* [2010] EWHC 113 (Comm), [2011] 1 All ER (Comm) 46 [93]–[96] (Christopher Clarke J); *Wright v Kelly* (1884) 5 LR (NSW) 297; *Nixon v Furphy* (1925) 25 SR (NSW) 151; *TA Sundell & Sons Pty Ltd v Emm Yannoulatos (Overseas) Pty Ltd* (1956) SR (NSW) 323; *J & S Holdings Pty Ltd v NRMA Insurance Ltd* (1982) 41 ALR 539; *White Rose Flour Milling Co Pty Ltd v Australian Wheat Board* (1944) 18 ALJR 324; *Carr v Gilsenan* [1946] St R Qd 44; *Re Hooper & Grass' Contract* [1949] VLR 269; *Footwear Design & Marketing (Aust) Pty Ltd v Jas Forwarding (Aust) Pty Ltd* (1988) 7 SR (WA) 160; *Hennigan v Futuris Automotive Interiors (Australia) Pty Ltd* [2009] AIRC 187; *Electricity Generation Corporation t/as Verve Energy v Woodside Energy Ltd* [2013] WASCA 36. In New Zealand, see *McIntyre v Nemesis DBK Ltd* [2009] NZCA 329, [2010] 1 NZLR 463 [28]–[32] (the Court).

[52] *Pao On v Lau Yiu Long* [1980] AC 614.

[53] ibid 635.

[54] ibid 636; cf *Carillion Construction Ltd v Felix (UK) Ltd* [2001] BLR 1, [36]–[40].

[55] Eg *Electricity Generation Corporation t/as Verve Energy v Woodside Energy Ltd* [2013] WASCA 36, discussed immediately below; *Mitchell v Pacific Dawn Pty Ltd* [2011] QCA 98 [51]–[52] (Fraser JA; Chesterman JA and Ann Lyons J concurring).

[56] *B & S Contracts and Design Ltd v Victor Green Publications Ltd* [1984] ICR 419, 426 (Griffiths LJ), 428 (Kerr LJ); *Huyton SA v Peter Cremer GmbH & Co* [1999] 1 Lloyd's Rep 620, 636 (Mance J); *DNSD Subsea Ltd v Petroleum Geo-Services ASA* [2000] BLR 530; *Carillion Construction Ltd v Felix (UK) Ltd* [2001] BLR 1.

fortitude required of the victim in response to pressure that the court has held to be illegitimate. It would be invidious if a 'weak' (susceptible or vulnerable) person who had succumbed to proven illegitimate pressure should be denied relief because a more courageous person could have withstood it and taken some other course of action.[57]

Secondly, the requirement of no reasonable alternative to illegitimate pressure has its source in *R v Southerton*,[58] an 1805 case concerning the crime of menaces. In that case, Lord Ellenborough CJ held that:

> To obtain money under a threat of any kind, or to attempt to do it is no doubt an immoral action; but to make it indictable the threat must be of such a nature as is calculated to overcome a firm and prudent man.[59]

However, this restriction was quickly reinterpreted in *R v Thomas Smith* to mean something quite different:

> That rule must be understood to refer rather to the nature of the threat, than to its probable consequences in any particular case. Whether a threat be criminal or no, cannot be taken to depend on the nerves of the individual threatened, but on the general nature of the evil with which he is threatened. Threats attended with duress, or threats of duress, or of other personal violence, or of great injury ... will come within the rule.[60]

Since that date, there has been no suggestion that the crime of menaces requires a plaintiff to have had 'no reasonable alternative'. Nor is the requirement found in the tort of intimidation, which itself evolved from common law duress.[61] Adopting the requirement in the modern doctrine of illegitimate pressure ignores the intermingled roots and development of these three related sources of liability and introduces an unjustified inconsistency in the law.

Finally, as David Donaldson QC (sitting as a deputy judge of the High Court of England and Wales) observed in *Adam Opel GmbH v Mitras Automotive UK Ltd*,[62] over-emphasis on the existence of alternatives leads irresistibly to a 'line of argument ... worthy of admission to Alice's wonderland'. In that case, the defendant was the sole supplier of the front bumper of certain models of van developed by the claimant car manufacturers. The claimants decided to alter the bumper design, which would be produced by a process Mitras was not equipped to do. They gave notice to the defendant that it would cease to be the supplier. The defendant responded with a series of financial demands for 'recompense', threatening to suspend supplies if the demands were not met. After negotiations failed, the defendant refused supply. The claimants capitulated, fearing catastrophic consequences. They later relied on the illegitimate pressure to rescind the varied contract of supply and to recover the payments. Counsel for the defendant argued that the clear threatened and actual breach of the original supply contract meant that 'a court would have beyond all doubt have granted

[57] C Mitchell, P Mitchell and S Watterson (eds), *Goff and Jones: The Law of Unjust Enrichment*, 8th edn (London, Sweet & Maxwell, 2011) [10-52]; cf *Pharmacy Care Systems Ltd v Attorney-General* [2004] NZCA 187, (2004) NZCCLR 187 [95]–[98] (the Court); *McIntyre v Nemesis DBK Ltd* [2009] NZCA 329, [2010] 1 NZLR 463 [67] (the Court).

[58] *R v Southerton* (1805) 6 East 126, 102 ER 1235.

[59] ibid 140, 1240.

[60] *R v Thomas Smith* (1849) 1 Den 510, 514; 169 ER 350, 352 (Wilde CJ).

[61] *Allen v Flood* [1898] AC 1.

[62] *Adam Opel GmbH v Mitras Automotive UK Ltd* [2007] EWHC 3205, [2008] Bus LR D55 [32].

an injunction compelling supply'.[63] It followed, Counsel argued, that there was a practical alternative to payment and the claimants' claim of illegitimate pressure must fail. Acting Justice David Donaldson QC rejected the argument saying: 'the more blatantly unjustified and illegal the action threatened, the more readily the defendant would escape liability in duress'.[64]

For these reasons, the presence of alternative courses of action, protest or independent advice should not affect assessment of the illegitimacy of pressure. Nor should the question of illegitimacy be affected by an assessment of economic benefit. Although it has been argued that it is in society's economic interest for contracts to be renegotiated or abandoned, economic factors are not the only matters relevant to whether a contract is a legitimate and beneficial activity. What may seem on the face of it to have been a 'bad bargain' may once have supported important and desired non-pecuniary benefits, such as a valued long-term relationship, positive market exposure, and so on.[65] Further, these economic arguments are disputed and courts are not well equipped to develop the law based on complex arguments of economic theory. It is also difficult to see why the benefits of an agreement should be assessed only in economic terms: what about an attempt to renegotiate based on improvements to social, environmental, or even personal benefits?

The better approach is to adhere to the existing legal rules concerning what constitutes a 'threat'. Many attempts to renegotiate contracts will not involve threats but will involve warnings, requests or offers, or some combination of the three. For example, a warning of a probable breach, coupled with an offer of how to avoid that consequence, will not give rise to a threat if the warning party has no control over the predicted consequences that will follow if the offer is not accepted.[66] Likewise, if an offer is welcome to a party at the time it is made and acted upon, that party cannot subsequently claim it was a threat by proving that at a later stage, the offer became undesirable. By contrast, a threat to breach a contract should only be legitimate in the exceptional circumstance that statute has made the threat lawful, as may be the case with a threat to strike.[67]

A good example of the approach advocated here is found in *Electricity Generation Corporation t/as Verve Energy v Woodside Energy Ltd*.[68] An explosion at the Apache Energy gas production plant in Western Australia radically cut the supply of gas to that state's market. Woodside was the other main gas supplier and quickly found itself in a position where demand outstripped supply. The price of gas skyrocketed. Woodside refused to provide 'supplemental' gas energy nominated by the plaintiff pursuant to an existing supply contract (the original contract). Instead, it offered to supply gas to the plaintiff under new,

[63] ibid [32].

[64] ibid [32].

[65] See further Ch 11 p 274.

[66] *McIntyre v Nemesis DBK Ltd* [2009] NZCA 329, [2010] 1 NZLR 463 [32] (the Court): 'care must be taken to distinguish between (illegitimate) threats and (legitimate) warnings. Where one party warns the other that, as a matter of commercial reality, it will not be able to perform its contractual obligations unless changes are agreed to, this does not amount to a threat'. Cf Burrows' argument that a threat of breach made in circumstances closely analogous to frustration will not be 'in bad faith' and thus illegitimate: AS Burrows, *The Law of Restitution*, 3rd edn (Oxford, Oxford University Press, 2011) 274–75.

[67] *Universe Tankships Inc of Monrovia v International Transport Workers Federation (The Universe Sentinel)* [1983] 1 AC 366.

[68] *Electricity Generation Corporation t/as Verve Energy v Woodside Energy Ltd* [2013] WASCA 36 [24] (McLure P; Newnes JA concurring).

short-term contracts, at a price many times greater than that originally payable.[69] Under protest, the plaintiff agreed. Woodside later conceded in proceedings that, during the relevant period, it had sufficient gas to have supplied the nominated supplemental gas. Woodside's advice that no further supplemental gas would be supplied therefore did not constitute a 'warning', as it had control over the decision not to supply further gas.[70] Nor could the 'offered' replacement contracts be regarded as desirable to the plaintiff, given their highly disadvantageous terms. The Court of Appeal in Western Australia unanimously held that the pressure exerted on the plaintiff by the threatened breach of contract was unlawful and therefore prima facie illegitimate. The Court of Appeal's decision was overturned by the High Court, but this point was not addressed.[71] In the leading judgment on this point in the Court of Appeal, Murphy JA rejected Woodside's argument that threatened or actual breaches of contract might not be illegitimate if the threats were made in good faith.[72] The fact that a defendant had acted in bad faith might inferentially support the requirements of illegitimate pressure or causation of or contribution to the plaintiff's decision, but it is not a material fact on which the cause of action depends.[73] It followed that the defendant's undisputed belief that it was not acting in breach could not negate the finding of illegitimate pressure. In reaching this conclusion, Murphy JA drew support from the doctrine of duress *colore officii*, which likewise does not require that the defendant had acted in bad faith,[74] and to which we now turn.

iv. Threats of Refusals to Perform Statutory Duties

A fourth possible type of unlawful threat that has been held to amount to an illegitimate pressure is a threat by a public official to act contrary to duty or abstain from acting when there is a duty to act. That threat is wrongful, and the action can generally be compelled by a writ of mandamus. In general, the duty must be one owed to the plaintiff.[75] This category has been described as duress *colore officii* (by colour of office). One distinction between this type of illegitimate pressure and others is that in cases of duress *colore officii*, causation or contribution to the decision-making process is rebuttably presumed upon proof of the official position of the defendant and the unlawful demand.[76] It is also presumed that when an official makes a demand for payment or performance by the plaintiff, there is an implicit threat of sanction if payment or performance is not forthcoming.[77] Those presumptions

[69] The point that the short-term agreements may have been unsupported by fresh consideration and accordingly void was not argued by the plaintiff: *Electricity Generation Corporation t/as Verve Energy v Woodside Energy Ltd* [2013] WASCA 36 [204] (Murphy JA).

[70] ibid [199]–[200] (Murphy JA).

[71] *Electricity Generation Corporation t/as Verve Energy v Woodside Energy Ltd* [2014] HCA 7, (2014) 251 CLR 640.

[72] *Electricity Generation Corporation t/as Verve Energy v Woodside Energy Ltd* [2013] WASCA 36 [184]–[200] (Murphy JA), [30] (McLure JA), [44] (Newnes JA).

[73] See also ibid [30] (McLure JA).

[74] *Electricity Generation Corporation t/as Verve Energy v Woodside Energy Ltd* [2013] WASCA 36 [192], citing *Mason v New South Wales* [1959] HCA 5, (1959) 102 CLR 108, 141 [8] (Windeyer J).

[75] Eg *Mason v New South Wales* [1959] HCA 5, (1959) 102 CLR 108, 118–19 [3], [7] (McTiernan J), 140 [5] (Windeyer J); *Steele v Williams* (1853) 8 Ex 625, 155 ER 1502; *Morgan v Palmer* (1824) 2 B & C 729, 107 ER 554.

[76] *Sargood Brothers v Commonwealth* [1910] HCA 45, (1910) 11 CLR 258, 301 (Isaacs J), adopted with approval by Kitto J in *Bell Bros Pty Ltd v Shire of Serpentine-Jarrahdale* [1969] HCA 63, (1969) 121 CLR 137, 146 [9] (Menzies J agreeing).

[77] *Mason v New South Wales* [1959] HCA 5, (1959) 102 CLR 108, 142 [12] (Windeyer J).

recognise the strength of the authority with which public officials are clothed by the state. Indeed, historically, duress *colore officii* was a common law misdemeanour. It was viewed as a form of official robbery, made all the more odious because it is perpetrated by a person in authority.[78]

The leading Australian case is *Mason v New South Wales*,[79] which recognised that these cases are concerned with illegitimate pressure.[80] The plaintiffs paid charges to the State to obtain vehicle permits for the purpose of interstate trade. The payments were made under threat of seizure of their vehicles. But the officers of the State did not have authority to seize vehicles that were used for interstate trade. The plaintiff relied upon the unjust factor of illegitimate pressure for restitution of the charges paid from the defendant. Although the plaintiffs might have relied upon duress to goods,[81] they pleaded their case as one in which the 'moneys were unlawfully demanded by the defendant *colore officii* and paid by the plaintiffs involuntarily'.[82]

The principle of duress *colore officii* has been applied beyond defendants who are, strictly speaking, public officers, to cases where the defendant is an arbitrator or umpire,[83] to suppliers of goods or services who are under a public duty to supply, to public corporations[84] or defendants who enjoy a monopolistic position under statute, such as public utilities.[85] This is the state of the law of duress *colore officii* in Australia. Australian[86] and New Zealand[87] authority continues to recognise the doctrine of duress *colore officii*.

In England, Professor Burrows has argued that the doctrine of *colore officii* has been overtaken by the decision of the House of Lords in *Woolwich Equitable Building Society v Inland Revenue Commissioners*[88] and is subsumed within a policy for restitution based on unlawful demands for taxation.[89] In that case, a majority of the House of Lords held that a plaintiff taxpayer could succeed in recovering tax paid in response to demands by the Revenue made pursuant to *ultra vires* regulations. There was no need to show that the plaintiff paid under illegitimate pressure, or as a result of a mistake. The fact that the demand was *ultra vires* was enough. We doubt whether *Woolwich* has abolished the doctrine of duress *colore officii* in England. Certainly, none of the judges in that case expressly contemplated that they were doing so. It would have been an error to do so. One reason why it would be an error is that the two principles are conceptually distinct. As we will see in Chapter 13, when restitution is awarded for reasons of policy independently of those concerns unique to the parties, then this is not part of the law of unjust enrichment. As between the parties there is no proof

78 ibid 139–40 [6] (Windeyer J).

79 ibid; see also *Intercontinental Packers Pty Ltd v Harvey* [1969] Qd R 159.

80 ibid 115–16 [9] (Dixon CJ), 125–28 [4]–[9] (Kitto J), 129–30 [1] (Taylor J), 134–35 [13]–[15] (Menzies J), 139–40 [3]–[8] (Windeyer J); see also *Lactos Fresh Pty Ltd v Finishing Services Pty Ltd (No 2)* [2006] FCA 748 [94]–[97] (Weinberg J).

81 See, eg, *Mason v New South Wales* [1959] HCA 5, (1959) 102 CLR 108, 115–16 [9] (Dixon CJ), 129–30 [1] (Taylor J), 127 [7] (Kitto J), 132–33 [10]–[14] (Menzies J), 144–46 [14]–[15] (Windeyer J).

82 ibid 138 [2] (Windeyer J).

83 Eg *Re Coombs and Freshfield and Fernley* (1850) 4 Ex 839, 841; 154 ER 1456, 1458 (Parke B); *Fernley v Branson* (1851) 20 LJQB 178; *Barnes v Hayward* (1857) 1 H & N 742, 743; 156 ER 1400, 1400 (Pollock CB); *Barnes v Braithwaite* (1857) 2 H & N 569, 157 ER 234.

84 *Bell Bros Pty Ltd v Shire of Serpentine-Jarrahdale* [1969] HCA 63, (1969) 121 CLR 137.

85 *Criterion Theatres Ltd v Melbourne and Metropolitan Board of Works* [1995] VLR 267.

86 *Aerolineas Argentinas v Federal Airports Corporation* [1995] FCA 1776, (1995) 63 FCR 100.

87 *Waikato Regional Airport Ltd v Attorney-General* [2003] UKPC 50, [2004] 3 NZLR 1.

88 *Woolwich Equitable Building Society v Inland Revenue Commissioners* [1993] AC 70.

89 AS Burrows, *The Law of Restitution*, 3rd edn (Oxford, Oxford University Press, 2011) 266–67.

of injustice. In contrast, cases of duress, including duress *colore officii*, involve an imperfect transaction between the parties and the plaintiff's reliance upon his or her vitiated consent. A second reason is that the boundaries of the two doctrines might differ. Even apart from the presumptions that arise in cases of duress *colore officii*, that unjust factor applies beyond taxing or, indeed, public authorities to a wide range of persons or bodies standing in positions of public power or duty. It is uncertain whether *Woolwich* will extend to all such cases.

Although threats *colore officii* only apply to cases involving public officials or entities occupying public positions of responsibility, an identical approach is taken in cases where the plaintiff is entitled under statute to performance of a service and the defendant threatens not to perform unless an amount is paid in addition to any prescribed sum. For example, in *Great Western Railway Co v Sutton*[90] a railway refused to carry the plaintiff's goods unless the plaintiff paid an amount in excess of the amount it charged others for an equivalent service. In so doing, it breached a statutory requirement that railways charge equivalent fees for similar services. The court held that the plaintiff was entitled to restitution of the money paid.

v. *Threats of Breach of Equitable Duties*

It is not only threatened breaches of statutory or common law duties that may constitute unlawful pressure. Threatened breaches of equitable duties may also do so. In *Ellis v Barker*,[91] a testator appointed the defendants as trustees of his interest as tenant from year to year in a farming property. Under the terms of the trust, the defendants were to enter a transaction whereby the tenancy and farming stock would be transferred to the testator's nephew, provided the landlord would consent to the nephew as tenant. The testator left two other properties to the nephew. The trustees concluded that the testator's estate was not sufficient to satisfy his legacies and, after securing the support of the landlord, threatened the nephew that the landlord would withhold his consent unless the nephew executed a deed conveying the two devised properties to the trustees to sell in order to satisfy the other legacies. Lord Justice James, with whom Mellish LJ concurred, set aside the deed, and set aside the personal rights conferred upon the trustees, because the threat made by the trustees was a breach of trust.

C. Exertion of Pressure by Lawful Threats

In *R v Attorney-General for England and Wales*[92] a majority of the Privy Council said that although the threat of unlawful action will always be illegitimate, 'the fact that the threat is lawful does not necessarily make the pressure legitimate'.[93] But it is extremely difficult to

[90] *Great Western Railway Co v Sutton* (1868–1869) LR 4 HL 226.

[91] *Ellis v Barker* (1871) LR 7 Ch App 104; see also *Harris v Jenkins* [1922] HCA 54, (1922) 31 CLR 341, 360–61 (Higgins J, dissenting).

[92] *R v Attorney-General for England and Wales* [2003] UKPC 22, [2003] EMLR 24.

[93] ibid [16] (Lord Hoffman, delivering the majority judgment); see also *Progress Bulk Carriers Ltd v Tube City IMS LLC* [2012] EWHC 273, [2012] 2 All ER (Comm) 855 [26]–[29] (Cooke J). Cf the tort of intimidation, which continues to require that the threat be unlawful: see, eg, *Berezovsky v Abramovich* [2010] EWHC 647 [161] (Colman J); J Edelman and E Dyer, 'A Defence of Duress in the Law of Torts?' in A Dyson, J Goudkamp and F Wilmot-Smith (eds), *Defences in Tort* (Oxford & Portland, Hart Publishing, 2015) ch 9.

know when a lawful threat will be illegitimate. This point was expressed neatly by Professor Birks, in a passage quoted by Steyn LJ in *CTN Cash and Carry Ltd v Gallaher Ltd*:

> Can lawful pressures also count? This is a difficult question, because, if the answer is that they can, the only viable basis for discriminating between acceptable and unacceptable pressures is not positive law but social morality. In other words, the judges must say what pressures (though lawful outside the restitutionary context) are improper as contrary to prevailing standards. That makes the judges, not the law or legislature, the arbiters of social evaluation.[94]

The prospect of developing an inherently uncertain doctrine of lawful act illegitimate pressure led the New South Wales Court of Appeal in *Australia and New Zealand Banking Group Limited v Karam* to reject its existence outright.[95] In that case the defendants were directors of a company in grave financial difficulties. They approached the plaintiff bank for financial accommodation and the bank agreed, subject to the directors executing documents acknowledging that they were personally liable for the company's debts. The bank insisted upon execution of the documents because it was concerned that the existing guarantees by the directors were unenforceable. In a joint judgment, the Court of Appeal limited illegitimate pressure to threatened or actual *unlawful* conduct. It suggested that if illegitimate pressure in this sense is not made out, an agreement may be set aside for undue influence, unconscionable conduct or on statutory grounds. But the Court regarded any concept of lawful but illegitimate pressure as too vague to be applied. Ironically, the Court went on to suggest that statutory provisions such as those found in both the Trade Practices Act (Cth) 1974 and Contracts Review Act (NSW) 1980 were more precise and thus a preferable avenue to relief.[96] Those provisions allow for a contract to be set aside if its provisions were not 'reasonably necessary for the protection of the legitimate interests' of the stronger party.[97] The irony arises because the statutory test of whether the conduct went beyond what was reasonably necessary for protection of legitimate interests, which was thought to be more precise, is identical to the test for disproportionality which underlies the lawful act economic duress cases. The same principle also operates to disqualify clauses that are void for being in restraint of trade: it 'recognises certain interests which it is legitimate for

[94] *CTN Cash and Carry Ltd v Gallaher Ltd* [1994] 4 All ER 714, 718, citing P Birks, *An Introduction to the Law of Restitution*, rev edn (Oxford, Oxford University Press, 1989) 177.

[95] *Australia and New Zealand Banking Group Ltd v Karam* [2005] NSWCA 344, (2005) 64 NSWLR 149 [66]–[67]; followed in *Canon Australia Pty Ltd v Patton* [2007] NSWCA 246, (2007) 244 ALR 759 [3] (Basten JA); *Maher v Honeysett & Maher Electrical Contractors Pty Ltd* [2007] NSWSC 12, (2007) Aust Contract R 90-249. Cf *A v N* [2012] NSWSC 354 [509] (Ward J). The trend in subsequent cases has been to rely on unconscionable dealing in preference to lawful act duress, but has not extinguished the independent concepts nor use of the labels of 'economic duress' and 'illegitimate pressure'. See, eg: *A Little Company Limited v Gregory Raymond Peters* [2007] NSWSC 833 [44]–[59] (Rein AJ); *Tsarouhi v Tsarouhi* [2009] FMCAfam 126, discussed immediately below; *Australian and New Zealand Banking Group Ltd v Aldrick Family Company Pty Ltd* [2010] NSWSC 1000, (2010) 15 BPR 28,519 [169]–[171] (Einstein J); *Mitchell v Pacific Dawn Pty Ltd* [2010] QSC 243 [149]–[158] (Douglas J), approved on appeal in *Mitchell v Pacific Dawn Pty Ltd* [2011] QCA 98 [51]–[52] (Fraser JA; Chesterman JA and Ann Lyons J concurring); *Winter v Winter* [2010] FamCA 933 [182]–[183] (Reilley J). Cf *Pharmacy Care Systems Ltd v Attorney-General* [2004] NZCA 187, (2004) NZCCLR 187 [90] (the Court) where the Court suggested at [91] that 'the particular threat will be illegitimate because what is threatened is in and of itself a legal wrong, or because the threat is wrongful, or because it is contrary to public policy'; *McIntyre v Nemesis DBK Ltd* [2009] NZCA 329, [2010] 1 NZLR 463 [30]–[32] (the Court).

[96] See now s 21(2)(b) of the Australian Consumer Law, found in the Competition and Consumer Protection Act 2010 (Cth) Sch 2; see also ss 12CB and 12CC of the ASIC Act 2002 (Cth) for equivalent provisions relating to the financial services. Cf Consumer Protection from Unfair Trading Regulations 2008 (UK) reg 7(2)(d).

[97] *Australia and New Zealand Banking Group Ltd v Karam* [2005] NSWCA 344, (2005) 64 NSWLR 149 [67].

a covenantee to seek to protect … so long as the covenant is not wider than is reasonably necessary to protect those interests.'[98]

The requirement of disproportionality between (i) the lawful threat and (ii) the defendant's legitimate interest in the demand it supports underlies all cases of lawful, but illegitimate pressure.[99] An example of lawful act duress, decided after *Karam* and which reflects the disproportionality test, is the Australian case of *Tsarouhi v Tsarouhi*.[100] A woman sought to rescind a settlement agreement entered into with her former husband on the ground of illegitimate pressure. During the marriage, she had repeatedly withdrawn money from their joint home loan account by forging her husband's signature. She claimed she consented to the settlement agreement under the threat of prosecution. Federal Magistrate Riley held that an attempt to recover a debt backed up by a threat of prosecution was neither illegal nor illegitimate. However, the agreement concerned amounts 'beyond those which the wife "justly owe[d] to [her] creditor"'.[101] The disproportionality between the subject of the agreement and the true size of the debt to which she was legitimately entitled was a major factor in determining that the agreement was voidable for illegitimate pressure.[102]

An earlier example of the same approach is *R v Attorney-General for England and Wales*.[103] The Crown, through the Ministry of Defence (MOD), threatened to 'return to unit' any member of the United Kingdom Special Forces who failed to sign a confidentiality agreement preventing unauthorised disclosure of information arising out of their service. The majority of the Privy Council was prepared to assume that R had entered the contract as a result of the pressure applied to him.[104] However, R still had to establish that the pressure applied was illegitimate. On this point, their Lordships noted:

> In this case, the threat was lawful. Although return to unit was not ordinarily used except on grounds of delinquency or unsuitability and was perceived by members of the SAS as a severe penalty, there is no doubt that the Crown was entitled at its discretion to transfer any member of the SAS to another unit.[105]

The contracts were introduced out of 'legitimate concerns' that unauthorised disclosures were 'threatening the security of operations and personnel and were undermining the effectiveness and employability of the UKSF.'[106] Not only was the threatened conduct lawful, but it was also proportionate to the goal which the MOD sought to achieve. This is why the Privy Council emphasised not only that the threat was lawful but also that the demand was 'reasonable'.[107]

This requirement of disproportionality between, on the one hand, the nature and extent of the threats being made and, on the other hand, the subject matter which is demanded

[98] *Ringrow Pty Ltd v BP Australia Pty Ltd* [2005] HCA 71, (2005) 224 CLR 656 [27] (Gleeson CJ, Gummow, Kirby, Hayne, Callinan and Heydon JJ), citing *Butt v Long* [1953] HCA 76, (1953) 88 CLR 476, 486 [7] (Dixon CJ).

[99] *Electricity Generation Corporation t/as Verve Energy v Woodside Energy Ltd* [2013] WASCA 36 [25] (McLure P; Newnes JA concurring). Cf ibid [176] (Murphy JA).

[100] *Tsarouhi v Tsarouhi* [2009] FMCAfam 126.

[101] ibid [21], citing *Flower v Sadler* (1882) 10 QBD 572 (CA) 576 (Cotton LJ).

[102] Other elements included the facts that the defendant knew both the true size of the debt and that the wife entered the agreement with the desire of avoiding prosecution, as to which see below p 219.

[103] *R v Attorney-General for England and Wales* [2003] UKPC 22, [2003] EMLR 24.

[104] ibid [15] (Lords Bingham, Steyn, Hoffmann and Millett).

[105] ibid [17].

[106] ibid [17].

[107] ibid [20].

and any legitimate interest that the defendant has in that subject matter, underlies the four examples of lawful but illegitimate pressure considered below of blackmail, abuse of legal process, exertions of economic pressure and emotional pressure.

i. Blackmail

A simple example of threat of lawful conduct where the threat is illegitimate is blackmail. The conduct threatened may be lawful but the demand is usually itself unlawful. As Lord Atkin said in *Thorne v Motor Trade Association*:

> The ordinary blackmailer normally threatens to do what he has a perfect right to do—namely communicate some compromising conduct to a person whose knowledge is likely to affect the person threatened ... What he has to justify is not the threat, but the demand of money.[108]

Although the blackmailer's threat relates to lawful conduct, the illegality of the blackmail (such as threats to report a person to the authorities, or to bring a prosecution against a person, or to publish information about the plaintiff unless the plaintiff enters a transaction that enriches the defendant) means that the conduct will always be disproportionate to the defendant's demand. The defendant has no legitimate interest in demanding the benefit. Although not characterised as blackmail, the same approach is implicit in *Norreys v Zeffert*.[109] In that case, threats to report a punter's betting defaults to the trade protection societies and his social clubs were, in obiter dicta, considered illegitimate because they were 'aimed merely at injuring'.[110] On the other hand, threats to report the defaults to Tattersalls were considered legitimate because they were 'aimed at protecting and furthering the interests of bookmakers'.[111]

ii. Abuse of Legal Process

It has been repeatedly said that there is nothing illegitimate in threatening to invoke the legal process in order to protect one's rights.[112] This statement requires some qualification. It is legitimate to make a threat which is proportionate to any right of the threatening party. Nor does it matter that the plaintiff's ultimate motive for bringing the claim is to secure some extraneous or consequential benefit which will follow from the successful prosecution

[108] *Thorne v Motor Trade Association* [1937] AC 797, 806.

[109] *Norreys v Zeffert* [1939] 2 All ER 187.

[110] ibid 190 (Atkinson J).

[111] ibid 190.

[112] See, eg, *William Whitely Ltd v The King* (1909) 101 LT 741, 745 (Walton J); *Werrin v Commonwealth* [1938] HCA 3, (1938) 59 CLR 150, 157–59 (Latham CJ); *Mason v New South Wales* [1959] HCA 5, (1959) 102 CLR 108, 135 [16] (Menzies J), 144 [14] (Windeyer J); *Air India v Commonwealth* [1977] 1 NSWLR 449, 455 (the Court); *J & S Holdings Pty Ltd v NRMA Insurance Ltd* (1982) 41 ALR 539, 556 (the Court); *Esso Australia Resources Ltd v Gas and Fuel Corporation of Victoria* [1993] 2 VR 99, 105 (Gobbo J); *McKay v National Australia Bank Ltd* [1998] 4 VR 677, 686 (Winneke P; Tadgell and Batt JJA agreeing); *Woolwich Equitable Building Society v Inland Revenue Commissioners* [1993] AC 70, 165 (Lord Goff); *Flower v Sadler* (1882) 10 QBD 572, 576 (Cotton LJ); *Scolio Pty Ltd v Cote* (1992) 6 WAR 475, 484 (Ipp J; Seaman J agreeing); *Tsarouhi v Tsarouhi* [2009] FMCAfam 126 [20]–[30] (Riley FM); *Carrier v Georges* [2013] NSWSC 401 [25] (Nicholas J). Cf *Pharmacy Care Systems Ltd v Attorney-General* [2004] NZCA 187, (2004) NZCCLR 187 [94]–[95] (the Court).

of the claim.[113] But the position is different when the plaintiff's purpose in threatening proceedings is not to prosecute them to a conclusion but to use them as a means of obtaining some advantage for which they are not designed or some collateral advantage beyond what the law offers.[114] Thus if the person threatened is not the person who owes the corresponding duty or if the legal process threatened is not for the purpose of genuine assertion of the legitimate right, then the threat will be disproportionate to any legitimate interest that the defendant has in the subject matter of the demand and, accordingly, illegitimate.[115]

In *Williams v Bayley*,[116] the plaintiff's son forged promissory notes and cashed them with the defendant bankers. When the forgery was discovered, the bankers insisted on the plaintiff being a party to any settlement with his son. The plaintiff consented and executed a guarantee secured by an equitable mortgage to pay the amount obtained by his son. When his son absconded, the plaintiff sought to avoid the agreement and delivery up of the title deeds. The plaintiff succeeded in his action based on illegitimate pressure in equity, because the implicit threat by the bankers was that unless he paid up his son would be prosecuted or reported to the authorities. Punishment for a successful forgery prosecution was transportation for life. Although the House of Lords emphasised that the bankers had acted in good faith throughout, it was not legitimate to hold the fear of prosecution of the son over the father's head, when the father was not responsible for the debt, in order to extract the desired benefit from him.[117] A similar example that arose in equity rather than common law was *Mutual Finance Ltd v John Wetton & Sons Ltd*.[118] In that case, Percy Wetton signed a guarantee to the defendant company in order to avoid its implicit threat to prosecute his brother for forgery. Percy feared that a prosecution of his brother would kill their father, who was very ill. The defendant company was aware of that fact and it constituted one of the reasons for approaching Percy. Justice Porter held that while the contract was enforceable at common law—common law duress at that time being limited to duress to the person—the contract was voidable in equity. Although Porter J described the case as 'undue influence', it is clear from his decision that the case was concerned with illegitimate pressure.

Like threats to report a matter to the police or to the prosecution, it will also be illegitimate to make threats in relation to the criminal process generally, particularly where the threats may have the effect of stifling prosecutions in which there is a public interest beyond

[113] *Williams v Spautz* [1992] HCA 34, (1992) 174 CLR 509, 526–27 [36] (Mason CJ, Dawson, Toohey and McHugh JJ).

[114] *Dowling v Colonial Mutual Life Assurance Society Ltd* [1915] HCA 56, (1915) 20 CLR 509, 524 (Isaacs J), cited with approval in *Williams v Spautz* [1992] HCA 34, (1992) 174 CLR 509, 526–27 [36] (Mason CJ, Dawson, Toohey and McHugh JJ).

[115] Cf *Grainger v Hill* (1838) 4 Bing NC 212, 224; 132 ER 769, 774 (Bosanquet J): where legal process is used for 'an ulterior purpose; to obtain property by duress to which the Defendants had no right' then that property must be returned. The decision itself appears squarely founded on illegitimate pressure: see, eg, ibid 219–20, 772–73 (Tindal CJ), 223–24, 774 (Vaughan J), 224, 774 (Bosanquet J).

[116] *Williams v Bayley* (1866) LR 1 HL 200.

[117] See in particular the discussion of the relevance of the identity of victim and debtor in *Flower v Sadler* (1882) 10 QBD 572, 576 (Cotton LJ); *Scolio Pty Ltd v Cote* (1992) 6 WAR 475, 484 (Ipp J; Seaman J concurring); *Tsarouhi v Tsarouhi* [2009] FMCAfam 126 [20]–[30] (Riley FM).

[118] *Mutual Finance Ltd v John Wetton & Sons Ltd* [1937] 2 KB 389; see also *Public Service Employees Credit Union Co-operative Ltd v Campion* (1984) 75 FLR 131.

those of the private parties involved.[119] The most blatant example of such illegitimate conduct is an illegal agreement to compromise criminal proceedings.[120]

Finally, a lawful threat to institute *civil* proceedings may also be illegitimate, if the threat is used to support a demand for a benefit unconnected or disproportionate to any legitimate interest the defendant has in the subject of the civil proceedings. In *Unwin v Leaper*,[121] for example, the defendant threatened the plaintiff with civil proceedings with respect to one matter, in order to compel a settlement in relation to another, unrelated matter. The court allowed restitution of the money paid for illegitimate pressure. Similarly, in *Smith v Cuff*,[122] a creditor threatened to enforce a debt unless the debtor agreed to pay an additional amount. In neither of these cases was the threat inherently unlawful, but it was illegitimate because the demand was unrelated and disproportionate to the right which the creditor was threatening to enforce.

iii. Economic Pressure

The label 'economic duress' has rightly been criticised as suggesting a homogeneous category, whereas cases of economic duress come in countless varieties.[123] Many cases of economic duress involve unlawful threats, such as threats to property[124] or threats to breach contracts.[125] They can, and should, be understood by reference to the unlawfulness of the pressure. However, in some cases the threat may be lawful, yet illegitimate. For example, a threat to call up a debt might amount to illegitimate pressure in some circumstances.[126] The test to be applied in these cases should be the same as that in other cases of lawful acts or threats: is there a reasonable connection between, on the one hand, the nature and extent of the threats being made and, on the other hand, the subject matter which is demanded and any legitimate interest that the defendant has in that subject matter?

Although a number of cases in the context of economic pressure refer to the 'good faith' of the defendant,[127] this is not a separate matter to be proved. It is simply a factor from

[119] *Windhill Local Board of Health v Vint* (1890) 45 Ch D 351, 363 (Cotton LJ); *Kerridge v Simmonds* [1906] HCA 66, (1906) 4 CLR 253, 258 (Griffith CJ), 261–63 (Barton J). In that event, there may be a policy-based claim for restitution, independent of unjust enrichment: see below at p 219.

[120] *Lound v Grimwade* (1888) 39 Ch D 605; see also *Williams v Bayley* (1866) LR 1 HL 200, 213 (Lord Cranworth LC); *Kerridge v Simmonds* [1906] HCA 66, (1906) 4 CLR 253, 258 (Griffith CJ), 261–63 (Barton J); *Kaufman v Gerson* [1904] 1 KB 591; *Mutual Finance Ltd v John Wetton & Sons Ltd* [1937] 2 KB 389, 395 (Porter J); *Public Service Employees Credit Union Co-Operative Ltd v Campion* (1984) 75 FLR 131, 138–39 (Kelly J); *Tsarouhi v Tsarouhi* [2009] FMCAfam 126 [20]–[30] (Riley FM).

[121] *Unwin v Leaper* (1840) 1 Man & G 747, 133 ER 533.

[122] *Smith v Cuff* (1817) 6 M & S 160, 105 ER 1203.

[123] See K Mason, 'Economic Duress' in S Degeling and J Edelman (eds), *Unjust Enrichment in Commercial Law* (Pyrmont, NSW, Lawbook Co, 2008) ch 14. See also K Mason, JW Carter and GJ Tolhurst, *Mason and Carter's Restitution Law in Australia*, 2nd edn (Chatswood, NSW, LexisNexis Butterworths, 2008) para 518.

[124] *Hawker Pacific Pty Ltd v Helicopter Charter Pty Ltd* (1991) 22 NSWLR 298; *Vantage Navigation Corporation v Suhail and Saud Bahwan Building Materials LLC* [1989] 1 Lloyd's Rep 138.

[125] *Atlas Express Ltd v Kafco (Importers and Distributors) Ltd* [1989] QB 833; *Adam Opel GmbH v Mitras Automotive UK Ltd* [2007] EWHC 3205, [2008] Bus LR D55 [25] (David Donaldson QC); *Kolmar Group AG v Traxpo Enterprises PVT Ltd* [2010] EWHC 113, [2011] 1 All ER (Comm) 46 [93]–[96] (Christopher Clarke J).

[126] Discussed immediately above.

[127] *DSND Subsea v Petroleum Geo-Services ASA* [2000] BLR 530, 545 (Dyson J); *Huyton SA v Peter Cremer GmbH & Co* [1999] 1 Lloyd's Rep 620, 637 (Mance J); *CTN Cash and Carry Ltd v Gallaher Ltd* [1994] 4 All ER 714, 718 (Steyn LJ); *Mitchell v Pacific Dawn Pty Ltd* [2011] QCA 98 [51]–[52] (Fraser JA; Chesterman JA and Ann Lyons J concurring).

which disproportionality between the lawful threat and any legitimate goal of the defendant can be inferred. A good example of the interrelation between good faith and lawful but illegitimate pressure is *Borrelli v Ting*.[128] Ting was chairman and CEO of a company that went into liquidation. Its liquidators proposed a scheme of arrangement to raise funds to resource the liquidation. Ting assiduously opposed the scheme of arrangement, through means fair and foul, in order to prevent his conduct from being the subject of further investigation. The implicit threat was that, unless the liquidators agreed to forego any investigation or action against Ting, he would continue actively to oppose the scheme, with disastrous consequences. Faced with the impending collapse of the scheme, the liquidators entered a 'settlement agreement' with Ting. In it, Ting agreed to discontinue his opposition to the scheme in return for the liquidators forgoing any claims against Ting and his associates, and ceasing all investigations against Ting. When evidence of massive misappropriations by Ting against the company surfaced, the liquidators sought to set aside the settlement agreement. The Privy Council held that the agreement was procured by economic duress because Ting's pressure was applied 'for no good reason'[129] and without '*bona fide* grounds'.[130] Importantly, that conclusion did not rest solely (or even chiefly) on the undoubted forgery and false evidence used by Ting to oppose the scheme (and thus compel entry by the liquidators into the settlement agreement). The conclusion also rested on Ting's unjustifiable delay tactics and active opposition to the scheme. The inference is that even had Ting not resorted to forgery and false evidence, the agreement would still have been voidable for duress or illegitimate pressure.

The trend of recent decisions suggests that a threat will not be illegitimate if it is purely economic and is being used to pursue a lawful commercial goal.[131] But in extreme cases, even economic threats for lawful commercial goals may be illegitimate where the pressure is disproportionate to the demand. The leading English example of lawful, but illegitimate, economic pressure is the decision of the House of Lords in *Universe Tankships Inc of Monrovia v International Transport Workers Federation*.[132] The House of Lords considered whether economic action taken to 'black' (prevent services to) a ship constituted illegitimate pressure. Prima facie, the blacking involved unlawful conduct (and the implicit threat of continued unlawful conduct) because those in charge of tugs were persuaded to refuse, in breach of their contracts, to tow the *Universe Sentinel* to sea. However, the Trade Union and Labour Relations Act 1974 gave immunity to unions in respect of certain tortious acts, provided they were committed in furtherance of a trade dispute. The conclusion reached by a majority of the House was that a threat to black a ship is legitimate if it is done in furtherance of a trade dispute. The provisions of the statute were a strong indication of where the line was to be drawn between legitimate (proportionate) union pressure and illegitimate pressure. On the other hand, a separate threat to black the ship unless money was paid into the union's welfare fund was illegitimate, because it was disproportionate to the legitimate goals of the defendant in the context of a trade dispute.

[128] *Borrelli v Ting* [2010] UKPC 21, [2010] Bus LR 1718.

[129] ibid [35], see also at [41] ('no bona fide grounds for opposing the scheme').

[130] ibid [41].

[131] For example, *Alf Vaughan & Co Ltd (in administrative receivership) v Royscot Trust plc* [1999] 1 All ER (Comm) 856; *Cox v Esanda Finance* [2000] NSWSC 502; *Denmeade v Stingray Boats* [2003] FCAFC 215; *Investec Bank (Channel Islands) Ltd v The Retail Group plc* [2009] EWHC 476.

[132] *Universe Tankships Inc of Monrovia v International Transport Workers Federation (The Universe Sentinel)* [1983] 1 AC 366.

Even less likely to constitute duress or illegitimate pressure are lawful threats not to enter into contractual relations. Such threats will almost invariably be proportionate to the defendant's legitimate commercial interests. The leading Australian authority is *Smith v William Charlick Ltd.*[133] In that case, the Australian Wheat Harvest Board threatened not to have any further business with the plaintiff miller unless the miller paid a surcharge with respect to wheat already sold, paid for and delivered to it. Although the Wheat Board had a monopoly on supply and the miller had no choice but to pay the surcharge if it wanted to keep in business, the pressure was not illegitimate. Whilst the decision was given at a time when duress was limited to duress to the person and duress to goods, the decision is consistent with an approach to lawful pressure that requires that the lawful threat be disproportionate to the legitimate concern that the demand seeks to protect. The Board's demanded surcharge was designed to redress an oversupply of discounted wheat to the miller, who had overstated his requirements. The surcharge was a justifiable demand to protect the interests of the Board as well as other wheat growers who benefited from the discount.[134]

The leading English case on threats not to continue business can also be understood in this way. In *CTN Cash and Carry Ltd v Gallaher Ltd*,[135] the plaintiffs ordered a consignment of cigarettes from the defendants. The cigarettes were delivered to the wrong warehouse and then stolen before redelivery was possible. Believing that the risk of loss of the cigarettes had passed to the plaintiffs, the defendants invoiced them for the cost of the cigarettes. The parties disputed the invoice for two years, after which the defendants threatened to withdraw the plaintiffs' credit facilities unless they paid. Although withdrawal of the facilities would have severely jeopardised the plaintiffs' business, the defendants were lawfully entitled, at their complete discretion, to withdraw their credit facilities. Lord Justice Steyn, giving the leading judgment, regarded as 'critically important' the fact that the defendants' demand for the money was made bona fide, and that the lawful pressure exerted on the plaintiffs was made in view of obtaining a sum that they considered due to them.[136] This again emphasises the need for disproportionality between the lawful threat and the legitimate concern that the demand seeks to protect.[137]

The general reluctance of courts to recognise lawful economic or commercial threats as disproportionate to commercial goals (and thus illegitimate) is to be applauded. Any other approach would cut across the statutory competition law rules which draw complex distinctions between lawful and unlawful commercial behaviour. An infringement of rules of competition law should be unlawful and illegitimate for the purposes of the unjust factor of duress. Only in the most exceptional circumstances, if at all, should it be illegitimate to threaten to engage in conduct which a plaintiff has a right to engage in and which is not proscribed by competition law. However, where the threatened conduct is non-commercial in nature, such as threats to publish information or threats to foster rumours about a company,[138] a finding that the threat is disproportionate and therefore illegitimate may be more readily made.

[133] *Smith v William Charlick Ltd* [1924] HCA 13, (1924) 34 CLR 38; see also *Peanut Marketing Board v Cuda* (1984) 79 FLR 368; *APN New Zealand Ltd v Scott* [2010] NZHC 1253 [46] (Associate Judge Bell): 'The ability of a contractor providing services to refuse to do further work when past work has not been paid for is an important commercial protection.'

[134] *Smith v William Charlick Ltd* [1924] HCA 13, (1924) 34 CLR 38, 51–52, 62 (Isaacs J).

[135] *CTN Cash and Carry Ltd v Gallaher Ltd* [1994] 4 All ER 714.

[136] ibid 718.

[137] See also ibid 719 (Sir Donald Nicholls VC).

[138] As alleged in *Equiticorp Financial Services Ltd v Equiticorp Financial Services (NZ) Ltd* (1992) 29 NSWLR 260.

iv. Emotional Pressure

A number of cases in the last decade have involved claims for duress by wives who acted as surety for their husband's debts.[139] In *Bank of Scotland v Bennett*,[140] a wife signed a guarantee under threat from her husband that, unless she did so, he would leave her and the family would be split up. The court found that the wife entered the transaction as a result of illegitimate pressure. This is commonly termed 'emotional blackmail'. But it will not always constitute duress for legal purposes. Considerable emotional pressure is a fact of family life: even more so where the family unit or marriage is under stress. Like other cases of lawful pressure, it will only be illegitimate if the lawful threat is disproportionate to the underlying legitimate concern that the demand seeks to protect. Thus a threat of divorce may well be legitimate where the demand it supports is directed at the continued physical, financial or emotional wellbeing of the couple or family members. But in *Bennett* it was disproportionate to the business of the husband.

D. 'Unilateral' Illegitimate Pressure?

The vast preponderance of illegitimate pressure cases concern illegitimate pressure exerted by the defendant (or, more rarely, a third party) on the plaintiff. Professor Burrows has argued that it is impossible to have unilateral illegitimate pressure, in contrast to mistake.[141] But, while very rare, there is some suggestion in the case law that pressure may sometimes be illegitimate, notwithstanding that it is not attributable to any particular threat or demand. For the reasons below, the concept of a threat should also extend to unilateral pressure, such as a perceived 'peril' or 'menace', rather than being necessarily attributable to an act of some party other than the plaintiff.

The chief examples of unilateral pressure concern illegitimate pressure involving the legal process. In most cases, the enrichment of the defendant was made by the plaintiff to avoid a threat of prosecution (of a son, brother or the plaintiff) by the authorities. This might suggest that the cases involve third party pressure, rather than unilateral pressure. However, the critical point is that the cases contemplated that the plaintiff could recover the enrichment notwithstanding that it was the plaintiff's *own actions or decision* that connected the entirely lawful threat of prosecution with the plaintiff's entry into a transaction for the transfer of an unrelated or disproportionate benefit to the defendant, thereby rendering the pressure illegitimate. In other words, the illegitimacy of the pressure did not arise from the conduct of the defendant or a third party. In this aspect, the cases are analogous to cases of unilateral mistake or unilateral undue influence.[142] Thus in the leading case of *Williams v Bayley*,[143] Lord Cranworth commented that it would have made no difference to the outcome of that case had the suggestion for the agreement come from the father, rather than the bankers. The bankers would still have been aware of the pressure and could not retain the benefit of

[139] See also *Tsarouhi v Tsarouhi* [2009] FMCAfam 126, discussed above at p 212 and immediately below.

[140] *Bank of Scotland v Bennett* [1999] 1 FLR 1115; appeal conjoined and allowed on another ground in *Royal Bank of Scotland plc v Etridge (No 2)* [2001] UKHL 44, [2002] 2 AC 773.

[141] AS Burrows, *The Law of Restitution*, 3rd edn (Oxford, Oxford University Press, 2011) 256.

[142] Discussed in Ch 10 p 248.

[143] *Williams v Bayley* (1866) LR 1 HL 200, 213.

an agreement resulting from it.[144] In *Mutual Finance Ltd v John Wetton & Sons Ltd*, Porter J affirmed that 'It is enough if the undertaking were given owing to a desire to prevent a prosecution and that desire were known to those to whom the undertaking was given.'[145] In *Tsarouhi v Tsarouhi*,[146] Riley FM said that the settlement agreement was still voidable for duress whether or not, as the husband alleged, the suggestion that any prosecution of the wife should be halted in exchange for the agreement came from the wife. An even clearer example would be where there was no actual threat of prosecution but the plaintiff perceived that there may be a prosecution in the future and took action to avoid that possibility by entering a transaction to confer a disproportionate benefit on the defendant. In that case, the illegitimate pressure would be entirely founded in the plaintiff's own decision-making. However, it should still be recoverable, subject to any applicable countervailing juristic reasons to retain the enrichment (such as illegality or that the payment was made pursuant to a contract which cannot be set aside as against the defendant).[147]

The comments in these prosecution cases can also be explained on the ground that the impugned agreement constituted an illegal agreement not to prosecute. Where this is so, there is an autonomous ground of restitution, namely illegality, which is not concerned to protect a plaintiff's vitiated consent but to prevent an overriding prohibition of the law from itself being undermined.[148] In those circumstances, it should be irrelevant whether the illegitimate pressure was unilateral or whether it arose from the defendant. However, although unilateral illegitimate pressure will be rare, the possibility of unilateral illegitimate pressure should not be too readily dismissed. We have seen in Chapter 8 that unilateral mistake is a common ground of restitution. We will also see in Chapter 10 that there are examples of unilateral undue influence,[149] although these are comparatively rare. Both involve scenarios where the plaintiff's consent is impaired independently of any act by the defendant or a third party. In that context, cases of unilateral illegitimate pressure should be possible as a matter of principle, even if clear examples in the case law are difficult to find.

IV. Causation and Contribution

A. The Test for Causation or Material Contribution

We saw in Chapter 8 that on one view, the concept of causation should only ever permit of one test: a test of necessity or 'but for' causation. On this approach, any departure from a requirement that an event was necessary for the outcome is to replace a test of causation within something else. But, we also saw in that chapter that Australian courts (to a greater extent) and English courts (to a lesser extent) have endorsed an alternative 'a factor test' in

[144] On the additional requirements of knowledge to rescind a contract on the grounds of illegitimate pressure, see Ch 7 pp 148–49.

[145] *Mutual Finance Ltd v John Wetton & Sons Ltd* [1937] 2 KB 389, 395.

[146] *Tsarouhi v Tsarouhi* [2009] FMCAfam 126, discussed above at p 212.

[147] In this scenario, the plaintiff must additionally show that the defendant was aware that the plaintiff entered the transaction as a result of illegitimate pressure: discussed in Ch 7 pp 148–49.

[148] Discussed in Ch 7 pp 148–49.

[149] Discussed in Ch 10 pp 248–50.

cases of contributions made by mistakes to the process of decision making. The Australian courts therefore use the compendious formula of 'causation or material contribution'.

In *Crescendo Management*, McHugh JA referred to the speech of Lord Cross from *Barton v Armstrong*[150] and said:

> It is unnecessary ... for the victim to prove that the illegitimate pressure was the sole reason for him entering into the contract. It is sufficient that the illegitimate pressure was one of the reasons for the person entering into the agreement. Once the evidence establishes that the pressure exerted on the victim was illegitimate, the onus lies on the person applying the pressure to show that it made no contribution to the victim entering into the agreement.[151]

This passage seems to make two points, both of which require preliminary comment. The first relates to the appropriate test for causation or contribution for the unjust factor of illegitimate pressure. We will see below that the courts in England and Australia appear to have diverged over the appropriate causal test for duress or illegitimate pressure. Australian courts follow *Barton v Armstrong* in requiring that the pressure be 'a' reason or 'a' factor which influenced the plaintiff's decision to enter the agreement. English courts have increasingly endorsed either a 'substantial cause' or, which is not the same thing, a 'but for' test in cases involving economic pressure. We will see that there is no justification for treating causation or contribution in duress or illegitimate pressure differently from causation or contribution in mistake or undue influence. Nor is there reason for distinguishing causation or contribution in cases involving economic pressure from other forms of duress or illegitimate pressure. The purpose of the enquiry is the same in all cases.

Secondly, the final sentence of the statement by McHugh JA might be read to suggest that proof of illegitimate pressure by a defendant raises a presumption of causation or contribution which must be rebutted by the defendant.[152] We will see in Chapter 10 that such a presumption arises in the context of undue influence once it is shown that there is enrichment of the defendant through a transaction with the plaintiff, in circumstances of influence, which calls for explanation.[153] But the presumption arises for particular reasons relating to influence. Apart from unusual cases like duress *colore officii*, it has no place in relation to the unjust factor of duress or illegitimate pressure just as it has no place in relation to mistake.[154] The better view is that McHugh JA was suggesting that although a plaintiff must prove causation or contribution in duress cases,[155] an inference of causation arises once certain evidence is given. In other words, once a plaintiff proves that she (a) was subject to illegitimate pressure and (b) complied with the demand (conferred the benefit), the natural inference is that the one event caused the other.[156]

Although it is sometimes difficult for a defendant to defend against the plaintiff's assertion that illegitimate pressure played a part in the plaintiff's decision, this defence is not

[150] *Barton v Armstrong* [1976] AC 104, 120.

[151] *Crescendo Management Pty Ltd v Westpac Banking Corporation* (1988) 19 NSWLR 40, 46.

[152] Eg *Huyton SA v Peter Cremer GmbH & Co* [1999] 1 Lloyd's Rep 620, 636, 638–39 (Mance J).

[153] Ch 10 pp 236–38.

[154] Ch 8 pp 189–94.

[155] *Mason v New South Wales* [1959] HCA 5, (1959) 102 CLR 108, 142 [12] (Windeyer J). See also *Huyton SA v Peter Cremer GmbH & Co* [1999] 1 Lloyd's Rep 620, 638–39 (Mance J); *Gould v Vaggelas* [1984] HCA 68, (1984) 157 CLR 215, 237 (Wilson J, discussing the question from the perspective of misrepresentation).

[156] *Barton v Armstrong* [1976] AC 104, 118 (Lord Cross); see also *Antonio v Antonio* [2010] EWHC 1199. The same analysis has been applied in the context of misrepresentation: *Gould v Vaggelas* [1984] HCA 68, (1984) 157 CLR 215, 237–38 (Wilson J).

impossible. In *Barton v Armstrong*[157] a minority rejected an inference that illegitimate pressure caused Barton's actions. In that case, Armstrong threatened to kill Barton if he did not enter into an agreement. Barton did so, but later sought to avoid it on the grounds of duress. Lords Wilberforce and Simon accepted that the test for causation or contribution was 'that the illegitimate means used was *a* reason (not *the* reason, nor the *predominant* reason nor the *clinching* reason) why the complainant acted as he did'.[158] But their Lordships relied on the rejection of much of Barton's evidence by the trial judge, Street J, whose finding—that Barton had entered into the contract because of sheer commercial necessity—they upheld.[159] In the New South Wales Court of Appeal, that finding had also been upheld. Justice Street had said: 'the conclusion … that Barton entered into this agreement because he wanted to and from commercial motives only is, I think undoubtedly correct.'[160]

B. The Same Test in Economic Pressure Cases

There is consistent authoritative support in Australia for the test of contribution for illegitimate pressure being whether the pressure was 'a factor which influenced the plaintiff'.[161] But a contrary line of English cases[162] suggests that in cases of economic duress, the test for causation or contribution is more stringent: the pressure must be a 'significant cause' or 'but for' cause of the plaintiff's decision to enter the impugned transaction. The test of a 'significant cause' stems from the statement of Lord Goff in *Dimskal Shipping Co SA v International Transport Workers Federation (The Evia Luck) [No 2]*[163] that economic pressure may amount to duress or illegitimate pressure where 'the economic pressure may be characterised as illegitimate and has constituted a significant cause inducing the plaintiff to enter into the relevant contract'. Given that Lord Goff cited both *Barton v Armstrong* and *Crescendo Management* in support of the test, it is possible that the adjective 'significant' was applied simply to signify that the pressure must be more than a negligible factor in

[157] *Barton v Armstrong* [1976] AC 104, 120.

[158] ibid 121 (emphasis in original).

[159] See also *Ford Motor Company of Australia Ltd v Arrowcrest Group Pty Ltd* [2003] FCAFC 313, (2003) 134 FCR 522 [147] (Lander J).

[160] Approved in *Barton v Armstrong* [1973] 2 NSWLR 598, 637 (Taylor AJA) and *Barton v Armstrong* [1976] AC 104, 124 (Lords Wilberforce and Simon).

[161] *Barton v Armstrong* [1976] AC 104; *Crescendo Management Pty Ltd v Westpac Banking Corporation* (1988) 19 NSWLR 40; *Ford Motor Company of Australia Ltd v Arrowcrest Group Pty Ltd* [2003] FCAFC 313, (2003) 134 FCR 522; *Bloomingdale Holdings Pty Ltd and Anor v 63 Buckley Street Pty Ltd* [2008] VSC 168 [427]–[428] (Hargrave J); *A v N* [2012] NSWSC 354 [504]–[505] (Ward J); *Electricity Generation Corporation t/as Verve Energy v Woodside Energy Ltd* [2013] WASCA 36 [24] (McLure P; Newnes JA concurring). See also *Pharmacy Care Systems Ltd v Attorney-General* [2004] NZCA 187, (2004) NZCCLR 187 [90] (the Court). In *News Ltd v Australian Rugby Football League Ltd* [1996] FCA 72, (1996) 58 FCR 447, 535–37, [277]–[284] Burchett J purported to apply the significant cause test, relying on both *Barton v Armstrong* and Lord Goff's judgment in *Dimskal Shipping*, apparently without being aware of the difference between the two tests there advocated.

[162] *Dimskal Shipping Co SA v International Transport Workers Federation (The Evia Luck) (No 2)* [1992] 2 AC 152, 165 (Lord Goff), ironically purporting to apply *Barton v Armstrong* [1976] AC 104, 121 and *Crescendo Management Pty Ltd v Westpac Banking Corporation* (1988) 19 NSWLR 40; see also *Huyton SA v Peter Cremer GmbH & Co* [1999] 1 Lloyd's Rep 620; *Carillion Construction Ltd v Felix (UK) Ltd* [2001] BLR 1; *Adam Opel GmbH v Mitras Automotive UK Ltd* [2007] EWHC 3205, [2008] Bus LR D55 [25] (David Donaldson QC); *Kolmar Group AG v Traxpo Enterprises PVT Ltd* [2010] EWHC 113, [2011] 1 All ER (Comm) 46 [92] (Christopher Clarke J).

[163] *Dimskal Shipping Co SA v International Transport Workers Federation (The Evia Luck) (No 2)* [1992] 2 AC 152, 165.

the decision-making process. That is, the requirement is that the illegitimate pressure be 'a factor' in the plaintiff's decision to enter the transaction that enriched the defendant. The test is certainly not consistent with adoption of a 'but for' test of causation. On this analysis, the English and Australian tests should align. But, as we explain immediately below, subsequent English authorities have not taken this view. English authorities also repeatedly suggest that in economic duress cases it is relevant to consider whether there were 'reasonable alternatives' open to the plaintiff, whether the defendant acted in good faith and whether the plaintiff protested.[164] We saw earlier that the presence or absence of good faith may inform the proportionality inquiry into the legitimacy of a *lawful* threat, by providing evidence which, when taken together with other circumstances, indicates disproportionality. Likewise, the presence of reasonable alternatives, good faith[165] and protest may inform the causation or contribution enquiry. However, none of them is critical to causation or contribution and they do not constitute independent elements of the claim in duress or illegitimate pressure.

i. Significant Cause and But For Cause

Because of a concern to protect 'normal commercial bargaining'[166] and uncertainty as to which circumstances give rise to duress or illegitimate pressure in a commercial context, some English judges have suggested that, in economic duress cases, the test for causation or contribution should be one of 'significant cause'[167] or 'but for' cause.[168] Thus, Mance J in *Huyton SA v Peter Cremer GmbH & Co* said:

> [The] relaxed ['a factor'] view of causation in the special context of duress to the person cannot prevail in the less serious context of economic duress. The minimum basic test of subjective causation in economic duress ought, it appears to me, to be a 'but for' test.[169]

Requiring that the pressure be a 'significant' reason (in the sense of substantial, or important, rather than simply non-trivial) or a 'but for' cause of the plaintiff's decision can lead to real problems. As for 'significant cause', there is considerable lack of clarity about the meaning of a 'significant' reason (or, which may be an oxymoron, a 'significant cause'). As we saw for mistake, there is no accurate method of measuring the relative weight of the factors that together bring about a plaintiff's decision to enter a transaction that enriches the defendant. Is the requirement that the pressure be a 'significant' reason to be assessed objectively or subjectively? If the former, on what basis are matters which are important to a plaintiff to be regarded as trivial by a Court? Is 'significant' cause a test for whether a matter is 'a factor' in the decision-making process or is it a 'but for' test? As for 'but for', such a test of

[164] *DSND Subsea Ltd v Petroleum Geo-Services ASA* [2000] BLR 530 [131] (Dyson J); *Harrison v Halliwell Landau* [2004] EWHC 1116 [91]–[98] (Judge Eccles QC.); *Capital Structures plc v Time and Tide Constructions Ltd* [2006] EWHC 591, [2006] BLR 226 [16] (David Willcox J); *Adam Opel GmbH v Mitras Automotive UK Ltd* [2007] EWHC 3205, [2008] Bus LR D55 [25]–[26] (David Donaldson QC); *Kolmar Group AG v Traxpo Enterprises PVT Ltd* [2010] EWHC 113, [2011] 1 All ER (Comm) 46 [92] (Christopher Clarke J).

[165] For a detailed discussion of the relevance of good faith and examples of its potential operation in relation to causation in illegitimate pressure, see *Electricity Generation Corporation t/as Verve Energy v Woodside Energy Ltd* [2013] WASCA 36 [184]–[200] (Murphy JA), [30] (McLure JA), [44] (Newnes JA), discussed above at 207–08.

[166] *DSND Subsea Ltd v Petroleum Geo-Services ASA* [2000] BLR 530 [131] (Dyson J).

[167] ibid [131].

[168] *Huyton SA v Peter Cremer GmbH & Co* [1999] 1 Lloyd's Rep 620, 636.

[169] ibid 636.

causation could make it more difficult to obtain restitution and would protect defendants involved in everyday commercial transactions. But explicit recognition of a limitation that pressure must be disproportionate to any lawful demand serves exactly the same purpose without the need to vary the test of causation or contribution in cases of economic pressure. Assuming that the 'a factor' test of contribution is appropriate for situations involving mental decisions (discussed in Chapter 8) the same test should apply, whatever the nature of the illegitimate pressure. It should be the same test as applied to cases of mistake and undue influence.

ii. 'No Reasonable Alternative'

English courts have repeatedly suggested that duress requires that a plaintiff must have had 'no reasonable alternative', or 'a lack of practical choice'.[170] On the other hand, whether the plaintiff has a reasonable alternative to complying with the demand has been held to be irrelevant to whether the pressure exerted is legitimate.[171] And the case law is replete with examples where transactions were found to have been entered into under duress notwithstanding that plaintiffs had alternative avenues open to them. In the leading decision of *Astley v Reynolds*,[172] it was no answer to the plaintiff's claim for recovery of money paid under duress of goods, that he had a reasonable alternative of recovery of the goods in an action in trover.[173] It was enough that a reason for his payment was the illegitimate pressure. In *Lactos Fresh Pty Ltd v Finishing Services Pty Ltd (No 2)*,[174] a tenant paid additional rent demanded by its landlord under threat of eviction. In finding that the payments were exacted under duress, Weinberg J held that 'the law does not limit restitution [for duress] where an applicant theoretically has other options.'[175] Although the tenant could have sought injunctive relief, the fact that he chose not to do so did not bar relief for duress.[176]

This does not mean that there is no role at all for evidence that there was a reasonable alternative to complying with the demand. The existence of a reasonable alternative is relevant evidence that might help to prove that the illegitimate pressure exerted was not a cause of, or did not contribute to, the plaintiff's decision to enter the transaction that enriched the defendant.[177] Conversely, as Christopher Clarke J noted in *Kolmar Group AG v Traxpo Enterprises PVT Ltd*: 'If there was no reasonable alternative, that may be very strong evidence in support of a conclusion that the victim of the duress was in fact influenced by the threat'.[178] But this is an evidentiary matter only. It is not a separate requirement for

[170] *Universe Tankships Inc of Monrovia v International Transport Workers Federation (The Universe Sentinel)* [1983] 1 AC 366, 400 (Lord Scarman); *Huyton SA v Peter Cremer GmbH & Co* [1999] 1 Lloyd's Rep 620, 636 (Mance J); *Adam Opel GmbH v Mitras Automotive UK Ltd* [2007] EWHC 3205, [2008] Bus LR D55 [25]–[26] (David Donaldson QC). See also discussion above at pp 205–07.

[171] *Carillion Construction Ltd v Felix (UK) Ltd* [2001] BLR 1 [36]–[40] (Lord Scarman).

[172] *Astley v Reynolds* (1731) 2 Str 915, 93 ER 939.

[173] ibid 916, 939 (the Court).

[174] *Lactos Fresh Pty Ltd v Finishing Services Pty Ltd (No 2)* [2006] FCA 748.

[175] ibid [97], citing *Mason v New South Wales* [1959] HCA 5, (1959) 102 CLR 108.

[176] The possibility of injunctive relief was also rejected as a bar to relief in *Kolmar Group AG v Traxpo Enterprises PVT Ltd* [2010] EWHC 113, [2011] 1 All ER (Comm) 46 [92] (Christopher Clarke J) and *Borelli v Ting* [2010] UKPC 21, [2010] Bus LR 1718.

[177] *Huyton SA v Peter Cremer GmbH & Co* [1999] 1 Lloyd's Rep 620, 638 (Mance J).

[178] *Kolmar Group AG v Traxpo Enterprises PVT Ltd* [2010] EWHC 113, [2011] 1 All ER (Comm) 46 [92].

causation or contribution. As Kitto J said in *Mason v New South Wales*, 'the critical question is not whether there was an alternative. It is whether the choice made between alternatives was made freely or under pressure'.[179]

iii. Protest

As with the issue of reasonable alternatives, the fact of protest is not an additional requirement in cases of economic duress but merely evidence from which it might be inferred that the exertion of illegitimate pressure did or did not influence the plaintiff's decision to enter the transaction that enriched the defendant. This limited role for protest was well expressed by Christopher Clarke J in *Kolmar*:

> [t]he presence, or absence, of protest, may be of some relevance when considering whether the threat had coercive effect. But, even the total absence of protest does not mean that the payment was voluntary.[180]

In *Mason v New South Wales*, Windeyer J further explained:

> A protest at the time of payment may of course 'afford some evidence, when accompanied by other circumstances, that the payment was not voluntarily made to end the matter' ... But there is no magic in a protest; for a protest may accompany a voluntary payment or be absent from one compelled ... Moreover the word 'protest' is itself equivocal. It may mean the serious assertion of a right or it may mean no more than a statement that payment is grudgingly made.[181]

V. A Separate Action for Wrongdoing

It has sometimes been suggested that duress is a 'legal wrong'.[182] Such statements should be viewed with great caution. As we have seen, duress or illegitimate pressure is not based on any wrongdoing, but is an unjust factor and part of a claim for unjust enrichment. We saw in Chapters 2 and 6 that the categories of wrongdoing and unjust enrichment are independent categories of law.[183]

Although the unjust factor of duress or illegitimate pressure is not a type of wrongdoing, this does not mean that there might not exist, on the same set of facts, a concurrent action for a tort or equitable wrong. A person who attacks another in order to pressure him into signing a contract commits the tort of battery as well as applying duress. The tort of

[179] *Mason v New South Wales* [1959] HCA 5 [8], (1959) 102 CLR 108, 128 [8]; cf *Spiteri v Commonwealth of Australia* [2003] NSWSC 391 [17]–[27] (Harrison M); *Bayview Gardens Pty Ltd v The Shire of Mulgrave* [1989] 1 Qd R 1, 6 (Connolly J; Kelly SPJ and Moynihan J agreeing).

[180] *Kolmar Group AG v Traxpo Enterprises PVT Ltd* [2010] EWHC 113, [2011] 1 All ER (Comm) 46 [92].

[181] *Mason v New South Wales* [1959] HCA 5, (1959) 102 CLR 108, 143 [13].

[182] *Universe Tankships Inc of Monrovia v International Transport Workers Federation (The Universe Sentinel)* [1983] 1 AC 366, 400 (Lord Scarman); *Smith v William Charlick Ltd* [1924] HCA 13, (1924) 34 CLR 38, 56 (Isaacs J); cited with approval in *Nixon v Furphy* (1925) 25 SR (NSW) 151, 160 (Long Innes J) and in *Hawker Pacific Pty Ltd v Helicopter Charter Pty Ltd* (1991) 22 NSWLR 298, 301 (Priestly JA); *Westpac Banking Corporation v Cockerill* (1998) 152 ALR 267, 292 (Kiefel J).

[183] Ch 2 pp 19–21; Ch 6 pp 127–30.

intimidation[184] or the equitable wrong of unconscionable conduct[185] will also sometimes be an alternative claim. The point of this section is simply that the unjust factor *itself* is not a claim for wrongdoing. There are three reasons why it is clear that the law has taken the position that duress or illegitimate pressure is not itself a type of wrongdoing: (1) compensation and disgorgement are not available remedies for illegitimate pressure unless it involves wrongdoing; (2) illegitimate but lawful pressure can be actionable notwithstanding that the lawful threat cannot amount to a wrong; and (3) a claim for duress or illegitimate pressure can be brought against an innocent, passive recipient. Once the unjust factor is clearly delineated from wrongdoing, we can immediately see that descriptions of the unjust factor of duress as requiring, or based upon, unconscionable or unconscientious conduct are mistaken.[186]

A. Compensation and Disgorgement are not Available

We saw in Chapter 3 that a claim for unjust enrichment does not give rise to a right to compensation or to disgorgement of profits.[187] The only remedy is restitution.[188] As Lord Diplock emphasised in *Universe Tankships Inc of Monrovia v International Transport Workers Federation*,[189] it is necessary to identify a tort separate from the unjust enrichment action for duress in order to recover compensation. More recently, in *Investec Bank (Channel Islands) Ltd v The Retail Group plc*, Sales J agreed:

> [T]he primary object of a plea of economic duress in relation to a contract is to avoid the contract, which is a legal consequence significantly different from establishing a cause of action in damages. So far as a cause of action in damages is to be made out, I can see no proper basis in principle why it should be on any basis other than a pleading of facts and matters sufficient to establish a cause of action for the tort of intimidation.[190]

B. Lawful Pressure might be Illegitimate but not Wrongful

It is possible that lawful pressure might be illegitimate for the purposes of a claim for restitution of unjust enrichment but not wrongful for the purposes of the law of torts or

[184] *Godwin v Uzoigwe* [1993] Fam Law 65; *Rookes v Barnard* [1964] AC 1129, 1205 (Lord Devlin); *Dusik v Newton* (1985) 62 BCLR 1, 39; (the Court); *Central Canada Potash Co Ltd v The Government of Saskatchewan* [1979] 1 SCR 42, 87 (Martland J); *Halpern v Halpern (Nos 1 & 2)* [2007] EWCA Civ 291, [2008] QB 195 [58], [59] (Carnwath LJ; Waller and Sedley LJJ concurring); *Kolmar Group AG v Traxpo Enterprises PVT Ltd* [2010] EWHC 113 (Comm), [2011] 1 All ER (Comm) 46 [119]–[121] (Christopher Clarke J).

[185] Ch 10 pp 242–45.

[186] See further Ch 2, pp 24–28.

[187] Ch 3 pp 31–35.

[188] Cf *Ruttle Plant Hire Ltd v Secretary of State for the Environment, Food and Rural Affairs* [2007] EWHC 2870, [2008] 2 All ER (Comm) 264, in which Ramsey J rejected the defendant's application to strike out the plaintiff's claim to rescind a settlement agreement for illegitimate pressure. The defendant had argued that since the plaintiff had not sought 'damages', its claim did not disclose a sufficient cause of action.

[189] *Universe Tankships Inc of Monrovia v International Transport Workers Federation (The Universe Sentinel)* [1983] 1 AC 366, 385, cited with approval in *Dimskal Shipping Co SA v International Transport Workers Federation (The Evia Luck) (No 2)* [1992] 2 AC 152, 166 (Lord Goff).

[190] *Investec Bank (Channel Islands) Ltd v The Retail Group plc* [2009] EWHC 476 [122].

equitable wrongdoing. For instance, as we saw above, in *Unwin v Leaper*,[191] the defendant threatened the plaintiff with civil proceedings with respect to one matter, in order to compel a settlement in relation to another, unrelated matter. The threat to institute proceedings was not itself unlawful but what made it illegitimate was that the threat was used to support a demand for a benefit unconnected or disproportionate to the defendant's legitimate interest in the subject of the civil proceedings. The court allowed restitution of the money paid for duress.

C. A Claim for Restitution Arising from Illegitimate Pressure can be Brought Against an Innocent Recipient

Finally, a claim in illegitimate pressure can be brought against an innocent defendant who receives an enrichment as a result of illegitimate pressure from a third party upon the plaintiff to enter into the transaction that enriches the defendant. Indeed, in such a case, as between the plaintiff and the defendant, the innocent defendant is in precisely the same position as an innocent recipient of a mistaken payment.[192] There are few examples of third party illegitimate pressure in the authorities. However, the prosecution cases of *Williams v Bayley*,[193] *Mutual Finance Ltd v John Wetton & Sons Ltd*[194] and *Tsarouhi v Tsarouhi*[195] all provide examples of how this scenario could arise. It will be recalled the defendants in those cases had threatened prosecution unless the plaintiff entered a transaction that conferred on them a benefit. In all these cases, the courts had also noted that it could make no difference whether the source of the illegitimacy was the defendant or plaintiff. The source of the illegitimate pressure was not relevant: what was relevant was that it had caused or contributed to the plaintiff's decision to enter into the transaction that enriched the defendant in circumstances where there was no justification for the defendant to retain the enrichment. Equally, as a matter of principle, it should make no difference if the source of the illegitimate pressure in those parties was a third party (for example, a local law enforcement official, or a solicitor): in all cases the unjust factor of illegitimate pressure would be established.[196] *O'Connor v Isaacs*[197] is another example of how such a claim could arise. In that case, the plaintiff was imprisoned several times for failure to pay maintenance to his wife following threats of imprisonment by magistrates for his failure. Subsequently it was discovered that the order for maintenance was invalid. The plaintiff sued the magistrates who imprisoned him for recovery of the moneys paid over under their order. His action in illegitimate pressure failed because the payment had been made to the collecting officer, to the use of the plaintiff's wife, rather than for the benefit of the magistrates. The plaintiff was only unable to proceed against his wife because of an undertaking he had given earlier in proceedings; had the action had been brought against his wife, it would have been an example of restitution from a third party that did not exert the unlawful pressure.

[191] *Unwin v Leaper* (1840) 1 Man & G 747, 133 ER 533.

[192] On the possibility of 'unilateral illegitimate pressure' as an equivalent to unilateral mistake, see above pp 218–19.

[193] *Williams v Bayley* (1866) LR 1 HL 200, 213 (Lord Cranworth).

[194] *Mutual Finance Ltd v John Wetton & Sons Ltd* [1937] 2 KB 389, 395 (Porter J).

[195] *Tsarouhi v Tsarouhi* [2009] FMCAfam 126.

[196] Ch 10 pp 246–50. See also Ch 2 pp 19–21.

[197] *O'Connor v Isaacs* [1956] 2 QB 288.

D. Duress or Illegitimate Pressure and 'Unconscionability'

In *Crescendo Management*,[198] McHugh JA said that, in order to be illegitimate, pressure must be unlawful or amount to 'unconscionable conduct'. The equitable wrong of unconscionable conduct is discussed and explained in the next chapter.[199] It arises 'whenever one party by reason of some condition of circumstance is placed at a special disadvantage vis-à-vis another and unfair or unconscientious advantage is then taken of the opportunity thereby created'.[200] Following the statement by McHugh JA, there has been academic[201] and judicial[202] support for the notion that illegitimate pressure is part of the equitable wrong of unconscionable conduct. In *Cox v Esanda Finance*,[203] the plaintiff claimed that the defendant finance company's misconduct in relation to funding of his property development had left him without physical or financial resources. He claimed that that conduct rendered illegitimate the finance company's threat of costly and lengthy litigation unless he agreed to enter into a deed of release. Although Hunter J rejected a claim for economic duress, he considered that it was 'better seen as an aspect of the doctrines of undue influence *and* unconscionability'.[204] If the suggestions that illegitimate pressure is part of the equitable wrong of unconscionable conduct were followed, illegitimate pressure would be treated as a type of wrongdoing or tort. If the approach of Hunter J were followed, the unjust factor of undue influence would be conflated into this wrong.[205]

Fortunately, in other cases, these suggestions have been rejected. In *Cockerill v Westpac Banking Corp*[206] a claim for illegitimate pressure was made against a bank that had exploited the applicants' 'parlous financial circumstances' to obtain a number of benefits. The trial judge found that the bank's conduct was 'unconscionable in the sense used by McHugh JA in *Crescendo* and constituted illegitimate pressure'.[207] On appeal, the Full Court found that the trial judge had been incorrect to apply the test for the equitable doctrine of unconscionable conduct to satisfy a claim pleaded as illegitimate pressure.[208] As Keifel J said in the leading judgment, the doctrine of unconscionable conduct looks to the quality of the conduct of the defendant, unlike illegitimate pressure, which looks to the quality of the plaintiff's intention.[209] As Gleeson CJ explained in *ACCC v CG Berbatis Holdings Pty Ltd*,[210]

198 *Crescendo Management Pty Ltd v Westpac Banking Corporation* (1988) 19 NSWLR 40.

199 Ch 10 pp 242–45.

200 *Commercial Bank of Australia Ltd v Amadio* [1983] HCA 14, (1983) 151 CLR 447, 462 [6] (Mason J); cited with approval by Gummow and Hayne JJ in *Australian Competition and Consumer Commission v CG Berbatis Holdings Pty Ltd* [2003] HCA 18, (2003) 214 CLR 51 [55] and clearly underlying the approaches of both Gleeson CJ and Callinan J, in preference to the broader formulation by Deane J in *Amadio* at 474 [12].

201 R McKeand, 'Economic Duress—Wearing the Clothes of Unconscionable Conduct' (2001) 17 *Journal of Contract Law* 1; A Phang, 'Economic Duress: Recent Difficulties and Possible Alternatives' (1997) 5 *Restitution Law Review* 53.

202 *Equiticorp Finance Ltd (in liq) v Bank of New Zealand* (1993) 32 NSWLR 50, 107 (Kirby P); cf *Australia and New Zealand Banking Group Ltd v Karam* [2005] NSWCA 344, (2005) 64 NSWLR 149 [66]–[67] (the Court), discussed above at pp 211–12.

203 *Cox v Esanda Finance* [2000] NSWSC 502.

204 ibid [146] (emphasis added).

205 The reasons why undue influence is distinct from wrongdoing are explained in Ch 10 pp 242–50.

206 *Cockerill v Westpac Banking Corporation* (1996) 142 ALR 227, 273 (Cooper J).

207 ibid 279.

208 *Westpac Banking Corporation v Cockerill* (1998) 152 ALR 267.

209 ibid 289; see also *Commercial Bank of Australia Ltd v Amadio* [1983] HCA 14, (1983) 151 CLR 447, 474 [13] (Deane J).

210 *Australian Competition and Consumer Commission v CG Berbatis Holdings Pty Ltd* [2003] HCA 18, (2003) 214 CLR 51 [18].

the equitable wrong of unconscionable conduct does not require illegitimate pressure although it may be part of the context in which pressure arises. Similarly, illegitimate pressure does not require unconscionable conduct, although that may assist to show that pressure in a commercial context is illegitimate.[211]

VI. Conclusion

Duress or illegitimate pressure is an unjust factor in the law of unjust enrichment. As McHugh JA observed in *Crescendo Management Pty Ltd v Westpac Banking Corporation*,[212] the categories of illegitimate pressure are not closed. Now that the law has broken free from the many historic restrictions on duress or illegitimate pressure, the authorities, both at common law and in equity, impose two requirements for a plaintiff to establish the unjust factor of illegitimate pressure: (1) an illegitimate exertion of pressure upon the plaintiff; (2) which causes or contributes to the plaintiff's decision to confer enter a transaction that enriches the defendant. Pressure will be illegitimate where it is unlawful or where lawful pressure is exerted which is unrelated or disproportionate to subject matter that is demanded and any legitimate interest that the defendant has in that subject matter. As to causation or contribution between the unjust factor and the impugned transaction, the test should be the same in all cases of alleged duress or illegitimate pressure. In Australia, the test is as follows: was the pressure *a factor* which influenced the plaintiff's decision to enter the transaction that enriched the defendant? In England, the 'but for' test has increasingly been adopted. In both jurisdictions proof by a plaintiff of illegitimate pressure on the part of a defendant will generally negate any juristic reason that justifies the defendant's retention of the enrichment.

[211] *Schipp v Cameron* [1998] NSWSC 997 [690] (Einstein J).

[212] *Crescendo Management Pty Ltd v Westpac Banking Corporation* (1988) 19 NSWLR 40, 46; see also *Woolwich Equitable Building Society v Inland Revenue Commissioners* [1993] AC 70, 165 (Lord Goff).

10

Undue Influence

Contents

I. Introduction

The previous chapter was concerned with the unjust factor of duress or illegitimate pressure. We saw that illegitimate pressure is well established as a reason for restitution in the law of unjust enrichment. Closely related to the unjust factor of illegitimate pressure is that of undue influence. As Carnwath LJ noted in *Halpern v Halpern*, 'duress and undue influence have much in common'.[1] This is because, as Deane J of the High Court of Australia has explained, 'Undue influence [in equity], like common law duress, looks to the quality of the consent or assent of the weaker party.'[2] We saw in the previous chapter that in a standard case involving a transfer of money from a plaintiff to a defendant, the plaintiff is entitled to

[1] *Halpern v Halpern (Nos 1 & 2)* [2007] EWCA Civ 291, [2008] QB 195 [70], [71] (Waller and Sedley LJJ concurring); cf *Royal Bank of Scotland plc v Etridge (No 2)* [2001] UKHL 44, [2002] 2 AC 773 [33] (Lord Nicholls).

[2] *Commercial Bank of Australia Ltd v Amadio* [1983] HCA 14, (1983) 151 CLR 447, 474 [13] (Deane J); see also *Halpern v Halpern* [2007] EWCA Civ 291, [2008] QB 195 [75], [76] (Carnwath LJ; Waller and Sedley LJJ concurring); *Bridgewater v Leahy* [1998] HCA 66, (1998) 194 CLR 457; *Electricity Generation Corporation t/a Verve Energy v Woodside Energy Ltd* [2013] WASCA 36 [175] (Murphy JA; McLure P and Newnes JA concurring on this point); Anthony Mason, 'The Impact of Equitable Doctrine on the Law of Contract' (1998) 27 *Anglo-American Law Review* 1, 6–8.

restitution from the defendant if the decision to enter the transaction was vitiated by duress or illegitimate pressure.[3] In undue influence cases, the plaintiff's decision is vitiated by the excessive or undue influence of another. This chapter focuses on the immediate defective transaction: Chapter 5 explains how subsequent causally linked transactions can also be the subject of a claim for unjust enrichment, including on the ground of undue influence.

We repeat the same observation in this chapter that we made in the previous one: the historical divide between common law and equity should not obscure the recognition of undue influence as an unjust factor within the law of unjust enrichment. As we saw in the last chapter, although duress at common law is well recognised as part of the law of unjust enrichment, illegitimate pressure in equity has been less recognised. The same is true of undue influence in equity. But there has been some recognition. In *David Securities v Commonwealth Bank of Australia*,[4] five justices of the High Court of Australia referred to both 'compulsion' and 'undue influence' when speaking of liability in unjust enrichment. In *Benedetti v Sawiris*,[5] Lord Neuberger cited undue influence alongside illegitimate pressure as examples of circumstances that may give rise to a claim in unjust enrichment. And, most recently, in the English Court of Appeal in *Hart v Burbidge*,[6] Vos LJ (Black and Richards LJJ concurring) approved the trial judge's characterisation of the juridical basis of undue influence as lying in unjust enrichment.

Although the unjust factors of illegitimate pressure and undue influence are closely related, they are distinct unjust factors. Unfortunately, in some cases a complaint of illegitimate pressure has been misdescribed by courts as one of undue influence.[7] Indeed, we saw in the previous chapter that almost all of the common law probate cases that are described as 'undue influence' are really cases involving illegitimate pressure.[8] Some recent English decisions have also gone so far as to suggest that all cases of 'actual undue influence' are cases of illegitimate pressure.[9] This tendency to merge the two unjust factors must be resisted. Cases of illegitimate pressure are usually characterised by a profound and conscious unwillingness on the part of the plaintiff who succumbs to the pressure to effect the impugned transaction. The hallmark of illegitimate pressure is therefore coercion.[10] Undue influence, on the other hand, typically manifests in an over-eagerness on the part of plaintiffs to enter into an impugned transaction without considering their own interests.

[3] Contracts, deeds and other juristic reasons call for further restrictions in the interests of coherence in the law: see Ch 7 pp 146, 149, 151 and 152–56.

[4] *David Securities Pty Ltd v Commonwealth Bank of Australia* [1992] HCA 48, (1992) 175 CLR 353, 374 [36] (Mason CJ, Dean, Toohey, Gaudron and McHugh JJ).

[5] *Benedetti v Sawiris* [2013] UKSC 50, [2014] AC 938 [175].

[6] *Hart v Burbidge* [2014] EWCA Civ 992 [43].

[7] See Ch 9 pp 200–01.

[8] Ch 9 p 201. For a recent example where illegitimate pressure was labelled 'actual undue influence' in both the probate and *inter vivos* contexts, see *Cattermole v Prisk* [2006] 1 FLR 693 [13] (Norris J): 'The essence of undue influence is *coercion* …'. The learned judge then, at [14], drew a distinction between actual undue influence in this form and 'presumed undue influence', the rationale of which was not wrongdoing, but one of public policy 'to prevent the influence arising from certain sorts of relationship being abused': see further below at pp 236, 240–41. Cf *Fletcher v Queensland Nursing Council* [2009] QCA 364, [2011] 1 Qd R 111 [32]–[33] (Muir J).

[9] See eg *Drew v Daniel* [2005] EWCA Civ 507, [2005] 2 FCR 365 [36] (Ward LJ): *Murphy v Rayner* [2011] EWHC 1 (Ch); *Howard v Howard-Lawson* [2012] EWHC 3258 [85] (Norris J); *Birmingham City Council v Beech (aka Howell)* [2014] EWCA Civ 830, [2014] HLR 38 [57] (Sir Terence Etherton C; Underhill and Briggs LJJ concurring). Cf *Davies v AIB Group (UK) Plc* [2012] EWHC 2178, [2012] 2 P & CR 19 [5], [9]–[12] (Norris J) and *Evans v Lloyd* [2013] EWHC 1725, [2013] WTLR 1137 [37] (Judge Keyser QC).

[10] *Leeder v Stevens* [2005] EWCA Civ 50 [17] (Jacob LJ; Gage LJ agreeing).

Its distinguishing trait is the plaintiff's lack of emancipation from a dominant influence, be it benign, welcome or otherwise. Although in rare cases both doctrines may be called into play by the one set of facts, this will be relatively unusual: 'People do not usually trust those who coerce them.'[11]

The plaintiff must negate any juristic reason (such as a contract, deed of gift or statute) that justifies retention of an enrichment conferred on the defendant as a result of undue influence. Proof of undue influence that negates a juristic reason for retaining the enrichment (such as avoiding a contract or deed[12]) will usually also establish an unjust factor for the purposes of restitution of any enrichment. In either case, the unjust factor of undue influence has two elements. First, the plaintiff must be subject to excessive influence from another person. Second, there must be a causal or contributing link between the influence and the plaintiff's decision to enter the transaction by which the defendant is enriched (the 'a factor' requirement that we discussed in Chapter 8). These requirements are explained in the first two sections of this chapter. The third section explains why this definition omits any requirement that the defendant must have exploited or abused their influence. That omission is intentional. Undue influence as an unjust factor requires no wrongdoing or breach of duty by the defendant. Indeed, the defendant need not even be the party that influences the plaintiff.[13] Exploitation or abuse of influence is a type of wrongdoing that is a wholly separate claim from the unjust factor of undue influence. It is therefore unfortunate that the same label of 'undue influence' is used both for the unjust factor of undue influence and the equitable wrong of abuse of influence. As we saw in Chapters 2 and 6, wrongdoing and unjust enrichment are entirely independent categories of claim. The final section of this chapter explores the differences between the two forms of 'undue influence'.

II. Excessive Influence

The first requirement for the unjust factor of undue influence is that the plaintiff must be subject to the excessive influence of another person or persons at the time of entering into the impugned transaction. The word 'excessive' is used instead of 'undue' simply to avoid any confusion: 'undue influence' is used to describe the completed unjust factor; proof of both excessive influence and the required link between the unjust factor and enrichment.

'Excessive' influence entails a level of influence that is very likely to interfere with the plaintiff's ability to exercise independent or emancipated judgment. By doing so it will impair the plaintiff's decision to enter a transaction that enriches the defendant. As Sir William Blackburne explained in *Hart v Burbridge*:

> It is not to be suggested that … everyday influences disable a person from freely exercising his or her will. The question only arises when the influences go beyond a point where the freedom of that

[11] *Thompson v Foy* [2009] EWHC 1076 (Ch), [2010] P & CR 16 [101] (Lewison J). See also discussion in Ch 9 pp 200–01.

[12] There may be other, additional factors that must be present to negate the particular juristic reason, such as knowledge or responsibility for the plaintiff's vitiated intention in cases of contract, discussed in Ch 7.

[13] *Anderson v McPherson (No 2)* [2012] WASC 19 [243] (Edelman J). The cases are discussed in detail below pp 246–50.

> person to act independently is compromised such that the court concludes that the transaction was not the act of a free agent. The identification of that point must obviously depend on the particular facts of the case.[14]

The level of influence that is regarded as excessive is that which contemporary society regards as a significant interference with a plaintiff's ability to exercise independent judgment.[15] This can vary over time, as societal values and trends change. For example, the growth of religious pluralism in nineteenth-century England coincided with recognition of a presumption of excessive influence in cases involving spiritualism,[16] Roman Catholicism[17] and the Plymouth Brethren.[18]

The existence of excessive influence can be proved in two ways.[19] The first involves proving facts which raise a presumption of excessive influence. The second involves proof by direct evidence or admission that, at the time of the impugned transaction, the plaintiff was subject to excessive influence.

A. Proof of Excessive Influence by Presumption

In England, certain categories of relationship are said, erroneously, to raise an 'irrebuttable'[20] presumption of excessive influence. These include the relationships of doctor and patient,[21] solicitor and client,[22] parent and child,[23] spiritual adviser and follower,[24] trustee and beneficiary and guardian and ward.[25] A presumption of influence is warranted in these categories of relationship because these are recognised relationships of great trust and confidence and 'It is natural to presume that out of that trust and confidence grows influence.'[26] However it is unnecessary and unhelpful to describe the presumption as irrebuttable: there is no justification for elevating a presumption of fact to an inflexible rule of law. A defendant should be entitled to adduce evidence to demonstrate that, although the relationship with the plaintiff is one commonly characterised by excessive influence, the instant relationship is entirely equal and uncharacterised by any influence.[27]

Not included in the list is the relationship of fiancé and fiancée. Although that relationship was historically treated as a relationship of presumed influence,[28] it is unlikely that

[14] *Hart v Burbridge* [2013] EWHC 1628 (Ch), [2013] WTLR 1191 [49].

[15] It has been described as a position 'in which it could fairly be said that the plaintiff's mind was in effect a mere channel through which the will of the defendant operated': *Tufton v Sperni* [1952] 2 TLR 516, 530 (Jenkins LJ), 532 (Morris LJ); *Bank of Credit and Commerce International SA v Aboody* [1990] 1 QB 923, 969 (Slade, Balcombe & Woolf LJJ); *Anderson v McPherson (No 2)* [2012] WASC 19 [248] (Edelman J).

[16] *Lyon v Home* (1868) LR 6 Eq 655.

[17] *Parfitt v Lawless* (1869–72) LR 2 P & D 462.

[18] *Morley v Loughnan* [1893] 1 Ch 736.

[19] *Anderson v McPherson (No 2)* [2012] WASC 19 [247] (Edelman J).

[20] *Royal Bank of Scotland plc v Etridge (No 2)* [2001] UKHL 44, [2002] 2 AC 773 [18] (Lord Nicholls).

[21] *Mitchell v Homfray* (1881) 8 QBD 587.

[22] *Wright v Carter* [1903] 1 Ch 27.

[23] *Lancashire Loans Ltd v Black* [1934] 1 KB 380.

[24] *Allcard v Skinner* (1887) 36 Ch D 145.

[25] *Hylton v Hylton* (1754) 2 Ves Sen 547, 28 ER 349.

[26] *Goldsworthy v Brickell* [1987] Ch 378, 404.

[27] Eg where a child is shown to have become 'emancipated' from the parent: *Tillett v Varnell Holdings Pty Ltd* [2009] NSWSC 1040 [80]–[81] (Brereton J).

[28] *Re Lloyd's Bank Ltd* [1931] 1 Ch 289; *Johnson v Buttress* [1936] HCA 41, (1936) 56 CLR 113, 134 (Dixon J).

this special protection for engaged women will be maintained for three reasons: (i) it was omitted from Lord Nicholls' list of 'irrebuttable' relationships of presumed influence in *Royal Bank of Scotland Plc v Etridge (No 2)*;[29] (ii) it is inconsistent with the exclusion of the relationship of husband and wife from the list;[30] and (iii) it reflects an unwarranted, sexist, assumption of dependence.

B. Proof of Excessive Influence by Evidence

A second method of establishing excessive influence is for the plaintiff to adduce evidence that a non-recognised relationship is characterised by the excessive influence of the defendant or influencing person or (seen from the other side) a want of emancipation on the part of the plaintiff. It must be shown that the influencing person has an ascendancy of judgment over the plaintiff and that the plaintiff is excessively dependent upon, or not emancipated from, the person in the position of influence.[31] This can be shown by the history of the relationship between the plaintiff and the influencer. For example, historically there have been numerous cases in which wives seeking to overturn commercial transactions into which they have entered have relied on a history of having abdicated their own judgment with respect to business matters in favour of that of their husband.[32] Where there is a proven history of excessive influence, the natural inference to draw is that, on the occasion in question when the impugned transaction took place, that influence was present.

Exceptionally, excessive influence may arise without the parties having any prior history of influence, such as when the alleged influence arises with respect to a single transaction.[33] For example, evidence may be led to demonstrate that the alleged influencer instructed the plaintiff to enter a transaction and, due to the circumstances and the nature of the influence involved with that transaction, the plaintiff submitted to that instruction without bringing an independent mind to bear on the transaction.[34]

[29] *Royal Bank of Scotland plc v Etridge (No 2)* [2001] UKHL 44, [2002] 2 AC 773 [18] (Lord Nicholls).

[30] As to which see *Howes v Bishop* [1909] 2 KB 390, 402 (Farrell LJ); *Yerkey v Jones* [1939] HCA 3, (1939) 63 CLR 649, 475 (Dixon J), cited by Lord Nicholls in *Royal Bank of Scotland plc v Etridge (No 2)* [2001] UKHL 44, [2002] 2 AC 773 [19].

[31] See, eg, *Johnson v Buttress* [1936] HCA 41, (1936) 56 CLR 113, 134–35 (Dixon J); *Goldsworthy v Brickell* [1987] Ch 378, 400–01 (Nourse LJ); *Popowski v Popowski* [2004] EWHC 668, [2011] WTLR 1011; *Smith v Cooper* [2010] EWCA Civ 722, [2010] 2 FCR 551 [50], [58] (Lloyd LJ; Wilson and Jacob LJJ agreeing); *Tulloch (deceased) v Braybon (No 2)* [2010] NSWSC 650 [51] (Brereton J); *Re Mahoney* [2015] VSC 600 [218]–[220] (McMillan J).

[32] See, eg, *Bank of Montreal v Stuart* [1911] AC 120; *Bank of Credit and Commerce International SA v Aboody* [1990] 1 QB 923; *Barclays Bank plc v Coleman* [2001] QB 20 affirmed in *Royal Bank of Scotland plc v Etridge (No 2)* [2001] UKHL 44, [2002] 2 AC 773; *Dailey v Dailey* [2003] UKPC 65, [2003] 3 FCR 369 [19]–[20] (Lord Hope delivering the advice of the Board); *Hewett v First Plus Financial Group plc* [2010] EWCA Civ 312, [2010] 2 P & CR 22.

[33] This was alleged but not established in *ANZ Banking Group Ltd v Alirezai* [2004] QCA 6, [2004] Q ConvR 54-601; see also *Khan v Khan* [2004] NSWSC 1189, (2004) 62 NSWLR 229; *Dailey v Dailey* [2003] UKPC 65, [2003] 3 FCR 369 [21] (Lord Hope delivering the advice of the Board); *Macklin v Dowsett* [2004] EWCA Civ 904, [2004] 2 EGLR 75; *Turkey v Awadh* [2005] EWCA Civ 382, [2005] 2 FCR 7 [10]–[12] (Chadwick LJ); *Thompson v Foy* [2009] EWHC 1076, [2010] P & CR 16 [100] (Lewison J). Contrast *Singla v Bashir* [2002] EWHC 883 (Ch) [25]–[26] (Park J).

[34] *Dailey v Dailey* [2003] UKPC 65, [2003] 3 FCR 369 [21] (Lord Hope delivering the advice of the Board); *Khan v Khan* [2004] NSWSC 1189, (2004) 62 NSWLR 229.

Whatever the particular circumstances, the key feature of the relationship must be that it is characterised by ascendancy and influence on the one hand, and dependence and trust on the other.[35] The kinds of circumstances that may be relevant to demonstrate the existence of excessive influence are infinitely varied.[36] In *Union Fidelity Trustee Co of Australia Ltd v Gibson*, for example, Gillard J said:

> The standard of intelligence and education, and the character and personality of the donor, are relevant matters. Age, state of health, blood relationship, experience, or lack of it, in business affairs of the donor, length of friendship or acquaintanceship between the donor and donee and the intricacy of their business affairs may be factors to influence a donor to depend upon the donee. Equally, the relative strength of character and personality of the donee, the period and closeness of the relationship and the opportunity afforded the donee to influence the donor in his business affairs are correlative considerations to the foregoing[.][37]

C. Factors Militating Against a Conclusion of Excessive Influence

The most common factor that will militate against a conclusion of excessive influence is evidence that shows that the relationship between the parties was commercial in nature, so that each party was acting in his or her own commercial self-interest.[38] Another circumstance that will militate against a finding of excessive influence is evidence that the plaintiff generally exercised an independent judgment in relation to his affairs or did so on the relevant occasion.[39] In *Yerkey v Jones*,[40] for example, Mrs Jones mistrusted her husband's business acumen and only grudgingly went along with the impugned transactions. Her subsequent claim that she entered into the transactions as a result of undue influence failed. Similarly, in *Commonwealth Bank of Australia v Cohen*, Cole J found that Mrs Cohen signed

[35] *Johnson v Buttress* [1936] HCA 41, (1936) 56 CLR 113, 134–35 (Dixon J).

[36] ibid 136 (Dixon J). See, eg, *Simpson v Simpson* [1992] 1 FLR 601 (wife–husband); *Tufton v Sperni* [1952] 2 TLR 516 (vendor–purchaser); *Goldsworthy v Brickell* [1987] Ch 378 (farm manager–farm owner); *Re Craig (deceased)* [1971] Ch 95 (housekeeper–owner); *Inche Noriah v Shaik Allie bin Omar* [1929] AC 127 (nephew–aunt); *Lloyds Bank Ltd v Bundy* [1975] QB 326 (bank–client); *O'Sullivan v Management Agency and Music Ltd* [1985] QB 428 (employer/manager–employee); *Nattrass v Nattrass* [1999] WASC 77 (former daughter-in-law and carer–elderly woman); *Commonwealth Bank of Australia v Ridout Nominees Pty Ltd* [2000] WASC 37 (parent–adult sons) and *Johnson v Buttress* [1936] HCA 41, (1936) 56 CLR 113 (trusted friends); *Bester v Perpetual Trustee Co Ltd* [1970] 3 NSWR 30 (uncle–niece).

[37] *Union Fidelity Trustee Co of Australia Ltd v Gibson* [1971] VR 573 [10], cited with approval in *Tranchita v Retravision (WA) Pty Ltd* [2001] WASCA 265; *Powell v Powell* [2002] WASC 105 [132] (McLure J). See also *Johnson v Buttress* [1936] HCA 41, (1936) 56 CLR 113, 137–38 (Dixon J); *Lee v Chai* [2013] QSC 136 [193]–[198] (Peter Lyons J). In England, see *Royal Bank of Scotland plc v Etridge (No 2)* [2001] UKHL 44, [2002] 2 AC 773 [33] (Lord Nicholls); *Cattermole v Prisk* [2006] 1 FLR 693 [14] (Norris J).

[38] *Xu v Lin* [2005] NSWSC 569, (2005) 12 BPR 23,131 [28] (Barrett J); *ANZ Banking Group Ltd v Alirezai* [2004] QCA 6, [2004] Q ConvR 54-601.

[39] *Re Estate of Brocklehurst* [1978] Ch 14. Good recent examples of the kind of detailed analysis called for to determine excessive influence is contained in *Papouis v Gibson-West* [2004] EWHC 396, [2004] WTLR 485 [26]–[34] (Lewison J: elderly aunt very fond of niece, but aunt was 'mentally robust' and independent in her decisions); *Thompson v Foy* [2009] EWHC 1076, [2010] P & CR 16 [103] (Lewison J: relationship between mother and daughter was supportive, but mother retained her independent judgement and was aware of the risks of the transaction) and *Christodoulou v Christodoulou* [2009] VSC 583, [104]–[105] (Kaye J: elderly, illiterate mother not conversant in English, who was abandoned by her husband and daughters, nonetheless remained a woman of 'independent disposition' and was not subject to any excessive influence from her admittedly supportive son).

[40] *Yerkey v Jones* [1939] HCA 3, (1939) 63 CLR 649.

a guarantee 'after discussion, and perhaps even argument with her husband'.[41] A similar pattern of independence characterised the wife's behaviour in *Bank of Scotland v Bennett*,[42] discussed in the previous chapter.[43] It was this very independence—following by sudden capitulation in the face of a threat of divorce—that showed the case was one of illegitimate pressure rather than undue influence. Although it is possible that a person of independent judgment might be able to show excessive influence of the person's spouse on a particular occasion, this will usually be difficult to prove.[44]

III. The Required Contributing Link Between the Influence and the Transaction that Enriched the Defendant

The second requirement for the unjust factor of undue influence is that there must be the requisite link between the excessive influence and the plaintiff's decision to enter the transaction that enriched the defendant. As we have seen with illegitimate pressure in the previous chapter, there are different views about what is required to establish the requisite link between the excessive influence and the impugned transaction. One view is that the link is a causal test of necessity or 'but for' causation. Another view is that the test is one of contribution to the process of decision making: an 'a factor' approach.

An example where the required link was 'but for' causation is *Bank of Credit and Commerce International SA v Aboody*.[45] Throughout her marriage, Mrs Aboody had entirely subordinated her judgment in all financial matters to that of her husband. Indeed, the English Court of Appeal found that her mind was, to that extent, 'a mere channel through which the will of [Mr Aboody] operated'.[46] When Mr Aboody asked his wife to sign various guarantee and charge documents in favour of the plaintiff bank to secure his company's borrowings, she dutifully agreed. She accompanied her husband to the bank so that her signature to the documents could be witnessed. There, a solicitor attempted to counsel her as to the dangers inherent in signing the documents, but she made it clear that she did not want to listen. Her husband had indicated that the documents were required in the interests of his company and she therefore just wanted to sign them. Notwithstanding this evidence, which would have satisfied the 'a factor' link, Mrs Aboody's claim was ultimately unsuccessful. Among other reasons given,[47] the court held that the 'but for' test of causation was

[41] *Commonwealth Bank of Australia v Cohen* (1988) ASC 55-681, 58,160.

[42] *Bank of Scotland v Bennett* [1999] 1 FLR 1115, appeal conjoined and allowed on another ground in *Royal Bank of Scotland plc v Etridge (No 2)* [2001] UKHL 44, [2002] 2 AC 773.

[43] Discussed in Ch 9 p 201.

[44] *Khan v Khan* [2004] NSWSC 1189, (2004) 62 NSWLR 229.

[45] *Bank of Credit and Commerce International SA v Aboody* [1990] 1 QB 923. Others are *Khan v Khan* [2004] NSWSC 1189, (2004) 62 NSWLR 229, considered Ch 7 p 149 and *Anderson v Anderson* [2013] QSC 8 (where the defendant was overheard prompting his mother to make certain decisions, to which urgings she immediately acceded).

[46] *Bank of Credit and Commerce International SA v Aboody* [1990] 1 QB 923, 969 (Slade LJ, delivering the judgment of the Court).

[47] One ground was that the transaction was not manifestly disadvantageous, as to which see below at p 237. Another was that the transaction was not wrongful, as to which see below at pp 242–50.

not satisfied.[48] The court found that, even if Mr Aboody had taken Mrs Aboody into his confidence, she still would have signed the documents. On that analysis, she had failed to satisfy the 'but for' test of causation.

In these cases of 'actual' undue influence, English courts have subsequently resiled from using the 'but for' test.[49] As was explained by Briggs J in *Hewett v First Plus Financial Group plc* (Leveson and Jacob LJJ agreeing):

> The right to set aside the transaction arises not because, on a but for causation analysis, it would otherwise have been avoided, but because of the equitable wrong ... was part of the process by which the victim's consent to it was obtained.[50]

Although using the language of an 'equitable wrong' rather than an 'unjust factor', this passage reflects the same 'a factor' approach to the required link that applies in cases of illegitimate pressure. As we will see below the 'a factor' approach to undue influence also applies where the link is proven by presumption.

The required 'a factor' link can be proved in two ways.[51] The first, and exceptional, method is for the plaintiff to lead direct evidence that the influence was 'a factor' in the plaintiff's decision to enter the transaction that enriched the defendant. When this is the approach taken, the claim is called one of 'actual undue influence'. The second, and far more common, method used by plaintiffs is to prove facts that raise a (rebuttable) presumption that the influence was 'a factor' in the plaintiff's decision to enrich the defendant. When this is done, the claim is called one of 'presumed undue influence'. They are not different forms of claim, but simply 'different ways of proving the same thing'.[52] We consider first the more common method of proving the required link, namely proof with the aid of a presumption.

A. Proof of the Contributing Link by Presumption

A presumption of an 'a factor' link will arise when a plaintiff who is in a relationship of excessive influence can show that she entered into a transaction 'calling for explanation'.[53] This presumption is separate from the presumption of excessive influence that arises when the plaintiff and defendant's relationship is one which is commonly characterised as giving rise to excessive influence. Rather, this presumption arises when (i) there is, or is presumed to be, a relationship of excessive influence, and (ii) a transaction occurs between the parties to that relationship which calls for explanation. The presumption that arises upon proof

[48] *Bank of Credit and Commerce International SA v Aboody* [1990] 1 QB 923, 970–71 (Slade LJ, delivering the judgment of the Court).

[49] *UCB Corporate Services Ltd v Williams* [2002] EWCA Civ 555, [2002] 3 FCR 448 [86]–[90] (Jonathan Parker LJ; Peter Gibson and Kay LJJ concurring); see also *Hewett v First Plus Financial Group plc* [2010] EWCA Civ 312, [2010] 2 P & CR 22 [34] (Briggs J).

[50] *Hewett v First Plus Financial Group plc* [2010] EWCA Civ 312, [2010] 2 P & CR 22 [34].

[51] *Allcard v Skinner* (1887) 36 Ch D 145, 171 (Cotton LJ).

[52] *Thompson v Foy* [2009] EWHC 1076, [2010] P & CR 16 [100] (Lewison J). See also *Papouis v Gibson-West* [2004] EWHC 396, [2004] WTLR 485 [5] (Lewison J); *Christodoulou v Christodoulou* [2009] VSC 583 [70], [74] (Kaye J); *Hart v Burbridge* [2013] EWHC 1628, [2013] WTLR 1191 [37] (Sir William Blackburne), upheld on appeal *Hart v Burbidge* [2014] EWCA Civ 992; *Daunt v Daunt* [2015] VSCA 58 [62] (the Court).

[53] *Papouis v Gibson-West* [2004] EWHC 396, [2004] WTLR 485 [5] (Lewison J); *Thompson v Foy* [2009] EWHC 1076, [2010] P & CR 16 [100] (Lewison J); *Curtis v Pulbrook* [2009] EWHC 782, [2011] WTLR 1503 [139] (Judge Sheldon QC).

of these two matters is that the excessive influence was a factor in the plaintiff's decision to enter the transaction. This presumption can be of great benefit to a plaintiff because evidence of an 'a factor' link independent of the plaintiff's testimony will be very rare.[54] And in cases where the plaintiff's claim is being brought by her estate, or where the plaintiff no longer has capacity, that direct evidence may be unavailable.

The requirement that the impugned transaction be one 'calling for explanation' was once described as a requirement that the transaction be 'manifestly disadvantageous' to the plaintiff. That label was criticised for being misleading and ambiguous about what a plaintiff must prove. The plaintiff does not need to prove any 'disadvantage'. Nor must the plaintiff prove that any disadvantage is 'manifest'. All that is required is that the transaction is 'not readily explicable by the relationship of the parties'.[55] Even transactions entered into for full value (and thus not 'manifestly disadvantageous' in an economic sense) may still call for explanation. For example, a very elderly plaintiff with no prospects of any other accommodation who suddenly decides to transfer his home for full value to a developer might be a transaction calling for explanation. On the other hand, small gifts to a person in a position of influence, for example, may well be explicable on the grounds of affection, gratitude or charitable intent. Thus, a small gift from a child to her parent, a client to his solicitor, or a religious adherent to her leader, is unremarkable and unlikely to be set aside.[56] Similarly, although substantial gifts between these parties might not be readily explicable by reference to normal motives of parties to that kind of relationship,[57] even in some relationships of proved excessive influence, a presumption of an 'a factor' link might not be applied. For instance, large gifts made by a wife to a husband are not generally subject to a presumption even if excessive influence is proved, because 'there is nothing unusual or strange in a wife from motives of affection or even of prudence conferring a large proprietary or pecuniary benefit upon her husband.'[58]

All the circumstances of a transaction must be considered before determining whether the transaction is one which calls for explanation. In *Quek v Beggs*,[59] Mrs Quek gave a sum of money to her pastor and his wife, which was relatively small in the context of her estate. She also gave several very large gifts which in total constituted virtually the whole of her estate. Mrs Quek had two teenage children and the intended effect of the gifts was to deprive them of any means of support following her (anticipated) death. The trial judge found that the small gift was explicable by reference to a natural desire on the part of Mrs Quek to support the defendants in their pastoral work, as well as motives of affection arising from the very strong personal friendship that had developed between the parties and refused to apply a presumption of an 'a factor' link. However, the larger gifts were not so explicable,

[54] Discussed below at pp 241–42.

[55] *Royal Bank of Scotland plc v Etridge (No 2)* [2001] UKHL 44, [2002] 2 AC 773 [21] (Lord Nicholls); see also *Goldsworthy v Brickell* [1987] Ch 378 401 (Nourse LJ): 'a gift ... or ... transaction so improvident, as not to be reasonably accounted for on the ground of friendship, relationship, charity or other ordinary motives on which ordinary men act'. See also *Macklin v Dowsett* [2004] EWCA Civ 904, [2004] 2 EGLR 75; *Turkey v Awadh* [2005] EWCA Civ 382, [2005] 2 FCR 7 [41] (Chadwick LJ).

[56] *Royal Bank of Scotland plc v Etridge (No 2)* [2001] UKHL 44, [2002] 2 AC 773 [24] (Lord Nicholls).

[57] See, eg, *Trevenar v Ussfeller* [2005] NSWSC 582 [53] (Gzell J).

[58] *Yerkey v Jones* [1939] HCA 3, (1939) 63 CLR 649, 675 (Dixon J). See also *Turkey v Awadh* [2005] EWCA Civ 382, [2005] 2 FCR 7 [20]–[32] (Buxton LJ), [39]–[41] (Chadwick LJ): unusual sale transaction explicable by reference to the particular familial context in which it took place and the circumstances of the parties to the transaction.

[59] *Quek v Beggs* (1990) 5 BPR 11,761; see also *McKeering v Rattle* [1995] QSC 75.

and were set aside for presumed undue influence. Similarly in *Cattermole v Prisk*,[60] a widow made two substantial gifts to her intimate companion and carer. The first was explicable by reference to their relationship and the personal and financial circumstances of the widow at the time, and was upheld. The second gift called for explanation: 'why give another sizeable gift so soon after the first and out of reduced means?'[61] In the absence of evidence from the defendant that the gift was made after 'full, free and informed'[62] thought, the gift was set aside for presumed undue influence.

B. Rebutting the Presumption

The presumption of an 'a factor' link between the excessive influence and the decision to enter the impugned transaction may be rebutted by evidence that shows that the plaintiff made her decision emancipated from excessive influence.[63] That is, the influence played no part, and therefore was not 'a factor' in the plaintiff's decision to enrich the defendant. However, that is a heavy burden placed on the defendant, once the presumption is raised. As Dixon J stated in *Johnson v Buttress*, it is incumbent upon the defendant to show that the gift 'cannot be ascribed to the inequality between [the plaintiff and defendant] which must arise from his special position'.[64] Another way of putting this is to say that the defendant must show that the influence made no contribution to—or was not a factor that affected—the plaintiff's decision to enter the transaction by which the defendant is enriched; the decision to must be the 'pure, voluntary, well understood, ac[t] of [the] mind' of the plaintiff.[65] This is the same 'a factor' link we have seen in cases of mistake[66] and illegitimate pressure.[67]

The most common method by which defendants attempt to rebut the presumption of an 'a factor' link is by showing that the plaintiff received full and independent legal advice prior to enriching the defendant.[68] However, the mere provision of advice about the mechanics of the transaction, or its legal features or consequences, will not suffice. It is commonplace that plaintiffs under excessive influence fully intend and understand what they are about to do: the question is not whether the intention existed but how it was produced.[69] The advice

[60] *Cattermole v Prisk* [2006] 1 FLR 693.
[61] ibid [85] (Norris J).
[62] ibid [85]–[86].
[63] See, eg, *Bester v Perpetual Trustee Co Ltd* [1970] 3 NSWR 30.
[64] *Johnson v Buttress* [1936] HCA 41, (1936) 56 CLR 113, 135.
[65] *Huguenin v Baseley* (1807) 14 Ves Jr 273, 296; 33 ER 526, 535 (Lord Eldon LC), quoted with approval by Latham CJ in *Johnson v Buttress* [1936] HCA 41, (1936) 56 CLR 113, 119. See also *Goldsworthy v Brickell* [1987] Ch 378, 401 (Nourse LJ); *Allcard v Skinner* (1887) 36 Ch D 145, 171 (Cotton LJ); *Christodoulou v Christodoulou* [2009] VSC 583, [77] (Kaye J); *Smith v Cooper* [2010] EWCA Civ 722, [2010] 2 FCR 551 [70] (Lloyd LJ; Wilson and Jacob LJJ agreeing); *Hart v Burbridge* [2013] EWHC 1628, [2013] WTLR 1191 [44]–[46] (Sir William Blackburne), upheld on appeal *Hart v Burbidge* [2014] EWCA Civ 992.
[66] Ch 8 pp 189–94.
[67] Ch 9 pp 219–24.
[68] *Jenyns v Public Curator (Qld)* [1953] HCA 2, (1953) 90 CLR 113, 131 [23] (the Court).
[69] *Hartigan v International Society for Krishna Consciousness Inc* [2002] NSWSC 810 [27] (Bryson J), citing *Huguenin v Basely* (1807) 14 Ves Jr 273, 300; 33 ER 526, 536 (Lord Eldon LC). See also *Bester v Perpetual Trustee Co Ltd* [1970] 3 NSWR 30, 36 (Street J); *Bullock v Lloyds Bank Ltd* [1955] Ch 317; *Smith v Cooper* [2010] EWCA Civ 722, [2010] 2 FCR 551 [70] (Lloyd LJ; Wilson and Jacob LJJ agreeing); *Hart v Burbridge* [2013] EWHC 1628, [2013] WTLR 1191 [130] (Sir William Blackburne), upheld on appeal *Hart v Burbidge* [2014] EWCA Civ 992.

must be effective to emancipate the plaintiff from the influence which exists in relation to the relevant transaction.[70] Effective, emancipating advice can come from any person, although it is common for a defendant to rely upon advice from a solicitor. As the Privy Council explained in *Inche Noriah v Shaik Allie bin Omar*:

> the nature and effect of the transaction [must have] been fully explained to the donor by some independent and qualified person so completely as to satisfy the Court that the donor was acting independently of any influence from the donee and with the full appreciation of what he was doing … [The advice] must be given with a knowledge of all relevant circumstances and must be such as a competent and honest adviser would give if acting solely in the interests of the donor.[71]

The operation of independent advice, and the need for it to be emancipating, can be seen in the facts of *Inche Noriah v Shaik Allie Bin Omar*,[72] an appeal to the Privy Council from the straits settlements of Singapore. In that case, an elderly Malay woman gave virtually all her property to her nephew. She was in bad health, illiterate and housebound. She relied on her nephew to look after her business dealings and to handle all of her domestic affairs. When she notified her nephew of her intention to make the gift, her nephew arranged for a lawyer to come to see her. The lawyer arranged for the nephew to be separately represented, so the aunt's lawyer would be truly independent. Notwithstanding her subsequent receipt of broad-ranging and independent legal advice, the Privy Council held that a presumption of excessive influence arose from the circumstances of the relationship. The presumption had not been rebutted.[73] The reason it had not been rebutted was because the independent solicitor was not aware that the intended gift constituted nearly all the old lady's property. Had he known that, he would have talked to her about the dangers inherent in taking her proposed course of action and advised her of the alternative means open to her of benefiting her nephew—for example, by leaving the property to him in her will.[74]

Another example is the Australian decision in *Quek v Beggs*, which was discussed in the previous section.[75] In that case, Mrs Quek actively sought advice from her solicitor about how best to deplete her estate before she died, with the conscious intention of depriving her children of an inheritance. However, that evidence was not sufficient to rebut the presumption of an 'a factor' link that arose in respect of the large gifts made by Mrs Quek to her pastor, Mr Beggs. Her solicitor understood her motives with respect to her children, but was unaware of the nature of the relationship between Mrs Quek and Mr Beggs.[76] Even had he been aware of the relationship of excessive influence, 'he may not have been equipped to free Mrs Quek from the effect of any influence arising from that relationship'.[77] The case demonstrates that independent legal advice may not be effective to emancipate the plaintiff

[70] See also *Royal Bank of Scotland plc v Etridge (No 2)* [2001] UKHL 44, [2002] 2 AC 773 [20] (Lord Nicholls); *Papouis v Gibson-West* [2004] EWHC 396, [2004] WTLR 485 [5] (Lewison J); *Thompson v Foy* [2009] EWHC 1076, [2010] P & CR 16 [99] (Lewison J); *Curtis v Pulbrook* [2009] EWHC 782, [2011] WTLR 1503 [143] (Judge Sheldon QC); *Hackett v Crown Prosecution Service* [2011] EWHC 1170, [2011] Lloyd's Rep FC 371 [61]–[74] (Silber J).

[71] *Inche Noriah v Shaik Allie bin Omar* [1929] AC 127 135–36.

[72] ibid.

[73] ibid 135–36.

[74] See also *Pesticcio v Huet* [2003] EWHC 2293, (2003) 73 BMLR 57.

[75] *Quek v Beggs* (1990) 5 BPR 11,761.

[76] See also *Bar-Moredecai v Hillston* [2004] NSWCA 65 [161] (Mason P, Tobias JA and Davies AJA).

[77] *Quek v Beggs* (1990) 5 BPR 11,761, 11,778 (McLelland J).

from the influence; much will depend on the nature of the influence, the identity of the plaintiff[78] and the nature of the advice.

There are other ways to rebut a presumption of an 'a factor' link than demonstrating that the plaintiff has received emancipating advice. For example, a defendant may be able to demonstrate that the plaintiff entered into the transaction for reasons entirely independent of any influence, such as to avoid inheritance tax,[79] for personal profit[80] or to preclude third parties from having access to the transferred benefit.[81] In *Daunt v Daunt*,[82] Mrs Daunt transferred her interest in a property held jointly with her husband to her son, Michael, who was also her primary carer. It was accepted that the relationship between mother and son was one of influence and that the onus lay upon Michael to show that the gift was the product of the exercise of an independent will. In a joint judgment, the Victorian Court of Appeal found that the evidence clearly showed that Mrs Daunt entered into the transaction in order to protect her pension entitlement and to enable her to continue to have access to the property.[83] The evidence therefore showed that she had entered into the transaction independently of Michael's influence, and the transaction stood.

C. Proof of the Contributing Link by Evidence

We saw earlier that cases where undue influence is proved by evidence rather than through operation of a presumption are called 'actual' undue influence. This label has caused great confusion. It has sometimes been used (inaccurately) in cases involving the quite distinct unjust factor of illegitimate pressure.[84] Some cases have also suggested that 'actual' undue influence involves wrongful influence, while 'presumed' undue influence is non-wrongful.[85] But this cannot be right. As we noted earlier, actual and presumed undue influence are not different forms of claim, but simply 'different ways of proving the same thing'.[86]

[78] See, eg, *Williams v Williams* [2003] EWHC 742, [2003] WTLR 1371, where the independent advice would have been effective for an 'ordinary person', but not the plaintiff, who was suffering a severe mental impairment and was dependent on the defendant.

[79] Cf *Hackett v Crown Prosecution Service* [2011] EWHC 1170, [2011] Lloyd's Rep FC 371, where the transaction was nonetheless considered to 'call for explanation' at [55]–[60] (Silber J).

[80] *Wilkinson v ASB Bank Ltd* [1998] 1 NZLR 674, 691 (Blanchard J); *ANZ Banking Group v Alirezai* [2004] QCA 6, [2004] Q ConvR 54-601 [75] (Jerrard JA).

[81] See, eg, *Christodoulou v Christodoulou* [2009] VSC 583 [107] (Kaye J: mother deliberately and spontaneously transferred her interest in her former matrimonial home to her son out of gratitude, affection and to prevent her daughters, who had 'deserted her in her hour of need' from having access to the property); cf *Quek v Beggs* (1990) 5 BPR 11,761, discussed immediately above.

[82] *Daunt v Daunt* [2015] VSCA 58.

[83] ibid [77]–[79]. It does not seem to have been of concern to the Court that the transaction might subvert the statutory scheme of pension entitlements: cf *Nelson v Nelson* [1995] HCA 25, (1995) 184 CLR 538, discussed in Ch 7 p 160, Ch 12 p 299 and Ch 13 pp 311–12.

[84] Ch 9 pp 200–01.

[85] *Randall v Randall* [2004] EWHC 2258, [2005] WTLR 119. An Australian equivalent may be *Maher v Honeysett & Maher Electrical Contractors Pty Ltd* [2007] NSWSC 12, (2007) Aust Contract R 90-249, compare [132] and [133]–[136] (Barrett J).

[86] *Thompson v Foy* [2009] EWHC 1076, [2010] P & CR 16 [100] (Lewison J). See also *Papouis v Gibson-West* [2004] EWHC 396, [2004] WTLR 485 [5] (Lewison J); *Christodoulou v Christodoulou* [2009] VSC 583 [70], [74] (Kaye J); *Hart v Burbridge* [2013] EWHC 1628, [2013] WTLR 1191 [37] (Sir William Blackburne), upheld on appeal *Hart v Burbidge* [2014] EWCA Civ 992; *Daunt v Daunt* [2015] VSCA 58 [62] (the Court).

Mr Swadling has identified a further difficulty with the label of actual undue influence.[87] The word 'actual' is usually used in law in contradistinction to 'constructive'. 'Constructive' signals a deemed fact that is accepted notwithstanding evidence to the contrary, as in constructive possession or constructive notice.[88] 'Actual' means that the fact really or genuinely exists. The labels of actual and presumed undue influence are therefore quite inapt: there is no doubt that cases of 'presumed' undue influence are addressing real or genuine cases of undue influence, albeit influence proved with the aid of a presumption rather than by evidence.

The view that the elements of undue influence can only be proved by presumption is incorrect. It is also nonsense to suppose that a matter that can be proved by presumption could not be proved by positive evidence. Although it is comparatively rare for both of the elements of undue influence to be proved without the benefit of a presumption, such cases exist. The main difficulty (and hence the rarity) of proving the 'a factor' link for undue influence without the benefit of presumptions lies in the difficulty of proof without the presumption that the excessive influence was 'a factor' in the plaintiff's decision to enter the transaction that enriched the defendant. A plaintiff will need to prove her motivations and the effect of the excessive influence upon her decision. There will rarely be direct evidence independent of the plaintiff's own account as to why she chose to do as she did. For instance, there will rarely be a statement contemporaneous with entry into the transaction that reveals the influence over the plaintiff operating on her decision to transfer. This can be contrasted with cases of illegitimate pressure, where the threat usually is linked to an objectively ascertainable demand that the plaintiff confer a benefit upon the defendant. In these cases, if the plaintiff is proved to have been the subject of a threat made for the purpose of inducing her to enter the transaction, and the plaintiff did enter the transaction, the obvious inference to draw is that the pressure was 'a factor' in the plaintiff's decision to enter the transaction.

A rare example of a case where there was direct evidence of both elements of the unjust factor of undue influence—that is, excessive influence and an 'a factor' link—is *Anderson v Anderson*.[89] In that case, an elderly mother, Roma, gave her family home (and sole significant asset) to one of her sons, Malcolm. Justice Dalton noted that although the relationship did not fall within one of the categories of presumed influence, the plaintiff (her other son and executor, John) had established by evidence that Malcolm was in a position of dominance over Roma.[90] That influence, together with the size of the gift, was sufficient to raise the presumption that Malcolm's influence was 'a factor' in Roma's decision to make the gift. But Dalton J also identified the direct evidence on this issue, as well as on the issue of influence. His Honour found that Roma was very frail and increasingly isolated from John by, and hence dependent on, Malcolm. His Honour found that, on numerous occasions, Malcolm had been heard during telephone conversations prompting or directing his mother to ask questions or make decisions. Rosa's diminishing mental capacity meant that

[87] W Swadling, 'Undue Influence: Lessons from America?' in C Mitchell and W Swadling (eds), *The Restatement Third: Restitution and Unjust Enrichment: Critical and Comparative Essays* (Oxford, Hart Publishing, 2013) 115–18.

[88] *Re Fewster* [1901] 1 Ch 447.

[89] *Anderson v Anderson* [2013] QSC 8. See also *Khan v Khan* [2004] NSWSC 1189, (2004) 62 NSWLR 229, discussed Ch 7 p 149.

[90] ibid [55].

she was, at the time of entering into the transaction, highly susceptible to Malcolm's directions. When Rosa and Malcolm went to see a new solicitor, Mr Hely, about changing her will, Malcolm was present and directed all discussion and decisions. Malcolm argued that Roma had been given independent advice on making the gift of the family home to him by Mr Hely, which advice was effective to rebut the presumption of a link between the excessive influence and the enrichment. Justice Dalton said:

> It was Mr Malcolm Anderson who suggested that the house be transferred to him and Mr Malcolm Anderson who gave the instructions for that to happen after Mr Hely attempted to discuss it with Mrs Roma Anderson. Far from assuaging any concerns about the impugned transaction, the descriptions given by Mr Hely as to his consultations with Mrs Roma Anderson demonstrate in my mind that in fact Mrs Roma Anderson was being dominated by and influenced by Mr Malcolm Anderson and not exercising her own free will and judgment as to the transactions.[91]

IV. Distinguishing Undue Influence from Abuse of Influence

A. Abuse of Influence: A Different Action based upon Wrongdoing

We saw at the beginning of this chapter that illegitimate pressure and undue influence are sometimes conflated, notwithstanding the distinct nature of the two unjust factors. Unfortunately, the confusion does not stop there. Another independent doctrine sometimes shelters under the label of undue influence. This is the equitable wrong of abuse of influence. The equitable wrong of abuse of influence is characterised by abuse or exploitation by the defendant of the trust and confidence reposed by the victim in the defendant, in order to extract some benefit from the victim.[92] The equitable wrong is indistinguishable from a tort, other than by its historical origins in the Court of Chancery. An analogous, but more specific, tort of sexual abuse of trust or influence has recently been recognised by the Irish High Court in *Walsh v Byrne*.[93] In that case, the defendant created a relationship of influence in order to prepare the plaintiff child for sexual abuse. As White J explained, recognition of this tort was required 'to cover what is now a well recognised and established pattern of wrongdoing, where a child is befriended, where trust is established and where that friendship and trust is used to perpetrate sexual abuse'.[94]

The equitable wrong of abuse of influence is very close to the equitable wrong of unconscionable conduct that was discussed briefly in Chapter 2.[95] In cases involving a plea of unconscionable conduct, the plaintiff must prove that he was at a special disadvantage in relation to the defendant and that the defendant exploited that disadvantage with a

[91] ibid [62]; see also [64].
[92] See eg *Birmingham City Council v Beech (aka Howell)* [2014] EWCA Civ 830, [2014] HLR 38 [57]–[59] (Sir Terence Etherton C; Underhill and Briggs LJJ concurring).
[93] *Walsh v Byrne* [2015] IEHC 414.
[94] ibid [22].
[95] Ch 2 p 21.

'predatory state of mind'[96] in a way that was not fair, just or reasonable.[97] All that would be required to assimilate the wrong of abuse of influence with the wrong of unconscionable dealing would be recognition that being subject to the excessive influence of another is a form of weakness/special disadvantage.[98] Indeed, the recognition in *Louth v Diprose*[99] that lovesickness was a form of special disadvantage shows that this is a simple step to take. In the context of the recent shift in focus towards a doctrine of abuse of influence, it is therefore not surprising that English courts have struggled to identify and apply a continuing distinction between the doctrines of unconscionable conduct and the wrong of undue influence.[100] It has been suggested that the distinction lies in the fact that unconscionable dealing is transaction-specific and requires no history of a relationship of disadvantage between the parties.[101] But neither should a wrong of exploitation of influence.

The very close relationship between the doctrines of abuse of influence and unconscionable conduct underscores the fundamental distinction between those wrongs and the unjust factor of undue influence. In Australia, the distinction between the unjust factor of undue influence and unconscionable dealing is well understood. Justice Kaye of the Victorian Supreme Court recently summarised the orthodox position:

> The doctrine of unconscionable conduct has some similarities to the doctrine of undue influence, but the underlying rationale of the two doctrines is quite different … [T]he principles relating to undue influence focus on whether the transaction was the product of the independent and voluntary will of the donor. By contrast, the doctrine of unconscionable conduct is concerned with circumstances where the will of the donor, while independent and voluntary, is the result of a special disadvantage or disability of the donor, of which the donee has taken unconscientious advantage. In other words, while undue influence focuses on the quality of the consent or assent of the donor, unconscionable dealing is concerned with the conduct of the donee or recipient in attempting to enforce, or retain the benefit of, a dealing with a person under a special disability '… in circumstances where it is not consistent with equity or good conscience that he should do so'.[102]

Unfortunately, in recent times, the language of an equitable wrong of abuse of influence has come to dominate English analysis of cases involving excessive influence.[103] Thus the House

[96] *Kakavas v Crown Melbourne Ltd* [2013] HCA 25, (2013) 250 CLR 392 [161] (the Court).

[97] *Commercial Bank of Australia Ltd v Amadio* [1983] HCA 14, (1983) 151 CLR 447, 462 [6] (Mason J).

[98] Cf *Royal Bank of Scotland plc v Etridge (No 2)* [2001] UKHL 44, [2002] 2 AC 773 [111] (Lord Hobhouse).

[99] *Louth v Diprose* [1992] HCA 61, (1992) 175 CLR 621.

[100] See, eg, *Royal Bank of Scotland plc v Etridge (No 2)* [2001] UKHL 44, [2002] 2 AC 773 [11] (Lord Nicholls: undue influence includes 'cases where a vulnerable person has been exploited'); *Macklin v Dowsett* [2004] EWCA Civ 904, [2004] 2 EGLR 75; *The Public Trustee v Bailey* [2005] EWHC 3524 [64] (Judge Weeks QC); *Evans v Lloyd* [2013] EWHC 1725, [2013] WTLR 1137 [76] (Judge Keyser QC). Compare *Thompson v Foy* [2009] EWHC 1076, [2010] P & CR 16 [99] (Lewison J: adopting Lord Nicholls' statement extending the analysis in *Papouis v Gibson-West* [2004] EWHC 396, [2004] WTLR 485 [5] (Lewison J)).

[101] *Irvani v Irvani* [2000] 1 Lloyd's Rep 412, 424 (Buxton LJ); applied in *Singla v Bashir* [2002] EWHC 883.

[102] *Christodoulou v Christodoulou* [2009] VSC 583 [78], citing *Commercial Bank of Australia Ltd v Amadio* [1983] HCA 14, (1983) 151 CLR 447, 474 [13] (Deane J); see also *Daunt v Daunt* [2015] VSCA 58 [62]-[63] (the Court); *Re Mahoney* [2015] VSC 600 [210] (McMillan J).

[103] Led by *Royal Bank of Scotland plc v Etridge (No 2)* [2001] UKHL 44, [2002] 2 AC 773, see, eg, [6], [32]–[33], [36] (Lord Nicholls), discussed below at p 244. See also *Davies v AIB Group (UK) Plc* [2012] EWHC 2178, [2012] 2 P & CR 19 [9]–[12] (Norris J); *Curtis v Pulbrook* [2009] EWHC 782, [2011] WTLR 1503 [158] (Judge Sheldon QC); *Brown v The NSW Trustee & Guardian* [2011] NSWSC 1203 [43]–[44] (Brereton J); *Birmingham City Council v Beech (aka Howell)* [2014] EWCA Civ 830, [2014] HLR 38 [57]–[59] (Sir Terence Etherton C; Underhill and Briggs LJJ concurring).

of Lords[104] and Privy Council[105] have repeatedly said in recent years that undue influence involves the wrongful use or abuse of influence; that it involves the exploitation of influence.[106] The leading English case, *Royal Bank of Scotland Plc v Etridge (No 2)*,[107] was not concerned with any allegation of wrongdoing by the banks. The issue was whether vitiating influence had been exerted upon the plaintiffs in a domestic context, in circumstances that impugned the plaintiff's transaction with the bank. But Lord Nicholls said:

> Undue influence has a connotation of impropriety. In the eye of the law, undue influence means that influence has been misused. Statements or conduct by a husband which do not pass beyond the bounds of what may be expected of a reasonable husband in the circumstances should not, without more, be castigated as undue influence.[108]

The language of wrongdoing is also present in the decision of a majority of the High Court of Australia in *Tanwar Enterprises Pty Ltd v Cauchi*[109] in which their Honours drew a contrast (albeit strictly in obiter dicta) between cases of 'alleged undue influence and catching bargains' and innocent misrepresentation. Their Honours took the view that, as to the former, the 'governing equitable principle … is concerned with the production *by malign means* of an intention to act'.[110]

The use of the language of 'wrongdoing' in these cases might suggest that undue influence is an unjust factor that requires proof of wrongful influence. The confusion has arisen because the equitable wrong of abuse of influence shares the same label as the unjust factor of undue influence. As we will see below, the two forms of claim have different elements, attract different defences[111] and give rise to different remedies. The failure to appreciate that an action for abuse of influence is a different category of claim can sometimes lead courts to refuse a claim for undue influence because there has been no abuse of the relationship of

[104] *Royal Bank of Scotland plc v Etridge (No 2)* [2001] UKHL 44, [2002] 2 AC 773 [6]–[11] (Lord Nicholls) followed in *Glanville v Glanville* [2002] EWHC 1587; *UCB Corporate Services Ltd v Williams* [2002] EWCA Civ 555, [2002] 3 FCR 448; *Singla v Bashir* [2002] EWHC 883; *Greene King plc v Stanley* [2001] EWCA Civ 1966, [2002] BPIR 491; *Rosenfeld v Ransley* [2004] EWHC 2962; *Royal Bank of Scotland plc v Chandra* [2010] EWHC 105, [2010] 1 Lloyd's Rep 677 [127]–[128] (Richards J), on appeal *Royal Bank of Scotland plc v Chandra* [2011] EWCA Civ 192, [2011] Bus LR D149 [32] (Patten LJ; Ward and Black LJJ agreeing); *Davies v AIB Group (UK) Plc* [2012] EWHC 2178, [2012] 2 P & CR 19 [9]–[12] (Norris J); *Curtis v Pulbrook* [2009] EWHC 782, [2011] WTLR 1503 [158] (Judge Sheldon QC); *Evans v Lloyd* [2013] EWHC 1725, [2013] WTLR 1137 [38]–[39] (Judge Keyser QC); *Birmingham City Council v Beech (aka Howell)* [2014] EWCA Civ 830, [2014] HLR 38 [57]–[59] (Sir Terence Etherton C; Underhill and Briggs LJJ concurring). See also *Barclays Bank plc v O'Brien* [1994] 1 AC 180, 189, 191, 194–95, 197–99 (Lord Browne-Wilkinson).

[105] *R v Attorney-General for England and Wales* [2003] UKPC 22, [2003] EMLR 24; *National Commercial Bank (Jamaica) Ltd v Hew* [2003] UKPC 51, [2004] 2 LRC 396 [28]–[35].

[106] This is also the position in New Zealand: *Wilkinson v ASB Bank Ltd* [1998] 1 NZLR 674; *R v Attorney-General for England and Wales* [2003] UKPC 22, [2003] EMLR 24; *Hogan v Commercial Factors Ltd* [2004] NZCA 269, [2006] 3 NZLR 618.

[107] *Royal Bank of Scotland plc v Etridge (No 2)* [2001] UKHL 44, [2002] 2 AC 773.

[108] ibid [32]; see also [5].

[109] *Tanwar Enterprises Pty Ltd v Cauchi* [2003] HCA 57, (2003) 217 CLR 315 [23] (Gleeson CJ, McHugh, Gummow, Hayne and Heydon JJ); see also *Freeman v Brown* [2001] NSWSC 1028 [65]–[73], [85]–86] (Barrett J); *Lai See Law by her Tutor the Protective Commissioner of New South Wales v Yan Mo* [2009] NSWSC 639 [79] (Bergin CJ).

[110] ibid (emphasis added). See also *Drew v Daniel* [2005] EWCA Civ 507, [2005] 2 FCR 365, where a very fine line is drawn between undue influence, illegitimate pressure and unconscionable dealing.

[111] For example, the wrong of abuse of influence does not attract the change of position defence, as does the unjust factor: see Ch 14 pp 332, 349 and 353–54.

influence. In other words, undue influence is rejected because it is thought that wrongdoing is required. In *R v Attorney-General for England and Wales*[112] the Privy Council rejected an argument by a soldier that he had been unduly influenced into signing a confidentiality agreement because the army had not exploited the influence that it had over the soldier. By focusing upon a lack of abuse of influence, the majority neglected the traditional model of undue influence based upon impaired intention. In contrast with the majority, Lord Scott, delivering the dissenting advice of the Privy Council, explained that exploitation was not required. His Lordship applied an unjust factor approach to the claim of undue influence, saying that it is 'the relationship ... between a soldier and that part of the Armed Services of which he is a member, that introduces the potentially vitiating element'.[113] Undue influence was present not because of any abuse of influence but because '[t]he essence of efficiency in a military unit is obedience to orders'.[114]

In order to avoid confusion between the equitable wrong of abuse of influence and the unjust factor of undue influence, the use of different terminology is essential. There is less danger of confusing illegitimate pressure or duress with the tort of intimidation when both have different labels. The same approach must be taken to abuse of influence and undue influence.

The two doctrines are very different. First, the wrong of abuse of influence requires active exploitation of influence by the defendant and, as a breach of duty, supports further remedies such as compensation and disgorgement. Secondly, the unjust factor of undue influence does not require the influence to come from the defendant but the wrong of abuse of influence requires the defendant to be a wrongdoer. These two points of difference are discussed below. The third distinction is that the defence of change of position is not generally open to a wrongdoer[115] and would not be available to a defendant who has abused her influence over the plaintiff. The defence is available in claims involving the unjust factor of undue influence. This third distinction is considered in Chapter 14, which examines the change of position defence.

B. Wrongful Abuse of Influence Permits Different Remedies from Undue Influence

An example of the equitable wrong of abuse of influence is *O'Sullivan v Management Agency and Music Ltd*.[116] The pop star Gilbert O'Sullivan entered into a series of transactions with the Management Agency as a result of the undue influence of his manager, Mr Mills (the third defendant). It was found that the Management Agency was aware of this influence and had also benefited from the undue influence exerted over O'Sullivan.

[112] *R v Attorney-General for England and Wales* [2003] UKPC 22, [2003] EMLR 24. See also *National Commercial Bank (Jamaica) Ltd v Hew* [2003] UKPC 51, [2004] 2 LRC 396 and *Mango Media Pty Ltd v Comitogianni* [2011] NSWSC 152 [230]–[231], [235]–[248]. In the latter case, Davies J regarded the plaintiff's strange willingness to agree to whatever the defendant wanted as negating any allegation of undue influence, 'coercion' or unconscionable dealing.

[113] *R v Attorney-General for England and Wales* [2003] UKPC 22, [2003] EMLR 24 [45].

[114] ibid [41].

[115] Discussed in Ch 14 pp 332 and 349.

[116] *O'Sullivan v Management Agency and Music Ltd* [1985] QB 428.

It was ordered to account for, and disgorge, the profits it had made. A central argument on appeal was that the appropriate award should not have been disgorgement of profits but instead (on the basis of evidence given by an expert, Mr Levison) should have been the sum that the Management Agency would reasonably have negotiated with O'Sullivan had he received independent advice. The Management Agency argued that this, less what had already been paid, was the restitution that should be made. As we saw in Chapter 4, this is the conventional method of measuring a restitutionary award. The English Court of Appeal disagreed and held that O'Sullivan was entitled to disgorgement of all of the profits made by the defendants (subject to an allowance in their favour for their skill and effort). The result is easily explicable on the basis that there was a fiduciary relationship between O'Sullivan and the defendants. But it was also decided on the basis of abuse of influence. The characterisation of the claim as one for a wrong of abuse of influence can be seen in the decision of Dunn LJ who spoke of the 'moral blame' of the defendants and described them as 'wrongdoers'.[117] In a similar approach, Fox and Walker LJJ rejected the submission because they considered that the doctrine of undue influence should be treated in the same way as the wrong of breach of fiduciary duty.[118] Characterisation of the undue influence claim as involving wrongdoing is also dictated by the remedy awarded. As we saw in Chapter 3 disgorgement of profits is a deterrent measure which often will be a different quantum from an award of restitution, as indeed it was in *O'Sullivan*.[119] The only basis for the award in *O'Sullivan* was that the court was not deciding the matter as a case of unjust enrichment but as one of wrongdoing.

Another example of a difference between a wrong involving abuse of influence and an unjust factor of undue influence is cases in which compensation has been awarded as a remedy.[120] Those cases equally cannot be explained as restitution in unjust enrichment for the unjust factor of undue influence. A good example of a loss-based claim for the wrong of abuse of influence is the Irish case of *Walsh v Byrne*, discussed earlier. In that case, the defendant abused his influence over the plaintiff by grooming the plaintiff as a child, in order to gain his trust for the purpose of carrying out sexual abuse, which he then carried out over a period of five years. In awarding compensation (including an amount by way of aggravated damages) White J observed that 'the mental trauma suffered by the plaintiff, is not just confined to the acts of assault and battery, but arises also as a result of the consequences of the breach of trust of the defendant who had played such an important role in the plaintiff's life'.[121]

C. Undue Influence does not Require Wrongdoing by the Defendant

There is a considerable weight of authority in support of the view that the unjust factor of undue influence does not require wrongdoing, or indeed any conduct at all, by the

[117] ibid 458.

[118] ibid 468, 472–73.

[119] See Ch 3 pp 34–5.

[120] *Mahoney v Purnell* [1996] 3 All ER 61; *Nattrass v Nattrass* [1999] WASC 77; *Smith v Glegg* [2004] QSC 443, [2005] 1 Qd R 561. See also JD Heydon, 'Equitable Compensation for Undue Influence' (1997) 113 *Law Quarterly Review* 8.

[121] *Walsh v Byrne* [2015] IEHC 414 [22].

defendant,[122] including a number of English decisions.[123] An early example is *Bridgeman v Green*,[124] where the excessive influence of Bridgeman's butler led to Bridgeman making payments to parties that included the butler, the butler's wife and the butler's brother. Lord Commissioner Wilmot, said:

> There is no pretence that [the butler's] brother, or his wife, was party to any imposition, or had any due or undue influence over the plaintiff; but does it follow from thence, that they must keep the money? No: whoever receives it, must take it tainted and infected with the undue influence and imposition of the person procuring the gift; his partitioning and cantoning it out amongst his relations and friends, will not purify the gift, and protect it against the equity of the person imposed upon. Let the hand receiving it be ever so chaste, yet if it comes through a corrupt polluted channel, the obligation of restitution will follow it[.][125]

A more recent example is *Hammond v Osborn*. An elderly bachelor, Mr Pritler, made a gift of almost £300,000, to a neighbour, Mrs Osborn, who had looked after him for over a year. The gift represented more than 90 per cent of his assets. He made the gift without any independent advice and in the context of a relationship in which he placed much trust and confidence in Mrs Osborn. In the English Court of Appeal, Ward LJ found that Mrs Osborn was not guilty of any 'reprehensible conduct'.[126] Although Sir Martin Nourse questioned her behaviour, he emphasised that he would have reached the same result even if her conduct were 'unimpeachable and that there was nothing sinister in it, that would be no answer to an application of the presumption.'[127] This point was reiterated by Mummery LJ in a later decision:

> Although undue influence is sometimes described as an 'equitable wrong' or even as a species of equitable fraud, the basis of the court's intervention is not the commission of a dishonest or wrongful act by the defendant, but that, as a matter of public policy, the presumed influence arising from the relationship of trust and confidence should not operate to the disadvantage of the victim, if the transaction is not satisfactorily explained by ordinary motives.[128]

[122] In Australia, see: *Scott v Briggs* (1991) 14 Fam LR 661; *Giarratano v Smith* (NSWSC, 24 October 1985); see also (1985) NSW ConvR 55-267; *Bailey v Tredrea* [2005] NSWSC 108 [82]–[104] (Nicholas J); *Hewitt v Gardner* [2009] NSWSC 1107 [61]–[64] (Ward J); *Barkley v Barkley Brown* [2009] NSWSC 76 [142]–[147] (Ward J); *Christodoulou v Christodoulou* [2009] VSC 583 [74] (Kaye J); *Darmanin v Cowan* [2010] NSWSC 1118 [318]–[344] (Ward J), in particular at [323]; *Varma v Varma* [2010] NSWSC 786, (2010) 6 ASTLR 152 [532]–[535] (Ward J); *A v N* [2012] NSWSC 354 [475]–[482] (Ward J); *Anderson v McPherson (No 2)* [2012] WASC 19 [242] (Edelman J); *Daunt v Daunt* [2015] VSCA 58 [62]–[63] (the Court). In the United Kingdom, see: *Bullock v Lloyds Bank Ltd* [1955] Ch 317, 323–25 (Vaisey J); *Wright v Proud* (1806) 13 Ves Jr 136, 33 ER 246; *Everitt v Everitt* (1870) LR 10 Eq 405; *Hammond v Osborn* [2002] EWCA Civ 885, [2002] WTLR 1125; *Padgham v Rochelle* [2002] EWHC 2747, [2003] WTLR 71; *Jennings v Cairns* [2003] EWCA Civ 1935, [2004] WTLR 361 [33]–[40] (Arden LJ; Lord Phillips MR and Dyson LJ concurring); *Niersmans v Pesticcio (Pesticcio v Huet)* [2004] EWCA Civ 372, [2004] WTLR 699 [20] (Mummery LJ); *Wright v Hodgkinson* [2004] EWHC 3091, [2005] WTLR 435 [151] (Judge Hegarty QC).

[123] For a pellucid account of undue influence consistent with the unjust enrichment analysis by an English judge, see *Hart v Burbridge* [2013] EWHC 1628, [2013] WTLR 1191 [37] (Sir William Blackburne), upheld on appeal *Hart v Burbidge* [2014] EWCA Civ 992 [43] (Vos LJ; Black and Richards LJJ concurring).

[124] *Bridgeman v Green* (1757) Wilm 58, 97 ER 22.

[125] ibid, 64–65, 25.

[126] *Hammond v Osborn* [2002] EWCA Civ 885, [2002] WTLR 1125 [61], applied in *Jennings v Cairns* [2003] EWCA Civ 1935, [2004] WTLR 361 [40] (Arden LJ); *Goodchild v Bradbury* [2006] EWCA Civ 1868, [2007] WTLR 463. Cf *Gorjat v Gorjat* [2010] EWHC 1537, (2010) 13 ITELR 312 [145]–[147] (Judge Asplin QC).

[127] *Hammond v Osborn* [2002] EWCA Civ 885, [2002] WTLR 1125 [32].

[128] *Niersmans v Pesticcio (Pesticcio v Huet)* [2004] EWCA Civ 372, [2004] WTLR 699 [20]. See also *Macklin v Dowsett* [2004] EWCA Civ 904, [2004] 2 EGLR 75 [10] (Auld LJ); *Hackett v Crown Prosecution Service* [2011] EWHC 1170, [2011] Lloyd's Rep FC 371 [64] (Silber J); *Hart v Burbridge* [2013] EWHC 1628, [2013] WTLR 1191 [51] (Sir William Blackburne).

An Australian example is *Giarratano v Smith*.[129] Mrs Giarratano created a trust of her land for herself and her children with herself as trustee. She was 'naive, unsophisticated, with no real business sense or deep understanding of matters of property … and a woman who would readily succumb to the pressure of any influence which was exerted upon her.'[130] She acted at the direction of her father-in-law, signing the Deed of Trust at his suggestion. Her father-in-law was found to have acted throughout with the honest intention of protecting her because he perceived her as being vulnerable and open to exploitation by others. He sought and received no advantage from the transaction. Nonetheless, the New South Wales Supreme Court found that Mrs Giarratano was entitled to rescission of the trust and restitution of the land (subject to a small interest in favour of the children due to a contribution by her father-in-law). This was because the transaction was the result of the undue influence of the father-in-law. It was irrelevant that the children were entirely passive recipients in their initial receipt and that the excessive influence had come not from them but from a third party (the father-in-law).[131]

There are many of these cases where a third-party recipient is liable to make restitution for the undue influence of another.[132] To characterise a third party recipient—especially a passive recipient even if that person later discovers the receipt—of an enrichment as a wrongdoer would be a bizarre legal characterisation. Even strict liability wrongs require some positive act (for example the tort of conversion, which requires an act by the defendant inconsistent with the ownership of the plaintiff.)

Three decisions of Bryson J in the Supreme Court of New South Wales underscore that the unjust factor of undue influence is independent of the equitable wrong of abuse of influence. In all three cases, it was likely that the plaintiff's donative intent was spontaneous and not initiated by the defendant.[133] At the most, where the defendant was the ascendant party,[134] the defendant was the source of the excessive influence but did not knowingly exert it. In terms of the analogy with mistake, the cases lie somewhere between the equivalent of a unilateral mistake and an innocent misrepresentation case.[135] Further, there were express findings in all three cases that neither the defendant, nor any other person in a position of influence, had sought to exploit, or had in fact exploited, the plaintiff's position to gain a benefit for themselves.[136] Given those findings, the wrong of abuse of influence could

[129] *Giarratano v Smith* (NSWSC, 24 October 1985) 5; see also *Giarratano v Smith* (1985) NSW ConvR 55-267; *Darmanin v Cowan* [2010] NSWSC 1118 [318]–[344] (Ward J); *Varma v Varma* [2010] NSWSC 786, (2010) 6 ASTLR 152 [532]–[535] (Ward J).

[130] *Giarratano v Smith* (NSWSC 24 October 1985) 5; see also *Giarratano v Smith* (1985) NSW ConvR 55-267.

[131] See also *Everitt v Everitt* (1870) LR 10 Eq 405; *Bullock v Lloyds Bank Ltd* [1955] Ch 317; *Bester v Perpetual Trustee Co Ltd* [1970] 3 NSWR 30; *Huguenin v Baseley* (1807) 14 Ves Jr 273, 33 ER 526.

[132] See, eg, *Huguenin v Baseley* (1807) 14 Ves Jr 273, 33 ER 526; *Cooke v Lamotte* (1851) 15 Beav 234, 51 ER 527; *Ellis v Barker* (1871) LR 7 Ch App 104; *Bainbrigge v Browne* (1881) 18 Ch D 188; *Morley v Loughnan* [1893] 1 Ch 736; *Liles v Terry* [1895] 2 QB 679; *Willis v Barron* [1902] AC 271; *Wright v Carter* [1903] 1 Ch 27; *Lancashire Loans Ltd v Black* [1934] 1 KB 380; *Bullock v Lloyds Bank Ltd* [1955] Ch 317; *Bester v Perpetual Trustee Co Ltd* [1970] 3 NSWR 30; *Smith v Kay* (1859) 7 HL Cas 750, 11 ER 299; *Hartigan v International Society for Krishna Consciousness Inc* [2002] NSWSC 810 [26] (Bryson J); *Verduci v Gorlotta* [2010] NSWSC 506, (2010) 15 BPR 28,865 [69]–[70] (Slattery J).

[133] *Hartigan v International Society for Krishna Consciousness Inc* [2002] NSWSC 810 [28]; *Reid v Reid* (NSWSC, 30 November 1998); *Smith v Smith* (NSWSC, 12 July 1996) 24.

[134] In *Hartigan* and *Smith*, it is likely that the influence came from a third party or parties; see discussion below.

[135] Cf the cases of 'unilateral illegitimate pressure,' discussed in Ch 9 pp 218–19.

[136] *Hartigan v International Society for Krishna Consciousness Inc* [2002] NSWSC 810 [37]; *Reid v Reid* (NSWSC, 30 November 1998) 17; *Smith v Smith* (NSWSC, 12 July 1996) 24.

not possibly have been satisfied. However, undue influence was established and, subject to defences, the transactions were liable to be set aside.

In the first of these cases, *Hartigan v International Society for Krishna Consciousness Incorporated,*[137] the plaintiff was an enthusiastic member of the Krishna Consciousness Movement and had received instruction in that religion from a number of its spiritual teachers. She gave her house (with surrounding farm) to the defendant corporation, which held property for the Movement. The property was virtually her only material possession and, at the time, she had two small children and was expecting another. Justice Bryson found the presumption of excessive influence was raised by those facts and had not been rebutted by the defendant. As to the required 'a factor' link, even though the plaintiff had formed a mistaken belief, independently of her teachers, that the religion required her to divest herself of her material possessions, her devotion to its tenets as perceived by her had produced a highly disadvantageous transaction which could not be explained by reference to ordinary motives of 'generosity, charity or religious feeling'.[138] That finding was reinforced by the fact that her property constituted virtually her only asset and that it would expose her and her young family to the possibility of homelessness.

In the second case, *Reid v Reid,*[139] a formerly independent young adult was injured in a car accident, resulting in permanent brain damage. Although the young man partly recovered under the devoted care of his mother, Bryson J held that 'he was in a position somewhat like an adolescent'.[140] He depended on help and guidance from his parents for every major decision in life as well as most minor and day-to-day matters. On receiving compensation, he made a number of investment decisions and purchased a home, in the joint names of himself and his mother, in which he and his parents lived.

Justice Bryson found that the circumstances of the case raised a presumption of excessive influence. The son was mentally a child, and in a relationship of real dependence on his mother. Further, the gift of a substantial beneficial interest in the property had to be seen against the son's very limited earning potential and his likely future need to have full access to all his resources. Even accepting that the plaintiff had understandable feelings of affection and gratitude for his mother arising out of her considerable support for him, these motives could not explain the size of the gift, which could leave him financially exposed in the future in the event that the filial relationship deteriorated, as did later occur. Justice Bryson noted that it made no difference to this conclusion whether the idea to purchase the house in joint names came from the son, his mother or indeed his father. His Honour went on to reject strongly the son's alternative claim of unconscionable conduct: 'There is nothing like victimisation in this case.'[141]

Finally, in *Smith v Smith*[142] a widow lived in her son's house with her son, her dependent retarded daughter and her son's wife. She was entirely dependent upon her son for the everyday care and management of her business interests. Upon the sale of her only property, she gave the proceeds to her son's child (ie her grandson, the first defendant).

[137] *Hartigan v International Society for Krishna Consciousness Inc* [2002] NSWSC 810.
[138] ibid [37].
[139] *Reid v Reid* (NSWSC, 30 November 1998).
[140] ibid 7.
[141] ibid 17.
[142] *Smith v Smith* (NSWSC, 12 July 1996).

This constituted the vast bulk of her estate and exposed both her and her dependent retarded daughter to almost complete financial dependency on her son. Justice Bryson found the relationship between the widow and her son[143] raised a presumption of excessive influence, and the nature of the gift raised a presumption that the influence was 'a factor' in her decision to enrich the defendant. Neither presumption was rebutted on the facts. However, restitution of the value of the gift was barred by the defences of acquiescence or laches.

V. Conclusion

The unjust factor of undue influence, like mistake and duress, applies where a plaintiff's decision to enter a transaction that enriches the defendant is vitiated. It does not require proof of abuse of influence or any form of breach of duty (wrongdoing). Instead, like mistake and duress, the focus of the claim is the effect of the excessive influence on the plaintiff's decision, not the defendant's conduct. Undue influence in its non-wrongful aspect is an unjust factor, just as mistake and duress are unjust factors. The doctrine concerning wrongful abuse of influence is a separate and distinct equitable wrong.

As with mistake and illegitimate pressure, the plaintiff must negate any juristic reason justifying the defendant's retention of the impugned enrichment. Provided this is satisfied, restitution of an enrichment will be ordered where the plaintiff demonstrates (i) she was subject to excessive influence that (ii) was 'a factor' in the plaintiff's decision to enter the transaction that enriched the defendant. As to the first element (excessive influence), certain categories of relationship are presumed to be characterised by excessive influence. Alternatively, the plaintiff may demonstrate excessive influence by pointing to features of the relationship or the instant transaction that demonstrate ascendancy and influence on the one hand and dependence and trust on the other. As to the second element (an 'a factor' link), a rebuttable presumption of the required link arises in the plaintiff's favour where the relationship is one of excessive influence and the impugned transaction calls for explanation. The onus then shifts to the defendant to show that the influence had no effect on the plaintiff's decision to enrich the defendant. Otherwise, the plaintiff can directly prove the required link by evidence that the undue influence was a factor that influenced her decision to enter the transaction that enriched the defendant.

[143] While there is passing reference to the grandson also being in a position of influence, his Honour's analysis of the facts concentrates on the relationship between the widow and her son.

11

Failure of Consideration

Contents

I. Introduction

In this chapter we see a shift from the nature of the unjust factors we have considered so far. Chapters 8, 9 and 10 were concerned with cases where the plaintiff's consent was impaired by (respectively) mistake, illegitimate pressure, or undue influence. This chapter is concerned with circumstances in which the plaintiff's intention to enter the transaction was unimpaired but was objectively qualified by a basis, purpose, or condition. The unjust factor, and the defect in the transaction, arises when that qualification fails.

In Chapter 6 we explained that there are two requirements for an enrichment to be 'unjust'. Like mistake, illegitimate pressure, and undue influence, the unjust factor of failure of consideration can operate to show injustice in each of these ways. The first is to show that there is an unjust factor which affects the plaintiff's consent. The second is to negate any juristic reason that the defendant asserts as an entitlement to retain the enrichment. Although the principles concerning the operation of failure of consideration are the same for each of these two manners of its operation, failure of consideration as an unjust factor is the main focus of this chapter. We saw in Chapters 6 and 7 its operation to negate a juristic reason. For instance, we saw in Chapter 7 that a juristic reason for the *receipt* of an enrichment might be that it was transferred under a contract. But the contract as a juristic reason to *retain* the enrichment can be negated by demonstrating that a fundamental basis of the transaction that enriched the defendant failed.[1] Another example of the use of failure of consideration to negate a juristic reason is that a plaintiff can prove that a contract is void if it was entered into as a result of a fundamental, objective basis which failed either immediately (common mistake)[2] or subsequently (frustration). In each case the contract may have provided a juristic reason to receive the benefit but it does not provide a juristic reason to retain the enrichment after the failure of basis.

With a focus on failure of consideration as an unjust factor, this chapter first considers the development of the modern unjust factor of failure of consideration in England and Australia. We then explain its operation in the law today and consider five difficult issues that arise in relation to this unjust factor. The simplest lesson of this chapter, as the High Court of Australia has repeatedly emphasised, is that failure of consideration means a failure of the underlying objective basis, purpose, or condition for the transaction that causes the defendant's enrichment.[3] We focus in this chapter only upon immediate transactions. Subsequent transactions, following the initially defective one, were considered in Chapter 5.

II. The Meaning and Development of Failure of Consideration in English Law

A. The Meaning of Consideration in the Unjust Factor of 'Failure of Consideration'

In *Hudson v Robinson*,[4] Lord Ellenborough CJ said that 'an action for money had and received is maintainable wherever the money of one man has, without consideration, got into the pocket of another'. There are four essential points to observe about the meaning of consideration when used in the context of the unjust factor of failure of consideration.

First, as Australian cases have emphasised, the meaning of consideration in the law of unjust enrichment is *not* the same as in the law of contract.[5] It means the basis, purpose, or condition of the transaction that enriches the defendant. This definition was recently adopted in the United Kingdom Supreme Court in *Crown Prosecution Service v Eastenders Group*[6] by Lord Toulson, with whom Lady Hale, and Lords Kerr, Wilson and Hughes agreed.

[1] *Roxborough v Rothmans of Pall Mall Australia Ltd* [2001] HCA 68, (2001) 208 CLR 516.

[2] *Great Peace Shipping Ltd v Tsavliris Salvage (International) Ltd* [2002] EWCA Civ 1407, [2003] QB 679.

[3] *Roxborough v Rothmans of Pall Mall Australia Ltd* [2001] HCA 68, (2001) 208 CLR 516, 525 [16] (Gleeson CJ, Gaudron and Hayne JJ), 557 [104] (Gummow J); *Equuscorp Pty Ltd v Haxton; Equuscorp Pty Ltd v Bassat; Equuscorp Pty Ltd v Cunningham's Warehouse Sales Pty Ltd* [2012] HCA 7, (2012) 246 CLR 498 [31]–[32] (French CJ, Crennan and Keifel JJ), [134] (Heydon J).

[4] *Hudson v Robinson* (1816) 4 M & S 475, 478; 105 ER 910, 911.

[5] Above n 3. See also *Nu Line Construction Group Pty Ltd v Fowler* [2014] NSWCA 51 [11] (Basten JA), [192] (Young AJA).

[6] *Crown Prosecution Service v Eastenders Group* [2014] UKSC 26, [2015] AC 1 [104]–[113].

Secondly, although the notion of a basis, purpose, or condition is central to the definition of 'consideration', this should not be confused with the label 'absence of basis' which was used by Professor Birks to describe the approach to unjust enrichment in jurisdictions which do not expressly recognise that unjust enrichment liability requires an 'unjust factor'.[7] As we saw in Chapter 6, those jurisdictions appear to treat liability as arising based *only* upon a lack of juristic reason. Unjust factors are present but they are submerged in the analysis.

Thirdly, the failed state of affairs upon which a transaction is conditioned may be factual or legal. And it may pertain to the past, present or future. As to it being legal as well as factual, we will see below that in one of the leading decisions, that of the High Court of Australia in *Roxborough*, the basis for the payment concerned a legal matter, namely the obligation of the wholesaler to pay tax to the government.[8] As to the basis concerning the future as well as the present, we will see that a frequent circumstance in which failure of consideration concerns a future failure is when parties commence services in anticipation of a contract that fails to materialise and they are not paid for their work, when payment was the basis upon which it had been performed. All such bases count for the purposes of the unjust factor.

Fourthly, in ascertaining the basis for the transaction that enriched the defendant, the condition or purpose is objectively determined. The leading authority in Australia is the New South Wales Court of Appeal decision in *Fostif Pty Ltd v Campbells Cash & Carry Pty Ltd*.[9] That case arose as a result of a class action brought by tobacco retailers against tobacco wholesalers in the aftermath of the decision in *Roxborough*. One issue before the New South Wales Court of Appeal was whether there was sufficient coincidence between the issues in each case to allow a class action. The wholesalers argued that there was not. They asserted that a failure of consideration required examination of the contemplated basis for the transaction and different retailers might have contemplated entirely different bases for their contracts. President Mason (with whom Sheller JA and Hodgson JA agreed) held that the consideration or 'basis' was not determined subjectively, but that it meant the 'common, objectively discernible basis of the earlier transaction'.[10] The same objective approach has been adopted in England.[11]

There is a strong reason of principle supporting this objective approach and the need for an objective common basis. A plaintiff who enters a transaction upon a subjective basis that is not apparent to the other party knowingly runs the risk of disappointment. As we

[7] P Birks, *Unjust Enrichment*, 2nd edn (Oxford, Oxford University Press, 2005).

[8] See also *Guinness Mahon & Co Ltd v Kensington and Chelsea Royal London Borough Council* [1999] QB 215, 240 (Robert Walker LJ), 226, 227–28 (Morritt LJ).

[9] *Fostif Pty Ltd v Campbells Cash & Carry Pty Ltd* [2005] NSWCA 83, (2005) 63 NSWLR 203 [226]–[227], issue not considered on appeal in *Campbells Cash and Carry Pty Ltd v Fostif Pty Ltd* [2006] HCA 41, (2006) 229 CLR 386 [39] (Gummow, Hayne and Crennan JJ). The objective approach has also been expressly adopted in *Woodgate v Keddie* [2007] FCAFC 129 [43]–[44] (Buchanan J; Edmonds J concurring); *Anderson v McPherson (No 2)* [2012] WASC 19 [236], [239] (Edelman J). See also *Equuscorp Pty Ltd v Haxton; Equuscorp Pty Ltd v Bassat; Equuscorp Pty Ltd v Cunningham's Warehouse Sales Pty Ltd* [2012] HCA 7, (2012) 246 CLR 498 [135] (Heydon J).

[10] *Fostif Pty Ltd v Campbells Cash & Carry Pty Ltd* [2005] NSWCA 83, (2005) 63 NSWLR 203 [239].

[11] *Giedo Van der Garde BV v Force India Formula One Team Ltd (formerly Spyker F1 Team Ltd (England))* [2010] EWHC 2373 (QB) [285]–[286] (Stadlen J); *DRL Ltd v Wincanton Group Ltd* [2010] EWHC 2896; *Killen v Horseworld Ltd* [2011] EWHC 1600. See also *Upton-on-Severn Rural District Council v Powell* [1942] 1 All ER 220, discussed in J Edelman, 'Liability in Unjust Enrichment Where a Contract Fails to Materialise' in A Burrows and E Peel (eds), *Contract Formation and Parties* (Oxford, Oxford University Press, 2010) 166.

saw in our discussion of mistake in Chapter 8, the courts undertake an evaluative exercise to determine whether a plaintiff has assumed the risk of being disappointed in making the transaction. That will be so where the plaintiff has subjectively mispredicted some future outcome which fails. But it will not be so if the plaintiff acts on a basis which is communicated with the defendant. These are the common cases of failure of consideration. For instance, a typical failure of consideration case involves a plaintiff who performs a service for the defendant on the basis that he will be paid. The objective, conditional nature of the transaction that enriches the defendant means that the plaintiff was not assuming the risk of non-payment. Conversely, where the basis on which the plaintiff proceeds is not one which is objectively manifested then restitution should be refused.[12] For example, in *Gilbert & Partners v Knight*,[13] surveyors performed extra work not covered by the contract in supervising additional work that a developer had requested the builders to do. The surveyors performed the additional supervision on the subjective basis that they would be paid for it, although they did not communicate this to their employer. Although the English Court of Appeal's reasoning was based on the rejected implied contract theory of restitution,[14] its refusal of restitution (a *quantum meruit*) is consistent with the need for an objective basis. Underlying the reasoning was the same concern that the surveyors should not recover because, not having communicated the basis of their work, they ran the risk of not being paid for it. A reasonable person in their position would understand that, in the absence of the basis being communicated to the defendant, the predicted payment may well fail to eventuate.[15] The same reasoning can be seen in *Burgess v Rawnsley*.[16] In that case, a widower and a widow met and bought a house as joint tenants, each providing half of the purchase price of £850. The widower bought the house as a matrimonial home in contemplation of marriage to the defendant, but never mentioned marriage to her. They did not marry, and the defendant did not move into the house. After the widower's death, the defendant claimed that the house was hers by survivorship. The widower's executor claimed that the basis on which the house had been bought (marriage) had failed and that the widower's interest should result back to the estate. A majority of the English Court of Appeal (Lord Denning MR dissenting) held that since the widower had not communicated that purpose to the defendant, there was no common purpose that had failed. That was the

[12] *Spaul v Spaul* [2014] EWCA Civ 679 [27], [44]–[47] (Rimer LJ; Sullivan and Kitchen LJJ concurring).

[13] *Gilbert & Partners v Knight* [1968] 2 All ER 248. See further F Maher, 'A New Conception of Failure of Basis' [2004] *Restitution Law Review* 96, 101.

[14] See Ch 2 pp 10–12.

[15] See also *Countrywide Communications Ltd v ICL Pathway Ltd* [1996] C No 2446 (Judge Strauss QC), referring to the relevance of negotiations stated to be 'subject to contract' compared to a case where there are indications or assurances that the other party will not withdraw, cited with approval in *MSM Consulting Ltd v United Republic of Tanzania* [2009] EWHC 121 [170] (Christopher Clarke J). The fact that a transaction is expressed to be subject to contract will not, however, preclude restitution where there is other evidence that services conferred prior to reaching contract were performed on the basis that they would not be gratuitous: *Whittle Movers Ltd v Hollywood Express Ltd* [2009] EWCA Civ 1189, [2009] 2 CLC 771 [22]–[23] (Waller LJ; Dyson and Lloyd LJJ concurring); *Cobbe v Yeoman's Row Management Ltd* [2008] UKHL 55, [2008] 1 WLR 1752 [42] (Lord Scott; Lords Hoffmann, Walker, Brown and Mance concurring on this point). And in *Valencia v Llupar* [2012] EWCA Civ 396, the English Court of Appeal regarded it as unarguable that payments made expressly 'subject to contract' (ie on condition that a contract was agreed) should be returned upon the failure of negotiations: see in particular ibid [51] (Mummery LJ, Black LJ and Dame Janet Smith).

[16] *Burgess v Rawnsley* [1975] Ch 429.

reason why the widower's estate failed in its claim for restitution in the form of the rights being held on resulting trust.[17]

B. The Development of Failure of Consideration in English Law

The traditional English approach to failure of consideration was exemplified by the decision of the Court of Appeal in *Chandler v Webster*.[18] The plaintiff contracted for provision of a room from which to view the coronation of Edward VII. Payment of £141 was to be made in advance, and the plaintiff paid £100 in advance. After Edward VII fell ill, the coronation was cancelled and the plaintiff brought an action for recovery of the sum of £100 for failure of consideration. The Court of Appeal held that the contract had been frustrated, which meant that contractual rights had been discharged for the future. However, the money paid in advance could not be recovered, because the defendant had an accrued contractual right to the money. The Master of the Rolls explained that failure of 'consideration' meant the failure of the condition upon which the money was paid. But, although the condition (the coronation) had failed, the existence of a valid contract and validly accrued rights prevented restitution. In his Lordship's view, it was only 'If the effect were that the contract were wiped out altogether ... that money paid under it would have to be repaid as on a failure of consideration'.[19] This decision was consistent with considerable authority.[20]

The *Chandler v Webster* approach was seen by many as particularly harsh.[21] Two decades later, in 1924, the issue came before the House of Lords in an appeal from Scotland, *Cantiare San Rocco SA v Clyde Shipbuilding and Engineering Co*.[22] A Scottish shipbuilding company had agreed to supply marine engines to an Austrian company. Payments were made in advance under the contract but then the outbreak of war frustrated the contract. The Scottish courts had followed *Chandler v Webster* and held that the prepayments were irrecoverable. The House of Lords, deciding the matter for Scottish law, unanimously rejected *Chandler v Webster* and held that an action for failure of consideration succeeded. Lord Birkenhead LC said:

> The rule may, I think, be fairly stated thus: A person who had given to another any money or other property for a purpose which had failed could recover what he had given, unless there had been no fault on the recipient's part and he had not been enriched thereby.[23]

In 1937, the English failure of consideration rule in cases of frustration was referred to the Law Revision Committee to consider whether the Scottish rule should be adopted in cases

[17] For discussion of the restitutionary nature of a resulting trust see Ch 3 pp 38–42. The executor, however, succeeded on the separate ground that an earlier oral agreement to sell had severed the joint tenancy.

[18] *Chandler v Webster* [1904] 1 KB 493.

[19] *Chandler v Webster* [1904] 1 KB 493, 499.

[20] *Stubbs v The Holywell Railway Company* (1867) LR 2 Exch 311; *Appleby v Myers* (1867) LR 2 CP 651; *Civil Service Co-Operative Society Limited v General Steam Navigation Company* [1903] 2 KB 756, 764 (Lord Halsbury LC; Lord Alverstone CJ and Cozens-Hardy LJ concurring); *Blakeley v Muller & Co* [1903] 2 KB 760. Cf *The Teutonia* (1871) LR 3 Ad & Ecc 394; *The Corsican Prince* [1916] P 195, decisions in admiralty where the principle was one of loss-sharing.

[21] See eg the judgment of Atkin LJ in *Russkoe Obschestvo d'lia Izgstovlenia Snariadov I'voennick Pripassov v John Stirk & Sons Ltd* (1922) 10 Lloyd's Rep 214.

[22] *Cantiare San Rocco SA v Clyde Shipbuilding and Engineering Company Limited* [1924] AC 226.

[23] ibid 235; see also 252 (Lord Shaw).

of frustration. The report of the Law Revision Committee came down strongly in favour of the rule, and led to the eventual introduction of the Law Reform (Frustrated Contracts) Act 1943, which established and extended the right to restitution following frustration of contracts.[24] Seen against this backdrop, the decision of the House of Lords in *Fibrosa Spolka Akcyjna v Fairbairn Lawson Combe Barbour Ltd*[25] was predictable.[26] The facts of *Fibrosa* were similar to those in *Cantiare*. A Polish company ordered textile machinery from a company in England and made a part-payment of £1000. The English company incurred significant expense in manufacturing the machines, but before the machines could be completed and sent to the Polish company, the outbreak of the Second World War frustrated the contract. The House of Lords was unanimous in overruling *Chandler v Webster* and finding that the Polish company was entitled to recover its payment. Lord Wright said that

> It is clear that any civilized system of law is bound to provide remedies for cases of what has been called unjust enrichment or unjust benefit, that is to prevent a man from retaining the money of or some benefit derived from another which it is against conscience that he should keep … [p]ayment under a mistake of fact is only one head of this category of the law.[27]

His Lordship explained that failure of consideration was another head within the category of unjust enrichment. The reason for restitution in *Fibrosa* was that 'The payment was originally conditional. The condition of retaining it is eventual performance. Accordingly, when that condition fails, the right to retain the money must simultaneously fail.'[28] In the words of Viscount Simon LC, 'The money was paid to secure performance and, if performance fails the inducement which brought about the payment is not fulfilled.'[29] The basis of the payment, which failed, was that the Polish company would receive the machines. Restitution was therefore allowed despite the fact that, like the contract in *Chandler v Webster*, the contract had only been terminated for the future. The characterisation of failure of consideration as an unjust factor within the law of unjust enrichment was recently and repeatedly affirmed by the UK Supreme Court in *Crown Prosecution Service v Eastenders Group*[30] and in *Menelaou v Bank of Cyprus UK Ltd*.[31]

Although *Fibrosa* clearly established the unjust factor of failure of consideration in England, confusion sometimes arises due to the diverse labels used to describe claims for failure of consideration. One example of that confusion is in *Cobbe v Yeoman's Row Management Ltd*,[32] a decision of the House of Lords. That case was brought by a developer in respect of services performed in obtaining council approval for redevelopment of the

[24] The historical events surrounding the report are fully examined in P Mitchell, '*Fibrosa Spolka Akcyjna v Fairbairn Lawson Combe Barbour Ltd* (1942)' in C Mitchell and P Mitchell (eds), *Landmark Cases in the Law of Restitution* (Oxford, Hart Publishing, 2006).

[25] *Fibrosa Spolka Akcyjna v Fairbairn Lawson Combe Barbour Ltd* [1942] UKHL 4, [1943] AC 32.

[26] Two of the Law Lords who sat in *Fibrosa* had integral roles in the passage of the Act. Lord Wright had been Chairman of the Law Revision Committee that had recommended the Act and Viscount Simon LC was responsible for the drafting of the legislation.

[27] *Fibrosa Spolka Akcyjna v Fairbairn Lawson Combe Barbour Ltd* [1942] UKHL 4, [1943] AC 32, 61 [17].

[28] ibid 65 [19].

[29] ibid 48 [7].

[30] *Crown Prosecution Service v Eastenders Group* [2014] UKSC 26, [2015] AC 1 [103]–[104] (Lord Toulson; Lady Hale, and Lords Kerr, Wilson and Hughes agreeing).

[31] *Menelaou v Bank of Cyprus UK Ltd* [2013] EWCA Civ 1960, [2014] 1 WLR 854 [18] (Lord Clarke; Lords Kerr and Wilson agreeing).

[32] *Cobbe v Yeoman's Row Management Ltd* [2008] UKHL 55, [2008] 1 WLR 1752.

defendant's properties.[33] The developer performed the services on the basis that he would receive title to the defendant's property and various profits. But the developer did not have an enforceable agreement with the defendant. Although there was no enforceable contract the developer was entitled to restitution of the value of the services performed. Lord Scott (Lords Hoffmann, Mance and Brown concurring) held that the claim for restitution arose due to the failure of the objective basis upon which the work was performed (ie, that it would be remunerated). But his Lordship also ordered restitution on the separate grounds of *quantum meruit* and unjust enrichment. This illustrates the confusion caused by different labels which can be used to describe the same phenomenon. *Quantum meruit* simply describes a form of action and says nothing about the underlying cause of action. It was a form of action that could be brought for claims in contract as well as for claims which would now fall within the category of unjust enrichment.[34] In this case, the label was simply the form of action in which failure of consideration claims might have been brought historically. As to the third of Lord Scott's categories, a claim for unjust enrichment is not a separate cause of action from failure of consideration. Failure of consideration, as we have seen, is part of a cause of action which is in turn part of the law of unjust enrichment. The three categories of claim described by Lord Scott were, on the facts of that case, one and the same.[35]

III. The Reception of Failure of Consideration in Australia

The English frustrated contracts legislation which mitigated the effect of *Fibrosa* in frustration cases was followed (and adapted) in only three Australian states.[36] The purpose of the legislation was the reform of the restitutionary claims and, in some instances, loss apportionment in cases of frustration. However, the decision in *Fibrosa* became part of general Australian law in states in which frustration legislation did not apply and also, in all contexts other than frustration, in those states in which it does.

There are two leading Australian cases which illustrate the operation of failure of consideration at general law. The first is *Roxborough v Rothmans of Pall Mall Ltd*.[37] It will be recalled from Chapter 7[38] that in *Roxborough*, tobacco retailers purchased cigarettes from wholesalers for a price that included a distinct payment representing the tax due from the wholesalers to the government. It was later discovered that the tax was unconstitutional, which meant that the wholesaler did not have to pay it to the government. The retailer brought an action for restitution against the wholesaler. A majority of the High Court of Australia allowed the claim. In a joint judgment, Gleeson CJ, Gaudron and Hayne JJ quoted from Mason CJ, who had said that this claim for restitution 'operates to restore to the

[33] The developer also sought relief pursuant to the doctrine of estoppel and by way of constructive trust.
[34] *Pavey & Matthews Pty Ltd v Paul* [1987] HCA 5, (1987) 162 CLR 221, 227 [10]–[11] (Mason and Wilson JJ), 256 [13]–[14] (Deane J).
[35] Explained in *Lampson (Australia) Pty Ltd v Fortescue Metals Group Ltd (No 3)* [2014] WASC 162 [94] (Edelman J).
[36] Australian Consumer Law and Fair Trading Act 2012 (Vic) Part 3.2; Frustrated Contracts Act 1978 (NSW); Frustrated Contracts Act 1988 (SA).
[37] *Roxborough v Rothmans of Pall Mall Australia Ltd* [2001] HCA 68, (2001) 208 CLR 516.
[38] Ch 7 p 150.

plaintiff what has been transferred from the plaintiff to the defendant whereby the defendant has been unjustly enriched'.[39] Their Honours held that 'consideration … embraces payment for a purpose which has failed as, for example, where a condition has not been fulfilled, or a contemplated state of affairs has disappeared'.[40] Hence, the action succeeded because 'The state of affairs, which was within the contemplation of the parties as the basis of their dealings, concerning tax liability, altered … in circumstances which permitted, and required, severance of part of the total amount paid for the goods.'[41] Justice Gummow also emphasised that 'consideration' in this unjust factor is *not* used in its contractual sense (ie as a promise for a promise): the unjust factor of failure of consideration permits restitution because of 'the failure to sustain itself of the state of affairs contemplated as a basis for the payments the appellants seek to recover'.[42]

In 2012, the unjust factor again came before the High Court for consideration. The facts of *Equuscorp Pty Ltd v Haxton*,[43] were broadly as follows. The appellant sought to recover money lent to the respondents as part of a failed blueberry farm investment scheme. In earlier proceedings in the Victorian Supreme Court of Appeal,[44] it was held that the loan agreements were in furtherance of an illegal purpose and hence unenforceable. Before the High Court, the appellant claimed that this conclusion meant that the basis on which the loans were made (namely, that they could be enforced) had failed from the outset. In considering that claim,[45] French CJ, Crennan and Kiefel JJ, accepted that argument. Their Honours explained the operation of failure of consideration as involving the failure of the basis for the payment. Their Honours also explained the need for the *retention* of the enrichment to remain unjust: 'Failure of consideration is one of the factors that makes retention of a benefit prima facie unjust.'[46] Justice Heydon, dissenting on other grounds, endorsed the same analysis.[47]

IV. The Operation of Failure of Consideration

A. An Unjust Factor at Common Law and in Equity

We saw above that an English case which considered a claim for failure of consideration in equity was *Burgess v Rawnsley*.[48] In that case, the widower's executor claimed restitution in

[39] *Roxborough v Rothmans of Pall Mall Australia Ltd* [2001] HCA 68, (2001) 208 CLR 516 529 [26]. See *Commissioner of State Revenue (Vic) v Royal Insurance Australia Ltd* [1994] HCA 61, (1994) 182 CLR 51, 75 [41].

[40] *Roxborough v Rothmans of Pall Mall Australia Ltd* [2001] HCA 68, (2001) 208 CLR 516, 525 [16].

[41] ibid 526 [17].

[42] ibid 557 [104].

[43] *Equuscorp Pty Ltd v Haxton; Equuscorp Pty Ltd v Bassat; Equuscorp Pty Ltd v Cunningham's Warehouse Sales Pty Ltd* [2012] HCA 7, (2012) 246 CLR 498 [31]. Justices Gummow and Bell preferred (at [112]) the formulation offered by Deane J in *Muschinski v Dodds* [1985] HCA 78, (1985) 160 CLR 583, 620 [14], set out and discussed below at p 259.

[44] *Haxton v Equuscorp Pty Ltd (formerly Equus Financial Services Ltd) (ACN 006 012 344)* [2010] VSCA 1, (2010) 28 VR 499.

[45] The claim ultimately failed on the ground of illegality, discussed in Ch 7 pp 161–62.

[46] *Equuscorp Pty Ltd v Haxton; Equuscorp Pty Ltd v Bassat; Equuscorp Pty Ltd v Cunningham's Warehouse Sales Pty Ltd* [2012] HCA 7, (2012) 246 CLR 498 [31].

[47] ibid [134].

[48] *Burgess v Rawnsley* [1975] Ch 429.

the form of the rights being held on resulting trust. One case, similar to *Burgess v Rawnsley*, that was cited with approval by the majority joint judgment in *Roxborough*, is *Muschinski v Dodds*.[49] This is another case involving failure of consideration in equity.[50] Ms Muschinski and Mr Dodds lived in a de facto relationship and purchased land as joint tenants. The purpose of their purchase was to share the land as part of their continuing relationship and use it as a home and an arts and crafts centre. That basis failed when their relationship ended. Ms Muschinski had contributed 10 times more than Mr Dodds to the acquisition and improvement of the land. The High Court of Australia declared that they held the joint ownership on trust as tenants in common in proportion to their contributions. Justice Deane (with whom Mason J agreed) said that the equitable principle was the counterpart of the common law doctrine of failure of consideration.[51] He continued, saying that

> the principle operates in a case where the substratum of a joint relationship or endeavour is removed without attributable blame and where the benefit of money or other property contributed by one party on the basis and for the purposes of the relationship or endeavour would otherwise be enjoyed by the other party in circumstances in which it was not specifically intended or specifically provided that the other party should so enjoy it.[52]

B. Fault is not an Independent Element of the Unjust Factor

We have seen in Chapter 8 that fault is not an independent element for the unjust factor of mistake. The same should be true where the defect in the transaction arises because an objective basis has failed. In that context, the reference to 'blame' by Deane J in the passage cited above has the potential to be a source of confusion in Australian courts. Fortunately, the notion of 'fault' in this context has been circumscribed. It was invoked by Gummow and Bell JJ in *Equuscorp* to distinguish unsuccessful claims for restitution involving illegality from those, such as *Roxborough*, where restitution was allowed.[53] In a series of New South Wales Supreme Court decisions, the requirement has also been marginalised to apply only in cases of 'gross' conduct 'involving criminality or similarly reprehensible behaviour.'[54] On this analysis, the requirement for 'fault' would better be described as 'stultification'. As explained in Chapter 7, and as was apparent in *Equuscorp* itself, courts must take into account the ramifications of illegality in relation to all unjust factors, including failure of basis, in order to ensure that the grant or denial of restitution for unjust enrichment does not stultify an overriding policy or prohibition of the law.[55] Given the

[49] *Muschinski v Dodds* [1985] HCA 78, (1985) 160 CLR 583.

[50] For a recent example of a thoroughly 'fused' application of the principles of failure of basis to a commercial joint venture see *John Nelson Developments Pty Ltd v Focus National Developments Pty Ltd* [2010] NSWSC 150; cf *McKay v McKay* [2008] NSWSC 177 [15] (Brereton J) and *Raulfs v Fishy Bite Pty Ltd* [2012] NSWCA 135 [73]–[89] (Campbell JA).

[51] *Muschinski v Dodds* [1985] HCA 78, (1985) 160 CLR 583, 618 [13].

[52] ibid [14].

[53] *Equuscorp Pty Ltd v Haxton; Equuscorp Pty Ltd v Bassat; Equuscorp Pty Ltd v Cunningham's Warehouse Sales Pty Ltd* [2012] HCA 7, (2012) 246 CLR 498 [112].

[54] *Bennett v Horgan* (NSWSC, 3 June 1994), Bryson J approved by Burchett AJ in *Kriezis v Kriezis* [2004] NSWSC 167 [23] and in *Hill v Hill* [2005] NSWSC 863 [35] (Campbell JA) and *McKay v McKay* [2008] NSWSC 177 [16] (Brereton J). See also *Raulfs v Fishy Bite Pty Ltd* [2012] NSWCA 135 [73]–[77] (Campbell JA; Meagher and Barrett JJA agreeing);

[55] Ch 7 pp 161–62.

ambiguous and emotive nature of the language of 'blame', it would be better to omit references to fault and to refocus the relevant enquiry on the broader issue of stultification. The short point is that there is no independent element of fault in the unjust factor of failure of basis: like mistake, liability arising from this unjust factor is strict. Considerations of 'fault' are only relevant where they inform the overriding issue of stultification or, put in another way, the principle of coherence within the law.

C. Failure of Consideration in Contractual and Non-Contractual Cases

As *Muschinski* shows, the unjust factor of failure of consideration can apply where a contract was never even contemplated. It can also apply where a contract is void, voidable or terminated. In *Roxborough*, Gummow J referred to other examples of non-contractual failure of consideration including payments made 'subject to contract' when no contract eventuates[56] or where a condition precedent to the existence of the contract is not fulfilled.[57]

Perhaps the most common instances in the cases which involve failure of consideration where no contract exists are cases in which a contract is contemplated but which never eventuates. We saw one example of this above in the decision of the House of Lords in *Cobbe v Yeoman's Row Management Ltd.*[58] Another well-known English case is *William Lacey (Hounslow) Ltd v Davis.*[59] In that case, the plaintiff had submitted the lowest tender for building work on the defendant's war-damaged premises. The defendant intimated that a contract would be entered into with the plaintiff and requested that the plaintiff work on a cost estimate for reconstruction. The defendant used the estimate and obtained an 'approved amount' for reconstruction from the War Commission. However, the premises were subsequently sold and the plaintiff was not remunerated for its work. The plaintiff succeeded in obtaining restitution of the value of the work done. Justice Barry observed that the work was not done 'gratuitously merely in the hope that the building scheme would be carried out and that the person who did the work would obtain the contract'.[60] It had been done on the basis that a contract would eventuate. When that basis failed, the defendant was liable to make restitution of its enrichment.

In similar circumstances, this decision was applied in the New South Wales Supreme Court in *Sabemo Pty Ltd v North Sydney Municipal Council.*[61] The plaintiff had successfully tendered for the construction of a civic centre for the defendant council. After the plaintiff had done the work to the value of $426,000, the defendant abandoned the project. The plaintiff succeeded in a claim for restitution of that sum. However, perhaps because unjust

[56] *Roxborough v Rothmans of Pall Mall Australia Ltd* [2001] HCA 68, (2001) 208 CLR 516, 541 [65]. In England, see *Chillingworth v Esche* [1924] 1 Ch 97; *Pan Ocean Shipping Co Ltd v Creditcorp Ltd* [1994] 1 WLR 161, 164, 165, 166 (Lord Goff); *MacDonald Dickens & Macklin v Costello* [2011] EWCA Civ 930, [2012] QB 244 [22]–[32] (Etherton LJ; Patten and Pill LJJ concurring).

[57] *Roxborough v Rothmans of Pall Mall Australia Ltd* [2001] HCA 68, (2001) 208 CLR 516 [65] (Gummow J). See *Wright v Newton* (1835) 2 Cr M & R 124, 150 ER 53; *Simmons v Heseltine* (1858) 5 CB NS 554, 141 ER 224.

[58] *Cobbe v Yeoman's Row Management Ltd* [2008] UKHL 55, [2009] 1 WLR 1752, discussed above at pp 256–57.

[59] *William Lacey (Hounslow) Ltd v Davis* [1957] 1 WLR 932. See also *Regalian Properties plc v London Docklands Development Corporation* [1995] 1 WLR 212.

[60] *William Lacey (Hounslow) Ltd v Davis* [1957] 1 WLR 932, 939.

[61] *Sabemo Pty Ltd v North Sydney Municipal Council* [1977] 2 NSWLR 880.

enrichment as a category of law had not yet been recognised in Australia (the case having been decided in 1977),[62] Sheppard J said that this was not a case of unjust enrichment.[63] However, Sheppard J described the principles he applied in exactly the same terms as the majority judgment in *Roxborough* explained failure of consideration:

> where two parties proceed upon the joint assumption that a contract will be entered into between them, and one does work beneficial for the project, and thus in the interests of the two parties, which work he would not be expected, in other circumstances, to do gratuitously, he will be entitled to compensation or restitution, if the other party unilaterally decides to abandon the project ...[64]

These cases were all applied in *Vivian Fraser & Associates Pty Ltd v Shipton*.[65] An architect, Fraser, and his company, were engaged by property developers to prepare preliminary drawings for a tender. Fraser set his price substantially below market rates and did additional work thinking it was a term of his contract that he would be appointed project architect if the developers won the tender. He intended to recoup his losses on the preliminary drawings in the contract that would follow a successful tender by the developers. But when the developers won the tender, they did not appoint Fraser as the project architect. Although the trial judge rejected the claim that it was a term of the contract that Fraser would be appointed project architect, he held that, 'in so far as they thought about the matter, both parties made a general assumption that they would enter into a contract of retainer, subject always to [the developers'] tender being successful'.[66] Fraser was entitled to restitution for the value of the additional work done that was within the scope of the anticipated future contract, because the basis for doing that work failed when he was not appointed project architect.[67] However, some of Fraser's work was well outside the (objectively ascertained) scope of the anticipated contract. Justice Lindgren held that Fraser had assumed the risk of not being paid for that extra work, so it could not be said that the objective basis for performing that work had failed.

V. Difficult Issues in Failure of Consideration Cases

Although it is now established that failure of consideration is a failure of a basis underlying the transaction, this unjust factor gives rise to further difficult issues. Five are considered here:

(1) How is the consideration or basis for the transaction to be identified?
(2) When does the basis for a transaction fail?

[62] See Ch 2 p 12.

[63] *Sabemo Pty Ltd v North Sydney Municipal Council* [1977] 2 NSWLR 880, 897.

[64] ibid 902–03.

[65] *Vivian Fraser & Associates Pty Ltd v Shipton* [1999] FCA 60. See also *Scheps v Cobb; Estate of Dagobert Scheps deceased* [2005] NSWSC 455 [31] (Burchett AJ); *Kronenberg v Bridge* [2013] TASSC 57 and *Nu Line Construction Group Pty Ltd v Fowler* [2014] NSWCA 51, discussed below at p 264.

[66] *Vivian Fraser & Associates Pty Ltd v Shipton* [1999] FCA 60 [337] (Lindgren J).

[67] '[W]hen the beliefs of the parties were falsified ... the law should imply an obligation—to pay a reasonable price for the services which had been obtained': *Vivian Fraser & Associates Pty Ltd v Shipton* [1999] FCA 60 [333], Lindgren J quoting *William Lacey (Hounslow) Ltd v Davis* [1957] 1 WLR 932, 939 (Barry J).

(3) Does the failure of consideration need to be 'total'?
(4) Can a party rely on failure of consideration to avoid a bad bargain?
(5) Can a party in breach of contract claim for failure of consideration?

A. Issue 1: Identifying the Basis for the Transaction

We saw above that Australian and English courts have explained that the meaning of 'consideration' is the basis or condition of the transaction by which the defendant was enriched. We have also seen that it is now well-established that the basis or condition is determined objectively. In contractual cases, the basis upon which a performance is rendered is usually the receipt of the promised counter-performance. As Lord Wright said in *Fibrosa*, 'The payment was originally conditional. The condition of retaining it is eventual performance. Accordingly, when that condition fails, the right to retain the money must simultaneously fail'.[68] However, as the majority of the High Court emphasised in *Roxborough*, cases where consideration can fail are not limited to counter-performance. Further, as we saw, the basis for a transaction can also occur outside a contractual context, as in *Muschinski v Dodds*[69] or in the cases of anticipated contracts or failure of a condition precedent to a contract.[70] In each case it is necessary first to identify whether the alleged condition is the basis of the transaction before considering whether it has failed. As Floyd LJ (Laws and Bean LJJ agreeing) said in *Gartell & Son (a firm) v Yeovil Town Football & Athletic Club Ltd* (a case where the alleged basis was a failure of contractual performance) 'the starting point in deciding whether there is a total failure of consideration (or "failure of basis" as it is sometimes called) is to determine what the contractual performance should have been'.[71]

Even in the usual failure of consideration case where the objective basis for performance is the receipt of counter-performance, it will not always be a simple matter to determine whether counter-performance has been received. It is important to characterise the precise nature of the objective basis. The question is what a reasonable person in the position of the parties would have understood to be the promised counter-performance. Pertinent considerations will include what the parties relevantly did and said, the apparent background circumstances and history of their dealings, and the terms of any related contractual or other documentation. In many contractual cases, the terms of the 'background' contract will be of primary importance.[72] It will be recalled that in *Fibrosa Spolka Akcyjna v Fairbairn Lawson Combe Barbour Ltd*,[73] the basis of the payment which failed was that the Polish company

[68] *Fibrosa Spolka Akcyjna v Fairbairn Lawson Combe Barbour Ltd* [1942] UKHL 4 [19], [1943] AC 32, 65.
[69] *Muschinski v Dodds* [1985] HCA 78, (1985) 160 CLR 583.
[70] Above pp 260–61.
[71] *Gartell & Son (a firm) v Yeovil Town Football & Athletic Club Ltd* [2016] EWCA Civ 62 [31].
[72] *Anderson v McPherson* (No 2) [2012] WASC 19 [235] (Edelman J); see also *Ansett Australia Ltd v Diners Club Pty Ltd* [2007] VSC 102 [238]–[241] (Hargrave J); *Woodgate v Keddie* [2007] FCAFC 129 [41]–[44] (Buchanan J; Edmonds J concurring); *Ideas Plus Investments Ltd v National Australia Bank Ltd* [2006] WASCA 215, (2006) 32 WAR 467 [75]–[76] (Steytler P; Buss JA concurring) [110] (McLure JA); *JD No 6 (Dava) Pty Ltd v P Battlay Holdings Pty Ltd* [2011] VSC 353 [46], [50] (Croft J); *The Leasing Centre (Aust) Pty Ltd v Rolepress Proplate Group Pty Ltd* [2010] NSWSC 282 [147]–[150] (Barrett J); *Sharma v Simposh Ltd* [2011] EWCA Civ 1383, [2013] Ch 23 [26], [28]–[55] (Toulson CJ; Laws and Black LJJ concurring).
[73] *Fibrosa Spolka Akcyjna v Fairbairn Lawson Combe Barbour Ltd* [1942] UKHL 4, [1943] AC 32.

would receive the machines. This basis was determined by close consideration of the contractual provisions addressing the conditions for payment. By contrast, in *Stocznia Gdanska SA v Latvian Shipping Co*[74] one question was whether an instalment payment in a contract for the design, building and delivery of a ship was recoverable for failure of consideration.[75] The purchasers argued that when the contract was terminated they had received no property right to any part of the uncompleted ship and therefore, like the Polish purchasers in *Fibrosa*, had received no counter-performance. The House of Lords rejected this argument, holding that the basis for the instalment had not failed because the basis was not the receipt of the ship, but the work to be performed: it was 'a contract under which the design and construction of the vessel formed part of the year's contractual duties, *as well as* the duty to transfer the finished object to the buyers'.[76] The contractual terms, in other words, revealed a different basis existed for the transfer, notwithstanding the broader factual similarities between the cases.

The contrast between *Fibrosa* and *Stocznia* illustrates that fine distinctions can exist when characterising the nature of promised counter-performance. In particular, in cases like *Fibrosa* and *Stocznia* the difficult issue is whether a reasonable person in the position of the parties would understand the basis of the promised counter-performance to be the performance of a service by the defendant or the transfer of the end product from that service, or both. An Australian example is the decision of the High Court of Australia in *Re Continental C and G Rubber Co Pty Ltd*.[77] The case was factually very similar to *Fibrosa*. A company called Anderson & Sons contracted to provide and erect machinery for the Continental C and G Rubber Company. Progress payments were made and work commenced, but no machinery was ever delivered because of the outbreak of war. The High Court held that the contract had been frustrated because Anderson & Sons was owned by enemy aliens. However, a claim by Continental for restitution of its progress payments was refused. The decision is weakened because it applied reasoning based on the implied contract theory of unjust enrichment. The decision also applied *Chandler v Webster*, which, as we saw above, was overruled in *Fibrosa*. But despite its factual similarity with *Fibrosa*, the result is probably still good law. Clause 22 of the contract between Continental and Anderson & Sons provided that the progress payments were to be made according to the progress of the work and upon receipt of an engineer's certificate. That single fact differentiates *Re Continental C and G Rubber Co Pty Ltd* from *Fibrosa* by showing that the basis for the progress payments was the work done, not the receipt of an end product.

Although receipt of the counter-performance is often the basis of a plaintiff's contractual performance, this is not always the case. Indeed, receipt of counter-performance will rarely be the *only* basis for a plaintiff's performance. In cases involving performance of a service under an entire obligation another basis will usually be that the defendant will not prevent the plaintiff from completing the service and earning the price. In *Planché v Colburn*,[78] the defendant contracted with the plaintiff for the plaintiff to write a book for a series

[74] *Stocznia Gdanska SA v Latvian Shipping Co* [1998] 1 WLR 574.

[75] The instalment had not been paid but the issue was whether it was recoverable because the defendants argued that if it were paid, as the plaintiffs sought, it would be immediately recoverable for failure of consideration.

[76] *Stocznia Gdanska SA v Latvian Shipping Co* [1998] 1 WLR 574, 588 (Lord Goff; Lords Hoffmann, Hope and Hutton concurring) (emphasis added). See also *Hyandai Heavy Industries Co Ltd v Papadopoulos* [1980] 1 WLR 1129.

[77] *Re Continental C and G Rubber Co Pty Ltd* [1919] HCA 62, (1919) 27 CLR 194.

[78] *Planché v Colburn* (1831) 8 Bing 14, 131 ER 305.

entitled *The Juvenile Library*.[79] When the defendant repudiated the contract, the plaintiff sued for restitution of the value of work done (*quantum meruit*) on the incomplete book and succeeded. We saw in Chapter 4 the difficulties this case presents for the enrichment enquiry.[80] But, in terms of the unjust factor,[81] one basis upon which the work was done was that the defendant would not prevent its completion and the earning of the price by the plaintiff.[82] A similar analysis is possible for the case of *Cobbe v Yeoman's Row Management Ltd*,[83] discussed earlier, in which one basis on which the plaintiff no doubt proceeded was that the defendant would not withdraw from contract negotiations in bad faith.

B. Issue 2: When does the Basis of a Transaction Fail?

In most cases of failure of consideration it is not difficult to determine when the basis failed. For example, in *Sabemo*[84] the basis failed with the date of abandonment of the project, and in *Vivian Fraser*[85] the basis failed at the date of the defendant's refusal to appoint Fraser as the architect. Other cases are more difficult. An example is *Nu Line Constructions Ltd v Fowler*.[86] In that case, the plaintiff paid various amounts to the defendants as deposits on the purchase of title to land. No contract for sale was ever finalised. Eight years later, the plaintiff sought to recover the payments. The New South Wales Court of Appeal held that the question was whether the anticipated agreement had objectively failed to materialise because the contract had been abandoned more than six years ago. If so, the failure of basis would have occurred outside the applicable limitation period of six years.[87] The timing of the failure of basis was difficult to determine. As Young AJA put it, 'It is very difficult to put a time on when something doesn't happen.'[88] Ultimately, Basten JA and Young AJA considered that the objective circumstances of the transaction indicated that the parties would reasonably be considered not to have abandoned the contract prior to the critical date, notwithstanding the delay that had occurred. This was because one third of the purchase price had been paid over, and both parties were commercially experienced and yet neither sought to terminate the relationship or to seek (or effect) return of the money until the present proceedings were commenced. The opposite view was reached by the trial judge and the dissentient on appeal, Barrett JA.

[79] For a detailed discussion of this case see C Mitchell and C Mitchell, '*Planché v Colburn* (1831)' in C Mitchell and P Mitchell (eds), *Landmark Cases in the Law of Restitution* (Oxford, Hart Publishing, 2006).

[80] Ch 4 pp 69–70.

[81] An alternative analysis is that the award was for the reliance loss as a result of the defendant's breach of contract. See R Childres and J Garamella, 'The Law of Restitution and the Reliance Interest in Contract' (1969) 64 *Northwestern University Law Review* 433, 437.

[82] See also *Appleby v Myers* (1867) LR 2 CP 651, 659 (the Court); *Slowey v Lodder* (1901) 20 NZLR 321, 356 (Edwards J) affirmed on different grounds in *Lodder v Slowey* [1904] AC 442.

[83] *Cobbe v Yeoman's Row Management Ltd* [2008] UKHL 55, [2008] 1 WLR 1752, discussed above at pp 256–57.

[84] *Sabemo Pty Ltd v North Sydney Municipal Council* [1977] 2 NSWLR 880.

[85] *Vivian Fraser & Associates Pty Ltd v Shipton* [1999] FCA 60.

[86] *Nu Line Construction Group Pty Ltd v Fowler* [2014] NSWCA 51.

[87] Limitation periods are discussed in Ch 15 pp 385–94.

[88] *Nu Line Construction Group Pty Ltd v Fowler* [2014] NSWCA 51 [193].

Difficulties also arise where the failed basis is a previous judicial decision.[89] We encountered this difficulty in Chapter 8 when we considered cases of mistake of law caused by the overruling of an earlier decision. We saw there that the best view is that the mistake occurs at the time of enrichment notwithstanding that the overruling decision came later.[90] The same issue arises in cases of failure of basis. For instance, suppose money is paid pursuant to a judgment debt. The basis for the payment is the judgment. If the judgment is later overturned, the retrospective nature of decision would generally mean that, according to the later decision, the basis must have failed at the time the payment was made pursuant to the erroneous judgment.[91] In other words, an action for restitution based on the unjust factor of failure of consideration accrued at the time that the payment that was made in reliance on the erroneous decision even though that earlier decision is only later overturned.

However, in Australia, this conclusion must now be qualified in light of *State of New South Wales v Kable*.[92] As we saw in Chapter 7,[93] the High Court of Australia held in that case that in the Australian constitutional context the decision of a superior court constitutes a valid and justifying ground for actions taken during the period the decision is in force, even if it is later overturned.[94] This means that the decision remains a valid basis for payment until it is reversed. In other words, the defendant had a juristic reason to receive the payment but no juristic reason to retain it after the decision is overturned. Since the lack of juristic reason to retain an enrichment will only arise when the decision is overturned, an action for unjust enrichment will not be complete until the decision is overturned. This means that there is unlikely to be any need for final resolution of the question of when the basis for the payment fails.

The authorities that have considered when the basis fails in this context have done so either in obiter dicta or by concession. In *Keelhall Pty Ltd t/as 'Foodtown Dalmeny' v IGA Distribution Pty Ltd*[95] the relevant dates were only 35 days apart, so the issue did not need to be decided. Nevertheless, Einstein J said 'it seems to me likely' that the argument that the action arises from the date of enrichment is 'the correct position'.[96] By contrast, in *British American Tobacco Australia Ltd v Western Australia*,[97] McHugh, Gummow and Hayne JJ referred to the cause of action accruing at the date of the later judgment, rather than the date of the payments. However, their Honours observed that this was an issue that had

[89] For the alternative analyses of the nature of the unjust factor in these cases, see Ch 13 pp 321–23.

[90] *Torrens Aloha Pty Ltd v Citibank NA* (1997) 72 FCR 581; *David Securities Pty Ltd v Commonwealth Bank of Australia* [1992] HCA 48, (1992) 175 CLR 353, 389 [4] (Brennan J).

[91] 'The adjudication of existing rights and obligations as distinct from the creation of rights and obligations distinguishes judicial power from non-judicial power': *Ha v New South Wales* [1997] HCA 34, (1997) 189 CLR 465, 504 (Brennan CJ, McHugh, Gummow and Kirby JJ); see also 515 (Dawson, Toohey and Gaudron JJ). Cf *National Westminster Bank Plc v Spectrum Plus Ltd (in liq)* [2005] UKHL 41, [2005] 2 AC 680.

[92] *State of New South Wales v Kable* [2013] HCA 26, (2013) 252 CLR 118.

[93] At p 165.

[94] *State of New South Wales v Kable* [2013] HCA 26, (2013) 252 CLR 118 [32]–[36] (French CJ, Hayne, Crennan, Kiefel, Bell and Keane JJ), [46]–[47] (Gageler J). Contrast statutory adjudications void for jurisdictional error, which are in general a nullity and of no effect: *BM Alliance Coal Operations Pty Ltd v BGC Contracting Pty Ltd* [2013] QCA 394, [2015] 1 Qd R 228 [62]–[77] (Muir JA, Holmes JA and Ann Lyons J concurring).

[95] *Keelhall Pty Ltd t/as 'Foodtown Dalmeny' v IGA Distribution Pty Ltd* [2003] NSWSC 816, (2003) 54 ATR 75.

[96] ibid [12].

[97] *British American Tobacco Australia Ltd v Western Australia* [2003] HCA 47, (2003) 217 CLR 30 [54].

been conceded. In *Fostif Pty Ltd v Campbells Cash & Carry Pty Ltd*,[98] Mason P, with whom Sheller JA and Hodgson JA agreed, said that in a case like *Roxborough* the consideration only fails when the scheme is struck down as unconstitutional.

C. Issue 3: A Requirement of 'Total' Failure of Consideration?

i. *The Rule*

The traditional requirement in the doctrine of failure of consideration has been that the failure be 'total'. That is, the basis of the transaction with the defendant must completely fail. In *Fibrosa*, Lord Porter said:

> If a divisible part of the contract has wholly failed and part of the consideration can be attributed to that part, that portion of the money so paid can be recovered, but unless this be so there is no room for restitution under a claim in indebitatus assumpsit. A partial failure of consideration gives rise to no claim for recovery of part of what has been paid.[99]

This requirement has been much criticised in academic writing.[100] The courts have sometimes noted those criticisms. In *Heckenberg v Delaforce*,[101] Mason P cited several of these criticisms and suggested that '[a] compelling case exists to reconsider it'.[102] In *Giedo Vander Garde BV v Force India Formula One Team Ltd*,[103] Stadlen J refused restitution of a proportion of a fee paid to the defendant, because the failure of the basis for the payment had not been total. In so doing, his Lordship noted, 'I am bound to say that I reach this conclusion with considerable regret, joining as I do the growing list of judges and academic writers who have expressed the view that the requirement of proof of total failure of consideration as a necessary condition for an award of restitution is unsatisfactory and liable in certain cases to work injustice.'[104] And in *Equuscorp*, Heydon J (dissenting) indicated a readiness to move away from the total failure requirement.[105] However, despite the academic criticisms

[98] *Fostif Pty Ltd v Campbells Cash & Carry Pty Ltd* [2005] NSWCA 83, (2005) 63 NSWLR 203 [14].

[99] *Fibrosa Spolka Akcyjna v Fairbairn Lawson Combe Barbour Ltd* [1942] UKHL 4 [28], [1943] AC 32, 77.

[100] See eg K Barker, 'Restitution of Passenger Fare: The Mikhail Lermontov' [1993] *Lloyd's Maritime and Commercial Law Quarterly* 291; P Birks, 'Failure of Consideration' in FD Rose (ed), *Consensus Ad Idem: Essays in the Law of Contract in Honour of Guenter Treitel* (London, Sweet & Maxwell, 1996) 195; P Birks, 'Equity in the Modern Law: An Exercise in Taxonomy' (1996) 26 *University of Western Australia Law Review* 1; E McKendrick, 'Total Failure of Consideration and Counter-Restitution: Two Issues or One?' in P Birks (ed), *Laundering and Tracing* (Oxford, Clarendon Press, 1995); J Edelman, 'The New Doctrine of Partial Failure of Consideration' (1997) 15 *Australian Bar Review* 229; F Wilmot-Smith, 'Reconsidering "Total" Failure' (2013) 72 *Cambridge Law Journal* 414.

[101] *Heckenberg v Delaforce* [2000] NSWCA 137 [41].

[102] See also G Jones (ed), *Goff and Jones: The Law of Restitution*, 5th edn (London, Sweet and Maxwell, 1998) 42, 502–04; JW Carter and GJ Tolhurst, 'Restitution for Failure of Consideration' (1997) 11 *Journal of Contract Law* 162; J Edelman, 'The New Doctrine of Partial Failure of Consideration' (1997) 15 *Australian Bar Review* 229. See now C Mitchell, P Mitchell and S Watterson (eds), *Goff & Jones: The Law of Unjust Enrichment*, 8th edn (London, Sweet & Maxwell, 2011) [12-16]–[12-23].

[103] *Giedo Van der Garde BV v Force India Formula One Team Ltd (formerly Spyker F1 Team Ltd (England))* [2010] EWHC 2373.

[104] ibid [367]. It is noteworthy that the feared injustice was avoided in that case by the ready availability of remedies for breach of contract.

[105] *Equuscorp Pty Ltd v Haxton; Equuscorp Pty Ltd v Bassat; Equuscorp Pty Ltd v Cunningham's Warehouse Sales Pty Ltd* [2012] HCA 7, (2012) 246 CLR 498.

and some judicial doubts, the requirement has continued to be applied consistently by English[106] and Australian[107] courts.

The difficulty in this area may not lie with the requirement of a total failure, but rather with a misunderstanding of what it means. All the justices in *Roxborough* accepted the total failure requirement but explained that it did not apply to the 'total' failure of a severable part of the performance.[108] As we will see below, once 'consideration' is understood to mean an objective 'condition', 'basis' or 'purpose', then there is no difficulty with a rule requiring a total failure of basis. Indeed, it is only when the requirement is maintained that the spectre of this unjust factor undermining contract is avoided. Where the objective evidence is that the parties had established a condition for their respective performance, any decision to award restitution for partial failure of consideration in a contractual context comes perilously close to a decision to rewrite the contractual allocation of risk.[109] While this is sometimes permitted by statute to achieve policy objectives (eg consumer protection),[110] it is not a legitimate step for the common law.[111]

The importance of the requirement for a total failure of consideration can be seen in an examination of the controversial decision in *Sumpter v Hedges*.[112] In that case, a builder repudiated a contract after completing part of two houses and stables on the defendant's land. Although the defendant completed the work and obtained the benefit from the builder's work, the builder's claim for restitution for the fair value of the work he had done (as a *quantum meruit*) was refused. *Sumpter v Hedges* has been heavily criticised.[113] But a powerful defence of it by Professors Stevens and Macfarlane argues that the result is defensible

[106] Eg *Stocznia Gdanska SA v Latvian Shipping Co* [1998] 1WLR 574, 590 (Lord Goff); *Goss v Chilcott* [1996] UKPC 17, [1996] AC 788, 797 [8] (Lord Goff); *DRL Ltd v Wincanton Group Ltd* [2010] EWHC 2896 [229] (Stephen Davies J); *Marks and Spencer plc v BNP Paribas Securities Services Trust Co (Jersey) Ltd* [2013] EWHC 1279, [2013] L & TR 31 [42] (Morgan J); *Crown Prosecution Service v Eastenders Group* [2014] UKSC 26, [2015] AC 1 [114] (Lord Toulson; Lady Hale, and Lords Kerr, Wilson and Hughes agreeing).

[107] Eg *Raulfs v Fishy Bite Pty Ltd* [2012] NSWCA 135 [88]–[89] (Campbell JA; Meagher and Barrett JJA agreeing); *Leasing Centre (Aust) Pty Ltd v Shepard* [2011] FCA 443 [20]–[22] (Robertson J); *John Nelson Developments Pty Ltd v Focus National Developments Pty Limited* [2010] NSWSC 150 [333]–[335] (Ward J); *JD (No 6) (Dava) Pty Ltd v P Battlay Holdings Pty Ltd* [2011] VSC 353 [45]–[50] (Croft J); *The Leasing Centre (Aust) Pty Ltd v Rolepress Proplate Group Pty Ltd* [2010] NSWSC 282 [142]–[151] (Barrett J); *Jaddcal Pty Ltd v Minson (No 3)* [2011] WASC 362 [236]–[242] (Le Miere J); *Luo v Zhai* [2015] FCA 350 [34] (Perram J).

[108] *Roxborough v Rothmans of Pall Mall Australia Ltd* [2001] HCA 68, (2001) 208 CLR 516, 527 [19] (Gleeson CJ, Gaudron and Hayne JJ), 557–58 [106] (Gummow J), 577–78 [165]–[167] (Kirby J), 589 [199] (Callinan J).

[109] Recognised in *PCE Investors Ltd v Cancer Research UK* [2012] EWHC 884, [2012] 2 P & CR 5 [54] (Peter Smith J).

[110] Eg under the *Australian Consumer Law* s 243 but also see the effects of the various Frustrated Contracts Acts and other similar legislation noted below at p 271.

[111] See for example *Myddleton v Lord Kenyon* (1794) 2 Ves Jr 391, 408; 30 ER 689, 698–99.

[112] *Sumpter v Hedges* [1898] 1 QB 673.

[113] GL Williams, 'Partial Performance of Entire Contracts, I' (1941) 57 *Law Quarterly Review* 373; G Jones (ed), *Goff and Jones: The Law of Restitution*, 6th edn (London, Sweet & Maxwell, 2002) 544–45; AS Burrows, *The Law of Restitution*, 3rd edn (Oxford, Oxford University Press, 2011) 356–61; G Treitel, *The Law of Contract*, 10th edn (London, Sweet & Maxwell, 1999) 765; P Birks, *An Introduction to the Law of Restitution*, rev edn (Oxford, Oxford University Press, 1989) 234; cf P Birks and C Mitchell, 'Unjust Enrichment' in P Birks (ed), *English Private Law*, vol II (Oxford, Oxford University Press, 2000) 564; A Tettenborn, *Law of Restitution in England and Ireland*, 2nd edn (London, Cavendish Publishing, 1996) 124–25; G Virgo, *The Principles of the Law of Restitution*, 3rd edn (Oxford, Oxford University Press, 2015) 342; C Mitchell, P Mitchell and S Watterson (eds), *Goff & Jones: The Law of Unjust Enrichment*, 8th edn (London, Sweet & Maxwell, 2011) para 17.08.

because the builder's obligation to perform the building work was entire.[114] In other words, the agreed basis upon which the builder performed was that he would only be entitled to payment when entire performance was rendered. Because the builder did not render entire performance, and because the defendant did not prevent the builder from completing, the basis upon which the builder performed the work could not be said to have failed. As Mansfield CJ remarked, in a case in which a builder sought restitution of the reasonable cost of his work performed (as a *quantum valebat)* after failing to complete a contract:

> Suppose you had come hither upon a quantum valebant only, could you have recovered on it? Certainly not. The Defendant would have said, 'I made no such agreement: I agreed to pay you if you would build my house in a certain manner, which you have not done[.]'[115]

The reasoning in *Sumpter v Hedges* is consistent with, and was expressly approved in, the decision of the High Court of Australia in *Steele v Tardiani.*[116] In that case, the plaintiffs agreed to cut firewood into sections of a particular length and width, for payment according to the tonnage cut. Much of the firewood cut was not the required length. The defendant accepted the firewood and sold it, but refused to pay the plaintiffs. The High Court held that the obligation as to the dimensions of the firewood was entire and, although succeeding on other grounds,[117] the plaintiffs were not entitled to restitution (a *quantum meruit*) for the failure of the basis on which they performed the work.[118] As Dixon J explained, the correct cutting of each length of firewood was an entire obligation so that 'no action is maintainable, if any part of the [plaintiffs' performance] has failed; for, being entire, by failing partially, it fails altogether'.[119] In other words, the basis of the plaintiffs' performance did not fail because the basis was that they would not be remunerated for any length of firewood unless their work on that length was completely performed.

In *Baltic Shipping Co v Dillon*[120] this reasoning was again applied by the High Court of Australia. Mrs Dillon was one of the passengers on the *Mikhail Lermontov*, a cruise ship that hit a rock and sank off the New Zealand coast, on the ninth day of a 14-day cruise. Mrs Dillon had prepaid the cruise price of $2204.50. Baltic Shipping refunded $787.50 (or 5/14th's) of the price. But Mrs Dillon sought restitution of her *entire* payment.[121] The High Court unanimously held that she was not entitled to restitution of the whole fare. The reason for this was that the Baltic Shipping company's obligation was not entire. She would have been entitled to restitution if she had paid only upon the basis of entire performance. But as Gaudron J explained, complete performance was not a condition precedent for entitlement to the fare: it 'was not merely a round-trip journey contract; it was a contract for a

[114] B McFarlane and R Stevens, 'In Defence of *Sumpter v Hedges*' (2002) 118 *Law Quarterly Review* 569.

[115] *Ellis v Hamlen* (1810) 3 Taunt 52, 53; 128 ER 21, 22. See also *Oliver v Lakeside Property Trust Pty Ltd* [2005] NSWSC 1040 [76] (Barrett J); appeal on another ground dismissed in *Oliver v Lakeside Property Pty Ltd* [2006] NSWCA 285.

[116] *Steele v Tardiani* [1946] HCA 21, (1946) 72 CLR 386. See also *Idameneo (No 123) Pty Ltd v Angel-Honnibal* [2002] NSWSC 1214, (2003) ATPR 41-918.

[117] The plaintiff succeeded on the basis that a fresh contract was to have been implied by the conduct of the defendant or alternatively that there was a waiver from precise performance.

[118] *Steele v Tardiani* [1946] HCA 21, (1946) 72 CLR 386, 393–94 (Latham CJ).

[119] ibid 401 (Dixon J).

[120] *Baltic Shipping Co v Dillon* [1993] HCA 4, (1993) 176 CLR 344.

[121] See also *Nea Pty Ltd v Magenta Mining Pty Ltd* [2005] WASC 106 [121]–[131] (EM Heenan J); appeal on another ground dismissed in *Nea Pty Ltd v Magenta Mining Pty Ltd* [2007] WASCA 70.

fourteen-day pleasure cruise'.[122] That basis did not totally fail. Mrs Dillon received nine days of the cruise. As Deane and Dawson JJ observed, the time spent aboard the pleasure cruise was not a mere incidental benefit, like a plane forced to turn back to the starting location after an inflight movie and dinner.[123] Nor could the entire consideration be apportioned 'on a day by day basis'.[124] It is to this possibility that we now turn.

ii. Total Failure of a Portion of the Basis

The so-called 'apportionment' exception to failure of consideration cases was recognised well before Lord Porter's famous obiter dictum in *Fibrosa*. In 1871, in *Whincup v Hughes*,[125] the plaintiff had paid a premium to a watchmaker to obtain a five-year apprenticeship for his son. When the watchmaker died two years later, the plaintiff sought to recover the premium. It was held that he could not recover it. A reason for this was that a failure of consideration must be total.[126] Chief Justice Bovill, in the leading judgment, said that where the consideration could be apportioned, such as in cases where the consideration was severable, an action would succeed:

> There may be some cases of partial performance which form exceptions to this rule, as, for instance, if there were a contract to deliver ten sacks of wheat and six only were delivered, the price of the remaining four might be recovered back. But there the consideration is clearly severable.[127]

The consideration could not be apportioned in the instant case because, as Bovill CJ observed, the first two years of instruction would clearly be more difficult for the watchmaker and the apprentice would receive much of the benefit in the early years.[128] Clearly, more than two-fifths of the premium should be paid for this period. But how much more? The court was of the view that there was no way accurately to apportion the premium over the five years.[129]

A similar quandary was faced by Stadlen J in *Giedo Vander Garde BV*.[130] In that case, an aspiring racing car driver entered into agreements with the defendant company, which

[122] *Baltic Shipping Co v Dillon* [1993] HCA 4, (1993) 176 CLR 344, 386 [9].

[123] ibid 378 [11]. See further below at p 273.

[124] ibid 377 [10] (Deane and Dawson JJ); see also ibid 353 [17]–[18] (Mason CJ, Brennan and Toohey JJ agreeing), 386 [9] (Gaudron J), 392 [9]–[12] (McHugh J).

[125] *Whincup v Hughes* (1871) LR 6 CP 78.

[126] *Baltic Shipping Co v Dillon* [1993] HCA 4, (1993) 176 CLR 344, 350 [12] (Mason CJ), 383 [1] (Toohey J), 387 [10] (Gaudron J), 388 [3]–[4](McHugh J); Deane and Dawson JJ found it 'unnecessary to consider that question' (377) [10]. See also *Rover International Ltd v Cannon Film Sales Ltd* [1989] 1 WLR 912, 923 (Kerr LJ); *David Securities Pty Ltd v Commonwealth Bank of Australia* [1992] HCA 48, (1992) 175 CLR 353, 382 [53] (Mason CJ, Deane, Toohey, Gaudron and McHugh JJ); *Copping v Commercial Flour & Oatmeal Milling Co Ltd* [1933] HCA 65, (1933) 49 CLR 332; *Fibrosa Spolka Akcyjna v Fairbairn Lawson Combe Barbour Ltd* [1942] UKHL 4, [1943] AC 32, 64–65 [19] (Lord Wright).

[127] *Whincup v Hughes* (1871) LR 6 CP 78, 81 (Bovill CJ). See also ibid 84 (Willes J), 85–86 (Montague Smith J), 86 (Brett J).

[128] ibid 81 (Bovill CJ), 85 (Montague Smith J).

[129] The same concern can be seen in the speech of Viscount Simon LC in *Fibrosa Spolka Akcyjna v Fairbairn Lawson Combe Barbour Ltd* [1942] UKHL 4, [1943] AC 32, 49 [7]. Viscount Simon LC argued that apportionment is a role for the legislature. However as Professor Birks points out, equity was always prepared to apportion interests in the dissolution of partnerships: P Birks, 'Equity in the Modern Law: An Exercise in Taxonomy' (1996) 26 *University of Western Australia Law Review* 1, 78.

[130] *Giedo Van der Garde BV v Force India Formula One Team Ltd (formerly Spyker F1 Team Ltd (England))* [2010] EWHC 2373. For a recent Australian example, see *Jaddcal Pty Ltd v Minson (No 3)* [2011] WASC 362 [236]–[242] (Le Miere J).

owned and operated a Formula One racing team. In return for a $3 million fee, the defendant was obliged to provide the plaintiff with 6000 km of test driving experience, valuable 'Friday night' driving experience, potentially 'reserved driver status' as well as various sponsor, travel, accommodation and other ancillary benefits.[131] The defendant breached its contractual obligations by providing only one-third of the 6000 km promised. It was accepted by Stadlen J that the 'essential commercial purpose' of the agreements was the provision of the 6000 km of Formula One driving experience in return for the fee.[132] His Honour also agreed that it was possible, in theory, to allocate a notional portion of the fee to each withheld kilometre. However, the contingent rights to participate in Friday driving and the reserve driver status were not collateral and cumulative to the promised driving experience. They were an essential aspect of it. The $3 million fee covered all driving experience rights, without distinction or apportionment. In those circumstances, it was impossible to apportion the consideration. The claim in unjust enrichment accordingly failed.[133]

In other cases, apportionment will not be difficult. In *Roxborough*, for example, the severable part of the contract price that failed was the tax component thought to be owing from the wholesaler to the government.[134] In explaining that there was a separate basis for that component, Callinan J said that this was not an exception to the requirement of total failure of basis: 'relevantly there has been a total failure of consideration, that is to say, a failure in respect of a discrete, clearly identified component of the consideration.'[135] Another example is *Goss v Chilcott*.[136] Goss mortgaged his land to obtain a loan. The mortgage was void. The lenders sought recovery of the loan and succeeded. The Privy Council held that restitution was possible for failure of consideration even though Goss had made two repayments of interest. Lord Goff said:

> even if part of the capital sum had been repaid, the law would not hesitate to hold that the balance of the loan outstanding would be recoverable on the ground of failure of consideration; for at least in those cases in which apportionment can be carried out without difficulty, the law will allow partial recovery on this ground.[137]

The basis for the loan was that repayment would be made and, if not, that it could be enforced. That basis failed. Even if Goss had repaid part of the capital, the basis failed with respect to the communicated assumption concerning the legal right to enforce a claim for the remainder.

Apportionment will therefore usually be easy when the parties themselves have apportioned the contract. In such cases, as Deane J said in *Commonwealth of Australia v Amann Aviation Pty Ltd*,[138] restitution may 'found a direct action for the excess of money paid ... over the value of any consideration actually received'.[139] Apportionment becomes much

[131] On the role of ancillary benefits in failure of basis claims, see below at pp 271–74.

[132] *Giedo Van der Garde BV v Force India Formula One Team Ltd (formerly Spyker F1 Team Ltd (England))* [2010] EWHC 2373 [331].

[133] The claims based on breach of contract, including one for restitutionary damages, succeeded.

[134] Cf *Roxborough v Rothmans of Pall Mall Australia Ltd* [2001] HCA 68, (2001) 208 CLR 516, 578–79 [169]–[172] in which Kirby J, dissenting, argues that the tax component was not a severable part of the contract.

[135] ibid 589 [199].

[136] *Goss v Chilcott* [1996] UKPC 17, [1996] AC 788. See also *PCE Investors Ltd v Cancer Research UK* [2012] EWHC 884, [2012] 2 P & CR 5.

[137] *Goss v Chilcott* [1996] UKPC 17, [1996] AC 788, 798 [10].

[138] *Commonwealth of Australia v Amann Aviation Pty Ltd* [1991] HCA 54, (1991) 174 CLR 64.

[139] ibid 117 [3].

more difficult, albeit not impossible,[140] when a contractual obligation is severable into parts but the parties have not themselves apportioned the consideration for each part. *Ferguson v Sohl*[141] is an example. In that case, the defendant builders 'left site' in breach of contract. At first instance, it was found that the building obligation was not entire, and that the builders had been overpaid £4673. Restitution of that sum was ordered because it was paid for a consideration that had wholly failed. This was approved by the English Court of Appeal. Judge Hicks QC, with whom the Court of Appeal agreed, said:

> First, the contract price should be ascertained and adjusted for any post-contract extras, omissions or other variations. From the adjusted price should be deducted (i) the value of any contract work not done, at contract prices, (ii) payments made on account of the contract price.[142]

A final type of apportionment case is where the legislature provides for apportionment, as in some jurisdictions following frustration of contract,[143] or in partnership cases where legislation now requires apportionment of fixed premiums, paid upon entry into a partnership for a fixed term, where the partnership dissolved before the end of that term.[144]

iii. Counter-Restitution of Incidental Benefits

One reason why commentators suggest that there is a doctrine of 'partial failure of consideration' is because the basis for the performance of a transaction by a plaintiff might totally fail even though the defendant has conferred some enrichment upon the plaintiff. Like apportionment cases, this is not really an exception to the requirement for total failure, but merely recognition that in cases of total failure, the basis might totally fail notwithstanding the conferral of some benefits for which counter-restitution must be made to the defendant.

An incidental benefit need not be a *small* benefit. But it must not be part of the basis of the transaction that enriched the defendant, which must entirely fail. An example is *Pavey & Matthews Pty Ltd v Paul.*[145] Pavey and Matthews Pty Ltd agreed to do building work for Mrs Paul under an oral contract that was unenforceable. The unenforceable agreement was that they would charge her a reasonable sum for their work, which the court determined to be approximately $62,000. Mrs Paul paid $36,000, but refused to pay any more. The basis for the builders doing their work was that they would be paid a reasonable rate for all of their work. Although she had paid part of the price, the basis for the builders' work totally failed. As Professor Burrows put it: 'The builders had not been paid at the prevailing rate as promised which was their basis for doing the work'.[146] When the fair value was not paid for the

[140] Cf *Giedo Van der Garde BV v Force India Formula One Team Ltd (formerly Spyker F1 Team Ltd (England))* [2010] EWHC 2373 [297] (Stadlen J).

[141] *DO Ferguson v Sohl* (1992) 62 BLR 95. See also 'Cases— *Cotter v Minister for Agriculture*' [1993] *Restitution Law Review* 144.

[142] *DO Ferguson v Sohl* (1992) 62 BLR 95, 96.

[143] Frustrated Contracts Act 1943 (UK); Australian Consumer Law and Fair Trading Act 2012 (Vic) Part 3.2; Frustrated Contracts Act 1978 (NSW); Frustrated Contracts Act 1988 (SA).

[144] See, for example, Partnership Act 1890 (UK) s 40 which reverses the decision in *Whincup v Hughes* (1871) LR 6 CP 78 in cases of partnership premiums. All Australian states and territories have corresponding provisions. This legislation reflects a long-standing Chancery rule: *Atwood v Maude* (1868) LR 3 Ch App 369; *Wilson v Johnstone* (1873) LR 16 Eq 606.

[145] *Pavey & Matthews Pty Ltd v Paul* [1987] HCA 5, (1987) 162 CLR 221.

[146] AS Burrows, *The Law of Restitution*, 3rd edn (Oxford, Oxford University Press, 2011) 383.

entirety of the work, the basis on which they performed their work totally failed. However, as the basis for the builders' work had failed, Mrs Paul was also entitled to 'counter-restitution' of the incidental benefit she conferred upon the plaintiff ($36,000), because the basis for that also failed. As six Justices of the High Court of Australia explained in *David Securities Pty Ltd v Commonwealth Bank of Australia,*[147] 'counter-restitution [of the incidental benefit] is relatively simple'.

Sometimes the receipt of some counter performance might not amount to an incidential benefit requiring any counter-restitution. For instance, the receipt of some of the requested performance will not prevent there being a failure of basis if the performance is so defective that the basis nevertheless fails. In *Gartell & Son (a firm) v Yeovil Town Football & Athletic Club Ltd,*[148] work performed on Yeovil's athletic pitches was so defective, and so lacking in skill and care, that it made no improvement to the playing surface. That was the basis of the contract and that basis failed, despite some performance being rendered. Sometimes the intense focus upon whether the basis for a benefit has failed can lead to neglect of the existence of a claim for restitution of incidental benefits. This can be seen in the case of *Rowland v Divall.*[149] Rowland, a car dealer, purchased a car from Divall. Two months later Rowland sold the car to Railsdon. After Railsdon had used the car for two months, it became apparent that the car had been stolen, and the police took possession of the car. Rowland claimed the price back from Divall, alleging a failure of consideration. Justice Bray held that the use of the car by Rowland and Railsdon for four months meant that the failure of the basis for the transaction was not total and the action failed. However, the English Court of Appeal unanimously reversed this decision on the basis that:

> The buyer has not received any part of that which he contracted to receive—namely, the property and right to possession—and, that being so, there has been a total failure of consideration.[150]

Rowland has been directly relied upon in numerous cases since.[151] In *Baltic Shipping,*[152] Mason CJ (with whom Brennan and Toohey JJ agreed) said that 'Where the buyer is entitled under the contract to good title and lawful possession but receives only unlawful possession … there is a total failure of consideration'. Although the basis of the transaction involving the purchase of the car (that Rowland would obtain good title pursuant to the transaction) had totally failed, there was still clearly an incidental benefit obtained by Rowland through his use of the car for two months. As we saw in Chapter 5, that benefit came at the expense of Divall. But unlike Mrs Paul in *Pavey & Matthews Pty Ltd v Paul,* Rowland was not required to make counter-restitution of this incidental benefit. The Court of Appeal did not explain the reason why no counter-restitution was required. The simple answer appears to be that it was not sought. If it had been sought there is a strong argument that it should have been made.

[147] *David Securities Pty Ltd v Commonwealth Bank of Australia* [1992] HCA 48, (1992) 175 CLR 353, 383 [55].

[148] *Gartell & Son (a firm) v Yeovil Town Football & Athletic Club Ltd* [2016] EWCA Civ 62.

[149] *Rowland v Divall* [1923] 2 KB 500.

[150] ibid 507 (Atkin LJ).

[151] *Karflex Ltd v Poole* [1933] 2 KB 251; *Warman v Southern Counties Car Finance Corporation Ltd* [1949] 2 KB 576; *Butterworth v Kingsway Motors Ltd* [1954] 1 WLR 1286; *Rogers v Parish (Scarborough) Ltd* [1987] QB 933.

[152] *Baltic Shipping Co v Dillon* [1993] HCA 4, (1993) 176 CLR 344, 351 [13].

Another example is *Rover International Ltd v Cannon Film Ltd.*[153] Cannon agreed to supply films to Rover, who would dub and distribute them in exchange for a substantial share of box office receipts. The agreement was void because Rover was not incorporated at the time of contracting. Rover never received a share of the box office receipts. Rover claimed for restitution of advance payments made under the void contract for failure of consideration. Rover also sought restitution (as a *quantum meruit*) for the work done in dubbing and distributing the films. Cannon conceded that restitution could be awarded for the work done but argued that Rover's claim for restitution of the advance payments should fail because there had been no total failure of consideration. Cannon pointed to the fact that Rover had had the benefit of possession and use of the films as provided by the contract and alleged that it had distributed one film for a substantial sum. The English Court of Appeal held that the 'relevant bargain' (or basis) was the opportunity to earn a substantial share of the gross receipts. The basis had totally failed because that opportunity was not available.[154] The possession and use of the films themselves was 'merely incidental' to the contract.[155] However, once again, Cannon had not argued that if a failure of consideration was found, counter-restitution of the value of the use of those films[156] should be made to it, so this point was not considered. In *David Securities*, the joint judgment in the High Court cited *Rowland* and *Rover* with approval,[157] but emphasised that where counter-restitution is relatively simple, it should be made. In cases such as *Rover* where an incidental benefit is transferred from the plaintiff to the defendant, counter-restitution should be ordered as a condition of restitution for failure of consideration.

In Chapter 15 we will see that there are unlikely to be any cases in which courts are unable to value incidental benefits for the purpose of requiring counter-restitution.[158] However, in some cases, incidental benefits will be of little or no value without reference to the main consideration and, if that has totally failed, there should be no requirement for counter-restitution. Passengers who have received a meal and seen an in-flight movie on a flight from Sydney to London should not be liable to make counter-restitution of the value of those services in the event that the flight is turned around half way.[159] Similarly, in *Giedo Vander Garde*, Stadlen J accepted that the ancillary sponsorship, accommodation, travel and 'paddock pass' benefits delivered to the plaintiff were of 'zero' value without the driving experience rights.[160] Another example is *Luo v Zhai*,[161] where the defendant had provided certain financial statements as required under an agreement, the main purpose of which

[153] *Rover International Ltd v Cannon Film Sales Ltd* [1989] 1 WLR 912. NH Andrews, 'Restitution and Void Contracts: The Unmeritorious Defendant Must Pay' (1990) 49 *Cambridge Law Journal* 15; J Beatson, 'Restitutionary Remedies for Void and Ineffective Contracts' (1989) 105 *Law Quarterly Review* 179.

[154] *Rover International Ltd v Cannon Film Sales Ltd* [1989] 1 WLR 912, 925 (Kerr LJ, Nicholls J agreeing).

[155] ibid 924.

[156] Which, as seen in Ch 4 pp 59–61, is not necessarily the same as the actual profits made.

[157] *David Securities Pty Ltd v Commonwealth Bank of Australia* [1992] HCA 48, (1992) 175 CLR 353, 383 [54].

[158] '[I]n several fields the judges are well accustomed to putting figures to intangibles, and I see no reason why the imprecision of the exercise should be a barrier, if that is what fairness demands': *Ruxley Electronics and Construction Ltd v Forsyth* [1996] AC 344, 361 (Lord Mustill).

[159] An example given in *Baltic Shipping Co v Dillon* [1993] HCA 4, (1993) 176 CLR 344, see immediately below.

[160] *Giedo Van der Garde BV v Force India Formula One Team Ltd (formerly Spyker F1 Team Ltd (England))* [2010] EWHC 2373 [336].

[161] *Luo v Zhai* [2015] FCA 350.

was the transfer of 40 per cent of the shares in exchange for $800,000. Justice Perram considered that the received benefits constituted a trivial and merely ancillary part of the substantive bargain, valueless in themselves. The consideration for the transaction had wholly failed.

D. Issue 4: Can Restitution for Failure of Consideration Allow Escape from a Bad Bargain?

The answer to this question is 'yes', with the heavy qualification that parties do not always bargain solely for price-related benefits; sometimes people will provide benefits below market price for other reasons. The essential reason why a party can escape a bad bargain by a claim for restitution based on failure of consideration is because the failure of the basis for a plaintiff's performance means that the contractual allocation of risk and value has also failed. In *Roxborough v Rothmans of Pall Mall Ltd,*[162] Gummow J explained that one reason why there is a continued insistence on the requirement of 'total' failure of the basis is because if restitution were generally allowed, it would 'cut across the compensatory principle' and allow parties to circumvent bad bargains.

The operation of the unjust factor of failure of consideration in the context of a 'bad' bargain can be illustrated by a simple example, based on a United States case.[163] X contracts with Y for the sale of 10 bags of wheat at $100 a bag. X pays the full price of $1000 in advance. But X has made a bad bargain. The market price of a bag of wheat is $50. Y only delivers six bags and X terminates the contract. If X sues for breach of contract for the failure to deliver four bags, the only financial loss he has suffered is $200, because he made a bad bargain. That is the additional cost of purchasing four bags. But X can argue that the basis upon which the $1000 was paid was apportioned to $100 per bag. Therefore, the basis for payment of $400 has totally failed as four bags have not been received, and restitution should be made of $400. In this way, X is allowed to circumvent the bad bargain he made by agreeing to purchase those four bags of wheat at $50 above market value. This is allowed because Y has not performed in exchange for the money. The allocation of price and risk for the bags of wheat depended upon the basis that Y would deliver them to X. When that basis fails so too does the contractual allocation of price. This result is orthodoxy. It has approval by the High Court of Australia,[164] and support in a long line of English cases on section 30(1) of the Sale of Goods Act 1893 (UK), which, providing for short delivery, derives from the action for failure of consideration.[165]

Failure of consideration cases that seem to allow escape from a bad bargain can, however, seem 'bizarre'[166] when they involve an agreement for services. In *Boomer v Muir,*[167]

[162] *Roxborough v Rothmans of Pall Mall Australia Ltd* [2001] HCA 68, (2001) 208 CLR 516, 557 [105] citing G Treitel, *The Law of Contract*, 10th edn (London, Sweet & Maxwell, 1999) 978.

[163] *Bush v Canfield* 2 Conn 485 (Conn 1818). Cf *Dutch v Warren* (1721) 1 Str 406, 93 ER 598 and *L Albert & Son v Armstrong Rubber Co* 178 F 2d 182 (CA 1949).

[164] *Roxborough v Rothmans of Pall Mall Australia Ltd* [2001] HCA 68, (2001) 208 CLR 516, 527 [20] (Gleeson CJ, Gaudron and Hayne JJ).

[165] See *Dawood Ltd v Heath Ltd* [1961] 2 Lloyd's Rep 512; *Behrend & Co Ltd v Produce Brokers Co Ltd* [1920] 3 KB 530.

[166] P Birks, *Unjust Enrichment*, 2nd edn (Oxford, Oxford University Press, 2005) 59.

[167] *Boomer v Muir* 24 P 2d 570 (Cal App 1933).

a contractor repudiated a contract and the subcontractor claimed restitution of the value of the work done on the construction project. Although only a small amount of work remained to be performed, the subcontractor was awarded restitution of the full value of his services less payments received under the contract. The difference was $238,000. Another example, which followed *Boomer*, is the decision of the New South Wales Court of Appeal in *Renard Constructions v Minister for Public Works*.[168] In that case, the New South Wales Court of Appeal allowed a claim for restitution (as a *quantum meruit*) for work done to a value of $285,000, although the total value of the *completed* contract was only $208,950. Justice Meagher (with whom Priestley JA and Handley JA agreed) said that it is well established that, following a repudiatory breach, the innocent party can claim the fair value of services provided.[169] Justice Meagher said of the submission by counsel that the valuation of the enrichment should be limited to the contract price, that there is nothing 'anomalous in the prospect that a figure arrived at on a *quantum meruit* might exceed, or even far exceed, the profit which would have been made if the contract had been fully performed'.[170] In refusing special leave to appeal from the decision, Deane J, speaking for the High Court of Australia special leave panel, said:

> In a context where the conclusion had been reached that the contract had been repudiated by the applicant and that that repudiation had been accepted by the respondent, the Court does not think that the decision of the Court of Appeal on that particular question of law is attended by sufficient doubt to warrant a grant of special leave to appeal to this Court.[171]

Finally, in *Sopov v Kane Constructions Pty Ltd (No 2)*,[172] a construction contract to renovate and to extend a boilerhouse was terminated by the plaintiff builder for the defendants' breach after 90 per cent of the contract work had been completed. The plaintiff claimed restitution (a *quantum meruit*) of the value of all work performed, less the progress payments made by the defendants. A unanimous Victorian Supreme Court of Appeal upheld the decision of the trial judge, Warren CJ, that the plaintiff was entitled to an award of restitution, although (like Warren CJ) the Court of Appeal referred to 'powerful' judicial criticisms and 'significant academic disapproval' of this conclusion.[173] These criticisms are considered below.

The result in these cases, and others like them,[174] can be defended if the performance obligation by the plaintiff contractors was entire. As we have explained above, an entire obligation is one in which entire performance is a precondition for counter-performance. If this were the case in *Renard* then the repudiation by the defendant prevented the plaintiff from earning any of the contract price and the basis for the work totally failed. The only question that then remains is whether the contract price should form a ceiling on the recovery.

[168] *Renard Constructions (ME) Pty Ltd v Minister for Public Works* (1992) 26 NSWLR 234.

[169] *Lodder v Slowey* [1904] AC 442; *United States, for Use of Susi Contracting Co v Zara Contracting Co* 146 F 2d 606 (CA 1944); *Re Montgomery's Estate* 6 NE 2d 40 (NY 1936).

[170] *Renard Constructions (ME) Pty Ltd v Minister for Public Works* (1992) 26 NSWLR 234, 277.

[171] *Minister of Public Works v Renard Constructions (ME) Pty Ltd* (1992) 13 Legal Rep SL 1 (Deane, Dawson, McHugh JJ).

[172] *Sopov v Kane Constructions Pty Ltd (No 2)* [2009] VSCA 141, (2009) 24 VR 510.

[173] ibid [11] (Maxwell P, Kellam JA and Whelan AJA); *Kane Constructions Pty Ltd v Sopov* [2005] VSC 237 [859] Warren CJ).

[174] *Appleby v Myers* (1867) LR 2 CP 651, 659 (the Court; *Slowey v Lodder* (1901) 20 NZLR 321, 356 (Edwards J) affirmed on different grounds *Lodder v Slowey* [1904] AC 442.

There is strong support for such a requirement from many commentators[175] including an article by the Reporter of the new United States Restatement of Restitution (Third),[176] the view of the Restatement itself,[177] and obiter dicta in at least one English decision.[178] In Chapter 4 we explained that this issue is a matter concerned with the quantum of enrichment; it is not concerned with whether there has been a failure of consideration.[179]

As mentioned, the decisions in *Renard*, *Boomer* and *Sopov* can only be justified on the basis that the contractors' obligations were entire. If a contractor's obligations are not entire—and in large building contracts they are invariably severable—then the basis of the entirety of the contractual performance will rarely fail if the contractor has not been given the opportunity to complete performance. This is because the contractor will have a right to the contract price for the severable part of the contract obligation which has been performed. The basis for that part of the performance has not failed.[180] In *Trimis v MINA* Mason P (Priestly and Handley JJA agreeing) said:

> Restitution respects the sanctity of the transaction, and the subsisting contractual regime chosen by the parties as the framework for settling disputes. This ensures that the law does not countenance two conflicting sets of legal obligations subsisting concurrently.[181]

Justice Finn found this to be an attractive proposition in *GEC Marconi Systems Pty Ltd v BHP Information Technology Pty Ltd*.[182] In that case, his Honour said that because 'rights are not divested or discharged which have already been unconditionally acquired' prior to the termination of the contract, those rights should be governed by the contract and not by the law of unjust enrichment.[183] These comments by Mason P and Finn J could not have been meant to suggest that a subsisting contractual regime could never be upset when the basis for performance by the plaintiff under the contract had wholly failed. They are merely insisting that where the basis for performance relied upon is counter-performance, then if the contractor has an accrued right to counter-performance, the basis will not have failed.

E. Issue 5: Can a Party in Breach Rely upon Failure of Consideration?

We saw earlier that fault is not an independent element of the unjust factor of failure of consideration. Consistently with this position, the previous section demonstrated that where a contract has been terminated for the defendant's breach, a plaintiff can escape the consequences of what might objectively appear to be a bad bargain if the basis for the plaintiff's

[175] Commentators that support such a contract ceiling valuation include H Mather, 'Restitution as a Remedy for Breach of Contract: The Case of the Partially Performing Seller' (1982) 92 *Yale Law Journal* 14, 48; GE Palmer, 'The Contract Price as a Limit on Restitution for Defendant's Breach' (1959) 20 *Ohio State Law Journal* 264; JM Perillo, 'Restitution in the Second "Restatement of Contracts"' (1981) 81 *Columbia Law Review* 37; P Birks, *Unjust Enrichment*, 2nd edn (Oxford, Oxford University Press, 2005) 59; AS Burrows, *The Law of Restitution*, 3rd edn (Oxford, Oxford University Press, 2011) 349–50.

[176] A Kull, 'Restitution as a Remedy for Breach of Contract' (1994) 67 *Southern California Law Review* 1465.

[177] American Law Institute, *Restatement of the Law (Third) Restitution and Unjust Enrichment* (St Paul, Minn, American Law Institute Publishers, 2011) §49(3)(d).

[178] *Taylor v Motability Finance Ltd* [2004] EWHC 2619 (Comm) [26] (Cooke J).

[179] At pp 81–84.

[180] *Taylor v Motability Finance Ltd* [2004] EWHC 2619 (Comm).

[181] *Trimis v Mina* [1999] NSWCA 140 [54].

[182] *GEC Marconi Systems Pty Ltd v BHP Information Technology Pty Ltd* [2003] FCA 50, (2003) 128 FCR 1 [651]–[666], [1569].

[183] ibid [651].

performance has wholly failed. The justification for this is not that the defendant is at fault, but that the defendant is not entitled to retain an enrichment without performance of the basis of the transaction by which she was enriched. Conversely, if the condition for a payment has wholly failed, in theory it should not matter that the failure occurred as a result of the plaintiff's breach. In *Baltic Shipping*,[184] McHugh J quoted from Professor Birks that 'once it does appear that the condition for retaining the money has failed the fact that it failed in response to the payer's own breach does not matter'.

However, in many cases a breach by the plaintiff may mean that the basis of the agreement has not failed. Assuming the contractors' obligations to have been entire in *Renard*, *Boomer* or *Sopov*, if the facts were reversed and the contractor were a repudiating party who had made a bad bargain, there would clearly be no failure of basis. It could not be said that the contractor had been prevented from completing the contract and earning the price. *Sumpter v Hedges* is a good example of this.[185] The basis was that the builder would perform the work and be paid on complete performance (the obligation of the builder was entire). Because the builder did not render complete performance, and because the defendant did not prevent the builder from completing in any way,[186] the basis upon which the builder performed the work did not fail. It is in this sense that Lord Wright stated in *Fibrosa* that failure of consideration requires a failure for a reason 'not involving fault on the part of the plaintiff'.[187] Similarly, in *Baltic Shipping*, Mason CJ, with whom Brennan and Toohey JJ agreed, said that 'There can, of course, be no such failure when the plaintiff's unwillingness or refusal to perform the contract on his or her part is the cause of the defendant's non-performance'[188] upon which the failure of consideration relies. These cases do not signify, therefore, some independent requirement of fault in the unjust factor of failure of consideration. Instead, they merely serve as emphasis for the need for the consideration to have wholly failed. This in turn is necessary to ensure that the claim in restitution does not undermine or contradict the contractual regime.

Although comparatively rare, there are some cases in which the basis upon which a plaintiff in breach has performed can still wholly fail, so as to permit restitution. These are cases in which the defendant's obligation to perform is not conditional upon complete performance, such as payment, by the plaintiff. In *Dies v British and International Mining and Finance Corporation*[189] a purchaser made an advance payment of £100,000 as part of a contract price of £270,000 for a delivery of rifles and ammunition. However, the purchaser failed to meet the next instalment and the vendor terminated the contract. The purchaser sued and recovered the £100,000. Justice Stable was of the opinion that 'the general rule is that the law confers on the purchaser the right to recover his money, and that to enable the seller to keep it he must be able to point to some language in the contract from which the inference to be drawn is that the parties intended and agreed that he should'.[190] He observed

[184] *Baltic Shipping Co v Dillon* [1993] HCA 4, (1993) 176 CLR 344, 390 [7].

[185] *Sumpter v Hedges* [1898] 1 QB 673. See also *Bolton v Mahadeva* [1972] 1 WLR 1009.

[186] See *Renard Constructions (ME) Pty Ltd v Minister for Public Works* (1992) 26 NSWLR 234; *Jennings Construction Ltd v QH and M Birt Ltd* (NSWCA, 31 January 1989); *Watkins Pacific Pty Ltd v Lezzi Constructions Pty Ltd* (QCA, 3 February 1993); *Pohlmann v Harrison* (QCA, 3 February 1993).

[187] *Fibrosa Spolka Akcyjna v Fairbairn Lawson Combe Barbour Ltd* [1942] UKHL 4, [1943] AC 32, 64–65 [19] (Lord Wright).

[188] *Baltic Shipping Co v Dillon* [1993] HCA 4, (1993) 176 CLR 344, 352 [15].

[189] *Dies v British and International Mining and Finance Corporation, Ltd* [1939] 1 KB 724.

[190] ibid 743.

that such recovery has long been recognised in contracts for the sale of land.[191] Unlike *Sumpter v Hedges*, the vendor's obligation in *Dies* was an independent obligation to deliver the rifles. It was not an entire obligation. In other words, entire payment by the purchaser was not a condition precedent to delivery of the rifles. Therefore when the purchaser did not receive the goods, the basis for the payment failed.

Although, in *Dies*, Stable J said that the right to restitution was not based upon failure of consideration,[192] later decisions have emphasised that failure of consideration is the best explanation of the case. One example is that in *Baltic Shipping Co v Dillon*,[193] where McHugh J rightly said that the 'best explanation' of *Dies* was that 'once it does appear that the condition for retaining the money has failed the fact that it failed in response to the payer's own breach does not matter'.

Two qualifications must be made to the above discussion. First, even in those cases where the party in breach is entitled to restitution, it must be remembered that the innocent party retains the right to sue for breach of contract, so there is no benefit for a party to a bad bargain seeking to avoid the bad bargain by repudiating the contract and seeking restitution of benefits conferred under the contract. Secondly, subject to equitable rules of relief against forfeiture,[194] it is open to the parties, by agreement, to exclude the right to restitution and provide that the defaulting party will forfeit any money paid or the value of work done upon breach of a condition or repudiation.[195]

VI. Conclusion

The most important lesson of this chapter is the meaning of 'failure consideration'. The message is that 'consideration' is not used in its contractual sense. Failure of consideration means the failure of the basis or condition of the transaction by which the plaintiff enriched the defendant. Once that is appreciated, it becomes possible to address the difficult issues that surround the unjust factor, such as the requirement that the failure of consideration be total, in a transparent and coherent manner. Adopting that approach, this chapter has shown that failure of consideration constitutes a well-established unjust factor both at common law and in equity. References to the role of 'fault' in cases of failure of consideration do not indicate an independent requirement of the unjust factor. We also saw that failure of consideration operates in contractual and non-contractual contexts. Where it operates in a contractual context, the key issue is to ensure that it does not undermine the contractual allocation of risk. As we saw in this chapter and in Chapter 7, the contractual risk will not be undermined when the consideration for the contract, or for a severable obligation in the contract, has wholly failed.

[191] *Palmer v Temple* (1839) 9 Ad & El 508, 112 ER 1304; *Mayson v Clouet* [1924] AC 980.

[192] *Dies v British and International Mining and Finance Corporation, Ltd* [1939] 1 KB 724, 744. See *Hyundai Heavy Industries Co Ltd v Papadopoulos* [1980] 1 WLR 1129, 1142 (Lord Edmund Davies).

[193] *Baltic Shipping Co v Dillon* [1993] HCA 4, (1993) 176 CLR 344, 390 [7]. Cf Mason CJ (Brennan and Toohey JJ agreeing) who preferred an explanation of *Dies* as based on a conditional contractual right (at 352 [15]).

[194] *Tanwar Enterprises Pty Ltd v Cauchi* [2003] HCA 57, (2003) 217 CLR 315.

[195] *McDonald v Dennys Lascelles Ltd* [1933] HCA 25, (1933) 48 CLR 457.

12

No Intention to Benefit the Defendant

Contents

I. Introduction

In previous chapters we considered unjust factors which involved an impaired intention to enter a transaction that enriched another (mistake, duress, undue influence) or an intention subject to a condition which is not satisfied (failure of consideration). So, if a plaintiff paid money to a defendant mistakenly believing that the money was owing, the plaintiff's intention would be impaired and there would be a prima facie right to restitution. If a plaintiff paid money to a defendant on the express condition that it would be used for the defendant's wedding, then the failure of the wedding to occur would prima facie entitle the plaintiff to restitution. But what about a situation where the plaintiff's intention to enter a transaction that enriched the defendant was not impaired or conditional, but was wholly *absent?* This chapter is concerned with unjust factors where there is a complete absence of intention to benefit the defendant through the impugned transaction.

At first impression, it might seem that there are stronger reasons to recognise unjust factors involving no intention than those well-established unjust factors where a plaintiff's intention is merely impaired.[1] If a plaintiff can recover when she makes a payment mistakenly, surely recovery should be possible when the payment is made from the plaintiff's funds without any knowledge of the plaintiff? So, if a shopkeeper who mistakenly overpays a customer $50 has a right to restitution (mistake), it would seem that the same shopkeeper should have a right to restitution if the customer steals the $50 by taking it without the shopkeeper's knowledge (ignorance). Indeed, there may be little difference of principle between such a case of ignorance and a case of lack of understanding based on the plea of *non est factum*, considered in Chapter 7.[2]

The same reasoning that requires recognition of 'ignorance' by analogy with mistake also explains why unjust factors of 'powerlessness' and 'anti-beneficial intention' should be recognised by analogy with illegitimate threats and failure of consideration. If a plaintiff can recover a payment made as a consequence of duress, then surely recovery should be possible when the plaintiff is entirely powerless to prevent the payment. So, if a shopkeeper obtains restitution after paying $50 to a customer due to an illegitimate threat, then the shopkeeper should also recover if he is bound to a chair while $50 is stolen by the customer (powerlessness). And if restitution is allowed when a plaintiff makes a payment to a defendant on a particular basis which fails (failure of consideration), restitution should also be allowed when a payment is made on the express basis that the defendant will not benefit from the use or enjoyment of the rights (anti-beneficial intention).

The justification for unjust factors of ignorance, powerlessness, and anti-beneficial intention therefore follows by analogy with the existence of the unjust factors of mistake, duress, and failure of consideration. But the analogy is not perfect. For instance, if title to a motor vehicle is mistakenly transferred by a plaintiff to a defendant the defendant obtains the title from the plaintiff, and the plaintiff's only action will be for unjust enrichment. In contrast, when a thief steals a chattel from a plaintiff who is ignorant of the theft, the plaintiff's title is unaffected. However, as we saw in Chapter 4, the defendant is enriched in both cases by the transaction. And although the plaintiff will have an action against the thief for the tort of conversion, the existence of an additional action for conversion does not mean that the action for unjust enrichment should be abolished.

The difficulty for these unjust factors should not be their existence. If the plaintiff was ignorant of the transaction, powerless to prevent it, or received the benefit on an anti-beneficial basis, then restitution should follow, in the absence of a reason to retain the enrichment. The difficulty usually concerns whether the defendant has a right to retain the enrichment. In cases involving no intention to benefit, that focus can overshadow everything else in the unjust enrichment enquiry, including the existence of the unjust factor. In these cases, if there is a right to retain the enrichment, then there is usually no need to ask whether an unjust factor exists. Equally, if there is no right to retain the enrichment, then courts rarely worry about whether the plaintiff (who never intended the transaction) can rely on any unjust factor. Unfortunately, the lack of focus in cases on the unjust factor has led to doubts about the existence of categories of unjust factor concerned with a lack of intention to benefit the defendant through the impugned transaction. For instance, an argument for an unjust factor of ignorance was made in the High Court of Australia in

[1] P Birks, *An Introduction to the Law of Restitution*, rev edn (Oxford, Oxford University Press, 1989) 141.
[2] Ch 7 pp 142–43.

Farah Constructions Pty Ltd v Say-Dee Pty Ltd, where counsel asserted that an alleged receipt of assets in breach of fiduciary duty was an 'enrichment [which] was unjust because it was without [the plaintiff's] knowledge or fully informed consent'. The High Court of Australia said that 'No case, even in England, has treated ignorance as a "reason for restitution".'[3]

II. Ignorance

A. The Meaning of an Unjust Factor of Ignorance

As with all the unjust factors considered in this chapter, the underlying principle is that the plaintiff had no intention to enter the transaction that enriched the defendant. Therefore, the unjust factor of ignorance is not concerned with a circumstance where a plaintiff intended the defendant to benefit from a transfer, but the plaintiff was ignorant of some material detail. As we have seen in Chapter 8, the scenario where the plaintiff is aware of the transaction but ignorant of a material matter falls to be considered within the unjust factor of mistake.

B. The Focus is on the Defendant's Right to Retain the Benefit

In many unjust enrichment cases involving an absence of the plaintiff's intention to benefit the defendant through the impugned transaction, the issue concerns the defendant's right to retain the benefit, in whole or in part. This is most commonly seen in ignorance cases where the plaintiff is a company. In some of these cases no knowledge of the transaction can be attributed to the company. The company is therefore ignorant of the transaction that enriched the defendant. But in those cases the key point, and the focus of the decision, is whether the plaintiff company can negate any juristic reason that the defendant asserts for the retention of the enrichment. For instance, where the defendant asserts that the enrichment was provided by contract, then the plaintiff company will need to prove that the contract was non-existent, void, or voidable. In *Criterion Properties plc v Stratford UK Properties LLC*, Lord Nicholls of Birkenhead explained that:

> If a company (A) enters into an agreement with B under which B acquires benefits from A, A's ability to recover these benefits from B depends essentially on whether the agreement is binding on A ... If, however, the agreement *is* set aside, B will be accountable for any benefits he may have received from A under the agreement ... A will have a personal claim against B for unjust enrichment, subject always to a defence of change of position.[4]

An example of a case where a company sought restitution of its assets dissipated without authority in a manner which it was powerless to stop, or ignorant of, is the decision

[3] *Farah Constructions Pty Ltd v Say-Dee Pty Ltd* [2007] HCA 22, (2007) 230 CLR 89 [156] (the Court).
[4] *Criterion Properties plc v Stratford UK Properties LLC* [2004] UKHL 28, [2004] 1 WLR 1846 [4].

of the English Court of Appeal in *Blue Station Ltd v Kamyab*.[5] The defendant company director signed a cheque to himself for £100,000. He had power to sign cheques, but was not authorised to make this payment to himself. The Court of Appeal upheld the order for restitution to the company. Lord Justice Chadwick said that in the circumstances 'the claimant company needed to prove only that the payment was one to which the payee was not entitled'.[6] The ignorance or powerlessness of the company was not a matter in any doubt. The Court of Appeal did not need to consider the unjust factor once the plaintiff company had established that the defendant had no right to retain the enrichment.

C. An Unjust Factor of Ignorance at Common Law: Principle

As we explained in the introduction to this chapter, the existence of an unjust factor allowing restitution for mistaken payments is a good reason for the recognition of an unjust factor based on ignorance. As a matter of principle, if a vitiated intention to enter the transaction that enriched the defendant permits restitution, then so should the complete absence of intention to benefit the defendant by an impugned transaction. Further, there will sometimes be a very fine line between cases that are based on the unjust factor of ignorance, and those based on the unjust factor of mistake. For instance, in *State Bank of New South Wales Ltd v Swiss Bank Corporation*,[7] a senior employee of the State Bank of NSW was part of an elaborate fraud that caused the State Bank to pay $20 million to the Swiss Bank, which the employee then withdrew from the Swiss Bank. No one in the State Bank was aware of this fraud, or the payment, at the time it was made, although the payment was registered in the bank's computers. The payment was treated by the New South Wales Court of Appeal as a case of unjust enrichment based on mistake. But it might also have been treated as a case of ignorance. This case contrasts with *Port of Brisbane Corporation v ANZ Securities Ltd (No 2)*,[8] which clearly is a mistaken payment case. In that case an employee defrauded the Port Corporation by having two general managers sign a cheque which they had been defrauded into mistakenly believing was an investment by the Port Corporation.

Another example which illustrates the fine line between mistake and ignorance is *Commonwealth of Australia v Davis Samuel Pty Ltd (No 7)*.[9] In that case, Refshauge J found that the Commonwealth had made a number of mistaken electronic transfers when a fraudster transferred moneys from its account to various third parties.[10] His Honour acknowledged the difficulty of characterising the case as one involving a mistake in circumstances in which the transaction was entirely electronic and there was, at the Commonwealth's bank, no actual person who made the mistake. He concluded that 'It may not now be necessary, with electronic commerce, for a human mind to be conscious of the error in the transaction for there to be a mistake which is actionable.'[11]

[5] *Blue Station Ltd v Kamyab* [2007] EWCA Civ 1073. See also *Russell Gould Pty Ltd v Ramangkura* [2014] NSWCA 310, (2014) 87 NSWLR 552.
[6] *Blue Station Ltd v Kamyab* [2007] EWCA Civ 1073 [18].
[7] *State Bank of New South Wales Ltd v Swiss Bank Corporation* (1995) 39 NSWLR 350.
[8] *Port of Brisbane Corporation v ANZ Securities Ltd (No 2)* [2002] QCA 158, [2003] 2 Qd R 661.
[9] *Commonwealth v Davis Samuel Pty Ltd (No 7)* [2013] ACTSC 146, (2013) 282 FLR 1.
[10] ibid [1690]–[1707].
[11] ibid [1707].

D. An Unjust Factor of Ignorance at Common Law: Authority

i. Ignorance of the Plaintiff of an Unauthorised Transaction

Several examples can be given involving an unjust factor of 'ignorance' where the plaintiff was ignorant of an unauthorised transaction by which the defendant received the plaintiff's assets. The first case is *Holiday v Sigil*,[12] involving the loss by Holiday of a £500 Bank of England note. Evidence was given that Sigil was seen picking it up, and had taken it to another banking house the following month. Holiday was entitled to recover from Sigil £500 in an action for money had and received, which we saw in Chapter 2 was a form of action which often was an action for unjust enrichment. The claim in *Holiday* was not brought for wrongdoing (trover), but was simply based upon the receipt by Sigil of Holiday's asset through the impugned transaction.

A second example is *Barros Mattos Junior v MacDaniels Ltd*.[13] In that case a Brazilian bank had millions of dollars stolen from it by fraudulent SWIFT transfers. The defendants received $8 million of the money, which they thought was for genuine foreign exchange transactions (a matter not challenged on the summary judgment application). They converted the money into foreign currency and paid it over, less their commission. The trial judge, Laddie J, held that the bank (by its assignee) was entitled to restitution. He said that the starting point was that 'someone who receives stolen money is placed under a legal obligation to hand it, or an equivalent sum, back to the rightful owner. If he does not, he will be unjustly enriched'.[14]

A third example is *Cressman v Coys of Kensington*.[15] In that case a car was sold at auction, but the auctioneer expressly disregarded instructions from the vendor not to sell valuable personal number plates worth £15,000. Due to the statutory registration system, the number plates passed to the purchaser without the knowledge of the vendor.[16] The Court of Appeal held that the purchaser had been unjustly enriched. The unjust factor relied upon by the vendor was simply that he had not intended to enter the transaction that enriched the purchaser: 'it was legally unjust for Mr McDonald to keep the registration mark, since it was an express term of the auction contract that he would not receive the vehicle's existing mark'.[17] In other words, the vendor was 'ignorant' of the transfer of his number plates.

Turning from England to Australia, a fourth example is the decision of the High Court of Australia in *Black v S Freedman & Co*.[18] Black stole cash from his employer and paid some of it into his bank account, which he then withdrew and paid into his wife's account. Other cash he stole was paid directly into his wife's account. Justice O'Connor said that Black held the money in his bank account (ie his rights against his bank) on trust for his employer and, consequently, Black's wife held her rights against her bank on trust for Black's employer.[19]

[12] *Holiday v Sigil* (1826) 2 C & P 176, 172 ER 81. See also *Neate v Harding* (1851) 6 Exch 349, 155 ER 577; *Moffatt v Kazana* [1969] 2 QB 152.

[13] *Barros Mattos Junior v MacDaniels Ltd* [2004] EWHC 1188, [2005] 1 WLR 247.

[14] ibid [15].

[15] *Cressman v Coys of Kensington (Sales) Ltd* [2004] EWCA Civ 47, [2004] 1 WLR 2775.

[16] Vehicle Excise and Registration Act 1994 (UK) s 21; Retention of Registration Marks Regulations 1993 (UK).

[17] *Cressman v Coys of Kensington (Sales) Ltd* [2004] EWCA Civ 47, [2004] 1 WLR 2775 [25] (Mance LJ; Wilson J and Thorpe LJ agreeing).

[18] *Black v S Freedman & Company* [1910] HCA 58, (1910) 12 CLR 105.

[19] ibid 110.

Putting to one side whether the proper restitutionary response was a trust,[20] the reason why Black and his wife (who was assumed to be innocent) were both liable to make restitution of the funds they held is best understood as unjust enrichment.[21] The unjust factor could only be the ignorance of the transaction by Black's employer. And neither Black nor his wife had any juristic reason to retain the money. The same approach was taken in *Shaw Building Group Pty Ltd v Narayan (No 2)*.[22] In that case, Mr Narayan used his authority as the financial controller of the plaintiff company to steal company funds, withdrawing them and using them for his own benefit. The Federal Court held that Mr Narayan was liable to make restitution of the money he had stolen as 'an independent restitutionary claim based upon unjust enrichment'.[23] The court held that although the claim was a personal one, it was another way of addressing the same issue which had been resolved in *Black* by the imposition of a trust.[24]

ii. Ignorance of the Plaintiff of an Unauthorised Use of the Plaintiff's Asset

A second category of ignorance concerns the ignorance of an unauthorised *use* of the plaintiff's assets by which the defendant is enriched. The classic obiter dictum recognising a claim for restitution of the value of the opportunity to use of a plaintiff's asset in circumstances of ignorance is that of Lord Mansfield in *Hambly v Trott*. In discussing actions which survive the death of a tortfeasor, Lord Mansfield said that although an action in tort would have been extinguished by the *actio personalis* rule:

> if a man take a horse from another, and bring him back again; an action for trespass would not lie against his executor ... but an action for the use and hire of the horse will lie against the executor.[25]

If the plaintiff is unaware that his horse has been taken and used, the action for the value of the opportunity to use and hire obtained by the defendant would be an action for unjust enrichment based on ignorance. A more modern Australian example is *Torpey Vander Have Pty Ltd v Mass Constructions Pty Ltd*.[26] Architects had prepared building plans for a development planned by a related company on a property it owned. When the company experienced financial difficulty, a liquidator was appointed and the property was sold at public auction. The purchaser developed the land using the architects' plans. The architects sought restitution of their professional fees from the purchaser. A majority of the New South Wales Court of Appeal dismissed their claim. Chief Justice Spigelman (with whom Foster AJA agreed) said 'In the absence of proof that it acquired a license to use the plans under the mortgage, it appears that the respondent received a benefit for which it did not pay.'[27] But Spigelman CJ held that there was a licence, so the purchaser had not been unjustly enriched. In dissent, Young J said that[28] 'the respondent held no such licence at the time of the trial

[20] See Ch 3 pp 36 and 39.

[21] See also *Evans v European Bank Ltd* [2004] NSWCA 82, (2004) 61 NSWLR 75 [113] (Spigelman CJ; Handley and Santow JJA agreeing), citing R Chambers, *Resulting Trusts* (Oxford, Clarendon Press, 1997) 22–23, 116–18.

[22] *Shaw Building Group Pty Ltd v Narayan (No 2)* [2015] FCA 585.

[23] ibid [37].

[24] ibid [41].

[25] *Hambly v Trott* (1776) 1 Cowp 371, 375, 98 ER 1136, 1138. Cf *Foster v Stewart* (1814) 3 M & S 191, 199, 105 ER 582, 585 (Lord Ellenborough CJ).

[26] *Torpey Vander Have Pty Ltd v Mass Constructions Pty Ltd* [2002] NSWCA 263, (2002) 55 IPR 542.

[27] ibid [34].

[28] ibid [113]–[114].

and the [architects] still held copyright and property in the drawings ... The grounds were thus made out for the claim that the respondent was unjustly enriched at the expense of the plaintiff.' Although the claim was refused on the facts, all of the judges recognised that the opportunity to use the architects' asset without their knowledge, and by which the respondent was enriched, was sufficient for a claim in unjust enrichment.

iii. Unauthorised Transactions Using the Plaintiff's Rights

A third example of an unjust enrichment claim based on ignorance is where the defendant receives an enrichment without the plaintiff's knowledge by a transaction involving an asset of the plaintiff's. In many older cases, claims for money had and received were allowed where the defendant had received money in exchange for an asset belonging to the plaintiff.[29] For instance, in *Oughton v Seppings*[30] a sheriff's officer mistakenly seized and sold Oughton's pony under a writ of *fi fa* against Winslove. It was held that Oughton was entitled to 'waive the tort' and bring a claim for money had and received for Winslove's proceeds of sale. The action was fictitiously described as an implied contract between Oughton and Winslove, but as we saw in Chapter 2, the implied contract fiction disguised an action for unjust enrichment in such cases.

An Australian example is *Creak v James Moore & Sons Pty Ltd.*[31] In that case, Watson stole cash and galvanised iron from his employer. The iron was sold to Creak and the proceeds deposited in Watson's bank account. Those funds were paid by the police to the employer. Despite receiving the proceeds, the employer also brought a claim against Creak for conversion of the iron. The question for the High Court was whether the employer could keep the proceeds from the sale of the iron and also sue for the loss suffered from the conversion of the iron. A majority of the High Court held that the employer could not sue for conversion. In the majority, the Chief Justice explained that the reason why the employer was entitled to the proceeds was because it had an equitable right to the proceeds. Watson's retention of the proceeds was 'unjustified'.[32] The unjust factor could only be the employer's ignorance of Watson's enrichment by an unauthorised transaction using the plaintiff's rights.

The landmark English decision in *Lipkin Gorman v Karpnale Ltd*[33] is another example of ignorance involving an unauthorised transaction with the plaintiff's assets. In that case, the House of Lords recognised that the action was based upon unjust enrichment. It will be recalled that Cass, a rogue partner of a firm of solicitors (Lipkin Gorman), withdrew £323,222 from the solicitors' client trust account. He deposited the money withdrawn into another account in his name, enriching himself by a debt from his bank through the unauthorised use of Lipkin Gorman's funds. That debt was then extinguished in exchange for cash which he gambled and lost at the Playboy Club (Karpnale). The solicitors succeeded in a claim against the Playboy Club for unjust enrichment. Although no unjust factor was

[29] *Lightly v Clouston* (1808) 1 Taunt 112, 127 ER 774; *Lamine v Dorell* (1705) 2 Ld Raym 1216, 92 ER 303; *Oughton v Seppings* (1830) 1 B & Ad 241, 109 ER 776; *King v Leith* (1787) 2 Term Rep 141, 100 ER 77; *Parker v Norton* (1796) 6 Term Rep 695, 101 ER 777; *Feltham v Terry* (1773) Lofft 207, 98 ER 613.

[30] *Oughton v Seppings* (1830) 1 B & Ad 241, 243, 109 ER 776, 777.

[31] *Creak v James Moore & Sons Pty Ltd* [1912] HCA 67, (1912) 15 CLR 426.

[32] ibid 432 (Griffith CJ).

[33] *Lipkin Gorman v Karpnale Ltd* [1991] 2 AC 548.

explicitly mentioned, the unjust factor must have been ignorance.[34] The solicitors were ignorant that money they had held for their clients had been taken without authority and used by a series of transactions to confer a benefit on the Playboy Club. Although it has not been analysed in great detail by any later judicial decision, the decision in *Lipkin Gorman* has been referred to with approval and applied in Australia.[35] An important part of the case was that Lipkin Gorman could negate any right that the Playboy Club asserted to retain the enrichment because gambling contracts were, at that time, void. Legislation in Victoria also reaches the same result. Section 2.6.3 of the Gambling Regulation Act 2003 (Vic)[36] provides that:

> If money is stolen or embezzled and paid to a person as or on account of a wager or bet, the person from whom it was stolen or embezzled may recover it, or a sum not exceeding its amount, in a court of competent jurisdiction from the person to whom it was paid.

Another example is *Vickery v JJP Custodians*.[37] In that case, JJP lent $50,000 to Christos. Christos was represented by his son, Donald, who purported to be Christos' attorney under power. The loan (principal and interest) was repaid by a payment of $77,400 to JJP from Dr Vickery, an associate of Donald's. However, Dr Vickery claimed he had been defrauded into paying the $77,400 and that it had not been paid to discharge Christos' debt. To complicate matters further, at trial Austin J found that Donald's power of attorney had been withdrawn at the time of the loan from JJP, so that the loan agreement did not bind Christos. Dr Vickery brought a claim against Christos in unjust enrichment. Because the legal nature of the agreement was a loan from JJP to *Donald*, and because Christos received no benefit from the loan, the claim failed. However, in obiter dicta, Austin J said that a claim for unjust enrichment by Dr Vickery might have succeeded if Donald had acted with his father's authority in taking the loan from JJP. The basis for such an action, Austin J explained, arises by analogy with mistaken payments. In other words, if a mistaken payment from A to B to C allows restitution, so too should restitution be allowed where a payment is made without authority to B who discharges a debt owed to C:

> If Donald had acted with his father's authority at all times, the case might have presented itself as a candidate for this kind of developmental analysis [unjust enrichment]. It would have been a case where A is induced by fraud to pay C, who appropriates the payment to discharge B's debt to C. The question would be whether, aided by principles of equity or the concept of unjust enrichment, the Court would allow recovery by A from B, although B is not the recipient of A's payment. In terms of unjust enrichment, B would have been enriched by the discharge of his debt, and it might be arguable that the enrichment was unjust, by analogy with cases on mistaken payments.[38]

[34] See P Birks, 'Misdirected Funds: Restitution from the Recipient' [1989] *Lloyd's Maritime and Commercial Law Quarterly* 296.

[35] *Spangaro v Corporate Investment Australia Funds Management Ltd* [2003] FCA 1025, (2003) 54 ATR 241; *Gertsch v Atsas* [1999] NSWSC 898, (1999) 10 BPR 18,431 [63] (Foster AJ); *Re Global Finance Group Pty Ltd* [2002] WASC 63, (2002) 26 WAR 385 [213] (McLure J); *Finlay v Silicon Industries Pty Ltd* [2003] SASC 236 [124] (Doyle CJ; Nyland and Lander JJ concurring); *Scenic Outlook Pty Ltd v Ocean Central Ltd* [2002] SASC 378 [80] (Judge Burley).

[36] Formerly the Lotteries Gaming and Betting Act 1966 (Vic), the equivalent section (s 67) of which is considered in *Davison Faulkner Pty Ltd v Totalizator Agency Board* [1971] VR 274. See also s 45 of the Unlawful Gambling Act 1998 (NSW), which, however, is confined to moneys stolen or misappropriated by a minor.

[37] *Vickery v JJP Custodians* [2002] NSWSC 782, (2002) 11 BPR 20, 333 [134].

[38] ibid [136].

E. An Unjust Factor of Ignorance in Equity

A controversial question is whether a claim can be brought in equity for restitution of unjust enrichment based on the unjust factor of ignorance. This question has already been answered where claims are brought by a company against a recipient of its assets. A claim brought by a company against a recipient of company assets is an equity claim. It was a claim brought in the Court of Chancery, which had jurisdiction over companies. As we have seen, these claims should be understood as part of the law of unjust enrichment, although the focus of these claims is rarely upon the ignorance or powerlessness of the impugned transaction on the part of the company (which is usually uncontroversial). Again, the focus is usually upon whether the transaction was authorised such that the recipient would have a right to retain the enrichment.

The question in equity becomes much more difficult when a trustee is involved. A common scenario is where a trustee pays trust funds to a third party without authority. Can a claim for unjust enrichment be brought by the beneficiary against the third party? The starting point is that the best-known claim that the beneficiary can bring against the third party is a claim for the equitable wrong of knowing receipt. This claim requires proof of a degree of fault or knowledge on the part of the recipient. The recipient is liable as a wrongdoer.[39]

It has been suggested that a difficulty with the recognition of a strict liability action in unjust enrichment is the existence of a fault requirement in the personal action for knowing receipt against a recipient wrongdoer. This requirement of knowledge has been long established. An example of the need to prove knowledge by the recipient is the decision in *Re Montagu's Settlement Trusts*.[40] In that case, trustees held chattels on trust for beneficiaries, who included the plaintiff, the eleventh Duke of Manchester. The trustees were required to select and make an inventory of the chattels after the ninth Duke died. In breach of trust, the chattels were released to the tenth Duke before the inventory was taken. The eleventh Duke brought an action in equity against the tenth Duke for receipt of his equitable property. It was held by Megarry VC that the tenth Duke was not liable, because he did not know that the chattels were subject to a trust.

The required degree of knowledge or fault on the part of the recipient has varied from case to case. Although Megarry VC in *Re Montagu's Settlement Trust* thought that only knowledge which amounted to dishonesty would suffice, other English cases have held that carelessness is sufficient.[41] The English courts appear to have settled on a requirement of 'unconscionable conduct' which could encompass either.[42] Australian courts have also insisted upon knowledge, although controversy remains about the required degree.[43]

The highest courts in Canada and Australia have both confronted, and rejected, arguments that the recipient of misdirected trust property should be strictly liable in unjust

[39] *Williams v Central Bank of Nigeria* [2014] UKSC 10, [2014] AC 1189 [31] (Lord Sumption JSC).

[40] *Re Montagu's Settlement Trusts* [1987] Ch 264.

[41] For instance *Belmont Finance Corporation v Williams Furniture Ltd (No 2)* [1980] 1 All ER 393; *International Sales and Agencies Ltd v Marcus* [1982] 3 All ER 551.

[42] *Bank of Credit and Commerce International (Overseas) Ltd v Akindele* [2001] Ch 437, 455 (Nourse LJ); *Arthur v The Attorney General of the Turks & Caicos Islands* [2012] UKPC 30 [33].

[43] *Grimaldi v Chameleon Mining NL (No 2)* [2012] FCAFC 6, (2012) 200 FCR 296 [263]–[264] (the Court).

enrichment without knowledge or fault. In Canada, this occurred in *Citadel General Assurance Co v Lloyds Bank Canada*.[44] An insurance company collected premiums for insurance policies and, after payment of commissions and claims, deposited the balance with Lloyds Bank Canada. The court found that the deposits with Lloyds Bank were held on trust for the underwriter, Citadel. In breach of trust, large sums were transferred from the insurance company's trust account with Lloyds Bank to its parent company, to reduce the overdraft of the parent company. The Supreme Court upheld the finding of the trial judge that the bank should have known that the transfer of the money from the insurance company to its parent was in breach of trust. An action by Citadel against the bank in unjust enrichment succeeded. Delivering the judgment of himself, Gonthier, Cory, McLachlin, Iacobucci and Major JJ, La Forest CJ explained that 'in restitutionary terms, there can be no doubt that the Bank received trust property for its own use and benefit'.[45] The Supreme Court of Canada held that restitutionary liability for receipt of the equitable property of another is not strict but requires constructive knowledge. This was satisfied because Lloyds Bank ought to have known that the transfers were in breach of trust.

In Australia, the rejection of strict liability occurred in *Farah Constructions Pty Ltd v Say-Dee Pty Ltd*.[46] In the circumstances of that case, the High Court of Australia rejected the coexistence of any strict liability action in unjust enrichment for receipt of misdirected trust assets.[47] The High Court said that the recognition of a liability in unjust enrichment was ahistorical and that in practice the recognition of a strict liability claim would

> erode the existing law, because it would tend to nullify the first limb [of *Barnes v Addy*]: for what plaintiff would wish to take on the burden of showing that the defendant had notice under the 'old' first limb if, by reliance on the new doctrine, that burden could be escaped and a contrary and even more onerous burden placed on the defendant?[48]

Despite this, however, there are significant reasons why a strict liability action for unjust enrichment should exist and why it would not nullify a *Barnes v Addy* action for knowing receipt against a defendant wrongdoer. One reason is that although there is no direct historical authority for a strict liability claim in unjust enrichment, there is substantial analogous authority that might support the recognition of a strict liability action in unjust enrichment for receipt of misdirected trust assets. Those analogies were partly what led Lord Millett to suggest, judicially, that such a claim should be recognised as well as, extrajudicially (following Professor Birks), Lord Millett, Lord Nicholls, Lord Hoffmann and Lord Walker.[49]

[44] *Citadel General Assurance Company v Lloyds Bank Canada* [1997] 3 SCR 805.

[45] ibid [30].

[46] *Farah Constructions Pty Ltd v Say-Dee Pty Ltd* [2007] HCA 22, (2007) 230 CLR 89 [140] (the Court).

[47] In other circumstances, see *Artcraft Pty Ltd v Dickson* [2014] SASC 108; *Fistar v Riverwood Legion and Community Club Ltd* [2016] NSWCA 81.

[48] *Farah Constructions Pty Ltd v Say-Dee Pty Ltd* [2007] HCA 22, (2007) 230 CLR 89 [153] (the Court).

[49] *Twinsectra Ltd v Yardley* [2002] UKHL 12, [2002] 2 AC 164 (Lord Millett). Extrajudicially: P Millett 'Proprietary Restitution' in S Degeling and J Edelman (eds), *Equity in Commercial Law* (Sydney, Lawbook Co, 2005); Lord Nicholls, 'Knowing Receipt: The Need for a New Landmark' in WR Cornish, R Nolan, J O'Sullivan and G Virgo (eds), *Restitution: Past, Present and Future: Essays in Honour of Gareth Jones* (Oxford, Hart Publishing, 1998); R Walker, 'Address—Dishonesty and Unconscionable Conduct in Commercial Life: Some Reflections on Accessory Liability and Knowing Receipt' (2005) 27 *Sydney Law Review* 187; L Hoffmann, 'The Redundancy of Knowing Assistance' in PBH Birks (ed), *The Frontiers of Liability*, vol 1 (Oxford, Oxford University Press, 1994) 29; P Birks, *An Introduction to the Law of Restitution*, rev edn (Oxford, Oxford University Press, 1989) 477–78; P Birks, 'Misdirected Funds: Restitution from the Recipient' [1989] *Lloyd's Maritime and Commercial Law Quarterly* 296; P Birks, 'Knowing Receipt: *Re Montagu's Settlement Trusts* Revisited' (2001) 1 *Global Jurist Advances* 20.

One analogy is with claims at common law based on tracing. An example is the case which recognised the law of unjust enrichment in England and which has been adopted in Australia. That case was considered above: *Lipkin Gorman v Karpnale Ltd*.[50] In that case, counsel for the Playboy Club submitted that liability could not be imposed because the club was an innocent recipient.[51] Counsel argued that the position in equity was that an innocent recipient of misappropriated trust funds is not liable so the same position should existed at common law.[52] This argument had particular force because the claim in *Lipkin Gorman* could also have been brought in equity. As Lord Goff observed, 'there is no doubt that, even if legal title to the money did vest in Cass immediately on receipt, nevertheless he would have held it on trust for his partners'.[53] The result in *Lipkin Gorman* was that the Playboy Club was liable. Counsel's argument can be turned on its head: why should the position in *equity* be any different? In other words, why should the Playboy Club be strictly liable to the partners of the law firm at common law but not in equity? Indeed, there were circumstances where the common law recognised and gave effect to a trust,[54] and this case might be best understood as another example of the common law giving effect to equitable rights. Although Lords Templeman and Goff held that Cass obtained title to the money he withdrew from the firm's account, Lord Templeman spoke throughout as Cass having obtained 'stolen' money, and reasoned that the Playboy Club should be liable in the same way as the High Court of Australia has held third party recipients of misdirected trust money liable.[55]

The second analogy which supports the recognition of a strict liability claim for unjust enrichment by the beneficiary of a trust is that equity already takes this stance in relation to claims by legatees against the innocent recipients of misdirected assets from an administered estate. In *Re Diplock*,[56] the executors of the deceased estate of Caleb Diplock mistakenly distributed the estate to certain charities, instead of the next of kin. Because their mistake was one of law and, at that time, mistakes of law did not allow restitution, the executors had no right of recovery against the charities. However, the Court of Appeal and House of Lords held that the innocent charities were strictly liable to make restitution of the money received to the true legatees subject to a restriction requiring exhaustion of claims against the personal representatives.[57] *Re Diplock* has been claimed to be analogous support for strict liability in unjust enrichment for all recipients of misdirected trust property.[58] There are differences between the claims. An expectancy from an unadministered estate

[50] *Lipkin Gorman v Karpnale Ltd* [1991] 2 AC 548.

[51] ibid 553: 'the club was an innocent recipient and had no knowledge that the money was stolen' (Lightman QC).

[52] ibid 554.

[53] ibid 572 (Lord Goff).

[54] *Winch v Keeley* (1787) 1 Term Rep 619, 623, 99 ER 1284, 1286 (Buller J and Ashurst J); *Scott v Surman* (1742) Willes 400, 402, 125 ER 1235, 1236 (Willes CJ); *Boddington v Castelli* (1853) 1 El & Bl 879, 885, 118 ER 665, 667 (Baron Parke).

[55] *Black v S Freedman & Company* [1910] HCA 58, (1910) 12 CLR 105.

[56] *Re Diplock; Diplock v Wintle* [1948] Ch 465. Upheld in the House of Lords: *Ministry of Health v Simpson* [1951] AC 251.

[57] *Ministry of Health v Simpson* [1951] AC 251, 266–67.

[58] P Birks, 'Misdirected Funds: Restitution from the Recipient' [1989] *Lloyd's Maritime and Commercial Law Quarterly* 296; P Birks, 'Gifts of Other People's Money' in PBH Birks (ed), *The Frontiers of Liability*, vol 1 (Oxford, Oxford University Press, 1994) 31; P Birks, 'Equity in the Modern Law: An Exercise in Taxonomy' (1996) 26 *University of Western Australia Law Review* 1, 72; P Birks, 'Property and Unjust Enrichment: Categorical Truths' [1997]

is not a beneficial interest in a trust. In 1965 the Privy Council held that a legatee under an unadministered estate had no proprietary interest.[59] But, in 1948, this point was not taken in the Court of Appeal or House of Lords. Much of the judgment in the Court of Appeal assumed that the beneficiaries did have an existing proprietary interest. For example, the Court of Appeal said that 'the payers in the present case (namely the executors) were handling not their own money but the money of others who had a proprietary interest unknown to and unrecognized by the executors'.[60] In later cases, the decision in *Re Diplock* has been thought to apply beyond the circumstances of deceased estates.[61]

However, even though there are arguments of principle and authority for the recognition of strict liability in unjust enrichment for receipt of misdirected trust assets, there is a significant reason why courts may be unlikely to *need* to recognise a strict liability claim based on the plaintiff's ignorance of a transaction that enriches a third party without juristic reason. This is because such an action will almost always be superfluous. In *Williams v Central Bank of Nigeria*, Lord Sumption (with whom Lord Hughes agreed) said that

> The essence of a liability to account on the footing of knowing receipt is that the defendant has accepted trust assets knowing that they were transferred to him in breach of trust and that he had no right to receive them. His possession is therefore at all times wrongful and adverse to the rights of both the true trustees and the beneficiaries ... There may also, in some circumstances, be a proprietary claim. But all this is simply the measure of the remedy. It does not make him a trustee.[62]

This passage from Lord Sumption JSC illustrates that other claims exist apart from a novel claim from unjust enrichment. We have already seen the potential for a claim for knowing receipt. The other claim mentioned is a strict liability 'proprietary' claim against the recipient of the trust asset if the asset or its proceeds remain in that person's hands.[63] This 'proprietary claim', described in Australia as 'orthodox',[64] leaves a potential need for a claim for unjust enrichment only where a trustee has transferred trust assets to the defendant recipient without authority *and* the defendant recipient no longer retains those assets or their traceable proceeds *and* the defendant recipient has no defence of change of position. But even in this very narrow circumstance, there may still be a recognised claim that a beneficiary could bring. The claim would be for restitution of the asset or its value based on the trustee's breach of fiduciary duty.[65] That claim would be properly brought by the trustee in breach (as joined by the beneficiary), or by a replacement trustee, to undo the consequences of a wrongful act. As a matter of principle, the existence of a claim against the recipient could have been left to the trustee or any replacement trustee. Indeed, for hundreds of years it was understood that a beneficiary did not have any direct action against a third party

New Zealand Law Review 623, 651–54. See also RP Austin, 'Constructive Trusts' in PD Finn (ed), *Essays in Equity* (Sydney, The Law Book Co Ltd, 1985) 217.

[59] *Commissioner of Stamp Duties (Queensland) v Livingston* [1965] AC 694, 712. But even after *Livingstone*, the result in *Re Diplock* can still be saved by the explanation given by Professor Birks: the money which the charities received was, as a matter of law, destined to go to the next of kin: P Birks, *Unjust Enrichment*, 2nd edn (Oxford, Oxford University Press, 2005) 76.

[60] *Re Diplock; Diplock v Wintle* [1948] Ch 465, 481. See also 517, 522, 525, 547.

[61] *GL Baker Ltd v Medway Building and Supplies Ltd* [1958] 1 WLR 1216; *Butler v Broadhead* [1975] Ch 97.

[62] *Williams v Central Bank of Nigeria* [2014] UKSC 10, [2014] AC 1189 [31].

[63] *Arthur v The Attorney General of the Turks & Caicos Islands* [2012] UKPC 30 [34]; *Fistar v Riverwood Legion and Community Club Ltd* [2016] NSWCA 81.

[64] *Farah Constructions Pty Ltd v Say-Dee Pty Ltd* [2007] HCA 22, (2007) 230 CLR 89 [140] (the Court).

[65] *Pitt v Holt* [2013] UKSC 26, [2013] 2 AC 108 [73] (Lord Walker JSC).

unless the beneficiary was able to show that the third party's receipt or conduct has constituted the third party a trustee for the beneficiary. For instance, in *Harrison v Pryse*[66] Lord Hardwicke had said that the trustee must be a defendant where a claim is brought following the conveyance to a third party of real estate held on trust. The erosion of this principle may have come as a consequence of the suggestion by the Lord Chancellor that the same principle did not apply to chattels.[67] A century later, in *Barnes v Addy*,[68] Lord Selborne said that a third party would be liable if he 'receive[d] and bec[a]me chargeable with some part of the trust property'. There was no longer any mention of the requirement that the trustee be joined to the action.

If the very narrow circumstance were to arise in which a strict liability claim for unjust enrichment were needed, then that claim would be distinct from a claim, based on wrongdoing, which alleged knowing receipt. One reason is that the action for knowing receipt might entitle the plaintiff beneficiary to recover consequential losses to the trust assets or to disgorge profits made by the defendant. An action for restitution of unjust enrichment would be confined to the enrichment of the defendant the value of which might be minimal or non-existent, or the receipt might not have been in a personal capacity, or which might be subject to change of position. Hence, it is unsurprising that a claim for knowing receipt can succeed where a claim for unjust enrichment fails.[69]

III. Powerlessness

A. The Meaning of Powerlessness

Professor Birks gave a simple example of powerlessness where 'I tear your purse from your grip, overcoming by force your physical power to prevent me'.[70] This is not a case of duress, because my intention to give you the purse has not been coerced by any pressure. I did not intend to give you the purse at all. This is the basic model of a claim based on powerlessness.

The most common instances involving claims for restitution of a benefit conferred as a result of powerlessness are cases of where the powerlessness comes as a result of the compulsion of the law. For instance, suppose A is legally compelled to pay money to B in order to discharge B's debt to C. The need for a plaintiff to negate a defendant's right to retain the benefit will mean that these claims will often fail, if brought against B. This is because B has a right to retain the benefit due to the court order. But what about a claim brought by A against C?

An example is *Exall v Partridge*.[71] Exall had left his carriage at Partridge's premises. Exall's carriage was seized by Partridge's landlord as distress for Partridge's failure to pay rent. Exall could only recover his carriage by paying the arrears of rent. Exall paid them and then sued

[66] *Harrison v Pryse* (1740) Barn Ch 324, 27 ER 664.
[67] ibid.
[68] *Barnes v Addy* (1874) LR 9 Ch App 244, 251–52.
[69] *Australasian Annuities Pty Ltd (in liq) (recs and mgrs apptd) v Rowley Super Fund Pty Ltd* [2015] VSCA 9, (2015) 318 ALR 302.
[70] P Birks, *An Introduction to the Law of Restitution*, rev edn (Oxford, Oxford University Press, 1989) 141.
[71] *Exall v Partridge* (1799) 8 Term Rep 308, 101 ER 1405.

Partridge for restitution of the arrears paid. The court held that, in the language of the old money counts of *indebitatus assumpsit*, the money was paid to the use of Partridge. Justice Grose said that '[Exall] could not have relieved himself from the distress without paying the rent: it was not therefore a voluntary, but a compulsory payment'.[72] In the words of a later case 'If a party making the payment is obliged to pay, in order to obtain possession of things to which he is entitled, the money so paid is not a voluntary, but a compulsory payment.'[73] Exall's payment to Partridge's landlord was not an unjust enrichment. Partridge's landlord had a right to retain the payment as a discharge of Partridge's debt. But Exall was powerless to prevent the transactions by which Partridge was enriched (the seizure and sale of the carriage). Exall did not voluntarily choose to enable the transaction that enriched Partridge. If he had not made the payment he would still have been powerless to prevent the enrichment of Partridge by the sale of his carriage, because the landlord had the power to sell the carriage and to use the proceeds to pay off Partridge's debt.[74] From Exall's perspective, such a situation is materially indistinguishable from his purse being torn from his grip by Partridge.

In England, actions for contribution or recoupment should be understood in the same way. They have been recognised as restitutionary[75] and based upon unjust enrichment.[76] For a time, Australian authority also generally supported that position.[77] But in *Bofinger v Kingsway Group Ltd*[78] the High Court emphasised that for cases of contribution 'the concept of unjust enrichment [is] not a principle supplying a sufficient premise for direct application in a particular case'. This does not deny that the doctrines can fall within the *category* of unjust enrichment.[79] Indeed, the High Court made the same point in a case involving a claim for restitution for a payment made by mistake of fact[80] and it is unlikely that the court, by these remarks, intended to reject a mistake of fact as falling within the law of unjust enrichment.[81] The reason for the importance of the note of caution by the High Court is the same as with ignorance cases. The unjust factor is rarely an issue in cases of

[72] ibid 311, 1406. See also *Johnson v Royal Mail Steam Packet Company* (1867) LR 3 CP 38, 44 (Willes J, delivering the judgment of the Court).

[73] *Shaw v Woodcock* (1827) 7 B & C 73, 85; 108 ER 652, 657 (Holroyd J; Littledale J concurring). See also 84; 657 (Bayley J).

[74] *Edmunds v Wallingford* (1885) 14 QBD 811.

[75] *Westdeutsche Landesbank Girozentrale v Islington London Borough Council* [1996] UKHL 12, 52, [1996] AC 669, 727 (Lord Woolf); *Berghoff Trading Ltd v Swinbrook Developments Ltd* [2009] EWCA Civ 413, [2009] 2 Lloyd's Rep 233 [24] (Rix LJ).

[76] *Dubai Aluminium Co Ltd v Salaam* [2002] UKHL 48, [2003] 2 AC 366 [76] (Lord Hobhouse).

[77] *Fitzpatrick v Waterstreet* (NSWCA, 17 December 1998) (Mason P); *Trade Practices Commission v Manfal Pty Ltd (No 3)* [1991] FCA 650, (1991) 33 FCR 382; *Austotel Management Pty Ltd v Jamieson* (FCA, 20 December 1995); *Halgido Pty Ltd v DG Capital Co Ltd* [1996] FCA 1123, (1996) 34 ATR 582; *Balkin v Peck* (1998) 43 NSWLR 706, 712 (Mason P; Priestley JA and Sheppard AJA concurring); *James Hardie & Co Pty Ltd v Wyong Shire Council* [2000] NSWCA 107, (2000) 48 NSWLR 679 [36] (Giles JA); *Cockburn v GIO Finance Ltd (No 2)* [2001] NSWCA 177, (2001) 51 NSWLR 624 [24] (Mason P; Davies AJA and Ipp AJA concurring); *AMP Workers' Compensation Services (NSW) Ltd v QBE Insurance Ltd* [2001] NSWCA 267, (2001) 53 NSWLR 35 [22] (Handley JA; Mason P and Beazley JA agreeing); *Belan v Casey* [2003] NSWSC 159, (2003) 57 NSWLR 670 [71] (Campbell J); *Lukey v Corporate Investment Australia Funds Management Pty Ltd* [2005] FCA 298 [335] (Emmett J).

[78] *Bofinger v Kingsway Group Ltd* [2009] HCA 44, (2009) 239 CLR 269 [85] (the Court). See also *Friend v Brooker* [2009] HCA 21, (2009) 239 CLR 129 [7]–[8] (French CJ, Gummow, Hayne and Bell JJ).

[79] *Burke v LFOT Pty Ltd* [2002] HCA 17, (2002) 209 CLR 282 [111]–[112] (Kirby J).

[80] *Australian Financial Services and Leasing Pty Ltd v Hills Industries Ltd* [2014] HCA 14, (2014) 253 CLR 560 [78] (Hayne, Crennan, Kiefel, Bell and Keane JJ).

[81] See Ch 2 pp 25–26.

powerlessness. The focus is almost invariably on whether the defendant has a right to retain the enrichment. Any attempt to apply directly principles of unjust enrichment might distract from the central importance in these cases of the enquiry into whether the defendant has a right to retain some or all of the benefit.

B. The Focus upon the Right to Retain in Powerlessness Cases

Like cases involving the unjust factor of ignorance of the transaction, there is rarely any dispute in cases where there is no intention to benefit a defendant that the plaintiff was powerless to prevent the transfer of the benefit. As explained above, cases involving ignorance of a transaction by a company will rarely involve dispute about the company's knowledge. The focus will be on whether the transaction was authorised. The same is true in cases of powerlessness. An example is the decisions of the New South Wales Supreme Court in *Break Fast Investments Pty Ltd v Giannopoulos (Nos 5 and 6)*.[82] Those decisions involved a director of Break Fast who made payments of $317,000 to Mr Giannopoulos without authority. The trial judge, Black J, explained that the claim for unjust enrichment depended on an allegation that the payments were made without the authority of the company.[83] The payments were also found to have been made without the knowledge of the other director.[84] There was, therefore, no dispute that the company was powerless to prevent the payments once the lack of a right to retain was proved.

Similarly, in the cases of recoupment or contribution considered below, there is almost never any dispute concerning whether the plaintiff was powerless to make the contribution. Almost invariably, the plaintiff will have been compelled, or be liable to be compelled, to engage in the transaction that enriches the defendant by operation of the legal process. The real question in these cases focuses upon the value of the benefit that the defendant has a right to retain. That is a question that is not susceptible to precise calculation. In *Mahoney v McManus*[85] Gibbs CJ (with whom Murphy and Aickin JJ agreed) said that the operation of contribution and recoupment 'should not be defeated by too technical an approach'.

C. Common Instances of Powerlessness: Principles of Contribution and Recoupment

This section considers the operation of common law and equitable principles of contribution and recoupment. It is far from a comprehensive examination of those doctrines which are now heavily based in statute in most jurisdictions. The purpose of the examination at common law and in equity is merely to illustrate another example of recognition at general law of an unjust factor based in notions of powerlessness. The statutes about which contribution is usually concerned have altered some of the common law and equitable rules

[82] *Break Fast Investments Pty Ltd v Giannopoulos (No 5)* [2011] NSWSC 1508, and *Break Fast Investments Pty Ltd v Giannopoulos (No 6)* [2012] NSWSC 286.

[83] *Break Fast Investments Pty Ltd v Giannopoulos (No 5)* [2011] NSWSC 1508 [34].

[84] ibid [39].

[85] *Mahoney v McManus* [1981] HCA 54, (1981) 180 CLR 370, 378 [18]; *Lavin v Toppi* [2015] HCA 4, (2015) 254 CLR 459 [34] (the Court).

but an understanding of the underlying principle of unjust enrichment may still assist. For instance, historically where the shared burden of the plaintiff and the defendant was a common liability arising from a judgment debt for wrongdoing, it was thought that no contribution was possible.[86] In *James Hardie & Co Pty Ltd v Wyong Shire Council*[87] Giles JA (with whom Heydon JA agreed) considered the New South Wales statute (one of many of which followed the United Kingdom model in altering the law),[88] and held that the statutory alteration made this area of contribution consistent with the other common law and equity cases which are 'now being brought within the concept of unjust enrichment'.[89] In that case, the words in the legislation permitting recovery of 'damage' from the other tortfeasor were not confined to recovery of part of the damages but included restitution of that part of the legal costs incurred in defending the action, because by defending the claim the other tortfeasor was enriched: 'If the plaintiff had sued the contributing tortfeasor instead of, or as well as, the tortfeasor found liable, the contributing tortfeasor would have been ordered to pay the costs.'[90]

Lord Mansfield said that cases arising from recoupment or contribution were based upon principles of natural justice,[91] a label he also applied to unjust factors such as mistake, failure of consideration, and duress.[92] The High Court of Australia has also reiterated that the source of recoupment and contribution lies in natural justice.[93] Cases like *Exall* (discussed above) share common features with the contribution cases which are sometimes described as 'recoupment' because the contribution is sought for 100 per cent recoupment of the amount paid. The common elements are that (1) the defendant has been enriched by the plaintiff's payment or performance of an obligation; (2) the obligation of the plaintiff to pay or perform work for the defendant's creditor is secondary to the defendant's obligation; and (3) the plaintiff is lawfully compelled to pay the defendant's debt or perform the defendant's obligation. The classic statement of principle that underlies these cases was made by Cockburn CJ in *Moule v Garrett*, who said that:

> Where the plaintiff has been compelled by law to pay, or, being compellable by law, has paid money which the defendant was ultimately liable to pay, so that the latter obtains the benefit of the payment by the discharge of his liability; under such circumstances the defendant is held indebted to the plaintiff in the amount.[94]

Very closely related to cases of restitution for recoupment is another type of powerlessness described in the cases as 'contribution'. To reiterate, recoupment is sometimes also described as a contribution of 100 per cent of the liability. The concept of contribution was explained by Willes J in *Moule v Garrett*:[95] 'where two persons are under an obligation to

[86] *Merryweather v Nixan* (1799) 8 Term Rep 186, 101 ER 1337.
[87] *James Hardie & Co Pty Ltd v Wyong Shire Council* [2000] NSWCA 107, (2000) 48 NSWLR 679.
[88] Law Reform (Miscellaneous Provisions) Act 1946 (NSW) s 5.
[89] *James Hardie & Co Pty Ltd v Wyong Shire Council* [2000] NSWCA 107, (2000) 48 NSWLR 679 [36].
[90] *James Hardie & Co Pty Ltd v Wyong Shire Council* [2000] NSWCA 107, (2000) 48 NSWLR 679 [40].
[91] *Godin v London Assurance Company* (1758) 1 Burr 489, 492, 97 ER 419, 420.
[92] *Moses v Macferlan* (1760) 2 Burr 1005, 1012, 97 ER 676, 681.
[93] *Albion Insurance Co Ltd v Government Insurance Office (NSW)* [1969] HCA 55, (1969) 121 CLR 342, 349–50 [5] (Kitto J); *Mahoney v McManus* [1981] HCA 54, (1981) 180 CLR 370, 378 [18] (Gibbs CJ; Murphy and Aickin JJ concurring); *Friend v Brooker* [2009] HCA 21, (2009) 239 CLR 129 [38] (French CJ, Gummow, Hayne and Bell JJ); *Lavin v Toppi* [2015] HCA 4, (2015) 254 CLR 459 [34] (the Court).
[94] *Moule v Garrett* (1872) LR 7 Ex 101, 104.
[95] ibid 103.

the same performance ... if both share the benefit which forms the consideration they must divide the burden'. The difference from recoupment is that in cases of contribution the liability of the plaintiff is not secondary to that of the defendant. In cases of recoupment, the plaintiff is entitled to restitution of the full value of the payment because that is the enrichment of the defendant whose debt is the primary debt. But in contribution cases the liability is joint and the plaintiff is only entitled to restitution of part of the value.

i. Principles of Recoupment

We have seen that there are three requirements for recoupment. As the High Court of Australia has emphasised, it is necessary that (1) the defendant is enriched ('derive[s] a benefit')[96] by the plaintiff's payment or performance of an obligation; (2) the obligation of the plaintiff to pay or perform work for the defendant's creditor is secondary to the defendant's obligation; and (3) the plaintiff is lawfully compelled to pay the defendant's debt or perform the defendant's obligation.

There are some difficult issues that arise in relation to enrichment (requirement (1)). The enrichment requirement usually means that the defendant's liability must have been discharged, or will be discharged by the plaintiff's performance or payment.[97] At common law, before restitution was awarded it was necessary for the plaintiff to have paid the money or performed the service.[98] But, prior to payment, equity granted a declaration of entitlement to restitution *quia timet* ('because he fears') which required the defendant to make restitution as soon as payment was made by the plaintiff.[99] This shows that the defendant's *liability* to make restitution existed from the moment that the creditor's right of recoupment was triggered even if the defendant's *duty* to make restitution did not arise until the plaintiff had actually made the payment.

Another difficult issue that can arise in relation to enrichment occurs in cases where a plaintiff attempts to pay off the defendant's debt without the defendant's knowledge or authority. This will not usually discharge the debt,[100] so it is necessary to show some other basis upon which it can be said that the payment enriched the defendant such as the defendant's choosing to take the benefit of the plaintiff's payment.[101]

The second requirement (ie (2) above) concerns the difference between enrichment in powerlessness cases of 'recoupment' and enrichment in powerlessness cases of 'contribution'. Where the liability of the plaintiff is secondary to that of the defendant, the defendant is

[96] *Lavin v Toppi* [2015] HCA 4, (2015) 254 CLR 459 [45] (the Court).

[97] *Esso Petroleum Co Ltd v Hall Russell & Co Ltd* [1989] AC 643, 663 (Lord Goff; Lord Templeman agreeing). See further Ch 4 p 57.

[98] *Walker v Bowry* [1924] HCA 28, (1924) 35 CLR 48; *Albion Insurance Co Ltd v Government Insurance Office (NSW)* [1969] HCA 55, (1969) 121 CLR 342, 351 [6] (Kitto J).

[99] *McLean v Discount & Finance Ltd* [1939] HCA 38, (1939) 64 CLR 312, 343 (Starke J).

[100] *Vickery v JJP Custodians* [2002] NSWSC 782, (2002) 11 BPR 20, 333 [76] (Austin J) citing *City Bank of Sydney v McLaughlin* [1909] HCA 78, (1909) 9 CLR 615, 633 (Isaacs J); *Lucas v Wilkinson* (1856) 1 H & N 420, 156 ER 1265; *Re Rowe* [1904] 2 KB 483; *Smith v Cox* [1940] 2 KB 558; *Guardian Ocean Cargoes Ltd v Banco do Brazil SA* [1991] 2 Lloyd's Rep 68, 87–88 (Hirst J); cf *Hirachand Punamchand v Temple* [1911] 2 KB 330. For a detailed analysis of the rules of when a payment to another's creditor discharges another's debt see C Mitchell, *The Law of Contribution and Reimbursement* (Oxford, Oxford University Press, 2003) 175–82.

[101] See Ch 4 p 71; *Cheeseman v Industries Assistance Board* (1926) 29 WALR 1; *Johnston v Arnaboldi* [1990] 2 Qd R 138; K Mason and J Carter, *Restitution Law in Australia* (Sydney, Butterworths, 1995) 261–63, para 846. Cf *City Bank of Sydney v McLaughlin* [1909] HCA 78, (1909) 9 CLR 615, 625.

enriched by the full value of the plaintiff's payment (recoupment). Where the obligations are joint and co-ordinate, the enrichment of the defendant is only to the extent to which the obligation should be borne by the defendant (contribution). The most common example of recoupment is suretyship. A guarantor who is legally compelled to discharge the debt of a primary debtor is entitled to full restitution from the debtor: 'A right of indemnity is a right of restitution'.[102]

It is the third requirement that establishes the unjust factor of 'powerlessness'. There is a distinction between a surety who is compelled to pay a principal debt and a surety who voluntarily discharges the debt. Restitution is allowed in the first case but not in the second. In the first case, the plaintiff is powerless to prevent the enrichment of the defendant. Her liability was only ever secondary to the defendant's liability; she intended to ensure that the creditor was paid but she did not intend to enrich the defendant. A difficult intermediate situation is where the plaintiff-surety voluntarily, and without request, takes on liability as a guarantor. Although the plaintiff may be later legally compelled to pay the primary debt, one English case, *Owen v Tate,*[103] has held that a plaintiff's assumption of suretyship without request by the primary debtor, and without any necessity to assume it, meant that the plaintiff's payment was 'voluntary'; he was not powerlessness to prevent the defendant's (primary debtor's) enrichment. Although this case has been referred to with approval in Australia,[104] *Owen v Tate* has been heavily criticised and is inconsistent with obiter dicta that deny the need for a request by the primary debtor.[105] As we saw above, such a request should not be necessary because the plaintiff may intend to act as a surety, and accept *secondary* liability, yet not intend to enrich the defendant. However, despite the controversial result, the reasoning of each of their Lordships focused upon the voluntary act of the plaintiff and rightly emphasised that the underlying inquiry is not the legal compulsion behind the payment from the plaintiff but that the plaintiff was powerless to prevent the transaction by which the defendant was enriched.

All that has been said so far in relation to payments of money applies equally to compelled performance of a *service*. In *Gebhardt v Saunders,*[106] the plaintiff was a tenant who was legally compelled by the Health Authority to carry out work to fix a blocked drain in his premises. The blockage was caused by a structural defect in the premises, which was the primary responsibility of the defendant landlord. The plaintiff was entitled to recover from the landlord for the performance of a service which discharged the landlord's liability. In contrast, in *Macclesfield Corp v Great Central Railway,*[107] a canal company had constructed a canal pursuant to a private Act of Parliament. The construction had involved building a bridge, which later fell into disrepair. The plaintiff highway authority requested the canal company to repair the bridge but the canal company refused. The highway authority then repaired the bridge itself and claimed restitution of the cost of repair. The Court of Appeal

[102] *Owen v Tate* [1976] QB 402, 409.

[103] *Owen v Tate* [1976] QB 402.

[104] *Re Gasbourne Pty Ltd* [1984] VR 801, 847–49 (Nicholson J).

[105] *Re A Debtor (No 627 of 1936)* [1937] Ch 156, 166 (Greene LJ; Romer LJ concurring); *Anson v Anson* [1953] 1 QB 636, 642–43 (Pearson J). It is also inconsistent with English legislation not cited to the court, the Mercantile Law Amendment Act 1856 (UK).

[106] *Gebhardt v Saunders* [1892] 2 QB 452. Referred to with approval in *Re Gasbourne Pty Ltd* [1984] VR 801, 844 (Nicholson J).

[107] *Macclesfield Corporation v Great Central Railway* [1911] 2 KB 528.

held that it was not entitled to restitution because there was no obligation for the highway company to make the repairs and therefore its act was voluntary;[108] it was not powerless to prevent the transaction that enriched the defendant.

ii. Principles of Contribution

Consider, for example, a judgment debt in tort where two tortfeasors, A and B, are found to be jointly and severally liable for a tort. Although the judgment creditor can call upon the plaintiff, tortfeasor A, to pay the whole of the debt the defendant, tortfeasor B, is partly responsible for the judgment debt liability. The assessment of the degree of responsibility and the extent to which contribution must be made is referred to by courts as the 'practical burden' or 'proper share'.[109] When P's payment to the creditor discharges D's debt, P enriches D to the extent of the discharge of that 'practical burden'. The payment to the creditor is intended (and legally compelled), but there is no intention to benefit by the impugned transaction the other judgment debtor whose debt is extinguished and who is enriched to the value of his proper burden.[110]

Like cases of recoupment, something more is also required than the fact 'that the claimant's payment has benefited or relieved the defendant financially'.[111] The requirements of an action for contribution are that the shared burden of the plaintiff and defendant of a common or co-ordinate liability is discharged by the plaintiff as a result of legal compulsion to enter into a transaction in circumstances in which it cannot be said that the plaintiff intended to benefit the defendant by that act.[112] Like recoupment, contribution claims can be brought at common law as well as *quia timet* in equity. They can be brought against a co-surety,[113] a joint contractor,[114] a partner in common partnership,[115] a co-trustee,[116] a co-director,[117] a co-owner[118] and co-insurers.[119] Again, the *quia timet* nature of an action means that the defendant's *liability* to make restitution exists from the moment that the creditor's right of recoupment is triggered even if the defendant's *duty* to make restitution does not arise until the plaintiff had actually made the payment. This is why a creditor

[108] ibid 536 (Vaughan Williams LJ), 539 (Farwell LJ), 540 (Kennedy LJ).

[109] *Davies v Humphreys* (1840) 6 M & W 153, 168–69, 151 ER 316, 367–68 (Parke B); *Dimdore v Leventhal* (1936) 36 SR (NSW) 378, 385 (Jordan CJ; Davidson and Stephen JJ concurring); *Albion Insurance Co Ltd v Government Insurance Office (NSW)* [1969] HCA 55, (1969) 121 CLR 342, 351 [6] (Kitto J); *Mahoney v McManus* [1981] HCA 54, (1981) 180 CLR 370, 376 [14] (Gibbs CJ; Murphy and Aickin JJ agreeing).

[110] 'The right arises at law when "one of several persons has paid more than his proper share towards discharging a common obligation"': *Albion Insurance Co Ltd v Government Insurance Office (NSW)* [1969] HCA 55, (1969) 121 CLR 342, 351 [6] (Kitto J).

[111] *Cockburn v GIO Finance Ltd (No 2)* [2001] NSWCA 177, (2001) 51 NSWLR 624 [30] (Mason P; Davies AJA and Ipp AJA concurring).

[112] *Albion Insurance Co Ltd v Government Insurance Office (NSW)* [1969] HCA 55, (1969) 121 CLR 342, 351–52 [6] (Kitto J).

[113] *Mahoney v McManus* [1981] HCA 54, (1981) 180 CLR 370.

[114] *Bartels v Behm* (1990) 19 NSWLR 257, 260 (Young J).

[115] Partnership Act 1892 (NSW) s 9; Partnership Act 1891 (Qld) s 12; Partnership Act 1891 (SA) s 9; Partnership Act 1891 (Tas) s 14; Partnership Act 1958 (Vic) s 13; Partnership Act 1895 (WA) s 16.

[116] *Chillingworth v Chambers* [1896] 1 Ch 685.

[117] *Ramskill v Edwards* (1885) 31 Ch D 100; *Cummings v Lewis* (1993) 41 FCR 559, 594–99 (Cooper J).

[118] *Dimdore v Leventhal* (1936) 36 SR (NSW) 378, 385 (Jordan CJ; Davidson and Stephen JJ concurring).

[119] *Albion Insurance Co Ltd v Government Insurance Office (NSW)* [1969] HCA 55, (1969) 121 CLR 342.

cannot defeat the plaintiff's existing power to obtain restitution from the defendant by subsequently undertaking not to sue the defendant.[120]

IV. Anti-Beneficial Basis

We have seen that the generic group of unjust factors described as 'no intention to benefit' include cases where a plaintiff is wholly ignorant of the transaction that enriches the defendant. She has no intention to enter the transaction because she never had an opportunity to consider the matter. We also saw that in cases of powerlessness, the plaintiff is allowed restitution where she has no intention to benefit the defendant through the impugned transaction but was legally compelled to pay a third party which directly enriched the defendant. If the plaintiff's act is voluntary, she is not powerless to prevent the defendant's enrichment because the enrichment is a consequence of her freely intended act. Unlike ignorance or powerlessness, the third unjust factor based upon no intention to benefit describes cases in which the plaintiff's act *was* voluntary. However, in these cases the very basis of the plaintiff's entry into the transaction was that the defendant would not benefit from it.

The usual legal answer where a plaintiff enters a transaction with the defendant on the manifest basis that the defendant will not benefit from it is that an express trust is created.[121] The defendant is not unjustly enriched because there is a juristic reason upon which the defendant holds the benefit, namely as an express trustee. But, exceptionally, cases arise where no express trust is created. In those cases, the defendant can be unjustly enriched by the receipt of the benefit through the impugned transaction. If a plaintiff is entitled to restitution for a transaction where he intends the defendant to benefit on some basis or condition which fails then the plaintiff should also be entitled to restitution where he never intends the defendant to benefit from the transaction at all. Also, like cases of failure of consideration, a basis that the defendant will not benefit from the transaction will need to be shared. Otherwise the plaintiff is simply taking a risk that the defendant will not benefit from the transfer. In other words, the manifested conduct of both the defendant and the plaintiff must show that the basis of the transaction with the defendant was that the defendant must not benefit from it.

An example is the decision in *Vandervell v Inland Revenue Commissioners*.[122] In that case a trustee company was given a valuable option to hold on trust. But the objects of the trust were not defined, so the trust failed. A majority of the House of Lords held that the benefit of the option should result back to the settlor by a resulting trust. Lord Reid dissented, because he considered that there was an intention that the trust company benefit from the use of the option. However, Lord Reid explained that the contrary argument for the Inland Revenue Commissioners was that 'there was no intention that the trust company or any of its three directors and shareholders should gain financially from the option and therefore the company was not intended to take beneficially'.[123] As a matter of principle, the reason

120 *Lavin v Toppi* [2015] HCA 4, (2015) 254 CLR 459.
121 *George v Webb* [2011] NSWSC 1608 [1]–[15], [258]–[283] (Ward J).
122 *Vandervell v Inland Revenue Commissioners* [1966] UKHL 3, [1967] 2 AC 291.
123 ibid 308.

why the resulting trust arose in the case was to prevent the unjust enrichment of the trustee company. The underlying right to restitution in these cases is stronger than cases of failure of consideration, where it is intended that the defendant benefit from a transfer, although that intention is conditional or qualified on some basis that fails. In these cases there is never any intention that the defendant benefit from the transfer.

In Australia, the leading example is the decision of the High Court in *Nelson v Nelson.*[124] In that case, Mrs Nelson transferred property into the names of her children so that she would be eligible for a subsidised government loan. When her children refused to return the property to her, she sought a declaration that they held the property on resulting trust for her. On one view, the case can be seen as one where the resulting trust gives effect to the express intention of Mrs Nelson that her children hold the property on trust. On another view, perhaps due to the express trust failing, the case is one where the resulting trust is a response to unjust enrichment because Mrs Nelson 'had no intention to confer on her children any beneficial interest in the ... property or in the proceeds of sale'.[125] Justices Deane and Gummow quoted from Scott and Fratcher, that 'If A cannot recover the property, B keeps it and is thereby [unjustly] enriched.'[126] Justice Toohey also spoke of the consideration of 'preventing injustice and the enrichment of one party at the expense of the other'.[127]

Another example is *Air Jamaica Ltd v Charlton.*[128] In that case, a company had established a pension plan for its employees in which substantial funds had accrued. Upon the sale by the government of its controlling interest in the company, the employees were made redundant and the plan was discontinued. Clause 13(ii) of the pension scheme created a trust of the contribution funds to the employees if the plan were discontinued. Clause 4 provided that no money contributed by the company was, under any circumstances, to be repaid to the company. The Privy Council held that clause 13(ii) was void in perpetuity and, notwithstanding the company's expressed intention in clause 4 that trust funds were not to be repaid to it, the funds were held on trust for the company when the clause 13(ii) trust failed. Plainly the company did not intend to create a trust for itself.[129] The trust arose because it did not intend to benefit the administrators of the pension plan through the impugned transaction who were the purported legal owners. As Lord Millett said in delivering the advice of the Privy Council:

> [A resulting trust] arises whether or not the transferor intended to retain a beneficial interest—he almost always does not—since it responds to the absence of any intention on his part to pass a beneficial interest to the recipient. It may arise even where the transferor positively wished to part with the beneficial interest[.][130]

In each of these three cases (*Vandervell, Nelson,* and *Air Jamaica*) the enrichment of the defendant was reversed by an order that the defendant hold rights on trust for the plaintiff. However, no other order was sought. The only order sought by the plaintiff was a trust. In other words, the plaintiffs did not seek an order in any of those cases that the defendants

[124] *Nelson v Nelson* [1995] HCA 25, (1995) 184 CLR 538.
[125] ibid 549 [33] (Deane and Gummow JJ), 586–87 [16] (Toohey J).
[126] ibid 564 [83].
[127] ibid 597 [45].
[128] *Air Jamaica Ltd v Charlton* [1999] 1 WLR 1399.
[129] *Re Vandervell's Trusts (No 2)* [1974] Ch 269.
[130] *Air Jamaica Ltd v Charlton* [1999] 1 WLR 1399, 1412. See also *Twinsectra Ltd v Yardley* [2002] UKHL 12, [2002] 2 AC 164 [92] (Lord Millett).

make restitution of the enrichment in the form of the *value* received rather than the *rights* received. As we saw in Chapter 3, an order for restitution only of the value is much more easily justified.[131]

V. Conclusion

The last five chapters have focused upon different unjust factors. Chapters 8, 9, 10 and 11 were all concerned with circumstances in which the plaintiff's intention to enter into the transaction that enriched the defendant was impaired, such as by mistake (Chapter 8), duress or illegitimate pressure (Chapter 9) or undue influence (Chapter 10). Chapter 11 was concerned with circumstances in which the plaintiff's intention to enter the transaction that enriched the defendant was qualified or conditional and where the qualification or condition failed. This chapter was concerned with circumstances in which the plaintiff had no intention to benefit the defendant by the impugned transaction at all. We saw that the cases recognise three unjust factors that arise in these circumstances of no intention to benefit: where the plaintiff is wholly ignorant of the defendant's enrichment at his expense; where the plaintiff is powerless to prevent the defendant's enrichment at his expense; and where the plaintiff transferred value to the defendant on the basis that the defendant would not benefit from it.

In each of these unjust factors the plaintiff has a stronger moral claim for relief than in cases of impaired intention. A plaintiff's claim to restitution of value transferred to a defendant from his assets without his knowledge (ignorance) is a stronger claim to restitution than in the case in which the defendant is enriched from his assets as a result of his mistaken payment. A plaintiff's claim to restitution of value transferred to a defendant from his assets which he is powerless to prevent is a stronger claim to restitution than in the case where the plaintiff is coerced (duress) or unduly influenced into transferring the value to the defendant. And finally, a claim to restitution of value transferred to the defendant on the basis that the defendant would not benefit from it (anti-beneficial basis) is stronger than a claim to restitution of value transferred to the defendant intending that the defendant benefit from the transfer but subject to a basis or condition which fails (failure of consideration).

All of these unjust factors in the last five chapters have therefore been concerned with transactions in which the plaintiff's intention to engage in them is imperfect. The next chapter is concerned with a collection of instances in which courts have allowed restitution for broad reasons of 'policy'. This miscellaneous collection of instances of restitution stands apart from all of the unjust factors considered so far because they have nothing to do with the intention of the plaintiff. They are not concerned with any considerations between the parties themselves. Nor are they cases of wrongdoing, so they cannot be classified as restitution for wrongs. Although courts and commentators have recognised these cases as part of the law of unjust enrichment, it is time to recognise that restitution is being awarded for a policy reason independent of considerations between the parties which are the concern of actions for unjust enrichment or wrongdoing.

[131] Ch 3 p 36.

13

Policy-Based Reasons for Restitution

Contents

I. Introduction

The unjust factors considered in Chapters 8 to 12 concerned circumstances where there was a vitiated intention to enter a transaction that enriches the defendant (mistake, illegitimate pressure, undue influence), a qualified intention to enter a transaction that enriches a defendant (failure of consideration), or no intention to enter a transaction that enriches the defendant (ignorance, powerlessness or an anti-beneficial basis). In each category, the unjust factor constituted a reason of interpersonal justice, between plaintiff and defendant, why the defendant's receipt of the enrichment was unjust. We saw that in these circumstances the defendant must make restitution of an enrichment to the plaintiff if the defendant has no right to retain the enrichment. The common feature of all these cases was that the plaintiff's intention to enter the transaction that enriched the defendant was imperfect.

The plaintiff's intention to enter the transaction that enriched the defendant will be perfect if none of the following factors is present: (i) impaired intention to enter the transaction that enriched the defendant; (ii) conditional intention to enter the transaction that enriched the defendant; or (iii) no intention to enter the transaction that enriched the defendant. As between the parties, the transaction is not unjust. However, there are other reasons why restitution might be required which are external to the perfectly intended transaction between the parties. These are reasons of policy. An example is the category of case involving restitution of unlawful taxes. As we will see below, the policy against taxation without legislation requires restitution of unlawful taxes even where the plaintiff's consent to the payment was unimpaired. A failure to appreciate this can lead to unwarranted analogies being drawn between the required elements for restitution of unjust enrichment and the requirements for restitution on the ground of policy. The proper approach was taken by Lord Walker in *FII Group Litigation v Revenue and Customs Commissioners*, where he referred, without mention of the plaintiff's intention, to the need for the tax paid to be 'in response to (and sufficiently causally connected with) an apparent statutory requirement to pay tax'.[1] However, the policy reason for restitution of unlawful tax is wholly independent of a plaintiff's consent.

Policy-based reasons for restitution are essentially different to unjust factors because the policy reason for restitution is extrinsic to the interpersonal interests of the particular parties to the claim. A policy is a standard that sets out some goal to be reached that is external to the parties: some improvement to a social, political or economic feature of the broader community, or protection of some existing feature of that community from change.[2] It is not a reason of interpersonal justice between the parties that requires restitution. Thus in *Holman v Johnson*, Lord Mansfield commented of the doctrine of illegality that it 'is founded in general principles of policy, which the defendant has the advantage of, contrary to the real justice, as between him and the plaintiff'.[3] The consequence is that core features of unjust enrichment law will be irrelevant or inappropriate in the context of policy-based claims for restitution. The significant schism between interpersonal reasons for restitution and 'policy' reasons for restitution has historically seen policy reasons usually treated separately from the law of unjust enrichment. This is appropriate. These policy reasons for restitution are concerned with fundamentally different norms. Further, we saw in Chapter 2 that not every instance of restitution is a response to unjust enrichment. For instance, restitution may be a response to a tort or breach of an equitable duty.

This chapter briefly considers six categories of policy-based reasons for restitution. The categories are: illegality, incapacity, reversal of judgment restitution, encouragement of intervention, prevention of accumulation, and free acceptance. The chapter does not

[1] *Test Claimants in the FII Group Litigation v Revenue and Customs Commissioners* [2012] UKSC 19, [2012] 2 AC 337 [79].

[2] See eg R Dworkin, *Taking Rights Seriously* (London, Duckworth, 2009) 22.

[3] *Holman v Johnson* (1775) 1 Cowp 341, 343, 98 ER 1120, 1121.

attempt to provide an exhaustive examination of each. Rather, it seeks to identify the nature of the policy underpinning each claim and in so doing illustrate the different considerations that motivate these claims compared to claims in unjust enrichment. Some of the policies are controversial. However, the recognition that these matters are not part of the law of unjust enrichment directs attention to whether the policy is a legitimate reason for restitution despite the perfect intention of the parties to the transaction.

Strictly, this chapter should not be included in this book any more than a chapter which is concerned with restitution for a tort or some other civil wrong. But, as we will see, there is some support in both academic writing and modern judicial decisions for the treatment of policy-based reasons for restitution as part of the law of unjust enrichment. This contrasts with instances of restitution for wrongdoing which, as we saw in Chapter 2, is now recognised as a remedy independent of the law of unjust enrichment. The single most important point of this chapter is that policy-motivated reasons for restitution should not be treated as part of the law of unjust enrichment. Restitution can be awarded for reasons of wrongdoing, unjust enrichment, or policy external to the parties. Each category of reasons for restitution is distinct.

II. Illegality and Legal Stultification

A. Illegality as a Reason for Restitution

The term 'illegality' is notoriously imprecise. It is used in this book because that is how the cases have labelled the concept both as a positive reason for restitution and as a defence.[4] But a more precise approach would be to speak of a policy to avoid irrationality or incongruity in the law or, to put it the other way, to promote coherence in the law.[5] This is a general policy applicable throughout the law,[6] and is not particular to the law of unjust enrichment or restitution. This is the meaning with which cases that speak of restitution for 'illegality' are concerned.

Illegality as a positive reason for restitution is engaged when another legal principle will be stultified unless the plaintiff is granted restitution.[7] In *David Securities Pty Ltd v Commonwealth Bank of Australia*,[8] Mason CJ, Deane, Toohey, Gaudron and McHugh JJ cited illegality as an example of 'a qualifying or vitiating factor' that would support a claim for restitution. But illegality does not qualify or vitiate a plaintiff's intention. The facts of that case can be used to illustrate this point. It will be recalled that David Securities entered into a contract of mortgage with the Commonwealth Bank. One clause of the mortgage required David Securities to pay withholding tax, for which the bank would otherwise be liable. Legislation provided that such a term was 'absolutely void.' We saw in Chapter 8 that David Securities sought restitution of the amounts paid pursuant to the clause, relying

[4] Ch 7 pp 140–41, 158–60.

[5] *Miller v Miller* [2011] HCA 9, (2011) 242 CLR 446.

[6] ibid. See also Ch 7 pp 140–41.

[7] *Boissevain v Weil* [1950] AC 327, 341 (Lord Radcliffe) discussed by P Birks, 'Recovering Value Transferred under an Illegal Contract' (2000) 1 *Theoretical Inquiries in Law* 155, 169.

[8] *David Securities Pty Ltd v Commonwealth Bank of Australia* [1992] HCA 48, (1992) 175 CLR 353, 379 [46].

upon the unjust factor of mistake. The High Court of Australia accepted that restitution would follow if David Securities had been mistaken and referred the case back to trial to determine whether the mistake had caused the payment.[9] As explained in Chapter 11, the payments had also been been made on a basis that wholly failed. So there were two potential claims in unjust enrichment that arose from the imperfect consent of the plaintiff on the facts of this case. However, the joint judgment also identified the need to avoid undermining the purpose of the applicable statute as an independent reason for restitution.[10] The purpose of the operative statute was to ensure that withholding tax was paid by the party who derived the income from an overseas transaction. The respondent bank was aware of the existence of the invalidating statute, and also drafted the offending clause with the statute in mind:

> In circumstances where the party in the best position to order its affairs in the light of specialist advice has deliberately chosen to charge a particular interest rate and seek additional amounts by virtue of separate provision in the loan agreement, there is no injustice to that party in ordering recovery. *Otherwise the policy of s 261 would be defeated.*[11]

As their Honours' reasoning reveals, in the context of claims for restitution, where conduct is illegal, the reason for restitution is independent of the intention of the plaintiff. Instead, the reason is to avoid the stultification of the law that would otherwise follow were restitution to be denied. Importantly, this reason exists even if there is no alternative claim in unjust enrichment arising from mistake, failure of consideration or other unjust factor. The reason for restitution is motivated by policy concerns extrinsic to the parties and is independent of all the claims in unjust enrichment based upon imperfect intention.

The specific issue of stultification that is identified as underlying the right to restitution will depend in any particular case on the nature of the operative prohibition or overriding policy. This will be as varied as the range of possible legislation or policies of the law. However, a number of classes of claims recur sufficiently frequently to merit individual examination.

B. Types of Illegality Claims

i. Restitution of Payments Made by a Person in a Protected Class

The first general group of illegality claims is where the plaintiffs form 'members of a class … for whose protection the infringed provisions were enacted'.[12] If illegality had been relied upon as the reason for restitution in *David Securities* it would have fallen into this category of case. Restitution would be required so that the protective purpose of the statute would

[9] *David Securities Pty Ltd v Commonwealth Bank of Australia* [1992] HCA 48, (1992) 175 CLR 353, 368, 385 (Mason CJ, Deane, Toohey, Gaudron and McHugh JJ), 403 (Dawson J). See also *Leisure Resort Holdings Pty Ltd v Leisure Resort Group Pty Ltd* (QCA, 2 September 1994).

[10] *David Securities Pty Ltd v Commonwealth Bank of Australia* [1992] HCA 48, (1992) 175 CLR 353, 384 [57] (Mason CJ, Deane, Toohey, Gaudron and McHugh JJ).

[11] ibid 384 [57] (Mason CJ, Deane, Toohey, Gaudron and McHugh JJ) (emphasis added).

[12] *Amadio Pty Ltd v Henderson* [1998] FCA 823, (1998) 81 FCR 149, 197 (the Court). See also *Browning v Morris* (1778) 2 Cowp 790, 98 ER 1364; *Barclay v Pearson* [1893] 2 Ch 154; *Gray v Southouse* [1949] 2 All ER 1019; *Kiriri Cotton Co Ltd v Dewani* [1960] AC 192; *South Australian Cold Stores Ltd v Electricity Trust of South Australia* [1965] HCA 67, (1965) 115 CLR 247, 257 [3] (Kitto J).

not be defeated for members of the class. The same point was emphasised by Kitto J in *South Australian Cold Stores Ltd v Electricity Trust of South Australia*.[13] In that case, the appellant had brought a claim for recovery of overpayments made in excess of the maximum price lawfully payable under the Prices Act 1948 (SA). His Honour treated the claim as one based on policy rather than mistake:

> The contention must be upheld or rejected according as the appellant is or is not a member of a class of persons for whose protection the prohibition in the [Act] is enacted ... If it is a member of such a class, it is entitled to succeed, in my opinion, whether or not the statute actually contemplates the recovery in a civil action.[14]

In rejecting the appellant's claim, Kitto J compared the case with the classic example of a 'protected class' in *Kiriri Cotton Co Ltd v Dewani*.[15] There, a landlord charged a premium for the grant to a tenant of a seven-year lease, unaware that he was thereby committing an offence under Ugandan rent legislation. When the tenant realised the position, he sought restitution of the premium. His claim succeeded. As Kitto J explained in *South Australian Cold Stores Ltd*, rent legislation is designed 'to prevent the owners of premises from profiting by the position of advantage which in the nature of things they enjoy over would-be tenants in bargaining about rent at a time when there is a shortage of housing or other forms of accommodation'.[16] Justice Kitto rejected the claim in *South Australian Cold Stores Ltd* because the Prices Act had the purpose of protecting the value of money, not a class of persons such as purchasers.

Both the High Court of Australia in *South Australian Cold Stores Ltd* and the Privy Council in *Kiriri Cotton Co Ltd v Dewani* described the issue as whether the parties were '*in pari delicto*':[17] where legislation is for the benefit of a protected class of person of which the plaintiff is one, the parties are not equally at fault and so the plaintiff should be able to recover. However, in *Kiriri Cotton Co Ltd v Dewani*,[18] Lord Denning, delivering the advice of the Privy Council, treated illegality *non in pari delicto* as a reason for restitution alongside mistake and failure of consideration. We have seen that one difficulty with this reasoning is that the 'illegality' is not concerned with the intention of the plaintiff, unlike mistake or failure of consideration; instead it is concerned with policy matters external to the parties. There is a further difficulty with this reasoning: fault is not the reason why the claim should be allowed.[19] For this reason, McHugh and Gummow JJ said in *Fitzgerald v FJ Leonhardt Pty Ltd*,[20] that issues of liability should not be approached by considering any general *in pari delicto* doctrine. Similarly, the High Court of Australia has recently eschewed the maxim as

[13] *South Australian Cold Stores Ltd v Electricity Trust of South Australia* [1965] HCA 67, (1965) 115 CLR 247.

[14] ibid 257–58 [3] (Kitto J).

[15] *Kiriri Cotton Co Ltd v Dewani* [1960] AC 192.

[16] *South Australian Cold Stores Ltd v Electricity Trust of South Australia* [1965] HCA 67, (1965) 115 CLR 247, 258 [4].

[17] The full maxim is '*in pari delicto potior est conditio defendis*' ('where the guilt is shared the position of the defendant is the stronger'). See also *Amadio Pty Ltd v Henderson* [1998] FCA 823, (1998) 81 FCR 149, 197 (the Court); *Browning v Morris* (1778) 2 Cowp 790, 98 ER 1364.

[18] *Kiriri Cotton Co Ltd v Dewani* [1960] AC 192, 205.

[19] WJ Swadling, 'The Role of Illegality in the English Law of Unjust Enrichment' in D Johnston and R Zimmermann (eds), *Unjustified Enrichment: Key Issues in Comparative Perspective* (Cambridge, Cambridge University Press, 2002) 302.

[20] *Fitzgerald v FJ Leonhardt Pty Ltd* [1997] HCA 17, (1997) 189 CLR 215, 229. See also *Nelson v Nelson* [1995] HCA 25, (1995) 184 CLR 538.

confusing and unhelpful, because it does not reveal the reasoning that leads to the conclusion that liability should be allowed or denied.[21] A better approach, present in the reasoning in *Kiriri Cotton Co Ltd v Dewani*, is to ask whether the plaintiff is a member of a class for whom the legislation was enacted to protect.

ii. Restitution of Unlawfully Exacted Taxes

In *Woolwich Equitable Building Society v Inland Revenue Commissioners*,[22] a majority of the House of Lords held that a plaintiff taxpayer could succeed in recovering tax paid in response to a demand by the Revenue made pursuant to *ultra vires* regulations. This claim was later described as being based upon the 'high constitutional importance of the principle that there should be no taxation without Parliament'.[23] Lord Goff described the principle as based upon the general policy, traceable in England to the Bill of Rights 1689 (Imp), that taxation should not be levied without the authority of Parliament.[24] Lord Goff also noted the coercive nature of demands made by the state, failure to comply with which invariably raises the fear of unwelcome economic and social consequences, as a further impetus.[25]

The development of the *Woolwich* principle extended the coverage of protection offered to taxpayers beyond the matters between the parties which are the concern of the law of unjust enrichment including the unjust factors of mistake,[26] illegitimate pressure (including the doctrine of duress *colore officii*)[27] and failure of consideration.[28]

However, Dr Williams has argued that the *Woolwich* principle, as a public law policy concerning exactions that are *ultra vires* the state, should replace the private law unjust factors in the public law Revenue context.[29] We agree with her assessment of the basis for *Woolwich* in public policy. However, it should not replace the *inter partes* unjust factors. The reason why the exaction was *ultra vires* in *Woolwich* reflected principles of public law due to the overriding principle that there should be no taxation without legislation. To the extent that imperfect intention unjust factors support, rather than undermine, this principle, there is no reason why public law should deprive private parties of their rights. The *Woolwich* claim

[21] *Miller v Miller* [2011] HCA 9, (2011) 242 CLR 446 [13] (the Court).

[22] *Woolwich Equitable Building Society v Inland Revenue Commissioners* [1993] AC 70. See also *British Steel plc v Customs and Excise Commissioners* [1997] 2 All ER 366 (right to restitution applied to unlawful refusal to grant relief from tax); *Norwich City Council v Stringer* (2000) 2 LGR 1102. A similar principle has been adopted in Canada: *Kingstreet Investments Ltd v New Brunswick (Finance)* [2007] 1 SCR 3, 2007 SCC 1. However, the principle is regarded as arising outside of the law of unjust enrichment: ibid [35] (Bastarache J; McLachlin CJC and Binnie, LeBel, Deschamps, Fish, Abella, Charron and Rothstein JJ, concurring).

[23] *Test Claimants in the FII Group Litigation v Revenue and Customs Commissioners* [2012] UKSC 19, [2012] 2 AC 337 [74] (Lord Walker).

[24] See also *Test Claimants in the FII Group Litigation v Revenue and Customs Commissioners* [2012] UKSC 19, [2012] 2 AC 337 [173] (Lord Sumption).

[25] *Woolwich Equitable Building Society v Inland Revenue Commissioners* [1993] AC 70, 172–73. See also *Test Claimants in the FII Group Litigation v Revenue and Customs Commissioners* [2012] UKSC 19, [2012] 2 AC 337 [173] (Lord Sumption).

[26] *Littlewoods Retail Ltd v HM Revenue & Customs* [2010] EWHC 1071, [2010] STC 2072, for example, involved mistaken payments of tax made pursuant to a long-standing and incorrect understanding of the requirements of a valid taxing statute.

[27] *Mason v New South Wales* [1959] HCA 5, (1959) 102 CLR 108.

[28] *Roxborough v Rothmans of Pall Mall Australia Ltd* [2001] HCA 68, (2001) 208 CLR 516.

[29] R Williams, *Unjust Enrichment and Public Law: A Comparative Study of England, France and the EU* (Oxford, Hart Publishing, 2010) chs 2–4.

is independent of the private unjust factors. It applies notwithstanding that the plaintiff was rightly convinced that the taxing statute was invalid, so was under no mistake,[30] and that no illegitimate pressure was applied to exact the payment.[31] We will also see below that it is not subject to the defence of change of position.[32] Conversely, unjust factors may offer potential advantages such as (for mistake) extended limitation periods[33] or different conflict of law rules. Moreover, they may reach situations not covered by *Woolwich*. For example, the doctrine of duress *colore officii* applies beyond taxing and, indeed, beyond public authorities to apply to a wide range of persons or bodies standing in positions of public power or duty.[34] For these reasons, the *Woolwich* principle should stand alongside the unjust factors, not supplant them. This is the conclusion that has now been reached in England in relation to mistake:[35] *Woolwich* constitutes an additional, non-exclusive, weapon to mistake in the taxpayer's armoury for restitution of unlawfully exacted tax. The same should be true of illegitimate pressure, duress *colore officii* and failure of basis.

Since recognition of the *Woolwich* principle, courts have clarified important issues regarding its scope and operation. In the early decision of *Test Claimants in the FII Group Litigation v Revenue and Customs Commissioners*,[36] Henderson J held that the claim is not subject to the change of position defence. His Honour correctly considered that the defence was automatically precluded in such claims because the right of a private citizen to recover unlawfully exacted tax should, as a matter of principle, be unfettered.[37] We have seen that the *Woolwich* principle reflects a long-standing and vital public interest in prohibiting unlawful exaction of taxes by public authorities.[38] This policy would be wholly undermined if the change of position defence was permitted to allow public authorities to retain the benefit of their unlawful demands.[39] In two important, subsequent cases his Honour has clarified that the 'explanation for the bar on the defence of change of position to *Woolwich* claims is to be found in the stultification principle'.[40]

[30] *Woolwich Equitable Building Society v Inland Revenue Commissioners* [1993] AC 70.

[31] *Test Claimants in the FII Group Litigation v Revenue and Customs Commissioners* [2010] EWCA Civ 103, [2010] STC 1251 [157]–[173]; *Test Claimants in the FII Group Litigation v Revenue and Customs Commissioners* [2012] UKSC 19, [2012] 2 AC 337 [64]–[83] (Lord Walker) [173]–[174] (Lord Sumption; Lords Hope, Clarke, Dyson, Brown and Reed concurring on this point).

[32] Whether the policy considerations that underpin this area are so strong that they should likewise exclude the defence where the claim is brought in unjust enrichment is considered in Ch 14 p 350.

[33] Discussed in Ch 15 pp 388–89, 393.

[34] Ch 9 p 209.

[35] Clarified in *Deutsche Morgan Grenfell Group plc v Inland Revenue Commissioners* [2006] UKHL 49, [2007] 1 AC 558; see also *FII Group Litigation v Revenue and Customs Commissioners* [2012] UKSC 19, [2012] 2 AC 337.

[36] *Test Claimants in the FII Group Litigation v Revenue and Customs Commissioners* [2008] EWHC 2893, [2009] STC 254.

[37] ibid [339], approved on appeal [2010] EWCA Civ 103, [2010] STC 1251 [109] (Arden LJ giving the judgment of the Court); cf *Littlewoods Retail Ltd v HM Revenue & Customs* [2010] EWHC 1071, [2010] STC 2072 [101], [108] (Vos J). See also *Bloomsbury International Ltd v Sea Fish Industry Authority* [2009] EWHC 1721, [2010] 1 CMLR 12 [134] (Hamblen J).

[38] Above, p 306.

[39] The same applies to any contention that the defence should be allowed to operate with respect to claims for restitution of the use benefit (interest) derived from taxation payments: cf *Littlewoods Retail Ltd v HM Revenue & Customs* [2010] EWHC 1071, [2010] STC 2072 [108] (Vos J).

[40] *Test Claimants in the FII Group Litigation v HM Revenue & Customs* [2014] EWHC 4302, [2015] STC 1471 [315]; see also *Prudential Assurance Co Ltd v Revenue and Customs Commissioners* [2013] EWHC 3249, [2014] 2 CMLR 10 [188].

Another important clarification is that the claim does not require that the Revenue has issued a demand for the taxation payment.[41] The claim extends to any case where tax had been unlawfully exacted from a person by virtue of a legislative requirement. Consistently with this approach, *Woolwich* claims have been recognised as encompassing not only claims for taxes unsupported by valid legislation, but overpayments of otherwise lawful tax, as evidenced by the long-running *Littlewoods*[42] litigation. As that litigation also attests, *Woolwich* claims are not limited to seeking restitution of the principal sums paid, but also of the value of the opportunity to use that principal (ie interest).

Currently, the main focus of litigation in the *Woolwich* sphere is on the efficaciousness or otherwise of various legislative measures put in place to try to minimise claims against the Revenue, chiefly through the imposition of very restrictive and often retroactive limitation periods. These are discussed in Chapter 15. There are four other outstanding issues in relation to the scope of the *Woolwich* principle. The first returns to the range of transactions that come within the scope of the principle requiring restitution of 'unlawfully exacted' taxes. A taxing statute may breach some independent legal or statutory obligation owed by the Revenue.[43] Or it may be entirely *ultra vires* the Revenue. Or it may be invalid in part or in whole, such as for a failure to comply with legislative procedures. Or a taxpayer may pay more tax than is properly due under a valid taxation statute, whether because of a mistake induced by the Revenue or for other reasons. The best approach to the meaning of 'unlawfully exacted' tax, consistent with the rationale of the *Woolwich* principle, is to ask whether the exaction that actually occurred was justified or supported by lawful legislation. If not, then it must be returned.[44] This was the approach taken by Lord Walker in *FII Group Litigation v Revenue and Customs Commissioners*, where he said: 'where tax is purportedly charged without lawful parliamentary authority, a claim for repayment arises regardless of any official demand (unless the payment was, on the facts, made in order to close the transaction)'.[45]

The second question is whether the *Woolwich* principle extends beyond governments to other bodies standing in a position of public power or duty. For example, where state utilities are privatised, or state functions are delegated to a private body, there will often be a controlling statute that dictates the terms and conditions on which the services must be provided. If the private entity charges more for these services than it is entitled to, does the *Woolwich* principle apply to require restitution of the overpayment? There should be no difficulty where the recipient is acting as agent of the state. The problem arises where the body is acting as a private principal. However, if the *Woolwich* principle is primarily grounded in a principle of no taxation without legislation, then extension to non-state

[41] *Test Claimants in the FII Group Litigation v Revenue and Customs Commissioners* [2012] UKSC 19, [2012] 2 AC 337 [10] (Lord Hope) [79] (Lord Walker) [172]–[174] (Lord Sumption).

[42] *Littlewoods Retail Ltd v HM Revenue & Customs* [2010] EWHC 2771, [2011] STC 171; *Littlewoods Retail Ltd v HM Revenue & Customs* [2010] EWHC 1071, [2010] STC 2072; *Littlewoods Retail Ltd v HM Revenue & Customs* [2014] EWHC 868, [2014] STC 1761; *Littlewoods Retail Ltd v HM Revenue & Customs* [2015] EWCA Civ 515, [2015] 3 WLR 1748.

[43] As in *Test Claimants in the FII Group Litigation v Revenue and Customs Commissioners* [2008] EWHC 2893, [2009] STC 254; appealed in *Test Claimants in the FII Group Litigation v Revenue and Customs Commissioners* [2010] EWCA Civ 103, [2010] STC 1251.

[44] As in *British Steel plc v Customs and Excise Commissioners* [1997] 2 All ER 366.

[45] *Test Claimants in the FII Group Litigation v Revenue and Customs Commissioners* [2012] UKSC 19, [2012] 2 AC 337 [79]; see also [10] (Lord Hope) [172]–[174] (Lord Sumption). On the role of settlement, see Ch 15 p 395.

authorities is clearly problematic.[46] Overcharging by a private corporation that has taken over (eg through a process of privatisation) what were formerly key government activities is a different matter from unlawful state taxation. Further, even where a private corporation has performed functions delegated to it by the state, it is arguable (absent any legislative provision to the contrary) that the only party with standing to sue in those circumstances is the state, not the citizen.

The third question is how the *Woolwich* principle interacts with other public policies, whether those other policies are expressed in legislative terms or are found in the general fabric of the common law. The difficult issue will be where two or more applicable policies conflict. In such cases, courts must determine which is the overriding policy. An example of a potential conflict with a legislative policy is where the *Woolwich* principle conflicts with the provisions of a statute that address recovery of tax.[47] An example of a possible conflict with a general common law policy is the public interest in promoting the peaceful settlement of disputes.[48] Where a payment of tax has been made to settle or compromise a dispute, and it is subsequently revealed that the tax was not supported by legislation, does the policy favouring finality of disputes trump the *Woolwich* principle? In Australia, there are strong expressions of support for a positive answer.[49] England has yet to address this question directly, however the Law Commission indicated support for the Australian position,[50] as do some dicta in *Woolwich*[51] and *FII Group Litigation v Revenue and Customs Commissioners*.[52] Another common law policy that potentially conflicts with the *Woolwich* principle concerns the policy to prevent 'fiscal chaos' and the security of government operations. Where the *Woolwich* principle has been adopted, it necessarily trumps the fiscal chaos concern.[53] This is because, otherwise, the more outrageous and exorbitant an unlawful fiscal impost is, the less likely it could be recovered because of the inevitable and deep disruption to public finances.

The fourth and final issue that remains to be addressed is the future of the *Woolwich* principle in Australia. The reasoning in *Woolwich* has not been adopted directly by Australian courts. *Woolwich* has been mentioned without criticism, and even with approval, in a

[46] A view supported by obiter dicta in the English Court of Appeal: *Woolwich Equitable Building Society v Inland Revenue Commissioners* [1991] 3 WLR 790, 797 (Glidewell LJ), 852 (Butler-Sloss LJ).

[47] See, eg, *Monro v Revenue and Customs Commissioners* [2008] EWCA Civ 306, [2009] Ch 69; *Test Claimants in the FII Group Litigation v Revenue and Customs Commissioners* [2010] EWCA Civ 103, [2010] STC 1251; *ACN 005 057 349 Pty Ltd v Commissioner of State Revenue* [2015] VSCA 332, the last discussed further below.

[48] See further Ch 15 p 395.

[49] Ch 15 p 399. Cf Wilson J in *Air Canada v British Colombia* [1989] 1 SCR 1161 [13].

[50] Law Commission, *Restitution of Payments Made under a Mistake of Law* (Law Com CP No 120, 1991) para 3.69; Law Commission, *Restitution: Mistakes of Law and Ultra Vires Public Authority Receipts and Payments* (Law Com No 227, 1994) paras 2.25–2.228.

[51] *Woolwich Equitable Building Society v Inland Revenue Commissioners* [1993] AC 70, 100 (Glidewell LJ), 204 (Lord Slynn).

[52] *Test Claimants in the FII Group Litigation v Revenue and Customs Commissioners* [2012] UKSC 19, [2012] 2 AC 337 [79] (Lord Walker).

[53] Fiscal chaos was accepted as a legitimate reason to deny restitution in *Air Canada v British Columbia* [1989] 1 SCR 1161 [93] (La Forest J); cf Wilson J (dissenting in part) at [14]. This policy interest was demoted in *Kingstreet Investments Ltd v New Brunswick (Finance)* [2007] 1 SCR 3, 2007 SCC 1 in favour of the same policy that underpins the *Woolwich* principle: [14], [20], [25] (Bastarache J; McLachlin CJC and Binnie, LeBel, Deschamps, Fish, Abella, Charron and Rothstein JJ concurring). See also *Woolwich Equitable Building Society v Inland Revenue Commissioners* [1993] AC 70, 175 (Lord Goff); *Commissioner of State Revenue (Vic) v Royal Insurance Australia Ltd* [1994] HCA 61, (1994) 182 CLR 51, 68 [26] (Mason CJ).

number of Australian cases.[54] Outside the immediate *Woolwich*, context, many cases involving statutory claims for reimbursement or writs of mandamus against taxing authorities have adopted approaches consistent with the *Woolwich* principle. Thus a number of cases have emphasised the duty of taxing authorities to collect the correct amount of tax: 'not a penny more, not a penny less'.[55] In *ACN 005 057 349 Pty Ltd v Commissioner of State Revenue*,[56] the Victorian Court of Appeal recently emphasised that taxing legislation, and in particular any statutory provisions regulating the recovery of taxation payments from public authorities, must be construed consistently with that underlying duty. In that case, a statutory power to amend land tax assessments was considered to carry with it an inherent power to refund any overpaid amounts. Viewed against the underlying duty, the Court held that both powers constituted duties that could be enforced by a writ of mandamus in circumstances where the taxing commissioner knew of errors in the original assessments but nonetheless refused to amend them or to repay the overpayments made pursuant to the original assessments.[57]

Although there are signs that Australian courts might adopt a *Woolwich* principle, it is much more likely that the Australian position will be tailored to the Australian constitutional context just as one of the factors relevant to *Woolwich* was the European constitutional context.[58] A claim for restitution (as money had and received) where an Australian state levies a tax based on an unconstitutional state law,[59] might easily be extended to taxes passed which are not supported by legislation. But many questions arise about how that restitutionary corollary of the constitutional principle might operate. In addition to the three questions discussed above concerning the *Woolwich* principle, there are questions concerning whether the Australian constitutional principle would operate to permit restitution *to* the Commonwealth, such as where the Commonwealth makes payments by reference to the executive power in section 61 of the Constitution but without empowering legislation.[60] Further, how would the Australian principle operate in light of the acceptance by Australian legislatures and courts of the 'fiscal chaos' policy as a legitimate reason for denying restitution of taxes? The High Court of Australia decision in *Thiess v Collector of Customs*[61] is a good example. In that case, customs officials miscalculated the tariff that should be paid by the plaintiff to import a yacht into Australia. The Court explained[62] that the particular

[54] Eg *State Bank of New South Wales v Federal Commissioner of Taxation* (1995) 62 FCR 371, 378 [16] (Wilcox J); *Chippendale Printing Co Pty Ltd v Commissioner of Taxation* [1996] FCA 1259 (1996) 62 FCR 347, 366 [20] (Lehane J); *SCI Operations Pty Ltd v Commonwealth* [1996] FCA 754, (1996) 69 FCR 346, 369–76 (Beaumont and Einfeld JJ); *Meriton Apartments Pty Ltd v Council of the City of Sydney (No 3)* [2011] NSWLEC 65, (2011) 80 NSWLR 541 [158]–[158] (Pepper J).

[55] *Lighthouse Philatelics Pty Ltd v Commissioner of Taxation* [1991] FCA 506, (1991) 32 FCR 148, 155 [33] cited in *Tourism Holdings Australia Pty Ltd v Commissioner of Taxation* [2005] NTCA 3, 15 NTLR 80 [4] (Mildren J) and *ACN 005 057 349 Pty Ltd v Commissioner of State Revenue* [2015] VSCA 332 [133]–[141] (the Court); see also *Commonwealth Agricultural Service Engineers Ltd (In Liquidation) v Commissioner of Taxes (SA)* [1926] HCA 30, (1926) 38 CLR 289, 294 (Isaacs J).

[56] *ACN 005 057 349 Pty Ltd v Commissioner of State Revenue* [2015] VSCA 332 [123] (the Court).

[57] ibid [139]–[143], [159], [162] (the Court).

[58] *Amministrazione delle Finanze Dello Strato v Spa San Georgio* [1983] ECR 3595.

[59] *Antill Ranger & Co Pty Ltd v Commissioner for Motor Transport* [1955] HCA 25, (1955) 93 CLR 83; *British American Tobacco Australia Ltd v Western Australia* [2003] HCA 47, (2003) 217 CLR 30 [42] (McHugh, Gummow and Hayne JJ).

[60] *Williams v The Commonwealth* [2012] HCA 23, (2012) 248 CLR 156.

[61] *Thiess v Collector of Customs* [2014] HCA 12, (2014) 250 CLR 664.

[62] ibid [31]–[32].

statutory provisions governing recovery of payments under the Customs Act 1901 (Cth) were a direct response to concerns raised by Isaacs J in *Sargood Bros v The Commonwealth*[63] that allowing restitution of tariffs paid by mistake would cause serious fiscal confusion at a time when customs duty accounted for more than half of all Commonwealth revenue. The legislative response substantially restricted recovery through an exhaustive claim process, itself subject to very short limitation periods. The legislation was clearly regarded by the High Court in *Thiess* as a proportionate response to that danger.[64] *Thiess* is an example of the widespread introduction of statutory regimes that provide exhaustive claim processes for the recovery of tax payments. There are numerous others.[65]

iii. Restitution After Withdrawing from the Illegality Prior to Completion

There is a final category of illegality case in which the reason for restitution is to prevent stultification of the law by positively encouraging respect for the law. Central to this category are the so-called 'repentance' cases (more properly described as 'withdrawal' cases), described in *Nelson v Nelson* by Deane and Gummow JJ as 'well recognised in this [High] Court.'[66] The same category is also well established under English law.[67] These cases allow restitution of benefits conferred pursuant to an illegal design if the plaintiff withdraws from the transaction before anything has been done to carry out the illegal purpose.[68] Until recently, it was unclear whether genuine subjective repentence was required,[69] or it was enough that the plaintiff withdrew from the illegal transaction before it was carried out. We considered *Parkinson v College of Ambulance*[70] in Chapter 7. It will be recalled that Lush J refused to order restitution of a payment made to secure a knighthood, for reasons of public policy. Another reason given by Lush J was that the plaintiff had withdrawn from the illegal transaction not because of repentance, but simply because he had failed to obtain the promised knighthood.[71] This suggests that genuine remorse is required. However, from the perspective of the principle of coherence, the better view is that withdrawal from illegal transactions is to be encouraged, whatever the motivation. Allowing recovery provides an incentive for plaintiffs to withdraw from their involvement in an illegal transaction before it is too late, thereby encouraging compliance with the law.[72]

63 *Sargood Bros v Commonwealth* [1910] HCA 45, (1910) 11 CLR 258, 303.

64 See in particular *Thiess v Collector of Customs* [2014] HCA 12, (2014) 250 CLR 664 [33] (the Court).

65 See, for example, the extensive list of examples involving federal taxing legislation and state stamp duty and payroll tax statutes discussed by Sloss J in *ACN 005 057 349 Pty Ltd v Commissioner of State Revenue* [2015] VSC 76 [65], [87]–[105]; on appeal, see *ACN 005 057 349 Pty Ltd v Commissioner of State Revenue* [2015] VSCA 332 [89] (the Court).

66 *Nelson v Nelson* [1995] HCA 25, (1995) 184 CLR 538, 562 [77]. The High Court authorities are collected in *Martin v Martin* [1959] HCA 62, (1959) 110 CLR 297, 305 [13] (the Court); see also *Payne v McDonald* [1908] HCA 40, (1908) 6 CLR 208, *Perpetual Executors and Trustees Association of Australia Ltd v Wright* [1917] HCA 27, (1917) 23 CLR 185, and *Miller v Miller* [2011] HCA 9, (2011) 242 CLR 446.

67 The primary authority is *Taylor v Bowers* (1876) 1 QBD 291, followed in cases such as *Kearley v Thomson* (1890) 24 QBD 742, *Tribe v Tribe* [1966] Ch 107, and *Patel v Mirza* [2014] EWCA Civ 1047, [2015] Ch 271. See also *Lipkin Gorman v Karpnale Ltd* [1991] 2 AC 548, 564, where Lord Templeman referred with approval to the decision of *Aubert v Walsh* (1810) 3 Taunt 277, 128 ER 110.

68 *Tribe v Tribe* [1966] Ch 107, 135 (Millet LJ); *Nelson v Nelson* [1995] HCA 25, (1995) 184 CLR 538.

69 *Bigos v Bousted* [1951] 1 All ER 92.

70 *Parkinson v College of Ambulance Ltd* [1925] 2 KB 1.

71 ibid 16.

72 P Birks, 'Recovering Value Transferred under an Illegal Contract' (2000) 1 *Theoretical Inquiries in Law* 155, 188–91; AS Burrows, *The Law of Restitution*, 3rd edn (Oxford, Oxford University Press, 2011) ch 19.

This was the approach adopted by the English Court of Appeal in *Patel v Mirza*,[73] a case also considered in Chapter 7. The case was very similar to *Parkinson*.[74] Mr Patel paid £620,000 to the defendant stockbroker to trade in shares on the basis of insider information. The agreement was contrary to the prohibition on insider trading in section 52 Criminal Justice Act 1993 (UK). Ultimately, the agreement was not executed because the expected insider information was not forthcoming. Mr Patel sought restitution of the enrichment for total failure of consideration. The Court split on the issue of whether the 'illegality defence' applied to the case. The majority concluded that the plaintiff necessarily advanced and relied upon the illegal transaction in order to establish his claim for restitution of the enrichment when that transaction failed. Accordingly, the defence in principle applied.[75] However, the Court was unanimous that remorse or 'genuine repentance' was not required in order for the plaintiff nonetheless to recover the payment on the basis that he had withdrawn from the illegal transaction before it had been carried out.[76]

As with the previous two cases of illegality, many repentance cases can alternatively be analysed as based on an independent unjust factor of imperfect intention. In all the cases cited by Deane and Gummow JJ in *Nelson v Nelson*,[77] the plaintiff had a separate ground of claim on which he relied. The evidence of illegal intention was raised by way of bar to that claim.[78] So too in *Patel v Mirza*. On appeal, Gloster LJ would have allowed the plaintiff's claim for restitution for total failure of consideration.[79] However, the policy of encouraging withdrawal from illegal transactions provides an additional, positive reason for restitution, in the same way as the 'protected class' policy in *David Securities* provided a reason for restitution additional to mistake and failure of consideration. Further, as with the 'protected class' cases, it will not always be the case that there will be an alternative, imperfect intention unjust factor available to the repentant plaintiff.

III. Incapacity

A. Incapacity as a Reason for Restitution

There are four main types of legal incapacity: the *ultra vires* doctrine, minority, mental incapacity, and intoxication. Professor Burrows argues that human incapacity should operate as an independent impaired consent unjust factor on the ground that, by analogy with

[73] *Patel v Mirza* [2014] EWCA Civ 1047, [2015] Ch 271.

[74] Oddly, not cited to the Court: see eg ibid [43] (Rimer LJ).

[75] *Patel v Mirza* [2014] EWCA Civ 1047, [2015] Ch 271 [20]–[22] (Rimer LJ) [102] (Vos LJ). See further Ch 7 p 159.

[76] *Patel v Mirza* [2014] EWCA Civ 1047, [2015] Ch 271 [45] (Rimer LJ) [96] (Gloster LJ), [118] (Vos LJ).

[77] *Payne v McDonald* [1908] HCA 40, (1908) 6 CLR 208; *Perpetual Executors and Trustees Association of Australia Ltd v Wright* [1917] HCA 27, (1917) 23 CLR 185, 193 (Barton ACJ); *Martin v Martin* [1959] HCA 62, (1959) 110 CLR 297, 303–08 (the Court).

[78] See also W Swadling, 'The Role of Illegality in the English Law of Unjust Enrichment' in D Johnston and R Zimmermann (eds), *Unjustified Enrichment: Key Issues in Comparative Perspective* (Cambridge, Cambridge University Press, 2002) 305–08; P Birks, 'Recovering Value Transferred under an Illegal Contract' (2000) 1 *Theoretical Inquiries in Law* 155, 188–91.

[79] *Patel v Mirza* [2014] EWCA Civ 1047, [2015] Ch 271 [70] (Gloster LJ).

mistake, 'the claimant who lacks capacity does not truly intend to benefit the defendant'.[80] This confuses two different concepts. Consider, for example, human incapacity by reason of minority. It is entirely possible that a four-year-old child might not truly intend to enter a transaction to enrich the defendant by agreeing to a large payment of money. In such a case there might be an unjust factor based on lack of intention. But the same might not be true of a 15-year-old minor. When restitution is awarded simply for the reason of incapacity by minority, there is no need to enquire into the mental processes of the plaintiff. The better approach, which is also consistent with the application of incapacity as a defence[81] and with policy-based reasons for restitution in general, is to ask whether the policies behind recognising incapacity, in each case in which it arises, require restitution to be made. This would also treat incapacity in exactly the same way as a policy-based reason for restitution based on illegality.

B. *Ultra Vires*

Many claims involving the doctrine of *ultra vires* involve unauthorised payments by public authorities. In this context, the *ultra vires* rule often reflects a policy that public funds should be protected, with the consequence that the authority must be entitled to recover the funds. The policy would be stultified if restitution of any unauthorised payment were to be denied. Thus, like illegality, the reason for restitution in cases of *ultra vires* transactions is to prevent stultification of the policy underlying the law's prohibition.

This approach can be seen in the decision of the Privy Council in *Auckland Harbour Board v R*.[82] In that case, the Privy Council considered whether £7500 paid *ultra vires* was recoverable by the Harbour Board. Delivering the advice of the Board, Viscount Haldane stated: 'Any payment out of the consolidated fund made without Parliamentary authority is simply illegal and *ultra vires*, and may be recovered by the Government if it can, as here, be traced.'[83]

In some cases, the particular policy of a statute may provide a reason for restitution *against* a public authority which has acted *ultra vires*. Thus in some of the swaps cases (which we considered in Chapter 6) restitution was ordered from the authority acting *ultra vires* because the legislation had a purpose of protecting the public and persons who dealt with the public authority. In this category of case, the claim of restitution against the authority must be permitted because otherwise the protective purpose of the statute would be undermined. As Legatt LJ said in one case:

> It is not the policy of the law to require others to deal at their peril with local authorities, nor to require others to undertake their own inquiries about whether a local authority has power to make particular contracts or types of contract.[84]

[80] AS Burrows, *The Law of Restitution*, 3rd edn (Oxford, Oxford University Press, 2011) 311. Burrows deals with payments and exactions made *ultra vires* a public authority separately from human incapacity, on the ground at least in part that the policy concerns are quite different; human incapacity being concerned to protect the *incapax*, while institutional incapacity generally operates to protect the public: 517.

[81] See Ch 7 pp 163–64.

[82] *Auckland Harbour Board v The King* [1924] AC 318.

[83] *Auckland Harbour Board v The King* [1924] AC 318, 327.

[84] *Westdeutsche Landesbank Girozentrale v Islington London Borough Council* [1994] 4 All ER 890, 967, approved in *Guinness Mahon & Co Ltd v Kensington & Chelsea Royal London Borough Council* [1999] QB 215, 233

The same, necessary enquiry into the reason for the law's restriction on a public body's powers underpinned our discussion in the previous section of the *Woolwich* principle and the *ultra vires* exactions in issue in that case. The common factor in cases involving *ultra vires* transactions is that the purpose for the restriction on the body's capacity or powers must be considered.

C. Minority

The approach taken by courts with respect to cases of minority is unfortunately less clear. There are three concerns involved in minority cases. First, there is a concern to protect minors from any youthful proclivity to act impulsively and without mature consideration.[85] Secondly, there is a policy to protect minors from exploitation. Thirdly, there is a policy to avoid the imposition of crushing personal liability on minors. It is only possible to navigate the complex rules concerning when restitution of benefits may be obtained by minors by keeping these three policies in mind.

After a minor rescinds a contract on the grounds of minority, he is entitled to restitution of the value of personal rights obtained by the other contracting party. However, to date, restitution of the value of proprietary rights transferred pursuant to the contract has only been granted where the minor has been able to demonstrate a total failure of consideration.[86] Thus, in *Steinberg v Scala (Leeds) Ltd*[87] the plaintiff, a minor, applied for shares in a company and paid the amount due on allotment. The company allocated her the shares. The minor subsequently paid further amounts due on allotment and on the first call. Some 18 months later, the minor repudiated the contract and sought recovery of the monies paid by her. The English Court of Appeal unanimously held that, in order for the minor to succeed, there must be a total failure of consideration.[88] The minor had received the shares for which she had bargained. She had the opportunity to sell them, to obtain dividends, and to attend meetings to vote. The fact that she had not sold the shares, nor received any dividend on them, nor attended any shareholders meetings, made no difference. Her claim for restitution failed.

This refusal of relief in cases involving property rights transferred by minors is hard to justify. It seems at odds with the protective policies underpinning the denial of contractual capacity to minors. However, it is arguable that a rationale for requiring a total failure of consideration might be to balance the interests of the minor and the defendant

(Waller LJ). See also R Williams, *Unjust Enrichment and Public Law: A Comparative Study of England, France and the EU* (Oxford, Hart Publishing, 2010) 56–59.

[85] See, eg, *Zouch d Abbot and Hallet v Parsons* (1765) 3 Burr 1794, 1801, 97 ER 1103, 1106–07 (Lord Mansfield). Cf Minors (Property and Contracts) Act 1970 (NSW), which adopts a presumption of capacity subject to a discretion to provide relief.

[86] *Valentini v Canali* (1889) 24 QBD 166; *Steinberg v Scala (Leeds) Ltd* [1923] 2 Ch 452; *Pearce v Brain* [1929] 2 KB 310; *Chaplin v Leslie Frewin (Publishers) Ltd* [1966] Ch 71; *English v Gibbs* (1888) 9 LR (NSW) 455; *Woolf v Associated Finance Pty Ltd* [1956] VLR 51; *Curruth v Ern Moro & Amoco Enterprises Pty Ltd* (1966) 60 QJPR 106.

[87] *Steinberg v Scala (Leeds) Ltd* [1923] 2 Ch 452. See also *Corpe v Overton* (1833) 10 Bing 252, 131 ER 901; *Holmes v Blogg* (1818) 8 Taunt 508, 129 ER 481.

[88] *Steinberg v Scala (Leeds) Ltd* [1923] 2 Ch 452, 458–61 (Lord Sterndale MR), 461–63 (Warrington LJ), 464–65 (Younger LJ).

in circumstances in which a claim by a defendant for counter-restitution might be barred. The reason why a defendant's claim for counter-restitution might be barred is because any claim by the defendant for counter-restitution of the value of benefits conferred on the minor[89] raises the danger of imposing crushing personal liability on the minor. Just as a claim *against* a minor is restricted to the benefit that the minor retained,[90] a claim against a minor for counter-restitution would also be restricted to the benefit retained by the minor. Hence, if the minor brings a claim for restitution of the value of a property right, restricting the minor's claim to situations of failure of consideration might ensure some protection to a defendant who might otherwise have had a right to counter-restitution.

There is also confusion over whether minority can constitute a basis for restitution in the case of gifts.[91] The best approach to take through this confusion, consistently with the approach taken to restitution of benefits conferred *ultra vires*, is to permit restitution of benefits conferred by minors where, otherwise, the protective policies of the law would be stultified. The third policy concern involving the imposition of crushing personal liability on minors would not be engaged in the gift context. However, it is likely that the other two policies will be stultified by a refusal to permit restitution in cases of gift, just as in cases of contract. In both cases, it might reasonably be expected that impulsive minors will require significant protection to prevent them from suffering the consequences of their immature judgment and from the threat of exploitation.

D. Mental Incapacity

The protective policies of the law in relation to mental incapacity (including severe intoxication) largely mirror those for minority. However, mental incapacity will only constitute a ground of restitution for benefits conferred pursuant to a contract where the defendant was aware of the mental incapacity.[92] This is because parties to a contract are generally entitled to presume that an adult with whom they are dealing has mental capacity. In cases of gift, by contrast, there is no additional requirement of knowledge on the part of the defendant, in cases of mental incapacity.[93]

[89] See eg *Valentini v Canali* (1889) 24 QBD 166, 167 (Lord Coleridge CJ; Bowen LJ concurring).

[90] *R Leslie Ltd v Sheill* [1914] 3 KB 607, 618. See also ibid 623–24 (Kennedy LJ), 627 (Lawrence J). *Re King Ex parte The Unity Joint Stock Mutual Banking Association* (1858) 3 De G & J 63, 44 ER 1192. Discussed in E Bant, 'Incapacity, Non Est Factum and Unjust Enrichment' (2009) 33 *Melbourne University Law Review* 368.

[91] See, generally, DJ Harland, *The Law of Minors in Relation to Contracts and Property* (Sydney, Butterworths, 1974) 11–15. Authorities in favour include *Gibbons v Wright* [1954] HCA 17, (1954) 91 CLR 423, 447 [18] (the Court), citing *Perkins' Profitable Book*. See also *Hearle v Greenbank* (1749) 3 Atk 695, 712, 26 ER 1200, 1208 (Lord Hardwicke); *Re D'Angibau; Andrews v Andrews* (1880) 15 Ch D 228, 241 (Cotton LJ); *Burnaby v Equitable Reversionary Interest Society* (1885) 28 Ch D 416, 424 (Pearson J). Authorities against include: *Earl of Buckinghamshire v Drury* (1761) 2 Eden 60, 72–73, 28 ER 818, 821 (Lord Mansfield) and *Taylor v Johnston* (1882) 19 Ch D 603, discussed by Harland at 14. See also Lord Chancellor's Department, *Report of the Committee on the Age of Majority* (Cmnd 3342, 1967) 98.

[92] *Molton v Camroux* (1848) 2 Exch 487, 154 ER 584; *The Imperial Loan Company Limited v Stone* [1892] 1 QB 599; *Gibbons v Wright* [1954] HCA 17, (1954) 91 CLR 423; *Hart v O'Connor* [1985] AC 1000.

[93] The case law is slight: see *Re Beaney* [1978] 1 WLR 770 (probably a case of *non est factum* rather than general incapacity). On the difference between *non est factum* and cases of general incapacity, see the discussions in *Gibbons v Wright* [1954] HCA 17, (1954) 91 CLR 423, 437–49 (the Court) and *Ford v Perpetual Trustees Victoria Ltd* [2009] NSWCA 186, (2009) 75 NSWLR 42 [36]–[90] (Allsop P and Young JA; Sackville AJA concurring).

Unfortunately the cases involving mentally incompetent people have been confused by a failure to distinguish between policy-based restitution and cases of restitution for the wrong of exploitation of weakness (unconscionable dealing), in which the mental incapacity of the plaintiff is exploited by the defendant.[94] We saw in Chapter 2 that the wrong of unconscionable dealing requires proof of exploitation by the defendant of a special disadvantage of the plaintiff and a predatory intent.[95] Although there is no doubt that that kind of claim *may* arise in cases of mental incapacity as an alternative to a claim for restitution based on policy grounds, courts often do not clarify the basis for the award of restitution.[96] An example is the decision of the Privy Council in *Hart v O'Connor*.[97] In that case, the Privy Council denied restitution to a mentally incapable 83-year-old plaintiff who entered into a contract for the sale of land to an unsuspecting defendant who was unaware of the plaintiff's disability. The Privy Council denied restitution, referring to both reasons of policy as well as the lack of 'victimisation' of the plaintiff.[98]

IV. Policies to Encourage Intervention by the Plaintiff

In general, restitutionary claims for unjust enrichment are often denied for benefits that are obtained by defendants without request: 'Liabilities are not to be forced upon people behind their backs any more than you can confer a benefit upon a man against his will.'[99] A defendant will not be enriched in those circumstances. But policy reasons for restitution are not based upon unjust enrichment. In cases of emergency or great need,[100] the law sometimes has the policy of encouraging intervention to protect the health or property of others. The range of circumstances in which this policy applies is limited and varied. One group of cases involves a right to reclaim the reasonable costs of burying a deceased based on 'common principles of decency and humanity' and 'in order to avoid what, if not provided against, may become an inconvenience to the public'.[101] There are also cases that allow medical professionals recovery of reasonable remuneration for providing urgent medical services to injured persons.[102]

The largest of these groups of cases concerns 'agents of necessity' and salvage cases, which reflect a policy of encouraging rescue.[103] While agency of necessity originated in cases of carriage by sea, in which the master of a ship acted in an emergency to save the crew or its

[94] See AH Hudson, 'Mental Incapacity in the Law of Contract and Property' [1984] *The Conveyancer and Property Lawyer* 32, discussing among others *Archer v Cutler* [1980] 1 NZLR 386.

[95] Ch 2 p 21.

[96] A classic example is *Blomley v Ryan* [1956] HCA 81, (1956) 99 CLR 362.

[97] *Hart v O'Connor* [1985] AC 1000.

[98] ibid 1024.

[99] *Falcke v Scottish Imperial Insurance Company* (1886) 34 Ch D 234, 248 (Bowen LJ).

[100] *Re F* [1990] 2 AC 1, 75 (Lord Goff).

[101] *Rogers v Price* (1829) 3 Y & J 28, 34 (Garrow B), 36 (Hullock B), 148 ER 1080, 1082 (Garrow B), 1083 (Hullock B). See also *Jenkins v Tucker* (1788) 1 H Bl 90, 126 ER 55; *Croskery v Gee* [1957] NZLR 586.

[102] *Matheson v Smiley* [1932] 2 DLR 787. See also *Re F* [1990] 2 AC 1, 74–79 (Lord Goff).

[103] Cf *Lumbers v W Cook Builders Pty Ltd (in liq)* [2008] HCA 27, (2008) 232 CLR 635 [80] (Gummow, Hayne, Crennan and Keifel JJ).

cargo,[104] it has also been applied to claims arising from land-based emergencies.[105] Thus in *Great Northern Rly Co v Swaffield*,[106] the defendant sent a horse by the plaintiffs' railway, but when it arrived at its destination it was not collected. The station master accordingly arranged for the horse to be stabled. The defendant refused to pay for the charges and the horse remained in the stables. Four months later, the plaintiffs paid the charges and delivered the horse to the defendant. They then sought recovery of the charges from the defendant. The action succeeded. Drawing an analogy between the instant case and the 'agency of necessity' cases involving carriage by sea, Kelly CB stated:

> [I]t has been held that a shipowner who, through some accidental circumstance, finds it necessary for the safety of the cargo to incur expenditure, is justified in doing so, and can maintain a claim for reimbursement against the owner of the cargo. This is exactly the present case. The plaintiffs were put into much the same position as the shipowner occupies under the circumstances I have described. They had no choice, unless they would leave the horse at the station or in the high road to his own danger and the danger of other people, but to place him in the care of a livery stable keeper, and as they are bound by their implied contract with the livery stable keeper to satisfy his charges, a right arises in them against the defendant to be reimbursed those charges which they have incurred for his benefit.[107]

In relation to the complex and voluminous law relating to salvage,[108] the law is that where a person, without pre-existing obligation,[109] assists in preserving a recognised subject of salvage from a real danger of loss or damage, that person is entitled to a salvage award.[110] Historically, the right to a salvage award arose in relation to the rescue of ships, persons and cargos in peril on the high seas. It is now usually extended by statute to tidal waters. It has not been applied beyond tidal waters, to non-tidal waters or to land-based claims.[111] There may be

[104] *Gaudet v Brown; Cargo ex 'Argos'* (1873) LR 5 PC 134; *Burns Philp & Co Ltd v Gillespie Brothers Pty Ltd* [1947] HCA 3, (1947) 74 CLR 148.

[105] Eg *Prager v Blatspiel, Stamp and Heacock Ltd* [1924] 1 KB 566; *Jebara v Ottoman Bank* [1927] 2 KB 254; *Sachs v Miklos* [1948] 2 KB 23; *China-Pacific SA v Food Corp of India (The Winson)* [1982] AC 939. See also cases dealing with the rights of a plaintiff who accept a bill of exchange 'for the honour' of the drawer: *Hawtayne v Bourne* (1841) 7 M & W 595, 151 ER 905. In England, the doctrine has also been raised (not always successfully) by salvors of stolen cars: see *Lambert v Fry* [2000] CLY 113; *Surrey Breakdown Ltd v Knight* [1999] RTR 84; *Eagle Recovery Services v Parr* [1998] CLY 3379; *Egertons v KGM Motor Policies at Lloyd's* [1997] CLY 3168; *Service Motor Policies at Lloyd's v City Recovery Ltd* [1997] EWCA Civ 2073, cf *Suburban Towing & Equipment Pty Ltd v Suttons Motor Finance Pty Ltd* [2008] NSWSC 1346, (2008) 74 NSWLR 77, declining to extend the doctrine to tow truck services. See also *Guildford Borough Council v Hein* [2005] EWCA Civ 979, [2005] LGR 797 [50]–[51] (Clarke LJ: council paying for kennel costs for dogs) and *Re Berkeley Applegate (Investment Consultants) Ltd; Harris v Conway* [1989] Ch 32, 62 (Edward Nugee QC: reimbursement and remuneration of liquidator from assets held by the insolvent company on trust), followed in *Shirlaw v Taylor* [1991] FCA 415, (1991) 31 FCR 222, but cf *Dean-Willcocks v Nothintoohard Pty Ltd (in liq)* [2006] NSWCA 311, (2007) 13 BPR 24,245. For a recent refusal by an Australian court to expand the application of the doctrine beyond the more traditional categories, see *Hawksford v Hawksford* [2005] NSWSC 463, (2005) 191 FLR 173 [73] (Campbell J).

[106] *Great Northern Railway Co v Swaffield* (1874) LR 9 Exch 132. See also *Re Berkeley Applegate (Investment Consultants) Ltd; Harris v Conway* [1989] Ch 32 62 (Edward Nugee QC).

[107] *Great Northern Railway Co v Swaffield* (1874) LR 9 Exch 132, 136.

[108] See, eg, FD Rose, *Kennedy and Rose: The Law of Salvage*, 6th edn (London, Sweet & Maxwell, 2002); J Reeder (ed), *Brice on Maritime Law of Salvage*, 4th edn (London, Sweet & Maxwell, 2003).

[109] For example, arising from contract or in fulfilment of a statutory duty.

[110] FD Rose, 'Restitution for the Rescuer' (1989) 9 *Oxford Journal of Legal Studies* 167, 171.

[111] *The Goring* [1988] AC 831 determined that in England, the statutory right of salvage did not extend to non-tidal waters. The maritime law of salvage was assumed not to apply to land-based claims in *Owners of the Tojo Maru v NV Bureau Wijsmuller; The Tojo Maru* [1972] AC 242, 268 (Lord Reid), and in *Sorrell v Paget* [1950] 1 KB 252, 260 (Bucknill LJ).

reasons why the policy should be different. Underlying the law of salvage is the policy need to encourage salvors to assist persons or property in peril.[112] Whether that policy should change with the tides, may depend on considerations peculiar to maritime law.

Unlike claims in unjust enrichment,[113] the remedies required to promote the policy favouring intervention include not only restitution, but also disgorgement or compensation awards, and in some case an additional amount by way of 'reward'. In many cases, courts do not clearly identify the nature of the award. Thus in *Matheson v Smiley*,[114] the Manitoba Court of Appeal considered a claim by a surgeon for reasonable remuneration for his services performed on a dying suicide. The Court did not consider the issue of enrichment, which was difficult on the facts.[115] So it is unclear that the award duly made by the Court was restitutionary in nature. It could have been by way of compensation or reward. The short point was that some award was necessary because the law takes the view that such services ought to be encouraged as a matter of public policy, in order to encourage intervention by appropriate persons. As Professor Honoré has said:

> If the law does not encourage rescue, it is sure to discourage it. If it does not compensate, it will indirectly penalize. If the rescuer who suffers injury or incurs expense or simply expends his skill goes without compensation, the law, so far as it influences conduct at all, is discouraging rescue.[116]

In this case, the considerable deterrent effect and possible ramifications of refusing remuneration were obvious and demanded relief whether framed as restitution, compensation or, indeed, reward.

The policy of encouraging intervention by appropriate persons often dictates the size and nature of the award. Professional salvors have been held to be entitled to a more generous amount by way of reward than lay persons.[117] For example, in considering the possible development of a general doctrine of necessitous intervention, Ralph Gibson LJ opined that any right to remuneration, as opposed to reimbursement of expenses, should be limited to services 'of a professional nature'.[118] This kind of favouritism makes sense from a policy perspective: the law may not want to encourage inexperienced or incompetent efforts at rescue, even if at the end of the day those efforts prove successful. On the other hand, courts appear to be conscious of the means and status of the recipient of the benefit when evaluating the extent of any award in cases of necessity.[119] The courts' approach can be justified by reference to the underlying policy: while there is a need to encourage

[112] Eg *Owners of the Tantalus v Owners of the Telemachus* [1957] P 47, 49 (Willmer J); *The St Blane* [1974] 1 Lloyd's Rep 557, 560 (Brandon J). The policy considerations are comprehensively examined in O Lennox-King, 'Laying the Mark to Port and Starboard: Salvage under Duress and Economic Duress at Contract Law' [2007] *Australian and New Zealand Maritime Law Journal* 32.

[113] See Ch 2 p 15.

[114] *Matheson v Smiley* [1932] 2 DLR 787.

[115] See also P Birks, *Unjust Enrichment*, 2nd edn (Oxford, Oxford University Press, 2005) 23.

[116] AM Honoré, 'Law, Morals and Rescue' in JM Ratcliffe (ed), *The Good Samaritan and the Law* (New York, Anchor Books, 1966) 232.

[117] *The Queen Elizabeth* (1949) 82 Ll L Rep 803.

[118] *The Goring* [1987] QB 687, 708.

[119] Eg *Matheson v Smiley* [1932] 2 DLR 787 (reasonable remuneration for surgeon), citing *Wood v McMartin* (1917) 54 Que SC 391 and *Gibson v Mackay* (1907) 10 OWR 1081; *Rogers v Price* (1829) 3 Y & J 28, 148 ER 1080; *Jenkins v Tucker* (1788) 1 H Bl 90, 94, 126 ER 55, 57 (Gould J: burial expenses). See also FD Rose, 'Restitution for the Rescuer' (1989) 9 *Oxford Journal of Legal Studies* 167, 171, 200 (salvage).

intervention by making an appropriate award, that award should not be crushing on the defendant.

Finally, in salvage cases, the courts' remedy usually includes a significant element of reward expressly 'for the encouragement of those who engage in so dangerous a service'.[120] This measure reflects an appreciation that the gravity of the peril faced by the intervenor should be considered in allocating the salvor's reward.[121] While peril to the rescuer may be less common in cases involving land-based emergencies, there is no reason why this policy should not extend to other cases of necessity, where the need for encouraging appropriate intervention is high and the danger to the intervenor particularly great.

V. Policy Against Accumulation

Professor Degeling has argued that in England where a plaintiff (1) receives a benefit, or has the right to recover a debt or damages from X, and (2) receives or has a right to receive value in respect of the same debt or damage from Y, then the plaintiff should rarely be able to retain both benefits. There is a policy against accumulation, and one transfer must be reversed. Degeling has identified this policy as a new and independent reason for restitution.[122]

The key case upon which this thesis rests is *Hunt v Severs*.[123] In that case, Hunt was a pillion passenger on a motorcycle being driven by her boyfriend, Severs. Hunt became a paraplegic as a result of an accident caused by Severs' negligence. As a result, Hunt required full-time care. Later, Hunt and Severs married and Severs took on the role of her primary carer. Hunt (via her insurer) successfully sued Severs for compensatory damages, which included an amount for the past and future value of carer services provided to her by Severs. Severs (via his insurer) appealed this award to the House of Lords. In obiter dicta, the House explained that the award of compensation for a carer's services is by way of recompense to the carer so that, as long as the carer is not a tortfeasor, the amount should be held by the plaintiff on trust for the carer. Severs' dual identity as carer and tortfeasor precluded that result. Lord Bridge said that 'there can be no ground in public policy or otherwise for requiring the tortfeasor to pay to the plaintiff, in respect of the services which he himself has rendered, a sum of money which the plaintiff must then repay to him'.[124] Dr Degeling argues that the imposition of a trust in respect of carers' components of compensation

[120] *Nicholson v Chapman* (1793) 2 H Bl 254, 257, 126 ER 536, 538 (Eyre CJ).

[121] AM Honoré, 'Law, Morals and Rescue' in JM Ratcliffe (ed), *The Good Samaritan and the Law* (New York, Anchor Books, 1966) 232.

[122] S Degeling, 'A New Reason for Restitution: The Policy against Accumulation' (2002) 22 *Oxford Journal of Legal Studies* 435; see also S Degeling, 'The Policy against Accumulation as an Unjust Factor' in EJH Schrage (ed), *Unjust Enrichment and the Law of Contract* (The Hague, Kluwer Law International, 2001); S Degeling, *Restitutionary Rights to Share in Damages: Carer's Claims* (Cambridge, Cambridge University Press, 2003).

[123] *Hunt v Severs* [1994] 2 AC 350; *Islington London Borough Council v University College London Hospital NHS Trust* [2005] EWCA Civ 596, [2006] PIQR P3; *Drake v Foster Wheeler Ltd* [2010] EWHC 2004, [2011] 1 All ER 63. See also *Dimond v Lovell* [2000] UKHL 27, [2002] 1 AC 384, and *Lord Napier and Ettrick v RF Kershaw Ltd (No 1)* [1993] AC 713, analysed by S Degeling, 'A New Reason for Restitution: The Policy against Accumulation' (2002) 22 *Oxford Journal of Legal Studies* 435, 449–60.

[124] *Hunt v Severs* [1994] 2 AC 350, 363 (Lord Bridge).

awards reflects a policy against accumulation on the part of the plaintiff which is a policy-based reason for restitution.[125]

In Australia, the High Court decision in *Kars v Kars*[126] has put an end to the possibility of this policy-based claim for restitution.[127] In that case, the High Court unanimously rejected the approach taken in *Hunt v Severs*. As Dawson J explained:

> [I]t cannot be said in Australia that the underlying rationale of awarding damages for services provided gratuitously is to enable the carer to receive proper recompense for his or her services. The damages are recoverable to compensate the plaintiff for the loss which is evidenced *by the need for the services* and it is a matter for the plaintiff whether they are used to recompense the person providing the services.[128]

On this approach, the payment by the tortfeasor is by way of compensation to the victim for his or her need for care and is not held on trust. The difference between the Australian and English approaches is based upon a different perception of the underlying policy of the award of compensation to the victim. The English approach sees the policy of compensation as one which allows recovery to recoup the costs of services. The Australian approach sees the policy as one which allows recovery to recoup the cost of the *need* for services.

VI. Reversal of Judgment Restitution

It is well established that a plaintiff is entitled to restitution of enrichment transferred in satisfaction of a judgment that is later reversed or set aside.[129] The juridical basis of that right is much less obvious and the different alternative possibilities are rarely canvassed in judicial decision.[130] The best approach is to recognise that there are several possible alternatives, only one of which is a policy-based reason for restitution.

[125] S Degeling, 'A New Reason for Restitution: The Policy against Accumulation' (2002) 22 *Oxford Journal of Legal Studies* 435, 441.

[126] *Kars v Kars* [1996] HCA 37, (1996) 187 CLR 354. See also *Grincelis v House* [2000] HCA 42, (2000) 201 CLR 321; *CSR Ltd v Eddy* [2005] HCA 64, (2005) 226 CLR 1.

[127] The case is considered in S Degeling, *Restitutionary Rights to Share in Damages: Carer's Claims* (Cambridge, Cambridge University Press, 2003).

[128] *Kars v Kars* [1996] HCA 37, (1996) 187 CLR 354, 360 (emphasis added); see also 370–72 (Toohey, McHugh, Gummow and Kirby JJ).

[129] *Heydon v NRMA Ltd (No 2)* [2001] NSWCA 445, (2001) 53 NSWLR 600 [12] (Mason P). It was described as 'reasonably well settled' by DM Gordon in his seminal article on the subject, 'Effect of Reversal of Judgment on Acts Done between Pronouncement and Reversal' (1958) 74 *Law Quarterly Review* 517. The principle dates back at least to *Eyre v Woodfine* (1590) Cro Eliz 278, 78 ER 533. The history and scope of operation of the action is examined in detail by Brooking J in *National Australia Bank Ltd v Bond Brewing Holdings Ltd* [1991] 1 VR 386, 591–605. The numerous modern Australian authorities are gathered and discussed by Steytler J (with whom Wheeler and Roberts-Smith JJ agreed) in *Easterday v Western Australia* [2005] WASCA 105, (2005) 30 WAR 122. See also *Ambulance Service of New South Wales v Worley (No 2)* [2006] NSWCA 236, (2006) 67 NSWLR 719 [25]–[34] (Basten JA, Tobias and McColl JJA agreeing); *Nationwide News Pty Ltd v Naidu (No 2)* [2008] NSWCA 71 [10] (Spigelman CJ); *Woolworths Ltd v Strong (No 2)* [2011] NSWCA 72, (2011) 80 NSWLR 445 [25] (Campbell JA; Handley AJA and Harrison J concurring).

[130] *Heydon v NRMA Ltd (No 2)* [2001] NSWCA 445, (2001) 53 NSWLR 600 [13] (Mason P). The alternative candidates and supporting case law are reviewed by AJ Papamatheos, 'What are the Juridical Bases of Reversal of Judgment Restitution?' (2004) 25 *Australian Bar Review* 268.

A. The Basis of the Right is not Wrongdoing

One suggestion can immediately be rejected. In *Rodger v Comptoir D'Escompte de Paris*[131] Lord Cairns (giving the opinion of the Privy Council) stated that 'one of the first and highest duties of all Courts is to take care that the act of the Court does no injury to any of the Suitors'.[132] His Lordship later referred to the fact that the defendant to the action for restitution had obtained the benefit of monies obtained 'by mistake and by wrong obtained possession of the money under a judgment which has been reversed'.[133] This language was clearly not meant to indicate an actionable wrong[134] such as would support, for example, a claim for compensation against the court. And even if it were, that would not avail the plaintiff against the defendant who, after all, cannot be held accountable for the mistakes of the court. It is precisely for these reasons that courts generally require, as a condition of granting an interlocutory injunction, that the party seeking the injunction give an undertaking as to damages. As Brooking J explained in *National Australia Bank Ltd v Bond Brewing Holdings Ltd*,[135] implicit in this practice is the recognition that, without the undertaking, the defendant will be left 'without remedy' in the event that the injunction turns out to have been incorrectly granted. It is not concerned with wrongdoing or compensation for any loss suffered.[136]

B. The Claim may be Based on the Unjust Factor of Powerlessness

A possible basis for restitution in these cases is the unjust factor of powerlessness in a claim for unjust enrichment. In some cases the courts speak of 'compulsion' in a sense which might suggest the operation of an unjust factor of powerlessness which we saw in Chapter 12.[137] The argument might be that the plaintiff's intention to enter a transaction that enriches the defendant is absent because the court has compelled the plaintiff to make the transfer. If the plaintiff does not, the successful claimant could execute against the plaintiff's assets. Usually, this powerlessness will not be sufficient for the plaintiff to bring a claim for restitution. There is an obvious right that the defendant will have to retain the enrichment: the court order. But once the court order is set aside that right no longer exists, at least for the purpose of retaining the capital sum.

[131] *Rodger v Comptoir d'Escompte de Paris* (1871) LR 3 PC 465.

[132] ibid 475.

[133] ibid 475.

[134] See *Woolworths Ltd v Strong (No 2)* [2011] NSWCA 72, (2011) 80 NSWLR 445 [35] (Campbell JA; Handley AJA and Harrison J concurring).

[135] *National Australia Bank Ltd v Bond Brewing Holdings Ltd* [1991] 1 VR 386, 600–03, cited with approval in *SmithKline Beecham v Apotex Europe Ltd* [2006] EWCA Civ 658, [2007] Ch 71 [56]–[60] (the Court).

[136] *National Australia Bank Ltd v Bond Brewing Holdings Ltd* [1991] 1 VR 386, 597; see also *Meerkin & Apel v Rossett Pty Ltd (No 2)* [1999] VSCA 10, [1999] 2 VR 31 [7] (Callaway JA; Charles and Batt JJA concurring), and *Burger King Corporation v Hungry Jack's Pty Ltd* [2001] NSWCA 187 [487]–[500] (the Court).

[137] *Commissioner for Railways (NSW) v Cavanough* [1935] HCA 45, (1935) 53 CLR 220, 225 (Rich, Dixon, Evatt and McTiernan JJ) quoting from *Dr Drury's Case* (1610) 8 Co Rep 141b, 143a, 77 ER 688, 691; *Caldwell v Hill* [2000] NSWCA 239 [56] (Mason P); cf *Aspect Contracts (Asbestos) Ltd v Higgins Construction plc* [2013] EWHC 1322, [2013] Bus LR 1199 [28], [47]–[48] (Mr Justice Akenhead), considering restitution of moneys paid pursuant to adjudication held under a statutory scheme; K Mason, JW Carter and GJ Tolhurst, *Mason and Carter's Restitution Law in Australia*, 2nd edn (Chatswood, NSW, LexisNexis Butterworths, 2008) para 701.

C. The Claim may be Based on the Unjust Factor of Mistake

Following the removal of the mistake of law bar,[138] mistake is another basis for restitution in these cases[139] and may have clear advantages for a plaintiff, particularly in terms of limitation periods.[140] On the other hand, if the plaintiff relies upon mistake as the unjust factor, there is authority that the claim will be subject to the change of position defence.[141] Whether the defence should be denied where it would undermine the concurrent policy basis for restitution, even where the claim is brought on the basis of mistake, is considered further in Chapter 14.

D. The Claim may be Based on Failure of Consideration

A third juridical basis for reversal of judgment restitution is failure of consideration: the shared basis of the transaction that enriched the defendant, namely the assumption of liability following the court order, failed. Thus in *Vasailes v Robertson*,[142] Davies AJA (with whom Hodgson JA and Pearlman AJA agreed) stated that:

> once the judgments of the first trial had been set aside, the respondents were entitled to recover the moneys paid thereunder. These moneys were moneys paid for a consideration which had wholly failed and the appellant was unduly enriched thereby. The respondents had a cause of action for restitution.[143]

Characterising the claim in this way would leave open the possibility (subject to as the issue of stultification discussed below) of the change of position defence in circumstances which might include an appeal brought out of time where the plaintiff believed he could dispose of the asset without the possibility of appeal.

E. The Claim may be Based on Reasons of Policy

The final possible reason for restitution following reversal of a judgment is one of policy. There is a clear policy interest in encouraging unsuccessful parties to comply with judicial orders and that policy is advanced by allowing restitution if the order is subsequently reversed or set aside.[144] As Professors Mason and Carter put it: 'The corollary of

[138] In *David Securities Pty Ltd v Commonwealth Bank of Australia* [1992] HCA 48, (1992) 175 CLR 353, discussed in Ch 8 p 185–89.

[139] *Rodger v Comptoir d'Escompte de Paris* (1871) LR 3 PC 465, 475 (Lord Cairns); *GH Varley Pty Ltd v Thomson* (NSWSC, 25 February 1998), and *Palmer v Blue Circle Southern Cement Ltd* [1999] NSWSC 697, (1999) 48 NSWLR 318.

[140] See further Ch 15 pp 388–89, 393.

[141] *Palmer v Blue Circle Southern Cement Ltd* [1999] NSWSC 697, (1999) 48 NSWLR 318.

[142] *Vasailes v Robertson* [2002] NSWCA 177.

[143] ibid [5].

[144] See generally B McFarlane, 'The Recovery of Money Paid under Judgments Later Reversed' [2001] 9 *Restitution Law Review* 1, cited with approval in *Woolworths Ltd v Strong (No 2)* [2011] NSWCA 72, (2011) 80 NSWLR 445 [35] (Campbell JA; Handley AJA and Harrison J concurring).

the obligation to obey an unstayed judgment or order is the right to be restored if it is reversed.'[145] Likewise, if a defendant's right to appeal is not to be rendered nugatory, the appellate court must have an inherent power to order restitution of any benefits transferred as a result of that incorrect judgment order.[146] To put it in another way, if Parliament's purpose in providing an appeal process is not to be stultified, courts must have an inherent power to award restitution.

This policy-based reason for restitution has significant support in Australian courts.[147] Since this claim for restitution is independent of unjust enrichment, an application of the defence of change of position would inevitably undermine the policy promoting restitution. This means that the defence should not apply. *White v Tomasel*[148] provides a good example of these concerns.[149] In that case, orders were set aside on appeal as irregular but, in the interim, White had transferred the property the subject of the dispute to Tomasel pursuant to the order. McMurdo J said:

> A successful appellant's right is a personal one in the sense that restitution can be ordered only against a party to the judgment. The risk that money paid or property transferred pursuant to a judgment will have been paid or transferred away by the respondent by the conclusion of the appeal often provides a basis for staying a judgment under appeal. But whether a stay is sought, of if sought is granted, does not affect an unsuccessful respondent's obligation to restore to the appellant what was the appellant's property prior to the judgment.[150]

VII. 'Free Acceptance': A Policy of Encouraging the Defendant to Reject Unrequested Benefits?

A. Introduction

The final policy-based reason for restitution which we consider in this chapter is free acceptance. Free acceptance, if it exists as an independent reason for restitution, must reflect a policy of requiring a defendant to take active steps to reject benefits from the plaintiff that have not been chosen by the defendant. We will see below, however, that this policy would be inconsistent with the refusal in private law to impose generalised positive obligations on

[145] K Mason and J Carter, *Restitution Law in Australia* (Sydney, Butterworths, 1995) 225, cited with approval by Williams JA in *White v Tomasel* [2004] QCA 89, [2004] 2 Qd R 438 [55]. See now K Mason, JW Carter and GJ Tolhurst, *Mason and Carter's Restitution Law in Australia*, 2nd edn (Chatswood, NSW, LexisNexis Butterworths, 2008) para 702.

[146] *Commonwealth v McCormack* [1984] HCA 57, (1984) 155 CLR 273, 276 [4] (the Court), citing with approval the dictum of Lord Field in *Cox v Hakes* (1890) 15 App Cas 506, 547 that *restitutio in integrum* is the right of every successful appellant; see also *Nykredit Mortgage Bank plc v Edward Erdman Ltd* [1997] 1 WLR 1627, 1637 (Lord Nicholls).

[147] Most recently, see *Woolworths Ltd v Strong (No 2)* [2011] NSWCA 72, (2011) 80 NSWLR 445 [31]–[35] (Campbell JA; Handley AJA and Harrison J concurring).

[148] *White v Tomasel* [2004] QCA 89, [2004] 2 Qd R 438.

[149] See also *Easterday v Western Australia* [2005] WASCA 105, (2005) 30 WAR 122 [40] (Steytler J; Wheeler and Roberts-Smith JJ concurring).

[150] *White v Tomasel* [2004] QCA 89, [2004] 2 Qd R 438 [67].

defendants. It would also contradict the law's otherwise pervasive policy against rewarding undue risk-taking by plaintiffs.[151] The conclusion must be that any such policy-based reason for restitution should be rejected. Further, most cases that have attracted the label of 'free acceptance' are better understood as cases of total failure of consideration.

Originally, the concept of free acceptance was proposed by Lord Goff and Professor Jones[152] to explain a number of older cases where awards of restitution were made. Professor Birks subsequently adopted the concept and argued that free acceptance was not only a test for enrichment but also an unjust factor.[153] He argued that the enrichment of the defendant is unjust if a defendant;

(1) knows a benefit is not conferred gratuitously;[154]
(2) has an opportunity to reject a benefit conferred by the plaintiff; and
(3) fails to take the opportunity to reject the benefit.

B. A Policy to Encourage Rejection of Unrequested Benefits Undermines Existing Policies of the Law

From its inception, the concept of free acceptance was trenchantly criticised by academic commentators.[155] As an unjust factor, it introduced an undesirable incoherence into the law of unjust enrichment. The focus on the mental state of the defendant, rather than any impairment of the plaintiff's intention, was obviously different from the imperfect intention unjust factors. The concept also ran counter to the traditional common law reluctance to impose on parties a positive duty to act (here, to reject a benefit). Thus there is no general duty to rescue in tort, nor a duty to reject unwanted offers in contract. These attacks precipitated a gradual retreat from, and finally abandonment of the concept as an unjust factor by one of its initially strongest defenders, Professor Birks.[156] One important factor in Birks' abandonment of the concept was Professor Burrows' analysis that the central cases which had been thought to be cases of free acceptance were better analysed as based

[151] See *Chief Constable of the Greater Manchester Police v Wigan Athletic AFC Ltd* [2008] EWCA Civ 1449, [2009] 1 WLR 1580 discussed immediately below.

[152] In the last edition, G Jones (ed), *Goff and Jones: The Law of Restitution*, 7th edn (London, Sweet & Maxwell, 2007) para 1-019: see now C Mitchell, P Mitchell and S Watterson (eds), *Goff and Jones: The Law of Unjust Enrichment*, 8th edn (London, Sweet & Maxwell, 2011) ch 17.

[153] P Birks, *An Introduction to the Law of Restitution*, rev edn (Oxford, Oxford University Press, 1989) 265–93. See also K Mason, JW Carter and GJ Tolhurst, *Mason and Carter's Restitution Law in Australia*, 2nd edn (Chatswood, NSW, LexisNexis Butterworths, 2008) para 1025, who reject the contrary analysis of failure of basis on the ground that there was only a partial failure of consideration in *Pavey & Matthews Pty Ltd v Paul* [1987] HCA 5, (1986) 162 CLR 221, as to which see Ch 11 pp 271–72.

[154] Cf the formulation by Goff and Jones, which imports an objective element: in the previous edition, see G Jones (ed), *Goff and Jones: The Law of Restitution*, 7th edn (London, Sweet & Maxwell, 2007) para 1-019; but now see C Mitchell, P Mitchell and S Watterson (eds), *Goff and Jones: The Law of Unjust Enrichment*, 8th edn (London, Sweet & Maxwell, 2011) paras 17-09–17-12.

[155] See, eg, AS Burrows, 'Free Acceptance and the Law of Restitution' (1988) 104 *Law Quarterly Review* 576. See now AS Burrows, *The Law of Restitution*, 3rd edn (Oxford, Oxford University Press, 2011) 335, 337–38. G Mead, 'Free Acceptance: Some Further Considerations' (1989) 105 *Law Quarterly Review* 460.

[156] P Birks, 'In Defence of Free Acceptance' in A Burrows (ed), *Essays on the Law of Restitution* (Oxford, Clarendon Press, 1991) 109; P Birks and C Mitchell, 'Unjust Enrichment' in P Birks (ed), *English Private Law*, vol II (Oxford, Oxford University Press, 2000) ch 15.

on the unjust factor of failure of consideration.[157] This conclusion is amply supported by consideration of those English and Australia cases said to support an unjust factor of free acceptance discussed below. However, the most fundamental problem for free acceptance as a free-standing ground of restitution is that it could only exist if it were supported by a policy reason for restitution. But the policy points in the opposite direction.

Suppose a plaintiff expects to be paid for work done but the defendant, having an opportunity to reject, accepts the work thinking that he was not obliged to pay for it. If the basis of the work was not objectively shared by the parties, then the plaintiff was proceeding on the basis of a secret, unilateral misprediction. To allow restitution in this context would reward her risk-taking behaviour. We have seen in Chapter 11 that this is precisely why, in relation to the unjust factor of failure of consideration, the law requires that the basis must be identified by reference to the objectively manifested behaviour of the parties.[158]

Another situation in which free acceptance would be contrary to other legal policy is where there is no shared understanding because, although a defendant understands that the plaintiff is to be paid, the plaintiff does not expect to be paid. In such a case, the plaintiff again is a risk-taker who should not be rewarded.[159] In an article entitled 'In Defence of Free Acceptance', Professor Birks accepted this, acknowledging that a defendant who stops to watch a street show is not obliged to pay when the hat is passed around.[160] Indeed, under the Australian Consumer Law, a plaintiff commits an offence if he even asserts a right to payment unless he or she 'has reasonable cause to believe that there is a right to the payment'.[161]

C. 'Free Acceptance' Cases can also Involve Failure of Consideration

The conclusion above that free acceptance cannot be justified on the basis of a policy for restitution raises the question of whether those legal decisions that appear to recognise free acceptance must be overruled. In England, free acceptance was recognised as an unjust factor in *R (Rowe) v Vale of White Horse District*.[162] In that case, Lightman J explained that, in the ordinary case, 'a householder who receives and uses services from a supplier such as the Council must reasonably expect to pay for such services and will know that he has the option to reject them, and he will accordingly be liable under the principle of free acceptance to pay for them'.[163] However, this reasoning equally fits the unjust factor of failure of consideration: the householder received the services on the basis (objectively ascertained) that he would pay for them. Conversely, where, as was in fact the case, the defendant was in the unusual position that he reasonably understood the services were free, there was

[157] AS Burrows, *The Law of Restitution*, 3rd edn (Oxford, Oxford University Press, 2011) 335–39. See also now C Mitchell, P Mitchell and S Watterson (eds), *Goff and Jones: The Law of Unjust Enrichment*, 8th edn (London, Sweet & Maxwell, 2011) paras 17-06–17-07.

[158] Ch 11 pp 253–54.

[159] Cf *Lumbers v W Cook Builders Pty Ltd (in liq)* [2008] HCA 27, (2008) 232 CLR 635 [46] (Gleeson CJ).

[160] P Birks, 'In Defence of Free Acceptance' in A Burrows (ed), *Essays on the Law of Restitution* (Oxford, Clarendon Press, 1991) 119, 121.

[161] Competition and Consumer Act 2010 (Cth) sch 2 (Australian Consumer Law) s 40.

[162] *R (on the application of Rowe) v Vale of White Horse District Council* [2003] EWHC 388 (Admin), [2003] 1 Lloyd's Rep 418 [13]–[14] (Lightman J).

[163] ibid [14] (Lightman J).

no shared condition of payment so as to support liability. Although Lightman J framed this conclusion in terms of free acceptance, it is entirely consistent with failure of basis reasoning.

In *Benedetti v Sawiris*,[164] Patten J at first instance also unequivocally accepted the unjust factor of free acceptance. In the Court of Appeal,[165] Etherton LJ (Rimer LJ concurring on this part) noted that the controversy over whether the ground of restitution was free acceptance or failure of basis was not the subject of appeal. The Supreme Court likewise noted that it was common ground and undisputed that the plaintiff had established a prima facie claim for restitution.[166] However, both Lord Reed[167] and Lord Neuberger[168] went on to characterise the operative unjust factor as failure of basis: in the words of Lord Reed JSC, 'the services were provided on the basis that arrangements would be agreed for Mr Benedetti to be rewarded, but no such arrangements eventuated'.

A final example of a 'free acceptance' case in England was *Chief Constable of the Greater Manchester Police v Wigan Athletic AFC Ltd*.[169] In that case, the Chief Constable provided policing to the defendant football club at a higher level than the club considered warranted. In the course of deciding that the club had not chosen the services, and therefore had not been enriched, Sir Andrew Morritt C and Maurice Kaye LJ adopted the language of free acceptance to describe the possible reason for restitution. Lord Kaye, dissenting, would have granted restitution based on an independent policy ground, namely the necessity under the relevant statute for the game to be policed at a certain level in order to maintain the required safety certificate and for the game to proceed.[170] This policy-based reason for restitution notably bears no resemblance to the proposed policy underpinning free acceptance.

The authority in England for free acceptance as an independent ground for restitution is therefore very slim. In every case where liability has been found the reasoning can be understood as turning upon the same considerations as failure of consideration.

In Australia, one case which is said to support free acceptance as a reason for restitution is the decision of the High Court of Australia in *Pavey & Matthews* Pty *Ltd v Paul*.[171] It will be recalled that a majority of the High Court recognised that the builders' successful action was based in unjust enrichment but did not specifically state the 'unjust factor' upon which they relied.[172] However, we saw in Chapter 11 that the case is easily understood as involving the unjust factor of failure of consideration.[173] All subsequent cases relying on

[164] *Benedetti v Sawiris* [2009] EWHC 1330 [574].

[165] *Benedetti v Sawiris* [2010] EWCA Civ 1427 [143]. Cf *Dry Bulk Handy Holding Inc, Compania Sud Americana de Vapores SA v Fayette International Holdings Limited, Metinvest International SA* [2012] EWHC 2107 [81]–[82] (Mr Justice Andrew Smith), appeal on other points dismissed in *Dry Bulk Handy Holding Inc v Fayette International Holdings Ltd* [2013] EWCA Civ 184, [2013] 1 WLR 3440.

[166] *Benedetti v Sawiris* [2013] UKSC 50, [2014] AC 938 [11] (Lord Clarke JSC; Lord Kerr and Wilson JJSC concurring) [86] (Lord Reed JSC) [151] (Lord Neuberger PSC).

[167] *Benedetti v Sawiris* [2013] UKSC 50, [2014] AC 938 [86] (Lord Reed JSC).

[168] ibid [175] (Lord Neuberger PSC).

[169] *Chief Constable of the Greater Manchester Police v Wigan Athletic AFC Ltd* [2008] EWCA Civ 1449, [2009] 1 WLR 1580.

[170] *Chief Constable of the Greater Manchester Police v Wigan Athletic AFC Ltd* [2008] EWCA Civ 1449, [2009] 1 WLR 1580 [65]–[69].

[171] *Pavey & Matthews Pty Ltd v Paul* [1987] HCA 5, (1987) 162 CLR 221.

[172] ibid 227 [9]–[11] (Mason and Wilson JJ), 255 [12] (Deane J).

[173] Ch 11 pp 271–72.

Pavey & Matthews as having established a ground of restitution for 'free acceptance' fall into the same fact pattern.[174]

The concept of free acceptance was also subject to criticism by the High Court of Australia in *Lumbers v W Cook Builders Pty Ltd (in liq)*.[175] A builder, W Cook & Sons Pty Ltd ('Sons'), entered into a contract with Warwick Lumbers and his son to build the Lumbers a house of a very specific design. Subsequently, Sons entered into an agreement with a related company, W Cook Builders Pty Ltd ('Builders'), pursuant to which Builders undertook to complete the work. The Lumbers never requested, were never advised of, nor agreed to, this change. Builders completed the house and sought payment from the Lumbers. The Lumbers refused.

A majority of the Full Court of the Supreme Court of South Australia accepted Builders' argument that the Lumbers had been incontrovertibly benefited by the receipt of its services and had 'freely accepted' its services, so that the Lumbers were obliged to make restitution for the fair value of Builders' services (a *quantum meruit*).[176] But as Gleeson CJ noted on appeal,[177] even assuming the existence of an unjust factor of free acceptance, it could not have applied on the facts of the case. Entirely ignorant of the arrangements between Sons and Builders, the Lumbers never had a reasonable opportunity to reject Builders' services.[178] In a joint judgment, Gummow, Hayne, Crennan and Keifel JJ went further. They rejected Builders' characterisation of *Pavey & Matthews* as supporting a concept of free acceptance. They explained that there was no issue in *Pavey & Matthews* about whether the plaintiff had a claim for restitution. The only question was whether the claim was defeated by a statutory provision.[179] The case therefore provided no direct support for Builders' submission in *Lumbers* that free acceptance of a benefit sufficed to found an action for restitution. Further, in strongly worded obiter dicta, they rejected as 'wrong' the reasoning of one Australian case that could be said to provide express support for an unjust factor of free acceptance.[180]

In the light of the plurality's decision in *Lumbers*, it might be doubted that the unjust factor of free acceptance has any future in Australia. However, at the level of a strike out application it cannot yet be said in Australia to be entirely without merit. In *Lampson (Australia) Pty Ltd v Fortescue Metals Group Ltd (No 3)*[181] one of us observed that the High Court

[174] Eg *Brenner v First Artists' Management Pty Ltd* [1993] 2 VR 221; *Angelopoulos v Sabatino* (1995) 65 SASR 1; *Upjay Pty Ltd v MJK Pty Ltd* [2001] SASC 62, (2001) 79 SASR 32; *ABB Power Generation Ltd v Chapple* [2001] WASCA 412, (2001) 25 WAR 158; *Damberg v Damberg* [2001] NSWCA 87, (2001) 52 NSWLR 492 [187]–[190] (Heydon JA; Spigelman CJ and Sheller JA agreeing); *Andrew Shelton & Co Pty Ltd v Alpha Healthcare Ltd* [2002] VSC 248, (2002) 5 VR 577; *Concrete Constructions Group v Litevale Pty Ltd (No 2)* [2003] NSWSC 411 [11], [26] (Mason P).

[175] *Lumbers v W Cook Builders Pty Ltd (in liq)* [2008] HCA 27, (2008) 232 CLR 635 [82], [84], [86] (Gummow, Hayne, Crennan and Keifel JJ). See also *BBB Constructions v Aldi Foods* [2010] NSWSC 1352.

[176] *W Cook Builders Pty Ltd (in liq) v Lumbers* [2007] SASC 20, (2007) 96 SASR 406 [72]–[88] (Sulan and Layton JJ; Vanstone J dissenting). Originally, Builders sued both Sons and the Lumbers for payment. However, due to Builders' failure to provide Sons with security for its costs, further proceedings against Sons were stayed. By the time the matter came before the High Court of Australia, Sons had been wound up and deregistered.

[177] *Lumbers v W Cook Builders Pty Ltd (in liq)* [2008] HCA 27, (2008) 232 CLR 635 [53].

[178] For the same reason, failure of consideration was likely unavailable. Cf *ABB Power Generation Ltd v Chapple* [2001] WASCA 412, (2001) 25 WAR 158.

[179] Discussed in Ch 7 p 161.

[180] *Angelopoulous v Sabatino* (1996) 65 SASR 1, rejected *Lumbers v W Cook Builders Pty Ltd (in liq)* [2008] HCA 27, (2008) 232 CLR 635 [90].

[181] *Lampson (Australia) Pty Ltd v Fortescue Metals Group Ltd (No 3)* [2014] WASC 162 [80].

in *Lumbers* did not mention an earlier High Court authority which could be regarded as supporting the concept of free acceptance.[182] In *Liebe v Molloy*, Griffiths CJ, delivering the judgment of the High Court, stated:

> When a man does work for another without any express contract relating to the matter, an implied contract arises to pay for it at its fair value. Such an implication of course arises from an express request to do work made under such circumstances as to exclude the idea that the work was covered by a written contract. So it would arise from the owner standing by and seeing the work done by the other party, knowing that the other party, in this case the contractor, was doing the work in the belief that he would be paid for it as extra work. If the umpire was of opinion that any of this work was done under such circumstances that the owner knew or understood that the contractor was doing the work in the belief that he would be paid for it as extra work, then the umpire might, and probably would, infer that there was an implied promise to pay for it.[183]

Unless that decision can be treated as turning upon a genuinely implied contract, lower courts in Australia are presented with the principled approach in *Lumbers* but a decision in *Liebe* where the result turned upon considerations which are identical to the factors involved in free acceptance.

In summary, although the label 'free acceptance' has been used to describe an unjust factor in English and Australian cases, the enquiry is usually one of whether the basis has failed and not the three-fold test for free acceptance that Birks originally explained. Free acceptance could only exist independently of failure of consideration if it were able to be supported on some policy ground. But reasons of policy point in exactly the opposite direction.

VIII. Conclusion

This chapter has identified the key characteristics of a number of policy-based claims that give rise to the remedy of restitution and clarified their relationship with the law of unjust enrichment. Some proposed policy reasons for restitution (free acceptance and, in Australia, accumulation) have been rejected as independent reasons for restitution or are close to rejection. Many of the remaining policy-based restitutionary claims, such as illegality, incapacity and reversal of judgment restitution, may involve facts that could give rise to an alternative claim based on an unjust factor relating to imperfect intention. But in those categories of case, the fact of the plaintiff's imperfect intention is irrelevant to the plaintiff's independent right to restitution, also recognised in those cases, based on policy.

Where restitution is sought on the basis of policy, the reason for restitution has little in common with unjust factors based on imperfect intention. Nor is the reason for restitution concerned with issues of interpersonal justice between the parties arising from the plaintiff's impaired consent. It is an external standard that sets out some social, political or economic goal to be reached that is external to the parties. Separating out policy-based reasons for restitution from the law of unjust enrichment is therefore critical to maintaining coherence both within the law of unjust enrichment and more broadly in private law.

[182] ibid [86].

[183] *Liebe v Molloy* [1906] HCA 67, (1906) 4 CLR 347, 354.

Part IV

Defences

14

Change of Position

Contents

I. Introduction

One of the great advances in the law of unjust enrichment has been the explicit judicial recognition of the defence of change of position.[1] The defence applies where a good faith defendant has so changed her position as a result of her receipt that she would suffer detriment if ordered to make restitution or restitution in full.[2] The defence operates *pro tanto*, relieving the defendant from the obligation to make restitution to the extent of her detrimental change of position. Thus, suppose a defendant made a gift of £200 to a charity, in reliance on a mistaken payment of £500. Application of the defence would reduce her restitutionary liability to £300. The defence of change of position is an important illustration of the existence of an independent claim based on unjust enrichment. Not only was it first recognised as a defence to unjust enrichment, but courts have also denied that the defence applies to claims against wrongdoers, even for wrongs of strict liability.[3] Further, the defence will not generally apply to policy-based reasons for restitution, such as the *Woolwich* principle.[4]

The first section of this chapter addresses the elements of the defence, namely the requirements of a detrimental change of position, a causal or contributing link between the change of position and the defendant's enrichment and the roles of good faith and fault in the defence. The second section explains that there is no independent bar to the defence except in circumstances of overriding statutory or public policy. The third section explains why, notwithstanding its general application to claims in unjust enrichment, the defence is most commonly associated with claims for personal restitution on the ground of mistake. The final section considers statutory defences of change of position.

II. Elements of the Defence

It is often said that, in order for the change of position defence to apply, the defendant must have so changed his position that it would be inequitable,[5] unconscionable[6] or

[1] *Lipkin Gorman v Karpnale Ltd* [1991] 2 AC 548; *David Securities Pty Ltd v Commonwealth Bank of Australia* [1992] HCA 48, (1992) 175 CLR 353. However, see also *Campbell v Kitchen & Sons Ltd and Brisbane Soap Co Ltd* [1910] HCA 50, (1910) 12 CLR 515 discussed in *Australian Financial Services and Leasing Pty Ltd v Hills Industries Ltd* [2014] HCA 14, (2014) 253 CLR 560 [89] (Hayne, Crennan, Kiefel, Bell and Keane JJ); *Commonwealth v Kerr* [1919] SALR 201; *Commonwealth Bank of Australia v Younis* [1979] 1 NSWLR 444; *Bank of New South Wales v Murphett* [1983] 1 VR 489; cf *National Mutual Life Association of Australasia Ltd v Walsh* (1987) 8 NSWLR 585.

[2] *Australian Financial Services and Leasing Pty Ltd v Hills Industries Ltd* [2014] HCA 14, (2014) 253 CLR 560 [77] (Hayne, Crennan, Kiefel, Bell and Keane JJ) [157] (Gageler J).

[3] *Lipkin Gorman v Karpnale Ltd* [1991] AC 548, 580 (Lord Goff); endorsed in *Test Claimants in the FII Group Litigation v Revenue and Customs Commissioners* [2008] EWHC 2893, [2009] STC 254 [320] (Henderson J); *Western Areas Exploratión Pty Ltd v Streeter (No 3)* [2009] WASC 213, (2009) 234 FLR 265 [40] (Heenan J). Cf *Cavenagh Investment Pte Ltd v Kaushik Rajiv* [2013] SGHC 45 [60]–[65] (Chan Seng Onn J) (defence applied in case of innocent trespass); see also *Kuwait Airways Corporation v Iraqi Airways Co (Nos 4 and 5)* [2002] UKHL 19, [2002] 2 AC 883 [79] (Lord Nicholls).

[4] Discussed at pp 351–52, 355.

[5] *Lipkin Gorman v Karpnale Ltd* [1991] 2 AC 548, 579 (Lord Goff); *Haugesund Kommune v Depfa ACS Bank* [2010] EWCA Civ 579, [2012] QB 549 [152] (Etherton LJ).

[6] *Niru Battery Manufacturing Co v Milestone Trading Ltd* [2003] EWCA Civ 1446, [2004] QB 985 [147]–[149] (Clarke LJ; Butler-Sloss P concurring).

unjust[7] to require restitution or restitution in full. A recent example is the High Court of Australia's decision in *Australian Financial Leasing Services Pty Ltd v Hills Industries Ltd*,[8] in which French CJ considered the defence in terms of a broad normative standard of 'inequitability',[9] Hayne, Crennan, Kiefel, Bell and Keane JJ spoke in interchangeable terms of 'inequitability'[10] and 'unconscionability'[11] and Gageler J referred to the circumstances that would render an order for restitution or restitution in full against the defendant 'inequitable or unjust'.[12] These labels describe the ultimate norm motivating the defence rather than a criterion for direct application. As French CJ went on to explain in *AFSL v Hills*: 'Guiding criteria are indispensable to judicial decision-making in the application of broad normative standards to particular classes of case.'[13] It is to the applicable guiding criteria for change of position, rather than the ultimate normative principle, that we now turn.

A. A 'Detrimental' Change of Position

i. Detriment is not 'Disenrichment'

In *David Securities Pty Ltd v Commonwealth Bank of Australia*, the High Court of Australia identified as the core requirement of the defence that 'the defendant has acted to his or her detriment on the faith of the receipt'.[14] The importance of detriment or 'disadvantage' was affirmed by Hayne, Crennan, Kiefel, Bell and Keane JJ in *AFSL v Hills*,[15] who considered that the defence would apply where 'the recipient has so far altered its position in relation to the receipt that it would be a detriment to it if it were now required to repay'. This emphasis lends support to the view that one rationale of the defence lies in the prevention of detriment or harm to the defendant.[16]

It is important to pinpoint what 'detriment' means in this context. There are two main views. Professors Birks and Burrows have consistently argued that the change of position defence is concerned with 'disenrichment'.[17] Only changes of position that lead to the loss of all or part of the value of the benefit received will count for the purpose of the defence. It is this loss of 'net' enrichment that makes it inequitable, unconscionable or unjust to require restitution or restitution in full. The disenrichment analysis has been received positively by

[7] *David Securities Pty Ltd v Commonwealth Bank of Australia* [1992] HCA 48, (1992) 175 CLR 353, 385 [59] (Mason CJ, Deane, Toohey, Gaudron and McHugh JJ); *Haugesund Kommune v Depfa ACS Bank* [2010] EWCA Civ 579, [2012] QB 549 [122] (Aikens LJ; Pill LJ concurring).

[8] *Australian Financial Services and Leasing Pty Ltd v Hills Industries Ltd* [2014] HCA 14, (2014) 253 CLR 560.

[9] ibid [1].

[10] ibid [65]–[77].

[11] ibid [65]–[76], [81].

[12] ibid [155].

[13] ibid [25]; see also [76] (Hayne, Crennan, Kiefel, Bell and Keane JJ).

[14] *David Securities Pty Ltd v Commonwealth Bank of Australia* [1992] HCA 48, (1992) 175 CLR 353, 385 [59] (Mason CJ, Deane, Toohey, Gaudron and McHugh JJ) (emphasis omitted).

[15] *Australian Financial Services and Leasing Pty Ltd v Hills Industries Ltd* [2014] HCA 14, (2014) 253 CLR 560 [77].

[16] The harm-based rationale is powerfully developed in H Dagan, *The Law and Ethics of Restitution* (Cambridge, Cambridge University Press, 2004) 46–47; see further E Bant, *The Change of Position Defence* (Oxford, Hart, 2009) 215–20.

[17] P Birks, *Unjust Enrichment*, 2nd edn (Oxford, Oxford University Press, 2005) 208–12; AS Burrows, *The Law of Restitution*, 3rd edn (Oxford, Oxford University Press, 2011) 526.

English courts[18] and unjust enrichment commentators.[19] Some commentators say that the disenrichment conception of the defence is necessary to avoid the defence collapsing into the exercise of unguided discretion.[20] In particular, the New Zealand statutory versions of the defence (which have greatly influenced the development of their common law counterpart)[21] compare the fault of the parties in determining the level of protection to be afforded to the defendant. This approach has been condemned as 'hopelessly unstable'.[22]

As we will see below, it is right to identify disenrichment as characteristic of change of position cases. The defendant who gives his received benefit to a charity has changed his position by disenriching himself in such a way as likely attracts the defence.[23] But as an overriding criterion, the concept is not consistent with the defence as it has developed in the authorities, nor with the concept of enrichment used for the primary claim. It is neither sufficient nor is it necessary. It is not sufficient because there are separate requirements that the defendant must have been acting in good faith and that his receipt of the impugned benefit must have caused or contributed to the defendant's change of position. Disenrichment is not a necessary requirement because there can be non-disenriching changes of position. Even Professor Birks, one of the staunchest defenders of the disenrichment concept of the defence, acknowledged that changes of position do not need to be inherently pecuniary in nature. He gave the example of the decision to have a child, although arguing that it had 'foundation[s] in disenrichment'.[24] But to label the conception and delivery of a child as relevantly 'disenriching' for the purposes of change of position stretches the concept well beyond its natural domain. As Allsop P observed in the New South Wales Court of Appeal decision in *Hills Industries Ltd v Australian Financial Services and Leasing Pty Ltd*:

> There are difficulties ... in using purely monetary and expenditure based considerations to decide upon change of position. Given the broad range of acts or omissions that may legitimately be done

[18] See, eg, *Dextra Bank & Trust Co Ltd v Bank of Jamaica* [2001] UKPC 50, [2002] 1 All ER (Comm) 193; *Test Claimants in the FII Group Litigation v Revenue and Customs Commissioners* [2014] EWHC 4302, [2015] STC 1471 [309]–[354] (Henderson J); *John Ruskin College v Harley* [2013] EWHC 3714 [41]–[46] (Bean J).

[19] Eg R Grantham and C Rickett, 'Change of Position in New Zealand' [1999] *New Zealand Business Law Quarterly* 75, 77–78; R Grantham and C Rickett, 'Change of Position and Balancing the Equities' [1999] *Restitution Law Review* 158, 162–63; AS Burrows, *The Law of Restitution*, 3rd edn (Oxford, Oxford University Press, 2011) 526; J Palmer, 'Chasing a Will-o'-the-Wisp? Making Sense of Bad Faith and Wrongdoers in Change of Position' [2005] *Restitution Law Review* 53, 55–58; cf G Virgo, 'Change of Position: The Importance of Being Principled' [2005] *Restitution Law Review* 34, 35–37.

[20] See, eg, the judgment of Munby J in *Commerzbank AG v Price-Jones* [2003] EWCA Civ 1663, criticised in A Burrows, 'Clouding the Issues on Change of Position' (2004) 63 *Cambridge Law Journal* 276, 279.

[21] *National Bank of New Zealand Ltd v Waitaki International Processing (NI) Ltd* [1999] 2 NZLR 211; cf *Saunders & Co v Hague* [2004] 2 NZLR 475, 491, where Chisolm J considered himself, arguably incorrectly, as bound by the Privy Council decision in *Dextra Bank & Trust Co Ltd v Bank of Jamaica* [2001] UKPC 50, [2002] 1 All ER (Comm) 193 to ignore considerations of relative fault. Now see *Karl v Accident Compensation Corporation* [2005] NZAR 97 and *Foai v Air New Zealand Ltd* [2012] NZEmpC 57, both affirming the continuing relevance of fault in the New Zealand statutory context notwithstanding *Saunders*: see also *Air New Zealand Ltd v Foai* [2012] NZCA 341, (2012) 9 NZELR 480 [14] (Glazebrook, White and Simon France JJ).

[22] *Dextra Bank & Trust Co Ltd v Bank of Jamaica* [2001] UKPC 50, [2002] 1 All ER (Comm) 193 [45], adopting the arguments of P Birks, 'Change of Position and Surviving Enrichment' in W Swadling (ed), *The Limits of Restitutionary Claims: A Comparative Analysis* (London, United Kingdom National Committee of Comparative Law, 1997) 41.

[23] Subject to the requirement of irreversibility, see below pp 335–38.

[24] P Birks, 'Change of Position: The Two Central Questions' (2004) 120 *Law Quarterly Review* 373, 375. See also P Birks, *Unjust Enrichment*, 2nd edn (Oxford, Oxford University Press, 2005) 260; AS Burrows, *The Law of Restitution*, 3rd edn (Oxford, Oxford University Press, 2011) 526.

> or not done on the faith of a receipt, to require the measurement of the payee's position in terms only of the currency of the payer's mistake may unfairly or mechanically restrict the just reconciliation of the competing rights.[25]

In *AFSL v Hills Industries* the High Court emphasised this point and rejected the disenrichment analysis.[26] While generally accepting (without analysing the question) that disenriching changes of position might well attract the defence, all justices were unanimous in rejecting the necessity of disenrichment, in particular because of its perceived tendency to exclude or marginalise non-pecuniary changes of position, and to require 'a mathematical assessment of enduring economic benefit'.[27] As French CJ put it, 'there may be changes of position which are difficult or even impossible to value which are not, on that account, irrelevant for the purpose of the defence'.[28] Justice Gageler likewise emphasised that the relevant question is whether

> by reason of having so acted or refrained from acting, the defendant would be placed in a worse position if ordered to make restitution of the payment than if the defendant had not received the payment at all. The detriment constituted by that difference in position need not, in every case, be financial or pecuniary. If financial or pecuniary, it need not, in every case, be established with precision. It can be an opportunity forgone. It must, in every case, be shown by the defendant to be substantial.[29]

ii. Detriment as 'Irreversible' Change

An alternative formulation of the requirement for a 'detrimental' change of position, which has been articulated by Australian courts, is that a relevant change must be irreversible.[30] As expressed by Buss JA of the Western Australian Court of Appeal (Steytler P concurring) in *Alpha Wealth Financial Services Pty Ltd v Frankland River Olive Co Ltd*,[31] this conception

[25] *Hills Industries Ltd v Australian Financial Services and Leasing Pty Ltd* [2012] NSWCA 380, (2012) 295 ALR 147 [153], Bathurst CJ concurring on this point.

[26] *Australian Financial Services and Leasing Pty Ltd v Hills Industries Ltd* [2014] HCA 14, (2014) 253 CLR 560 [22]–[25] (French CJ) [78]–[84] (Crennan, Kiefel, Bell and Keane JJ) [147]–[148] (Gageler J).

[27] ibid [84] (Crennan, Kiefel, Bell and Keane JJ).

[28] ibid [23].

[29] ibid [157] (citations omitted).

[30] In relation to recovery of tax paid in reliance on the receipt, see *K & S Corp Ltd v Sportingbet Australia Pty Ltd* [2003] SASC 96, (2003) 86 SASR 312 [161] (Besanko J); *Fazzolari v Couchouron* [2003] VCAT 503, [2003] V ConvR 58-572; *Hinckley and Bosworth BC v Shaw* (1999) 1 LGLR 385, 425 (Bell J); *Hillsdown Holdings plc v Pensions Ombudsman* [1997] 1 All ER 862, 904 (Knox J). Cf *Lokan v Defence Force Retirement and Death Benefits Authority* [2007] AATA 1652 [14]–[15] (Deputy President PE Hack SC). Outside the taxation context, see *Scottish Equitable plc v Derby* [2001] EWCA Civ 369, [2001] 3 All ER 818 [34] (Robert Walker LJ). See also *Jaffer v Commonwealth Bank of Australia Ltd* [2001] SASC 191 [61]–[67] (Perry J); *Eden Productions Pty Ltd v Southern Star Group Ltd* [2002] NSWSC 1166 [226] (Gzell J); *Day v Day* [2005] EWHC 1455 [49] (Mr L Henderson QC); *Estate of Karl v Accident Compensation Corporation* [2003] NZACC 274 [24] (Judge MJ Beattie). Similar requirements are found in estoppel, the agent's defence of payment over and arguably the requirement of *restitutio in integrum* found in rescission: see eg *Jones v Churcher* [2009] EWHC 722, [2009] 2 Lloyd's Rep 94 [69] (HHJ Havelock-Allan QC); *Citigroup Pty Ltd v National Australia Bank Ltd* [2012] NSWCA 381, (2012) 82 NSWLR 391 [109] (Barrett JA; Bathurst CJ, Allsop P, Meagher JA and Macfarlan JA agreeing on this point).

[31] *Alpha Wealth Financial Services Pty Ltd v Frankland River Olive Co Ltd* [2008] WASCA 119, (2008) 66 ACSR 594 [202]; see also *Fitzsimons v McBride, Minister for Liquor, Gaming and Racing (NSW)* [2008] NSWSC 782 [128]–[129] (McDougall J); *Glad Cleaning Service Pty Ltd v Vukelic* [2010] NSWSC 422 [51] (Slattery J); *Hills Industries Ltd v Australian Financial Services and Leasing Pty Ltd* [2012] NSWCA 380, (2012) 295 ALR 147 [162], [165] (Allsop P; Bathurst CJ at [1] and Meagher JA at [215] concurring on this point); *Comgroup Supplies Pty Ltd v Products for Industry Pty Ltd* [2016] QCA 88.

of the defence requires that 'the recipient must have changed his or her position, and the change must be legally or practically irreversible or there must be significant difficulties in reversing the change'.

The criterion of irreversibility was endorsed by the High Court of Australia in *AFSL v Hills*.[32] In that case, AFSL (a financier) was induced by a fraudster to make payments to a number of businesses, including the respondents, Hills and Bosch, for the purchase of non-existent equipment. The fraudster advised Hills and Bosch that the payments were for the discharge of debts owed to them by his companies. In reliance on their receipts, Hills and Bosch changed their position by, amongst other matters, continuing to trade with the fraudster's companies and giving up the opportunity to pursue remedies in enforcement proceedings against those companies. Both recipients also gave up the opportunity of taking other steps to better their position, such as by seeking security from third parties.

All members of the Court applied the defence in full, analogising with the concept of 'detriment' in equitable estoppel, where the defence includes non-pecuniary changes of position provided that they are substantial.[33] Applying this approach, French CJ[34] and the joint judgment[35] separately explained that the changes undertaken by the respondents were very substantial and relevantly irreversible (and hence detrimental to the respondents). This was because, by the time the fraud came to light and AFSL gave notice of its mistake, the various steps of enforcement or securing of the debt could no longer be taken.[36] Moreover, French CJ noted that any difficulty in proving the precise value of the changes (what would or even could have been obtained as a consequence of enforcement proceedings, or obtaining security from third parties, for example) were a direct consequence of the passage of time between the mistaken payment and the demand.

The approach which focuses upon irreversible detriment requires the court to assess the irreversible changes to the defendant's position and to offset that detriment against what would otherwise be the full measure of the defendant's restitutionary liability. Some cases will involve irreversible detriment, which will be a complete defence. An example is the contentious Canadian case of *RBC Dominion Securities Inc v Dawson*.[37] Mrs Dawson received a mistaken payment on the faith of which she refurbished some of her furniture and replaced other household and domestic goods with new items. The Newfoundland Court of Appeal accepted that Mrs Dawson remained enriched following her change of position.[38] Nonetheless, it held that the change of position defence applied to all but one new item, which she said she would have purchased in any event. The decision can be justified by the irreversibility requirement, which identifies the difficulties and expenses Mrs Dawson would face

[32] *Australian Financial Services and Leasing Pty Ltd v Hills Industries Ltd* [2014] HCA 14, (2014) 253 CLR 560 [23]–[31] (French CJ) [95] (Hayne, Crennan, Kiefel, Bell and Keane JJ).
[33] ibid [88] (Hayne, Crennan, Kiefel, Bell and Keane JJ) [150] (Gageler J); see also [23], [25] (French CJ).
[34] ibid [29]–[30].
[35] ibid [95].
[36] Cf ibid [166] (Gageler J) citing the same facts but without the language of irreversibility.
[37] *RBC Dominion Securities Inc v Dawson* (1994) 111 DLR (4th) 230.
[38] ibid 240.

in reversing her changes (including selling the goods, finding equivalent and acceptable second-hand furniture to that which she initially replaced, and reversing the refurbishing work carried out on retained furniture) as being key to the application of the defence.[39] Another example is *Corporate Management Services (Australia) Pty Ltd v Abi-Arraj*.[40] The defendant changed his position by extending and renovating the family home in reliance on a mistaken overpayment of worker's compensation that was later reduced. The court found that the work completed on the home had deteriorated and that there was no prospect of it being finished, so the defence applied completely.

In general, the requirement that a change of position be irreversible is strictly applied. Thus where a defendant purchases a saleable asset in reliance on his receipt, courts will regard any detriment as limited because the asset can be sold and thus the change reversed.[41] The value of the defence will be limited to any proven depreciation of the asset.[42] It has even been held that in cases involving the purchase of land (for which sale involves time and expense), the purchase is to be treated as analogous with 'the acquisition of a motor car' (which is reversible), rather than 'the purchase of a world cruise' (which is not).[43] Similarly, where a defendant has discharged a debt in reliance on his receipt, courts will generally assume that a lender will be able to be found on similar terms as previously existed, so as to return the defendant to his position of former indebtedness.[44] Cogent evidence will need to be brought that no willing lender now exists.[45] By contrast, there is implicit support in the cases for the view that where a defendant can only reverse a change of position through litigation, proof by the defendant that the claim will be contested will suffice to satisfy the irreversibility requirement.[46] This likely reflects the speculative, expensive and time-consuming nature of litigation.[47]

[39] See also *Saunders & Co v Hague* [2004] 2 NZLR 475, 495–96 (Chisolm J: defendant pleaded obstacles to selling house which were not established on the facts).

[40] *Corporate Management Services (Australia) Pty Ltd v Abi-Arraj* [2000] NSWSC 361.

[41] *Lipkin Gorman v Karpnale Ltd* [1991] 2 AC 548, 560 (Lord Templeman); *Credit Suisse (Monaco) SA v Attar* [2004] EWHC 374 [98] (Gross J), discussed by C Mitchell in 'Change of Position: The Developing Law' [2005] *Lloyd's Maritime and Commercial Law Quarterly* 168, 173; see also M McInnes, 'Enrichment Revisited' in JW Neyers, M McInnes and SGA Pitel (eds), *Understanding Unjust Enrichment* (Oxford, Hart, 2004) 197–98, citing *Sullivan v Lee* (1994) 95 BCLR (2d) 195; *Empire Life Insurance Co v Neufeld Estate* (1998) 4 CCLI (3d) 278. McInnes cites *RBC Dominion Securities Inc v Dawson* (1994) 111 DLR (4th) 230 as authority to the contrary.

[42] *Lipkin Gorman v Karpnale Ltd* [1991] 2 AC 548, 560 (Lord Templeman).

[43] *Campden Hill Ltd v Chakrani* [2005] EWHC 911 [87] (Hart J).

[44] *Boscawen v Bajwa* [1996] 1 WLR 328, 341 (Millett LJ); *Pearce v Lloyds TSB Bank plc* [2001] EWCA Civ 1907; *National Bank of Egypt International Ltd v Oman Housing Bank SAOC* [2002] EWHC 1760, [2003] 1 All ER (Comm) 246; *Hartigan v International Society for Krishna Consciousness Inc* [2002] NSWSC 810 [98] (Bryson J); *Datasat Communications Ltd v Swindon Town Football Company Limited* [2009] EWHC 859 [109] (Mr Gavin Kealey QC).

[45] As in *Gertsch v Atsas* [1999] NSWSC 898, (1999) 10 BPR 18,431 [88], [95] (Foster AJ).

[46] In particular, the cases where tax was paid on receipts, such as *K & S Corp Ltd v Sportingbet Australia Pty Ltd* [2003] SASC 96, (2003) 86 SASR 312 [161] (Besanko J); *Fazzolari v Couchouron* [2003] VCAT 503, [2003] V ConvR 58-572; *Hinckley and Bosworth BC v Shaw* (1999) 1 LGLR 385, 425 (Bell J); *Hillsdown Holdings plc v Pensions Ombudsman* [1997] 1 All ER 862, 904 (Knox J). See also the position taken in estoppel: *Deutsche Bank (London Agency) v Beriro and Co Ltd* [1895–99] All ER Rep 1164.

[47] Cf *Australian Financial Services and Leasing Pty Ltd v Hills Industries Ltd* [2014] HCA 14, (2014) 253 CLR 560 [28]–[30] (French CJ).

In *AFSL v Hills*, the High Court confirmed that the concept of irreversible detriment includes irreversible decisions *not* to act[48] or to forgo a benefit[49] even though they entail no outflow of wealth. The High Court's approach also emphasised that the scale of the detriment for the purposes of the defence is assessed at the time the plaintiff seeks restitution of the received benefit, not at the time of the original change of position.[50] This explains why 'remoteness' considerations are irrelevant to the defence.[51] Provided that the change was caused by or contributed to by the original receipt, the reason why it has since become irreversible does not matter. Thus, in *Gertsch v Atsas*[52] a defendant changed his position in reliance on his receipt by purchasing a car which was uninsured and later stolen.[53] The change of position defence was held to apply. A comparable example, derived from an estoppel context, is where a defendant invests the amount of an overpayment in a company that subsequently goes into liquidation.[54]

B. Causation or Contribution

In order for the defence to apply, the defendant's detrimental change of position must have caused or contributed to the impugned transaction.[55] This is most clearly demonstrated by

[48] *Council of the City of Sydney v Burns Philp Trustee Co Ltd (in liq)* (NSWSC, 13 November 1992); *Gilsan (International) Ltd v Optus Networks Pty Ltd* [2004] NSWSC 1077 [260] (McDougall J), approved on this point on appeal in *Optus Networks Pty Ltd v Gilsan (International) Ltd* [2006] NSWCA 171 [79] (Hodgson JA; Beasley and McColl JJA concurring); *Eastbourne Borough Council v Foster* (QB, 20 December 2000), appealed on another point *Eastbourne Borough Council v Foster* [2001] EWCA Civ 1091, [2002] ICR 234. The example given in *Sempra Metals Ltd (formerly Metallgesellschaft Ltd) v Inland Revenue Commissioners* [2007] UKHL 34, [2008] 1 AC 561 [233] (Lord Mance) of a defendant hiding a mistaken payment under her bed, and thus omitting to invest the money so as to obtain commercial rates of interest for its use, is another example of this category of change: see *Sempra Metals Ltd (formerly Metallgesellschaft Ltd) v Inland Revenue Commissioners* [2007] UKHL 34, [2008] 1 AC 561 [119] (Lord Nicholls). See also *Test Claimants in the FII Group Litigation v Revenue and Customs Commissioners* [2014] EWHC 4302 (Ch), [2015] STC 1471 [414]–[415] (Henderson J).

[49] *Killham v Banque Nationale de Paris* (VSC, 28 June 1994) [50] (Hedigan J); *Palmer v Blue Circle Southern Cement Ltd* [1999] NSWSC 697, (1999) 48 NSWLR 318 [33]–[34] (Bell J); *Scottish Equitable plc v Derby* [2001] EWCA Civ 369, [2001] 3 All ER 818 [32]–[33] (Robert Walker LJ); *Commerzbank AG v Price-Jones* [2003] EWCA Civ 1663 [71]–[72] (Munby J); *Ethnic Earth Pty Ltd v Quoin Technology Pty Ltd (in liq) (No 3)* [2006] SASC 7, (2006) 94 SASR 103 [86] (Bleby J); *Kinlan v Crimmin* [2006] EWHC 779, [2007] BCC 106; *Moore v National Mutual Life Association of Australasia Ltd* [2011] NSWSC 416; *TRA Global Pty Ltd v Kebakoska* [2011] VSC 524. Cf *National Westminster Bank plc v Somer International (UK) Ltd* [2001] EWCA Civ 970, [2002] QB 1286 [47] (Potter LJ).

[50] *Australian Financial Services and Leasing Pty Ltd v Hills Industries Ltd* [2014] HCA 14, (2014) 253 CLR 560 [23]–[24] (French CJ) [85]–[88] (Hayne, Crennan, Kiefel, Bell and Keane JJ), [157] (Gageler J), noting the equivalence to estoppel and in particular the statement in *Grundt v Great Boulder Pty Gold Mines Ltd* [1937] HCA 58, (1937) 59 CLR 641, 674–75 (Dixon J); see also *Hills Industries Ltd v Australian Financial Services and Leasing Pty Ltd* [2012] NSWCA 380, (2012) 295 ALR 147 [158] (Allsop P; Bathurst CJ at [1] and Meagher JA at [215] agreeing on this point).

[51] Cf AS Burrows, *The Law of Restitution*, 3rd edn (Oxford, Oxford University Press, 2011) 531; R Nolan, 'Change of Position' in P Birks (ed), *Laundering and Tracing* (Oxford, Clarendon Press, 1995) 149–51.

[52] *Gertsch v Atsas* [1999] NSWSC 898, (1999) 10 BPR 18,431.

[53] The relevance of the fault of the defendant in changing his position is considered below pp 348–49.

[54] *Holt v Markham* [1923] 1 KB 504; see also *United Overseas Bank Ltd v Jiwani* [1976] 1 WLR 964, 968 (MacKenna J).

[55] *Ovidio Carrideo Nominees Pty Ltd v The Dog Depot Pty Ltd* [2004] VSC 400 [42]–[43] (Kaye J); *Scottish Equitable plc v Derby* [2001] EWCA Civ 369, [2001] 3 All ER 818 [31] (Robert Walker LJ); *Philip Collins Ltd v Davis* [2000] 3 All ER 808, 827 (Jonathan Parker J), cited with approval in *Commerzbank AG v Price-Jones* [2003] EWCA

Scottish Equitable plc v Derby,[56] in which the English Court of Appeal explained that it was irrelevant that the defendant pensioner would suffer undeniable and even crushing hardship if required to make restitution of a mistaken payment. The hardship was irrelevant, because the mistaken payment had played no role in bringing about his misfortunes.

In most cases, the required link is a link between the receipt of the benefit and the subsequent change of position.[57] In *Commerzbank AG v Price-Jones*,[58] Mummery LJ (Sedley LJ concurring) warned against adopting the 'mass of learning on causation questions generated by the cases on the recoverability of damages for tort', preferring a simple requirement that there be a 'relevant connection' between the change of position and the receipt.[59] Similar sentiments were expressed by Munby J.[60] These concerns may be overstated. This section demonstrates that, with the assistance of some straightforward but crucial distinctions between defendant-instigated and independent changes of position, the requirement of some causal or contributing link can be readily understood and applied in a principled and consistent manner.

i. *Defendant-Instigated Changes of Position*

One situation of change of position can arise from the defendant's decision to act or not to act. Such a 'defendant-instigated' change of position requires the link between receipt and change of position to be established by the concept of reliance.[61] As Moore-Bick J said in *Standard Bank London Ltd v Canara*:

> [I]n order to establish a change of position … it will normally be necessary for the payee to be able to show that the receipt of the money operated on his mind and caused him to act as he did.[62]

The role of reliance in establishing the defence has been widely recognised by the courts.[63] Less attention has been paid to the relevant test that applies to determine whether the defendant relied on her receipt. Consistently with the role of reliance in areas such as estoppel, in

Civ 1663 [58]–[59] (Munby J); *Heperu Pty Ltd v Belle* [2009] NSWCA 252, (2009) 76 NSWLR 230 [133] (Allsop P; Campbell JA and Handley AJA concurring); *Bloomsbury International Ltd v Sea Fish Industry Authority* [2009] EWHC 1721, [2010] 1 CMLR 12 [137] (Hamblen J). See also *Colliers CRE plc v Pandya* [2009] EWHC 211 [72] (Judge Richard Seymour QC).

[56] *Scottish Equitable plc v Derby* [2001] EWCA Civ 369, [2001] 3 All ER 818 [31] (Robert Walker LJ); cf *Bloomsbury International Ltd v Sea Fish Industry Authority* [2009] EWHC 1721, [2010] 1 CMLR 12 [137]–[142] (Hamblen J).

[57] Anticipatory changes of position are considered below at pp 341–42.

[58] *Commerzbank AG v Price-Jones* [2003] EWCA Civ 1663.

[59] ibid [43].

[60] ibid [58]–[59].

[61] *Citigroup Pty Ltd v National Australia Bank Ltd* [2012] NSWCA 381, (2012) 82 NSWLR 391 [6] (Bathurst CJ, Allsop P and Meagher JA), [84]–[86] (Barrett JA, Macfarlan JA concurring on this point).

[62] *Standard Bank London Ltd v Canara Bank* [2002] EWHC 1032 [104]; see also *Glad Cleaning Service Pty Ltd v Vukelic* [2010] NSWSC 422 [51] (Slattery J).

[63] *Australian Financial Services and Leasing Pty Ltd v Hills Industries Ltd* [2014] HCA 14, (2014) 253 CLR 560 [81] ((Hayne, Crennan, Kiefel, Bell and Keane JJ: citing *Scottish Equitable plc v Derby* [2001] EWCA Civ 369, [2001] 3 All ER 818; *Commerzbank AG v Price-Jones* [2003] EWCA Civ 1663). See also *Littlewoods Retail Ltd v HM Revenue & Customs* [2010] EWHC 1071, [2010] STC 2072 [114], [121]–[122] (Vos J). Cf *Test Claimants in the FII Group Litigation v Revenue and Customs Commissioners* [2008] EWHC 2893, [2009] STC 254 and *Bloomsbury International Ltd v Sea Fish Industry Authority* [2009] EWHC 1721, [2010] 1 CMLR 12 [137]–[138] (Hamblen J), discussed in *Littlewoods Retail Ltd v HM Revenue & Customs* [2010] EWHC 1071, [2010] STC 2072 [119]–[123] (Vos J).

cases of change of position, reliance breaks down into two stages of enquiry: (1) the receipt must have caused or contributed to the defendant's assumption regarding the receipt, and (2) the defendant must have acted on that assumption. A causal or contributing link must be established at both stages of the enquiry. As we saw in Chapter 8,[64] there are two tests commonly employed by courts to determine the required link: the 'but for' and 'a factor' tests. Both have also been employed to establish this link in the change of position context.[65] Application of the 'a factor' test in the context of change of position is consistent with the approach taken to the analogous defence of estoppel.[66] Where there is an established pattern of behaviour by a defendant, the 'but for' test has been applied.[67] For example, where a defendant uses a mistaken payment to pay his rent or usual weekly shopping, the 'but for' test applies to exclude the receipt as causally irrelevant and to deny the defence of change of position.[68] Conversely, if the defendant can show that, relying upon the receipt, he changed his weekly shopping habits to include additional or more expensive items, the financial difference between the pre-receipt and post-receipt levels of expenditure will be taken into account for the purposes of the defence.[69]

ii. Independent Changes of Position

We turn then to changes of position arising from the actions of a third party or a natural event. There is significant support for the application of the defence to this type of independent change of position.[70] But, as we have seen,[71] the High Court of Australia in *David Securities* framed the defence in terms of detrimental changes made 'on the faith of' the receipt. If this were applied to all changes of position, then there could never be an independent change of position. For instance, if a defendant receives a mistaken payment and spends it in reliance upon a lavish party, then she will have a defence of change of position. But she will not have a defence if the money is stolen. Australian courts have yet to address this question directly.[72] It might be doubted whether the High Court in *David Securities*

[64] At pp 189–94.

[65] See eg *Southage Pty Ltd v Vescovi* [2015] VSCA 117, (2015) 321 ALR 383 [76]–[79] (the Court).

[66] *Amalgamated Investment & Property Co Ltd (in liq) v Texas Commerce International Bank Ltd* [1982] QB 84, 104–05 (Robert Goff J); *Sidhu v Van Dyke* [2014] HCA 19, (2014) 251 CLR 505 [71]–[78] (French CJ, Kiefer, Bell and Keane JJ).

[67] Eg *Citigroup Pty Ltd v National Australia Bank Ltd* [2012] NSWCA 381, (2012) 82 NSWLR 391 [6] (Bathurst CJ, Allsop P and Meagher JA) [86] (Barrett JA). See also *Skandinaviska Enskilda Banken AB (Publ), Singapore Branch v Asia Pacific Breweries (Singapore) Pte Ltd* [2009] 4 SLR(R) 788 [329] (Belinda Ang J), upheld on appeal to the Court of Appeal.

[68] As in *Scottish Equitable plc v Derby* [2001] EWCA Civ 369, [2001] 3 All ER 818.

[69] As in *Philip Collins Ltd v Davis* [2000] 3 All ER 808.

[70] *Lipkin Gorman v Karpnale Ltd* [1991] 2 AC 548, 560 (Lord Templeman) 580–81 (Lord Goff); *Scottish Equitable plc v Derby* [2001] EWCA Civ 369, [2001] 3 All ER 818 [32] (Robert Walker LJ) [46] (Keane and Simon Browne LJJ concurring); *Dextra Bank & Trust Co Ltd v Bank of Jamaica* [2001] UKPC 50, [2002] 1 All ER (Comm) 193; *Cressman v Coys of Kensington (Sales) Ltd* [2004] EWCA Civ 47, [2004] 1 WLR 2775; *Test Claimants in the FII Group Litigation v Revenue and Customs Commissioners* [2008] EWHC 2893 (Ch), [2009] STC 254 [325] (Henderson J); *Bloomsbury International Ltd v Sea Fish Industry Authority* [2009] EWHC 1721 (QB), [2010] 1 CMLR 12 [134]–[137] (Hamblen J); *Test Claimants in the FII Group Litigation v Revenue and Customs Commissioners* [2014] EWHC 4302 (Ch), [2015] STC 1471 [343]–[347] (Henderson J); *T & L Sugars Ltd v Tate & Lyle Industries Ltd* [2015] EWHC 2696 [134]–[137] (Simon J).

[71] Above p 333.

[72] *Alpha Wealth Financial Services Pty Ltd v Frankland River Olive Company Ltd* [2008] WASCA 119, (2008) 66 ACSR 594 [203] (Buss JA; Steytler P concurring).

intended to exclude all cases involving independent changes of position. The facts of *David Securities* itself involved only a defendant-instigated change of position. It was unnecessary to consider the position of independent changes of position. However, in *Citigroup Pty Ltd v National Australia Bank Ltd*[73] Barrett JA considered in obiter dicta that it was not open to the New South Wales Court of Appeal to adopt a wider version of the defence that took into account non-reliance changes, in light of the High Court's pronouncement. On this view, and if reliance is always required, independent changes of position must fall outside the ambit of the defence.[74] This conclusion is further supported by obiter dicta in *AFSL v Hills*.[75] On the other hand, the High Court has emphasised the 'equitable' foundations of the defence of change of position, and the High Court has not yet confronted directly, as the English courts have, cases of independent change of position. When this issue is confronted directly, it is difficult to see any reason of principle or policy which would prevent the High Court from adopting the English approach to recognise an independent change of position in cases such as loss, theft, or depreciation. These independent changes of position have also been recognised in both Australia and England in the context of determining orders for restitution (*restitutio in integrum*) consequent upon rescission.[76] The same should apply to the defence of change of position.

iii. Anticipatory Changes of Position

Suppose a defendant is informed she has won the lottery. She changes her position by making an irrecoverable donation to a charitable cause in reliance on her win. She receives the award in due course but is later told that it was made by mistake. Does she have a change of position defence to the payer's claim in unjust enrichment?[77]

It is clear that, as a matter of logic, a prior ('anticipatory') change of position cannot be caused by or contributed to by a subsequent receipt.[78] However, it is also increasingly clear that courts are not prepared to distinguish between anticipatory and subsequent changes

[73] *Citigroup Pty Ltd v National Australia Bank Ltd* [2012] NSWCA 381, (2012) 82 NSWLR 391 [64] (but cf Bathurst CJ, Allsop P, Meagher JA at [6], seemingly leaving the question open).

[74] This is the best explanation of a series of English cases where wives were denied the defence because the relevant change (withdrawal of money from a joint account) had been carried out by their husbands: *Streiner v Bank Leumi (UK) plc* (QB, 31 October 1985); *Euroactividade AG v Moeller* (CA, 1 February 1995). See also *Credit-Suisse (Monaco) SA v Attar* [2004] EWHC 374 [98] (Gross J); C Mitchell, 'Change of Position: The Developing Law' [2005] *Lloyd's Maritime and Commercial Law Quarterly* 168, 178–79.

[75] *Australian Financial Services and Leasing Pty Ltd v Hills Industries Ltd* [2014] HCA 14, (2014) 253 CLR 560 [81] (Hayne, Crennan, Kiefel, Bell and Keane JJ) [142] (Gageler J).

[76] On the obligation to make counter-restitution in relation to a deteriorated asset, see *Alati v Kruger* [1955] HCA 64, (1955) 94 CLR 216, 225 [11] (Dixon CJ, Webb, Kitto and Taylor JJ); *Cheese v Thomas* [1994] 1 WLR 129, 135 (Sir Donald Nicholls VC); *Armstrong v Jackson* [1917] 2 KB 822; *Balfour & Clark v Hollandia Ravensthorpe NL* (1978) 18 SASR 240, 258 (Hogarth J); *Akron Securities Ltd v Iliffe* (1997) 41 NSWLR 353, 370 (Mason P; Priestley JA agreeing). The point rarely arises in practice against defendants: as Lord Wright commented in *Spence v Crawford* [1939] 3 All ER 271, 289, the 'plaintiff who seeks to set aside the contract will generally be reasonable in the standard of restitution which he requires'.

[77] The example is derived from P Birks, 'Change of Position and Surviving Enrichment' in W Swadling (ed), *The Limits of Restitutionary Claims: A Comparative Analysis* (London, United Kingdom National Committee of Comparative Law, 1997) 51.

[78] As argued in the first edition of this work: J Edelman and E Bant, *Unjust Enrichment in Australia* (South Melbourne, Oxford University Press, 2006) 328. Cf *South Tyneside Metropolitan Borough Council v Svenska International plc* [1995] 1 All ER 545.

of position.[79] Thus in *Dextra Bank & Trust Co Ltd v Bank of Jamaica*,[80] the Privy Council suggested that a defendant could change his position in reliance on a receipt even if the change was made in anticipation of a payment, provided that the payment was subsequently received.[81] The Privy Council used the word 'receipt' to mean 'eventual receipt'. The Privy Council's view was unanimously accepted by the English Court of Appeal in *Commerzbank AG v Price-Jones*.[82]

The judicial extension of the defence to anticipatory changes of position has clear attractions as a matter of practice. It removes the need to make invidious distinctions in cases involving series of payments, where the defendant may have changed his position sometimes before and sometimes after receipt, in the reasonable expectation of the regular and ongoing receipt of benefits from the plaintiff.[83] Further, there are no strong policy objections to the extension. The law is not being asked to enforce the defendant's expectations, thereby usurping the role of contract.[84] This is because the defence will only be available if the anticipated receipt has been received (that is, the defendant has been enriched) and thus where the defendant's expectations have already been met. Finally, as a matter of principle, the change of position might not be caused or contributed to by the later payment but it is, nevertheless, a transaction which is linked to the later payment, because the anticipated payment caused or contributed to the change of position. This explains why the defence failed in *Commerzbank AG v Price-Jones*.[85] In that case, the defendant anticipated receipt of a bonus. However, what he received was an entirely coincidental mistaken payment. In those circumstances, any change of position made by the defendant was not made in anticipation of the benefit that was subsequently received. Accordingly there was no sufficient link between the defendant's expectation, change of position and subsequent receipt to support the defence.

C. Good Faith

Good faith on the part of the defendant has always formed an important aspect of the change of position defence.[86] Good faith is a normative standard that, in the context of change of position, directs attention to the relationship between the defendant's change

[79] The distinction was ignored in *Lipkin Gorman v Karpnale Ltd* [1991] 2 AC 548, *Philip Collins Ltd v Davis* [2000] 3 All ER 808, and *Thomas v Houston Corbett and Co* [1969] NZLR 151. See also *Alpha Wealth Financial Services Pty Ltd v Frankland River Olive Co Ltd* [2008] WASCA 119, (2008) 66 ACSR 594 [39] (Pullin JA) [204] (Buss JA; Steytler P concurring); *Fitzsimons v McBride, Minister for Liquor, Gaming and Racing (NSW)* [2008] NSWSC 782 [125] (McDougall J). Cf *Lokan v Defence Force Retirement and Death Benefits Authority* [2007] AATA 1652 [16] (Deputy President PE Hack SC).

[80] *Dextra Bank & Trust Co Ltd v Bank of Jamaica* [2001] UKPC 50, [2002] 1 All ER (Comm) 193.

[81] ibid [38].

[82] *Commerzbank AG v Price-Jones* [2003] EWCA Civ 1663 [38] (Mummery LJ; Sedley LJ concurring) [64] (Munby J).

[83] *Philip Collins Ltd v Davis* [2000] 3 All ER 808.

[84] AS Burrows, *The Law of Restitution* (London, Butterworths, 1993) 425; but withdrawn in AS Burrows, *The Law of Restitution*, 2nd edn (London, Butterworths, 2002) 517–19; see now AS Burrows, *The Law of Restitution*, 3rd edn (Oxford, Oxford University Press, 2011) 532–35.

[85] *Commerzbank AG v Price-Jones* [2003] EWCA Civ 1663.

[86] *Lipkin Gorman v Karpnale Ltd* [1991] 2 AC 548, 579–80 (Lord Goff).

of position and the 'state of mind reasonably engendered'[87] in the recipient by the broader context of the receipt.

A line of Australian cases has emphasised that the defendant must have 'a foundation of information obtained in connection with the receipt to justify acting on the basis of the receipt'.[88] It follows that it will not be acting in good faith for a defendant irreversibly to change her position in reliance on the fact of receipt alone. The defence failed for this reason in the leading Australian case of *State Bank of New South Wales Ltd v Swiss Bank Corporation*.[89] The plaintiff bank paid $20 million to the defendant bank on the basis that it would be credited to a customer's account, but failed to indicate the relevant customer. The defendant credited the $20 million to a particular customer on the advice of a third party, although only the plaintiff could have identified the intended payee. The New South Wales Court of Appeal held that the defence did not apply, because the bank could only 'bring itself within the change of position defence if it shows that at the time of disbursement it knew or thought it knew more than the fact of receipt standing alone'.[90]

The requirement that a defendant have a foundation of knowledge to justify her change of position directs attention not only to what the defendant knows, but whether her act is consistent with that knowledge. For example, if a defendant recipient knows of the payer's mistake and pays the money away nonetheless, she may well not have acted in good faith.[91] Consistently with this analysis, the defence has been denied in a number of 'failure of consideration' cases where the defendant acted inconsistently with the known condition of the receipt.[92] However, all the circumstances surrounding the receipt of the benefit and the defendant's change of position must be considered in assessing the question of good faith. In *National Bank of New Zealand Ltd v Waitaki International Processing (NI) Ltd*,[93]

[87] *Citigroup Pty Ltd v National Australia Bank Ltd* [2012] NSWCA 381, (2012) 82 NSWLR 391 [95]; see also [70]–[83], [95]–[102] (Barrett JA), and concurring analysis at [4]–[6] (Bathurst CJ, Allsop P and Meagher), and at [17] (Macfarlan JA).

[88] *Perpetual Trustees Australia Ltd v Heperu Pty Ltd* [2009] NSWCA 84, (2009) 76 NSWLR 195 [139] (Allsop P and Campbell JA; Handley AJA concurring, explaining and endorsing *State Bank of New South Wales Ltd v Swiss Bank Corporation* (1995) 39 NSWLR 350). A similar analysis was pressed, in obiter dicta, in *Hills Industries Ltd v Australian Financial Services and Leasing Pty Ltd* [2012] NSWCA 380, (2012) 295 ALR 147 [204]–[205] (Meagher JA). See also *Commerzbank AG v Price-Jones* [2003] EWCA Civ 1663 [186]–[187] (Sedley LJ).

[89] *State Bank of New South Wales Ltd v Swiss Bank Corporation* (1995) 39 NSWLR 350. Cf *Port of Brisbane Corporation v ANZ Securities Ltd (No 2)* [2002] QCA 158, [2003] 2 Qd R 661 [15]–[17], [21]–[23] (McPherson JA; Davies JA and Mullins J concurring), where the Queensland Court of Appeal found that the instruction was received by the true payer, and so the issue in *Swiss Bank* did not arise; contrast *Port of Brisbane Corporation v ANZ Securities Ltd* [2001] QSC 466 [39]–[69] (Chesterman J).

[90] *State Bank of New South Wales Ltd v Swiss Bank Corporation* (1995) 39 NSWLR 350, 356 (the Court). Cf *Bank Tejarat v Hong Kong and Shanghai Banking Corporation (CI) Ltd* [1995] 1 Lloyd's Rep 239, 246 (Tuckey J), where, in the circumstances, it was reasonable for the defendant to believe the instructions related to and came from its client.

[91] *Lipkin Gorman v Karpnale Ltd* [1991] 2 AC 548, 580 (Lord Goff); *Cressman v Coys of Kensington (Sales) Ltd* [2004] EWCA Civ 47, [2004] 1 WLR 2775 [41] (Mance LJ; Thorpe LJ and Wilson J concurring).

[92] *State Bank of New South Wales Ltd v Swiss Bank Corporation* (1995) 39 NSWLR 350; *Goss v Chilcott* [1996] UKPC 17, [1996] AC 788, 799 [13] (Lord Goff); *Sanwa Australia Finance Ltd v Finchill Pty Ltd* [2001] NSWCA 466 [29]–[30] (Davie AJA; Beazley and Heydon JJA concurring); *Gilsan (International) Ltd v Optus Networks Pty Ltd* [2004] NSWSC 1077 [358]–[381] (McDougall J), cf on appeal *Optus Networks Pty Ltd v Gilsan (International) Ltd* [2006] NSWCA 171 [79] (Hodgson JA; Beasley and McColl JA concurring); *Saba Yachts Ltd v Fish Pacific Ltd* [2006] NZHC 1452, (2006) 3 NZCCLR 963 [59]–[62] (Winklemann J); *Haugesund Kommune v Depfa ACS Bank* [2010] EWCA Civ 579, [2012] QB 549 [127] (Aikens LJ; Pill LJ concurring).

[93] *National Bank of New Zealand Ltd v Waitaki International Processing (NI) Ltd* [1999] 2 NZLR 211, where the statutory defence only foundered in these circumstances because it required reliance on 'the validity of' the receipt: Judicature Amendment Act 1958 (NZ) s 94B, discussed below at pp 360–61.

for example, the plaintiff bank made a mistaken payment to the defendant, notwithstanding the latter's repeated attempts to notify the bank of its error. The defendant invested the amount to preserve the fund pending the bank coming to its senses. The investment failed and the money was lost. Although the New Zealand Court of Appeal took the view that the defendant had been careless in the choice of investment and discounted the defence accordingly,[94] it was unanimous that the defendant had acted throughout in good faith. The defendant's actions were justified by the known circumstances of his receipt. The position would have been different had the defendant invested the sum in the hope of making a windfall profit. Good faith will be similarly satisfied where a defendant receives a benefit that he has grounds for believing is payable to a third party, and acts in accordance with that basis.[95]

The authorities are also increasingly clear that a defendant may fail to act in good faith even if he is not dishonest. In England, the leading authority is *Niru Battery Manufacturing Co v Milestone Trading Ltd*.[96] In a decision upheld by the English Court of Appeal, Moore-Bick J at first instance held that the defendant bank failed to establish good faith because, although not dishonest, it acted in a manner involving 'sharp practice' when it paid money under a letter of credit for a shipment of lead that it knew did not exist. In coming to this conclusion, Moore-Bick J explained that bad faith 'is capable of embracing a failure to act in a commercially acceptable way and sharp practice of a kind that falls short of dishonesty as well as dishonesty itself'. Later in the same passage, also approved by the English Court of Appeal, the trial judge said:

> Greater difficulty may arise, however, in cases where the payee has grounds for believing that the payment may have been made by mistake, but cannot be sure. In such cases good faith may well dictate that an enquiry be made of the payer. The nature and extent of the enquiry called for will, of course, depend on the circumstances of the case, but I do not think that a person who has, or thinks he has, good reason to believe that the payment was made by mistake will often be found to have acted in good faith if he pays the money away without first making inquiries of the person from whom he received it.[97]

On this approach it remains possible for a defendant to change her position in good faith reliance on her receipt, although she knows there is a risk that the transfer was vitiated. This will be so where her doubts are diminished by other circumstances of her receipt, including

[94] Discussed below at pp 361–62.

[95] As in *Thomas v Houston Corbett and Co* [1969] NZLR 151; *Orix Australia Corporation Ltd v M Wright Hotel Refrigeration Pty Ltd* [2000] SASC 57, (2000) 155 FLR 267; *Dextra Bank & Trust Co Ltd v Bank of Jamaica* [2001] UKPC 50, [2002] 1 All ER (Comm) 193.

[96] *Niru Battery Manufacturing Co v Milestone Trading Ltd* [2002] EWHC 1425, [2002] 2 All ER (Comm) 705 [135] (Moore-Bick J); on appeal, *Niru Battery Manufacturing Co v Milestone Trading Ltd* [2003] EWCA Civ 1446, [2004] QB 985 [164]–[165] (Clarke LJ; Butler-Sloss P concurring); followed in *Abou-Rahmah v Abacha* [2006] EWCA Civ 1492, [2007] 1 All ER (Comm) 827; *Armstrong DLW GmbH v Winnington Networks Ltd* [2012] EWHC 10, [2013] Ch 156 [106]–[110], [123] (Judge Morris QC). See also *Cavenagh Investment Pte Ltd v Kaushik Rajiv* [2013] SGHC 45 [68]–[72] (Chan Seng Onn J).

[97] *Niru Battery Manufacturing Co v Milestone Trading Ltd* [2003] EWCA Civ 1446, [2004] QB 985 [164]–[165] (Clarke LJ; Butler Sloss LJ concurring); see also [186]–[187] (Sedley LJ); followed in *Fea v Roberts* [2005] All ER (D) 69 [104] (Hazel Williamson QC); *Jones v Churcher* [2009] EWHC 722 (QB), [2009] 2 Lloyd's Rep 94 [46] (HHJ Havelock-Allan QC); *Armstrong DLW GmbH v Winnington Networks Ltd* [2012] EWHC 10 (Ch), [2013] Ch 156 [110], [122]. Cf *US International Marketing Ltd v National Bank of New Zealand Ltd* [2004] 1 NZLR 589 [8]–[11] (Tipping J); contrast [67]–[69] (Anderson J) and [78]–[79] (Glazebrook J); *ASB Securities Ltd v Geurts* [2005] 1 NZLR 484; *Port of Brisbane Corporation v ANZ Securities Ltd (No 2)* [2002] QCA 158, [2003] 2 Qd R 661 [21]–[22] (McPherson JA; Davies JA and Mullins J concurring).

statements made by the payer.[98] In this scenario, the question becomes whether (to echo the extracted passage in *Niru*) the 'nature and extent of the enquiry called for' has been satisfied.

Although the core content of good faith is increasingly settled, it remains unclear whether the normative standard of good faith in change of position extends to some obligation to act reasonably, as it has been said to, for example, in the context of contractual duties of good faith.[99] It would be possible, for example, for the law to require the defendant to have a reasonable foundation of knowledge to justify acting on the basis of her receipt.[100] Justice Gummow (as he then was), writing extrajudicially, has argued further that good faith for the purposes of the change of position defence requires 'the exercise of caution and diligence to be expected of a person of ordinary prudence placed in the situation in question'.[101] On this analysis, the repeated recognition by English courts that a defendant who fails to act in a 'commercially acceptable way' does not act in good faith, is reflective of this more demanding standard of prudence.[102] In *AFSL v Hills*, Gageler J left the question open, noting that 'Whether the defendant needs also to have acted reasonably is a question which does not now arise for determination'.[103]

On the other hand, in *AFSL v Hills* Gageler J also stated that the defence did not involve an enquiry into the parties' 'relative fault'.[104] Similarly, Hayne, Brennan, Kiefel, Bell and Keane JJ stated that the defence does not 'invite a balancing of competing equities as between the parties, based on considerations such as fault'.[105] These statements clearly endorse the position taken by the Privy Council in *Dextra Bank and Trust Co Ltd v Bank of Jamaica*[106] in which the Board refused to consider the relative fault of the parties in applying the defence. In so doing, their Lordships adopted the criticisms of Professor Birks[107] levelled at the relative fault approach adopted in New Zealand. The first criticism was that taking into account the parties' relative fault was inconsistent with the strict liability approach otherwise applicable in the law of unjust enrichment. Their Lordships agreed that, given that fault on the part of the plaintiff is irrelevant to establishing her prima facie claim, it should not be relevant for the purposes of the defence. However, while it can be accepted that fault is irrelevant for the purposes of establishing a prima facie claim for restitution of the defendant's enrichment, her claim is then subject to defences such as change of position. At this second stage of analysis,[108] the defendant's position has irreversibly changed with the result

[98] Compare *Scottish Equitable plc v Derby* [2001] EWCA Civ 369, [2001] 3 All ER 818 [30] (Robert Walker LJ) and *Commerzbank AG v Price-Jones* [2003] EWCA Civ 1663 [79]–[82] (Munby J).

[99] *Macquarie International Health Clinic Pty Ltd v Sydney South West Area Health Service* [2010] NSWCA 268 [12] (Allsop P).

[100] *Commerzbank AG v Price-Jones* [2003] EWCA Civ 1663 [79]–[82] (Munby J); *Commerzbank AG v Price-Jones* [2003] EWCA Civ 1663 [186]–[187] (Sedley LJ).

[101] Hon Justice WMC Gummow, '*Moses v Macferlan*: 250 Years On' (2010) 84 *Australian Law Journal* 756, 763.

[102] ibid 763.

[103] *Australian Financial Services and Leasing Pty Ltd v Hills Industries Ltd* [2014] HCA 14, (2014) 253 CLR 560 [157].

[104] ibid [145]–[146].

[105] ibid [69].

[106] *Dextra Bank & Trust Co Ltd v Bank of Jamaica* [2001] UKPC 50, [2002] 1 All ER (Comm) 193 [45].

[107] P Birks, 'Change of Position and Surviving Enrichment' in W Swadling (ed), *The Limits of Restitutionary Claims: A Comparative Analysis* (London, United Kingdom National Committee of Comparative Law, 1997) 41.

[108] *Australian Financial Services and Leasing Pty Ltd v Hills Industries Ltd* [2014] HCA 14, (2014) 253 CLR 560 [138], [143] (Gageler J).

that either the defendant or plaintiff will be left (as a result of application or refusal of the defence) in a worse position than they occupied prior to the transaction. At that second stage, considerations of fault are, at the least, not obviously irrelevant,[109] a view reflected in most statutory forms of the defence.[110] However, a further consideration that weighs against the adoption of a relative fault approach is the uncertainty and instability of relative fault enquiries (again all too familiar from the statutory context of applying contributory negligence and apportionment provisions based on considerations of relative fault). In this regard, their Lordships agreed that the

> New Zealand courts have shown how hopelessly unstable the defence ... becomes when it is used to reflect relative fault ... the reader has the impression of judges struggling manfully to control and to contain an alien concept.[111]

It remains to be seen whether a requirement of reasonable reliance can or should be incorporated into the defence in a principled way, which will not dissolve into an impressionistic exercise in loss apportionment on the basis of fault.[112]

D. Onus and Standard of Proof

i. Onus of Proof

It is uncontroversial that, as a defence, the onus of establishing change of position rests with the defendant. In cases of defendant-instigated changes of position, this is an onus to prove good faith reliance.[113] In *Abou-Rahmah v Abacha*[114] the defendant bank had opened an account for a client, notwithstanding its suspicions that the client might be involved in money laundering. It subsequently received a payment from the claimant to the account of its client. The bank paid over the amount of the deposit to a third party, in accordance with its client's instructions. It later transpired that the claimant had been the victim of a fraud to which the bank's client was a party. The English Court of Appeal struggled to determine whether the bank had acted in good faith, even in the extended sense of 'commercially acceptable conduct' employed in *Niru Battery Manufacturing Co v Milestone Trading Ltd*.[115]

[109] *National Bank of New Zealand Ltd v Waitaki International Processing (NI) Ltd* [1999] 2 NZLR 211, 229 (Thomas J); *Commerzbank AG v Price-Jones* [2003] EWCA Civ 1663 [192] (Sedley LJ).

[110] Discussed below pp 361–62.

[111] *Dextra Bank & Trust Co Ltd v Bank of Jamaica* [2001] UKPC 50, [2002] 1 All ER (Comm) 193 [45].

[112] Cf *Commerzbank AG v Price-Jones* [2003] EWCA Civ 1663 [79]–[82] (Munby J), simultaneously rejecting relative fault enquiries while adopting a requirement of reasonable reliance. For a discussion of the issues, see E Bant, *The Change of Position Defence* (Oxford, Hart, 2009) 151–55, 179–83.

[113] *Standard Bank London Ltd v Canara* [2002] EWHC 1032 [104] (Moore-Bick J), discussed above at p 339. In *Lipkin Gorman v Karpnale Ltd* [1991] 2 AC 548, Lord Goff referred to good faith both as part of the positive defence and also identified 'bad faith' as a bar to the defence. However, cases since *Lipkin Gorman* have proceeded on the basis that it forms part of the positive defence and that the onus of proof thus rests with the defendant: *Philip Collins Ltd v Davis* [2000] 3 All ER 808, 827 (Jonathan Parker J); *Scottish Equitable plc v Derby* [2001] EWCA Civ 369, [2001] 3 All ER 818; *Cressman v Coys of Kensington (Sales) Ltd* [2004] EWCA Civ 47, [2004] 1 WLR 2775. In Australia, there is no doubt that the onus lies on the defendant: see *Alpha Wealth Financial Services Pty Ltd v Frankland River Olive Company Ltd* [2008] WASCA 119, (2008) 66 ACSR 594 [39] (Pullin JA) [210]–[212] (Buss JA; Steytler P concurring); *Glad Cleaning Service Pty Ltd v Vukelic* [2010] NSWSC 422 [51] (Slattery J).

[114] *Abou-Rahmah v Abacha* [2006] EWCA Civ 1492, [2007] 1 All ER (Comm) 827.

[115] *Niru Battery Manufacturing Co v Milestone Trading Ltd* [2003] EWCA Civ 1446, [2004] QB 985, discussed earlier at p 344.

Ultimately, the Court divided on the issue. Lady Justice Arden (with whom Pill LJ concurred in a separate judgment)[116] held that, in order for the defendant not to have acted in good faith (or 'inequitably'), it must have particular suspicions relating to the specific transactions in question.[117] Further, her Ladyship took the view that the bank could not be said to have acted other than in good faith: it had complied with the relevant requirements of Nigerian law in opening the account and, in the absence of suspicions relating to the specific transactions in question, no more was required. Since the onus lies on the defendant to prove good faith reliance, the majority was accordingly wrong to make an 'assumption' of good faith in favour of the defendant. Lord Justice Rix, dissenting, held that the bank's general suspicion as to the use of the client's account must attach to each and every transaction and, accordingly, the bank had failed to act in accordance with an objective standard of good faith.[118] Lord Justice Rix's approach is to be preferred. As soon as the defendant bank admitted that it had suspicions that the account might be being used to launder money, it must have been aware of the risk that its receipt of any monies through that account was insecure. In those circumstances, and in the absence of some good reason for believing the particular impugned transactions were clean, the bank could not be said to have acted in good faith reliance upon its receipt.[119]

ii. Standard of Proof

Courts have adopted a generous approach to the standard of proof required to establish the change of position defence. As the court in *RBC Dominion Securities Inc v Dawson* explained:

> to require that a private individual, who believed she was spending her own money, prove her expenditures as if she were claiming damages in an action for negligence would be most unfair. It was the plaintiff's error that put her in the funds in the first place and led her to believe that the funds were hers to spend without having to account to anyone for her expenditures.[120]

In such circumstances, the court could be 'satisfied with reasonable approximations'.[121] This approach was emphatically endorsed by the High Court justices in *AFSL v Hills Industries*,[122] who were unanimous that approaches to calculations of loss (including loss of opportunity) derived from tort or contract had no place in the change of position context.

[116] *Abou-Rahmah v Abacha* [2006] EWCA Civ 1492, [2007] 1 All ER (Comm) 827 [99]–[103].

[117] ibid [81], [84], [87].

[118] ibid [50]–[55], [58].

[119] *Maersk Air Ltd v Expeditors International (UK) Ltd* [2003] 1 Lloyd's Rep 491 [47]–[49] (Alton J); *ASB Securities Ltd v Geurts* [2005] 1 NZLR 484 [63]–[64].

[120] *RBC Dominion Securities Inc v Dawson* (1994) 111 DLR (4th) 230, 240.

[121] ibid. See also *Philip Collins Ltd v Davis* [2000] 3 All ER 808, 827 (Jonathan Parker J), approved in *Bloomsbury International Ltd v Sea Fish Industry Authority* [2009] EWHC 1721, [2010] 1 CMLR 12 [135]–[137] (Hamblen J); *Scottish Equitable plc v Derby* [2001] EWCA Civ 369, [2001] 3 All ER 818 [33] (Robert Walker LJ); *Fea v Roberts* [2005] All ER (D) 69 [111]–[112] (Hazel Williamson QC); *Test Claimants in the FII Group Litigation v Revenue and Customs Commissioners* [2008] EWHC 2893, [2009] STC 254 [343]–[344] (Henderson J); *Foai v Air New Zealand Ltd* [2012] NZEmpC 57 [79] (AD Ford J), leave to appeal refused in *Air New Zealand Ltd v Foai* [2012] NZCA 341, (2012) 9 NZELR 480. Cf *Qingyi Chong v Hong Wei Wu* [2010] NSWCA 10 [10]–[17] (MacFarlan JA; Young JA and Handley AJA concurring).

[122] *Australian Financial Services and Leasing Pty Ltd v Hills Industries Ltd* [2014] HCA 14, (2014) 253 CLR 560 [28]–[30] (French CJ) [84] (Hayne, Crennan, Kiefel, Bell and Keane JJ), [150] [157] (Gageler J).

While courts have adopted a generous approach to the required standard of proof, a simple assertion by the defendant that he has changed his position will not suffice: the court must be in a position to determine that a change took place and the extent to which an order for restitution would, in the light of that change, place the defendant in a worse position than he occupied prior to his receipt. Thus in *Commerzbank AG v Price-Jones*,[123] the defendant claimed that he had changed his position as a result of a large overpayment of a salary bonus, by failing to seek employment elsewhere. A majority of the English Court of Appeal held that this alleged change was 'not sufficiently significant, precise or substantial in extent to be treated as a change of his position'.[124] While the majority did not elaborate further, there are two reasons that support this conclusion. First, there was little independent evidence before the court as to the likelihood that the defendant would have obtained better employment conditions elsewhere (for example, a better wage, job stability or career prospects). Thus Mummery LJ drew a contrast with the situation where a defendant has turned down a firm offer of a better-paid job, which might well qualify as a relevant change.[125] Given its very speculative nature, the value of the alleged lost opportunity was nil. Secondly, if the defendant had merely demonstrated a good chance of obtaining 'similar' employment elsewhere, the value of any change would have been nil.

III. Possible Bars to the Defence

A. Fault

We have seen that there remain questions over whether the requirement of good faith includes some obligation of reasonableness on the part of the defendant. However, there are two further ways in which the defendant's fault might play a role in the defence.

i. Fault in Losing the Received Benefit

The first example of fault as a possible bar to change of position is where the defendant is at fault in *losing* the received benefit. In general, the defendant's fault is irrelevant to such cases.[126] Provided that the defendant has acted consistently with his knowledge of the basis of his receipt, then it does not matter if he has acted foolishly or carelessly. The defendant's interest in the security of his receipt must apply no matter what risks he takes with the benefit. A defendant who has a foundation of knowledge that leads him to believe his receipt is secure is entitled to gamble it away at hopeless odds if he wishes.

However, the defendant's right to the security of his receipt is qualified where he knows that, in due course, the benefit must be paid over to the plaintiff or to another. The defendant's knowledge of the third party's better right affects the scope of protection offered by

[123] *Commerzbank AG v Price-Jones* [2003] EWCA Civ 1663.

[124] ibid [40] (Mummery LJ; Sedley LJ concurring). See also *MGN Ltd v Horton* [2009] EWHC 1680 [33] (Tugendhat J).

[125] *Commerzbank AG v Price-Jones* [2003] EWCA Civ 1663 [39].

[126] *Port of Brisbane Corporation v ANZ Securities Ltd (No 2)* [2002] QCA 158, [2003] 2 Qd R 661 [23] (McPherson JA; Davies JA and Mullins J concurring).

the defence.[127] This restriction could be characterised as an independent bar,[128] but, as we have seen, it will usually be accommodated through the requirement that the defendant must act in good faith.

ii. Fault in Inducing the Plaintiff's Vitiated Decision

It is possible that a defendant whose behaviour has caused or contributed to his enrichment should be made to bear the risk of its loss.[129] This question arises where the defendant has 'knowingly contributed to the making of the payment [to him]'[130] such as when the benefit was transferred by the plaintiff as a result of the defendant's innocent misrepresentation,[131] undue influence[132] or duress.[133] Of course, if the defendant's conduct amounts to an actionable tort or equitable wrong then the plaintiff could seek restitution for the wrong. The question in that context is whether application of the defence of change of position would undermine the law's prohibition of the wrong.[134] But, as we saw in Chapter 3, this book is concerned with actions for restitution of unjust enrichment not actions for restitution for wrongdoing.

There is no obviously correct answer to this issue in the unjust enrichment context. On the one hand, it does seem unduly harsh to deny the defence to a party who has committed no wrong. On the other hand, it is clearly arguable that, having interfered with the plaintiff's autonomy, the defendant could be regarded as losing the right to protection of his own autonomy. On this analysis, the bar would operate to exclude the defence completely. A less severe approach is to assess the comparative fault of plaintiff and defendant in the manner adopted in the Restatement (Third) of Unjust Enrichment and Restitution § 52(3), which provides that a defendant who is 'primarily responsible' for his unjust enrichment may not assert the change of position defence.[135] This approach allows courts to consider the respective natures of the parties, for example that the plaintiff is a sophisticated banking institution or insurance company, as compared to a private individual.[136] An incidental benefit of this approach is that it would provide a strong incentive to institutional payers to take reasonable precautions to prevent mistakes in their transfer transactions.

[127] Eg *National Bank of New Zealand Ltd v Waitaki International Processing (NI) Ltd* [1999] 2 NZLR 211; *Citibank Ltd v Department of Public Works and Services* [2001] NSWSC 1066 [31] (Newman AJ) and in rescission, in *Alati v Kruger* [1955] HCA 64, (1955) 94 CLR 216, 225–26 (Dixon CJ, Webb, Kitto and Taylor JJ), 228 (Fullagar J).

[128] E Bant, *The Change of Position Defence* (Oxford, Hart, 2009) 188–91.

[129] Cf American Law Institute, *Restatement of the Law of Restitution: Quasi Contracts and Constructive Trusts* (St Paul, Minn, American Law Institute Publishers, 1937) ch 8, § 142(2), which states that: 'Change of circumstances may be a defense or a partial defense if the conduct of the recipient was not tortious and he was no more at fault for his receipt, retention or dealing with the subject matter than was the claimant.' Cf comments (a) and (g) to § 65 of the *Restatement of the Law (Third) Restitution and Unjust Enrichment*, 2 vols (St Paul, Minn, American Law Institute Publishers, 2011), explaining that the defence will be denied where 'the defendant rather than the claimant is primarily responsible for the defendant's unjust enrichment': § 52(3).

[130] *Rogers v Kabriel* [1999] NSWSC 368 [67] (Young J).

[131] *Larner v London County Council* [1949] 2 KB 683, 688–89 (Denning LJ), followed on this point in: *Avon County Council v Howlett* [1983] 1 WLR 605, 620 (Slade LJ); *Secretary of State for Employment v Wellworthy Ltd (No 2)* (1976) ICR 13, 25 (Nield J); *Saronic Shipping Co Ltd v Huron Liberian Co* [1979] 1 Lloyd's Rep 341.

[132] *Allcard v Skinner* (1887) 36 Ch D 145; *Hartigan v International Society for Krishna Consiousness Inc* [2002] NSWSC 810.

[133] *Waikato Regional Airport Ltd v Attorney-General* [2001] 2 NZLR 670, 715 (Wild J).

[134] *Cavenagh Investment Pte Ltd v Kaushik Rajiv* [2013] SGHC 45 [60]–[65] (Chan Seng Onn J).

[135] See also commentary (g) and (h) to § 65.

[136] Eg *Scottish Equitable plc v Derby* [2001] EWCA Civ 369, [2001] 3 All ER 818.

B. Illegality and Stultification

The change of position defence should not be allowed where its application would undermine or stultify an overriding policy or prohibition of the law.[137] This rule reflects what the High Court of Australia has described as the overriding principle of 'coherence'.[138] It is for this reason why 'wrongdoers' who breach some common law or equitable duty will often not be allowed to avail themselves of the defence.[139] But the principle is one of general application that applies well beyond claims of civil wrongdoing. In *O'Neil v Gale*,[140] the defendant had assisted her husband to run an illegal Ponzi scheme (a criminal offence under the Financial Services and Markets Act). She had done so in a small but significant way by allowing him to use her bank account and to open a betting account for his sole use. Being a declared bankrupt, he was not permitted to do either of those things personally. The defendant knew the intended use of the accounts, but acted throughout in good faith, unaware of the illegality of her husband's investment scheme. The claimant was an investor who had lost $300,000 in the scheme. She brought a claim in unjust enrichment against the defendant, who argued that she had changed her position in good faith. The English Court of Appeal affirmed the decision at first instance that the defence must 'inescapably'[141] fail. In so finding, Vos LJ (Laws and Jackson LJJ concurring) agreed with the observation of the trial judge that it would be very strange if the very acts that were 'themselves unlawful under legislation designed to protect just such investors' could operate in aid of a defence against the claimant's action.[142] In the language adopted in this section, to allow the defence in such circumstances would directly undermine the statutory prohibition.

The operation of this bar has been obscured in England by overly rigid and formulaic approaches to cases where defendants have been involved in illegal conduct. Three cases exemplify the problem. In *Barros Mattos Junior v Macdaniels Ltd*,[143] the defendants changed their position in good faith by exchanging currency received from the defendant. However, the exchange occurred pursuant to a foreign exchange contract that was illegal under Nigerian law. Laddie J held that the illegality prevented reliance by the defendants upon a change of position defence. However, the result is very difficult to justify. If the defendants were indeed the innocent recipients of the proceeds of fraud and had irreversibly changed their position in good faith, it seems very harsh that their 'technical infraction'[144] of the Nigerian exchange laws (which did not appear to subvert the purpose of the statute) should deny them the defence.

[137] *Jeffrey v Fitzroy Collingwood Rental Housing Association Ltd* [1999] VSC 335 [44] (Harper J), where allowing the defence would have undermined the protection afforded to tenants under the statute. Cf *Tonkin v Cooma-Monaro Shire Council* [2006] NSWCA 50, (2006) 145 LGERA 48.

[138] *Miller v Miller* [2011] HCA 9, (2011) 242 CLR 446. This is the same approach that informs the substantive defence of illegality: *Nelson v Nelson* [1995] HCA 25, (1995) 184 CLR 538, discussed in Ch 7 p 160. See also *Garland v Enbridge Gas Distribution Inc* [2004] 1 SCR 629, 2004 SCC 25 [66] (Iacobucci J, delivering the judgment of the Court); *Equiticorp Industries Group Ltd v The Crown (No 47)* [1998] 2 NZLR 481, 654, 730 (Smellie J).

[139] See p 332.

[140] *O'Neil v Gale* [2013] EWCA Civ 1554, [2014] Lloyd's Rep FC 202.

[141] ibid [29].

[142] ibid [28].

[143] *Barros Mattos Junior v MacDaniels Ltd* [2004] EWHC 1188 (Ch), [2005] 1 WLR 247.

[144] A Tettenborn, 'Bank Fraud, Change of Position and Illegality: The Case of the Innocent Money-Launderer' [2005] *Lloyd's Maritime and Commercial Law Quarterly* 6, 9.

The second English case that considered the change of position defence in the context of an illegal transaction is the Court of Appeal decision in *Abou-Rahmah v Abacha*,[145] discussed earlier. The majority considered the relevance of the bank's suspicions of its client's activities, and the illegality of the transaction in which the bank had taken part, only in the context of determining whether the defendant had acted in good faith. However, good faith and illegality are distinct concepts, albeit ones that tend to overlap factually in case scenarios. The majority ought to have separately addressed the significance of the illegality of the transaction at the heart of the pleaded defence. Further, on the legal stultification approach to the bar, there were strong policy reasons for denying the defence. As Rix LJ, dissenting, pointed out, the effect of allowing the defence was to undermine Nigeria's attempts to stop the 'vice of money laundering'.[146] Thus, even were the primary elements of the defence satisfied, it is arguable that public policy considerations should have operated to deny the bank the defence.

The final case in the trilogy is the 2008 decision of Henderson J in *Test Claimants in the FII Group Litigation v Revenue and Customs Commissioners*.[147] The plaintiffs had paid tax to the Revenue pursuant to the mistaken belief that the applicable taxation regime was lawful. Alongside their mistake claims, the claimants also brought independent *Woolwich*-style[148] claims against the Revenue arising out of its unlawful taxation demands. Justice Henderson correctly considered that the change of position defence was automatically precluded in such claims because the right of a private citizen to recover unlawfully exacted tax should, as a matter of principle, be unfettered.[149] We have seen that the *Woolwich* principle reflects a longstanding and vital public interest in prohibiting unlawful exaction of taxes by public authorities.[150] This policy would be wholly undermined if the change of position defence was permitted to allow public authorities to retain the benefit of their unlawful demands.[151] Unfortunately, however, because the bar was reasoned in terms of 'wrongdoing' rather than as an independent stultification bar, it was not appreciated that the same policy may also be undermined if the Revenue is allowed to switch to a mistake-based claim and thereby gain the benefit of the change of position defence.[152]

These three cases failed to engage directly with the problem of stultification. However, more recently, in *Prudential Assurance Co Ltd v Revenue and Customs Commissioners*[153] Henderson J returned to the point and on this occasion considered that it was arguable that the same factors that rendered the defence inapplicable in *Woolwich* cases, should apply 'with equal force, and should lead to the same conclusion, where the claim is founded on

[145] *Abou-Rahmah v Abacha* [2006] EWCA Civ 1492, [2007] 1 All ER (Comm) 827.

[146] ibid [50], [55].

[147] *Test Claimants in the FII Group Litigation v Revenue and Customs Commissioners* [2008] EWHC 2893, [2009] STC 254.

[148] *Woolwich Equitable Building Society v Inland Revenue Commissioners* [1993] AC 70, discussed in Ch 13 pp 306–11.

[149] *Test Claimants in the FII Group Litigation v Revenue and Customs Commissioners* [2008] EWHC 2893, [2009] STC 254 [339], approved on appeal [2010] EWCA Civ 103, [2010] STC 1251 [109] (Arden LJ giving the judgment of the Court); cf *Littlewoods Retail Ltd v HM Revenue & Customs* [2010] EWHC 1071, [2010] STC 2072 [101], [108] (Vos J). See also *Bloomsbury International Ltd v Sea Fish Industry Authority* [2009] EWHC 172, [2010] 1 CMLR 12 [134] (Hamblen J).

[150] Ch 13 pp 306–11.

[151] The same applies to any contention that the defence should be allowed to apply with respect to claims for restitution of the use benefit (interest) derived from taxation payments: cf *Littlewoods Retail Ltd v HM Revenue & Customs* [2010] EWHC 1071, [2010] STC 2072 [108] (Vos J).

[152] Discussed immediately below.

[153] *Prudential Assurance Co Ltd v Revenue and Customs Commissioners* [2013] EWHC 3249, [2014] 2 CMLR 10.

a mistake about the lawfulness of the overpaid tax'.[154] In *Test Claimants in the FII Group Litigation v HM Revenue & Customs*,[155] a successor to the 2008 decision, Henderson J further examined the relevant arguments but refrained from expressing a final view on jurisdictional grounds. However, after addressing the criticisms made by commentators of the 'wrongdoing' reasoning employed in his 2008 decision, his Honour agreed that 'a better explanation for the bar on the defence of change of position to *Woolwich* claims is to be found in the stultification principle'.[156] This is a vastly preferable approach and supports his Honour's earlier view taken in *Prudential Assurance*. Taken together with the English Court of Appeal's decision in *O'Neile v Gale*, the cases may reflect a growing appreciation of the role of the principle of coherence (or stultification, viewed from the other perspective) within the law of unjust enrichment.

C. Impact on Third Parties

Third parties may be prejudiced by an order for restitution made against the defendant. For example, a third party may have extended credit to the defendant on the basis of his apparent assets and be prejudiced by an order that the defendant restore part of those assets to the plaintiff.[157] A slight variant is the problem of inter-generational equity, raised where the burden of the order for restitution effectively falls on third party successors to the original recipient.[158] However, the position as a matter of general law seems to be that the defence is established according to whether repayment is 'inequitable' to the defendant[159] and that the potentially adverse impact on a third party cannot influence the outcome.[160]

IV. Ambit of Operation

A. Application to Claims for Unjust Enrichment not Based on Mistake

Notwithstanding that the change of position defence is a general defence to claims in unjust enrichment,[161] the requirement of good faith will usually restrict the defence to cases involving mistaken payments. For example, a defendant who knows of, or sufficiently suspects, the circumstances of the unjust factor (as occurs in many cases in which

[154] ibid [188].
[155] *Test Claimants in the FII Group Litigation v HM Revenue & Customs* [2014] EWHC 4302, [2015] STC 1471 [316]–[341].
[156] ibid [315].
[157] E Bant and P Creighton, 'The Australian Change of Position Defence' (2002) 30 *University of Western Australia Law Review* 208, 221.
[158] See, eg, *Air Canada v British Columbia* [1989] 1 SCR 1161 [92] (La Forest J: burden of funding restitution of unlawful tax would fall on a new generation of taxpayers), but rejected in *Hartigan v International Society for Krishna Consciousness Inc* [2002] NSWSC 810 [96]–[97] (Bryson J).
[159] *Lipkin Gorman v Karpnale Ltd* [1991] 2 AC 548, 580 (Lord Goff).
[160] The position under some Australian statutory defences is considered below at p 361.
[161] *Lipkin Gorman v Karpnale Ltd* [1991] 2 AC 548, 579–80 (Lord Goff); *Haugesund Kommune v Depfa ACS Bank* [2010] EWCA Civ 579, [2012] QB 549 [122] (Aikens LJ; Pill LJ concurring); *David Securities Pty Ltd v Commonwealth Bank of Australia* [1992] HCA 48 [59], (1992) 175 CLR 353, 385 (Mason CJ, Deane, Toohey, Gaudron and McHugh JJ).

the defendant exerts undue influence or duress) will struggle to satisfy the requirement of good faith. The same is true of a defendant who knows that the enrichment was conferred on a conditional basis (as occurs in most cases of failure of consideration) and acts as if his receipt were unconditional. However, where good faith is made out, the defence may apply. An example of where the defence of change of position should apply in the context of a claim of failure of consideration is *Fibrosa Spolka Akcyjna v Fairbairn Lawson Combe Barbour Ltd.*[162] In that case, the defendant purchaser was ordered to make restitution of a pre-payment for machinery following frustration of the contract of sale caused by the outbreak of war. Although the consideration for the payment failed because the machinery was not delivered, the defendant company had incurred costs for the purposes of performing the contract in reliance upon its receipt of the pre-payment. Whilst the change of position defence had not been recognised in 1943, the defence would now apply in such circumstances in those jurisdictions which do not have frustration legislation.[163]

Although omitting the modern terminology of change of position, courts of equity have also long applied an analogous conception to change of position in the context of rescission for undue influence. An early example concerning undue influence is *Allcard v Skinner.*[164] Although the *ratio* of the case was that the plaintiff failed to recover the value of her assets made over to the defendant on the basis of laches or acquiescence, Lindley LJ also recognised in obiter dicta that a change of position defence should apply:

> I cannot come to the conclusion that nothing has been done on the faith of the money being the property of the sisterhood. It is contrary to human nature to suppose that the Plaintiff's money was not for years regarded as the money of the sisterhood, and that the sisterhood did not act on that assumption and make their arrangements accordingly.[165]

Another example of the recognition of a defence equivalent to change of position for undue influence is *Cheese v Thomas.*[166] The plaintiff paid £43,000 towards the purchase of a house by his great nephew (the defendant). The parties had agreed that the plaintiff would be entitled to live in the house for the rest of his life. The defendant was to pay all the mortgage instalments on the house. When the defendant failed to make the mortgage payments, the plaintiff sought rescission of the transaction and restitution of the value of his contribution. However, the value of the house had plummeted since its acquisition. The English Court of Appeal held that the loss of value should be borne proportionately to the amount contributed by each to the purchase of the house. Although not described as a change of position defence, this was precisely the effect of reducing the awards of restitution and counter-restitution by reference to the detrimental change of position in the market value of the house. As Sir Donald Nicholls VC (with whom Butler-Sloss and Peter Gibson LJJ agreed) said:

> It is axiomatic that, when reversing this transaction, the court is concerned to achieve practical justice for both parties, not the plaintiff alone. The plaintiff is seeking the assistance of a court of equity, and he who seeks equity must do equity.[167]

[162] *Fibrosa Spolka Akcyjna v Fairbairn Lawson Combe Barbour Ltd* [1942] UKHL 4, [1943] AC 32.

[163] Indeed, some frustration legislation allows a statutory change of position defence to apply in such circumstances: see below at pp 356–58.

[164] *Allcard v Skinner* (1887) 36 Ch D 145.

[165] ibid 188–89.

[166] *Cheese v Thomas* [1994] 1 WLR 129, discussed in M Chen-Wishart, 'Loss Sharing, Undue Influence and Manifest Disadvantage' (1994) 110 *Law Quarterly Review* 173.

[167] *Cheese v Thomas* [1994] 1 WLR 129, 136.

A third example is *Quek v Beggs*,[168] in which the defendant took out a mortgage over one of the given properties and used that money to improve the property of a third party. The defendant later discharged the mortgage through sale of another of the given properties. When the plaintiff later sought to rescind the transaction, McLelland J, citing *Allcard v Skinner*, held that it would be inequitable to make the defendant account for the sums used to improve the third party's property, as he would be unable to be restored to his original position.

Finally, in *Hartigan v International Society for Krishna Consciousness Incorporated*,[169] Bryson J considered a claim raised by the defendant association, to the effect that it had changed its position by applying the proceeds of sale of the donated property in reducing its debt. The defendant cited *Allcard v Skinner* and *Quek v Beggs* in support of its claim. Justice Bryson rejected the defence but only because the defendant had received a considerable financial benefit by discharging the debt early so that it would not be inequitable for it to be returned to the 'relative position of indebtedness which it would have been in if it had not received the proceeds of the sale'.[170]

B. Application to Claims for Restitution of Rights

As a general defence to unjust enrichment, the defence ought in principle to be available where a plaintiff obtains an order for restitution of rights rather than restitution of value for unjust enrichment.[171] In many cases, however, the question will not arise. This is because where the change detrimentally affects the benefit to which the right relates (for example, a unique chattel devalues or is destroyed), any order requiring restitution of the right will automatically encompass that change.

The need for a discrete defence in cases of restitution of rights is therefore most acute in cases of 'defendant-instigated' changes of position, where the change of position does not affect the claimed right. For example, if a defendant receives title to a house by way of gift and, in good faith reliance on his receipt, gives away his right to subsidised council accommodation, the defence should be available whether the claim is to the value of the house or to restitution of the right pursuant to a trust or power to obtain reconveyance of the right.[172] At present, the authorities are unclear whether restitution of rights pursuant to a trust is subject to the defence.[173] A key issue is whether allowing the defence will undermine, or be inconsistent with, the law's protection generally afforded to vested rights held by the plaintiff, such as through the doctrine of conversion. On the other hand, the rescission case law provides ample support for the view that where an equitable power to obtain

[168] *Quek v Beggs* (1990) 5 BPR 11,761.

[169] *Hartigan v International Society for Krishna Consciousness Inc* [2002] NSWSC 810.

[170] ibid [98]; see also *McCulloch v Fern* [2001] NSWSC 406 [89]–[113] (Palmer J).

[171] Cf *Armstrong DLW GmbH v Winnington Networks Ltd* [2012] EWHC 10, [2013] Ch 156 [103] (Stephen Morris QC), taking the view that the defence did not apply to a 'proprietary restitutionary claim'.

[172] This is consistent with the position under the Trustees Act 1962 (WA) s 65(8), discussed below at p 359.

[173] Cf, eg, *Williams v Williams* [2003] EWHC 742 (Ch), [2003] WTLR 1371 [52]–[54] (Kevin Garnett QC); *Re Diplock; Diplock v Wintle* [1948] Ch 465, 546 (the Court). See also *Armstrong DLW GmbH v Winnington Networks Ltd* [2012] EWHC 10, [2013] Ch 156 [103] (Stephen Morris QC.)

reconveyance of a right arises, changes of position made prior to the exercise of the power (and thus prior to the vesting of the right) might be taken into account for the purposes of determining the parties' restitutionary and counter-restitutionary liabilities.[174] The four cases examined in section IVA above provide good examples of this approach in practice.

C. Application to Public Authorities and the Defence of 'Exhaustion of Benefits'

The defence applies to all unjust enrichment defendants, whether they are private individuals or public authorities such as the Revenue.[175] For this reason, some courts have assumed that the defence may apply, for example, to diminish or defeat claims for restitution of overpaid tax.[176] However, in the case of public authorities, the stultification bar assumes particular importance. We saw previously[177] that in *Claimants in the FII Group Litigation v Revenue and Customs Commissioners*, Henderson J rightly concluded that the defence could never apply to *Woolwich* claims made against the Revenue. The conclusion rested on the assumption that the Revenue was a 'wrongdoer' in those circumstances. With respect, that characterisation is not always accurate: the taxation may simply have been unauthorised rather than imposed in breach of some legal or equitable duty. Nonetheless, the ultimate conclusion is correct: as Henderson J noted in a subsequent case in that litigation, to allow the defence would undermine the policy requiring restitution that underpins *Woolwich* claims.[178] The *Woolwich* claim was not a claim for restitution of unjust enrichment. It was a claim for restitution for reasons of policy. Where reasons of policy require restitution, and where those reasons of policy do not restrict the claim to restitution of only extant enrichment, there is no scope for a defendant to point to his or her own personal circumstances to circumvent the general policy.[179] Nor is the problem of the defence of change of position operating to stultify policy-based reasons for restitution avoided by relabelling the defence one of 'exhaustion of benefits'.[180]

[174] Eg *Armstrong v Jackson* [1917] 2 KB 822; *Brown v Smitt* [1924] HCA 11, (1924) 34 CLR 160, 173–74 (Knox CJ, Gavan Duffy and Starke JJ); *Alati v Kruger* [1955] HCA 64, (1955) 94 CLR 216, 229–30 (Dixon CJ, Webb, Kitto and Taylor JJ); *Balfour and Clark v Hollandia Ravensthorpe NL* (1978) 18 SASR 240, 254–255 (Bray CJ; Hogarth and Zelling JJ agreeing on this point); *Akron Securities Ltd v Iliffe* [1997] NSWSC 106, (1997) 41 NSWLR 353, 370 (Mason P; Priestley JA agreeing); *Munchies Management Pty Ltd v Belperio* [1988] FCA 413, (1988) 58 FCR 274, 289 [39]–[40](the Court); *Coastal Estates Pty Ltd v Melevende* [1965] VR 433, 440–41 (Sholl J).

[175] *Test Claimants in the FII Group Litigation v Revenue and Customs Commissioners* [2008] EWHC 2893, [2009] STC 254 [302]–[352], [445] (Henderson J); *Littlewoods Retail Ltd v The Commissioners for Revenue and Customs* [2010] EWHC 1071.

[176] Eg *Commissioner of State Revenue (Vic) v Royal Insurance Australia Ltd* [1994] HCA 61, (1994) 182 CLR 51, 64 [20] (Mason CJ); considered *ACN 005 057 349 Pty Ltd v Commissioner of State Revenue* [2015] VSCA 332 [168]–[171] (the Court).

[177] Above p 351.

[178] *Test Claimants in the FII Group Litigation v HM Revenue & Customs* [2014] EWHC 4302, [2015] STC 1471 [310]–[315] (Henderson J).

[179] *Prudential Assurance Co Ltd v Revenue and Customs Commissioners* [2013] EWHC 3249, [2014] 2 CMLR 10 [188] (Henderson J).

[180] *Littlewoods Retail Ltd v HM Revenue and & Customs* [2010] EWHC 1071, [2010] STC 2072 [126]–[131] (Vos J). Cf *Littlewoods Retail Ltd v HM Revenue & Customs* [2014] EWHC 868 [412] (Henderson J).

V. Statutory Defences of Change of Position

This section considers defences analogous to the change of position defence that arise both in England and in Australia pursuant to frustrated contracts legislation, before turning to consider a variety of other Australian statutory defences of change of position.[181]

A. Frustrated Contracts Acts

Some frustrated contracts legislation is expressly concerned with loss apportionment.[182] However, the Law Reform (Frustrated Contracts) Act 1943 (UK) contains provisions that modify the restitutionary liability of the parties to a frustrated contract in a manner that is broadly analogous to the change of position defence. Victorian legislation modelled on the Act has recently been repealed, redrafted in 'plain English' and eventually re-enacted as part of the state's Consumer Law and Fair Trading Act.[183] However the revised provisions remain consistent with their UK counterparts in all material respects. The following discussion will therefore adopt the original UK legislation as its principal point of reference.

i. Similarities Between Section 1(2) and the Common Law Defence

The legislation governs restitution of benefits transferred pursuant to certain classes of frustrated contracts.[184] Section 1(2) of the UK Act applies where a party has received a money benefit (which includes an accrued right to a sum):

> All sums paid or payable to any party in pursuance of the contract before the time when the parties were so discharged (in this Act referred to as 'the time of discharge') shall, in the case of sums so paid, be recoverable from him as money received by him for the use of the party by whom the sums were paid, and, in the case of sums so payable, cease to be so payable: *Provided that, if the party to whom the sums were so paid or payable incurred expenses before the time of discharge in, or for the purpose of, the performance of the contract, the court may, if it considers it just to do so having regard to all the circumstances of the case, allow him to retain or, as the case may be, recover the whole or any part of the sums so paid or payable, not being an amount in excess of the expenses so incurred* [emphasis added].

[181] Trustee Act (NT) s 50AA(2)(c); Trusts Act 1973 (Qld) s 109(3); Succession Act 1981 (Qld) s 53(5); Perpetuities and Accumulations Act 1992 (Tas) s 24(2)(c); Trustees Act 1962 (WA) s 65(8); Property Law Act 1969 (WA) s 125.

[182] Frustrated Contracts Act 1978 (NSW) and Frustrated Contracts Act 1988 (SA).

[183] Australian Consumer Law and Fair Trading Act 2012 Part 3.2, previously Fair Trading Act 1999 (Vic) ss 32ZE–32ZO, originally Frustrated Contracts Act 1959 (Vic). The 2012 provisions were applied in *Foley v Afonso Building Solutions Pty Ltd (Building and Property)* [2014] VCAT 1640.

[184] The Acts do not apply if there is a contractual provision to the contrary. This suggests they are intended to operate as a code. The UK legislation excluded charterparties, contracts for the carriage of goods by sea other than by charterparty, contracts of insurance and contracts for the sale of goods where the goods have perished. The Victorian legislation extends to contracts for the sale of goods that have been 'avoided' under s 12 of the Goods Act 1958 (Vic).

Although some have suggested that the proviso is concerned with loss apportionment,[185] the better view, as expressed by Robert Goff J in *BP Exploration Co (Libya) v Hunt (No 2)*, [186] is that it operates as a change of position defence. First, the proviso operates as an independent enactment, the onus lying on the party seeking to rely on the proviso to satisfy its requirements.[187] Secondly, it provides a ceiling to relief by reference to the value of the benefit received and restricts that relief to the value of the expenses incurred. These limitations suggest that the proviso operates as a defence of change of position rather than as an independent source of rights to compensation or as a means of apportioning loss, for example. Finally, the proviso is only triggered where the relying party has received a monetary benefit in the form of a sum paid or payable and has incurred expenditure 'in, or for the performance of the contract'. This formulation is both consistent with a reliance requirement and is sufficiently broad (through the use of the phrase 'for the performance of') to encompass anticipatory changes of position.

The proviso invests in a court considering the position of a qualified recipient a broad discretion to allow relief to a qualified recipient 'if it considers just to do so, having regard to all the circumstances of the case'. Although apparently unfettered, it is highly desirable that the same considerations and principles that inform the more developed common law defence should also inform (and restrict) the statutory discretion. A uniform approach will both give definite content to the discretion and will ensure coherent treatment of like cases. Further, the few cases to date that have invoked the discretion have seen it exercised in a principled manner consistent with the common law defence. Thus, in the Victorian case of *Lobb v Vasey Housing Auxiliary (War Widows Guild)*,[188] Hudson J considered that the proviso would not apply where the defendant's change of position (building a flat in reliance on the receipt of a contractual payment) could be reversed by selling the asset so as to recover the value of the benefit originally received. This reasoning echoes the core irreversibility requirement of the common law defence.

The sole English case on point, *Gamerco SA v ICM/Fair Warning (Agency) Ltd*,[189] is likewise grounded in familiar restitutionary principles. In that case, a rock concert to be held in Spain was cancelled at the last moment because the proposed venue was declared unsafe. The claimants had paid some $412,000 to the defendants and owed them a further sum by the date frustration occurred. Both claimants and defendants had incurred expenditure in preparation for the concert. Although purporting to exercise a 'broad' discretion unfettered by change of position considerations, Garland J effectively set off the parties' expenses to conclude that the defendant should not be entitled to any relief pursuant to the proviso. The

[185] Eg AM Haycroft and DM Waksman, 'Frustration and Restitution' [1984] *Journal of Business Law* 207; AS Burrows, *The Law of Restitution*, 3rd edn (Oxford, Oxford University Press, 2011) 364. Burrows' conclusion rests on the assumption that receipt of an accrued right to payment, as opposed to the payment itself, does not constitute a benefit; a view which is rejected in Ch 4 p 57.

[186] *BP Exploration Co (Libya) v Hunt (No 2)* [1979] 1 WLR 783, 800 (Robert Goff J), affirmed on other grounds in *BP Exploration Co (Libya) Ltd v Hunt (No 2)* [1981] 1 WLR 232, and *BP Exploration Co (Libya) Ltd v Hunt (No 2)* [1983] 2 AC 352. Contra is *Gamerco SA v ICM/Fair Warning (Agency) Ltd* [1995] 1 WLR 1226 1237 (Garland J), although the reasoning is entirely consistent with a change of position defence: see immediately below.

[187] *Lobb v Vasey Housing Auxiliary (War Widows Guild)* [1963] VR 239, 247 (Hudson J); *Gamerco SA v ICM/Fair Warning (Agency) Ltd* [1995] 1 WLR 1226, 1236 (Garland J).

[188] *Lobb v Vasey Housing Auxiliary (War Widows Guild)* [1963] VR 239.

[189] *Gamerco SA v ICM/Fair Warning (Agency) Ltd* [1995] 1 WLR 1226.

result is largely consistent with the application of a change of position defence in favour of both parties with respect to each party's claim and counter-claim for restitution of benefits conferred pursuant to the frustrated contract.

ii. Differences Between Section 1(2) and the Common Law Defence

Notwithstanding its similarities, the proviso has a far narrower ambit of operation than its common law counterpart. Not only is it restricted to certain classes of frustrated contract, the proviso applies only to reliance expenditure, which must have been made in or for the purposes of the contract. It follows that non-pecuniary changes of position, and reliance expenditure that relates to matters outside the contract, do not count as relevant changes of position. Thus a party who receives a payment pursuant to a frustrated contract and changes his position in reliance on his receipt by spending the money on a holiday cruise would not be able to avail himself of the statutory defence.

iii. Relationship to Section 1(3)(a) and (b)

Section 1(3) addresses restitution of non-money benefits. It reads:

> Where any party to the contract has, by reason of anything done by any other party thereto in, or for the purpose of, the performance of the contract, obtained a valuable benefit (other than a payment of money to which the last foregoing subsection applies) before the time of discharge, there shall be recoverable from him by the said other party such sum (if any), not exceeding the value of the said benefit to the party obtaining it, as the court considers just, having regard to all the circumstances of the case and, in particular,—(a) the amount of any expenses incurred before the time of discharge by the benefited party in, or for the purpose of, the performance of the contract, including any sums paid or payable by him to any other party in pursuance of the contract and retained or recoverable by that party under the last foregoing subsection, and (b) the effect, in relation to the said benefit, of the circumstances giving rise to the frustration of the contract.

There is an obvious symmetry between this subsection and section 1(2). There is the same requirement that a party has received a benefit, albeit in non-monetary form. The value of any just sum is again limited by the value of the benefit received. And the wording of section 1(3)(a) reflects the proviso in section 1(2) relating to the recipient party's change of position. The relationship between the two subsections is highlighted by the direction that the court must take into account any award under section 1(2) so as to avoid double counting of expenses incurred. Given the close connection between the subsections, the starting point in interpreting section 1(3) must be that it introduces the same kind of claim, subject to the same sort of statutory change of position defence as applies under section 1(2).

The major substantive difference between the provisions stems from section 1(3)(b). Professor Burrows argues persuasively that section 1(3)(b) addresses the case where the received benefit is destroyed due to a frustrating event, as where a partly built house is destroyed by fire.[190] The proviso allows a court to take into account such independent changes of position and accordingly extends the potential scope of the statutory defence beyond solely reliance-based changes of position.

[190] AS Burrows, *The Law of Restitution*, 3rd edn (Oxford, Oxford University Press, 2011) 368.

However, *BP Exploration Co (Libya) v Hunt (No 2)*[191] presents a significant obstacle to that interpretation. In that case, Robert Goff J identified section 1(3)(a) as a statutory change of position defence.[192] His Lordship treated section 1(3)(b) as going to the logically prior issue of the identification of the valuable benefit to which any statutory change of position would then relate.[193] Notwithstanding this interpretation, the structure of the provision as a whole strongly suggests that it naturally divides into two parts: the first dealing with the non-discretionary identification of a received benefit and the second, with the valuation of the 'just sum' in which discretion (in the sense discussed previously) plays an important role. That is, the section requires that there must be an identified benefit before subsections (a) and (b) can apply. In that context, the simpler reading of the section is that section 1(3) is the counterpart of section 1(2) and its subsections both raise change of position considerations. On this approach, section 1(3)(b) simply makes it clear that independent changes of position caused by the frustrating event may properly be taken into account in determining the 'just sum'.

B. Other Statutory Change of Position Defences

Australia boasts a significant number of additional statutory defences of change of position. They arise with respect to different types of mis-payment and mis-distributions and in different contexts—for example, trust and estate distributions,[194] mistaken payments generally,[195] and cy-près distributions.[196] An example of the statutory defences is contained in section 125 of the Property Law Act 1969 (WA):

> Relief ... shall be denied wholly or in part if the person from whom relief is sought received the payment in good faith and has so altered his position in reliance on the validity of the payment that in the opinion of the Court, having regard to all possible implications in respect of the parties (other than the plaintiff or claimant) to the payment and of other persons acquiring rights or interests through them, it is inequitable to grant relief or to grant relief in full.

This following discussion is not a comprehensive examination of each of the statutory defences as the application of each turns upon their particular statutory context. Instead it is a broad outline of the general similarities and differences between the common law and statutory defences.

i. Similarities to the Common Law Defence

Each statutory defence requires that the defendant receive a benefit in good faith and alter his position so that it is 'inequitable' to grant relief wholly or in part. There is nothing in the provisions that requires the concepts of good faith and change of position to be

[191] *BP Exploration Co (Libya) Ltd v Hunt (No 2)* [1979] 1 WLR 783, 800 (Robert Goff J), affirmed on other grounds [1981] 1 WLR 232 and [1983] 2 AC 352.

[192] *BP Exploration Co (Libya) Ltd v Hunt (No 2)* [1979] 1 WLR 783, 800, 804.

[193] ibid 801–03.

[194] Trusts Act 1973 (Qld) s 113(3); Succession Act 1981 (Qld) s 53(5); Trustees Act 1962 (WA) s 65(8).

[195] Property Law Act 1969 (WA) s 125.

[196] Trustee Act (NT) s 50AA(2)(c); Perpetuities and Accumulations Act 1992 (Tas) s 24(2)(c).

treated differently from their common law counterparts.[197] The requirement of inequitability can be read consistently with the common law defence as demanding that the change be irreversible.

It is unclear whether the statutory defences will extend to anticipatory changes of position. The order of words, namely that the defendant has 'received the payment in good faith and has so altered his position in reliance on the validity of the payment' may suggest that the changes of position must follow receipt. On the other hand, considerations of principle and of consistency with the common law position favour allowing anticipatory changes of position, as does certain New Zealand authority.[198] Further, as we saw earlier, the Privy Council in *Dextra Bank & Trust Co Ltd v Bank of Jamaica*[199] used 'receipt' to mean 'eventual receipt'.

ii. Differences from the Common Law Defence

There are three major points of distinction between the common law and statutory defences:

a. Reliance on the Validity of the Receipt

Each statutory defence requires that the defendant acted in reliance on the assumption that there was *no ground* for reversing the transaction by which the benefit was conferred.[200] In other words, the defendant must have acted on the basis that his receipt of the benefit was 'free from challenge or attack'[201] by the plaintiff. This requirement of reliance on the *validity* of the receipt may be more demanding than the common law defence and may be a reason for a defendant to plead instead the common law defence in preference to (or at least in the alternative to) its statutory counterpart.[202] We saw that at common law it is possible for a defendant to change his position by acting in reliance on his receipt, even if he knows of the existence of a vitiating factor, provided that he acts consistently with the known basis of his receipt.[203] In contrast, the defendant's knowledge of an unjust factor will prevent the application of any of the statutory defences. For example, in *National Bank of New Zealand*

[197] *Wendt v Orr* [2004] WASC 28 [213]–[234] (Commissioner Johnson QC), addressing the provisions of Trustees Act 1962 (WA) s 65(8); see also *Meltzer v Axiom International Ltd* [2001] NZCA 209 [30]–[38] addressing the provisions of Companies Act 1955 (NZ) s 270(3).

[198] *Thomas v Houston Corbett and Co* [1969] NZLR 151; *Re Island Bay Masonry Ltd (in liq); Firth Industries Ltd v Gray* (1998) 8 NZCLC 261, 751 discussed by P Watts, 'Company Law' [1999] *New Zealand Law Review* 23, 39–40, is another possible example.

[199] *Dextra Bank & Trust Co Ltd v Bank of Jamaica* [2001] UKPC 50, [2002] 1 All ER (Comm) 193 confining *South Tyneside Metropolitan Borough Council v Svenska International plc* [1995] 1 All ER 545 to its facts. See also *Philip Collins Ltd v Davis* [2000] 3 All ER 808, 827.

[200] For example, in Trustees Act 1962 (WA) s 65(8) the defendant recipient must have 'altered his position in reliance on his having an indefeasible interest in the assets or interest'. Under the Property Law Act 1969 (WA) s 125(1) the recipient must have 'altered his position in reliance on the validity of the payment'. The same notion is expressed in the Trusts Act 1973 (Qld) s 109(3) and the Succession Act 1981 (Qld) s 53(5), as acting in reliance on 'the propriety of the payment or distribution', and in the Administration Act 1969 (NZ) s 51 as acting in the reasonable belief that 'the distribution was properly made and would not be set aside'.

[201] *National Bank of New Zealand Ltd v Waitaki International Processing (NI) Ltd* [1999] 2 NZLR 211, 217 (Henry J).

[202] The statutory defences are unlikely to have been intended to cover the field and oust their common law counterpart. The practice has been to argue both in the alternative: *National Bank of New Zealand Ltd v Waitaki International Processing (NI) Ltd* [1999] 2 NZLR 211; *Alpha Wealth Financial Services Pty Ltd v Frankland River Olive Co Ltd* [2008] WASCA 119, (2008) 66 ACSR 594.

[203] Above p 344.

Ltd v Waitaki International Processing (NI) Ltd,[204] a case dealing with section 94B of the Judicature Act 1908 (NZ)—the terms of which are substantially mirrored in section 125 of the Property Law Act 1969 (WA)—a majority of the Court of Appeal of New Zealand found that the defendant's knowledge of the mistake meant that the statutory defence failed.

Although the statutory defences insist that the defendant have no knowledge of any unjust factor, they do not require that the defendant consider himself entitled to the benefit received. Thus, in *Thomas v Houston Corbett and Co*,[205] the plaintiff was induced by a dishonest employee, Cook, to pay £1,381 to the defendant. Cook told the defendant that he was entitled to keep £541 of this amount for himself, but that the balance was payable to other parties. Relying on this, the defendant paid the balance to Cook. The New Zealand Court of Appeal found that the defendant had acted in reliance on the validity of the payment for the purposes of section 94B of the Judicature Act 1908 (NZ), even though he believed he was entitled only to part of it.

b. Third Party Interests

Once the defendant has established the prerequisites for the particular statutory defence, the court must assess whether it would be inequitable to grant relief, in part or in whole, against the defendant: whether the defendant has 'so altered his position … that … it is inequitable to grant relief'.[206] The test to be applied is not an idiosyncratic test of fairness. For instance, a defendant could not rely on his impecunious state, unless his poverty were attributable to the change of position.[207] A difference from the common law defence, however, is that some of the statutory defences require the court to have regard to the implications for other persons in assessing whether it would be inequitable to grant relief.[208] For example, in *Alpha Wealth Financial Services Pty Ltd v Frankland River Olive Co Ltd*,[209] Commissioner Sanderson of the Western Australian Supreme Court considered the application of section 125 of the Property Law Act 1969 (WA) in the context of mistaken payments made under an investment scheme. His Honour noted that if the defendant were required to make restitution there was a real prospect that the investment scheme would fail entirely, affecting the rights of third parties under the scheme. This was regarded as a factor that strongly supported the application of the statutory defence.

c. Fault

The third distinction between the common law and statutory defences is that under the statutes, the issue of whether it would be inequitable to grant relief clearly includes the

[204] *National Bank of New Zealand Ltd v Waitaki International Processing (NI) Ltd* [1999] 2 NZLR 211.

[205] *Thomas v Houston Corbett and Co* [1969] NZLR 151.

[206] See, eg, Property Law Act 1969 (WA) s 125(1).

[207] *Wendt v Orr* [2004] WASC 28 [220] (Commissioner Johnson QC), addressing the provisions of Trustees Act 1962 (WA) s 65(8). However, in *Menzies v Bennett* (Napier SC (NZ) 14 August 1969), noted in RJ Sutton, 'Case and Comment: More on Money Paid under Mistake' [1970] *New Zealand Law Journal* 5, Beattie J did take into account the defendant's financial hardship in applying the Judicature Amendment Act 1958 (NZ) s 94B.

[208] Trustee Act (NT) s 50AA(2)(c); Perpetuities and Accumulations Act 1992 (Tas) s 24(2)(c); Trustees Act 1962 (WA) s 65(8); Property Law Act 1969 (WA) s 125. Contrast Trusts Act 1973 (Qld) s 109(3) and Succession Act 1981 (Qld) s 53(5), which contain no direction.

[209] *Alpha Wealth Financial Services Pty Ltd v Frankland River Olive Co Ltd* [2006] WASC 70, (2006) 199 FLR 91, reversed on another ground [2008] WASCA 119, (2008) 66 ACSR 594.

defendant's fault in causing the original enrichment or contributing to its loss.[210] For example, New Zealand courts have held that under the statute, it is not inequitable for the defendant to bear a loss which was attributable to his own carelessness. In *Thomas v Houston Corbett and Co*,[211] the New Zealand Court of Appeal assessed the relative fault of the plaintiff and defendant in allowing the plaintiff's employee, Cook, to perpetrate his fraud. Finding that the defendant bore a minor share of the blame, the court reduced by one-third the defence otherwise available in respect of the £840 that had been paid to Cook and thereby lost.

VI. Conclusion

The change of position defence is the primary defence to a claim in unjust enrichment. The defence is gradually taking shape through a series of important, and largely consistent, judicial determinations. Since its recognition in 1991 the *pro tanto* common law change of position defence has developed three core elements:

a. a detrimental change of position;
b. caused or contributed to by the receipt; and
c. good faith on the part of the defendant.

We saw that a key criterion in determining the element of detriment is whether the effects of the change of position are irreversible. Additionally, the chapter has shown that, in changing her position, the defendant must have acted in accordance with good faith conduct. The analysis also demonstrates that, except when some overriding public policy or statutory policy would be stultified by application of the defence, there are no independent bars to the defence. There are related requirements for statutory defences of change of position.

This chapter was devoted entirely to change of position because of the central role that the defence plays in unjust enrichment. Recognition of the defence, which protects defendants from harm which might otherwise arise from reversal of the impugned transaction, has allowed unjust factors such as mistake to evolve beyond their historical limitations. In contrast with change of position, the next, and final, chapter of this book considers a large selection of other possible defences. Unlike change of position, none of these is fundamental to unjust enrichment.

210 Trustee Act (NT) s 50AA(2)(c) and Perpetuities and Accumulations Act 1992 (Tas) s 24(2)(c) both refer to the need for the defendant to have altered his position 'reasonably.' See also Administration Act 1969 (NZ) s 51, Companies Act 1993 (NZ) s 296(3), and Insolvency Act 1967 (NZ) s 58(6)(a).

211 *Thomas v Houston Corbett and Co* [1969] NZLR 151; see also *National Bank of New Zealand Ltd v Waitaki International Processing (NI) Ltd* [1992] 2 NZLR 211.

15

Other Defences

Contents

I. Introduction

The previous chapter explored the most important defence to a claim in unjust enrichment, namely change of position. This chapter considers eight other possible defences. This chapter does not seek to explain their operation in comprehensive detail. Many of them have had entire books devoted to their operation. They are general defences, not limited to unjust enrichment. This chapter is simply an introduction and outline of some of the other significant Anglo-Australian defences to claims for unjust enrichment.

The eight defences considered in this chapter are good consideration (which label conceals at least five different principles), counter-restitution being impossible, bona fide purchase for value without notice, estoppel, ministerial receipt, delay, dispute resolved, and passing on.

II. Good Consideration

In *Barclays Bank Ltd v WJ Simms, Son and Cooke (Southern) Ltd*,[1] Robert Goff J said that a claim to recover a mistaken payment may fail where:

> the payment is made for good consideration, in particular if the money is paid to discharge, and does discharge, a debt owed to the payee (or a principal on whose behalf he is authorised to receive the payment) by the payer or by a third party by whom he is authorised to discharge the debt.[2]

What Robert Goff J meant by 'good consideration' has been a matter of ongoing speculation. The difficulty is that there are at least five different possible principles[3] harboured under the umbrella of 'good consideration'. Each has its own distinct rationale and elements.

The first possibility, which we saw in Chapter 7, is that 'good consideration' refers to circumstances where the defendant has a juristic reason to retain the benefit. For instance, a defendant will generally have a juristic reason to retain a benefit if the defendant paid the benefit with the effect that it discharged a debt or obligation owed to the defendant. For clarity of analysis, in Chapter 7 we described this principle as 'receipt in satisfaction of a right'. An example is *Lloyds Bank plc v Independent Insurance Co Ltd*.[4] In that case, the plaintiff bank's mistaken payment discharged its client's debt to the defendant creditor. Restitution was refused. Similarly, in *Aiken v Short*,[5] a bank acquired property from a third party which the bank thought was subject to a charge in favour of the defendant. The bank paid the defendant to discharge the third party's debt and remove the charge. However, the third party from whom the bank acquired the property did not have good title to it. This meant that the bank had discharged a debt in order to remove a charge which did not exist. The bank sought recovery of the money paid to the defendant on the ground of mistake. A majority[6] held that the defendant had given good consideration for the payment by discharging the debt owed by the third party.

1 *Barclays Bank Ltd v WJ Simms Son & Cooke (Southern) Ltd* [1980] QB 677.

2 ibid 695.

3 Cf American Law Institute, *Restatement of the Law (Third) Restitution and Unjust Enrichment* (St Paul, Minn, American Law Institute Publishers, 2011) § 62, approximating our defence of receipt in satisfaction of right; § 67, incorporating discharge of debt; and §§ 27 and 63(d), which together address counterclaims for failure of consideration.

4 *Lloyds Bank plc v Independent Insurance Co Ltd* [2000] QB 110.

5 *Aiken v Short* (1856) 1 H & N 210, 156 ER 1180.

6 ibid 214–15, 1181–82 (Pollock CB and Platt B). Bramwell B held that the mistake, not being as to the bank's liability to pay, did not support the claim: see Ch 8 p 183.

A second possibility considered by some cases is that 'good consideration' is an application of the defence of change of position.[7] We saw in the last chapter that the core elements of this defence are: (1) an irreversible change of position; (2) that was caused or contributed to by the receipt of a benefit; and (3) good faith on the part of the defendant. The defence operates to prevent a defendant from being placed unjustifiably in a worse position than she occupied prior to her receipt.

A third possibility sees the label as describing the defence of payment in satisfaction of a legal claim.[8] This defence, which is concerned with the finality of disputes, is considered later in this chapter.

A fourth, separate, category of case that shelters under the umbrella term of 'good consideration' is a counterclaim by way of set-off for failure of consideration. Very recently, a fifth principle has been proposed: a defence of 'bona fide discharge of debt'. It is the fourth and fifth defensive principles that will be the subject of analysis in this section.

A. Failure of Consideration

The fourth manifestation of the defence of good consideration was considered in *David Securities Pty Ltd v Commonwealth Bank of Australia.*[9] Having cited the formulation of the defence in *Barclays Bank Ltd v WJ Simms, Son and Cooke (Southern) Ltd*,[10] the joint judgment of Mason CJ, Deane, Toohey, Gaudron and McHugh JJ went on to consider the defence as a defence of *failure of consideration*. The joint judgment said that 'In this context, consideration means the matter considered in forming the decision to do the act, "the state of affairs contemplated as the basis or reason for the payment."'[11] For example, suppose a plaintiff mistakenly paid money to a defendant and, overjoyed at this act of kindness, the defendant later waived a debt that the plaintiff owed to him. If a claim for restitution of the mistaken payment were brought against the defendant, the defendant would have a defence in the nature of a set-off for restitution of the value of the debt that was waived on the basis (consideration) that he was entitled to keep the plaintiff's payment.

The rationale of the defence is that the plaintiff must not be unjustly enriched by an order for restitution.[12] As Lord Wright said in *Spence v Crawford* in the context of rescission:

> Though the defendant has been fraudulent, he must not be robbed, nor must the plaintiff be unjustly enriched, as he would be if he both got back what he had parted with and kept what he had received in return.[13]

This defence has been manifest in the common law and equitable doctrines of rescission for hundreds of years. In equity, the requirement is often couched in terms of 'doing equity'.[14]

[7] *Lloyds Bank plc v Independent Insurance Co Ltd* [2000] QB 110, 125–26 (Waller LJ). See also *K & S Corp Ltd v Sportingbet Australia Pty Ltd* [2003] SASC 96, (2003) 86 SASR 312 [161] (Besanko J).

[8] *Hookway v Racing Victoria Ltd* [2005] VSCA 310, (2005) 13 VR 444 [39] (Ormiston J).

[9] *David Securities Pty Ltd v Commonwealth Bank of Australia* [1992] HCA 48, (1992) 175 CLR 353, 380 [48].

[10] *Barclays Bank Ltd v WJ Simms Son & Cooke (Southern) Ltd* [1980] QB 677.

[11] *David Securities Pty Ltd v Commonwealth Bank of Australia* [1992] HCA 48, (1992) 175 CLR 353, 382 [52]; see also Brennan J ibid 400 [16].

[12] *Smith New Court Securities Ltd v Citibank NA* [1997] AC 254; *Spence v Crawford* [1939] 3 All ER 271.

[13] *Spence v Crawford* [1939] 3 All ER 271, 288–89.

[14] Eg *Maguire v Makaronis* [1997] HCA 23, (1997) 188 CLR 449, 474–75 (Brennan CJ. Gaudron, McHugh and Gummow JJ).

Whether characterised as an equitable condition on recovery or as a common law counter-claim based on unjust enrichment, the defensive principle remains the same.[15] Where a plaintiff rescinds a transaction to recover the benefit transferred to the defendant, the basis on which the defendant transferred any benefits to the plaintiff (that is, enjoyment of the plaintiff's counter-performance) fails. The plaintiff must accordingly make counter-restitution to the defendant as part of the process of mutual restitution and counter-restitution.

As the earlier example demonstrates, the defence also arises outside the rescission context. In *Ovidio Carrideo Nominees Pty Ltd v The Dog Depot Pty Ltd*,[16] the Victorian Court of Appeal held that a landlord had a defence of 'good consideration' to a claim by its tenant for restitution of money paid to it by mistake. In separate judgments, Chernov JA and Nettle JA (with whom Ashley JA agreed) considered that the landlord had a good counter-claim against the tenant for the use and occupation of its premises for the disputed period, in an amount 'broadly equivalent'[17] to the amount mistakenly paid by the tenant.[18] The landlord's claim for counter-restitution[19] was a complete defence to the tenant's claim. This analysis has subsequently been approved and applied on numerous occasions.[20]

The onus of proving the defence of set-off for failure of consideration is on the defendant.[21] The defendant must prove that the basis upon which a counter-enrichment was conferred on the plaintiff would fail if restitution of the defendant's enrichment were ordered.[22] Negligence or even fraud of the defendant is irrelevant. However, the *plaintiff* may seek to rely on defences such as the change of position defence in relation to a defendant's set-off for failure of consideration.[23]

B. Bona Fide Discharge of Debt

The fifth manifestation of the defence of good consideration was proposed by Allsop P in *Hills Industries Ltd v Australian Financial Services and Leasing Pty Ltd.*[24] In that case, the

[15] *Plan B Trustees Ltd v Parker (No 2)* [2013] WASC 216, (2013) 11 ASTLR 242 [89]–[91] (Edelman J).

[16] *Ovidio Carrideo Nominees Pty Ltd v The Dog Depot Pty Ltd* [2006] VSCA 6, (2006) V ConvR 54-713.

[17] ibid [21] [22] (Chernov JA).

[18] ibid [2006] VSCA 6 [21] (Chernov JA) [32]–[48] (Nettle JA); (2006) V ConvR 54-713 [22] (Chernov JA) [34]–[50] (Nettle JA).

[19] ibid [2006] VSCA 6 [47] (Nettle JA), (2006) V ConvR 54-713 [49] (Nettle JA).

[20] *R & C Mazzei Nominees Pty Ltd v Aegean Food Import Export Pty Ltd* [2006] VSC 210, (2006) V ConvR 54-721 [45] (Osborn J); *Kiwi Munchies Pty Ltd v Nikolitsis* [2006] VCAT 929, (2007) V ConvR 58-580 [23]; *Fensford Pty Ltd v Nour Pty Ltd* [2006] VSCA 118 [40] (Nettle JA; Chernov and Ashley JJA concurring); *Ragi Pty Ltd v Kiwi Munchies Pty Ltd* [2007] NSWADT 108 [145]–[146] (the Tribunal); *Cook's Construction Pty Ltd v SFS 007.298.633 Pty Ltd* [2009] QCA 75, (2009) 254 ALR 661 [139]–[140] (Fraser JA; Daubney JA concurring with Fraser JA and Keane JA); *Adrenaline Pty Ltd v Bathurst Regional Council* [2015] NSWCA 123, (2015) 322 ALR 180 [78]–[86] (Leeming JA; Macfarlan and Ward JJA agreeing). Distinguished in *Lactos Fresh Pty Ltd v Finishing Services Pty Ltd (No 2)* [2006] FCA 748 [104]–[109] (Weinberg J).

[21] *David Securities Pty Ltd v Commonwealth Bank of Australia* [1992] HCA 48, (1992) 175 CLR 353, 383 [56] (Mason CJ, Deane, Toohey, Gaudron and McHugh JJ); *Cook's Construction Pty Ltd v SFS 007.298.633 Pty Ltd* [2009] QCA 75, (2009) 254 ALR 661 [140] (Fraser JA Daubney JA concurring with Fraser JA and Keane JA).

[22] See Ch 11 pp 252–53.

[23] For equivalent considerations in the context of rescission, see eg *Brown v Smitt* (1924) 34 CLR 160, 165–66 (Knox CJ, Gavan Duffy and Starke JJ); *Alati v Kruger* [1955] HCA 64, (1955) 94 CLR 216, 229-30 (Dixon CJ, Webb, Kitto and Taylor JJ).

[24] *Hills Industries Ltd v Australian Financial Services and Leasing Pty Ltd* [2012] NSWCA 380, (2012) 295 ALR 147 [83].

appellant companies Hills and Bosch received mistaken payments from AFSL, which had been induced to pay by a third party fraudster. The fraudster misled Hills and Bosch into believing that the payments were by way of repayment of debts owed to them by his companies. In reliance on the receipt, Hills and Bosch (amongst other matters)[25] discharged those debts. The Court of Appeal held that the change of position defence applied.[26] However, in a separate judgment, Allsop P also considered that the defence of good consideration applied.[27] His Honour analogised the defence of good consideration with that of bona fide purchase and found that it was rooted in the need for security and certainty in certain business transactions.[28] In particular, his Honour approved certain US decisions on the defence of 'discharge for value' which had held that it would introduce intolerable risk and uncertainty into commercial transactions if discharges of debts for value were liable to be undone.[29] In that context, it did not matter that AFSL had not actually intended its payments to discharge debts owed by the third party companies to Hills and Bosch. Nor did it matter that the debts were not owed to Hills and Bosch by AFSL or some principal of AFSL. As we saw, if they had been so owed, the defence of receipt in satisfaction of right would have clearly applied.

Justice Meagher disagreed with this analysis. His Honour considered that the case did not fall within the defence of good consideration as traditionally conceived. His Honour further rejected that the scope of the defence should be broadened in the manner suggested by Allsop P. Again reviewing the American authorities, Meagher JA considered that the illustrations of the discharge of debt cases that fell outside receipt in satisfaction of right could be better characterised on Anglo-Australian law as instances of the defence of payment over[30] and a particular manifestation of the change of position defence.[31]

On appeal, the High Court of Australia did not need to address this aspect of the case at any length. A joint judgment of Hayne, Crennan, Kiefel, Bell and Keane JJ very briefly endorsed Meagher JA's view that the case did not fall within the 'good consideration' defence (in the sense of receipt in satisfaction of right) as articulated by Goff J because AFSL's payments were not made to discharge the companies' debts to Hills and Bosch.[32] To that extent, any future development of a bona fide discharge defence will not occur under the umbrella label of 'good consideration'—a positive outcome which will assist to avoid the conflation of different concepts under the same label. However, the future development and recognition of a bona fide discharge defence may be unlikely. The defence as proposed by Allsop P

[25] The full changes made in reliance on the receipt are discussed in Ch 14 p 336.

[26] Discussed in Ch 14 pp 334–36.

[27] *Hills Industries Ltd v Australian Financial Services and Leasing Pty Ltd* [2012] NSWCA 380, (2012) 295 ALR 147 [76]–[145].

[28] ibid [83].

[29] See in particular the discussion at ibid [107]–[112], drawing on *Stephens v Board of Education of Brooklyn* 79 NY 183, 186–88 (Ct App 1879) (Andrews J delivering the judgment of the New York Court of Appeals) and the work of scholars, including Andrew Kull as author of American Law Institute, *Restatement of the Law (Third) Restitution and Unjust Enrichment* (St Paul, Minn, American Law Institute Publishers, 2011) § 67.

[30] *Hills Industries Ltd v Australian Financial Services and Leasing Pty Ltd* [2012] NSWCA 380, (2012) 295 ALR 147 [195]. On the defence of payment over, see below p 381.

[31] ibid [198]–[199].

[32] *Australian Financial Services and Leasing Pty Ltd v Hills Industries Ltd* [2014] HCA 14, (2014) 253 CLR 560 [100]–[101].

is similar in many respects to a receipt in satisfaction of a right.[33] Where it differs is that it is dependent on the defendant's purported discharge being effective immediately and conclusively. If, as Hayne, Crennan, Kiefel, Bell and Keane JJ observed,[34] discharges brought about as a result of a third party's fraud are liable to be reversed, then this model of automatic and conclusive discharge cannot be sustained.

III. Counter-Restitution Impossible

A defence closely related to the defence of set-off for 'failure of consideration' is the defence of counter-restitution impossible. If a defendant has a right to counter-restitution from the plaintiff (for example, for failure of basis), the plaintiff's inability to make counter-restitution traditionally operates as a bar or defence to the plaintiff's primary claim for relief.

At common law, restitution[35] was conditional on the plaintiff making precise counter-restitution to the defendant of benefits received by the plaintiff pursuant to the transaction.[36] This requirement of precise counter-restitution provided a defence if benefits provided by a defendant could not be returned *in specie*.[37] For example, in *Hunt v Silk*[38] the plaintiff was a tenant who terminated a lease for fundamental breach and sought restitution of his deposit for failure of consideration. The court rejected the claim, as the tenant had had the benefit of a few days' occupation. The court did not contemplate setting off the monetary value of the benefit of occupation received by the tenant against the value of the deposit. The tenant's inability to effect counter-restitution *in specie* afforded the landlord a complete defence.

In equity, by contrast, there was no such difficulty. In *Spence v Crawford*,[39] Lord Wright said of *Hunt v Silk* that 'the form of action at law in that case was different from the equitable jurisdiction'. In the leading English case of *Erlanger v New Sombrero Phosphate Co*,[40] the plaintiffs sought to rescind a contract for the purchase of an island containing a phosphate mine, on the ground of breach of fiduciary duty.[41] However, the mine had been worked extensively by the plaintiffs since its purchase and had significantly depreciated in value.

[33] *Hills Industries Ltd v Australian Financial Services and Leasing Pty Ltd* [2012] NSWCA 380, (2012) 295 ALR 147 [114], [116]–[117].

[34] *Australian Financial Services and Leasing Pty Ltd v Hills Industries Ltd* [2014] HCA 14, (2014) 253 CLR 560 [101].

[35] Including rescission of contractual rights as well as restitution of property rights. See Ch 3 p 38, Ch 4 p 47.

[36] *Clarke v Dickson* (1858) EB & E 148, 120 ER 463. Cf *Ruttle Plant Hire Ltd v Secretary of State for the Environment, Food and Rural Affairs* [2007] EWHC 2870, [2008] 2 All ER (Comm) 264 [87]–[90].

[37] E McKendrick, 'Total Failure of Consideration and Counter-Restitution: Two Issues or One?' in P Birks (ed), *Laundering and Tracing* (Oxford, Clarendon Press, 1995) 221, citing *Whincup v Hughes* (1871) LR 6 CP 78.

[38] *Hunt v Silk* (1804) 5 East 449, 102 ER 1142; see also *Clarke v Dickson* (1858) EB & E 148, 120 ER 463; *Fullers' Theatres Ltd v Musgrove* [1923] HCA 12, (1923) 31 CLR 524. For a good example of the contrasting approach in equity to occupation of a premises during the period prior to rescission, see *Koutsonicolis v Principe (No 2)* (1987) 48 SASR 328.

[39] *Spence v Crawford* [1939] 3 All ER 271, 290.

[40] *Erlanger v New Sombrero Phosphate Co* (1878) 3 App Cas 1218.

[41] ibid 1236 (Lord Cairns), 1243 (Lord Hatherley), 1245–46 (Lord O'Hagan), 1277 (Lord Blackburn), 1284 (Lord Gordon). Lord Penzance considered the case to be one of undue influence, and Lord Blackburn also spoke of misrepresentation, 'corruption' and undue influence as alternative bases for rescission, at 1264–65.

The plaintiffs could not, accordingly, return it to the defendants in the same condition as it was received. In the course of considering whether rescission was barred for *laches*, Lord Blackburn stated:

> a Court of Equity could not give damages, and, unless it can rescind the contract, can give no relief. And, on the other hand, it can take accounts of profits, and make allowance for deterioration. And I think the practice has always been for a Court of Equity to give this relief whenever, by the exercise of its powers, it can do what is practically just, though it cannot restore the parties precisely to the state they were in before the contract.[42]

The House of Lords accordingly affirmed that the contract of sale should be rescinded subject to counter-restitution.

Lord Blackburn's analysis was cited with approval in the leading decision of the High Court of Australia in *Alati v Kruger*.[43] In that case, the respondent purchased a business from the appellant in reliance on the appellant's fraudulent misrepresentations about the weekly takings of the business. The respondent went into possession and for reasons unrelated to the misrepresentations, the business deteriorated. Thus it was not possible to return the business to the appellant precisely in the same condition in which it had been transferred. Nor could the use by the respondent of the premises be returned *in specie*. In a joint judgment, Dixon CJ, Webb, Kitto and Taylor JJ observed that either of these points might have meant that, under the common law approach, the plaintiff was not entitled to rescission and restitution of the purchase price, but the plaintiff succeeded in equity.[44]

Another approach sometimes taken in equity is to make the primary order for restitution conditional[45] upon the plaintiff giving counter-restitution of the value of the benefit received from the plaintiff.[46]

Equity's willingness to make counter-restitution of the value of non-monetary benefits is not limited to cases where the property the subject of the claim has remained in the hands of a party to the case. It has also been used to defeat the traditional bar that rescission and restitution of enrichment is not available where third party interests have intervened. In *Hartigan v International Society for Krishna Consciousness Inc*,[47] the plaintiff gave her house (with surrounding farm) to the defendant corporation which held property for the Krishna Consciousness movement. Justice Bryson found that the gift should be rescinded on the

[42] ibid 1278–79. See also *Lagunas Nitrate Co v Lagunas Syndicate* [1899] 2 Ch 392, 456 (Rigby LJ); *Spence v Crawford* [1939] 3 All ER 271, 288 (Lord Wright); *O'Sullivan v Management Agency and Music Ltd* [1985] QB 428.

[43] *Alati v Kruger* [1955] HCA 64, (1955) 94 CLR 216. See also *Vadasz v Pioneer Concrete (SA) Pty Ltd* [1995] HCA 14, (1995) 184 CLR 102, 113 [26] (Deane, Dawson, Toohey, Gaudron and McHugh JJ); *Hartigan v International Society for Krishna Consciousness Inc* [2002] NSWSC 810 [25] (Bryson J).

[44] *Alati v Kruger* [1955] HCA 64, (1955) 94 CLR 216, 224 [10] (Dixon CJ, Webb, Kitto and Taylor JJ).

[45] *Boscawen v Bajwa* [1996] 1 WLR 328, 340–41 (Millet LJ), discussing *Re Diplock; Diplock v Wintle* [1948] Ch 465; *Gertsch v Atsas* [1999] NSWSC 898, (1999) 10 BPR 18,431 [95] (Foster AJ): see also M Bryan, 'Rescission, Restitution and Contractual Ordering: The Role of Plaintiff Election' in A Robertson (ed), *The Law of Obligations: Connections and Boundaries* (London, UCL Press; Portland, Or, Cavendish Publishing, 2004) 69; J Poole and A Keyser, 'Justifying Partial Rescission in English Law' (2005) 121 *Law Quarterly Review* 273.

[46] *Maguire v Makaronis* [1997] HCA 23, (1997) 188 CLR 449; see also *Winefield v Clarke* [2008] NSWSC 882 [82] (Barrett J).

[47] *Hartigan v International Society for Krishna Consciousness Inc* [2002] NSWSC 810; see also NY Nahan, 'Rescission: A Case for Rejecting the Classical Model?' (1997) 27 *University of Western Australia Law Review* 66, 74–76, also seeking to explain *Mahoney v Purnell* [1996] 3 All ER 61 and the older case of *McKenzie v McDonald* [1927] VLR 134 on this basis. For a comprehensive examination, see B Häcker, 'Rescission and Third Party Rights' [2006] *Restitution Law Review* 21.

ground of undue influence.[48] The defendant pleaded that it had sold the property to reduce its level of debt, with the consequence that restitution *in specie* was no longer possible.[49] Justice Bryson rejected the plea, on the basis that personal remedies are available against a donee who has directly received property from a donor, even if specific assets cannot be restored.[50]

There are today few circumstances in which a defence of counter-restitution being impossible should continue to be recognised. One circumstance where it may apply is where the plaintiff refuses to or will be incapable of making counter-restitution.[51] An example is *Streeter v Western Areas Exploration Pty Ltd*,[52] where Murphy JA (McLure P and Buss JA concurring on this point), concluded that rescission was denied because, inter alia, the mining tenements the subject of the claim had grossly increased in value due to the defendant's efforts and skill. It would be highly unlikely that the plaintiff would be in a position to make counter-restitution of the value of that increase. In the circumstances, an order that the asset be held on trust for the plaintiff would 'unjustly advantage' the plaintiff. The same conclusion was reached on relevantly similar facts by a unanimous Full Court of the Federal Court in *Grimaldi v Chameleon Mining NL (No 2)*.[53] However, in most cases, if a defendant has a defence of counter-restitution (such as for a failure of consideration, as seen above)[54] then there will be no reason why the unavailability of counter-restitution of the precise right that the defendant has conferred upon the plaintiff should mean that the plaintiff's primary claim is denied. Adoption of this more flexible approach to counter-restitution at common law is also supported by the statement in the joint judgment in *David Securities Pty Ltd v Commonwealth Bank of Australia*[55] that '[i]n cases where consideration can be apportioned or where counter-restitution is relatively simple, insistence on total failure of consideration can be misleading or confusing.' Since courts undertake complex valuation exercises every day, there should be very few cases in which counter-restitution is not relatively simple at common law.[56] This is further evidenced by experience in England and Australian states which have enacted legislation providing for counter-restitution to be made in cases that involve a failure of consideration after frustration of contract.[57]

Consistently with this analysis, the English Court of Appeal has recently held that the requirement of counter-restitution should now operate at common law in the same flexible way as it has always done in equity. In *Halpern v Halpern*,[58] members of a family entered into an agreement to compromise an inheritance dispute. The defendants later alleged that they entered into the compromise as a result of illegitimate pressure and sought to rescind

[48] See Ch 10 p 249.
[49] *Hartigan v International Society for Krishna Consciousness Inc* [2002] NSWSC 810 [25].
[50] ibid [98].
[51] *Campbell v Backoffice Investments Pty Ltd* [2008] NSWCA 95, (2008) 66 ACSR 359 (reversed on other grounds in *Campbell v Backoffice Investments Pty Ltd* [2009] HCA 25, (2009) 238 CLR 304; *Chint Australasia Pty Ltd v Cosmoluce Pty Ltd* [2008] NSWSC 635, (2008) 14 BPR 26,279 [127]–[133] (Einstein J).
[52] *Streeter v Western Areas Exploration Pty Ltd (No 2)* [2011] WASCA 17, (2011) 278 ALR 291 [682].
[53] *Grimaldi v Chameleon Mining NL (No 2)* [2012] FCAFC 6, (2012) 200 FCR 296 [680].
[54] See above p 365.
[55] *David Securities Pty Ltd v Commonwealth Bank of Australia* [1992] HCA 48, (1992) 175 CLR 353, 383 [55] (Mason CJ, Deane, Toohey, Gaudron, and McHugh JJ).
[56] See also P Birks, 'Equity in the Modern Law: An Exercise in Taxonomy' (1996) 26 *University of Western Australia Law Review* 1, 79.
[57] See Ch 14 pp 356–59.
[58] *Halpern v Halpern (Nos 1 & 2)* [2007] EWCA Civ 291, [2008] QB 195.

the agreement. The compromise had required them to destroy certain documents. The plaintiffs argued that, on the assumption that this had been done, *restitutio in integrum* was impossible. The documents could not be restored and no amount of monetary payment could restore the plaintiffs to the position (vis-à-vis the documents) they occupied prior to entering into the compromise. Lord Justice Carnwath (with whom Waller LJ and Sedley LJ agreed) refused to accept that, even with the destruction of the documents, the court exercising its common law jurisdiction lacked the ability to do 'practical justice' between the parties.

A more difficult question is how to reconcile the defendant's traditional right to full (pecuniary) counter-restitution with the plaintiff's countervailing right to plead that she has changed her position in reliance on her receipt of the benefit from the defendant. Suppose, for example, a plaintiff purchases title to a car as a result of the defendant's innocent misrepresentation. When she discovers the mistake, she seeks to rescind the transaction and recover the purchase price. What is the legal position if the car has, in the interim, been damaged in an accident? On the one hand, the defendant's right to full counter-restitution dictates that the plaintiff's recovery of the purchase price will be conditional on her returning the car, together with a payment to make good the amount by which the car has depreciated. On the other hand, her change of position was suffered in good faith and in reliance on her receipt, and would ordinarily attract the defence of change of position. How are these competing rights reconciled?

With some limited exceptions (that are themselves consistent with a change of position analysis),[59] the traditional position was that the balance was struck by requiring the plaintiff to make full counter-restitution. If the plaintiff could not do so, she could not rescind. This result, however, seems highly arbitrary. There is no obvious reason why the defendant's right to counter-restitution should trump the plaintiff's right to protection resulting from her change of position. A better reconciliation is to give full effect to the defendant's counter-claim and recognise that, like any other claim in unjust enrichment, it is prima facie subject to the change of position defence.

IV. Bona Fide Purchase for Value Without Notice

The bona fide purchase defence is available to a purchaser of an asset, in good faith for value and without notice[60] from a person whose title to the asset is defective or absent.[61]

[59] Eg in cases where an asset received by the plaintiff deteriorated without fault on the part of the plaintiff, due to the inherent nature of the asset or was the result of independent market forces: *Alati v Kruger* [1955] HCA 64, (1955) 94 CLR 216, 225 [11] (Dixon CJ, Webb, Kitto and Taylor JJ); *Cheese v Thomas* [1994] 1 WLR 129, 135 (Sir Donald Nicholls VC); *Balfour and Clark v Hollandia Ravensthorpe NL* (1978) 18 SASR 240, 258 (Hogarth J); *Akron Securities Ltd v Iliffe* (1997) 41 NSWLR 353, 370 (Mason P; Priestley JA agreeing). See also *Coastal Estates Pty Ltd v Melevende* [1965] VR 433, 440–41 (Sholl J) (a good faith plaintiff who did not occupy the received property should not be required to pay rent for the period following receipt).

[60] *Sinclair Investments (UK) Ltd v Versailles Trade Finance Ltd* [2011] EWCA Civ 347, [2012] Ch 453 [109] (Lord Neuberger), approved *Papadimitriou v Crédit Agricole Corpn and Investment Bank* [2015] UKPC 13, [2015] 1 WLR 4265 [14]–[15], [18]–[20] (Lord Clarke), see also at [33] (Lord Sumption).

[61] The elements of the defence in equity are comprehensively summarised in JD Heydon, MJ Leeming and PG Turner, *Meagher Gummow and Lehane's Equity Doctrines and Remedies*, 5th edn (Chatswood, NSW, LexisNexis Butterworths, 2015) paras [8-240]–[8-285].

The function of the bona fide purchase defence is, as an exception to the general rule of property *nemo dat quod non habet* (one cannot give that which one does not have), to grant the defendant good title to an asset in circumstances where otherwise that title would be defective. It operates therefore in cases including those brought for unjust enrichment where more than two parties are involved. The requirement for more than two parties is because in the simple two-party case the transferor usually has good title.[62] A standard example is if a thief steals the plaintiff's money and spends it by buying something from R (the recipient). The defence of bona fide purchase extinguishes the plaintiff's original title to the notes and grants the ownership of them to R. The defence favours R's security of purchase over the original owner's security of title and prevents a claim by the plaintiff against R for conversion, unjust enrichment or to vindicate a property right to an asset in the defendant's possession.[63]

The defence differs from change of position in four significant ways. First, the defendant's interest in receipt is stronger because the requirement is that the receipt be *purchased*. Indeed, the consideration for the purchase must be valuable and not merely nominal.[64] It follows that changes of position that would qualify for the change of position defence—such as irreversible non-pecuniary changes or wasted expenditure on a third party—do not satisfy the purchase requirement. Secondly, reflecting the stronger interest at stake, the defence operates as a complete defence, not merely a defence to the extent of the change of position. Thirdly, bona fide purchase operates as a defence by conferring a fresh, non-derivative title on the defendant and extinguishing the plaintiff's title. This is in stark contrast with change of position, the operation of which is strictly limited by reference to the benefit originally received by the defendant. Finally, as we will see immediately below, the defence of bona fide purchase is less concerned with protecting the particular defendant than the class of commercial transaction in which he was involved. Accordingly, while the defences may bear some superficial similarities, and may on occasion function to similar effect, they are and should remain distinct.

The most common example of the defence at common law is in cases involving passage of money into currency.[65] When a defendant provides goods or services in honest exchange

[62] *Barclays Bank plc v Boulter* [1999] 1 WLR 1919, 1924 (Lord Hoffmann; Lords Slynn, Nolan, Steyn and Hutton agreeing). Cf *Armstrong DLW GmbH v Winnington Networks Ltd* [2012] EWHC 10, [2013] Ch 156 [105], where Stephen Morris QC considered that the defence did not extend to claims in unjust enrichment precisely because title needed to pass for the defendant to be enriched.

[63] *Foskett v McKeown* [2000] UKHL 29, [2001] 1 AC 102, 129 (Lord Browne-Wilkinson); *Papamichael v National Westminster Bank plc (No 2)* [2003] EWHC 164, [2003] 1 Lloyd's Rep 341 [214] (Judge Chambers QC); *Armstrong DLW GmbH v Winnington Networks Ltd* [2012] EWHC 10, [2013] Ch 156 [99]–[101] (Stephen Morris QC). See generally R Chambers, *An Introduction to Property Law in Australia*, 3rd edn (Sydney, Thomson Reuters, 2013) para 29.15–29.85; W Swadling, 'Restitution and Bona Fide Purchase' in W Swadling (ed), *The Limits of Restitutionary Claims: A Comparative Analysis* (United Kingdom National Committee of Comparative Law, 1997); G Virgo, *Principles of the Law of Restitution*, 3rd ed (Oxford, Oxford University Press, 2015) 656. Cf K Barker, 'After Change of Position: Good Faith Exchange in the Modern Law of Restitution' in P Birks (ed), *Laundering and Tracing* (Oxford, Clarendon Press, 1995); A Burrows, *The Law of Restitution*, 3rd edn (Oxford, Oxford University Press, 2011) 573–80.

[64] *Park v Dunn* [1916] NZLR 761; *Nurdin & Peacock plc v DB Ramsden & Co Ltd (Rectification Claim)* [1999] 1 EGLR 119, 123 (Neuberger J); *Patroni v Conlan* [2004] WASC 16 [15] (Pullin J). In *Lipkin Gorman v Karpnale Ltd* [1991] 2 AC 548 the right to use chips to purchase food and drink was not sufficiently valuable consideration for the money exchanged.

[65] The other, where it still applies, is the doctrine of market overt: W Swadling, 'Restitution and Bona Fide Purchase' in W Swadling (ed), *The Limits of Restitutionary Claims: A Comparative Analysis* (United Kingdom National Committee of Comparative Law, 1997) 82–89.

for stolen money, the plaintiff's ownership of the money is extinguished, even where the actual notes or coins are still identifiable.[66] This rule reflects the common law's recognition of the defence as essential to the efficient operation of a market economy.[67] Other instances of bona fide purchase at common law (such as sale of goods in market overt) have the same rationale.

In equity, the defence operates generally to protect good faith purchase of *legal* title for value without notice. It also operates to defeat a plaintiff's restitutionary right to rescind a transaction, such as in cases involving fraud or mistake.[68] The defence does not operate to protect a good faith purchaser of an equitable estate.[69] In such cases, equity assumes that the transfer is innocent 'in the sense of being intended to pass that which the conveyor is justly entitled to and no more'.[70] Although it has been said that the basis of the defence in equity is a lack of jurisdiction to interfere with the legal title,[71] this rationalisation does not explain the broader operation of the defence. An explanation based on protection of security of purchase is more coherent. Although the defence primarily applies with respect to claims for restitution of particular rights, it must also apply to claims for restitution of value:[72] any other conclusion would undermine or stultify the purpose of the defence to protect the security of defendants' purchases.

It will be apparent from the above discussion that the bona fide purchase defence is not a general defence to a claim for unjust enrichment. In unjust enrichment, the bona fide purchase defence operates only in relation to a three-party situation in which the defendant is a *subsequent* purchaser from a third party whose title to an asset is defective.[73] For instance, suppose A mistakenly transfers a unique asset (such as an heirloom) to B. We saw in Chapter 3 that in addition to A's personal right to restitution of the value of the mistaken transfer, the asset may also be held on constructive trust for A.[74] Suppose that B then transfers the asset to C in exchange for the delivery of valuable goods from C. As we saw in Chapter 5, A can bring a claim against C for unjust enrichment at his expense because of C's receipt of an enrichment through a series of causally connected transactions where each transaction could be rescinded and therefore is not supported by a juristic reason.[75] But another way to terminate the tracing process through causally connected transactions is by the defence of

[66] *Orton v Butler* (1822) 5 B & Ald 652, 106 ER 1329; *Foster v Green* (1862) 7 H & N 881, 158 ER 726; *Miller v Race* (1758) 1 Burr 452, 457; 97 ER 398, 401 (Lord Mansfield, delivering the judgment of the Court).

[67] W Swadling, 'Restitution and Bona Fide Purchase' in W Swadling (ed), *The Limits of Restitutionary Claims: A Comparative Analysis* (United Kingdom National Committee of Comparative Law, 1997) 82–85; D Fox, 'Bona Fide Purchase and the Currency of Money' (1996) 55 *Cambridge Law Journal* 547, 565. For a recent judicial endorsement of this analysis, see *Hills Industries Ltd v Australian Financial Services and Leasing Pty Ltd* [2012] NSWCA 380, (2012) 295 ALR 147 [83] (Allsop P).

[68] *Phillips v Phillips* (1861) 4 De GF & J 208, 215; 45 ER 1164, 1166 (Lord Westbury); *Latec Investments Ltd v Hotel Terrigal Pty Ltd (in liq)* [1965] HCA 17, (1965) 113 CLR 265.

[69] *Cave v Cave* (1880) 15 Ch D 639; *Rice v Rice* (1854) 2 Drew 73, 61 ER 646; *Latec Investments Ltd v Hotel Terrigal Pty Ltd (in liq)* [1965] HCA 17, (1965) 113 CLR 265.

[70] *Latec Investments Ltd v Hotel Terrigal Pty Ltd (in liq)* [1965] HCA 17, (1965) 113 CLR 265, 278 [9] (Kitto J).

[71] *Pilcher v Rawlins*(1871–72) LR 7 Ch App 259.

[72] Implicit in the treatment of the defence in *Lipkin Gorman v Karpnale Ltd* [1991] 2 AC 548 and *Dextra Bank & Trust Co Ltd v Bank of Jamaica* [2001] UKPC 50, [2002] 1 All ER (Comm) 193.

[73] *Dextra Bank & Trust Co Ltd v Bank of Jamaica* [2001] UKPC 50, [2002] 1 All ER (Comm) 193 [47].

[74] Ch 3 p 38.

[75] Ch 5 pp 98–100.

bona fide purchase.[76] If C is a purchaser for good faith for value without notice, this will be a complete defence to either a claim for restitution of value or of rights because C's title is created by his bona fide purchase for value and is therefore not at A's expense.

V. Estoppel

A. The Varieties of Estoppel

The doctrines of estoppel *per rem judicatum*, issue estoppel and *Anshun* estoppel are all relevant as defences to claims in unjust enrichment. However, their rationales and characteristics are quite distinct from the other varieties of estoppel and thus are considered separately.[77] Other types of estoppel include estoppel by deed (which prevents a party to an action on the deed from resiling from any statement of fact contained within the deed), promissory estoppels, and proprietary estoppels (including estoppels by acquiescence and encouragement).

The main categories of estoppel that are relevant to claims in unjust enrichment are estoppel by representation and estoppel by convention (although promissory estoppel is also capable of being a defence). In each case, the defendant relies upon an 'estoppel by conduct' when a plaintiff, by words or conduct, or on the basis of an agreed or assumed state of facts or law,[78] which neither can deny,[79] represents (or promises) to the defendant that the latter is entitled to his receipt, and the defendant relies on that representation to his detriment.

B. The Core Elements of Estoppel by Representation

The primary example of estoppel by conduct, namely estoppel by representation, originated in the Chancery courts and was later adopted into the common law. The result is that its constituent elements are the same both at law and in equity.[80] The estoppel has three essential features:

(1) The plaintiff must have made a *representation of existing fact*, and possibly also a representation of existing *law*, to the defendant.[81] The representation may be explicit or

[76] *Papadimitriou v Crédit Agricole Corpn and Investment Bank* [2015] UKPC 13, [2015] 1 WLR 4265 [21] (Lord Clarke) [33] (Lord Sumption).

[77] Considered below pp 395–98.

[78] *Hilton Hotels (Australia) Pty Ltd v Sunrise Resources (Australia) Pty Ltd* [2000] NSWSC 46, (2000) 9 BPR 17,495 [71] (Hodgson CJ); *Santos v Delhi Petroleum Pty Ltd* [2002] SASC 272 [471]–[489] (Lander J: estoppel by convention extends to mutual mistake as to private legal rights); *Powercor Australia Ltd v Pacific Power* [1999] VSC 110 [450] (Gillard J); *Greer v Kettle* [1938] AC 156; *Cardigan v Moore* [2012] EWHC 1024, [2012] WTLR 931 [23] (Newey J).

[79] *Con-Stan Industries of Australia Pty Ltd v Norwich Winterthur Insurance (Australia) Ltd* [1986] HCA 14, (1986) 160 CLR 226, 244 [22] (Gibbs CJ, Mason, Wilson, Brennan and Dawson JJ).

[80] *Jorden v Money* (1854) 5 HL Cas 185, 10 ER 868.

[81] *Legione v Hateley* [1983] HCA 11, (1983) 152 CLR 406, 431 [3] (Mason and Deane JJ); *Waltons Stores (Interstate) Ltd v Maher* [1988] HCA 7, (1988) 164 CLR 387, 398 [17]–[18] (Mason CJ and Wilson J), 415 [12]–[15]

implicit, in words or conduct, as long as it is clear and unambiguous.[82] Thus a mere payment does not contain an implicit representation that the defendant is entitled to it. It is only where the plaintiff is under a duty of accuracy,[83] or where being aware of the defendant's mistake gives rise to a duty to speak,[84] that a representation will be implicit in the fact of the payment.

(2) The defendant must have acted in *reasonable reliance* on that representation.[85] The standard of reasonableness includes essential characteristics of the defendant, his position and state of knowledge. Thus, a defendant with little experience in financial matters may be found to have acted reasonably in reliance on an express statement of his entitlement from an experienced financial firm, notwithstanding that a person of ordinary financial aptitude would have suspected immediately that the statement was incorrect.[86]

(3) The defendant will suffer *detriment* if the plaintiff is allowed to resile from her representation. The focus of this enquiry is on what detriment the defendant would incur as a result of his change of position, should the plaintiff be permitted to resile from her representation.[87] Detriment is not restricted to financial loss.[88] In *Commonwealth v*

(Brennan J), 458-59 [17]-19] (Gaudron J); *Commonwealth v Verwayen* [1990] HCA 39, (1990) 170 CLR 394, 499–500 [29] (McHugh J); *Steria Ltd v Hutchison* [2006] EWCA Civ 1551, [2007] ICR 445 [89] (Neuberger LJ).

[82] *Low v Bouverie* [1891] 3 Ch 82, 106, 113 (Bowen LJ); *Newbon v City Mutual Life Assurance Society Ltd* [1935] HCA 33, (1935) 52 CLR 723, 738 (Starke J); *Western Australian Insurance Co Ltd v Dayton* [1924] HCA 58, (1924) 35 CLR 355, 375 (Isaacs ACJ); *Byron Shire Council v Vaughan (No 2)* [2000] NSWLEC 216, (2000) 110 LGERA 424 [25] (Lloyd J).

[83] *Skyring v Greenwood* (1825) 4 B & C 281, 107 ER 1064.

[84] *Holt v Markham* [1923] 1 KB 504; *Moorgate Mercantile Co Ltd v Twitchings* [1977] AC 890; *Pacol Ltd v Trade Lines Ltd (The Henrik Sif)* [1982] 1 Lloyd's Rep 456, 465 (Webster J); *The Stolt Loyalty* [1993] 2 Lloyd's Rep 281, 289–90 (Clarke J); *India v India Steamship Co Ltd (The Indian Endurance and The Indian Grace) (No 2)* [1996] 3 All ER 641, 654–55 (Staughton LJ); *Trenorden v Martin* [1934] SASR 340; *Williams v Frayne* [1937] HCA 16, (1937) 58 CLR 710, 736 (Dixon J); *Nigel Watts Fashion Agencies Pty Ltd v GIO General Ltd* (1995) 8 ANZ Insurance Cases 61-235, 651 (Handley JA).

[85] The leading English authorities include: *Freeman v Cooke* (1848) 2 Ex 654, 681, 154 ER 652, 663 (Parke B); *Seton, Laing, & Co v Lafone* (1887) 19 QBD 68, 73 (Lord Esher MR); *Low v Bouverie* [1891] 3 Ch 82; *Canada and Dominion Sugar Co Ltd v Canadian National (West Indies) Steamships Ltd* [1947] AC 46, 55–56 (Lord Wright, delivering the judgment of the Court); *Sidney Bolsom Investment Trust Ltd v E Karmios & Co (London) Ltd* [1956] 1 QB 529, 540 (Denning LJ); *Steria Ltd v Hutchison* [2006] EWCA Civ 1551, [2007] ICR 445 [93] (Neuberger J). Australian authorities include: *Waltons Stores (Interstate) Ltd v Maher* [1988] HCA 7, (1988) 164 CLR 387, 397 [13] (Mason CJ and Wilson J); *Commonwealth v Verwayen* [1990] HCA 39, (1990) 170 CLR 394, 414 [39]–[40] (Mason CJ), 445 [21] (Deane J); *Valbirn Pty Ltd v Powprop Pty Ltd* [1991] 1 Qd R 295, 297–98 (de Jersey J; Macrossan CJ and Sheperdson J concurring); *Standard Chartered Bank Aust Ltd v Bank of China* (1991) 23 NSWLR 164, 180–81 (Giles J); *Australian Securities Commission v Marlborough Gold Mines Ltd* [1993] HCA 15, (1993) 177 CLR 485, 506 [41] (Mason CJ, Brennan, Dawson, Toohey and Gaudron JJ); *Murphy v Overton Investments Pty Ltd* [2001] FCA 500, (2001) 112 FCR 182 [68] (Branson J) [96] (RD Nicholson J), decision overturned on appeal on another point in *Murphy v Overton Investments Pty Ltd* [2004] HCA 3, (2004) 216 CLR 388; *Voss v Suncorp-Metway Ltd (No 2)* [2003] QCA 252, [2004] 1 Qd R 214; *Galaxidis v Galaxidis* [2004] NSWCA 111 [94], [113]–[116] (Tobias JA; Giles and Hodgson JJA concurring on this point); *Macquarie Bank Ltd v Lin* [2005] QSC 221 [258] (McMurdo J); *Pacific National (ACT) Ltd v Queensland Rail* [2006] FCA 91.

[86] *Scottish Equitable plc v Derby* [2001] EWCA Civ 369, [2001] 3 All ER 818.

[87] *Grundt v Great Boulder Pty Gold Mines Ltd* [1937] HCA 58, (1937) 59 CLR 641, 674 (Dixon J), endorsed in *Sidhu v Van Dyke* [2014] HCA 19, (2014) 251 CLR 505 [80]–[81] (French CJ, Kiefel, Bell and Keane JJ); *Gillett v Holt* [2001] Ch 210, 232–33 (Robert Walker LJ); and *Cadbury Schweppes plc v Halifax Share Dealing Ltd* [2006] EWHC 1184, [2006] BCC 707 [30] (Lindsay J). See also *Central Newbury Car Auctions Ltd v Unity Finance Ltd* [1957] 1 QB 371, 380 (Lord Denning MR); *James v Heim Gallery (London) Ltd* [1979] 2 EGLR 91, 93 (Thomas J).

[88] *Newbon v City Mutual Life Assurance Society Ltd* [1935] HCA 33, (1935) 52 CLR 723, 732–35 (Rich, Dixon and Evatt JJ).

> *Verwayen*[89] for example, several members of the High Court of Australia accepted that the potential psychiatric harm of the defendant through the plaintiff's withdrawal of a benefit could constitute detriment sufficient to support a claim in estoppel.[90]

Although estoppel by representation requires a representation by the plaintiff, the primary focus of the doctrine is on the effect of the representation on the defendant, rather than the intention of the plaintiff in making the representation.[91] The nub of the defendant's plea is that she has changed her position in reliance on some assumption induced by the claimant, whether as a result of some representation or other equivalent conduct.[92] Knowledge by the plaintiff of the truth of the representation is irrelevant. Nor is there any requirement that the plaintiff have intended to mislead the defendant.[93] Although references to 'unconscionability' as the basis for the defence of estoppel by representation are occasionally made, these should be avoided.[94]

C. The Operation of Estoppel by Representation

Estoppel by representation traditionally operates to protect the defendant from the harm that otherwise would flow from the latter's change of position if the plaintiff were permitted to resile from her representation. It does so by preventing the plaintiff from relying on evidence that is inconsistent with the representation. The consequence is that the plaintiff is kept to her representation and the estoppel operates as a complete defence to the claim. This 'all-or-nothing' operation of the defence has troubled courts. In particular, if the rationale of the defence is to protect the defendant from the harm that would flow from his change of position, it seems inequitable to deny the plaintiff's claim entirely if the defendant would suffer minimal inconvenience or, indeed, no harm at all were the plaintiff's claim to succeed.

These concerns are reflected in the leading English authority of *Avon County Council v Howlett*.[95] In that case, an employer brought an action for restitution of money mistakenly overpaid to its employee. For the purposes of the appeal, the employee was treated as having spent only part of the overpayment in reliance on the employer's express assurances that he

[89] *Commonwealth v Verwayen* [1990] HCA 39, (1990) 170 CLR 394.

[90] Mason CJ only rejected Verwayen's allegation of psychological harm because it was not made out on the evidence, not because it was not a legitimate head of detriment.

[91] *Freeman v Cooke* (1848) 2 Ex 654, 663, 154 ER 652, 656 (Parke B); *Craine v Colonial Mutual Fire Insurance Co Ltd* [1920] HCA 64, (1920) 28 CLR 305, 327 and authorities cited therein; *Vaughan v Byron Shire Council* [1999] NSWCA 235, (1999) 103 LGERA 321 [21] (Handley JA; Powell JA agreeing). A significant source of confusion appears to be statements such as that made by Sir George Jessel MR in *Redgrave v Hurd* (1881) 20 Ch D 1, 21 that there must have been 'a material representation calculated to induce [a party] to [act]'. However, the expression 'calculated to' means naturally tending to or apt, not 'intended': see *Seton, Laing, & Co v Lafone* (1887) 19 QBD 68, 72, 73 (Lord Esher MR).

[92] *Grundt v Great Boulder Pty Gold Mines Ltd* [1937] HCA 58, (1937) 59 CLR 641, 674–77 (Dixon J), cited with approval in *Australian Financial Services and Leasing Pty Ltd v Hills Industries Ltd* [2014] HCA 14, (2014) 253 CLR 560 [85]–[87] (Crennan, Kiefel, Bell and Keane JJ) [149] (Gageler J); *Sidhu v Van Dyke* [2014] HCA 19, (2014) 251 CLR 505 [80] (French CJ, Kiefel, Bell and Keane JJ) [89] (Gageler J agreeing on this point).

[93] *Vaughan v Byron Shire Council* [1999] NSWCA 235, (1999) 103 LGERA 321 [21] (Handley JA; Power JA agreeing) and *Byron Shire Council v Vaughan (No 2)* [2000] NSWLEC 216, (2000) 110 LGERA 424 (Lloyd J).

[94] *Ryan v Moore* [2005] 2 SCR 53, 2005 SCC 38 [74] (Bastarche J; McLachlin CJ and Major, Lebel, Deschamps, Abella and Charron JJ concurring).

[95] *Avon County Council v Howlett* [1983] 1 All ER 1073.

was entitled to the amount. The question was whether estoppel by representation operated as a complete defence to the plaintiff's claim. By a majority, the court held that the doctrine operated as a rule of evidence, and therefore it barred the plaintiff's claim completely.[96] However, each member of the majority expressly qualified the finding and acknowledged that in some circumstances this could work injustice.[97] In the minority, Cumming-Bruce LJ simply refused to consider the matter hypothetically and held in favour of the defendant on the basis that, on the true facts, the defendant had spent all the money. His Lordship further declared that he did not consider that 'where on the facts it would be clearly inequitable to allow a party to make a profit by pleading estoppel, the court will necessarily be powerless to prevent it'.[98]

Subsequent English decisions have sought to escape the 'all-or-nothing' approach of the estoppel defence to claims for unjust enrichment in three ways.[99] None of these is convincing. First (and most contentious) is the argument that if the change of position defence is available, it should be used in preference to, or to the exclusion of, estoppel because as a *pro tanto* defence it is a fairer method of protecting the defendant's interest in his security of receipt.[100] Although this approach has been adopted in Canada,[101] it has the objectionable consequence that a defence which is a general defence to all claims both at common law and in equity is uniquely excluded from the law of unjust enrichment.[102] It also incorrectly assumes that estoppel and change of position share the same purpose.[103]

Secondly, English courts have focused on the reference to 'unconscionability' by the court in *Avon County Council v Howlett* and have suggested that it is unconscionable for the defendant to rely on the defence to defeat the plaintiff's claim completely where the amount sought to be recovered bears no relation to the detriment that the defendant could possibly have suffered.[104] As Professor Burrows observes, this approach leads to the odd result that the exception swallows up the all-or-nothing rule because, subject to *de minimis* cases, it will always be 'unconscionable' for a defendant to retain a windfall benefit.[105] Further, as Hazel Williamson QC, sitting as a Chancery judge, has observed in relation to this defence, the danger of the language of unconscionability is that it degenerates 'into a discretionary analysis of "justice" on a case by case basis'.[106]

Thirdly, there is the argument, described by the English Court of Appeal as 'ingenious' and 'convincing',[107] advanced by junior counsel on appeal in *Scottish Equitable plc v Derby*.

[96] ibid 1087 (Slade LJ), 1078 (Eveleigh J).

[97] ibid 1078 (Eveleigh LJ), 1089 (Slade LJ).

[98] ibid 1076.

[99] 'Judicial discomfort [with the all or nothing approach] was obvious': *Fea v Roberts* [2005] All ER (D) 69 [70] (Hazel Williamson QC).

[100] *Lipkin Gorman v Karpnale Ltd* [1991] 2 AC 548, 579; *Phillip Collins Ltd v Davis* [2000] 3 All ER 808, *Scottish Equitable plc v Derby* [2000] 3 All ER 793.

[101] *RBC Dominion Securities Inc v Dawson* (1994) 111 DLR (4th) 230.

[102] *TRA Global Pty Ltd v Kebakoska* [2011] VSC 480, (2011) 209 IR 453 [44] (Osborn J).

[103] ibid [58] [69]–[70] (Osborn J). See below p 378.

[104] *Scottish Equitable plc v Derby* [2001] EWCA Civ 369, [2001] 3 All ER 818 (Robert Walker LJ); *National Westminster Bank plc v Somer International (UK) Ltd* [2001] EWCA Civ 970, [2002] QB 1286 [48] (Potter LJ) [76] (Peter Gibson LJ). The exception was also noted by the learned trial judge (citing *Avon County Council v Howlett* [1983] 1 All ER 1073 and the Victorian case of *Riseda Nominees Pty Ltd v St Vincent's Hospital (Melbourne) Ltd* [1998] 2 VR 70) but was not argued in *TRA Global Pty Ltd v Kebakoska* [2011] VSC 480, (2011) 209 IR 453 [75]–[77] (Osborn J).

[105] AS Burrows, *The Law of Restitution*, 3rd edn (Oxford, Oxford University Press, 2011) 557.

[106] *Fea v Roberts* [2005] All ER (D) 69 [76] (Hazel Williamson QC).

[107] *Scottish Equitable plc v Derby* [2001] EWCA Civ 369, [2001] 3 All ER 818 [45]–[47] (Robert Walker LJ).

This argument was that if one assessed the detriment suffered by the defendant as at the date of trial, any 'detriment' which might otherwise flow from the plaintiff resiling from her representation would be negated *by application of the change of position defence*, with the result that the defendant would not be able to make out the defence of estoppel. In this way, it was said, the defence of change of position pre-empts and negates the estoppel defence.

While Robert Walker LJ was beguiled by this argument, as were others after him,[108] it was rightly rejected by Osborn J in the Victorian decision in *TRA Global Pty Ltd v Kebakoska*.[109] As His Honour noted, the argument makes application of the estoppel defence conditional on the prior application of another defence. But there is no justification for change of position applying prior to estoppel—other than it may free the court from having to apply the estoppel defence. Indeed, as a general rule of evidence, one might think there is some case for awarding estoppel priority over change of position. Nor is there any reason for thinking that the nature of the estoppel defence has suddenly changed from one which looks to the detrimental acts of the defendant in reliance on the representation of the plaintiff, to one which looks to the effect of a legal finding on the defendant's position. Defences operate by reference to the facts of the case, not by reference to a court's assessment of the availability of a separate defence—which may or may not be pleaded. A finding that the change of position defence applies is not a 'fact' on which the estoppel defence should be assessed.

There are two further reasons why the 'ingenious argument' should be rejected. The first is that detriment for the purposes of estoppel is assessed at the time the plaintiff seeks to resile from her representation, not at the time of trial.[110] Secondly, detriment in estoppel is determined by the harm that would be suffered as a result of the defendant's change of position if the plaintiff were permitted to resile from her representation. The point of reference in determining detriment is therefore the represented position. We saw in the previous chapter that change of position, by contrast, assesses the detrimental change of position by reference to the position the defendant occupied prior to his receipt. The two points of reference will not always be the same. There is accordingly no reason to think that the measures of detriment will always correspond.

Two final methods of avoiding the all-or-nothing operation of estoppel have been suggested by commentators. The first applies where there has been a representation which causes multiple payments. It has been suggested that an estoppel defence operates separately in relation to each payment so that the representation is treated as having been made on multiple occasions and reliance must be established separately for each occasion.[111] However, to deny a defendant protection because of want of evidence of particular acts of reliance seems particularly harsh, given that it will often be the plaintiff's general representation of entitlement to the benefit that will have lulled the defendant into thinking that the

[108] AS Burrows, *The Law of Restitution*, 3rd edn (Oxford, Oxford University Press, 2011) 555.

[109] *TRA Global Pty Ltd v Kebakoska* [2011] VSC 480, (2011) 209 IR 453 [73]–[74] (Osborn J).

[110] *Grundt v Great Boulder Pty Gold Mines Ltd* [1937] HCA 58, (1937) 59 CLR 641, 674–75 (Dixon J), endorsed, for example, by AK Turner (ed), *Spencer Bower and Turner: The Law Relating to Estoppel by Representation*, 3rd edn (London, Butterworths, 1977) 110, in turn approved in *Gillett v Holt* [2001] Ch 210, 232–33 (Robert Walker LJ) and *Cadbury Schweppes plc v Halifax Share Dealing Ltd* [2006] EWHC 1184, [2006] BCC 707 [30] (Lindsay J). See also: *Central Newbury Car Auctions Ltd v Unity Finance Ltd* [1957] 1 QB 371, 380 (Lord Denning MR); *James v Heim Gallery (London) Ltd* [1979] 2 EGLR 91, 93 (Thomas J); KR Handley, *Estoppel by Conduct and Election* (London, Sweet & Maxwell, 2006) para 5-016.

[111] AS Burrows, *The Law of Restitution*, 3rd edn (Oxford, Oxford University Press, 2011) 555; KR Handley, *Estoppel by Conduct and Election* (London, Sweet & Maxwell, 2006) paras 5-026–5-027, 5-033.

benefit was his to spend without keeping strict records.[112] Accordingly, it should only be in cases where the plaintiff's representations are genuinely discrete that they should be treated as independent sources of an estoppel.

The other suggested method of restricting the operation of estoppel by representation, proposed by Professor Birks, is to regard representations as generally subject to a condition of revocability. Birks argued that a reasonable person would understand most representations of entitlement as 'prospectively revocable in the event of the representor's discovering a mistake'.[113] Prior to being notified of the mistake, the defendant would be protected by the estoppel. Once notified of a mistake, however, the estoppel would end. Any subsequent changes of position would not be made in reasonable reliance on an assumption induced by the claimant. On this approach, recognition of an estoppel would rarely produce results disproportionate in comparison with the change of position defence. However, it is debatable that reasonable people faced by an unconditional statement, 'We have checked this out and you may rely on us that all is in order',[114] would think it is subject to the implied condition 'unless and until we notify you to the contrary'.[115] Moreover, as *Avon County Council* itself demonstrates, the practice of the courts has not been to find, or find readily, this sort of implication.

D. Estoppel and Change of Position

Since the defence of estoppel by representation is not otiose in cases of unjust enrichment, estoppel and change of position should continue to have a separate, albeit overlapping existence. This has generally been the case in Australian courts.[116] An example is the Victorian Supreme Court decision of *TRA Global Pty Ltd v Kebakoska*.[117] An employee was mistakenly advised by her employer that she was entitled to a redundancy payment, which was subsequently paid to her. In reliance upon both the representation and upon her receipt,

[112] KR Handley, *Estoppel by Conduct and Election* (London, Sweet & Maxwell, 2006) paras 5-027, 5-033. The point echoes the Canadian Court of Appeal's concerns in *RBC Dominion Securities Inc v Dawson* (1994) 111 DLR (4th) 230 in the context of the change of position defence, discussed in Ch 14 p 347. See also *TRA Global Pty Ltd v Kebakoska* [2011] VSC 480, (2011) 209 IR 453 [58] (Osborn J): '[T]he factual situation which develops in consequence of a representation may be one in which it would not be equitable to require a defendant to strictly prove retrospectively every element of change of position'.

[113] P Birks, *Unjust Enrichment*, 2nd edn (Oxford, Oxford University Press, 2005) 235–36.

[114] ibid 236.

[115] ibid 236.

[116] *David Securities Pty Ltd v Commonwealth Bank of Australia* [1992] HCA 48, (1992) 127 CLR 353, 385 [59] (Mason CJ, Deane, Toohey, Gaudron, and McHugh JJ). Both change of position and an estoppel were pleaded by way of defence in *Council of the City of Sydney v Burns Philp Trustee Co Ltd (in liq)* (NSWSC, 13 November 1992) (estoppel by representation); *Civil Aviation Authority v Jorm* (1994) 56 IR 89 (estoppel by representation); *Commonwealth v Webster* (VSC, 27 July 1995) (estoppel by representation); *National Australia Bank Ltd v Budget Stationery Supplies Pty Ltd* (1997) 217 ALR 365 (estoppel by representation); *Australian Breeders Co-operative Society Ltd v Jones* (1997) 150 ALR 488 (estoppel by representation); *Gilsan (International) Ltd v Optus Networks Pty Ltd* [2004] NSWSC 1077 (estoppels by representation and convention); *Woodgate v Keddie* [2006] FCA 1728 (estoppel by representation); *Ethnic Earth Pty Ltd v Quoin Technology Pty Ltd (in liq) (No 3)* [2006] SASC 7, (2006) 94 SASR 103 (estoppel by representation); *Alpha Wealth Financial Services Pty Ltd v Frankland River Olive Company Ltd* [2008] WASCA 119, (2008) 66 ACSR 594 (estoppel by convention). Estoppel and change of position were mentioned as independent defences in *Ovidio Carrideo Nominees Pty Ltd v The Dog Depot Pty Ltd* [2004] VSC 400 [38] (Kaye J) and *Perpetual Trustees Victoria Ltd v Ford* [2008] NSWSC 29, (2008) 70 NSWLR 611 [116] (Harrison J).

[117] *TRA Global Pty Ltd v Kebakoska* [2011] VSC 480, (2011) 209 IR 453 [41]–[83] (Osborn J).

she disclosed the fact of her redundancy payments to the relevant social security authority and was accordingly denied unemployment benefits. Since she had no other source of income, she spent a large proportion of the redundancy payments on living expenses before eventually finding re-employment. Justice Osborn of the Victorian Supreme Court upheld the magistrate's findings that she was entitled to a partial defence of change of position. Moreover, in a careful and full review of the arguments, his Honour rejected arguments made by the employer that the defence of estoppel by representation has been displaced by change of position, or must operate *pro tanto*, and held that estoppel by representation operated in the circumstances to defeat the employer's claim completely.

The position has not yet been settled. In the New South Wales Court of Appeal decision of *Citigroup Pty Ltd v National Australia Bank Ltd*,[118] Barrett JA suggested that the defence of estoppel 'may have been subsumed' in the defence of change of position. However, Justice Macfarlan disagreed with Barrett JA, holding that an estoppel properly and independently arose on the facts, although it produced on the facts of the case the same result as application of the change of position defence. Chief Justice Bathurst, Allsop P and Meagher JA jointly considered that the issue did not need to be resolved in the case.

Finally, in the High Court in *AFSL v Hills Industries*,[119] although Gageler J found estoppel a potent source of analogical reasoning (a view we share), his Honour stated his preference for the view that change of position is but a particular instance of estoppel. That is, rather than taking the view, as English courts have done, that estoppel should be merged with change of position, his Honour considered that change of position might be merged into estoppel. His Honour expressed that the purpose of this merger was to identify the 'commonality of principle'[120] found in change of position and estoppel. On this approach, the defence of change of position is established where (1) the defendant has acted or refrained from acting 'in good faith on the assumption that the defendant was entitled to deal with the payment' and (2) as a result, 'the defendant would be placed in a worse position if ordered to make restitution … than if the defendant had not received the payment at all'.[121]

This conception of the defence as operating consistently with estoppel underpinned his Honour's view (discussed in Chapter 14) that change of position is likely limited to reliance-based changes of position. However, it also had other consequences. Thus his Honour stated:

> Where the defence [of change of position] is so established, the prima facie entitlement of the defendant is *to maintain the assumption on which the defendant acted and, on that basis, to retain the whole of the payment*. That entitlement is qualified to the extent that retention of the whole of the payment can be shown to be disproportionate to the degree of the detriment. Where the detriment is financial or pecuniary, can be quantified, and is less than the amount received, the entitlement of the defendant to retain the payment is reduced pro tanto.[122]

[118] *Citigroup Pty Ltd v National Australia Bank Ltd* [2012] NSWCA 381, (2012) 82 NSWLR 391 [130] (but cf Bathurst CJ, Allsop P, Meagher JA at [5], [13]–[14], noting differences between change of position and estoppel but leaving the question open).

[119] *Australian Financial Services and Leasing Pty Ltd v Hills Industries Ltd* [2014] HCA 14, (2014) 253 CLR 560.

[120] ibid [156].

[121] ibid [157].

[122] ibid [158] (emphasis added).

While this model would certainly reconcile the practical effect of change of position and estoppel,[123] it reverses the usual *pro tanto* operation of change of position. On Gageler J's approach, the defence operates completely unless shown to be disproportionate. It is unclear whether this assimilation would still allow a defence where, as we saw in Chapter 14, the defendant knew (or thought she knew) that she was not entitled to the received benefit but changed her position in good faith consistently with that belief. An example is where a defendant receives a payment knowing it was conferred by mistake and, pending its return to the payer, places the money for safekeeping with a bank that subsequently fails.[124] Another relatively common example from the cases is where a defendant pays the value of the benefit to a third party in the reasonable belief that the third party is entitled to the sum.[125]

VI. Ministerial Receipt

There are two forms of defence that are commonly engaged in the case of agents. One, the agent's defence of 'payment over', is an early form of change of position defence and should be subsumed within that defence.[126] The other is a distinct defence of ministerial receipt. The key to understanding the distinction between the two defences is the issue of when an agent will be enriched by receipt of a benefit.

We saw in Chapter 4 that when an agent receives an asset as a minister for another (that is, on behalf and for the benefit of another), the agent will not be enriched unless he appropriates the asset to his own use and benefit.[127] If the agent chooses the benefit in his personal capacity, he has no defence of ministerial receipt. However, in this situation, the agent may still have a defence if, after appropriating the benefit to his use, he changes his position in good faith by irreversibly paying the enrichment over to his principal. There are a large number of cases in equity that apply the agent's defence of payment over.[128] This defence

[123] Meeting the concerns of courts in cases such as *Scottish Equitable plc v Derby* [2001] EWCA Civ 369, [2001] 3 All ER 818; *National Westminster Bank plc v Somer International (UK) Ltd* [2001] EWCA Civ 970, [2002] QB 1286, and *RBC Dominion Securities Inc v Dawson* (1994) 111 DLR (4th) 230.

[124] Cf *National Bank of New Zealand Ltd v Waitaki International Processing (NI) Ltd* [1999] 2 NZLR 211, discussed in Ch 14 pp 343–44.

[125] As in *Thomas v Houston Corbett and Company* [1969] NZLR 151; *Dextra Bank & Trust Co Ltd v Bank of Jamaica* [2001] UKPC 50, [2002] 1 All ER (Comm) 193; *Orix Australia Corporation Ltd v M Wright Hotel Refrigeration Pty Ltd* [2000] SASC 57, (2000) 155 FLR 267, discussed in Ch 14 p 344.

[126] *Lipkin Gorman v Karpnale Ltd* [1991] 2 AC 548, 578 (Lord Goff); *Hills Industries Ltd v Australian Financial Services and Leasing Pty Ltd* [2012] NSWCA 380, (2012) 295 ALR 147 [198] (Meagher JA).

[127] Ch 5 p 78.

[128] *Agip (Africa) Ltd v Jackson* [1990] Ch 265, 291–92 (Millett J); approved on appeal *Agip (Africa) Ltd v Jackson* [1991] Ch 547; *El Ajou v Dollar Land Holdings plc* [1994] 2 All ER 685, 700 (Hoffmann LJ); *Eagle Trust plc v SBC Securities Ltd* [1993] 1 WLR 484, 490, 501 (Vinelott J); *Nimmo v Westpac Banking Corporation* [1993] 3 NZLR 218, 224–25 (Blanchard J); *Air Canada v M & L Travel Ltd* [1993] 3 SCR 787; *Citigroup Pty Ltd v National Australia Bank Ltd* [2012] NSWCA 381, (2012) 82 NSWLR 391 [7]–[11] (Bathurst CJ, Allsop P and Meagher JA) [16]–[17] (Macfarlan JA) [106]–[126] (Barrett JA); *Citadel General Assurance Co v Lloyds Bank Canada* [1997] 3 SCR 805 [24] (La Forest J, delivering judgment of La Forest, Gonthier, Core, McLaughlin, Iacobucci, and Major JJ); *Gold v Rosenberg* [1997] 3 SCR 767 [40] (Iacobucci J), cited and discussed by J Moore, 'Restitution from Banks' (DPhil thesis, University of Oxford 2000) 167–68. Moore's thesis is discussed and adopted by C Mitchell, 'Assistance' in P Birks and A Pretto (eds), *Breach of Trust* (Oxford, Hart, 2002) 184–87. See also *Evans v European Bank Ltd* [2004] NSWCA 82, (2004) 61 NSWLR 75 [166]–[168] (Spigelman CJ; Handley and Santow JJA agreeing, citing in

is best understood as an early and isolated example of the defence of change of position.[129] In most cases, as courts have repeatedly acknowledged, a defence of payment over will replicate change of position.[130] This is because the requirement of an irreversible payment over made without notice of the plaintiff's claim is the same as the requirements for the change of position defence. The only point of distinction between the two lies in the putative requirement for the payment over defence that the principal must be disclosed.[131] But where an agent knows that the principal has not been disclosed, the agent must be aware that the payment is proceeding under a mistake and will generally be unable to satisfy the change of position defence in any event.

The dominant position at common law of agents who receive benefits in a ministerial capacity and not for their own use and benefit was summarised by Millett LJ in *Portman Building Society v Hamlyn Taylor Neck (a firm):*

> The true rule is that where the plaintiff has paid money under (for example) a mistake to the agent of a third party, he may sue the principal whether or not the agent has accounted to him, for in contemplation of law the payment is made to the principal and not to his agent. If the agent still retains the money, however, the plaintiff may elect to sue either the principal or the agent, and the agent remains liable if he pays the money over to the principal after notice of the claim. If he wishes to protect himself, he should interplead. But once the agent has paid the money to his principal or to his order without notice of the claim, the plaintiff must sue the principal.[132]

Consistently with the approach to enrichment explained in Chapter 4, the first sentence of Millett LJ's analysis suggests that the rationale underlying the 'defence' of ministerial receipt is that the agent has not been enriched: the payment is made to the principal *and not to the agent.* The proper party to be sued is the principal, who is enriched as soon as the agent receives the benefit on the principal's behalf. That is so whether or not the agent has paid over the benefit to the principal. The agent never chose the benefit personally. Further, the agent is immediately liable to account to the principal for the receipt and, accordingly, is never enriched.[133] However, the balance of Millett LJ's analysis, which accurately reflects

support *Stephens Travel Service International Pty Ltd v Qantas Airways Ltd* (1988) 13 NSWLR 331); *Gray v Johnston* (1868) LR 3 HL 1; *International Sales and Agencies Ltd v Marcus* [1982] 3 All ER 551, 557 (Lawson J); *Westpac Banking Corporation v Savin* [1985] 2 NZLR 41, 69 (Sir Clifford Richard); *Cigna Life Insurance New Zealand Ltd v Westpac Securities Ltd* [1996] 1 NZLR 80, 87 (Greig J); *Uzinterimpex JSC v Standard Bank plc* [2008] EWCA Civ 819, [2008] Bus LR 1762 [39] (Moore-Bick LJ; Laws LJ and Clarke MR concurring); cf *Foxton v Manchester and Liverpool District Banking Co* (1881) 44 LT 406; *Citadel General Assurance Co v Lloyds Bank Canada* [1997] 3 SCR 805, discussed and approved by R Stevens, 'Why Do Agents "Drop Out"?' [2005] *Lloyd's Maritime and Commercial Law Quarterly* 101, 113.

[129] *Lipkin Gorman v Karpnale Ltd* [1991] 2 AC 548, 578 (Lord Goff); *Hills Industries Ltd v Australian Financial Services and Leasing Pty Ltd* [2012] NSWCA 380, (2012) 295 ALR 147 [198] (Meagher JA).

[130] *Jones v Churcher* [2009] EWHC 722, [2009] 2 Lloyd's Rep 94 [78] (Judge Havelock-Allan QC); *Citigroup Pty Ltd v National Australia Bank Ltd* [2012] NSWCA 381, (2012) 82 NSWLR 391 [12] (Bathurst CJ, Allsop P and Meagher JA) [16]–[17] (Macfarlan JA) [109]–[113] (Barrett JA).

[131] Compare *Portman Building Society v Hamlyn Taylor Neck (a firm)* [1998] 4 All ER 202, 207 (Millett LJ) endorsing a disclosure requirement with *Transvaal & Delagoa Bay Investment Co Ltd v Atkinson* [1944] 1 All ER 579 (defence applied notwithstanding that the principal was undisclosed).

[132] *Portman Building Society v Hamlyn Taylor Neck (a firm)* [1998] 4 All ER 202, 207; for a recent application, see *Jones v Churcher* [2009] EWHC 722, [2009] 2 Lloyd's Rep 94.

[133] See also *Australia and New Zealand Banking Group Ltd v Westpac Banking Corp* [1988] HCA 17, (1988) 164 CLR 662; *National Westminster Bank Ltd v Barclays Bank International Ltd* [1975] QB 654; *Chase Manhattan Bank NA v Israel-British Bank (London) Ltd* [1981] Ch 105.

the prevailing position at common law, suggests that the agent is only protected through the more limited defence of 'payment over'.

The view that there is no defence of ministerial receipt apart from payment over (change of position) was taken by Judge Havelock-Allan QC in *Jones v Churcher*.[134] In that case a bank had credited a mistaken payment to its customer's account. The trial judge held that the bank had no agency defence to the plaintiff's claim for restitution, because the credit entry could be reversed. In the trial judge's words, the defence of ministerial receipt required the money to have been transferred 'in an irrevocable fashion from the agent (the collecting bank) to the principal (the customer)'.[135] The stronger defence of ministerial receipt was rejected because it would mean that 'no collecting bank receiving money by CHAPS transfer could ever be named as defendant to a restitutionary claim'.[136]

As a matter of authority, the support for this conclusion is equivocal. Early common law cases applied the strong ministerial receipt defence and held that the agent was not liable even where he retained money received for his principal. Hence, in *Sadler v Evans*[137] an agent received money on behalf of his principal, Lady Windsor. The payer brought a claim for restitution from the agent. The trial judge non-suited the plaintiff's claim against the agent because the payment to the agent constituted payment to his principal and thus the action ought to have been brought against her.[138] This decision was approved on appeal. Lord Mansfield, giving the judgment of the court, said this:

> [The] money was paid to the known agent of Lady W. He is liable to her for it; whether he has actually paid it over to her, or not: he received it for her. … [W]here 'tis to a known agent … the action ought to be brought against the principal, unless in special cases, (as under notice, or malâ fide).[139]

This approach was followed in several cases.[140] Although, 12 years after *Sadler v Evans*, Lord Mansfield changed his mind and held that the agent could be sued while he retained the enrichment,[141] exceptions developed including in the case of deposits where payment to the agent is an instantaneous payment to the principal.[142]

As a matter of principle, imposing liability upon an agent who retains money received ministerially is capable of being onerous, and of causing insoluble difficulty. For instance, in *Australia and New Zealand Banking Group Ltd v Westpac Banking Corp*,[143] ANZ mistakenly paid $100,000 to Westpac for the credit of Westpac's account holder, Jakes. Three days later ANZ notified Westpac of its mistake. Westpac conceded that it was liable to ANZ from that time for the mistaken payment, so that it should have dishonoured all cheques drawn

[134] *Jones v Churcher* [2009] EWHC 722 (QB), [2009] 2 Lloyd's Rep 94.

[135] ibid [77].

[136] ibid [76].

[137] *Sadler v Evans* (1766) 4 Burr 1984, 98 ER 34.

[138] ibid 1985: 34 (Perrot B).

[139] ibid 1986; 35.

[140] *Greenway v Hurd* (1792) 4 TR 553, 555, 100 ER 1171, 1172 (Lord Kenyon CJ); *Miller v Aris* (1800) 3 Esp 231, 233, 170 ER 598, 599 (Lord Kenyon).

[141] *Buller v Harrison* (1777) 2 Cowp 565, 98 ER 1243.

[142] Eg *Duke of Norfolk v Worthy* (1808) 1 Camp 337, 339, 170 ER 977, 978 (Lord Ellenborough); *Hurley v Baker* (1846) 16 M & W 26, 30, 153 ER 1083, 1085 (Rolfe B); *Edgell v Day* (1865) LR 1 CP 80, 84 (Erle CJ); *Christie v Robinson* [1907] HCA 19, (1907) 4 CLR 1338, 1350 (O'Connor J); *Burt v Claude Cousins & Co Ltd* [1971] 2 QB 426, 435 (Lord Denning).

[143] *Australia and New Zealand Banking Group Ltd v Westpac Banking Corp* [1988] HCA 17, (1988) 164 CLR 662. Another good example of the dilemma is found in *US International Marketing Ltd v National Bank of New Zealand Ltd* [2004] 1 NZLR 589.

by Jakes on the account.[144] The High Court pointed out the difficulty associated with that concession:

> one is led to speculate about what Westpac's position vis-à-vis Jakes would have been if it had, of its own initiative, dishonoured those cheques. ... Certainly, its position would have been a somewhat difficult one if it had subsequently turned out that ANZ's claim for repayment could be met by a good defence on the part of Jakes.[145]

In other words, the concession that an agent like Westpac, which receives ministerially, is liable to a payer like ANZ, creates what Dr Moore has termed the 'agent's dilemma'.[146] The agent may find himself at the centre of a claim by the payer for restitution of benefits transferred pursuant to a mistake, as well as a claim from his principal to account for those benefits. What is an agent to do? Once the agent has notice of the claim he may not be protected by the defence of ministerial receipt (or change of position) if he pays over and the claim turns out to be correct. However, he is subject to significant fiduciary, and often contractual, obligations to pay over the benefit to his principal. Interpleading is not a satisfactory answer because, as Dr Moore explains:

> Even if interpleader could conceivably protect the bank from a subsequent action brought against it by the account holder, who is to protect the account holder from the disastrous consequences which might flow from the dishonour of its cheque?[147]

Another difficulty of principle that arises without the defence of ministerial receipt is that imposing liability for benefits received ministerially can be inconsistent with the enrichment requirement of a claim in unjust enrichment. We saw in Chapter 4 that an agent who can prove that he has received the benefit ministerially, and who never appropriates the payment to his own benefit, is not personally enriched by his receipt.[148] This is illustrated by the recent decision of Mr Justice Sales in *Jeremy D Stone Consultants Ltd v National Westminster Bank plc.*[149] In that case, Mr Stone was induced by a rogue into investing in a hotel business, which turned out to be a front for a Ponzi scheme. The sums were paid into an account held with the defendant bank. The rogue and his associate circulated large sums in and out of the account to create the illusion of a successful business for further investment. The plaintiff's claim for restitution of the mistaken payments failed because Natwest was found not to have been enriched by its receipt. As his Honour explained, the increase in the bank's assets through receipt of the payments was immediately offset by a countervailing liability to its customer in the form of a debt for the sum received. Although the bank's countervailing liability was a mere book entry, the bank had a defence of 'ministerial receipt'.[150] There was no argument in that case that the bank had been enriched by its choice to *use* the money (by the process of creation of credit) so that the enrichment could be measured as including the benefit of the use value of the money.[151]

In summary, where the defendant has received ministerially, the proper defendant to any claim in unjust enrichment is the principal, whether the claim is brought at common law or

[144] *Australia and New Zealand Banking Group Ltd v Westpac Banking Corp* [1988] HCA 17, (1988) 164 CLR 662, 677–78 [17] (the Court).

[145] ibid 678 [17].

[146] J Moore, 'Restitution from Banks' (DPhil thesis, University of Oxford 2000) 277–78.

[147] ibid 283.

[148] Ch 4 p 78.

[149] *Jeremy D Stone Consultants Ltd v National Westminster Bank plc* [2013] EWHC 208.

[150] ibid [242]–[245].

[151] Ch 4 pp 59–61.

in equity. Thus the New South Wales Court of Appeal, in the context of an equitable claim, has stated the principle in broad terms that a 'deposit which, on the evidence, will, in the normal course of banking, be paid by the bank, directly or indirectly [to the principal] … involves the ministerial role of a "mere depository" or "channel"'.[152] In a similar vein is *Vella v Permanent Mortgages Pty Ltd*,[153] where Young CJ held, citing *Australia and New Zealand Banking Group Ltd v Westpac Banking Corp*,[154] that a bank which received a mistaken payment did so as a 'mere conduit' and thus was not prima facie liable to make restitution on a count for 'money had and received'. By contrast, where the agent has accepted and appropriated the enrichment to her own use and benefit, a claim for restitution may properly be brought against the agent. The agent will be able to rely on the change of position defence (often described in this context as 'payment over') if, after appropriating the benefit to her use, the agent changes her position in good faith (such as by irreversibly paying the enrichment over to the principal).

VII. Delay

A. The Rationale of the Defence

There are clear reasons in favour of imposing some limitation on the commencement of actions.[155] Actions become more difficult to prove and thus defend as time passes: memories fade, witnesses move or pass on, and documents get lost. Further, the longer the delay, the more likely defendants may have irreversibly changed their position in reliance on being free from the threat of litigation.[156] The justifications for the defence therefore extend to claims in unjust enrichment in exactly the same way as they do to claims based on contract, tort or equitable wrongdoing. Unfortunately, different limitation rules apply depending upon whether the claim in unjust enrichment is brought at common law or in equity. The rules also differ depending upon the nature of the unjust factor and the factual circumstances.

Historically, there were no limitation periods at common law.[157] They were first introduced in England by statute.[158] This legislation and its successors[159] established periods

[152] *Evans v European Bank Ltd* [2004] NSWCA 82, (2004) 61 NSWLR 75 [175] (Spigelman CJ; Handley and Santow JJA concurring). The point was left open in *Nicholson v Morgan (No 3)* [2013] WASC 110, (2013) 8 ASTLR 277 [4] (Edelman J).

[153] *Vella v Permanent Mortgages Pty Ltd* [2008] NSWSC 505, (2008) 13 BPR 25,343 [462]–[463] (Young CJ); *Citigroup Pty Ltd v National Australia Bank Ltd* [2012] NSWCA 381, (2012) 82 NSWLR 391 [12] (Bathurst CJ, Allsop P and Meagher JA) [16]–[17] (Macfarlan JA). See also *Equuscorp Pty Ltd (formerly Equus Financial Services Ltd) v Bassat* [2007] VSC 553, (2007) 216 FLR 1 [132] (Byrne J), overturned on other grounds on appeal in *Haxton v Equuscorp Pty Ltd (formerly Equus Financial Services Ltd) (ACN 006 012 344)* [2010] VSCA 1, (2010) 28 VR 499 and proposition cited without disapproval at [115] (Dodds-Streeton JA; Ashley and Neave JJA concurring).

[154] *Australia and New Zealand Banking Group Ltd v Westpac Banking Corp* [1988] HCA 17, (1988) 164 CLR 662.

[155] P Handford, *Limitation of Actions: The Laws of Australia* 3rd edn (Sydney, Thomson Reuters, 2012) 63.

[156] *Hawkins v Clayton* (1986) 5 NSWLR 109, 118 (Kirby P).

[157] There remain considerable lacunae in the law, see for example *Fisher v Brooker* [2009] UKHL 41, [2009] 1 WLR 1764 (no limitation period provided for claims to copyright).

[158] Limitation Act 1623 (21 Jac 1 c 16).

[159] For Australia, see P Handford, *Limitation of Actions: The Laws of Australia* 3rd edn (Sydney, Thomson Reuters, 2012) 67.

within which an action must be commenced. In Australia, limitation periods for all common law actions are regulated through each state and territory's limitation legislation.[160] As we will see, even in a unitary jurisdiction such as England, the statutory framework seems often to work in an entirely arbitrary and unprincipled way. In Australia, the patchwork of state legislation only exacerbates the problem.

B. Delay in Equity: The Doctrine of Laches

In contrast with the common law, equity developed a principled approach to delay that was simple, flexible and effective. The defence in equity is usually described as *laches* and has two limbs: delay with acquiescence and delay with prejudice.[161] The former is really an umbrella label which is used in cases where the plaintiff has waived or abandoned his claim, or as a result of his conduct is estopped from bringing a claim. Acquiescence in this sense often accompanies, but is not dependent on, proof of delay.[162] Delay with prejudice, by contrast, is concerned with the effects of delay, in particular the possible prejudice it may cause to the defendant's right to a fair hearing and other consequences to the defendant (and third parties)[163] that may flow from the lapse of time.[164] A classic example of prejudice is where the defendant has reasonably acted to his or her detriment in reliance on the plaintiff's delay.[165] To this extent, the operation of the defence overlaps with change of position. Another is where witnesses have died or evidence which may have cast a different complexion on the matter has been lost or destroyed.[166]

In determining the weight to be given to the effects of delay, consideration is given to the length of the delay, the nature of the claim and the plaintiff's reason for delay. The doctrine of laches operates only once the plaintiff becomes aware, or ought to be aware, of his rights.

[160] For a full description of the legislative history of each state, see P Handford, *Limitation of Actions: The Laws of Australia* 3rd edn (Sydney, Thomson Reuters, 20012) 67.

[161] *Lindsay Petroleum Co v Hurd* (1874) LR 5 PC 221, 239–40 (Lord Selborne); *Erlanger v New Sombrero Phosphate Co* (1878) 3 App Cas 1218, 1279 (Lord Blackburn); *Walker v Melham* [2007] NSWSC 264 [64] (White J); *Streeter v Western Areas Exploration Pty Ltd (No 2)* [2011] WASCA 17, (2011) 278 ALR 291 [635] (Murphy JA; McLure P and Buss JA concurring on this point); *Gillespie v Gillespie* [2013] QCA 99, [2013] 2 Qd R 440 [80] (Margaret Wilson J; Margaret McMurdo P and White JA concurring). Cf *Fisher v Brooker* [2009] UKHL 41, [2009] 1 WLR 1764 [64] (Lord Neuberger; Lord Mance and Lord Walker concurring) below n 165.

[162] See, eg, *Glasson v Fuller* [1922] SASR 148, 161–63 (Poole J); *Cashman v 7 North Golden Gate Gold Mining Co* (1897) 7 QLJ 152, 153–54 (Griffith J).

[163] See, eg, *Orr v Ford* [1989] HCA 4, (1989) 167 CLR 316.

[164] *Lindsay Petroleum Co v Hurd* (1874) LR 5 PC 221, 239–40 (Lord Selborne); *Barker v Duke Group Ltd (in liq)* [2005] SASC 81, (2005) 91 SASR 167 [142] (Perry J; Duggan and White JJ concurring) affirming *The Duke Group Ltd (in liq) v Alamain Investments Ltd* [2003] SASC 415 (Doyle CJ) and cases cited therein; *The Bell Group Ltd (in liq) v Westpac Banking Corporation (No 9)* [2008] WASC 239, (2008) 39 WAR 1 [2967]–[2968] (Owen J););; *Streeter v Western Areas Exploration Pty Ltd (No 2)* [2011] WASCA 17, (2011) 278 ALR 291 [674]–[676] (Murphy JA; McLure P and Buss JA concurring on this point).

[165] *Lindsay Petroleum Co v Hurd* (1874) LR 5 PC 221, 239–40 (Lord Selborne); *Lamshed v Lamshed* [1963] HCA 60, (1963) 109 CLR 440, 452–53, 455 [10] (Kitto J; Windeyer J concurring). *Fisher v Brooker* [2009] UKHL 41, [2009] 1 WLR 1764 [64] ('Although I would not suggest that it is an immutable requirement, some sort of detrimental reliance is usually an essential ingredient of laches': Lord Neuberger; Lord Mance and Lord Walker concurring, [71].

[166] *Orr v Ford* [1989] HCA 4 [21], (1989) 167 CLR 316, 330 (Wilson, Toohey and Gaudron JJ); *Walker v Melham* [2007] NSWSC 264 [56]–[57] (White J); *Waller v Waller* [2008] WASC 51 [149]–[151] (Simmonds J); *Gillespie v Gillespie* [2013] QCA 99, [2013] 2 Qd R 440 [93]–[94] (Margaret Wilson J; Margaret McMurdo P and White JA concurring).

In relation to unjust enrichment, this means that the defence will not apply to a claim by a plaintiff who delays only because he is not in a position to assess whether or not to proceed with a claim, or is not aware of his claim, because of the effects of an equitable unjust factor such as mistake, pressure or undue influence.[167]

C. Delay Under Statute: The Introduction of Limitation Periods

Unfortunately, the clear and principled approach adopted in equity was adversely affected by the introduction of limitation statutes. The statutes often apply piecemeal, and to an uncertain extent, to equitable claims. It is thus often difficult to determine which approach to delay—statutory or equitable—applies to equitable claims and to what effect.[168] An initial question is how to apply statutory limitation periods. In general, it is necessary to identify the date when the claim for unjust enrichment was complete.[169] The statutory time limit will apply from that date, unless the commencement date is postponed for some further, exceptional reason.[170]

For unjust enrichment claims based on unjust factors of vitiated or absent intention such as mistake[171] and illegitimate pressure,[172] the claim will usually be complete at the date of enrichment. Where the unjust factor is failure of consideration, the date of accrual will depend upon whether the basis of the transaction has already failed at the point at which the defendant is enriched[173] (in which case unjust enrichment is complete from the moment of enrichment)[174] or whether the basis of the transaction fails *subsequently*, such as if a condition fails to materialise or where a contract is terminated or frustrated, in which case the unjust enrichment only arises at that later date.[175]

i. Statutory Limitation Periods—England

The main source of statutory limitation periods for claims in unjust enrichment in England is the Limitation Act 1980.[176] Most personal claims in unjust enrichment are subject to a

[167] *Brooksbank v Smith* (1836) 2 Y & C Ex 58, 60, 160 ER 311, 311; *Denys v Shuckburgh* (1840) 4 Y & C Ex 42, 160 ER 912; *Baker v Courage & Co* [1910] 1 KB 56, 63–64; *Gillespie v Gillespie* [2013] QCA 99, [2013] 2 Qd R 440 [83] (Margaret Wilson J; Margaret McMurdo P and White JA concurring).

[168] The difficulties are well-described by Owen J in *The Bell Group Ltd (in liq) v Westpac Banking Corporation (No 9)* [2008] WASC 239, (2008) 39 WAR 1 [9271].

[169] *Torrens Aloha Pty Ltd v Citibank NA* (1997) 72 FCR 581; *Nu Line Construction Group Pty Ltd v Fowler* [2012] NSWSC 587, (2012) 16 BPR 31,011 [276]–[277] (Ward J). Special provisions relating to tax often alter this base position: see below pp 389–90, 393–94.

[170] As in cases of fraud and mistake, see below pp 388–89 and 393.

[171] *Baker v Courage & Co* [1910] 1 KB 56; *Torrens Aloha Pty Ltd v Citibank NA* (1997) 72 FCR 581.

[172] *Maskell v Horner* [1915] 3 KB 106.

[173] As where the benefit is transferred pursuant to a void contract. The position of benefits transferred on the basis of a judgment subsequently overturned, or transferred on a basis that is found to have failed pursuant to a judicial decision, is considered in Ch 11 p 265. Cf *Chidiac v Matouk* [2010] NSWSC 386 [258]–[259] (Ward J), applying *Torrens Aloha Pty Ltd v Citibank NA* (1997) 72 FCR 581.

[174] As in *Coshott v Lenin* [2007] NSWCA 153, followed in *Sharjade Pty Ltd v RAAF (Landings) Ex-Servicemen Charitable Fund Pty Ltd* [2008] NSWSC 1003 and *Adamson v Miller* [2008] FMCA 1173.

[175] *Guardian Ocean Cargoes Ltd v Banco Do Brasil SA (No 3)* [1992] 2 Lloyd's Rep 193; *Nu Line Construction Group Pty Ltd v Fowler* [2012] NSWSC 587, (2012) 16 BPR 31,011 [276]–[289] (Ward J); upheld on this point in *Nu Line Construction Group Pty Ltd v Fowler* [2014] NSWCA 51.

[176] Taxing statutes in particular often impose specific, and generally much shorter, limitation periods, see further below pp 389–90, 393–94.

limitation period of six years pursuant to section 5 of the Act. This is because they are treated (artificially, but by dint of a history of association with 'quasi-contract') as arising under 'simple contracts'.[177] The Act occasionally provides defined limitation periods for certain unjust enrichment claims, the lengths of which vary markedly and without obvious reason. For example, claims to recover benefits transferred pursuant to the Law Reform (Frustrated Contracts) Act 1943, as 'any sum recoverable by virtue of any enactment', are subject to a six-year period under section 9 of the Limitation Act. Claims for statutory contribution are restricted to two years pursuant to section 10. Actions to recover land are given a far more generous period of 12 years under section 16.

There is considerable potential for overlap, confusion and inconsistency arising from this patchwork of provisions. For example, a personal claim for restitution arising out of a receipt of a mistaken transfer of land is subject to a limitation period of six years, whereas a proprietary claim enjoys a 12-year limitation period. Following the Supreme Court decision in *Williams v Central Bank of Nigeria*,[178] claims for 'knowing receipt' and *Re Diplock* (section 22) claims attract quite different limitation periods, notwithstanding that they may share virtually identical underlying fact patterns. Finally, section 36(1)(b) states that the time limits applicable under section 5 for actions founded on a simple contract will not apply in cases where what is sought is 'equitable relief'. In those cases, the equitable doctrine of laches applies. This provision clearly covers cases of rescission for undue influence, for example. But the position of equitable remedies for common law claims, such as equitable rescission for fraud[179] or illegitimate pressure, or a trust arising in response to the plaintiff's mistake, is far less clear. The problem lies in the ambiguity of the language and the overlay of precedent affecting its operation. Similar anomalies and ambiguities infect the Australian legislation, as we will see below.

The position is further complicated by the fact that the relevant limitation period may be postponed on various grounds, including disability,[180] fraud,[181] acknowledgment and part payment of a debt[182] and where the defendant has deliberately concealed any fact relevant to the plaintiff's right of action.[183] The most important provision from an unjust enrichment perspective is section 32(1)(c). It provides that where the action is for 'relief from the consequences of a mistake', the period of limitation shall not begin to run until the plaintiff has discovered the mistake or could with reasonable diligence have discovered it. It was this provision that motivated the successful challenge to the mistake of law bar in *Kleinwort Benson Ltd v Lincoln City Council*.[184] The plaintiffs sought restitution of payments made pursuant to a fully executed but void swaps transaction on the ground that the payments had been made pursuant to a mistake of law, in order to invoke the extension provisions.

[177] *Re Diplock; Diplock v Wintle* [1948] Ch 465, 514 (Lord Greene MR); *Westdeutsche Landesbank Girozentrale v Islington London Borough Council; Kleinwort Benson Ltd v Sandwell Borough Council* [1994] 4 All ER 890, 942–43 (Hobhouse J); *Kleinwort Benson Ltd v Lincoln City Council* [1998] UKHL 38, [1999] 2 AC 349; *Test Claimants in the FII Group Litigation v Revenue and Customs Commissioners* [2010] EWCA Civ 103, [2010] STC 1251 [231] (Arden LJ, delivering the judgment of the Court).

[178] *Williams v Central Bank of Nigeria* [2014] UKSC 10, [2014] AC 1189.

[179] Eg *Molloy v Mutual Reserve Life Insurance Co* (1906) 94 LT 756.

[180] Limitation Act 1980 s 28.

[181] ibid s 32(1)(a).

[182] ibid s 29(5).

[183] ibid s 32(1)(b).

[184] *Kleinwort Benson Ltd v Lincoln City Council* [1998] UKHL 38, [1999] 2 AC 349, discussed in Ch 8 pp 185–87.

The House of Lords held that all payments, including those made more than six years prior to the commencement of proceedings, could be recovered because the action had been brought within six years of its earlier decision[185] that had first established that the swaps transactions were *ultra vires* the council and thus void.

The boundaries of section 32(1)(c) became a matter of great importance in a series of cases against the UK Revenue for restitution of unlawfully exacted tax.[186] The common feature of the cases was that taxation payments had been made over many years, sometimes decades. The obvious consequence was that the usual limitation period of six years had long expired, and with it the plaintiffs' rights. However, if the actions could be brought within section 32(1)(c), then payments dating back 30 years or more could, in many instances, survive. There was no theoretical difficulty in applying the provision where the relevant claim was one for restitution of a mistaken payment. The problem for taxpayers was that mistake-based claims could well have been extinguished or unavailable for other reasons.[187]

The question then became whether the protection offered by section 32(1)(c) could extend to other causes of action (such as *Woolwich*-based claims) in which mistake did not form a necessary element of the cause of action, but had been causally significant to the events triggering the claim. This broader operation was rejected by the United Kingdom Supreme Court in a case where it held that the subsection applies only where the mistake is an essential ingredient of the cause of action.[188] An important consideration was the perceived difficulty in imposing any principled limit to the reach of the provision on its broader interpretation. This was seen to be of more concern than any anomalies which may flow from a more limited interpretation.[189]

Even with the restricted interpretation of section 32(1)(c) which limits it to mistake-based claims, the Revenue's potential tax liability arising from mistaken payments of tax has been enormous. In an attempt to cut down, or cut off, this liability, the UK government has introduced a variety of statutory amendments to reduce applicable time limits and in particular

185 *Hazell v Hammersmith and Fulham London Borough Council* [1992] 2 AC 1.

186 The most important for present purposes are: *Marks & Spencer plc v Customs and Excise Commissioners* [2002] ECR I-6325, [2003] QB 866; *Deutsche Morgan Grenfell Group plc v Inland Revenue Commissioners* [2006] UKHL 49, [2007] 1 AC 558; *Test Claimants in the FII Group Litigation v Revenue and Customs Commissioners* [2008] EWHC 2893, [2009] STC 254, appealed in *Test Claimants in the FII Group Litigation v Revenue and Customs Commissioners* [2010] EWCA Civ 103, [2010] STC 1251; *FJ Chalke Ltd v Revenue and Customs Commissioners* [2010] EWCA Civ 313, [2010] STC 1640.

187 In particular because (due to the independent existence of a *Woolwich* claim or other avenue for relief) mistake-based claims might not be regarded as necessary for the 'equivalent' and 'effective' protection of restitutionary rights to repayment of charges levied in breach of Community law required under the *San Giorgio* principle, and could therefore be excluded or restricted by legislative intervention: see, eg, *Test Claimants in the FII Group Litigation v Revenue and Customs Commissioners* [2008] EWHC 2893, [2009] STC 254 [260]–[262] (Henderson J), overturned in *Test Claimants in the FII Group Litigation v Revenue and Customs Commissioners* [2010] EWCA Civ 103, [2010] STC 1251 [157] (Arden LJ, delivering the judgment of the Court).

188 *Test Claimants in the FII Group Litigation v Revenue and Customs Commissioners* [2012] UKSC 19, [2012] 2 AC 337 [62] (Lord Walker, recanting from his earlier attraction to the broader approach) [184]–[185] (Lord Sumption, delivering the judgment of the Court on this issue and upholding *Test Claimants in the FII Group Litigation v Revenue and Customs Commissioners* [2010] EWCA Civ 103, [2010] STC 1251 [236]–[245] (Arden LJ, delivering the judgment of the Court) and approving *Phillips-Higgins v Harper* [1954] 1 QB 411, 419 (Pearson J) and *Malkin v Birmingham City Council* (CA, 12 January 2000) [23] (Aldous LJ; Laws LJ concurring).

189 That anomalies would be generated by the restrictive reading of the section was accepted in *Test Claimants in the FII Group Litigation v Revenue and Customs Commissioners* [2010] EWCA Civ 103, [2010] STC 1251 [240] (Arden LJ, delivering the judgment of the Court), but refuted in *Test Claimants in the FII Group Litigation v Revenue and Customs Commissioners* [2012] UKSC 19, [2012] 2 AC 337 [184]–[185] (Lord Sumption).

to exclude the effect of section 32(1)(c) in taxation cases.[190] Many of these amendments purport to operate retroactively. In Case C-362/12 *Test Claimants in the FII Group Litigation v Revenue and Customs Commissioners (formerly Inland Revenue Commissioners)*,[191] the European Court of Justice considered the operation of section 320 of the Finance Act 2004. The provision purported to operate retroactively to exclude section 32(1)(c) in proceedings for the recovery of sums paid under a mistake of law when the action related to a taxation matter. The Court rejected the Commissioners' case that section 320 did not breach the Community law principles of effectiveness, equivalence, legal certainty and legitimate expectation because there remained open to plaintiffs the *Woolwich*-based claim, which (on the current restricted reading) is not subject to the new limitation periods.[192] The Court held that the combination of the retroactive operation of the section and legislative failure to provide transitional arrangements, meant that section 320 must be disapplied.[193] The clear implication of the decision is that with adequate transitional provisions, these sorts of legislative curtailments of the protections afforded to taxpayers by the *Woolwich* principle and the law of unjust enrichment may well succeed.

In summary, the existing UK limitation framework is becoming increasingly fractured, difficult to construe and ultimately conducive to inconsistent treatment of like cases. There is as yet no sign of amending (and consolidating) legislation that might begin to rectify the position. And at least while the current suite of litigation rages over the effects of and restrictions upon limitation periods affecting the UK Revenue's enormous potential restitutionary liability, that situation is unlikely to change.[194]

ii. *Statutory Limitation Periods—Australia*

In Australia, the statutory position is complicated by the multiplicity of jurisdictions. Each state and territory limitations statute contains reference to a category of cause of action sufficiently wide to encompass personal claims in unjust enrichment, although the language adopted is generally arcane.[195] In relation to unjust enrichment claims at common

[190] See, eg, Finance Act 2004, s 320, Finance Act 2007, s 107 and Taxes Management Act 1970, s 33, together the subject of consideration in *Test Claimants in the FII Group Litigation v Revenue and Customs Commissioners* [2008] EWHC 2893, [2009] STC 254 [403]–[439] (Henderson J); *Test Claimants in the FII Group Litigation v Revenue and Customs Commissioners* [2010] EWCA Civ 103, [2010] STC 1251 [217]–[229], [246]–[268] (Lady Justice Arden, giving the judgment of the Court); *Test Claimants in the FII Group Litigation v Revenue and Customs Commissioners* [2012] UKSC 19, [2012] 2 AC 337 [14]–[22] (Lord Hope) [92]–[120] (Lord Walker) [121]–[125] (Lord Brown) [126]–[139] (Lord Clarke) [149]–[169] [197]–[205] (Lord Sumption) [228]–[245] (Lord Reed) and Case C-362/12 *Test Claimants in the FII Group Litigation v Revenue and Customs Commissioners (formerly Inland Revenue Commissioners)* [2014] AC 1161. For a brief history and analysis of the government's legislative response up to 2005, see M Chowdry, 'The Revenue's Response: A Time Bar on Claims' (2005) 121 *Law Quarterly Review* 546.

[191] Case C-362/12 *Test Claimants in the FII Group Litigation v Revenue and Customs Commissioners (formerly Inland Revenue Commissioners)* [2014] AC 1161.

[192] *Marks & Spencer plc v Commissioners of Customs & Excise* [2002] ECR I-6325, [2003] QB 866 [36]–[40], [246]–[268]; *Test Claimants in the FII Group Litigation v Revenue and Customs Commissioners* [2010] EWCA Civ 103, [2010] STC 1251 [217]–[229], [246]–[268] (Lady Justice Arden, giving the judgment of the Court).

[193] Case C-62/100 *Marks and Spencer v Customs and Excise Commissioners* [2002] ECR I-6325, [2003] QB 886.

[194] Cf Law Commission, *Limitation of Actions* (Law Com CP No 151, 1998) paras [1.47]–[1.49]; Law Commission, *Limitation of Actions* (Law Com No 270, 2001) paras [2.48]–[2.51], [4.76]–[4.79].

[195] In *Re Diplock; Diplock v Wintle* [1948] Ch 465, the Court of Appeal held that the words 'actions founded on simple contract' in the Limitation Act 1939 s 2(1)(a) covered such claims.

law, a number of statutes expressly provide limitation periods with respect to claims in 'quasi-contract',[196] and some for contracts 'implied in law'.[197] By contrast, section 38(1) of the Limitation of Actions Act 1936 (SA) provides a specific limitation period for claims for recovery of money 'based on restitutionary grounds'.[198] It is unclear whether the section extends to cases seeking recovery of the value of non-monetary benefits. The focus of the section on money payments would seem to indicate that it would not. This seems a strange result, and would throw non-monetary benefits claims back onto section 35(a) of the Act, relating to 'actions founded upon any simple contract express or implied'. The Australian Capital Territory has a 'catch-all' provision which would encompass claims in unjust enrichment.[199] In all jurisdictions except the Northern Territory, the operative limitation period is six years from the date of accrual of the cause of action. In the Northern Territory, the period is three years. Consistently with the treatment of unjust enrichment claims at common law, under the Victorian frustrated contracts legislation, claims for restitution of benefits conferred pursuant to contracts later discharged for frustration are 'taken to be founded on simple contract'[200] and hence subject to the usual six-year limitation period.[201]

Beyond these complex, but relatively certain, starting positions, the legislative frameworks rapidly lose their coherence. Almost all limitation statutes in Australia contain a provision preserving the equitable jurisdiction to *refuse* relief on the grounds of laches, acquiescence or otherwise.[202] However, as in the United Kingdom, the equitable *extensions* have not survived for those unjust factors to which the statutes apply.[203] Numerous anomalies and different treatment for the various unjust factors to which the statutes apply have been introduced. Further, anomalies arise for the same unjust factor depending upon the factual circumstances in which it arose and whether the relief sought is personal or proprietary. It is not the function of this brief overview to examine comprehensively the different limitation regimes in all the states. It suffices to observe five of these anomalies that have developed as a result of the statutory limitation defences to claims in unjust enrichment.

First, in relation to equitable unjust factors, the statutes apply to some but not to others. Where statutes do not apply to an equitable unjust factor, if the equitable claim is very similar to a common law cause of action for which a statutory limitation period applies (for instance an action based on the unjust factor of mistake, failure of consideration or

[196] Limitation Act 1981 (NT) s 12(1)(a); Limitation of Actions Act 1974 (Qld) s 10(1)(a); Limitations Act 1969 (NSW) s 14(1)(a), discussed in *Coshott v Lenin* [2007] NSWCA 153 [13]–[17] (Mason P; Spigelman CJ and Campbell JA concurring); see also *Nu Line Construction Group Pty Ltd v Fowler* [2014] NSWCA 51.

[197] Limitation of Actions Act 1958 (Vic) s 5(1)(a); Limitation Act 1974 (Tas) s 4(1)(a); Limitation Act 1935 (WA) s 38. The new Limitation Act 2005 (WA) s 13 (which only operates prospectively) provides a 'catch-all' limitation period of six years unless otherwise specified.

[198] Limitation of Actions Act 1936 (SA) s 38(1).

[199] Limitation Act 1985 (ACT) s 11. See also Limitation Act 2005 (WA) s 13.

[200] Australian Consumer Law and Fair Trading Act 2012 (Vic) s 43.

[201] ibid s 44 and Limitation of Actions Act 1958 (Vic) s 5(1)(a).

[202] Limitation Act 1985 (ACT) s 6; Limitation Act 1981 (NT) s 7; Limitation Act 1969 (NSW) s 9; Limitation of Actions Act 1974 (Qld) s 43; Limitation of Actions Act 1936 (SA) s 26; Limitation Act 1974 (Tas) s 36; Limitation of Actions Act 1958 (Vic) s 31; Limitation Act 1935 (WA) s 28; Limitation Act 2005 (WA) s 80.

[203] Limitation Act 2005 (WA) s 27 contemplates application of these rules, but only where the instant claim is not analogous to a common law claim.

illegitimate pressure in equity), that limitation period may[204] be applied by analogy.[205] The uncertainty infects the treatment of even the most straightforward equitable claims. A good example is the tortured reasoning contained in the judgments in the *Bell* litigation.[206] Like the UK Supreme Court case of *Williams*, the *Bell* litigation also concerned claims of knowing receipt. In *Bell*, the breaches of what were described as 'fiduciary' duties were said to have been committed by the directors of The Bell Group Ltd.[207] The reasoning and conclusion reached by Owen J at first instance and the majority on appeal bears a superficial similarity to the reasoning in *Williams*. In both cases a distinction was recognised between true (express) trusts and constructive trusts imposed as a formula for equitable relief.[208] Justice Owen concluded that, as a result of that distinction, the equivalent provision to section 21(1)(a)—section 47 of the Limitations Act 1935 (WA)—only applied to true trusts.[209] This conclusion, however, led to the further deduction that the limitation statute did not apply to cases of knowing receipt at all.[210] This in turn required his Honour to consider whether the statute should be applied by analogy to other nominated causes of action[211] (decided in the negative), with the result that the matter became one of the application of the equitable doctrine of laches. On appeal, Lee AJA considered that fiduciaries acting in fraudulent breach of trust were to be considered true trustees for the purposes of the Act, and that those knowingly in receipt of assets as a result of that breach also should be caught

[204] The court retains a discretion as to whether to apply the stipulated period: see *The Duke Group Ltd (in liq) v Alamain Investments Ltd* [2003] SASC 415 [135]–[142] (Doyle CJ), affirmed *Barker v Duke Group Ltd (in liq)* [2005] SASC 81, (2005) 91 SASR 167. See also *Williams v Minister, Aboriginal Land Rights Act 1983* (1994) 35 NSWLR 497, 509–11 (Kirby P; Priestley JA in agreement); *The Bell Group Ltd (in liq) v Westpac Banking Corporation (No 9)* [2008] WASC 239, (2008) 39 WAR 1 [9267]–[9268] (Owen J).

[205] *Motor Terms Co Pty Ltd v Liberty Insurance Ltd (in liq)* [1967] HCA 9, (1967) 116 CLR 177, 184 [7] (Kitto J); *Barker v Duke Group Ltd (in liq)* [2005] SASC 81, (2005) 91 SASR 167 [81]–[83] (Perry J; Duggan and White JJ concurring) affirming *The Duke Group Ltd (in liq) v Alamain Investments Ltd* [2003] SASC 415 (Doyle CJ) and cases cited therein; *The Bell Group Ltd (in liq) v Westpac Banking Corporation (No 9)* [2008] WASC 239, (2008) 39 WAR 1 [9267]–[9268] (Owen J); *Gerace v Auzhair Supplies Pty Ltd (in liq)* [2014] NSWCA 181, (2014) 87 NSWLR 435; *Amaca Pty Ltd v CSR Ltd* [2015] VSC 582 [461] (Macauley J, applying by analogy the limitations period for a claim of 'simple contract' applicable to claims in unjust enrichment to a claim of contribution). HM McLean, 'Limitation of Actions in Restitution' (1989) 48 *Cambridge Law Journal* 472, 491.

[206] *The Bell Group Ltd (in liq) v Westpac Banking Corporation (No 9)* [2008] WASC 239, (2008) 39 WAR 1 [9274]–[9284] (Owen J); on appeal *Westpac Banking Corporation v The Bell Group Ltd (in liq) (No 3)* [2012] WASCA 157, (2012) 44 WAR 1 [2673] (Lee AJA; Drummond AJA concurring on this point).

[207] An immediate point of contention should have been that the directors were not 'trustees' so as to attract the operation of the Act, a point noted but not addressed by Owen J in *The Bell Group Ltd (in liq) v Westpac Banking Corporation (No 9)* [2008] WASC 239, (2008) 39 WAR 1 [9260], who went on to find that the provisions did not apply to the banks as constructive trustees. Cf on appeal, where Lee AJA found that the directors were de facto trustees, citing amongst others *Barker v Duke Group Ltd (in liq)* [2005] SASC 81, (2005) 91 SASR 167 [75]–[77] (Perry J), and *Paragon Finance plc v DB Thakerar & Co* [1999] 1 All ER 400, 408 (Millett LJ); *Soar v Ashwell* [1893] 2 QB 390, 398 (Bowen LJ); *Westpac Banking Corporation v The Bell Group Ltd (in liq) (No 3)* [2012] WASCA 157, (2012) 44 WAR 1 [1183]. It followed that the provision applied. However, Perry J found precisely the contrary in *Barker v Duke Group Ltd (in liq)* [2005] SASC 81, (2005) 91 SASR 167 [78]. See also *Clay v Clay* [2001] HCA 9, (2001) 202 CLR 410, on the need to find an express trustee in order for the statutory provision to apply.

[208] *The Bell Group Ltd (in liq) v Westpac Banking Corporation (No 9)* [2008] WASC 239, (2008) 39 WAR 1 [9264] (Owen J); *Westpac Banking Corporation v The Bell Group Ltd (in liq) (No 3)* [2012] WASCA 157, (2012) 44 WAR 1 [1176] (Lee AJA) [2673] (Drummond AJA concurring).

[209] *The Bell Group Ltd (in liq) v Westpac Banking Corporation (No 9)* [2008] WASC 239, (2008) 39 WAR 1 [9261]–[9265].

[210] ibid [9265].

[211] Including the torts of conspiracy to injure by unlawful means, conspiracy to defraud and conversion, examined at ibid [9267]–[9296].

by the exception.[212] Whether or not this is correct, and whether or not the claim of knowing receipt forms part of the law of unjust enrichment,[213] the important point for current purposes is that the complex interplay between the statutory and equitable regimes resulted in highly divergent reasoning and conclusions concerning the relevant limitation period for a common form of claim.

The second category of anomaly apparent in the Australian context is that the legislative limitation periods vary in their treatment of extension or postponement depending on the unjust factor and circumstances surrounding the defendant's unjust enrichment. For example, most (but not all) jurisdictions' limitation legislation makes special provision for the postponement of the commencement of the limitation periods in cases involving fraud and mistake, to run from the time when the fraud or mistake was or could with reasonable diligence have been discovered.[214] In *Australia and New Zealand Banking Group Ltd v Paciocco,*[215] the ANZ argued that claims for restitution of bank fees paid pursuant to a mistake of law were not covered by the equivalent provision found in section 27(c) of the Limitation of Actions Act 1958 (Vic). The bank argued that the provision is limited to mistakes of fact on the basis that it is to be interpreted as a 'fixed time provision' and therefore cannot take account of developments in the law relating to restitution for the unjust factor of mistake. In the Full Court of the Federal Court, Besanko J held that the provision is ambulatory in nature and that the words of the provision are sufficiently general to accommodate mistakes of law. In this respect at least the statutory and equitable law of delay are more coherent. However, with the possible exception of South Australia, the same statutory extension provisions do not extend to circumstances where the effect of pressure or undue influence leads to the delay in bringing the action.[216]

Thirdly, as we have seen occurring recently in the UK, many of the Australian state limitation statutes contain special limitation provisions that apply to actions to recover overpayments of tax or payments of tax pursuant to what subsequently turns out to be an invalid statute.[217] The limitation periods in that context are significantly reduced, most often to between six and 12 months, and usually run from the date of payment rather than the date of accrual of the cause of action. We saw an example in Chapter 13. In *Thiess v Collector of Customs,*[218] customs officials miscalculated the tariff that should be paid by

[212] *Westpac Banking Corporation v The Bell Group Ltd (in liq) (No 3)* [2012] WASCA 157, (2012) 44 WAR 1 [1183]–[1186].

[213] See Ch 12 pp 287–91.

[214] *Torrens Aloha Pty Ltd v Citibank NA* (1997) 72 FCR 581; *Australia and New Zealand Banking Group Ltd v Paciocco* [2015] FCAFC 50 [396] (Besanko J). Limitation Act 1985 (ACT) ss 33, 34; Limitation Act 1969 (NSW) ss 55, 56; Limitation Act 1974 (Tas) s 32; Limitation Act 1981 (NT) ss 42, 43; Limitation of Actions Act 1958 (Vic) s 27; Limitation of Actions Act 1974 (Qld) s 38. The Western Australian provisions are very restrictive. The 1935 provisions apply only to claims in equity for the recovery of land and rent and in the case of concealed fraud: Limitation Act 1935 (WA) s 27. The 2005 provisions are limited to cases of 'fraudulent or other improper conduct': Limitation Act 2005 (WA) s 38(2); cf Limitation of Actions Act 1936 (SA) s 49.

[215] *Australia and New Zealand Banking Group Ltd v Paciocco* [2015] FCAFC 50 [396] (Besanko J).

[216] Limitation of Actions Act 1936 (SA) s 49. Limitation Act 2005 (WA) s 27 contemplates a delay in the commencement of time running against the defendant 'on equitable principles', but only where the instant claim is not analogous to a common law claim.

[217] Limitation Act 1985 (ACT) ss 21A, 54; Limitation Act 1981 (NT) ss 35D, 35E; Limitation of Actions Act 1974 (Qld) s 10A; Limitation of Actions Act 1936 (SA) s 38; Limitation Act 1974 (Tas) s 25D; Limitation of Actions Act 1958 (Vic) s 20A; Limitation Act 1935 (WA) s 37A; Limitation Act 2005 (WA) s 28.

[218] *Thiess v Collector of Customs* [2014] HCA 12, (2014) 250 CLR 664.

the plaintiff to import a yacht into Australia. The High Court explained[219] that the introduction of a highly restrictive statutory framework governing restitution of tariffs paid by mistake under the Customs Act 1901 (Cth) sought to address the perceived danger of fiscal chaos at a time when customs duty accounted for more than half of all Commonwealth revenue.[220] The limitation period for recovery under the Act is six months from the date of payment. A number of statutes further dictate that recovery is conditional on the court being satisfied that the amount paid by way of tax has not been recovered from or charged to another person.[221] That is, the statutes impose a passing-on defence, albeit restricted to a taxation context.

Fourthly, most limitation statutes confer a generous limitation period of 12 or 15 years with respect to actions to recover land.[222] Land is generally defined to include equitable interests in land, which means that a claim in unjust enrichment (mistake, undue influence, no intention to benefit) usually will have two applicable limitation periods: one in respect of the personal claim, the other for the claim that the land is held on trust. The arbitrary limitation consequences for identical causes of action have been highlighted by two New South Wales Supreme Court decisions addressing cases of total failure of consideration. In one, the plaintiff successfully obtained a declaration of constructive trust with respect to land, with the result that a limitations period of 12 years applied.[223] In the other, the claim of constructive trust was denied. It followed that the plaintiff's claim for personal restitution, which otherwise would have succeeded, was statute-barred after the passage of six years.[224]

Finally, even between states and territories there are very different treatments of identical unjust factors. For instance, in relation to claims based upon an unjust factor of no intention to benefit, such as for a share of a deceased estate, as in *Re Diplock*,[225] in Queensland and Tasmania, the limitation period is 12 years from the date on which the right to receive the share or interest accrued,[226] in Victoria the period is 15 years,[227] and in South Australia and in Western Australia for actions to which the 1935 Act apply,[228] the limitation period is limited to claims with respect to 'legacies' (chattels), leaving claims with respect to real property the subject of the general provisions regarding claims for the recovery of land.[229] New South Wales, the Australian Capital Territory, the Northern Territory and the 2005 Western Australian legislation deal with claims to a share of an estate by defining 'trustee' for the purposes of the trusts provisions as including executors, with the consequence that the limitation provisions follow those for a claim for receipt of trust assets.

[219] ibid [31]–[32] (the Court).

[220] *Sargood Brothers v Commonwealth* [1910] HCA 45, (1910) 11 CLR 258, 303 (Isaacs J).

[221] Limitation of Actions Act 1958 (Vic) s 20B; Limitation Act 1974 (Tas) s 25C; Limitation Act 1935 (WA) s 37B; Limitation Act 2005 (WA) ss 86, 87.

[222] Limitation Act 1981 (NT) s 21; Limitation Act 1969 (NSW) s 27; Limitation of Actions Act 1974 (Qld) s 13; Limitation of Actions Act 1958 (Vic) s 8; Limitation Act 1935 (WA) s 4; Limitation Act 2005 (WA) s 19.

[223] *Payne v Rowe* [2012] NSWSC 685, (2012) 16 BPR 30,869 [99] (Ball J).

[224] *Nu Line Construction Group Pty Ltd v Fowler* [2012] NSWSC 587, (2012) 16 BPR 31,011 [276]–[289] (Ward J). Unintentionally underlining the irrationality of the position, Ward J noted at [265] that the causes of action were indistinguishable, whereas Ball J refused to accept the same proposition, put by counsel for the defendant in that case, at [97]–[98].

[225] *Re Diplock; Diplock v Wintle* [1948] Ch 465.

[226] Limitation of Actions Act 1974 (Qld) s 28; Limitation Act 1974 (Tas) s 25.

[227] Limitation of Actions Act 1958 (Vic) s 22.

[228] See Limitation Act 2005 (WA) s 4.

[229] Limitation of Actions Act 1936 (SA) ss 4, 33; Limitation Act 1935 (WA) ss 4, 32.

VIII. Dispute Resolved

A. The Rationale of the Defence

There is a strong public interest in the finality of disputes, whether achieved by way of judicial determination, contractual settlement, compromise in the face of legal proceedings or through submission to an honest claim. Such mechanisms prevent the reopening of disputes that already have been resolved and protect defendants from the threat of recurring or indeterminate litigation.[230] The relationship between these defences is very close, with a tendency to overlap. They also intersect with, but are independent of and more limited than the broader doctrine of abuse of process.[231] Although also concerned with considerations of finality and fairness, abuse of process is, 'capable of application in any circumstances in which the use of a court's procedures would be unjustifiably oppressive to a party or would bring the administration of justice into disrepute'.[232] It can, for example, extend to preventing a party from bringing a claim or raising an issue that has already been, or should have been litigated in earlier proceedings, even where the party was not involved in the earlier proceedings.[233]

B. *Res Judicata*, and Cause of Action Estoppel

The doctrine of *res judicata* ('a thing decided') is a rule that if a final judgment has been given, no further proceedings can be brought with respect to that cause of action unless and until the original judgment has been set aside.[234] As Lord Mansfield explained in *Moses v Macferlan*,[235] 'the merits of a judgment can never be over-haled by an original suit, either at law or in equity'. The rationale of the doctrine is that there must be an end to litigation in the interests of public policy and for the sake of the litigants.[236]

There are two aspects to the doctrine of *res judicata* which are usually treated separately in Australia. If a legal claim is successful, the cause of action is said to merge in the judgment and to have no further independent existence.[237] Thus, where a later claim seeks an

230 *Tyne v UBS AG* [2016] FCA 5 [326] (Greenwood J).
231 *Tomlinson v Ramsey Food Processing Pty Ltd* [2015] HCA 28, (2015) 323 ALR 1 [24]–[26] (French CJ, Bell, Gageler and Keane JJ). For an example of this interplay, compare *Zurich Insurance Co plc v Hayward* [2011] EWCA Civ 641, [2011] CP Rep 39 and *Hayward v Zurich Insurance Co plc* [2015] EWCA Civ 327, [2015] CP Rep 30.
232 *Tomlinson v Ramsey Food Processing Pty Ltd* [2015] HCA 28, (2015) 323 ALR 1 [25] (French CJ, Bell, Gageler and Keane JJ).
233 ibid [26] (French CJ, Bell, Gageler and Keane JJ); applied in *Tyne v UBS AG* [2016] FCA 5 [343]–[352], [414]–[423](Greenwood J). The application of estoppels to parties to an action or their 'privies' is discussed below p 397.
234 *Jackson v Goldsmith* [1950] HCA 22, (1950) 81 CLR 446, 466 [5] (Fullagar J dissenting); cited with approval in *Port of Melbourne Authority v Anshun Pty Ltd* [1981] HCA 45, (1981) 147 CLR 589, 597 [17]–[18] (Gibbs CJ, Mason and Aickin JJ); *Chamberlain v Deputy Commissioner of Taxation* [1988] HCA 21, (1988) 164 CLR 502, 510–11 [21] (Deane, Toohey and Gaudron JJ).
235 *Moses v Macferlan* (1760) 2 Burr 1005, 1009; 97 ER 676, 678.
236 *Port of Melbourne Authority v Anshun Pty Ltd* [1981] HCA 45, (1981) 147 CLR 589, 609 [11] (Brennan J).
237 *Thoday v Thoday* [1964] P 181, 197–98 (Diplock LJ); *Port of Melbourne Authority v Anshun Pty Ltd* [1981] HCA 45, (1981) 147 CLR 589, 597 [17]–[18] (Gibbs CJ, Mason and Aickin JJ); *Chamberlain v Deputy Commissioner of Taxation* [1988] HCA 21, (1988) 164 CLR 502, 507–08 [9]–[11] (Deane, Toohey and Gaudron JJ), 512

alternative remedy arising from the original cause of action, the later claim will be barred by the judgment because the cause of action has been merged in the judgment and thereby extinguished.[238] The second aspect of *res judicata* arises if the claim is rejected. In such a case, the parties are estopped from claiming that the cause of action exists.[239] It is this aspect of *res judicata* that is commonly called 'cause of action estoppel'.[240]

In *Tomlinson v Ramsey Food Processing Pty Ltd*,[241] French CJ, Bell, Gageler and Keane JJ considered that cause of action estoppel is independent of the doctrine of *res judicata*, although both are informed by 'similar considerations of finality and fairness'.[242] Their Honours explained that, unlike *res judicata*, cause of action estoppel 'is not confined to an exercise of judicial power; it also operates in the context of a final judgment having been rendered in other adversarial proceedings'.[243] However, due to its close relationship with res judicata, the estoppel will be 'largely redundant'[244] in circumstances where that doctrine applies.

One difficulty in deciding when the defence of *res judicata* applies concerns whether further proceedings have been brought in respect of the same, or a different, cause of action. In *Port of Melbourne Authority v Anshun Pty Ltd*[245] Brennan J observed that 'cause of action' can mean either (1) the series of facts which the plaintiff must allege and prove to substantiate a right to judgment, or (2) the legal right which has been infringed, or (3) the substance of the action as distinct from its form. *Moses v Macferlan*[246] illustrates these difficulties. Moses owed money to Macferlan. In settlement of the matter, he entered into an agreement to pay to Macferlan part of what was owed and, in satisfaction of the balance, to sign over to Macferlan a number of promissory notes made in Moses' favour by a third party. As part of that agreement, Macferlan indemnified Moses for any liability on the notes and released Moses from the balance owed. When his action against the third party to recover on the notes was unsuccessful, Macferlan successfully sued Moses in the local Court of Conscience on the promissory notes.[247] As Gummow J noted in *Roxborough v Rothmans of Pall Mall Australia Ltd*,[248] Moses could have sought to enforce specifically the indemnity agreement, or brought an action at common law for breach of the agreement. He did neither of those

[1]–[2] (Dawson J); *Tomlinson v Ramsey Food Processing Pty Ltd* [2015] HCA 28, (2015) 323 ALR 1 [20] (French CJ, Bell, Gageler and Keane JJ).

238 *United Australia Ltd v Barclays Bank Ltd* [1941] AC 1, 27–28 (Lord Atkin).

239 *Trawl Industries of Australia Pty Ltd (in liq) v Effem Foods Pty Ltd* (1992) 36 FCR 406, 409 (Gummow J), affirmed *Effem Foods Pty Ltd v Trawl Industries of Australia Pty Ltd (recs and mgrs apptd) (in liq)* (1993) 43 FCR 510; *Thoday v Thoday* [1964] P 181, 197–98 (Diplock LJ); *Dublin Corporation v Building and Allied Trade Union* [1996] 1 IR 468.

240 On the distinction between and nomenclature for the two effects, see KR Handley, *Spencer Bower, Turner and Handley: The Doctrine of Res Judicata*, 4th edn (London, LexisNexis, 2009) 1–2.

241 *Tomlinson v Ramsey Food Processing Pty Ltd* [2015] HCA 28, (2015) 323 ALR 1.

242 ibid [21].

243 ibid [21].

244 ibid [22].

245 *Port of Melbourne Authority v Anshun Pty Ltd* [1981] HCA 45 [16]–[17], (1981) 147 CLR 589, 611.

246 *Moses v Macferlan* (1760) 2 Burr 1005, 97 ER 676.

247 The Court of Conscience for the County of Middlesex, established by 23 Geo II c 33 (1750). See *Roxborough v Rothmans of Pall Mall Australia Ltd* [2001] HCA 68, (2001) 208 CLR 516 [77] (Gummow J).

248 *Roxborough v Rothmans of Pall Mall Australia Ltd* [2001] HCA 68, (2001) 208 CLR 516 [77].

things. Instead, he sought to rely by way of defence on the agreement. The Court refused to entertain the defence, as it raised the possibility of issues going beyond the monetary limits of the Court's jurisdiction. Moses satisfied the judgment of the Court, then successfully sued Macferlan in the Court of King's Bench to recover the amount paid over in an action for money had and received. This judgment has been the subject of criticism[249] on the basis that it should have been barred pursuant to the doctrine of *res judicata*. However, the earlier cause of action the subject of decision was based on Macferlan's rights arising from the promissory notes whereas the latter decision was based on Moses' right to restitutionary damages which arose as a result of Macferlan's breach of contract in suing Moses. Further, as Gummow J noted, the Court below had not heard Moses on the subject of the agreement, as it considered itself without jurisdiction to do so. Thus the claim was not barred on the basis of 'issue estoppel' or '*Anshun* estoppel', which are addressed below.

Another difficult issue is common to cause of action estoppel, issue estoppel and *Anshun* estoppel. As the High Court explained in *Tomlinson v Ramsey Food Processing Pty Ltd*,[250] all three forms of estoppel have the potential to operate to restrict assertions made between parties to litigation or their 'privies'. The 'basic requirement of a privy in interest is that the privy must claim under or through the person of whom he is said to be a privy'.[251] However, the precise extent of the required connection has been elusive. The English approach requires 'a sufficient degree of identification between the two to make it just to hold that the decision to which one was party should be binding in proceedings to which the other is party'.[252] As Nettle J observed in *Tomlinson*, this formulation has the disadvantages of being circular and a category of indeterminate reference.[253] In *Tomlinson*, French CJ, Bell, Gageler and Keane JJ identified at least two bases on which a party (A) can be privy in interest with a party to an earlier proceeding (B):

> One basis is that A might have had some legal interest in the outcome of the earlier proceeding which was represented by B, or that B has some legal interest in the outcome of the later proceeding which is represented by A ... The other basis is that, after that earlier proceeding was concluded by judgment, A might have acquired from B some legal interest in respect of which B would be affected by an estoppel which A then relies on in the later proceeding.[254]

On either basis, the privy's interest must be legal in nature: it is not enough that it is an economic interest in the outcome of earlier proceedings conducted by B, for example.[255] The rationale of the privity principle is that the person who takes the benefit of a final judgment should also bear the burden of it.[256]

[249] *Phillips v Hunter* (1795) 2 H Bl 402, 126 ER 618; *Marriot v Hampton* (1797) 7 TR 269, 101 ER 969.

[250] *Tomlinson v Ramsey Food Processing Pty Ltd* [2015] HCA 28, (2015) 323 ALR 1 [23] (French CJ, Bell, Gageler and Keane JJ).

[251] *Ramsay v Pigram* [1968] HCA 34, (1968) 118 CLR 271, 279 [19] (Barwick CJ), approved *Tomlinson v Ramsey Food Processing Pty Ltd* [2015] HCA 28, (2015) 323 ALR 1 [17], [35] (French CJ, Bell, Gageler and Keane JJ) [92]–[93] (Nettle J).

[252] *Gleeson v J Wippell & Co Ltd* [1977] 1 WLR 510, 515 (Megarry VC).

[253] See eg *Tomlinson v Ramsey Food Processing Pty Ltd* [2015] HCA 28, (2015) 323 ALR 1 [97] (Nettle J).

[254] ibid [28], [33].

[255] ibid [28], [35] (French CJ, Bell, Gageler and Keane JJ).

[256] ibid [28], [29]–[30] (French CJ, Bell, Gageler and Keane JJ).

C. Issue Estoppel

As we saw above, a final judgment by a court is a conclusive determination of all the factual and legal issues that were fundamental or necessary steps to the decision[257] or final orders of the court.[258] Once an issue has thus been determined, the parties cannot dispute it in later proceedings between the same parties, even if the later proceedings are brought to pursue some other cause of action.[259] In England, issue estoppel forms part of the doctrine of *res judicata*.[260] However, although its rationale is identical to that of *res judicata*, it is not a defence of 'a thing decided'. The better view is the Australian position which, following the decision of Dixon J in *Blair v Curran*,[261] treats it separately as 'issue estoppel'.

D. *Anshun* Estoppel

Under this doctrine, named after the leading authority in Australia, *Port of Melbourne Authority v Anshun Pty Ltd*,[262] parties in subsequent proceedings may be prevented from raising causes of action or issues which they *could have* and *should have* raised in the former litigation, but did not do so. This doctrine serves to encourage parties to raise all issues relevant to a dispute at the first opportunity, so that they can all be settled by the one action. This clearly has the objective of saving the court system time and money. It also serves to prevent courts from making conflicting or contradictory decisions. On the other hand, it is undesirable to expand litigation unnecessarily, by requiring parties to raise every conceivable matter in dispute between them. Reflecting the need to balance these competing interests, the test applied in cases of *Anshun* estoppel is not merely whether the matter *could* have been raised in the earlier proceedings. The party's failure to raise a relevant matter must have been unreasonable.[263] In assessing this, courts have regard to all the relevant facts, but give particular weight to preventing the possibility of conflicting judgments.

E. Contractual Resolution

Another 'dispute resolved' defence to a claim (including a claim for unjust enrichment) is where the dispute has been resolved by contract. We saw in Chapter 7 that a valid contract constitutes a juristic reason to retain a benefit. There are various different types of

[257] *Blair v Curran* [1939] HCA 23, (1939) 62 CLR 464, 510 (Starke J), 531–32 (Dixon J); *Jackson v Goldsmith* [1950] HCA 22, (1950) 81 CLR 446, 466 [5] (Fullagar J dissenting); *Port of Melbourne Authority v Anshun Pty Ltd* [1981] HCA 45, (1981) 147 CLR 589, 597 [17]–[18] (Gibbs CJ, Mason and Aickin JJ); *Carl Zeiss Stiftung v Rayner & Keeler Ltd* [1967] 1 AC 853; *Tyne v UBS AG* [2016] FCA 5 [332] (Greenwood J);

[258] On the different treatments of consent as compared to 'Tomlinson' orders, compare *Zurich Insurance Company plc v Hayward* [2011] EWCA Civ 641, [2011] CP Rep 39 [23]–[25] (Smith LJ) and [48].

[259] *Blair v Curran* [1939] HCA 23, (1939) 62 CLR 464, 532 (Dixon J); *Jackson v Goldsmith* [1950] HCA 22, (1950) 81 CLR 446, 460 [2] (Williams J); *Azzopardi v Bois* [1968] VR 183, 187 (Adam J).

[260] But see *Zurich Insurance Company plc v Hayward* [2011] EWCA Civ 641, [2011] CP Rep 39 (Smith LJ).

[261] *Blair v Curran* [1939] HCA 23, (1939) 62 CLR 464.

[262] *Port of Melbourne Authority v Anshun Pty Ltd* [1981] HCA 45, (1981) 147 CLR 589.

[263] *Tomlinson v Ramsey Food Processing Pty Ltd* [2015] HCA 28, (2015) 323 ALR 1 [22] (French CJ, Bell, Gageler and Keane JJ).

contractual resolution. The parties might enter into a contract of settlement of the dispute pursuant to which they agree not to litigate. Alternatively, if litigation has begun the contract of settlement might be filed with the court as a compromise of the proceedings. Closely related to these cases of contractual resolution are cases in which parties provide in the contract that the dispute is to be resolved by arbitration rather than litigation. All of these defences reflect the position that a valid contract of settlement constitutes a juristic reason to retain the benefit. As Mackinnon LJ said in *Racecourse Betting Control Board v Secretary for Air*:

> the court makes people abide by their contracts, and, therefore, will restrain a plaintiff from bringing an action which he is doing in breach of his agreement with the defendant that any dispute between them shall be otherwise determined.[264]

A restrictive approach to rescission of settlement agreements, in particular in cases of mistake, promotes and is consistent with the public interest in the finality of disputes.[265] For this reason, courts will assess closely whether, in entering the transaction, the plaintiff assumed the risk of mistake in entering into the transaction, an enquiry that will often be answered in the affirmative given the known uncertainties of litigation and the law.[266]

F. Payment or Performance in Satisfaction of an Honest Claim

Where a dispute or disputed issue has been resolved by the submission of a defendant to a plaintiff's claim that has been formally commenced in the courts, it is well established that the same interest in finality of disputes gives rise to a defence if the defendant later seeks to bring a claim against the plaintiff even in the absence of a contract or judgment.[267] A common example is where proceedings are discontinued without a contract of settlement but following capitulation by the defendant. If the defendant later seeks to recover the payment or performance capitulated, then this defence will apply. Although this defence has been referred to as a defence of 'voluntariness',[268] this term has been powerfully criticised by Professors Mason and Carter as 'apt to mislead'.[269] The primary rationale of the defence has nothing to do with voluntariness but is based on the fact that the defendant who now

[264] *Racecourse Betting Control Board v Secretary of State for Air* [1944] Ch 114, 126. See also *AWA Ltd v Daniels* (NSWSC, 24 February 1992); *Allco (Steel) Queensland Pty Ltd v Torres Strait Pty Ltd* (QSC, 12 March 1990); *Aiton Australia Pty Ltd v Transfield Pty Ltd* [1999] NSWSC 996, (1999) 153 FLR 236 [28]–[29] (Einstein J).

[265] *Hayward v Zurich Insurance Co plc* [2015] EWCA Civ 327, [2015] CP Rep 30 [16],[19], [25] (Underhill LJ) [32]–[35] (Beatson LJ) [37] (King LJ, agreeing with both judgments); distinguished in *Gohil v Gohil* [2015] UKSC 61, [2015] 3 WLR 1085 [21]–[22] (Lord Wilson; Lord Neuberger, Lady Hale, Lord Clarke, Lord Sumption, Lord Reed and Lord Hodge agreeing) and currently on appeal to the UK Supreme Court.

[266] Discussed in Ch 8 pp 177–79 and 188–89.

[267] *Werrin v Commonwealth* [1938] HCA 3, (1938) 59 CLR 150, 159, 168 approved in *David Securities Pty Ltd v Commonwealth Bank of Australia* [1992] HCA 48, (1992) 175 CLR 353, 373–74 (Mason CJ, Deane, Toohey, Gaudron and McHugh JJ).

[268] ibid.

[269] K Mason and J Carter, *Restitution Law in Australia* (Sydney, Butterworths, 1995) 62, approved in *Hookway v Racing Victoria Ltd* [2005] VSCA 310, (2005) 13 VR 444 [24] (Ormiston JA). Now see K Mason, JW Carter and GJ Tolhurst, *Mason and Carter's Restitution Law in Australia*, 2nd edn (Chatswood, NSW, LexisNexis Butterworths, 2008) para [168].

seeks to bring a claim (including a claim for unjust enrichment) had the opportunity of defending the original action and chose not to do so. The law will not permit the defendant later to bring an action for unjust enrichment on the basis of matters that could have been clarified by way of defence.[270] A second, related rationale underlying the rule is that a defendant who chooses to pay rather than contest the plaintiff's claim does so knowing that there is a risk that he is not liable. The law provides a mechanism for eliminating that risk through the legal process. Given his choice to pay rather than litigate, there is no good reason for transferring the risk of his mistake to the plaintiff, which would be the result if the defendant were allowed to bring a claim seeking restitution of any enrichment transferred to the plaintiff by submission to the plaintiff's claim.

Although this defence is clear, its boundaries are in dispute. On the one hand, the defence and its rationale clearly apply to cases in which the defendant submits to an honest claim once proceedings have been brought even if there is no contract of settlement or judgment entered.[271] More doubtful is the case where submission occurs after threats of, or to forestall, proceedings. In *Brennan v Bolt Burdon*[272] Sedley LJ observed that although raising different policy considerations, he could 'see no principled way of distinguishing a compromise of extant litigation from a compromise of threatened litigation'. On the other hand, in the leading judgment in *Hookway v Racing Victoria Ltd*[273] Ormiston JA said that the defence should not apply where the plaintiff paid 'in ignorance of the legal position and in circumstances where it has not been shown that some such conscious decision has been made [to take the risk that he is not liable]'. The approach of Ormiston JA is more finely tailored to the second rationale of this defence. A similar analysis led Debelle J in *Re Magarey Farlam Lawyers Trust Accounts (No 3)*[274] to find the defence was established when partners of a law firm made a series of payments to clients to forestall any claims against the firm arising out of defalcations in the firm's client trust account. Critical to his Honour's reasoning was the fact that the partners made the payment taking a risk that no further liabilities would be discovered.[275]

In relation to cases where no proceedings are brought or threatened, but a payment is mistakenly made, the defence should not apply.[276] The two rationales for a defence of submission to an honest claim (finality of disputes and risk running) do not extend to this case. There is no independent defence of 'honest receipt'.[277]

[270] *Moore v Vestry of Fulham* [1895] 1 QB 399.

[271] *Wigan v Edwards* (1973) 47 ALJR 586; *Hookway v Racing Victoria Ltd* [2005] VSCA 310, (2005) 13 VR 444 [41].

[272] *Brennan v Bolt Burdon* [2004] EWCA Civ 1017, [2005] QB 303 [61].

[273] *Hookway v Racing Victoria Ltd* [2005] VSCA 310, (2005) 13 VR 444 [41].

[274] *Re Magarey Farlam Lawyers Trust Accounts (No 3)* [2007] SASC 9, (2007) 96 SASR 337 [169], [174].

[275] ibid [172]–[173]. The payments were also found to have been received in satisfaction of the client's rights: see Ch 7 pp 156–58. His Honour also found that either there was no mistake, or the mistake did not cause the payments: see Ch 8 p 174; see also *Lahoud v Lahoud* [2010] NSWSC 1297 [178]–[182] (Ward J); *Salib v Gakas; Newport Pacific Pty Ltd v Salib* [2010] NSWSC 505 [331]–[336] (Ward J).

[276] *Brennan v Bolt Burdon* [2004] EWCA Civ 1017, [2005] QB 303. See AS Burrows, *The Law of Restitution*, 3rd edn (Oxford, Oxford University Press, 2011) 603; Law Commission, *Restitution: Mistakes of Law and Ultra Vires Public Authority Receipts and Payments* (Law Com No 227, 1994) paras [2.25]–[2.38].

[277] *Hookway v Racing Victoria Ltd* [2005] VSCA 310, (2005) 13 VR 444 [55]–[59] (Ormiston J), discussing the proposition made in *David Securities Pty Ltd v Commonwealth Bank of Australia* [1992] HCA 48, (1992) 175 CLR 353, 399 [13] (Brennan J).

IX. Passing On

It is now well established under Australian law that there is no general defence to a claim in unjust enrichment that the plaintiff has 'passed on' or recouped from a third party the value of the enrichment transferred to the defendant.[278] The English Court of Appeal followed the Australian authorities in rejecting the defence in *Kleinwort Benson Ltd v Birmingham City Council*.[279] The reason lies in the meaning of the 'at the expense of' requirement, examined in Chapter 5. That chapter explained that the requirement reflects the need for the plaintiff to prove that the defendant was enriched by a defective transaction with the plaintiff, or one which was causally related to an initially defective transaction with the plaintiff. There is no need to prove, additionally, that the plaintiff suffered a loss *corresponding to* that enrichment.[280]

However, there are still two major ways in which a defence of passing on might operate. The first is by statute. There are a number of discrete statutory provisions in Australia[281] and England[282] that impose passing on defences to claims for restitution of tax. By contrast with general law versions of the defence found in other common law jurisdictions,[283] and statutory versions in England and the European Union,[284] the Australian provisions usually impose upon the plaintiff the onus of proving that the taxation burden *has not* been passed on to third parties. The most likely reasons for the change in onus in the statutory defences are that the provisions are designed to deter systematic 'profiteering' in tax,[285] to protect government finances and because the plaintiff has the most ready access to information about its pricing policies. The provisions therefore do not reflect a different parliamentary view of the 'at the expense of' requirement for the general claim in unjust enrichment.

The second way in which a defence of passing on may operate is if a third party has an unjust enrichment claim against the plaintiff arising from the passing on of the plaintiff's

[278] *Roxborough v Rothmans of Pall Mall Australia Ltd* [2001] HCA 68, (2001) 208 CLR 516, 529 [25] (Gleeson CJ, Gaudron and Hayne JJ), citing *Commissioner of State Revenue (Vic) v Royal Insurance Australia Ltd* [1994] HCA 61, (1994) 182 CLR 51, 75 [41] (Mason CJ); *Mason v New South Wales* [1959] HCA 5, (1959) 102 CLR 108, 146 [18] (Windeyer J).

[279] *Kleinwort Benson Ltd v Birmingham City Council* [1997] QB 380, approving *Commissioner of State Revenue (Vic) v Royal Insurance Australia Ltd* [1994] HCA 61, (1994) 182 CLR 51, and *Mason v New South Wales* [1959] HCA 5, (1959) 102 CLR 108.

[280] Cf the Canadian position, where enrichment and loss must coincide and thus the defence is permitted: *Air Canada v British Columbia* [1989] 1 SCR 1161, 1202 (La Forest J). Dr Rush notes that the defence has not received universal approval in Canada, but rather has tended to be restricted to public authorities: M Rush, *The Defence of Passing On* (Oxford, Hart, 2006) 50–52.

[281] Eg *Sales Tax Assessment Act 1992* (Cth), considered in *Avon Products Pty Ltd v Federal Commissioner of Taxation* [2005] FCAFC 63, (2005) 59 ATR 592. See also Limitation of Actions Act 1958 (Vic) s 20B; Limitation Act 1974 (Tas) s 25C; Limitation Act 1935 (WA) s 37B; Limitation Act 2005 (WA) ss 86, 87.

[282] Eg Value Added Tax Act 1994 s 80, as amended by the Finance Act 1997 ss 46–47, considered in *Customs and Excise Commissioners v National Westminster Bank plc* [2003] EWHC 1822, [2003] STC 1072; *Marks & Spencer plc v Customs and Excise Commissioners (No 1)* [2000] STC 16; both cases were discussed in *Avon Products Pty Ltd v Federal Commissioner of Taxation* [2005] FCAFC 63, (2005) 59 ATR 592.

[283] In Canada, see *Air Canada v British Columbia* [1989] 1 SCR 1161.

[284] It is contrary to European Union law for the plaintiff to have the onus to negate the defence by proving that unlawful charges have *not* been passed on: *Les Fils de Jules Bianco SA v Directeur Général des Douanes et Droits Indirects* [1988] ECR 1099, [1989] 3 CMLR 36.

[285] *Avon Products Pty Ltd v Federal Commissioner of Taxation* [2005] FCAFC 63, (2005) 59 ATR 592 [5] (Ryan and Merkel JJ) [32]–[34] (Conti J).

loss. There have been suggestions in Australia that if the defendant can prove that the plaintiff has been enriched at the expense of the third party the plaintiff will hold the proceeds of judgment against the defendant on constructive trust for the third party.[286] For instance, in *Commissioner of State Revenue (Vic) v Royal Insurance Australia Ltd*[287] money was paid by mistake from an insurance company, Royal, to a revenue authority in the form of overpaid stamp duty. The revenue authority was required to make restitution of the overpayments, even though the amount had been passed on to policyholders. Justice Brennan, with whom Toohey and McHugh JJ agreed, said:

> It may be that, if Royal recovers the overpayments it made, the policy holders will be entitled themselves to claim a refund from Royal ... However that may be, no defence of 'passing on' is available to defeat a claim for moneys paid by A acting on his own behalf to B where B has been unjustly enriched by the payment and the moneys paid had been A's moneys.[288]

One possible way to short-circuit the possibility of two actions (ie Royal against the defendant and the policyholders against Royal) would be for the insurance company to hold the proceeds of judgment on trust for the policyholders. This possibility was expressly endorsed by Mason CJ in a separate judgment.[289] However, although such a conditional order is possible,[290] Dr Rush has observed that there are considerable and unresolved difficulties involved in the recognition of such a limited version of the passing on defence.[291] What duties would the plaintiff be under as a constructive trustee? Does the plaintiff have a duty to invest? How can all the beneficiaries be identified? How much time and money must the plaintiff spend to identify all the beneficiaries? What standard of proof is required to accept a claim that a person is a beneficiary? Even if all beneficiaries can be identified, should the money be held on trust until it has all has been refunded?

X. Conclusion

It will be recalled from Chapter 1 that an understanding of the nature of a claim for unjust enrichment requires consideration of four questions:[292]

(1) Was the defendant enriched?
(2) Was the defendant's enrichment at the plaintiff's expense?
(3) Was the enrichment 'unjust'?
(4) What defences apply?

[286] Dr Rush also considers and rejects the possibility that courts should be capable of making a direct award in favour of third parties: M Rush, *The Defence of Passing On* (Oxford, Hart, 2006) 211–13. To do so contravenes the basic principle that awards should not be made for or against non-parties because to do so denies them the opportunity to present their claims in the manner and before the court they themselves choose and because the non-parties may have elected to waive their claims.

[287] *Commissioner of State Revenue (Vic) v Royal Insurance Australia Ltd* [1994] HCA 61, (1994) 182 CLR 51.

[288] ibid 90–91 [19] (Brennan J; Toohey and McHugh JJJ concurring). See also *Mutual Pools & Staff Pty Ltd v Commonwealth* [1994] HCA 9, (1994) 179 CLR 155, 177 [4] (Brennan J); see also 191 [17] (Deane and Gaudron JJ).

[289] ibid 75–76 [44].

[290] See, eg, the conditional order for judgment made in *Nelson v Nelson* [1995] HCA 25, (1995) 184 CLR 538.

[291] M Rush, *The Defence of Passing On* (Oxford, Hart, 2006) 214–15.

[292] See Ch 1 p 6.

This final chapter has provided an outline of some important defences, apart from change of position, to a claim for unjust enrichment. Most of the eight defences considered in this chapter are not limited to claims in unjust enrichment, but this chapter has shown how they operate in the law of unjust enrichment. A recurrent issue is to determine whether each defence is truly independent (for example, the various manifestations of the 'good consideration' defence), or is better understood as an instance of a broader defence (such as payment over and change of position), or as a circumstance where some aspect of the primary claim is absent (for example, enrichment in the case of ministerial receipt).

Developing the four-fold approach and explaining and clarifying each of its inquiries, enables us, in the words of the Chief Justice of the United States Supreme Court (in a different context), to limit 'discretion according to legal standards [and] promote the basic principle of justice that like cases should be decided alike'.[293]

[293] *Martin v Franklin Capital Corporation* 546 US 132, 139 (2005) (Roberts CJ for the Court), citing HJ Friendly, 'Indiscretion about Discretion' (1982) 31 *Emory Law Journal* 747, 758.

INDEX

www.ingramcontent.com/pod-product-compliance
Ingram Content Group UK Ltd.
Pitfield, Milton Keynes, MK11 3LW, UK
UKHW051449290926
15471UKWH00008B/1096

9 781841 133188